Aborigines and change: Australia in the '70s

Aborigines and change:

AUSTRALIA IN THE '70s

Edited by R. M. Berndt

Social Anthropology Series No. 11

Australian Institute of Aboriginal Studies, Canberra

Humanities Press Inc., New Jersey, U.S.A.

1977

Papers presented to a symposium at the 1974 meeting of the
Australian Institute of Aboriginal Studies

Library of Congress Catalog number 77-76827
National Library of Australia card number and ISBN 0 85575 059 6 hard cover
0 85575 060 X soft cover

U.S.A. edition ISBN 0 391 00726 2 hard cover
0 391 00727 0 soft cover

Typeset and printed in Australia by Typographics Communications Pty. Ltd., Sydney
8.77.3000

Contents

v

Preface

Late in 1973, I was asked by the Australian Institute of Aboriginal Studies to arrange and to convene a symposium on Social and Cultural Change for the 1974 Biennial Conference, to be held in Canberra. It was not intended to be in any way an ambitious venture: and the relevant committee planning this conference decided that our 'resource contributors' should be drawn from Australia, without overseas representation. Our main aim at that time was to face up to some of the problems inherent in the situation of Aborigines adapting to Australian-European society, to underline some of the difficulties involved in that process, and to demonstrate the Institute's vital concern for research into these particular areas. This was in no sense a new departure for the Australian Institute of Aboriginal Studies. From its inception (in 1961), it had emphasised both interest and research into such issues. What some of us wished to do, as social anthropologists, was to make that focus clearer.

The response from a range of persons who were involved in such studies was quite outstanding. We were not able to accommodate all of them, but twenty-eight papers were presented at the symposium (on 23-24 May 1974); only one was read *in absentia,* and one other had joint authors. The symposium was divided into six sections: General; Traditionally-oriented areas, Part I, the Western Australian Experience; Traditionally-oriented areas, Part II, Changing Frames of Reference; Education; Identity and Urban Situations; and Law and Politics. These sections were chaired by myself as convener (Sections 1 and 2), Dr L. R. Hiatt (Section 3), Professor Leonard Broom (Section 4), Professor Colin Tatz (Section 5) and Professor Charles Rowley (Section 6). I take this opportunity to thank each of the chairmen personally for the time and effort they put into this task, so helping to ensure a successful meeting. We originally planned to include the chairmen's introductory remarks, but this proved not to be feasible. Because the time available was limited, discussion after the presentation of each paper had to be limited too. Nevertheless, there was opportunity for comment from the main body of the audience. This was audio-visually recorded, and the material is stored at the Australian Institute of Aboriginal Studies.

Of those who originally spoke to their papers at the symposium, only two (Dr Marie Reay and Mr M. Lofgren) found it impossible to finalise their contributions for inclusion here. To replace them, I asked Mr Noel Wallace for a paper he was completing on Western Desert decentralisation, to complement one by Mr Gray on decentralisation in Arnhem Land: and Dr Nicolas Peterson kindly offered his paper on Aboriginal economic involvement.

Virtually all of the contributions have been revised or otherwise amended by their authors. My task as editor has been an agreeable and fairly painless one. I have taken it seriously on several counts, but have made changes only where I considered them absolutely necessary, and have been especially careful in each case to preserve the author's tone and sense. My touch has been light. As editor, I am not responsible—nor is the Institute—for personal opinions expressed by the authors. But the task, as I say, has been pleasurable and rewarding because this volume has collected together a wide range of authoritative studies, most of which are based on solid social scientific research, and some on considerable experience in the Aboriginal field. It is true that Marie Reay (ed.) *Aborigines Now* (1964) set the pattern for this kind of 'composite' work. The present volume is not intended to take its place. I would, however, like to feel that this one not only complements it but amplifies some of its basic themes, revealing, more clearly than was possible in 1964, the implications of beliefs and actions that had gone before. In that *one* decade, much has changed. Trends which were then quite blurred and not easily identified, have come more sharply into focus. It is these which the present papers bring out and discuss. Moreover, our volume has, spatially, a much wider coverage: all the Australian States are represented, except for Tasmania and, indirectly, Victoria.The theme of change takes into account traditionally-oriented Aborigines and those living in urban and rural environments.

The order of the papers included here is not the same as in the actual symposium. My concern, in arranging them, was to range from traditionally-oriented groups on one hand to urban living on the other. To achieve this has meant separating myself and my wife, providing a 'sandwich' effect. Both of us, in different ways, underline the same problems facing Aboriginal people—their quest for social and personal identity and involvement in their *own* affairs. These two issues are to us paramount; and the intervening papers, in their different ways, say the same things. This commonalty of approach—in spite of methodological variations and differing standpoints—is a reasonably true mirror of the situation today, a mirror in which reflections for the future may be seen, at times quite clearly.

It would be invidious for me to comment on the various contributions because, while there are common themes, there are many extensions which provide small 'islands' focusing on specific problems: questions relevant to education, legal advice, political action and economic adjustment, communication difficulties, the eroding influence of excessive liquor drinking, lack of employment and resources, prejudice and dissatisfaction, and so on. In spite of pious statements from administrative officials and others about the integrity of traditional culture, and about the right of people of Aboriginal descent to choose for themselves how they want to live, it is clear that any choices they do make are quite circumscribed. The overall impact of the multifaceted pressures now impinging on them allows little leeway in that respect. The move toward decentralisation in parts of Arnhem Land, Central Australia and the Western Desert, as in the Victoria River Downs district, does not necessarily signify trends toward Aboriginal traditionalism— although that ingredient may well be present. Just as obvious is the creation of miniature 'settlements' structurally similar to the larger ones from which the re-settlers have moved. Nevertheless, the pull of 'one's own country' is a powerful incentive, linked as it is with ideas of occupancy and protection from alien intrusion, as well as with land-rights claims.

The winds of change have strengthened, and many (both traditionally-oriented Aborigines and people of Aboriginal descent living in urban and near-urban settings) have begun to feel that, unless they are very careful indeed, the force of those winds can destroy much that they consider significant for themselves and for the on-coming generations—if Aboriginality is to have any positive meaning. Decentralisation is one way of coping, or trying to cope, with that situation. And it can in some instances be interpreted as 'an escape' from the tensions and upsets of larger community living and direct external control. On the other hand, Aborigines in the cities and country towns, particularly in the south, have approached the 'strengthening winds' head-on, by attempting to achieve, and to some extent achieving, political and economic independence. That process is far from completed; but because of their linkages with the wider Australian society and the impossibility of breaking with these at this juncture, it could be a long-drawn-out affair, and could be less than satisfactory. In that rests a dilemma (which I touched on in a small volume I edited, *A Question of Choice: an Australian Aboriginal Dilemma,* 1971). It does not involve only Aborigines living in cities and country towns. For various reasons—not least because all Aborigines of whatever descent are classified as Aborigines and identify themselves mostly in that way—it means inevitably that *all* must face that particular issue, sooner or later.

Aborigines have not, in the past, placed such a positive value on change as so many Australian-Europeans have—or, for that matter, as some social scientists have. Aborigines, being on the receiving end, are in a better position to evaluate practically the results of far-reaching changes which are taking place in almost all areas of socio-cultural activity and belief. While being forced to adapt, they are at the same time not convinced that all the changes which are imposed upon them are congenial and beneficial. Within the context of Western society, which is essentially epitomised by industrial-ised and technologically-focused urban configurations, change is increasingly being considered as something that is essentially good *in itself.* This is not the place to provide examples from all facets of Aboriginal life today, but those examples are myriad and are easy to find. One only has to look at the various reports, documents, directives and so forth produced in great profusion by the Department of Aboriginal Affairs and its State satellites (independent or otherwise), Social Services and Community and Welfare, Royal Commissions and Sitting (or Standing) Committees, etc.

It is unfair, perhaps, to select one particular document of this nature for consideration, but the 'Program for Yuendumu and Hooker Creek' (a *Report on Visit to Yuendumu and Hooker Creek,* by H. C. Coombs and W. E. H. Stanner in March 1974, Council for Aboriginal Affairs, Canberra, 1974) is a case in point. Recognising the existence of a dilemma, and the dangers of retrogression as a contrary trend in the face of positive governmental action *vis-à-vis* Aboriginal advancement and development, that document exemplifies the quite blatant, but probably unintentional, march of bureau-cratisation, in relation to Aboriginal communities: consultants and advisers of varying hues, community development and services, the building up of

the social and productive capital of communities, training Aborigines to be
effectively employed, contributing to their income-earning capacity, improving transport and communication facilities, the creation of social clubs,
progress associations, etc., establishing rules and regulations and constitutions
for local Aboriginal councils, training 'white' personnel, and so on. Each of
these may be laudable in itself. But in combination and in overall impact
they constitute rigid administrative control which, increasingly, provides
little opportunity for Aboriginal manoeuvre. How, in the face of such
pressures, can a people take advantage of the well-meaning statement noted
in that particular document (*ibid.*:3): 'that Aborigines be allowed and
helped to adapt freely to their own requirements and circumstances such
white Australian practices as they consider to be of value to them'? Realistically, what options do they have?

We need to ask ourselves, as Aborigines are now asking themselves,
'Change for what?' Change can be both negative and positive. The view
that change is something which is good in itself is influenced and intensified
by economic demands and economic pressures. One outcome has been a
continued trend toward de-humanisation, toward a subordination of human
values in contrast to purely materialistic and economic ones; increasing
dissatisfaction with existing conditions, manifested in social and political
agitation. (See R. Berndt, A Perspective on Social Anthropology, *Indian
Anthropologist*, Vol. 4, No. 2, 1974:71–80.) 'An emotionally-charged belief
in the social value of change: change of some kind—any kind—irrespective
of what it is, and regardless of the outcome . . . can and often does have
disastrous results . . . without consideration of context and without working
out the implications, or the *human* consequences of what is happening.'
(*Ibid.*:78.) Aborigines have realised this, and they see the erosion of their
human values, but the embracing bonds of bureaucratisation have them
virtually helpless.

What is required is a slackening of those bonds, a re-evaluation of change.
Self-regulation, self-control, and self-determination on the part of Aborigines,
are not really possibilities *unless* more provision is made for choices—*unless*
change is muted, and *unless* the people themselves are given more opportunities
to learn by their own mistakes. Bureaucratic machinery is perhaps, within
the structure of contemporary society, an essential feature which cannot
be entirely scrapped—but it has the tendency to create its own momentum
and pace and, more tellingly and less advantageously to those caught
within it, to subject people to increasing control. From an Aboriginal standpoint, we may well ask (as Catherine Berndt has done): 'are we indeed
back to square one?' And, in many cases, this seems to be what is happening.
But the pity of it is that it need not be so. It is, therefore, important that much
more attention—both on the part of Aborigines and administrations—be
paid to social scientific research. This is not in any sense the area in which
final answers will be found, nor ultimate satisfactions—those may be found
only in human attitudes and values and adaptations. One thing however is
clear, and to my way of thinking is demonstrated at least to some extent
in the contributions within this volume: that all of us (Aborigines and
non-Aborigines) do need to know a great deal more about the socio-cultural
situations within which we interact (in varying capacities), and much more
about human aspirations. There are many misconceptions about what

Anthropology (for instance) does, and what it aims to do, and what use can be made of its findings. These misconceptions are current among both Aborigines and non-Aborigines, and especially among the 'bureaucrats'. How these misconceptions can be corrected, how Anthropology can be put to work practically without damaging its scientific fabric, are not questions which I propose to explore here. But they do need to be explored soon.

One theme which appears in so many papers in this volume is that of Aboriginal social and personal identity. This is not posed as a question, but is considered as a reality, as a positive element which contributes toward Aboriginal socio-cultural integrity and Aboriginal self-respect. In 1964, when Marie Reay edited *Aborigines Now,* the administrative fashion then in vogue was 'guided assimilation'. It is true that in some of the papers published in her volume at that time this was questioned, at least implicitly—for example, by Fay Gale (*ibid.*:110) and Katrin Wilson (*ibid.*:145–6). Less than a decade after that, Aboriginal identity, in terms of pan-Aboriginality, with emphasis on nurturing and/or creating an Aboriginal heritage, had become a positive feature of all Aboriginal action. However, that identity is not a thing in itself, separated or separable from the wider context. One thing it does do, is to focus on the Aboriginal side of the picture and to rely on human values and human aspirations, in contrast to levelling pressures of a socio-economic and administrative nature which, unless they are relegated to their proper place (that is, unless they are seen in balance against other equally important imperatives), can at the worst eradicate Aboriginal identity, or at the best change it into something entirely different—a super-imposed identity which does not rely, necessarily, on an Aboriginal past or present, but simply on a contrived Aboriginal future. The issues here are not as clear as they should be; nor are they clear to the Aborigines themselves.

On 27 November 1974 I circulated all contributors regarding a possible title for this book. My suggested title was 'Aborigines in Crisis: Australia in the '70s'; several other alternative titles were also suggested. Twenty-two contributors responded, thirteen agreeing to my first suggestion. However, since that time, I myself have moved away from the idea of 'crisis'. I agree with Ken Maddock that Aborigines have always been faced with one crisis or another over the whole course of their contact with aliens—although the crisis they face today is, in my view, much greater than ever before, and one that has far-reaching implications for them as a people. Instead, I have chosen the one which is now used—'Aborigines and Change: Australia in the '70s', for two reasons: to emphasise (1) that virtually all the contributions concern themselves with what is taking place now, and (2) that it is not so much Aborigines 'in' change, as the fact that they are attempting to cope with rapid change and to carve out an identity of their own in the face of heavy adverse pressures.

Now a comment regarding participation.

From its beginnings, a major focus of the Institute was on research; and the understanding was that, ideally at least, such research and the presenta-tion of results would be based on recognised professional standards. Also, and notwithstanding an interest in changing circumstances, and on Aboriginal contact with the outside world, its major concentration was on traditional

Aboriginal life—on those features that were distinctively Aboriginal as contrasted with something else.

Aborigines who were actively involved in that life or otherwise truly knowledgeable about it were mostly not fluent in English, and were also locally oriented. Young people in such situations were not interested, or did not realise the importance of sustaining and conserving Aboriginal traditions that were under threat of extinction. People of Aboriginal descent in urban areas and country towns mostly took the same line, though not necessarily for the same reasons. And because of the long-drawn-out and pervasive and still in some ways continuing colonial era, most Aborigines until very recently lacked both opportunity and incentive to take part in tertiary education or to engage in professional social scientific or other scientific research.

This situation has been changing—in what has been, despite some claims to the contrary, a very slow process except where the erosion of traditional aspects is concerned. More people of Aboriginal descent have at last been moving into the sphere of post-primary and post-secondary education— although in doing so they have also moved further away from firsthand involvement in the remaining traditional core. Although a few will, it is hoped, proceed to research—serious, systematic research—into aspects of traditional culture, the majority are more likely to turn their attention to issues (socio-political, economic) that they see as being of more immediate relevance in the contemporary scene. For increasing numbers of the Aboriginal population in general, identification as 'Aborigines' or as 'Blacks' does not point to content so much as to alignment—identification as against 'European', or 'white'. The content, the substance of Aboriginal culture, is symbolic, giving meaning to the label.

So, the question of Aboriginal inclusion in Institute affairs as more than 'token' participants raises the matter of representation or representativeness (and definitions of this), of their direct as well as variously mediated contributions to professional research, and of the criteria that are or may be or should be applied to them *and* to other members and participants. It is not enough for them simply to 'be Aborigines' in this context: other qualifications and particular kinds of expertise are needed too, unless the Institute is to be entirely reconstituted. On the other hand, it is true that many non-Aboriginal members (etc.) of the Institute would appear to have little interest in and little knowledge of traditional Aboriginal life *per se:* to be content with a superficial picture (maybe without even realising this), or with bits that they regard as appropriate to their own particular fields of specialisation—whether these be archaeological, for instance, linguistic, medical, educational or psychological, or centred on contemporary political and welfare problems. In their case, a grounding in scientific research methods, broadly interpreted, is also not enough in itself.

There are several implications, which obviously cannot usefully be explored here. My main point, at this juncture, is that in future symposia on this and related topics (e.g. education and other socio-cultural subjects), I would expect Aboriginal participation to be taken for granted, articulate, and certainly equivalent in standard to the range of what has been forthcoming in the past from non-Aboriginal participants.

Finally, I thank all contributors to this volume, and the Australian Institute of Aboriginal Studies for holding its original symposium and for publishing these proceedings. Our major debt inevitably lies with the Aborigines of whom we write: and the expiation of that debt must surely be found in these contributions themselves—in their practical use, in providing descriptions and explanations of a fairly wide range of typical problem areas which are of direct concern to Aboriginal people, and directly as well as indirectly to others.

Ronald M. Berndt

Department of Anthropology
University of Western Australia

October 1975

1 Aboriginal identity: reality or mirage

Ronald M. Berndt

The question of social/personal identity, in any circumstance, is a multi-faceted one, not easily resolved—often shifting obliquely, and heavily influenced by outside opinion. Today, especially in industrialised-urban living, pressures of one kind or another (often predominantly political) are brought to bear on persons and on sub-groups in order to proclaim the uniqueness of one in contrast to another. Correlated with this is real or unfounded anxiety—anxiety about social or even physical survival in the face of a perceived threat; for example, where long-established beliefs and customary modes of behaviour are believed to be in jeopardy. Probably, all peoples have at some time been concerned with this particular problem, but both the content and the context have varied quite widely.

Conversely, assertions regarding identity are often grounded in a situation of relative security—where there seems to be a feeling of belonging securely within a particular social order that is taken for granted, accepted without any serious or consistent expressions of doubt. In such conditions, socio-cultural and personal identification is none the less significant. It helps to provide contrasts between those 'within' and those 'outside'. But it does more than provide an assortment of boundary-markers. In one sense, it serves as a protective crust—a significant factor in internal cohesion. Stress and strain were not absent from this kind of self- and other-identification, but they were minimal; so were pressures toward any major *re*-definition of identity. This is how it was, generally speaking, in traditional Aboriginal Australia, and how it still is for those persons who are still traditionally-oriented or still emphasise that perspective. But over much of the continent, the odds were heavily against its continuation. Through the vicissitudes of harsh and unsympathetic contact with people who were initially alien to them, many Aborigines lost their traditional heritage and in the process lost too their own socio-cultural identity and their sources of socio-cultural identification. What survived of these, came to depend on assumptions and premises dissimilar to those held by traditional Aborigines. In spite of their closer physical and cultural, but not necessarily social assimilation into the wider Australian society, they continued to be dominated by non-Aborigines, and this engendered varying degrees of insecurity and anxiety on a range of fronts. One response to this was an attempt, by some, to establish a commonalty of interests and experiences which could be taken to mark them off from non-Aborigines—again, in spite of the similarities between them. In this respect they were aided by non-Aborigines who, with few exceptions, categorised part-Aborigines as 'Aborigines'. Within the setting of these mutually-sustaining attitudes, a new form of identity emerged, which the policies of the last few years have encouraged. It is these two aspects of identification that I propose to discuss.

A. The traditional focus

Social identification in traditional Aboriginal society was, primarily, directed toward essentially non-political ends. It depended on the way life was organised. One of the difficulties that faced anthropologists looking at the social dimension lay in locating criteria that could be used to define the widest social entity: or, to put it another way, to determine the widest spatial recognition of likeness and, more importantly, the expectation of meaningful interaction between those within. The concept of the 'tribe' was sometimes assumed to be appropriate here. It soon became clear, however, that being a member of a 'tribe' or a larger language-community did not necessarily involve social commitment or face-to-face contact: that identity in this respect, was often vague, or not universally recognised. The rule of law was rarely if ever co-extensive for all the local units that might for some other reasons have been included; and the degree to which all members of a 'tribe' could rely on one another was minimal. Nevertheless, this wider fictional form of identification was significant, and was used by Aborigines to demarcate, very broadly, one kind of person from another. Further, it emphasised ethnocentric attitudes, through a variety of devices: defining 'us' as 'man' or 'human being' in contrast to others; emphasising regional association, or behavioural and linguistic differences or peculiarities, as seen from one point of view. These socio-cultural and language fences, although they were in no sense hard and fast, were sufficient to keep persons from mixing freely over a wide range: they helped to limit social interaction and restrict communication. Where there were exceptions, as in north-eastern Arnhem Land and in the Western Desert, it was the spread of a common language which was important. But even then, spatial restrictions were emphasised or obliquely suggested by dialectal variation. The overall result was to force people to rely on their own resources and to enhance their feeling of social independence. In one way, we can conceptualise the idea of 'tribe' as providing socio-psychological insulation, underlining traditional Aborigines' concentration on their own affairs.

Within that smaller frame, the matter of identifying persons in relation to other persons was clearly stipulated. Membership in specific categories (moieties, sections, sub-sections, semi-moieties, etc.) and in social units (local descent groups, clans, dialectal units, etc.) was determined basically through the medium of matri- and patri-descent. There was no form of category or unit in traditional Aboriginal Australia which was 'open' or to which one could belong voluntarily through purely individual choice. Religiously and economically, people were placed quite firmly within the total system—no room was left for an uncommitted, floating population. It did allow for trading partners and other visitors to be accommodated as, at least, nominal members: but they were assumed to have their own home social/territorial anchorages. On one hand, the social unit which in one form or another can be described as a local descent group, whether or not it possessed a specific label, defined and confirmed the mytho-spiritual linkages of its members to the land—specific land. That form of identification was unique to persons belonging to that unit, and could not be duplicated. However, such social units were linked to others by virtue of mytho-ritual ties, because many mythic beings moved over fairly wide stretches of country and most rituals were not confined solely to a particular mythic segment. So, a broader religious identification was possible. The fact remains, that primary social identification rested on the local descent group.

On the other hand, social categories also provided broader ways of identifying particular sorts of persons, outside the social units themselves. Or they bound together, in terms of kinship, members of different but structurally similar social units for purposes of co-operation. These social categories were devices which not only labelled persons in contrast to others, but also provided patterns for interpersonal interaction. That interaction was organised largely on the basis of kin positioning which, in turn, enunciated responsibilities and obligations, rights and duties between persons.

There are two significant features here. The first has to do with what can be called the primary functional unit, where co-operation was at its maximum. This was the socio-economic group which focused on food-collecting and on hunting, *and* on domesticity. It has variously been called the 'horde' or band, a co-resident or a land-utilising group. Throughout Aboriginal Australia, no formal label was used to designate such a group, and its criteria of membership rested on identification in the descent units. In spite of that, it was the only truly visible interactory group in ordinary everyday circumstances; it fluctuated in size, and was mobile—both of these factors being influenced by the natural environment. The principle of co-operation on a basis of real or assumed kinship held people together, but also provided opportunities to form and re-form into new groups as the occasion demanded. In so far as politics were significant in traditional Aboriginal life, this was the unit in which they were most clearly visible.

The second feature concerns social categories, particularly sections and subsections. While these were not present throughout the whole of Aboriginal Australia, traditionally they were relevant over large stretches of territory, and among many different 'tribes'. Such categories were readily identifiable at the inter-cultural and inter-language levels. Outside the religious linkages, they were the only social devices that could potentially bridge ethnocentric structures. The fact that they were organised in terms of descent, not simply of 'category', meant that 'outsiders' could be incorporated only on a personal basis and in relation to kinship.

Traditional Aboriginal identification was intensely localistic, and interests were turned inward rather than outward. One reason was the problem of obtaining a living, a problem that was not seen simply as a matter of applying skills and techniques. It included also activities that were designed to perpetuate the conditions which made exploitation of the natural environment possible. This is reflected in the two basic forms of identification I mentioned: one, the kind of social unit that was defined in terms of patri-lineal descent and/or of mythic association with a small area or territory; two, the use of an identifying label that placed a person within a specific category *vis-à-vis* others. The first, while being social, pointed toward the cultural component. It gave substance to identity and can be thought of as being relevant to common interests (that is, common to the members of that social unit), which might under certain conditions be extended to other units within a wider constellation. Those interests were religious, and were a dominant focus of traditional Aboriginal society.

The second, also social, provided connections between persons assumed to have common interests. Or, where that linkage extended beyond the 'kindred' or persons who already acknowledged close consanguineal ties, it presupposed an expectation of such interests. Structurally, as well as practically, this made possible the development of a 'community', on the basis of the food-collecting unit. It brought together an admixture of persons whose main bases of identification lay elsewhere—in local descent groups and in various social categories. Within that community were represented cross-cutting interests—interests which could be complementary but were just as often conflicting. Co-operation was at a premium, as it had to be in this situation; but interpersonal friction was also an inevitable ingredient.

There is no point in expanding on these issues here, except to say that social living of this kind appears to have been taken for granted and to have remained virtually unquestioned. The good and the bad were essential elements of that life: it was *there*, as a given totality, and Aborigines were part of it. Being an Aboriginal meant commitment to a particular belief system which identified him/her within a mythic scheme that had direct relevance to the present. That identification was both physical and spiritual. This is one of the reasons why the secret-sacred dimension is so vitally important in traditional Aboriginal Australia, and why traditionally-oriented Aborigines today feel strongly about safeguarding their interests in this respect—because this defines their *real* identity. Being an Aboriginal meant, also, interaction with others, within the context of social-personal identification. And those others were 'significant others', particular persons having defined responsibilities and obligations—not just *any* other person. All of this magnified the importance of what went on within a fairly small-scale situation, with little concern for what might be happening outside.

Generally, traditional Aboriginal identity rested on personal involvement and experience, on actual participation, on ways of thinking and acting, within an integrated and closed system which provided maximal security. It removed identification from the area of cross-cutting interests, where politics could have flourished. To a very large extent, this militated against the growth of political organisation on any large scale; and that, in turn, diminished the possibility of concerted resistance to alien intrusion.

Full commitment and identification in traditional Aboriginal terms, in the way I have conceptualised it, is no longer a reality. It has been replaced by another sort of reality, which includes something of the traditional, but much less than before. However, a fair amount has survived in a number of regions (in Arnhem Land and the Western Desert, for instance); and because of this we can continue to speak of the people there, in general, as being traditionally-oriented. This is one way of saying that they are oriented toward their *own* traditions: that traditional Aboriginal aspects of belief and action seem to be more significant to them than any others. Even so, in relation to identification, the two traditional forms I mentioned before (briefly, local descent and other groups, and social categories) have become much more compartmentalised. The intervening entity that has been called 'the community', previously to some extent a fluctuating-membership unit, has become more independent of the others and, consequently, less exclusive.

Further, it has become less mobile and less dependent on its own socio-economic resources. These two features alone have implications for the local descent unit and for 'membership' of social categories. That aside, personal and social identification has become more diffused. Being an Aboriginal, although it still rests on traditional identifications, also involves other factors.

Nevertheless, in spite of intrusive elements, the actuality of traditionally-oriented Aboriginal life is something which can be appreciated only (1) by a person born into it; and (2), in a different way, by an anthropologist. There is, of course, no substitute for first-hand experience, and we should not pretend that there is. The matter of feeling, of being in it, and of commitment to specific ways of thinking and living are qualities which cannot be simulated —not without parody. On the other hand, an anthropologist, through his research, should ideally come close to this. In one respect he goes beyond it, since his analysis of socio-cultural and psychological materials provides him with an interpretative frame which gives him an opportunity to understand and explain the phenomena he observes, in social scientific terms. This is true whether the society is Aboriginal or non-Aboriginal. These are differing levels of social awareness. There are, too, different levels of explanation, and Aborigines in their traditionally-oriented situation sought explanation mainly in mythic terms. So that, if a distinction can be drawn between these two approaches, the first may be said to be concerned with 'living within' and the other with 'understanding about'. These two should not be confused, although they often are. In certain circumstances they can be combined, but usually they are not.

B. The non-traditional focus

The 'reality' of traditional Aboriginal life, then, has to do with first-hand experience within it, and with particular kinds of identification. It was and is a unique situation, which cannot be merely assumed by someone outside the system. Further, as traditional ties are modified or broken and new ones are included, the position as it existed before cannot be re-created. There is no archaic memory which can make this possible for a person of Aboriginal descent or otherwise. The hard facts of socialisation within the traditional system *per se* are the only processes which are available for knowledge and feeling to be transmitted in that respect. Nevertheless, it is possible to have a particular perspective based on what is assumed to be an Aboriginal way of life—that is, to have an idea or vision of it. Whether we think of this as a 'mirage' or not is really beside the point. Certainly it is a mirage in relation to traditional Aboriginal life as it existed in the past or continues to exist today in some regions. But as a viable view, believed in by those who wish to believe in it, it has a reality of its own.

No assessment has yet been made of the actual number of Aborigines who may be regarded as being traditionally-oriented; there are inherent difficulties in making such an assessment. Nevertheless it is quite clear that (a), those who have been organised along traditional lines are becoming much less so; and (b), by far the greater number of persons who are now labelled 'Aboriginal' are not Aboriginal in this traditional sense.

The traumatic history of Aboriginal-European contact throughout this continent, with few exceptions, left in its wake small aggregations of people identified as being of Aboriginal descent. In some cases, these were small collections of persons acknowledging kin ties and common interests; in other cases, they were mixed-origin communities; and in others again, they were scattered through the wider Australian society, some of them merged within it. Those who were visible, visible *as Aborigines*, and who continued to be categorised as 'Aboriginal' by themselves and by others, remained locally anchored (in spite of trends toward seasonal mobility)—without opportunities and without an inclination to unite, to band together or to form an over-arching collective identity. Policies, official and unofficial, came and went: the people remained, diffused, almost atomistic. The reasons for this are to be found (a), in the nature of traditional Aboriginal aspects which survived, in a modified or even a distorted form, and (b), in the kind of contact they were subjected to over the years. These two orientations were sufficient to provide a layer of resistance. What happened in the past in so far as they were concerned, with its wastage of human life and aspiration, did at least enable small pockets of persons of Aboriginal descent to survive into the present, possessed of characteristics which marked them off from traditional Aborigines and from non-Aborigines. Whether this was a good or bad thing is not the issue. The fact remains that this is what took place. That they should have survived in this way, implies a measure of self-identity on their part, which was reinforced by feelings of insecurity. The issue is, how did this collective sense of identity take shape, what did it specifically involve, and to what extent was it significant?

We know a great deal about the history of Aboriginal-European contact, and the disastrous consequences for those on the receiving end—socially dispersed, culturally deprived, and relegated to the lowest rungs of the socio-economic ladder(s) in the wider Australian society. Along with this went indifferent or minimal educational opportunities. They were reduced from independence to dependence, subjugated to a dominant and politically powerful society. Descriptive accounts are explicit on all these points. There is less information on the actual mechanisms that led to this: how they functioned and developed their own patterns, in contradistinction to those of other members of the wider society.

Present government policies assume differences between Aborigines and other Australians, when the bases of those differences have been only partly explored; they assume that a stabilised economy with an acquisition of skills and a modicum of education can overcome immediately years of deprivation on virtually all social fronts; and they assume that rapid change is an essential feature, without any real awareness of the heritage of the past. They also assume a number of other things associated with the retention of aspects of traditional Aboriginal life, its cultures and its languages, as being relevant to all persons of Aboriginal descent and to all Australians.

It is not my purpose to be over-critical of a relatively liberal (small 'l') Aboriginal policy. And it is obvious that I cannot deal with all these problems here, even in summary. However, I suggest that two issues are undervalued. One is the importance of systematic research, and the other relates to the will of the people (Aboriginal people). As regards the first, there is no need for me to spell out the prevalence of slipshod and short-range research projects carried out by (for example) commercial consultant firms and/or by inadequately trained or inadequately prepared social scientists who have little first-hand experience in the field of Aboriginal studies. The second issue is crucial in a different way. I do not suppose that all persons who recognise Aboriginal identity are all *the same*: that because of that assumed identity, all are automatically in a position to know what is needed for themselves and for others who are Aborigines. We have enough experience in Australian-European society to realise that people, generally, are quite ignorant and uninformed in this respect. 'Aborigines' (using this label generally) require more than their own localistic opinions, more than governmental pre-digested directions. They require research results which specifically point out the alternative implications of different kinds of action which may or may not be recommended. It is for them to choose what course of action should be taken—but in full, or reasonably full, knowledge and understanding of the implications. That, ideally, is the real force of informed decision-making, which depends on research and not on personal opinion or on political expediency.

Be this as it may, and to return to my main theme. As I said before, although some Aborigines are still traditionally-oriented, many others are very far indeed from that kind of perspective. The gradual and not-so-gradual disappearance of traditional life as a living reality left them insecure—unsure of themselves as persons and as members of a group (or groups). Networks of social relations, often articulated in terms of kinship, continued to be significant, but the associated behavioural patterns were less pressing. And those groups which did emerge were defined, not so much in terms of common action and of descent, but rather in an acknowledgement of shared experiences within contact situations, where hostile pressures blocked personal and group initiative—except in relation to alien-approved forms. They became more and more dependent on the wider society, but simultaneously cut off from the main stream of that society. It was not so much that they were 'in between'. On the contrary, most Australian-Europeans classified them together with traditional Aborigines, with whom they had few ties; and they had limited social access to those (other Australians) to whom they had become increasingly similar—culturally, if not socially. This meant that their identification continued to have a traditional Aboriginal slant or flavour, and that they constituted an 'Aboriginal' sub-group. This sub-group contained elements primarily European in origin. However, these were arranged in a particular way which suggested that they were put to different uses and patterned in rather different ways.

That patterning, as I have said elsewhere, depended on there having been an Aboriginal past—the fact that linkages of some sort, which could be traced to that background, were still acknowledged—and on the conditions that their immediate forbears had experienced. These two aspects affected nearly all areas of living: socialisation, marriage and family life, education, socio-economic conditions, and attitudes toward the law etc. What was taking place (not just in this context, but also among traditionally-oriented Aborigines) was an Aboriginalisation of certain aspects of the wider Australian society and culture, moulded to fit into their own frames of reference. These patterns were reinforced by pressures from the outside, and by feelings of insecurity on the part of those within. This structure has continued into the present day, but with one major difference.

Changes in state and federal Aboriginal-policies over the last few years have provided opportunities for greater communication between what were, in the immediate past, mixed local groups. It became possible for Aborigines to identify common experiences and to broaden their frame of action. It also meant that spatial mobility was increased, and that the artificial boundaries which had been maintained for a long period were at last broken down. That is the position today: and it is symbolised by the National Aboriginal Congress and other national Aboriginal organisations.

However, the gap between these 'Aborigines' and those others who are still traditionally focused has not been adequately bridged—in spite of formal statements to the contrary. A major difference between them rests on the contrast between insecurity and security, between differing experiences of alien contact, in the past as well as in the present. It is true that all Aborigines have experienced alien contact to some degree. But over the years that contact has varied. Some Aborigines have, until quite recently, been 'protected' from its more corrosive manifestations. However, for many this was not humanly possible. This resulted in many localised groups of Aborigines, each with its own regional focus, and consequently, in many different identities—derived from the Aboriginal past and also from their own unique experience of contact with outsiders. This contact, traumatic, oppressive, and often disastrous, became part of their identity. Although they were socially and culturally far removed from traditional Aborigines, they were identified by those outside as 'Aborigines'—but in a negative, not a positive sense. Internal identity involved commitment to particular behavioural patterns which were essentially composite: and what they themselves identified as 'Aboriginal' was little more than a shell of what was so identified even a few decades ago, with the contents of that shell made up of something quite different.

Communication between these various local groups or local 'worlds' of this kind is beginning to replace them with one world defined in terms of pan-Aboriginality. With this has come the forging of a common Aboriginal identity that is seen as being relevant to common political action, and can be used as a rallying point to mark off those so identified from members of the wider Australian society.

C. The Aboriginal heritage

The bringing together of a wide range of local perspectives in order to weld these into some kind of commonalty, is essentially a contrived task—and it is no less contrived for being motivated by political aspirations, or being haphazardly advocated. However, it is generally accepted by people of Aboriginal descent that emotional stability can be achieved only through acknowledgement of a common set of experiences that differ from those of other Australians. Further, a significant factor here is the crucial issue of re-evaluating Aboriginal society and culture. That exercise is not an easy one. Most of those who are active in advocating a greater appreciation of past and present traditional Aboriginal life have little first-hand knowledge of it; and those who do have such knowledge, the traditionally-oriented Aborigines themselves, have little wish to share its essential substance with others, even though those others may be classified as 'Aborigines'.

But 'sharing in' involves participation and commitment, and it is not really these which are normally desired by those who advocate Aboriginality. Their concern is really for recognition of the significance of traditional society and culture for all Australians, including themselves. In the past, Aboriginal life was considered 'primitive', with little to offer the sophisticated. That view has changed drastically, mainly because of the writings of anthropologists. Today, a large part of emergent Aboriginal identity is based on selection of traditional elements that can be used in the contemporary scene. This is where difficulties arise. For one thing, it is an idea or vision of traditional life which is required, not its reality—a kind of digest or telescoping of the many different traditional societies and cultures into a generalised and abstract frame, focused on specific elements in contrast to others. If this is regarded as important, and there is every indication that it is, then it is helpful here to turn to anthropologists.

Anthropologists who have specialised in Aboriginal studies have in mind not only the canons of their own discipline but also the welfare of the people with whom they work. I do not want to go into details about what they do and the uses to which the material they collect and analyse is put. However, the direct relevance of their studies to Aborigines is not always appreciated. Perhaps this is because almost anyone who has a passing association with an Aboriginal or collects any information at all about Aborigines is regarded as an 'anthropologist' by members of the general public, and by the news media. Aborigines are, therefore, not always in a position to separate out the 'sheep' from the 'goats'. Perhaps, too, this is because professional anthropologists usually couch their writings in ways which are not readily usable by or explicable to non-anthropologists—although there are some well-known exceptions.

Increasingly, social anthropologists are concerned about the practical relevance of their research. But, between them and its application stand intermediaries who are neither anthropologists, nor anthropologically-oriented. The 'new' anthropological perspective is really only a re-emphasis of an older one. In short, it rests on systematic and professional research. There is a need for anthropologists to consider the practical implications of specific problems which emerge from fieldwork, and, in their recommendations, to ensure that these are mediated through the people themselves: that the choices between alternative forms of action and the decisions relevant to them should be made by Aborigines themselves—particular Aborigines, those actually involved in the situations studied. Administration machinery and officials, which in the past and even today have stood between anthropologists and Aborigines, should be subordinated to their functional role— that of activating *after* research has been carried out and *after* decisions have been made by Aborigines. Anthropologists have, through the very nature of their work, built up close ties between themselves and the people with whom they have worked. In their research, Aborigines have always been directly involved. In a sense, an anthropologist has been a kind of human machine into which Aborigines have fed information. His training enables him to process that information and, ideally, to put it together into meaningful patterns which can provide explanations to specific questions, that are not answerable simply at the level of raw information. And to repeat, for anthropologists who have had a continuing interest in Aboriginal Australia, welfare considerations have been no less significant than 'straight' research.

I mentioned the importance of Aborigines themselves making choices from a range of alternative possibilities presented by anthropologists. In order to evaluate the material and come to a decision, it is important that Aboriginal people should be better acquainted with anthropological and social scientific procedures. This, in turn, means that more need to be trained in those terms, and that social scientists themselves will have to spell out their recommendations and so forth in a more direct and understandable style. It seems to me that this is the only way, if informed decisions are to be made by Aborigines and if administrative or bureaucratic structures are to be relegated to their proper place in the scheme of things.

More specifically in relation to the main theme of this paper, Aboriginal identity in a traditional sense was something which was accepted unconditionally and which involved religious commitment. It could not be assumed or discarded at will: it was irrevocable. With increasing alien contact, demolishing or forcing changes in traditional Aboriginal structures and belief systems, an identity based on religion was diffused to become more directly associated with a generalised way of life. We could call this the secularisation of social identity. In consequence, the edges or boundaries between communities became less conspicuous. Social interaction spread over a wider area, among people who were now regarded as having a broadly similar if not identical life style, and with whom it was possible to identify on that basis.

This 'openness'—or trend toward acknowledging a traditionally-based 'sameness'—is rapidly gaining ground. It is a unifying process, which in one sense is a political necessity. But it is also, and not necessarily by design, a *levelling* process. And this aspect cannot easily be checked. Too many influences are contributing to it. Apart from the steady stream of various official visits to such 'traditional' areas, there are the expansion of educational facilities; the mounting of government projects of an economic nature; the formation of 'village' councils; the impingement of mining and other activities; the formalisation of land rights; and the activities of, for example, the Aboriginal Arts Board in encouraging local arts and crafts and the Northern Territory Theatre Foundation in assembling dancers and singers for professional performances within and outside their own indigenous regions. These forces, and others, even where they intend the exact opposite, have modified or destroyed large sections of traditional life, which cannot be recaptured. Never before, in the whole history of Aboriginal-European contact, has change been effected so rapidly and with such far-reaching results. And this has taken place within a general climate of interest in traditional Aboriginal culture, and—more recently—in a wish on the part of Australians generally and Aborigines particularly to retain and sustain that life, or at least some aspects of it. However, although these changes cannot be deflected (without asking whether they should be), it is the task of anthropologists to help traditionally-oriented Aborigines to become more aware of what is happening and to provide them with 'know-how' which could conceivably aid them in deciding, if they wished, to slow down that process and what could be done about it.

While social identity at the traditional level is expanding or contracting, depending on the view we take, other (non-traditionally-based) populations have been coalescing to form an embracing concept of Aboriginality, which has as its central theme an identity composed of two features.

Firstly, southern Aborigines are especially interested in their traditional Aboriginal antecedents. That background was, as I have noted, downgraded in the past. Such a response in the present follows as a natural reaction to what has gone on before. That this should be at the expense of their European or non-Aboriginal heritage is not significant, because it is the Aboriginal and not the European heritage which will provide the distinctiveness they are searching for. However, the Aboriginal background has virtually been obliterated or has survived only in modified forms. Therefore, it has to be re-created. So far, that re-construction has been unsystematic. It is impossible to restore the totality of traditional Aboriginal life as a living reality or for those involved to return to it, even if they wanted to do so. What *is* possible, is the nurturing of a general idea of traditional Aboriginal life at two levels: (a) in terms of social relations, developing social links with all who claim to be Aborigines, and (b) selecting aspects of traditional or quasi- or pseudo-traditional Aboriginal culture which might respond to being re-vamped and placed within a different context. Not all traditional aspects are so transferable. One aspect which is not, and which is (incidentally) basic to the Aboriginal heritage, is Aboriginal religion—namely, its sacred, and especially its secret-sacred dimension. That dimension was and still is crucial to traditional Aboriginal identity—but not outside the area of personal-social commitment. In such circumstances, for those who have lost that vital traditional linkage, that encompassing sphere remains elusive—a mirage which is not amenable to transmutation.

Nevertheless, there is much of generalised traditional Aboriginal culture that is transferable. In this respect, more use could be made of anthropological studies. Without such studies virtually nothing would be known of a large number of traditional Aboriginal cultures and societies. Anthropologists have been the only non-Aboriginal persons who have seriously and consistently taken Aboriginal life into account, not with a view to change or conversion but as something worthwhile in itself, in its own right. Anthropological studies are therefore significant in helping to establish a tangible system of values and concepts which together could add up to contemporary 'Aboriginal' identification.

Secondly, present-day identity does not rest solely on the first point, which may stem from what can be called 'traditional Aboriginal'. Equally important, is that part of the Aboriginal heritage which is derived from the long and painful process of Aboriginal-European contact. All persons of Aboriginal descent, either themselves or their immediate forbears, have been subject to prejudice, discrimination, maltreatment and misdirection, among other things. The shadow of that past, and of the near-present, has not been eradicated. Further, it was in that context that emergence into an entirely different situation took place. It is part of the history of Aboriginal people, as it is of other Australians, and not something that can be shrugged aside or forgotten. The experiences of the past have implications for the present and for the future. They are part of an Aboriginal heritage which in that respect is just as significant, just as vital, as traditional Aboriginal life. In fact, it is much closer to most persons of Aboriginal descent. This consideration should be made to work positively: not as an ever-bleeding wound which remains unhealed, but as a body of information and knowledge which epitomises the Aboriginal struggle against often insurmountable odds, toward equality (social, economic and political) and, importantly, toward emotional security.

It is in the fusing of these two facets that the *real* Aboriginal identity of today may be forged: not as a figment of the imagination, but as something which has a real basis, which has (or could have) a purpose, and which has meaning for all of the people concerned,.

The 'new' Anthropology of which I have spoken can—through the medium of the Australian Institute of Aboriginal Studies and other research institutions where professional Anthropology has some standing—serve appreciably in transforming that vision into a reality, and can dissipate the present mirage by helping to replace it with a more substantial and meaningful image.

2 Two laws in one community

Kenneth Maddock

Aborigines on the Beswick Reserve in the Northern Territory, certain of whose modern political concepts I wish to discuss, live after the manner neither of their ancestors nor of the white people. The understanding of their way of life is to found in the changeable meaning and relation of what they distinguish as 'blackfellow law' and 'whitefellow law', terms that may tentatively be taken to refer to the native Aboriginal and introduced British cultures respectively.

A blackfellow (*biji*) is a person of Aboriginal descent and blackfellow law is the body of law or lore transmitted to the present from the Aboriginal past: most of it is said to have originated in The Dreaming. A whitefellow (*munanga*) is a person of European descent and whitefellow law is the body of law or lore associated with people like him. In addition to black- and whitefellows, there are yellowfellows, but although these terms, and also black- and whitefellow law, are in common use, I cannot recall ever having heard of yellowfellow law. A yellowfellow is a person of Asian, usually Chinese, or of mixed Aboriginal and non-Aboriginal descent.

Some part-Aboriginal yellowfellows have been brought up in the black-fellow camps and are to all intents and purposes blackfellows themselves: they are thought of as within the pale of blackfellow law and, if male, are admitted in the usual way to religious cults; I am unaware of Aboriginal prejudice against them on account of their mixed ancestry. I know also of one or two part-Aboriginal yellowfellows who are accepted as within the pale even though they do not share camp life and belong occupationally and economically among whitefellows; they are accepted because they take part in ceremonies. The part-Aboriginal yellowfellow who shares neither the camp nor the ceremonial life of blackfellows is apt to be looked upon with disfavour and to be, at least behind his back, the target of prejudiced utterances, for example that he is like a dog. This dislike seems not to extend to Asians. The impression conveyed by the admittedly infrequent allusions to them is that they are harmless people, well-disposed to blackfellows and purveyors of such good things as curry and, in the old days, opium.

The Aborigines on the Reserve, then, conceptualise in colour their social universe. People are black or white or yellow and these descriptive terms form an idiomatic Aboriginal way of talking about race or race difference. But the social universe is conceptualised more abstractly as including also the possibility of adherence to a rule-bound way of life. People may follow blackfellow or whitefellow law or live instead like dogs and by using these expressions Aborigines are able to talk about culture or culture difference.

13

Australia is a country—South Africa and New Zealand are others—in which race differences and culture differences often coincide. The Aborigines about whom I am writing obviously are aware of these coincidences in their social universe, but they do not suppose that race determines culture. This is shown by their wish to master whitefellow law while keeping blackfellow law; by their recognition that a few Aborigines have gone, or would like to go, the 'whitefellow way', which means living in accord with whitefellow law and giving up blackfellow law; and by their recognition that it is possible to finish up leading a life without law. Thus colour and law, race and culture, are independent terms that can stand in more than one relationship to each other, even though, until recently, one colour was paired with one law and another colour with another law.

It may be wondered why part-Aboriginal yellowfellows living outside blackfellow law are not accepted as having their own law. They do behave and they do possess things. Does not all this qualify them for recognition as having a way of life, a culture, a law? The answer, I think, can only be that the concept of law is used prescriptively as well as descriptively, that as well as asserting regularities of behaviour it asserts that they are good to follow and ought to be followed. Blackfellow law has this value by virtue of its connection with The Dreaming and the world-creative powers who then shaped nature and culture; whitefellow law by virtue of the power and ingenuity with which it endows its followers. And each law has its mysteries that must be learned. Obviously one cannot say that part-Aboriginal yellowfellows in the north of the Northern Territory have a law comparable to those of black- and whitefellows; accordingly there is nothing to value in their ways.

Thus the situation on the Reserve is that two cultures associated historically with two races, are co-present. Their relation is felt, here as apparently everywhere else in Australia, to be a problem crying out for a solution. Australia is anything but unusual in this. Why else concepts like integration and biculturalism in New Zealand or *apartheid* in South Africa? Notice that these notions, too, are prescriptive as well as descriptive: just as much as the assimilation and two-laws concepts do they point to a state of affairs that might or might not exist (assuming that the terms are exact enough for this to be investigated) *and* that it would be desirable to bring about or keep in existence or prevent from existing.

The strain arising out of the co-presence of two cultures understandably bears more acutely upon Aborigines. Blackfellow law is part of them and its decay or loss would be change in them, a disorientation calling for the working out of a new view of things, while whitefellow law, too, has been taken to heart, even though, as Aborigines readily admit, they understand it imperfectly. For their part whites undoubtedly find the relation problematical. That reserves exist at all proves that once upon a time a problem was felt and a solution worked out. Both have changed while reservations have remained to be in their turn experienced as a problem in need of a solution.

In the period of the Reserve the white Australian solution to the first problem, that of the co-presence of two cultures, has been most often expressed as one of assimilation. The end of this policy was to end all that is culturally Aboriginal. Aborigines, by contrast, never seem to have felt that the two were mutually incompatible. Again and again I heard people say they wanted to keep blackfellow law and learn whitefellow law. Clearly, whites and Aborigines have had different problems; equally clearly, the conception that each people has had of its own mission has made difficulties for the other. While the staff of the Welfare Branch worked in the direction of weakening and expunging Aboriginal culture, the Aborigines thought to keep their hold on the old law and to get a hold on the new.[1]

What I propose to do in this paper, which is offered as a contribution to the understanding of Aboriginal political thought, is to look first at the historical past of the Reserve, secondly at the kind of life lived on it by Aborigines, thirdly at the nature of the relation between the two laws, and finally at the bearing of the two-laws concept on concepts formulated elsewhere about the relation between persons of different race and culture.

History of the Beswick Reserve

The Reserve, this scene of concepts in conflict, covers 3405 square kilometres (1315 square miles). Much is rolling savannah country well suited to cattle rearing. The greater part, known then as Beswick Station, was bought in 1947 by the Commonwealth Government to be used in giving pastoral training to Aborigines. Pieces of Mataranka and Veldt Stations later were added. In 1953 the whole was gazetted as an Aboriginal Reserve.

The Reserve has two centres of population. Bamyili, formerly Beswick Creek, Settlement was founded in 1951 to replace Tandandjal Compound, a few miles to its east, which had been condemned as unhealthy. Tandandjal itself had been set up in 1948 to take the people from King River Compound, the abandonment of which had been made desirable by water shortages and fever outbreaks. King River Compound dated from 1945. It had superseded a settlement at Maranboy, a tin field that had been in disuse for some years before my first arrival in the area, but that had in its heyday before the Second World War supported a large Aboriginal population. Maranboy has a police station (there is none on the Reserve) and until the late 1960s a sawmill operated. The handful of whites and Aborigines at these two establishments were the Reserve's nearest neighbours. The official objectives of this series of settlements were to control Aborigines and, increasingly after 1951, to prepare them for entry into the general economy. The former objective comes out clearly in the description of Maranboy Settlement's purposes and effects in the Northern Territory Administration's *Annual Report* (1945/46:27):

> . . . controlling drift of natives from Arnhem Land Reserve to town and military centres along the North-South road . . . preventing contact of natives with miners and Australian Works Council camps in the Maranboy district . . . as a dispersal depot for natives when they were discharged from Army native settlements at Larimah, Mataranka and Katherine.
>
> Before the War no supervised depot existed in this area and abuses of native employment and undeterred drift to town centres were rife. At Katherine uncontrolled native elements were addicted to opium and methylated spirits drinking and undesirable contact with Europeans was rampant. These abuses have been entirely eliminated by the establishment of this depot.

The War had seen the first introduction for these southern Arnhem Land Aborigines of the sedentary life in government institutions that has continued to the present day. The Army set up camps and put noncommisioned officers in charge. Morris (1965:3) says that these camps were:

> . . . partly to enable effective Army control of the nomadic Aboriginal population in the area and partly to ensure that the Aborigines could be given healthy living conditions and proper medical care, which was otherwise difficult under wartime conditions . . . the Aborigines . . . were employed by the Army and did useful work.[2]

Beswick Station is the only other population centre on the Reserve. The Station's core is the homestead of the pastoral property the government bought in 1947. It is from here that cattle raising on the Reserve is managed.

The Register of Wards, a document published on 13 May 1957, showed Bamyili (as it now is) to have 282 Aborigines belonging to twenty-four 'tribes'[3] and Beswick Station to have 53 belonging to ten 'tribes', three of which were unrepresented at the Settlement. Since then the population has grown to more than five hundred. I am unaware of any estimate as to the pre-European population densities in this area, but it may be doubted that the 3405 square kilometres (1315 square miles) of the Reserve would have supported more than the present number.[4]

Allowing for a steady trend upward because of an excess of births over deaths, the population changes also through the restlessness of its members. It is rare for anyone to take up life in the bush, even for a few days, but there is much coming and going between the Reserve and cattle stations (especially to the south and east), towns (especially Katherine), Christian missions (especially Oenpelli and Ngukurr, as it now is, when it was one) and government settlements (especially Maningrida and Ngukurr). People travel usually by road and in motor vehicles driven by whites, though occasionally they walk through the bush. Aboriginal-owned cars have too short a life to do much to satisfy people's craving for transport.

I did not ever stay longer than overnight at Beswick Station, where the population is not only smaller than at Bamyili but more active in productive work. The account which follows refers accordingly to the Settlement. There the Aborigines are numerous enough to carry out even the largest traditional activities, namely religious ceremonies, on their own.

Everyday life on the Beswick Reserve

A visitor to the Settlement might easily form the impression that its population is divided into two parts, one of which is decidedly superior to the other. As one enters Bamyili from the west, the direction in which one sets out to reach the towns of Katherine and Mataranka or the more nearby Maranboy, one discovers that it is bisected by a road that used to be part of the highway running east to Beswick, Mountain Valley and Mainoru Stations (nowadays the highway passes a little to the north of the Settlement). North of this road houses of suburban type occupied by Welfare Branch staff and their families are set pleasantly amid gardens and trees. These buildings have two or three bedrooms and are supplied with electricity, generated on the Settlement, and running water, pumped from a nearby spring. Two houses answering to this description recently were built just south of the road.

The Aboriginal 'village', as the local whites call it, is south of the road and presents a dreary contrast to the residential quarters on the other side. Here the dwellings stand close together in rows laid out on level ground which by now is largely devoid of trees and grass. Most have one room, a concrete floor and unlined walls and roof of corrugated metal. A few three-roomed houses are enlargements of the one-roomed variety. At any time there are likely also to be a few humpies occupied by people for whom there are no permanent dwellings. None of the Aboriginal houses has electricity and only the expanded ones have running water or washing and toilet facilities. The occupants of all the rest must use communal taps, laundries and latrines. During most of the year domestic life is conducted in the small yards of the dwellings, often around a fire, for people are disinclined to move indoors unless it is cold or rainy. Except for the few who own beds, people sleep on the ground in their 'swags' (ground sheet and blankets). They rarely cook for themselves as meals are provided from a communal kitchen, though sometimes game is caught and cooked and often a billy is boiled for tea.

Service and administrative buildings, including a communal kitchen and diningroom where three meals a day are served, workshops, store, canteen, office, hospital and school, cluster about the western end of the road. They form in effect a zone between the two residential quarters. The two sorts of resident do most of their interacting in this zone during working, school and canteen hours. They seldom associate outside those times, though certainly there is no official barrier to closer relations. What Long (1964:80) has said about Papunya, a settlement in central Australia, applies also to Bamyili:

> In the settlement situation today the white community is large enough for its members to keep for the most part to themselves and they are inclined to maintain social distance between themselves and the native community.

To this may be added that whites and blacks have little in common so that, even were 'snobbery' missing, they could be expected to keep to themselves much of the time. Thoreau remarked disparagingly of the new telegraph line from Maine to Texas that as far as he knew Maine and Texas had nothing to say to each other: one is tempted to remark the same of black- and whitefellows on the Beswick Reserve. Snobbery and the wish to maintain distance are, in any case, by no means to be found only on the white side. Cult performers like to invite a new superintendent to view some of their secret rites, but draw the line at less important members of staff. Men told me how much they disliked having staff walking about the village at night.

Thus, in this spot of Anglicised landscape set remotely in the Australian bush, a social pattern manifests itself spatially with a clarity of outline as sharp as that recorded by Howitt in the traditional encampments of the Wotjobaluk. What is ordered is different, for no longer is it a matter of moieties composed of clans, but the organisation remains dual and still, perhaps coincidentally, orients itself according to the east-west axis so that, as Durkheim and Mauss (1903:51) remarked of Howitt's data, one has 'une phratrie du Nord et une phratrie du Midi'.

Although the Settlement population is racially divided, with blackfellows in the south and whitefellows in the north, probably it is sounder to think of the spatial dualism as complementary opposition in social function than as race discrimination. To the south live those whose function it is to be administered. To the north live those whose function it is to administer. The social distinction is, of course, correlated with a racial distinction, but not exactly, because sometimes it happens that people are to be found dwelling in one residential quarter who in appearance are more like those in the other. Two white men who were on the staff during some of my stays had part-Aboriginal wives and for a while the staff included an Aboriginal. The latter, together with his family, was put in a large but old and dilapidated house hard by the mechanical workshop, that is to say, in the zone separating the two residential quarters. How appropriate for a marginal man![5] Some village children are so light in colour that in different circumstances they could pass for white.

While living at the Settlement nearly all men and many women of working age are employed for cash and keep at various unskilled or semiskilled jobs, such as stockman, driver, domestic, gardener, farm or kitchen hand, labourer, hospital or mechanic's assistant. The work they do is anything but arduous. It is mainly by payment for these tasks, which includes subsidised meals, and social service benefits that the Aborigines subsist. Rarely does an Aboriginal seek employment outside the Reserve or an employer come to the Reserve in search of labour. Income from handicrafts is negligible, though occasionally a few bark paintings or other objects are sold, and now and again men visit Darwin or, once, Sydney, to perform 'corroboree dances' semi-professionally. I do not know the *per capita* income of working adults, but it may be presumed that, when allowance is made for meals and medical attention supplied free or at nominal charges, some men earn the basic wage or more. The larger a man's family of dependants the higher his real income, because they, too, are fed and receive medical care. Single and childless men are relatively the worst off, but I have never known a complaint on this score.

Meals are of British-Australian food prepared after a British-Australian manner. They are eaten collectively in a dining room attached to the kitchen: cooking and eating have thus been removed from the individual group and put in an 'institutionalised' setting. This is justified on the grounds that it makes for a balanced diet and gives Aborigines the chance to eat like white people. Game is relished, but forms only a small part of the diet, and is cooked and eaten away from the communal kitchen and diningroom. I doubt that anyone bothers to make special trips to collect plant foods, though they may be eaten by people who are out in the bush for other reasons.

People are clothed almost all the time whether on or off the Settlement. For men this means shirt and trousers, long or short, and for women a dress, with sometimes shoes or boots, a hat, pullover or jacket. It seems uncommon to wear underclothes. Only during corroborees and ceremonies is one likely to see a change, for then men like to put on the loincloth called *naga* and, especially in ceremonies, to paint their bodies. But even on these occasions some men will continue to wear their European clothes or will take off only so many of them as is needed to expose the parts of the body that are to be painted.

Some of the more noticeable recreations of the people patently are not of Aboriginal derivation. Each weekend after the fortnightly pay, which is given out on a Friday afternoon, the village is gripped in a frenzy of gambling with cards during which considerable amounts of money change hands. The stake sometimes consists of marbles, to which a money value is assigned, but seldom if ever of anything else. Since the removal in 1964 of the legal prohibition on supplying liquor to Aborigines listed, as nearly all were, as wards, some men have taken to spending pay weekend in town. Usually there is a rush to board the bus which arrives on Saturday mornings from Katherine especially for this purpose. Often a taxi will have come the evening before to pick up the really keen drinkers. By 1970 a wet canteen had been established to sell restricted amounts of beer, but I do not know whether this has led to a falling off of interest in town visits. Liquor may legally be drunk on Aboriginal Reserves only on premises in respect of which a permit has been issued. This regulation applies to dwellings and, as far as I know, permission has only once been granted for an Aboriginal-occupied house. The permit-holder was the man we have encountered already as a marginally-placed member of staff. Welfare Branch staff seem always to get a permit if they want one and so do visiting contractors. Apart from gambling and drinking many men like to play European sports, usually in a sporadic and unorganised way, though during the basketball season teams visit Katherine one night a week to compete against local sides.

The language most often used is English which here, as in Katherine and Mataranka, is the *lingua franca*. It is spoken with varying degrees of proficiency, sometimes excellently, and is the only language spoken by all Aborigines. Some speak no other. No Aboriginal tongue is spoken by more than a minority. English is the language of instruction in the schools at Bamyili and Beswick Station, which children of school age attend pretty regularly, and necessarily is used between Aborigines and white Australians. The breakdown of Aboriginal languages on the Settlement is due, I think, neither to these causes nor to official discouragement, but to the number of different tongues spoken by the people who have made the Reserve their home. None has a sufficient number of local speakers to be assured of a future as a living language and none looks like catching on as a *lingua franca*. It often happens that adults, even man and wife, must speak in English if they are to communicate with each other. Children growing up at Bamyili or in Katherine appear to learn English alone.

This account of accommodation, work, diet, recreation and the like may well have built up a picture of Aboriginal assumption of the forms of white Australian life, albeit at a poorer level and with less personal independence than is usual for others. These deficiencies might be seen as unfortunate but inevitable for a people in transition between two ways of life. Assimilation, after all, cannot be expected to happen overnight. A casual visitor to the Reserve might draw just these conclusions. If, however, he allowed his acquaintance with the Reserve to deepen he might come to distrust his first impressions and feel the need to revise his opinions. He could realise that he had failed to see, and therefore left out of account, the shaping influence of Aboriginal culture in some areas of life. This realisation would not, in itself, enable him to predict any outcome. The people on the Reserve are subject to the pull of competing models of conduct, the blackfellow and the white-fellow, but there is no way in which the strength of the pull might be measured.

Moreover, the future course of events will be affected profoundly by decisions over which Aborigines will have little control, deeply though they are interested in them. The issue of land rights is a case in point.

The persistence of Aboriginal culture is evident enough in speech and recreation. Aboriginal languages are spoken, though not exclusively. On many nights corroborees are sung, though less often danced. But it is true to say that, just as Aboriginal languages are giving way to English, Aboriginal forms of recreation fail to inspire the enthusiasm obvious among gamblers and drinkers. Less apparent is the ordering of personal relationships by norms of kin, clan and class. To show how these affect action would take too much space; here marriage and country may briefly be mentioned to suggest what is happening to Aboriginal culture.

It is usual for man and wife to belong to the classes between whose members marriage is licit and to have stood to each other before marriage as *gagali*, as the Dalabon say, or by its cognate or equivalent in other languages. *Gagali* may be translated as 'potential wife'; mother's mother's brother's daughter's daughter is as close a genealogical specification as you can get for it. These rules are constricting, in that they exclude as a man's partners most women in his social universe. They are not upheld positively by the white authorities, who indeed seem if anything to be ignorant of their existence, but rather are indirectly discouraged. For example, white authority has virtually put an end to the resort to violence in defence of personal rights and interests without substituting any means by which an Aboriginal can stand up against infringement and encroachment. Aborigines are under the impression that polygyny and early bestowal are opposed by the Welfare Branch. Thus the persisting preponderance of licit marriage must be due entirely to impelling forces springing from Aboriginal culture in spite of the unfavourable environment in which it now finds itself.[6] But marriage has not remained the same, for polygyny and infant bestowal are in an advanced state of decay and the age discrepancy between men and women at first marriage would seem to be less than it must have been when their ancestors were free from alien control. Women finish school before marrying and men in their twenties have wives younger than themselves.

Let us turn now to country. Most Aborigines on the Reserve live far from their clan's territory. Many younger adults have never seen 'their' country and when I visited the territories of clans around the Wilton River I found that reliable guides were middle-aged. Even some of them had trouble in finding their way to places they had earlier told me about. Nevertheless, people will testify unhesitatingly to their country's plenitude and desirability, they regard themselves as its true owners and are familiar, if only by hearsay, with its totemic geography. A young man on his first visit might know the order in which places follow one another, without being able to guide you to those places. Aborigines, then, are absent owners who remained tied spiritually and sentimentally to their land. But they are not tied to it in such a way that the use of other land is ruled out. Some of the people from what is now Arnhem Land Reserve wanted a cattle station to be established for them around the Bulman Waterhole—I put their request to the authorities in Canberra—and this, if ever actualised, would have taken them back into the country over which their ancestral clansmen must have ranged, but several of them hoped to see a tin mine opened on the Beswick Reserve itself. They thought to take the 'old people' there to live and to gouge enough ore to support a small community (many of the Bamyili men who now are in early middle age or older have experience on the Maranboy tin field); if this venture had been brought off they would have been exploiting not their own but other people's land. People are inclined to think of reserves as belonging to Aborigines and thus they were disturbed when they heard that the saw-millers at Maranboy were cutting timber in the Arnhem Land Reserve itself, but they think of themselves as having also special rights in their clan's territory *and* in Bamyili if they have been living there for a long time. The latter feeling of proprietorship can give rise to a verbal denial of rights to Aborigines regarded as outsiders: I recall that on one occasion after a disagreement over blackfellow law some men from the Arnhem Land Reserve long resident at Bamyili expressed to me the sentiment that people from the mission (as it then was) at Roper River should go back there if they wanted to follow another law. All these people, whether from the Arnhem Land Reserve or the Roper River, were immigrants to the Beswick Reserve, yet the former, simply by virtue of length of residence, felt they had superior rights at Bamyili.

That Aboriginal culture should have been worn away and changed in many of its parts is unsurprising in view of the long history of contact between black- and whitefellows in the area from which the Reserve has drawn most of its people.[7] Contact occurred as early as 1844 when Leichhardt made his journey from the Roper River to Darwin. He would have passed just to the east of the Reserve. More serious disturbances set in by the last quarter of the nineteenth century. Whites then were beginning to settle in the region, variously to mine, raise cattle, serve the government or engage in commerce. In response to these events, which both attracted Aborigines and disrupted some conditions of their former mode of existence, the parents and grand-parents of the present generation of young adults started to settle around whites. In the first years after the Second World War there were still some people who spent much time in the bush, but they could hardly be described as 'unchanged'. They paid frequent visits to missions like Oenpelli and Ngukurr, allegedly for tobacco, to stations like Mainoru and to the tin field at Maranboy. Most of the people now on the Reserve were born at white centres or were taken to them as children.

The effects of white settlement have, of course, been exacerbated by recent assimilationism. This has consciously set out to replace one way of life by another. When to these forces is added the language diversity to which the Register of Wards bears witness, it is to be wondered at how much of Aboriginal culture has survived in people's lives. A necessary saving factor has surely been that most people on the Reserve, despite belonging to different clans and speaking different languages, perform close variants of the same ceremonies and conceptualise social and cosmic relations in comparable ways. This majority, drawn from southern and central Arnhem Land, has kept alive much in its tradition. The minority, whose members are from as far afield as Darwin and Alice Springs, understandably has been less suc-cessful. Their ceremonies could not be performed locally, even if there were a will to it, simply for want of actors.

Problems in the relation between two laws

The Aborigines say they want to have both laws, that is they aspire neither to revert to a pre-European past nor to assimilate themselves in conformity to government policy. Whatever exactly they might mean, their thought is independent, for there is no precedent known to them for what they strive after. The staff live according to whitefellow law, which Aborigines understand poorly, and practically ignore blackfellow law. I have been asked by Aborigines how whites were able to have such large houses—they knew nothing of rent and this had to be explained to them—and whom whites had to marry—they seemed convinced that whites have a system of kin relationships comparable to their own (I do not think that I succeeded in convincing them to the contrary)—and how the electoral and parliamentary system worked—they could not understand why, if a local representative supported some measure, such as an advantage for Aborigines, it might nonetheless fail to become law. As for white understanding of Aboriginal culture, a staff member might own a recording of Aboriginal music or express himself sympathetically concerning Aboriginal religion, but this comes nowhere near adopting part of the outlook or way of behaving of the other culture. Aborigines, then, are on their own when they aspire to lead a life that somehow comprehends two laws and they cannot expect guidance from outside.

I have suggested that visitors to the Reserve would at first be impressed more by change than by continuity in Aboriginal life but that, as their familiarity with local conditions grew, so, too, would their appreciation of the force of blackfellow law. They might be tempted to conceive of whitefellow law as a veneer over the other, hiding it from view but not doing away with it. This conception, however, will not meet the Beswick situation. For one thing, some traditionally Aboriginal activities are apparent on the surface of life: speech and corroborees are examples. For another, some white-induced changes have sunk deep roots in Aboriginal conduct. The marriage alterations to which I referred are a case in point. It is improbable that they would be reversed even if Aborigines became much more independent: people do seem to accept the principle of one man one wife, even though polygyny is by no means outlawed, and to accept that men will marry while still young and that men and women will exercise choice in whom they marry. Bestowals are not a thing of the past, but evidently need to be 'ratified' by the consent of the prospective spouses.

Equally it is unsatisfactory to think of the two laws as having united in a new synthetic culture. Aborigines certainly do not think so; if they did, what point would there be in saying that you wish to keep one law and learn the other? Furthermore, some parts of life are referred to one law and some to the other: medicine, literacy, machinery and legal and parliamentary arrangements are part of whitefellow law; ceremonies and all of the lore associated with the countryside are part of blackfellow law. It looks from this as though Aborigines want to live in accord with two laws kept apart in thought and action.

The trouble with this wish is the comprehensiveness of each law. One or the other could exist by itself as a people's way of life. When the two are brought together it will inevitably be found that in many situations they dictate conflicting courses of action. On occasion the conflict might be resolved by appealing to a 'transcendant' criterion in the light of which both laws may be judged. Perhaps the criterion of efficiency is one such. Thus given a choice between a stone axe and a steel axe for chopping into a tree to get at a wild bees' nest the answer is given by the principle of least effort. I have never known stone axes to be used, so we may assume that this particular issue has long been settled. But the example is a bad one, because if people disagreed each could take his own way: one using a stone and the other a steel axe.

What of suppositions governing situations in which, if agreement fails, some impose their will on others? Consider, for example, the conflicting black- and whitefellow approaches to religious lore and ritual. Aborigines hedge the religious domain about with all sorts of restrictions and deceits the effect of which is to stop general access and knowledge. Men's cults have a secret core from which women and children are excluded and to which men normally are admitted only after a novitiate. Women's cults exclude men altogether. Among whites it is usual for religious knowledge to be open to all irrespective of age or sex. This difference undoubtedly is part of the more general opposition between local mystery cults and universal pro-selytising faiths. The understanding of death is another example: on the one hand it is presumed that sorcerers cause it and on the other that natural causes are at work. The former conflict is not a problem at present, because Aborigines at Bamyili know and care little about Christianity and are preoccupied with their own cults. The latter is not much of a problem, partly because white control has suppressed native legal and political processes wherever these include violence, and partly because whites have assumed responsibility for dealing with death. Sick people are treated by the Settlement's nursing sister and serious cases are sent to hospital in Katherine or Darwin. People who die in hospital are buried by the white authorities which leaves little for the bereaved to do except carry out post-mortuary ceremonies. But the question of causation remains and one can readily imagine that were people once again to accept responsibility for the dying and the dead they would have to pay more attention to causes of death. Their present opinion is that people can die from old age or from a tumour or heart trouble (all uncaused by human agency) but that most people die from sorcery. There seems no criterion for deciding whether a death falls within one class or the other, and it is obscure why sorcerers, who can cause road accidents, cannot cause tumours to grow or hearts to fail.

A conflict which might come up at once should the Bamyili people ever get their cattle station or tin mine, would arise from the tension between their traditional economic attitudes and the demands of capital maintenance and accumulation. I remember vividly a man's complaint that he was unwanted and unwelcome at a certain cattle station, despite the work he had put into its fences and stockyards. That work should be paid for once and for all seemed strange to him; he understood it to give rise to a lasting relationship entitling him to visit the station Aborigines whenever he and they pleased. Another told me that a white man, for whom he had agreed to break in horses at the rate of payment usual for white contractors, had paid him at half rates when the work was done. He explained his failure to take the matter up with the Welfare Branch (his official protector) by saying that perhaps the white man had run out of money and therefore it would have been mean to put pressure on him. These cases have it in common that, at least on the Aboriginal side, consideration for the wishes and circumstances of others is thought to flow from an economic relationship. This traditional attitude has been imported, to Aboriginal disadvantage, into dealings of a sort that would never have arisen traditionally. But it would be wrong to leave the impression that Aborigines are imbued with an outlook that is bound always to make them lose out: I have heard people comment contemptuously on the 'humbug' of a man whose failing was to be too assiduous and efficient in cleaning the latrines; and on another occasion a man obtained murmurs of assent when he said that whites who complained because he did not work 'lively' had better pay him a 'lively' wage.

Difficulties like these would not go away if the Aborigines formed, as many would like, a community living on its own land, but might be felt more acutely than ever before, if only because people would have to face their own problems and come to terms with competing models of conduct in a way they are spared while controlled by whites. There seems little point in speculating about how an independent community would resolve these puzzles of existence or whether its resolutions would be genuine or spurious. The point to be stressed is that the conflicts mentioned, and others like them, rule out a concord of laws unless one or the other is reformed.

The finding to which these observations lead may seem to be that Aboriginal life on the Reserve is an untidy jumble of bits from one culture and pieces from the other. This has some truth in it, yet it is not wholly acceptable because there are complicated activities organised by Aborigines themselves in which the two laws have been grafted together after a fashion. To show this I shall look at the ways in which the two laws (or cultures) have interacted in the religious domain to produce the Yabuduruwa and Gunabibi cults in their present form.

As far as I can make out, myths, rites and symbolic understandings belonging to these cults have not been modified to accommodate British religious notions or precedents. Even the wide experience the Aborigines have of things European seems not to have affected mythical and ritual imagery, in which respect the situation on the Reserve differs from that described by Worsley (1967:147-50) amongst the Groote Eylandt Wanindiljaugwa into whose 'totemic myth-complexes' borrowed images, such as flying boats, had entered by 1953. Obvious changes have been brought about by whitefellow law, but these, with the exception of language, are in timing of performances, in attachment between cult and other features of life, and in materials used.

Aborigines now perform their ceremonies as permitted by work, gambling and drinking, which means that weekdays and pay weekends are unavailable. It is true that during a Gunabibi some men may go into the bush to sing for a few hours at night, but only once have I known a rite to be danced on a week night. Because Gunabibi and Yabuduruwa performances require six or seven days at least to be devoted to ritual dancing, it is usual for them to stretch out over a period of two or more months. In the days before Aborigines became subject to labour demands, cult performances presumably would have ended much more quickly. Thus the Yabuduruwa Elkin (1961) saw in 1949 at Tandandjal Compound took only eight days, during which as many rites were danced as in the performances I saw.

My informants told me that during the 1950s Welfare Branch staff had stopped cult performances, but I was unable to discover whether this was because they were staged on work days or because the assimilation policy was construed to require religious repression. Berndt (1951:206) says that during the War the civil and military authorities tried to suppress the Gunabibi because it interrupted 'normal work'. Often, then, what Aborigines have wished to do with their time has conflicted with what whites have wished to do with Aboriginal labour power. White political and legal superiority, Aboriginal craving for introduced goods and the absence of a realistic way in which Aborigines might force their wishes to be taken into account, have led to the present situation in which cult performances are tolerated if they do not interfere with work.

Pre-conquest ceremonial life appears to have made for a heightened social life in which scattered groups came together to arrange marriages, settle disputes and exchange goods as well as hold ceremonies. Today on the Reserve the cults are celebrated by people who live together all the year round and outsiders, though welcome, are unnecessary. The other matters that used to be attended to at the great gatherings may now be dealt with at any time. Sedentary existence in large numbers at a white-controlled centre has thus detached the cults from other interests and responsibilities bound up with them in earlier days. Perhaps this local self-sufficiency, which is to be found also at other places, will stimulate diverging traditions, but I cannot think of any way in which to determine whether the rate of change has accelerated.

When adorning their bodies and making paraphernalia, men substitute some introduced materials for those formerly in use. Feathers and wild cotton have largely given way to kapok and cotton wool, hair string to manufactured string and the fat of animals killed in the hunt to butter and margarine. Paperbark sometimes is replaced by cardboard and pipeclay by flour. These substitutes may easily be had from the Bamyili kitchen or canteen or from shops in town. Their use makes for a labour saving that must be all the more appreciated in view of the pressure work, gambling and drinking put on ceremonial time.

Conceptual shifts brought about by the growing use of English in communication among Aborigines should also, I think, be allowed for. Thus the concept *bolung,* which I need not enter into here since I have examined it elsewhere (1970:444-6, 1972:120-25), informs all of Aboriginal religious thought, but it cannot be conveyed in a single English word or phrase without losing its peculiarly comprehensive and evocative cluster of meaning. Another interesting example is *molo,* which means tail and penis and is also the name of certain cult objects. There is reason to think that these objects derived an ambiguous significance from their uncertain reference, but this intellectual play is lost in English, though it would not be in German, which has *der Schwanz. Molo* is a restricted and down to earth concept compared to *bolung,* but the principle of change is the same in each case: the inability of Aborigines, at a time when their own languages are breaking down, to express key ideas integrally in English. Aboriginal thought accordingly is changing through translation into a foreign language, which is different from changing through acceptance of the ideas held by the foreign bearers of that language.

Changes of the sort described do not imperil the near future of the cults. Perhaps they do the more distant future, because already the connections between rites and the rest of social life have been weakened or severed and it is conceivable that this will make the cults, the core of which has always been clothed in secrecy, seem more and more alien to human concerns. Yet it is only fair to add that cult performances were recently in danger of cessation: that they managed to gather strength shows that at present the cults are satisfying real human concerns. The danger came from high mortality during the 1950s when most of the ritual activists died. Aborigines talking about that time will remark that ceremonies almost ended. The situation was not entirely hopeless, however, because younger men did succeed in taking over ceremonial initiative from their rapidly disappearing elders. Probably the position on the Reserve was never as bad as among the Murinbata a little earlier (Stanner 1963:251).

> The collapse of the old ritual life came about by a conjunction of three things: persistent pressure by the missionaries to put an end to all pagan ceremonies, the decay of the external structure of tribal life, and the onset of a general sophistication. But the process was a slow one. The older Murinbata condoned it, in the first place, from motives of expediency, not from loss of enthusiasm, although a decline of interest set in once the impairment of the external and internal structures—a progressive trend—had reached a certain stage. The pressures to bend before a new, single authority, against which there was no appeal, were too insistent to be resisted except by a common front for which the men had no genius. The value placed on European goods—of which there was no other source—weakened everyone's will. The flow of candidates for initiation dried up when all infant males were circumcised at the mission hospital and, as they came to a right age, were withheld from the other rites. The number of visitors fell off when, because of their interference with the work of the mission, they were made to feel unwelcome, and because the shrunken ceremonies were a disappointment.

Despite these dejecting circumstances, Stanner felt able to add:

> But, in my judgement, it would have been possible to revive the entire ritual complex as late as the early 1950's, since there were still alive a sufficient number of older men possessing both the secrets and the interest. After that time, many deaths occurred among the ritual leaders, and a new set of influences became ascendant.

Meggitt (1962:333) has conjectured that the assimilationist and welfare dispensation, by saving the Walbiri from having to collect their own food, enabled them to give more time 'to singing and dramatizing the dreamings, to gossiping and brawling, to love-making and match-making—activities dear to Walbiri hearts'. My evidence is that the big ceremonies have been celebrated more regularly and often since about 1960 than in the 1940s or 1950s. The Gunabibi and Yabuduruwa are both performed each year now, but I do not know how this compares with the frequency of performance when the forbears of the Beswick people lived free from white control.

On the Reserve, then, as amongst the Walbiri in their settlements to the south, we have an instance of what de Josselin de Jong (1972:97-106) discusses as 'paradoxen van cultuurcontact'. The paradox consists in this: that even where non-Western societies accept Western influence, the influence itself may call up forces that work against Westernisation. This effect may be unexpected, and perhaps unintended, by the native population. In some Australian instances, as de Josselin de Jong points out, Aborigines have been encouraged to settle down by holding out to them such material inducements as easy food. The object of the offer was to detach Aborigines from their traditional ways, but an effect of it has been to allow them more free time than before, thereby facilitating traditional religious observances. One might add to de Josselin de Jong's account that the remoteness of many missions and settlements, together with the desire of their administrators to control and restrict Aboriginal contacts with the population at large, has saved the inmates from the disintegration that has overtaken so many of their fellows in town.

The religious cults in their present form and content evidently owe much more to black- than whitefellow law. Marriage, however, would seem to show the influence of whitefellow law much more, since the predominance of monogamy and the tendency to accept a free choice of partner (albeit within the class and kin rules) have greatly altered the profile this institution used to show. Blackfellow law has been displaced almost entirely from the productive economy, since about the only traditional objects still made are those needed for corroborees or ceremonies. These examples show that it is impossible to draw up one formula to express the relation of black- and whitefellow law in all parts of life; they suggest also that when Aborigines speak of having both laws they really mean that they want some of one law and some of the other, too, without being able to say, in a general way, just what it is they want from each.

If I am right, the question arises of why Aborigines say they want both laws. My opinion is that two-laws talk is significant, not so much as a description of what life actually is like or as a clear conception of what life might be like, but as an affirmation of the dignity and value of Aborigines themselves and of their traditional culture. Aborigines will say that black- and white-fellows have differently coloured skins but the same blood and that without their law (the blackfellow) Aborigines would be nothing. These I interpret as idiomatic assertions of human equality and cultural value and of the need to remain in touch with one's past if one is to remain truly human (cf. the prejudice against yellowfellows). Two-laws talk is politically significant because it shows that Aborigines have taken stock of their relation to people of another race and culture, have the will to be consulted and taken into account and have the will to shape their future and community instead of leaving their future and community in the hands of others. The two-laws concept accordingly is profoundly opposed to the assimilation concept. It is important that the two-laws concept has been thought and expressed; it is less important that it has yet to be thought out clearly.

When seen from this perspective religious cults like the Gunabibi and Yabuduruwa turn out to be especially significant to the modern Aboriginal orientation. The only large activities Aborigines are able to organise without white interference, they must be deeply satisfying for people who have so often been meddled with. Always the most dramatic and comprehensive activities in Aboriginal culture, nothing else weaves together and symbolically manifests so many social and cosmic relationships. That the cults continue bears witness to the living force of blackfellow law; should they be abandoned the two-laws concept would lose its plausibility. Nooy-Palm's rhetorical prognosis, that 'In de Atoomtijd is geen plaats voor de Droomtijd' (1964:386), is thus just the reverse of the truth at the present time, for some Dreamtime phenomena are proving to be essential to Aboriginal self-thought and self-orientation.

A comparative perspective

I should like in closing to place the two-laws concept among the other concepts formulated to explicate relations between persons who differ in race and culture. An examination of some of these will show that Aborigines on the Beswick Reserve have contributed, unwitting and unheard, to a widely recognised problem.

The Australian concept of assimilation, which seems to have been given up now, envisaged the withering away of everything distinctively Aboriginal and the merging of black- and whitefellows in 'one people'. But all the cultural concessions were to have been on the black side, because the 'one people' were to be culturally white Australian. Australians abroad sometimes heard their country's policy likened to *apartheid*, but the comparison was absurd and stemmed from the ignorance of those making it. Assimilation and *apartheid* are diametrically different, since one calls for cultural uniformity, the other for cultural variety. There is no need, I think, to discuss assimilation further, because it is well-known, at least in this country, and has been criticised from divergent positions by eminent Australianists, for example by Stanner (1965), Rose (1962) and Hiatt (1961).

New Zealand discussion has tended in another direction. There, as in Australia, a racial minority native to the country has made many cultural borrowings from a racial majority of relatively recent immigrants and their descendants, but the majority has borrowed little from the minority. The majority, at least in academic discussion and political policy, does not, however, envisage the disappearance of the minority culture as something to be desired and engineered. This majority acceptance of two cultures evidently agrees with minority wishes. Thus Schwimmer (1966:148) speaks of 'the Maori preference for separateness in social life' and Harré (1968:129) of a Maori 'desire to keep their group racially and culturally distinct'.

Schwimmer accordingly has put forward the notion of biculturalism. He says (1968:14) that a bicultural person is one who owes primary allegiance to the culture he learned in childhood, but accepts, and is familiar with, the values of a second culture. Most Maoris are bicultural. To be bicultural you must be able consciously to confront and reconcile the two systems of values. This is necessary because he who is familiar with a second culture often finds himself in situations where he must choose between alternative actions, each of which is correct in one culture.

Another concept used in New Zealand is integration. This means different things to different people: in the influential Hunn Report (1961:15) it means 'To combine (not fuse) the Maori and pakeha elements to form one nation wherein Maori culture remains distinct', but to Piddington (1968:260) it is a confused term and its users probably have assimilation uppermost in their minds. Furthermore, people differ in their evaluation of integration and biculturalism. Oppenheim (1973:35-6) thinks that policy-makers should aim at equality and not worry about things like integration and biculturalism, but he raises the possibility that ethnic culture may come to be seen as a mark of an educated person rather than as a sign of rural lack of sophistication. If this is to happen it will be necessary, he thinks, for Maori intellectuals to give more time to articulating the critical points of their culture and world view and less time to sentimentalising about them. The first condition such an ethnic culture will have to satisfy is the ability of its most visible parts to stand up to the same critical norms as are applied to other cultures. A second condition is that it must not restrict the middle-class person who lives by the majority norms. Piddington (1968) pleads for 'emergent development', by which he means the positive and spontaneous emergence of new types of social institution within cultures undergoing change. Elements from both cultures are combined in these developments and any explicit ideology that may be formulated with reference to them envisages neither reversion to pre-European practice nor assimilation to the politically and economically dominant European culture.

I suspect that many Aborigines would find concepts like biculturalism and emergent development attractive. Even the people of the Beswick Reserve, all of whom suffer from 'rural lack of sophistication' when it comes to whitefellow law, have a biculturalist's appreciation of the different answers given by the two cultures to frequently occurring problems. The sorts of movement I have elsewhere described (1972:1-20) are attempts at emergent development. But let us turn to South Africa.

Apartheid is a Dutch and Afrikaans word meaning apartness, separateness or distinctness. An interesting rational discussion of this concept in South African policy is to be found in Tatz's paper on 'Education and land rights: Australian and South African ideologies' read to the 1971 ANZAAS conference in Brisbane. But as my interest here is the concept itself and not the role it may play at any given time in government policy, I shall limit myself to its portrayal by Stoker, a philosopher who writes mostly in Afrikaans.

According to him (1967:212-13), *apartheid* is a concept limited in its application to South Africa alone because that country shows a 'pattern of humanity' found nowhere else. It has to do with relations between racially and culturally distinct groups rather than with relations between individuals and it stresses that each such group, having as it does its own physical traits, language, social organisation, history, attitude to life and so forth, should develop on the basis of these rather than on the basis of some other group's language, social organisation, etc. This does not mean that a group should cut itself off from others: Stoker (1967:136) remarks that for Afrikaners to promote their own culture calling or vocation (*kultuurroeping*) in isolation from other parts of the population and as their only goal would be nothing but enslavement to the idol of Afrikanership; and he asks (1967:51) whether the *apartheid* policy or, as he prefers to call it, the policy of differentiated development (*gedifferensieerde ontwikkeling*), while doing sufficient justice to the diverseness of peoples, has failed to do so to their mutual interrelatedness. But, like Piddington in New Zealand, Stoker fears that integration means nothing but assimilation.

Afrikaans is a Dutch-derived language and South Africa, so far as its culture is Afrikaner, is to be regarded as a 'province' of Dutch civilisation. South African thought about relations between groups of persons who differ in race and culture appears to be consistent with ideas held in the Netherlands, for example the Calvinist notion that creation is a coherent or interconnected diversity and the political-religious principle of 'sovereignty in own circle' (*souvereiniteit in eigenkring*). Each of these supports the other and both support and are supported by the singular variety of pluralism (the *verzuilingen*) to be found in the Netherlands. Accordingly it is interesting to find that these ideas, which Stoker shares, are appealed to by one of his critics, Stellingwerff (1971), in order to reject forced apartness and forced integration alike and to vindicate each race group's right to choose its own measure of differentiated development.

I have shown in this paper that assimilation is contrary to the two-laws concept of the Beswick Aborigines and I have suggested that biculturalism or emergent development would be congenial to them. Differentiated development would also attract them as it does the Kimberley Aborigines described by Kolig (1973*a*, 1973*b*), who speaks expressly of *apartheid*. These concepts all have it in common with the two-laws idea that, in opposition to assimilation, they look forward to different racial and cultural groupings persisting within a national boundary and that they prefer to adapt existing cultural traditions to the demands of new situations than to replace one tradition by another. Whether such aspirations are practicable need not concern us, for we cannot predict the future of the world's cultures, and in any case the question of feasibility may be raised also against the aspiration to assimilate all to one.

Acknowledgements

Although the invitation, in response to which this paper was submitted, came after my return from the Netherlands Institute for Advanced Study in the Humanities and Social Sciences, where I held a fellowship during the 1972-73 northern academic year, most of the work was carried out, with an eye to a different use, at the Institute to which I am greatly indebted for its admirable amenities in Wassenaar. The field data reported here were collected on several occasions between 1964 and 1970 under the auspices of the Australian Institute of Aboriginal Studies. It is to that period that everything I say may be referred unless my text makes the contrary evident.

Notes

1. Since my last visit to the Reserve the Australian Labor Party had taken office. Some of its pronouncements show that it views Aboriginal land rights and cultural persistence with favour, but whether the steps taken thus far really have improved the prospects of blackfellow law or merely have the effect of continuing the assimilation policy is a matter of doubt to me at the time of writing (August, 1974).

2. The 'useful work' consisted of helping to build the Stuart Highway, the sealed all-weather road from Darwin to Alice Springs. As Morris's account implies that Aborigines were not at liberty to leave, it may be worth mentioning that Aborigines who talked with me about the camps conveyed the impression of having enjoyed the life.

3. 'Tribe' is a controversial concept when the reference is to traditional life. But Aborigines use the word quite often when discussing their affiliations and organisation. In their usage it means a language and an area whose owners speak that tongue. Aborigines who come from that area (or whose parents came from it) and speak that language (or whose parents spoke it) do not form a solid political or residential or religious bloc at the Settlement. It is common for man and wife to belong to different tribes and evidently

there is no sentiment that one belongs to a tribe to the exclusion of all others, since many a man will, over a period of time, assert membership of several. To which he lays claim seems to be a function of context. Aborigines sometimes liken their tribes to the different European nationalities with which they have become familiar through post-war immigration.

4. Hiatt (1965:17) estimates the coastal Gidjingali to have lived at two to the square mile. Rose (1961:525) estimates the Groote Eylandt Wanindiljaugwa to have lived at one to three square miles. The Reserve, however, is inland. According to Specht (1958:482), the Arnhem Land population was concentrated along the coast because inland the food supply was poor.

5. I was struck one evening in the canteen by an illuminating instance of staff assertion of this man's marginality. His wife (let us call her Mary Smith) was being served by a senior white man. Instead of addressing her as Mary, which would have been normal had she been the wife of any other Aboriginal, or as Mrs Smith, which would have been normal had she been a married white woman, he called her Mrs Mary!

6. The staff on the Reserve, despite their official role as agents of assimilation, were not necessarily against Aboriginal culture. There was once a mild disturbance among some of the Aboriginal men because a young man proposed to marry a girl who stood in the wrong relation to him and who had already been promised to another. The matter was put before the acting-superintendent. The young man pleaded that as he wished to go 'whitefellow way' he could ignore marriage rules and promises. The acting-superintendent took the view that an Aboriginal who wished to live according to whitefellow law was out of place on the Reserve and had better leave it. The end of it all was that the illicit intrigue collapsed.

7. Bauer (1964) gives a history of the larger region of which the Reserve forms part.

References

BAUER, F. H. 1964 *Historical geography of white settlement in part of northern Australia: Part 2, the Katherine-Darwin region.* CSIRO, Canberra.
BERNDT, R. M. 1951 *Kunapipi.* Cheshire, Melbourne.
DURKHEIM, E. *and* M. MAUSS 1903 De quelques formes primitives de classification, *L'Année Sociologique,* 6:1-72
ELKIN, A. P. 1961 The Yabuduruwa, *Oceania,* XXXI:166-209.
HARRÉ, J. 1968 Maori-Pakeha intermarriage. In *The Maori people in the nineteen-sixties* (E. Schwimmer ed.), pp. 118-31. Blackwood and Janet Paul, Auckland.
HIATT, L. R. 1961 Big Brother in the Northern Territory. In Libertarian Society at Sydney University, *Broadsheet,* (19):2-5.
——1965 *Kinship and Conflict.* Australian National University, Canberra.
HUNN, J. K. 1961 *Report on Department of Maori Affairs.* Government Printer, Wellington.
JOSSELIN DE JONG, P. E. DE 1972 *Contact der continenten: bijdrage tot het begrijpen van niet-westerse samenlevingen.* Universitaire Pers, Leiden.
KOLIG, E. 1973a Progress and preservation: the Aboriginal perspective, *Aboriginal News,* 1(4): 18-20.
——1973b Tradition and emancipation: an Australian Aboriginal version of nativism. In *Supplement to Newsletter,* Aboriginal Affairs Planning Authority, Western Australia:1(6).
LONG, J. P. M. 1964 Papunya: westernization in an Aboriginal community. In *Aborigines now* (M. Reay ed.), pp. 72-82. Angus and Robertson, Sydney.
MADDOCK, K. 1970 Imagery and social structure at two Dalabon rock art sites, *Anthropological Forum,* 2:444-63.
——1972 *The Australian Aborigines: a portrait of their society.* Allen Lane, Penguin Press, London.
MEGGITT, M. J. 1962 *Desert people.* Angus and Robertson, Sydney.
MORRIS, F. R. 1965 The war efforts of Northern Territory Aborigines, *Australian Territories,* 5(1):2-10.
NOOY-PALM, C. H. M. 1964 De bewoners van Australië. In *Panorama der volken* (P. van Emst ed.), 1:347-86. Romen, Roermond.
NORTHERN TERRITORY ADMINISTRATION 1945-6 *Annual report.* Northern Territory Administration, Darwin.
OPPENHEIM, R. 1973 The idea of equality, *University of Auckland News,* 3(5):3-5, 34-6.
PIDDINGTON, R. 1968 Emergent development and 'integration'. In *The Maori people in the nineteen-sixties* (E. Schwimmer ed.), pp. 257-69. Blackwood and Janet Paul, Auckland.
ROSE, F. G. G. 1961 The Indonesians and the genesis of the Groote Eylandt society, northern Australia. In Veröffentlichungen des Museums für Völkerkunde zu Leipzig, *Beitrage zur völkerforschung: Hans Damm zum 65 geburtstag,* Akademie-Verlag, Berlin:524-31.
——1962 Grundlage und entstehung der 'Northern Territory Welfare (Native) Ordinance' von 1953, *Ethnographie-Archaologie Zeitschrift,* 3:59-71.

SCHWIMMER, E. 1966 *The world of the Maori*. Reed, Wellington.
——1968 The aspirations of the contemporary Maori. In *The Maori people in the nineteen-sixties* (E. Schwimmer ed.), pp. 9-64. Blackwood and Janet Paul, Auckland.
SPECHT, R. L. 1958 An introduction to the ethno-botany of Arnhem Land. In *Records of the American-Australian scientific expedition to Arnhem Land*, 3 (R. L. Specht *and* C. P. Mountford eds), pp. 479-503. Melbourne University Press, Melbourne.
STANNER, W. E. H. 1963 On Aboriginal religion, VI, cosmos and society made correlative, *Oceania*, XXXIII:239-73.
——1965 Religion, totemism and symbolism. In *Aboriginal Man in Australia* (R. M. Berndt *and* C. H. Berndt eds), pp. 207-37. Angus and Robertson, Sydney.
STELLINGWERFF, J. 1971 Gezag en vrijheid in het licht van Gods woord. In *Waarheid en werklikheid: wysgerige perspektiewe op die werklikheid*, De Jong, Braamfontein:176-90.
STOKER, H. G. 1967 *Oorsprong en rigting*, Band 1. Tafelberg, Kaapstad.
WORSLEY, P. 1967 Groote Eylandt totemism and *Le totémisme aujourd'hui*. In *The structural study of myth and totemism* (E. R. Leach ed.), pp. 141-59. Tavistock, London.

3 From tribesman to citizen?

Change and continuity in social identities among south Kimberley Aborigines

Erich Kolig

Jedes ist darin dem Anderen gleich, worin es sich ihm entgegengesetzt hat. Sein Sichunterscheiden von Anderen ist daher ein Sichgleichsetzen mit ihm und es ist Erkennen ebendarin . . . wie es im Anderen sich anschaut, als sich selbst weiss.

Hegel (Realphilosophie II)

(Free translation: self-definition is based on separation, contrast, which at the same time is inclusion, oneness.)

Man's identity is a theme of 'a thousand and one nights'. To state that the concept of identity has an infinite number of facets is more than a trite saying. It is an admission of the utility of dialectics. As Dahrendorf says (1973:88), 'there is no generally compelling image of man; there are at best convincing attacks on the problem from various angles'. Two fundamental, and in a way contrasting, aspects of the identity concept can be isolated, as Dahrendorf, for instance, has done. *Homo sociologicus* seems to stand in unbridgeable contrast to psychological man; the social self that stands against man as the unique individual—a conflict notorious and ancient at least in the teutonic realm of thought and exemplified by the incompatability of Kant's moral man and Hegel's societal man.

One traditional way of looking at man seems to go back to Kant's transcendental dialectic, in which the identity of the self is defined as an *a priori* existing entity of the transcendental (Habermas 1968:30). This concept appears to have given rise to psychological, psychoanalytical and pseudo-psychological images of identity as the *true self*; as being as one *really* is. And this is seen as contrasting with role playing in society and maintaining a social façade.

Fundamentally different is the sociological, or anthropological, view: man's social existence *is* his identity. This approach, I believe, issues ultimately from Hegel's philosophy—epitomised in the motto above—and has been introduced into the socioanthropological tradition by Durkheim's *de la Division du Travail social*, 1893, and his other writings, in which identity is understood as an entirely social matter. The identity of the self constitutes itself through a dimension of social embedment and the conduct of social roles.

The emphasis in my analysis is on the social self of man; on that identity which binds him to others, rather than separates him as individually unique. I presume that man in all societies is concerned with linking his personal existence to that of others and to find meaning, or part of an overall meaning, in identification with others. Hegel's maxim epitomises the broadest possible basis. This probably goes as far as one can *a priori* generalise cross-culturally, as there conceivably is an enormous variety of perspectives and interpretations. So Hegel pro-

vides, in the widest sense, my framework of analysis and sets the stage for
my heuristic.

The concept of social identity is variably used by anthropologists.
Linton (1936:113ff.), Merton (1957:369) and Goodenough (1965),
with slight differences, understand it as the role pattern, in terms of
reciprocal rights and duties, held by a group of persons within a given
cultural framework. For Goodenough, who has probably reconsidered
this concept most concisely (1965), social identity is the position a
person selects (or is ascribed) from an identity-set, in relation to specific
others. In the maintenance of his social *persona*, a person continuously
and unceasingly selects culturally prescribed clusters of behaviour and
strategies *vis-à-vis* other categories of role-carriers (i.e., social identities).
Social identity, therefore, is a behaviour regulator, to some extent
measurable and predictable. Indeed, the sum of the clustering of roles,
cultural inventory, social system and interrelationship *as experienced* by a
group of persons forms one major aspect of the concept of social identity.
These criteria define the 'we-feeling' and their awareness generates a
like-mindedness with others, a knowing 'where one stands'. However, I
stress here an aspect of social identity which, though inherently present
in Goodenough's formulation, deviates somewhat from that with which
he operates. I see social identity here mainly as a 'mental artefact'; an
artefact not only, and not primarily, as a pragmatically oriented tool to
deal with sets (or categories) of people, but in the first place as persons'
intellectual means of ordering their socioculture and, in a wider perspective, their universe—especially in relation to human beings contained in these entities. In so far as this entails behavioural group
strategies, defined through convention (rights, duties, privileges, etc.)
vis-à-vis other categories of people, I meet again with Goodenough's
primary understanding of the concept.

Complex societies offer a host of possibilities for identifications which
rely both on intra- and extra-society oneness and contrast. For social
identity is based as much on imaginary oneness as on imaginary contrast.
In less complex societies the most eminent social identity is contained in
ethnocentrism. Among the various definitions of 'we', the one which
coincides with ethnic boundaries is held as the most important of all.
Ensuing feelings of solidarity and sentiments are socioculturally introvert
(in the sense of Weber's *Vergemeinschaftung*; Bendix (1966:288). Apart
from its purely affective implications, ethnic identity strongly influences
definitions of humanity and shapes decisively the wider perception of
the cultural and physical order of mankind.

Analytically, I attribute three dimensions to 'identity': width,
structure and conceptual basis. By width I mean the range of persons
subsuming themselves, or being subsumed by others, under one identity
label. Identity structure is the specific interaction pattern, the social
interrelationships operating between entities of one identity. This is the
society's awareness of, and reaction to, the third identity dimension,
which is the truly creative and regulative force of identity. The third
dimension is the conceptual basis, the intellectual matrix from which
identity springs. Social identity does not exist *a priori*, but is a creation,
an artefact, of mind. As any classification of reality it does not exist
'outside' man, but issues from socially given intellectual modes. Thus,
for instance, Hegel's maxim is not only an objective framework of
analysis—a fragment of reality—but at the same time is itself a socially
produced, socially relevant and culture-specific artefact. I intend to
stress the third identity dimension, the conceptual basis, *vis-à-vis* the

other two, width and structure. The conceptual basis, itself a product of sociocultural intellect, is lastly responsible for the manifestation of the other two dimensions.

The identity quest of Australian Aborigines

The emergence of an Australian Aboriginal identity in recent years has occupied the thoughts of anthropologists, politicians and scholars in other fields of social studies, though for different reasons. (See, for instance, R. M. Berndt 1970:5; 1971:41; D. Tugby 1973.) The understanding and analysis of this identity is of paramount importance in many respects. Needless to emphasise the overall significance of it for those who accept it for themselves. It is of no lesser importance for those to whom it is ascribed—and this may not always coincide with self-identification. Yet, a much wider circle of persons is involved and ultimately the whole of the Australian society cannot stand aloof from what goes with this identity. Modes of coexistence of Aborigines and non-Aborigines—of those who identify as Aborigines and those who do not or cannot do so—are strongly influenced by, if not contingent upon, the emergence of this identity. In particular in a situation which finds Aborigines on the threshold of gaining control over their own affairs—a situation which intimately interlocks with matters concerning the wider society—this identity must certainly be of vital concern to the whole society.

In considering Aboriginal identity and its emergence, one has to distinguish between southern, urban Aborigines on the one hand and 'tribal', tradition-oriented, northern Aborigines on the other. Any generalised notion spanning the two factions without conceding differences, must be inflicted with severe shortcomings. Among southern Aborigines this identity surely has a meaning totally different from that among northern Aborigines. While this is irrelevant to this identity concept—which is emphatically aimed at breaking down current differences and at welding 'Aborigines' of quite different background together—for an analysis such a distinction has to be upheld. Consequently, my argument refers to tradition-oriented Aborigines—in so far as it potentially transgresses the confinement of a regional consideration—and I see a marked contrast here to urban Aborigines. (I shall briefly return to this contrast in the final section of this paper.)

The problem I propose to deal with in this paper is related to what C. H. Berndt (1961) has referred to as the identity quest of Australian Aborigines. As Berndt remarks, small *Gemeinschaft*-type units break up under the impact of mass-society, and this happens everywhere in the world. The Australian Aboriginal is a case in point of the helpless man 'who has no effective voice in major decisions affecting his very existence, and no real hope of influencing them. He is caught within the orbit of perhaps largely benevolent but also largely impersonal forces which are engaged in deliberate and concerted attempts to change his whole style of living, in short, to redefine his identity' (C. H. Berndt *ibid.*:17). In other words, external forces, on which the Aboriginal has little if any influence, define and prescribe his new identity for him. D. Tugby (1973:1), seemingly arguing in a similar vein, speaks of Aboriginality as a 'looking glass identity'. He sees it as, essentially, a 'white image'; a mirror held up by Europeans to those considered inflicted with the 'blemish' of Aboriginal ancestry. As von Sturmer says (1973:16): ' 'Aboriginality' is a fiction which takes on meaning only in terms of white ethnocentrism'.

The truth of these statements seems, at first sight, poignantly obvious. Yet I propose to scrutinise here one particular aspect which seems at least implicitly present in these views: that Aborigines in their search for new identities in the post-contact era have so awkwardly fallen victim of a 'white' fiction, when they do search for meaning in a common Aboriginality. Certainly, pan-Aboriginality is a 'white product'—it would be foolish to deny this. To be sure, the whole existence of Aborigines is undergoing drastic change. European pressure did force upon Aborigines the acceptance of pan-Aboriginality as a fact of life in the modern Australian society; but it has not succeeded in prescribing *how* Aborigines have to define, and conceive of, their Aboriginality. *Their* Aboriginality is neither a 'white' mirage, nor a fiction, nor a jest of the fate that has always favoured the 'white man'. I will argue that, although the necessity for redefinition has not been engendered by their own free choice, Aborigines in arriving at new definitions of them-selves are not just driven by external alien forces. Aboriginal man— at least as I know him—has reserved to himself a narrow margin, humble though it may be, within which he retains choice in defining his self-identity.

Aboriginal man's ethnocentrism, traditionally parochial and therefore seemingly highly vulnerable, has not been crushed by the massive Western impact. As Aborigines, under pressure, progress to ever widening horizons of a *Weltbild*, traditional elements of thought and concepts are retained and meaningfully adjusted. A distinct traditional flavour of ethnocentrism is preserved, notwithstanding the vast expansion of the known geographic world and the variety of human beings in it. Aborigines, though subdued by heavy-handed Western dominance, have at least in one tiny section remained masters of their life. Admittedly, it is a narrow section and it is a mental one, not directly observable in social life. Trivial as it may seem, this reserve is vital. On this basis, Aborigines do not just float helplessly on the tide of change but, in their own terms, they meaningfully and significantly adjust. They retain, at least intellectually, the upper hand. They identify; they are not just identified.

New identities emerge and they are not accidental, arbitrary and senseless, but are representative of, and meaningfully adjusted to, stages of change that came in the wake of Western influence. Aborigines' mental and behavioural patterns, strategies and self-definitions are causally co-ordinated. This suggests that new ways of self-identity among post-contact Aborigines are not coincidental, but reflect continuity with tradition and purposeful adaptation in new socio-environmental conditions. Aborigines did not permit themselves to be swallowed wholly by the vortex of acculturation from which they would either be released re-born as Australians, distinguishable only by complexion, or which would thrust them into desperate identity crises. Klapp (1969:15) predicts an 'explosion of identity needs' whenever accul-turation sets in. An acute groping for new identities would be engendered by culture contact; and Wallace (1966:212f.) generalises quite similarly. When culture contact had in fact assumed the guise of a culture clash, as was the case in Australia, one would presume even greater acuteness and desperation in the identity quest. As I shall attempt to demonstrate, nothing of the kind has happened in the area I am familiar with. Aborigines have indeed looked for new identities—and they have found them, in an 'orderly' way, without violent schisms and sectarianism. There are dissidents: for instance, a very few Aboriginal Christians, who have set out in search of an identity, separate from the majority. But they tend, with very few exceptions, to regard this identity as of minor importance and consequence. On the whole, there is certainly no acute gropings, no desperate need for identities as yet unfound.

I believe that the retention of traditional conceptual elements is mainly responsible for the prevention of an identity dilemma. Although surrendering traditionally narrow divisions of self-other identifications, Aborigines, by retaining traditional principles of order, reform their identity along relatively clear and to them familiar lines. So it would appear that, while all the cited authors are correct in some sense, the problem of reaching new identities for Aborigines is less grave than might be expected. As Aborigines have not been victimised in their search for new identities, their quest has not reached crisis proportions. In other words, Aborigines do not experience identity problems because of *ideational continuity*.

My thesis is then that the preservation of parts of the traditional ideological superstructure has facilitated the orderly and smooth adjustment of identities; or rather, has set the stage for an orderly sequence of changing identities adjusted to new conditions. The isolation of those parts of the superstructure, which I hold mainly responsible for this development, does not seem too difficult. Although cognitive processes of Aborigines are doubtlessly changing, certain pivots of the traditional superstructure are apparently retained. As long as these are retained the appearance of continuity is given to Aborigines and they can comprehend changes against a familiar background. Crises are avoided. Only when the pivots are removed or dissolved do the violent convulsions of intellectual reformation, identity crises, ensue. Of necessity this train of thought involves oversimplification. The intellectual pivots do not stand alone but are intertwined with other intellectual and conceptual factors which *in toto* form a complex network. I am aware that an analysis that rests on the isolated and independent treatment of intellectual elements is necessarily inflicted with the stigma of simplicity. Therefore, this presentation does not lay claim to be more than a preliminary consideration.

The setting As the 'raw material' of my presentation serves the Fitzroy area in the southern Kimberleys and its Aboriginal population.[1] The present Aboriginal population of this area is, strictly speaking, a conglomerate. Aborigines of quite disparate origins, of many different linguistic and cultural backgrounds, have met and mingled.

When European colonisation of the fertile Fitzroy River basin commenced late last century, Aboriginal 'tribes' were living there who today are termed Bunaba, Njigina and Gunian. The onslaught of early European settlement had a disastrous effect on the indigenous population and caused a severe reduction in their numbers. The descendants of these 'tribes' today form a minority of the Aboriginal population. From around the turn of the century until one or two decades ago, Aborigines from farther south, the Desert fringe and Desert areas, arrived in various waves. These groups, that today are retrospectively labelled Wolmadjeri and Julbaridja, and their descendants form the current majority. While many descendants of the indigenes are highly acculturated, the immigrants from the south, upholding

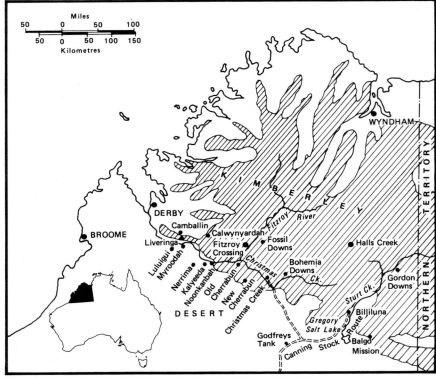

Figure 1 : *Map of the Kimberley Region of Western Australia.*

indigenous Aboriginal traditions, dominate the traditional religio-cultural life among the Fitzroy Aborigines. Most of the Njigina and Gunian became Wolmadjerised—i.e. they assimilated to the Desert culture and were culturally and physically absorbed by the immigrants. Today, they can hardly be traced through genealogical methods or through self-identification. Culturally, they are not distinguishable from their Desert neighbours among whom they live. The Bunaba who live north of the Fitzroy River and therefore were less exposed to the Desert immigration, retained their independence. They did not accept Desert culture. Having lost most of their own indigenous traditions and rejecting the last fragmented parts of their cultural heritage, most Bunaba are fairly deculturated—i.e. they have become weak imitations of Europeans.

Synchronically, there are various and partly overlapping (ethnic) identities in use among Fitzroy Aborigines. A person, though preferably emphasising one identity, may employ also other identities. In this self-identification a person usually has a choice among congenial identities and his selection depends on which one seems more appropriate or advantageous in the particular situation. Not unusually identification through third persons does not coincide with the self-identification as often prestige or derogation go with identities. Identities are frequently used as political 'weapons' for they are keenly subtle strategies in inter-personal relationships.

The identities reflect various levels of priority: some identities are clearly relics of the past, with very little significance today, others are highly *en vogue* and of acute importance, and yet others are an anticipation of the future. The variety of identities can be ordered in a chronological development. Preference for identities, or alternatively their rare usage nowadays, are indicative of a developmental (or micro-evolutionary) sequence that conforms with socio-environmental stages of change. Identity phases do not coincide with socio-environmental conditions a hundred per cent temporally precise. Nevertheless, I presume a causal conjunction of the two factors. Causality seems in any case of greater import to my argument than mere temporal precision.

The hypothetical pre-contact situation The premise of my further argument lies in eliciting a hypothesis on the pre-contact situation of spatial arrangement coupled with ethnocentrism. Present-day retrospection of Aborigines is, to put it mildly, unreliable. I am therefore unable to present empirical and conclusive evidence for the close conformity of my heuristic model to past realities.

In setting forth the narrowest ethno-perspective of a pre-contact social unit (a unit that is larger than the ego and the nuclear family) I purposely decline to correlate this unit with any known social grouping, as doing so would be arbitrary and incidental to my purpose. My hypothetical core-unit has obviously not much to do with land-tenure—i.e. it does not coincide with the land-owning group which was a genealogical and not a residential unit as far as we assume. My core-group would perhaps be more readily identifiable as a land-using unit, as my consideration of the ethno-perspective rests on spatial and residential criteria. From the perspective of such a core-group, neighbouring groups were regarded as closely congenial and were termed *djandu*. The classification implies sameness in language, custom, cultural inventory, social structure and ideological like-mindedness. The term *djandu* stems from the present-day Wolmadjeri language which is spoken as the *lingua franca* by Aborigines throughout much of the southern Kimberleys. Aborigines who have some command of English translate the term as 'countryman.' Traditionally, there exist various synonyms in other Aboriginal languages. (For instance, the term *(bundu) waldja,* in some Julbaridja languages.)

Groups that differed obviously in language, custom, etc. were classified as *ngai*, 'strangers' or aliens. *Ngai*, when seen from the limited perspective of a core-group, were removed from ordinary contact; but they were known through 'inter-tribal' meetings. In such large-scale religious gatherings groups from a wider geographic radius often participated. In the distinction between *djandu* and *ngai* the criteria of custom, religious belief, values, etc. played a prominent role. Predictability of cultural and behavioural reactions, and the likeness (or sameness) of custom and values, and alternatively the absence of such predictability were major criteria for the division. But probably the main determinant was linguistic communication.

Language, traditionally, is seen by Aborigines as of pre-eminent importance and as a determinant of full humanity. Somebody not speaking the same language was not only considered significantly different, but also fundamentally different. The importance of intelligible language as constitutive of full humanity, in the physical and cultural sense, is reflected in current linguistic usage. The term *bina* literally means ear and, one feels tempted to say, logically derived *bina-garin* means to listen, to hear. (It is interesting to note in this context that among Eighty Mile Beach Aborigines the word *bina-bina* refers to the spinal cord and is regarded as the seat of a person's personality; see H. Petri 1959:21f.) *Bina-nguru* and *bina djadi* (literally, belonging to the ear) means intelligent, knowledgeable, versatile and prominent in religion. The antonym *wangada* refers to deafness as well as to stupidity and states of madness, trance—i.e. in general socially unaccept-able behaviour. (This conforms to Gunwinggu practice: see R. and C. Berndt 1970:157.) Pathologically deaf persons, deaf-mutes (not however senile deafness) were considered mad as well as socially intolerable; for hearing and speaking as forms of meaningful social communication, were not considered purely 'physiological processes' but were seen as expression of physico-cultural humanity.

In abstraction, the realm of *djandu* approximates the anthropological concept of the dialectal unit which has been coined for the Western Desert by R. M. Berndt (1959) to replace the inadequate notion of the 'tribe'. (I refer here also explicitly to the Western Desert situation, as information on the pre-contact conditions among the indigenous Fitzroy population is by far too scanty to be included here.) The difference between the anthro-pological order, derived from the concept of the dialectal unit, and that based on the concept of *djandu,* lies in that the former bears the charac-teristics of an absolute and stable order, while the latter is highly relative.

It is noted that in the Western Desert, traditionally, no sharp demarcations existed between groups. (Sociocultural differences of some sort were given in that some groups had adopted the subsection system, while others had retained the section system.) Linguistic differences existed mainly in terms of slightly differing vocabulary or locally confined idioms. Seen from a fictitious point anywhere in the Western Desert, and proceeding from it into almost any direction, at first no significant linguistic differences are apparent. Only after a considerable distance has been covered, do language differences become noticeable and finally pronounced. While a difference now becomes noticeable between the point of origin and the end-point, there is no sharp break between as there is only a gradual transformation. Since no linguistic demarcations existed, neighbouring groups had every reason to consider each other *djandu. Ngai* were those at some distance where language differences were already noticeable to a significant extent and transgressed the occur-rence of a few local idioms.

As this is the core-point of my argument, I shall illustrate it with a simple sketch. A cluster of core-groups is represented by circles. For demonstration the core-groups A, B and C are singled out. Seen from core-group A, other groups gather around it in concentric arrangement according to the circular world perception which derives from primary observation. (See Mühlmann 1964; I have referred to this ethnocentric cosmology, 1972:6.)

Based on the ethno-perspective of a core-group, the following classifi-cation would derive: A refers to B as well as to C as *djandu*; and both B and C in turn call A *djandu*. But B would regard C as *ngai* and *vice versa*, in recognition of noticeable linguistic differences and other features of strange-ness. The same principle of order would pertain to all other core-groups of

the sketch and beyond it. The immediate ethnocentre was formed by the
core-group itself, and by a first step of amplification, the ethnocentre was
extended on to those groups considered *djandu*. The realm of *ngai* was external
to the ethnocentre based on strict cultural and linguistic considerations. Yet,
in a somewhat different sense *ngai* was partly inclusive. By a definition of
humanity which rested mainly on physical aspects, and partly ignored
cultural and linguistic criteria, groups beyond the ethnocentric were included
though perhaps considered of somewhat lesser humanity. Those *ngai* with
whom superficial and occasional contacts were maintained were classified
as *bi:n*, human beings (in the physical sense).[2]

Sketch

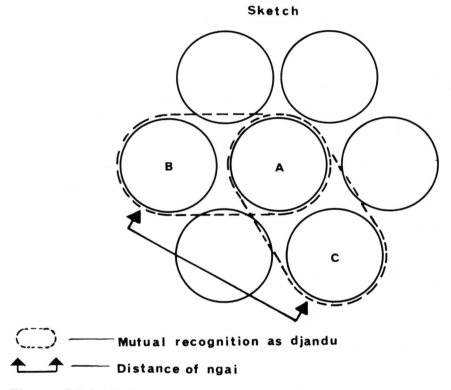

   ——— **Mutual recognition as djandu**

↑ ↑ ——— **Distance of ngai**

Figure 2: Relationship between core-groups

Notwithstanding the undoubted humanity of *ngai*, they were considered
inferior and to a lesser or larger extent detrimental features were associated
with them. The more distant a group was from the narrow perspective of a
core-group, the more abominable the characteristics which were attributed
to it. For those groups of whom only vague and second-hand information
existed, it was considered doubtful whether they were really *bi:n*. Treachery,
lechery, cannibalism, anomalies of sexual organs and sexual behaviour,
despicable social habits, etc., were commonly attributed to them. (See e.g.
R. and C. Berndt 1942:325; Meggitt 1962:43.)

For easier reference the aliens were usually summarised in larger categories according to the compass:

Woringari, waringari, waringadi: people to the north.
Wonaiga, wonajaga: people to the east.
Wondbada, wodeabul: people to the west.
Burngana: people to the north-east.
Bidungu: people to the south-west.
Wilangu: people to the north-west.
Julbaridja: people to the south.
Warmala, wormala, walmala: people to the south.
Djilbada: people to the far south (semi-ghost beings).

This order was of course not everywhere the same. These classes stand here
as a representative example.[3]

A group did not classify its neighbours in this way, as these categories
imply more or less strong notions of inferiority and derogation. So, for instance,
a group would not refer to its immediate neighbours to the south as Julbaridja.
Julbaridja were those living at some distance to the south. The *ngai* of the
known universe, though being *bi:n*, were already seen as of lesser human
quality. Even more so, the aliens summarised by the wider labels were
strongly doubtful as to their human status. These distant groups merge into
the sphere of the cosmological periphery: the sphere on the fringe of the
cosmos with forms of life and culture different from the known world (see
Kolig 1972:6f.).

To recapitulate briefly. The narrow ethnocentre was the forum of *djandu*;
and this was based on cultural considerations. The concept of *bi:n* extends
beyond it and while this realm does not show an abrupt margin, as does the
realm of *djandu*, it becomes gradually thinner with distance. The concept of
bi:n is based on physical considerations. The classification based on this
concept relied also on primary observation, but encompassed to some extent
also secondary relationships (second-hand information, long-distance trade
and exchange, etc.). Both images, the one of *djandu* and that of *bi:n*, were
highly ethnocentric in so far as they assumed the self as the measure of all
things and relied on the radial extension of the ego-perspective mostly through
primary, naive observation. The two images had, however, slightly differing
radii of application.

The two realms, the narrow one of *djandu* and the more liberal one of
bi:n, do not emerge as a consequence of a strict differentiation between
cultural and physical aspects of one concept of humanity, as may appear.
Aborigines hardly have made such a distinction. The dilemma of nomen-
clature here arises from the fact that Aborigines did not have a concise
concept of humanity. Seemingly Aborigines thought in terms of similarities
and dissimilarities, but they were not concerned with a clear-cut definition
of humanity that would have imposed abrupt limitations in classification.
Priority was simply given to cultural considerations and cultural criteria
were taken quite seriously. Physical similarity, though acknowledged, was
of lesser concern and the image of *bi:n* was accordingly both wide and relatively diffuse in its geographic application. One might say, Aborigines were
more apathetic *vis-à-vis* this concept and this is important to note, because
this, I believe, has influenced post-contact identities and behaviour. The
major self-other definitions continued to be sought in cultural similarities-

dissimilarities, in terms of *djandu-ngai;* while a *bi:n*-non-*bi:n* (i.e. European) contrast was of lesser concern. This might account for the absence of a racial conflict identity so far.

Internal confrontation With the advent of Europeans and the establishment of settlements in the Fitzroy area, Aborigines commenced to congregate at these centres in increasing numbers. Pastoral stations, mission settlements, government depots, police stations, telegraph posts, etc. exercised quite distinct attractions on Aborigines. Initially only locally relevant Aborigines gathered there. But later groups from ever distant and varying origins arrived. Disparate groups lived side by side on the settlements where some form of peaceful co-existence was enforced by European control. Newly arrived groups, in particular those from the Desert areas, often remained at first peripheral to the settlements, camping in 'the bush' nearby. The already settled Aboriginal population often was terrified of the proximity of these wild 'bush fellows'. But sooner or later some form of integration of the various groups was achieved.

When the groups of such distant and disparate origins met face-to-face on the settlements, the old order based on pre-contact ethnocentric notions had to be revised. Definitions of similarity and dissimilarity were placed on a wider basis, though in strict accord with pre-contact concepts. It was at this initial phase of Aboriginal confrontation that a comprehensive 'tribal order' was devised. Nowadays, when asked about pre-contact conditions, Aborigines would liberally refer to this 'tribal order'. But it seems obvious that the narrow geographic notions of pre-contact times did not permit the evolution of a comprehensive 'tribal order' which usually covers the entire southern Kimberleys and reaches down into the central Western Desert.

The basis of the 'tribal order' was given by the division in *djandu* and *ngai*, but the division now gained a far more comprehensive implication. Recognition was given to a wide variety of different groups. Those who considered themselves culturally and linguistically alike (i.e. were *djandu*), formed the members of a 'tribe'. And from their perspective, the culturally different ones (the aliens, *ngai*), were allotted to other 'tribes'. The label of *ngai*, of any tribal affinity, continued to apply the tinge of strangeness and oddity. Some of the 'tribal' labels are therefore quite derogatory, although *ngai* were now considered undoubtedly human. The radius of (physical) humanity became extended. For instance, those Julbaridja who lived now on the pastoral stations were conceded the status of full humanity. And many others who previously had been suspected of being semi- or sub-human were now classified as *bi:n* without reservation. Aliens remaining remote from the newly extended geographic perception, were still not attributed equal human status. At least the taint remained for them of having bad, inferior and morally depraved customs and beliefs (see e.g. Meggitt 1962:251f.;34) and contagion by their malignant and virulent 'law' was feared (see Petri 1968:303).

The 'tribal order' was far from being a stable and absolute one, as it was born out of the pre-contact notion of the *djandu-ngai* contrast. Consequently, many of the 'tribal' labels, being manifestations of *ngai*, retained a slight tinge of inferiority and detestation. (The label Julbaridja, for instance, carries cryptically the meaning of barbarian.) Moreover, the pre-contact relativity of classification was retained, as the basis of the order was still the relative viewpoint of a comparatively small group of persons who considered themselves culturally congenial. Aborigines who stem from the area around Godfrey's Tank and Gregory Salt Lake refer to traditionally distant groups in the south-east as Gugadja. As such, the label Gugadja indicates only that these groups use the term *guga* for meat. Implicit in the label is, however, the meaning of flesh-eater, cannibal. The groups thus denoted, therefore, prefer for themselves other labels, while attributing the label Gugadja to even more distant groups in the east or south-east. The Gugadja preferably refer to themselves as Wonggadjunga (probably from *wangga,* talk or speech, and *djunga,* straight or correct; the label 'correct-speakers' would conform to the language-based traditional ethnocentrism); or, if their origin lies farther in the east, as Ngadi or Ngambladj. The relativity of the label Gugadja can be documented further. Gugadja is the accepted identity nowadays at Balgo. Fitzroy Aborigines, however, who have come from there, maintaining close kinship ties to Balgo Aborigines, and express themselves ordinarily in a language conforming to that labelled Gugadja at Balgo (Peile n.d.) indignantly refute this label and attribute it to other groups.

Aborigines who are sometimes teasingly labelled Mandjildjara (which conveys also a derogatory meaning) are quick to emphasise that they are Wonggadjunga and that Mandjildjara, traditionally, have lived much farther south from their own 'territory'. Wolmadjeri stemming from areas south of the Fitzroy River region, maintain that Aborigines from the Sturt Creek area and south of it, around Gregory Salt Lake, were noticeably different from them. Language and people from these areas are called heavy or half Wolmadjeri, or Njanjan. Njanjan, as far as I can determine, seems to mean babbling, stammering, speaking inarticulately. The people thus denoted, as might be expected, heartily disapprove of this label and allocate it to groups in the far east.[4]

The 'tribal' label Djualin refers to various groups. So-called Wonggadjunga sometimes call their traditional northern 'neighbours' Djualin. But these people attach this label to groups in the western coastal areas, the so-called light Wolmadjeri. (Petri equates the terms Djualin and Wolmadjeri which seems to be the practice among Eighty Mile Beach Aborigines. Tjiwali, which sounds identical with Djualin, is given by Oates [1970] as a synonym of Mangala. Fitzroy Aborigines usually distinguish between Djualin and Mangala, although here again a wide variety of different conventions is noticeable). The 'tribal' labels are seemingly quite often not self-given labels, for obvious reasons. For instance, I think it likely that the label Wolmadjeri (or Walmadjeri, Walmahari, Wolmeri. etc.) was originally not a self-denotation. The label possibly derives from Warmala, Walmala or Walmadja the denotation for the southern Desert areas and its inhabitants, when seen from the perspective of more northern groups (cf. Kaberry 1937:93; Capell 1940:423).

I believe there is evidence to assume that the 'tribal' labels developed from the concept of *ngai.* In other words, self-identification was, traditionally, simply in terms of *djandu* or linguistic equivalents. More specific labels ('tribal' labels) are identifications through others. There was a definite need for this specification in the post-contact confrontation of various groups of disparate origins. While some labels became acceptable, others, being strongly derogatory, were not accepted and remained an exclusive matter of identification through third persons. The intellectual basis for 'tribal' identification was given by the concepts of *djandu* and *ngai* respectively. And the first experimental step toward the extension of the traditional ethnocentre was made along traditional principles. This being logically developed from pre-contact modes of identification, no serious rupture arose.

Conglomeration and internal accommodation Presumably the phase of initial confrontation had planted the seed for a development in which narrower identities were abandoned in favour of wider, more comprehensive ones. The search for, and acceptance of, common forms of life, common means of linguistic communication, coexistence and accruing mutual appreciation, must surely have encouraged the acceptance of 'supra-tribal' identities. The development of common religious modes expressed in the formation of extended sacred lodges (Kolig n.d.) and the acceptance of a *lingua franca* were certainly conducive to this if not a primary cause. Notions of prestige associated now with particular 'tribal' labels enticed persons to identify with these labels, usually with the approval of the relevant 'tribal' members. In other words, the concept of *djandu*, still relying on criteria of culture and language, by extension covered now a much wider number of persons.

Birdsell sees this development from a somewhat different angle. To him a momentum of pragmatism seems important. Certainly, this may have come into it. Birdsell refers to the situation he observed at Gogo Station, which lies in the Fitzroy area, in 1954, some 15 years before the onset of my research.

> Thus Gogo Station . . . was located in traditional Konean country, and it initially appeared to me that most of the older people dependent upon the station for support were indeed members of the Konean tribe. Detailed genealogical investigations quickly revealed, however, that the Konean as a group had passed almost to extinction, and had been replaced by incoming natives from a variety of sources. First some of the Djaru, whose traditional country lay to the east, had come down Christmas Creek to Gogo. Some decades later, Walmadjari tribesmen came in from the desert to the south to the river country and Gogo Station. Newly arrived, ignorant and incapable of communicating with their European masters, many had learned to speak the Konean language in order to have communication access to the Whites through the older stratum of established native servitors. In 1954 the Walmadjari were numerically preponderant at the station, and had come into effective Aboriginal power position. In their turn, they mediated between their European overlords and the final waves of desert-dwellers coming in from the wells of the middle of the Canning Stock Route. The latter, of the Wonkadjunga and Kokatja tribes, like all underprivileged minorities, tried to identify themselves with an acceptable semi-dominant group. They labeled themselves as Walmadjari, and indeed spoke that language as a second language in order to facilitate their absorption at Gogo. Dialectical changes of this sort are common in post-contact situations, and reflect rational behaviour. (Birdsell 1970:118.)

A phase in which the Gunian identity formed the dominant one must, according to my information, have been both very brief and locally confined to Gogo Station; and indeed this seems to be Birdsell's opinion too. For the

Wolmadjeri identity has for some considerable time now been the dominant and widely accepted one, throughout the entire Fitzroy area and beyond it.[5] (Concerning the particular situation at Gogo Station, my data suggest that already thirty or forty years ago Wolmadjeri was the dominant identity there, as so-called Gunian had learned the Wolmadjeri language and almost wholly relinquished Gunian. This means that at that time, the Wolmadjeri were already sufficiently established to influence previously arrived Aborigines.)

Desert Aborigines today conventionally identify partly as Wolmadjeri and partly as Julbaridja, though the latter also prefer the label of Wolmadjeri. At first sight this division seems to link up with residential criteria and a rough temporal sequence of immigration: the first waves having brought Wolmadjeri and later waves their southern neighbours the Julbaridja. This is, however, most probably an over-simplification. Of course, the first to arrive in large numbers were Aborigines from the Desert fringe areas, the Wolmadjeri, before 'the southerners' came from the region farther south. But I think that at an early stage Julbaridja elements arrived together with Wolmadjeri; and these Julbaridja were readily absorbed and could soon identify as Wolmadjeri, which was at that time already the dominant identity. In other words, the division of the Desert immigrants in Wolmadjeri and Julbaridja is the first result of the movement toward wider identities; and this already lies some time back.

The acceptance of a Wolmadjeri identity is not only defined by speaking the relevant language. It also means adherence to a specific cultural background. Indeed, as mentioned before, the descendants of the indigenous Njigina and Gunian have been thoroughly Wolmadjerised. Wolmadjeri-sation is, however, not the assimilation to the indigenous, unchanged Wolmadjeri background. What is today seen as Wolmadjeri traditional heritage encompasses a wide variety of cultural features. A wide cultural heterogeneity goes with the label of Wolmadjeri. The label encompasses cultural elements of the Wolmadjeri *and* the Julbaridja. Both groups have more or less fused their indigenous heritage and it now forms one consistent medium. There the heterogeneity does not stop, as various post-contact cultural acquisitions are equally regarded as integral parts of current Aboriginal traditions. On the other hand, acculturation has extracted its toll, resulting in the loss of many pre-contact cultural elements. All this forms part of the current Wolmadjeri identity. (See Kolig n.d.)

Wolmadjeri and the emphasis on religious traditions   The vernacular labelled Wolmadjeri by Aborigines is currently spoken as a *lingua franca* by Aborigines throughout the southern Kimberleys. (In accordance with traditional notions the label Wolmadjeri refers not only to the linguistic medium itself, but also to the people who speak it, as language and identity are one.) In general, Aborigines under the age of thirty do not speak any other Aboriginal languages. The use of this language as a generally accepted communication medium extends in a compact belt from Billiluna and Balgo Mission in the south-east of the Kimberleys as far west as settlements along the lower Fitzroy River. Through migration of Wolmadjeri speakers, this vernacular is nowadays also in use (together with other languages) outside this region. Thus Wolmadjeri is also spoken in settlements along the Eighty Mile Beach, called there Djualin. Wolmadjeri is occasionally also used in the coastal townships of Derby and Broome, and in settlements east of Sturt Creek, due to migration of Wolmadjeri speakers. According to the vast extension of the usage of Wolmadjeri the range of linguistic variation is considerable. Considerable variation is also provided by the fact that it is spoken by large numbers of people who originally spoke languages different from 'proper Wolmadjeri'. Some of these people often had only to adapt their language more or less, without completely abandoning their linguistic background, in order to communicate with other Wolmadjeri speakers. In a strict linguistic and historic sense what is presently termed 'Wolmadjeri' most certainly does not form one consistent language. Wolmadjeri speakers of any linguistic background, however, do not experience major difficulties in communication.

In recent years the communication network linking distant Aboriginal communities together has been enormously extended. Flourishing religious trade connects Aboriginal communities all over the southern Kimberleys. Routes of trade and exchange extend from the coastal area of the Eighty Mile Beach right across the southern Kimberleys into the Northern Territory. Large numbers of religious items, material as well as non-material ones, together with other goods, are regularly exchanged along these routes. Interlocked with this development is a noticeable residential mobility of Aborigines. Messengers, participants of large-scale religious festivals and employment-seeking Aborigines move freely over this area, but rarely outside it. In the southern Kimberleys Wolmadjeri as *lingua franca*—although local and regional versions thereof may differ noticeably—facilitates unimpaired linguistic communication between distant communities. The religio-cultural exchange is vastly increasing, suggesting for the future a fairly homogenous cultural medium throughout the southern Kimberleys (Kolig n.d.).

As a result of the close religio-cultural relationships, the concept of *djandu* is extended now to include the entire southern Kimberleys. With the exception of groups at the Eighty Mile Beach who have retained at least linguistic independence (Garadjeri, Njangomada), all south Kimberley Aborigines speaking Wolmadjeri as they do, are acceptable now as *djandu*. A man from Billiluna for instance may traverse the entire southern Kimberleys and he will be welcomed as a 'countryman' everywhere including Eighty Mile Beach settlements where there are strong contingents of Djualin and other Wolmadjeri migrants. The Wolmadjeri speakers all over the southern Kimberleys are encompassed now—and this is the contemporary state of affairs—by the concept of *djandu*. They are identified as Wolmadjeri and most accept this as a self-identification. *Djandu* contrasts now with Aborigines outside the wide Wolmadjeri realm—i.e. mainly people outside the southern Kimberleys. These others remain the *ngai*, aliens, and some suspicion *vis-à-vis* them is seen as still appropriate. At the same time, *ngai* are also represented within the Fitzroy area. Here a contrast between Wolmadjeri and non-Wolmadjeri has sharpened alongside a specific cultural development which might be termed religious nativism.

There is an increasing emphasis now on the perpetuation and partial revival of indigenous religious cultural traditions of the Desert repertoire. Fitzroy Aborigines share a relatively uniform religiosity which is mostly based on Desert traditions, i.e. traditions of the Wolmadjeri and Julbaridja.

The conglomerate of Wolmadjerised Aborigines in the Fitzroy area and cognate communities all over the southern Kimberleys accept this religious background as a common denominator, and religious exchange moves against this background. Some Aborigines in the Fitzroy area—and probably also elsewhere—remain crass outsiders. They have no wish to share in the Desert religiosity and they are treated accordingly as hostile aliens, *ngai*. These are the descendants of the indigenous 'tribe' of the Bunaba. The Bunaba had their traditional 'territory' north of the Fitzroy River, which formed a natural barrier, for some time, against the expansion of Desert Aborigines. The infiltrating Desert Aborigines had initially remained on the settlements along the southern fringe of the Fitzroy area, until they were pushed farther north by later arrivals. Desert Aborigines started to cross the Fitzroy River in greater numbers only ten to fifteen years ago. (E.g. the prevalent element at the United Aborigines Mission at Fitzroy Crossing when it was established in 1952 was Bunaba. Today, Desert Aborigines form the majority and that goes for most other settlements north of the Fitzroy River. The northward and westward movements of the Desert immigrants and their descendants have not yet come to a halt.)

While the indigenes south of the Fitzroy River, the Gunian and Njigina, have been thoroughly Wolmadjerised, the Bunaba retained their cultural independence. As mentioned before, the Bunaba have almost totally relinquished their indigenous traditional background—and partly did so by doctrinal rejection of that part of their cultural heritage that had not been destroyed as a consequence of culture contact. They did not see a valid reason in recent years, when contacts with Desert Aborigines became closer, to accept the Desert cultural background which they superstitiously fear as evil and dangerous, and at the same time despise as barbaric and crude. Bunaba see themselves deliberately and doctrinally apart from Wolmadjeri religiosity. (There are moves toward a reconciliation which seem to usher in the next stage: one of a common and uniform Aboriginality. In pragmatic terms Bunaba realise a certain advantage in emphasising a cultural Aboriginality. See Kolig 1974:35.)

From the Wolmadjeri perspective, the Bunaba are the foes of 'the tradition'. They are not only linguistically different, but also religiously different—a criterion which is seen now as of much importance. They could never be *djandu*. Bunaba are considered *bi:n*, of course. But the most important criterion of self-definition in the phase of religious nativism remains the cultural *djandu-ngai* distinction. And this distinction is sharpened by the acute religio-cultural opposition.

The counter-citizen?

Aborigines gradually come to orient their existence mainly in relation to Western society and they link themselves directly, though not kindly, with it. Partly by their own insight, partly by the import of ideas mainly from southern urbanised Aborigines, Aborigines begin to define themselves now mainly by comparison with Europeans. This tendency, for it is not more than a tendency at the moment, is most clearly expressed with younger Aborigines, under twenty-five years of age. For these the 'tribal' and 'supra-tribal' identities have largely become devoid of meaning and the identity is sought beyond these labels. Thus gradually an Aboriginal identity, an emphasis on common Aboriginality, emerges. While the previous stages of changing identities have relied on redefinitions of the concept of *djandu* (representing the cultural ethnocentre), the now emergent stage rests on the redefinition of the concept of physical likeness, the image of *bi:n*. The concept of *djandu*, which emphasised a relatively narrow, defined ethnocentre becomes redundant. The concept of *bi:n* comes into the foreground in its stead. Similar to the modern mass-society, the ethnocentre and the relevant identity now encompass primary and secondary relationships equally. *Bi:n* is extended and embraces not only all Australian Aborigines, but also, though perhaps less emphatically, dark-skinned and equally suppressed populations all over the world: an expression of racial solidarity (see Kolig 1972:7f.).

The emphasis on an all-Aboriginal identity is not engendered by a friendly attitude *vis-à-vis* the European society. It stems from oppositional feelings, from the awareness of deprivation, discrimination and suppression. The emergent Aboriginal identity is one of socio-political contrast *vis-à-vis* the unwanted dominance by racial aliens. It entails rejection of European inter-ference, a trend to isolate and emancipate and the attempt toward breaking the Europeans' monopoly of power. (This syndrome may be summarised as political nativism; Kolig 1974.) R. M. Berndt (1971:42) has termed this identity a 'status-seeking device'.

As a common Aboriginal identity gradually formulates itself, it has not been engendered solely by an awakening awareness of acute politico-racial contrast—although this has undoubtedly played an important role. The Aboriginal identity appears as the logical final stage in a development of expanding traditional identity concepts. I cannot agree with Wentworth (1973:9) who, probably expressing popular notions, states that Aborigines originally 'saw themselves as members of a tribe or group of tribes . . . or of a group whose minimal cohesion depended upon the sharing of specific cere-monies. In a sense, the creation of an 'Aboriginal identity' is in itself a very un-Aboriginal process, for which there is no historical substructure'. If not to be taken in a merely socio-political sense or in a conveniently loose rhetoric sense—which is analytically quite worthless—Wentworth's statement is incorrect. There is a historical substructure, although this is to be found in the depth of the mind, and not on the surface of socio-political appearance. Wentworth may have a point in so far as urban Aborigines are concerned. Through loss of their intellectual traditions, they cannot draw on any conceptual precedences and they could not harmoniously develop these precedences to fit the new requirements, as northern Aborigines have done. As the latter arrive at a seeming pan-Aboriginality, they rely on indigenous traditions of thought which have been developed from embryonic beginnings and form now the present condition of their Aboriginality.

The relevant differences between urban and northern Aborigines probably cannot be overestimated. The development of an Aboriginal identity with the two factions seems to have proceeded from different roots (though mutual stimulus has certainly had part in the process). The end products, by con-vergence, bring both factions together. As R. M. Berndt succinctly remarks (1971:41):

> People of Aboriginal descent, especially in the southern areas, are much more articulate than they were a couple of decades ago. While the

majority of those represented in this category are for all practical purposes Australian-Europeans, their knowledge of the traditional Aboriginal/heritage is not at first hand and indeed for most of them it is far removed. Yet they seek common social identity in that Aboriginal past—in the idea of it, because anything else, anything closer to traditional actuality, would find them completely at sea.

How different is the northern Aborigines' position. Even as they abandon culture-based identities and move toward an identity that relies on physical likeness more than anything else—and only on this basis can northern Aborigines embrace urban ones and dark-skinned populations elsewhere—they do not jeopardise their cultural heritage, or what they see as it. (See Armstrong 1971, about the relevant situation among Arnhem Land Aborigines.) Indeed intra-Aboriginal cultural contrasts become watered down, tend to be overlooked for the sake of a wider identity—and yet, northern Aborigines build upon a vast cultural heritage of customs and thought structures and this sets them distinctly apart from urban Aborigines.

Northern Aborigines have found a new frontier. They are manning the racial front-line. Yet there is no identity problem. The overcoming of identities which were based on introspective cultural criteria and the emphasis on a racial identity may usher in the long expected era of acute racial friction. Contrast is no longer experienced in intra-Aboriginal terms, but identity is sought and found in contrast to another 'foe', the 'white man'. The Aboriginal identity, emergent now, is bound in its extrovert orientation to collide with the contrast-group. It is a racial conflict identity.

I have elaborated on the two traditional identity concepts of *djandu* and *bi:n*: culturally and physically perceived identity. Aborigines have, briefly speaking, by retaining these concepts but gradually enlarging their implications, step by step adjusted their identification processes until the present-day result presents itself as 'their Aboriginality'! (The overcoming of a *djandu*-based identity, which traditionally had priority over the *bi:n*-based identity—as cultural criteria were considered pre-eminent—perhaps in itself indicates a step in the destruction of the traditional thought structure.) Aboriginality for Aborigines, strictly speaking, is perhaps not one identity— but two: cultural and physical. Only in combination do the two approximate to a pre-conceived Western image of Aboriginality. The incongruity between Aboriginal Aboriginality and European Aboriginality is expressed also in the dimension I have called the identity width. At first sight both images seem to coincide and this is probably the main reason for seeing one as the reflection of the other. Indeed width and structure have to some extent been prescribed by the dominant European society; but this impulse has been re-directed by Aborigines employing their indigenous identity concepts. A closer look reveals this. The culturally based Aboriginality tends to be strongly selective and excludes non-traditional and anti-traditional Aborigines. As Aborigines tend nowadays to lean more heavily on the physical aspect, they tend to over-shoot the target. They tend to include also dark-skinned populations outside Australia.

Finally, perhaps a word about the importance attributed to an identity. In a sense, importance is the mortar that joins together the three identity dimensions in actual observable reality. Only if high importance is conceded to a specific conceptual basis will structure and width, relevant to this basis, be readily observable and significant in everyday life. So far I have said little about the importance of the Aboriginal identity in the eyes of Aborigines themselves. In general, I would agree with the opinion that tradition-oriented Aborigines in conflict-situations rely on identifications with smaller units. But this is not unusual in all societies. After all, postulating 'pure' identities comes from a process of abstraction which is in this form probably specific to socio-anthropological thought. Everyday-life-reality, socially and intellectually, does not of course strictly conform to anthropological reality. In other words, man rarely, if ever, thinks in terms of 'pure' identities—unless ideologically incited—and never acts accordingly, as innumerable other 'pure' identities, personal interests, aspirations, obligations and possibly also individual psychic constellations intersect.

Identity is something eminently and completely social: identity formulates itself from *social* intellect and it finds expression in a *social* milieu. Aborigines embedded in a wider society as they are now, have to find identity in relation to 'the others' and this situation really is induced or even enforced. But as Aborigines do so, they draw on *their* social intellect and the result ultimately is *their* Aboriginality, and not a by-product of white encroachment.

Aborigines, on the whole, are no exception to other *gemeinschaft*-type units that break up and are welded into larger entities; and that entails shifts in identities. But Aborigines, perhaps unlike other people in similar circumstances, are more fortunate. They control their identity through the familiar usage of traditional concepts. Gradually and harmoniously they have transferred, preserved and developed pre-contact elements of thought and thus they have expanded their ethnocentre without bursting it.

Despite ecological discontinuity (drastic socio-environmental changes, geographical dislocation, rearrangement of material and economic life style), Aborigines have succeeded in preserving intellectual continuity. The question stands out, then, how that should have been possible in the face of the profound transformation of their whole life style. Traditional Aboriginal culture emanates the savour of a highly 'intellectual culture'. For Aborigines intellectual modes of existence had priority over material-economic ones. The points in which Aboriginal culture has unfolded most impressively and richly are immaterial, intellectual ones. Only material aspects immediately associated with belief, the religious symbolism, are more elaborate, while the material-economic side as such was comparatively crude and simple. Aborigines, therefore, seem to have lived in a predominantly intellectual medium, in a highly intellectualised world and one might say naïvely: how else could they have sustained themselves mentally in an environment and in conditions which rank amongst the harshest and most trying of the world. This may account for the fact that the elaborate ideological superstructure could relatively easily be detached from the simple groundwork of everyday life style and transferred to new socio-environmental conditions. While life changed 'around them', Aborigines continued to exist undisturbed in their basically traditional and highly intellectually oriented milieu.

It surprises me that so far as modern change among Aborigines has been made an object of studies—the primary concern of Australian Aboriginal Anthropology seems to be traditionally with reconstructing the past—the importance of mental continuity *versus* discontinuity has remained relatively neglected. Surely, the study of what Lévi-Strauss (1953:526f.) has called *conscious models,* the intellectual artefacts, which survive, should prove most rewarding. (Social continuity *and* social change can best be understood against the intellectual background, as Leach [1954] has demonstrated.) Aborigines with their traditional emphasis on intellectual life must have been vitally interested in preserving intellectual traditions, notwithstanding being uprooted in most other respects. Their 'home-made' models of pre-contact times, give them a sense of continuity in the face of profound change in other areas. Without this continuity the radical transformation of their lives would have made them mental non-entities, mere hulls mimicking Western behaviour like freaks. Appreciating this intellectual continuity means understanding Aborigines in their present form of existence, which often appears grossly maladjusted at first sight.

Acknowledgements

I thank Professor P. J. Wilson, Department of Anthropology, University of Otago, for some stimulating comments on the initial draft. The map and the sketch have been prepared by Mr M. Seden.

Notes

1. Field research was carried out from 1970 until 1972, under the auspices of the Australian Institute of Aboriginal Studies and the Department of Anthropology, University of Western Australia. I collected additional data while associated with the Aboriginal Affairs Planning Authority of Western Australia, from 1972 to 1973.

2. Walbiri ethnography shows a quite similar distinction into an exclusive concept *walaldja,* countryman, and a more inclusive one, *jaba,* human being (Meggitt 1962:67ff. 233).

3. Petri (1959:5ff.) has given an example of such a wider group orientation from the Eighty Mile Beach perspective. His example differs somewhat from mine, but is clearly based on the same general principle. In some areas these wider categories appear as so-called 'tribal' labels. (See, for instance, Meggitt 1966:89; *Wonaiga* and *Walmala.* C. Strehlow 1907, III, map; *Waringari.*) According to Elkin (1936:522) and Gould (1969:210), Desert Aborigines refer to non-secret war parties as *warmala.*

4. The few linguistic data, which I can reasonably identify as so-called Njanjan, seem to occupy a middle position between the usual Wolmadjeri and Balgo Gugadja. Njanjan may perhaps be identical with Capell's eastern Wolmadjeri or Buna:ra (Capell 1940:244).

5. The preferred identity at Balgo is nowadays Gugadja. As mentioned before, Fitzroy Aborigines who are closely related to Balgo Gugadja, call themselves Wolmadjeri and determinately refute the label Gugadja. This shows that a preferential 'tribal identity' emerges as a local convention and is accepted by all local residents regardless of their real origins.

References

ARMSTRONG, G. 1971 Current development among Arnhem Land Aborigines. In *A question of choice* (R. M. Berndt ed.), pp. 53-60. University of Western Australia Press, Perth.
BENDIX, R. 1966 *Max Weber.* University Paperbacks: Methuen, London.
BERNDT, C. H. 1961 The quest for identity: the case of the Australian Aborigines, *Oceania,* XXXII (1):16-33.
BERNDT, R. M. 1959 The concept of 'the tribe' in the Western Desert of Australia, *Oceania,* XXX (2):81-106.
——1970 Introduction. In *Australian Aboriginal Anthropology* (R. M. Berndt ed.), pp. 1-17. University of Western Australia Press, Perth.
——1971 The concept of protest within an Australian Aboriginal context. In *A question of choice* (R. M. Berndt ed.), pp. 25-43. University of Western Australia Press, Perth.
BERNDT, R. M. *and* C. H. BERNDT 1942 A preliminary report of field work in the Ooldea Region, Western South Australia, *Oceania,* XII (4):305-30.
——*and*——1970 *Man, land and myth in north Australia.* Ure Smith, Sydney.

BIRDSELL, J. B. 1970 Local group composition among the Australian Aborigines: a critique of the evidence from fieldwork conducted since 1930, *Current Anthropology*, 11 (2):115-42.

CAPELL, A. 1940 The classification of languages in North and North Western Australia, *Oceania*, X (3-4):241-72, 404-33.

DAHRENDORF, R. 1973 *Homo Sociologicus*. Routledge and Kegan Paul, London.

ELKIN, A. P. 1936 Australian tribal names, *Oceania*, VII (4):522.

GOODENOUGH, W. 1965 Rethinking 'Status' and 'Role': towards a general model of the cultural organisation of social relationships. In *The relevance of models for social anthropology* (M. Banton ed.), pp. 1-24. A.S.A. Monographs 1. Tavistock, London.

GOULD, R. A. 1969 *Yiwara*. Collins, London-Sydney.

HABERMAS, J. 1968 *Technik und Wissenschaft als 'Ideologie'*. Edition Suhrkamp.

KABERRY, P. M. 1937 Notes on the languages of East Kimberley, North-West Australia, *Oceania*, VIII (1):90-103.

KLAPP, O. E. 1969 *Collective search for identity*. Holt, Rinehart and Winston, New York.

KOLIG, E. 1972 Bi:n and Kageja: an Australian Aboriginal model of the European society as a guide in social change, *Oceania*, XLIII (1):1-18.

——1974 Tradition and emancipation: an Australian Aboriginal version of 'Nativism'. *Supplement to Newsletter*, Aboriginal Affairs Planning Authority, Western Australia, 1 (6): 1-42.

——(in press) The changing law: religious organization and Western influence among Aborigines of the Fitzroy Area, Southern Kimberleys.

LEACH, E. R. 1954 *Political systems of Highland Burma*. Athlone Press, London.

LEVI-STRAUSS, C. 1953 Social structure. In *Anthropology today* (A. L. Kroeber ed.), pp. 524-53. University of Chicago Press, Chicago.

LINTON, R. 1936 *The study of man*. Appleton-Century, New York.

MEGGITT, M. 1962 *Desert people*. University of Chicago Press, Chicago.

——1966 *Gadjari among the Walbiri Aborigines of Central Australia*. Oceania Monograph, 14. Sydney.

MERTON, R. K. 1957 *Social theory and social structure*. Free Press, Glencoe.

MUHLMANN, W. E. 1964 Erfahrung und Denken in der Sicht des Ethnologen, *Paideuma*, 10 (1):11-21.

OATES, W. and L. OATES 1970 *A revised linguistic survey of Australia*. Australian Institute of Aboriginal Studies, Canberra.

PEILE, A. n.d. Introduction to Gugadja. (Unpublished manuscript.)

PETRI, H. 1959 Geographisches Weltbild und zwischenstammliche Handelsverbindungen nordwestaustralischer Eingeborenen-Gruppen. *Wiener Völkerkundliche Mitteilungen*, 7,II, Nos. 1-4:3-22.

——1968 Nachwort. In *Die Religionen der Südsee und Australiens* (H. Nevermann, E. A. Worms, H. Petri eds.), pp. 298-311. Kohlhammer, Stuttgart.

STREHLOW, C. 1907 *Die Aranda-und Loritja-Stamme in Zentral-Australien*. Frankfurt/Main.

VON STURMER, J. 1973 Changing Aboriginal identity in Cape York. In *Aboriginal identity in contemporary Australian society* (D. Tugby ed.). Jacaranda Press. Brisbane.

TUGBY, D. (ed.) 1973 *Aboriginal identity in contemporary Australian society*. Jacaranda Press, Brisbane.

WALLACE, A. F. C. 1966 *Religion: an anthropological view*. Random House, New York.

WENTWORTH, W. C. 1973 Aboriginal identity, government and the law. In *Aboriginal identity in contemporary Australian society* (D. Tugby ed.), pp. 7-15. Jacaranda Press, Brisbane.

4 Old country, new territory:

some implications of the settlement process

Susan Tod Woenne

Broadly speaking, this paper is an investigation into the nature of the changes which occur when Desert Aborigines who traditionally[1] lived a semi-nomadic life in small groups of fluctuating size and composition commit themselves to living permanently in larger groups which, relatively speaking, are stable in size and composition.

The implications of the problem are, of course, wide-ranging and complex; as are the possible approaches one might adopt in order to define and explicate it. Indeed, it could be fairly asserted that most of the work concerned with traditionally oriented Aborigines in the desert areas, both past and present, deals implicitly or explicitly with facets of this general theme, whether discussion is of the (ethnographic) 'present' or of a reconstructed past, or whether the almost universal dislocation of the patterns of man-to-land relationships is explicitly acknowledged or obscured by other emphases. My intention here is to set out some of the factors involved with the spatial and conceptual location and re-location of traditionally defined man-to-land and man-to-man relationships *as they are modified by* a specific Settlement situation.

The specific focus of this paper is Docker River[2], a non-Mission affiliated Government Welfare Settlement in the south-western corner of the Northern Territory (see map). The Settlement was established recently, and all of the Aborigines who came to Docker River with the intention of residing there came from settlement-like places elsewhere in the Northern Territory as well as in Western Australia and South Australia.

Most people who came to Docker River in the first two years of its establishment asserted that they were coming back to live in, or near, their 'country'. The act of returning to one's country constitutes, among other things, an important social statement; and, generally speaking, that anyone's 'country' was Docker River was sufficient reason for returning to live there. Specific relationships to 'country', however, were based on a wide range of disparate affiliatory criteria; so, although reasons for returning to Docker were based primarily upon traditional criteria by which people are related to land, they were continually subject to dispute and negotiation. Such disputes were largely concerned with the right to reside permanently at the Settlement; and that right was derived from pre-settlement relatedness to Docker River within the context of the wider western Central Ranges area. Disputes seldom involved the question of who belonged on the Settlement *instead* of someone else; rather the question was who belonged there *more* than someone else. Negotiation seldom involved actual affiliations of people to land; rather it involved the relative weight of affiliations in terms of stronger or weaker claims to the right of permanent residence at Docker River.

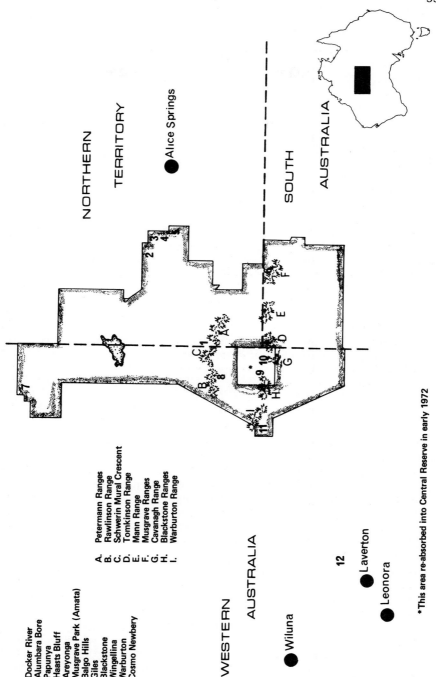

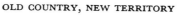

1. Docker River
2. Alumbara Bore
3. Papunya
4. Haasts Bluff
5. Areyonga
6. Musgrave Park (Amata)
7. Balgo Hills
8. Blackstone
9. Wingellina
10. Warburton
11. Cosmo Newbery
12.

A. Petermann Ranges
B. Rawlinson Range
C. Schwerin Mural Crescent
D. Tomkinson Range
E. Mann Range
F. Musgrave Ranges
G. Cavanagh Range
H. Blackstone Ranges
I. Warburton Range

*This area re-absorbed into Central Reserve in early 1972

Figure 1 : Locations from which Aborigines came to settle at Docker River

What follows, then, is based largely on the people's answers to their own questions of one another: Whose Settlement — whose 'country' — is Docker River? By what rights? Which people are Docker River people? In terms of which criteria? And relative to which social and territorial contexts? It will be useful to deal first with the matter of context in general.

Government settlements, missions and pastoral stations have been part of the scene for decades, affecting the lives, perceptions, and expectations of Aborigines variously and, in a sense, irrevocably. With very few exceptions a settlement-like situation of one kind or another comprises a large part of the living experience of all Aborigines in the Centre. Installations of this sort are part of the environment, for better or for worse; and, for those people born during the past thirty years or so, such places have, literally, *always* been there, have *always* constituted some part of their everyday experience of living.

Two assumptions basic to this discussion, then, are:
(1) The Settlement (in this case, Docker River) must be considered as part of people's everyday living context, part of their effective environment.
(2) Participation in what the people themselves define as traditional, i.e. pre-settlement, activities is an integral part of participation in a settlement-like situation.

As regards these assumptions, consider Meggitt's (1963:216) assertion that,

> . . . information and inference about traditional society which emerge from field work can have an evidential value if they are part of the pattern of social attitudes of contemporary Aborigines. That is, we need not be concerned with the absolute (and probably unknowable) validity of such propositions as statements of the actual characteristics of inter-relations of certain elements of the indigenous society; but we can usefully examine the Aborigines' own beliefs . . . about these phenomena if such beliefs condition the people's behaviour in, or adaptation to, the current society.

Self-conscious reconstruction and assertion of local pre-settlement conditions was a conspicuous and much-engaged-in activity at Docker River in the early years of its establishment. Also conspicuous was that the Settlement itself constituted a spatial and conceptual reference point in terms of which much reconstruction of the pre-settlement, traditional, past was carried out.

In order to determine how the Aborigines themselves define the inter-relationships between pre- and post-settlement Docker River, we must consider three inter-related areas of investigation:
(1) What are the multiple interpretations seen by the Aborigines to be appropriate to and arising from the Settlement itself?
(2) What is the significance to the Aborigines of the location of the Settlement in terms of territorial and social contexts relevant to the area in traditional times?
(3) How do the Aborigines define and order the inter-relationships of land and people in a context of a permanently settled place which is within traditionally settled 'country'?

It is necessary at this point to present some background material to underline what is considered by the Aborigines to be a unique set of relationships between a definable population, the specific Settlement with which that population is primarily associated, and the location of that Settlement with respect to pre-settlement distribution of the defined population throughout the area. I will then proceed, in the light of the above points, to discuss some aspects of the content of those relationships.

The area of reference is the central and eastern central part of the Western Desert bloc (see Berndt 1959), which comprises the western portion of the Central Ranges, together with some areas of more typical desert or semi-desert country to the west, north-west, and south of the Ranges. Docker River Government Settlement is located at the foot of the Dean Ranges in the Petermann complex in the extreme south-western corner of the Northern Territory. The Petermanns lie within the Petermann Reserve which comprises the southern one-third of the large Southwest Reserve. The Southwest Reserve, in turn, comprises part of the Central Reserve which extends into Western Australia and South Australia and is in the vicinity of 260,000 square kilometres (100,000 square miles) in total area. Bidjanjdjadjara, Ngaadjadjara, Ngaanjadjara, and Bindubi are spoken at Docker River, although dialect usage does not correspond to any specific, self-defined group in residence there[3].

Docker River's first full year as an established settlement was 1968[4]. Located in a part of the Reserve which had been virtually uninhabited for many years, it attracted gradually increasing numbers of people who considered the Settlement to be their 'country', or part of their 'country', or more their 'country' than their places of previous residence.

From an administrative point of view, Docker River was established to ease serious problems of overcrowding and the consequent lack of 'adequate' facilities and services on other south-western Northern Territory installations.[5] Choice of site in the Petermanns was well advised, as a number of people at settlements and missions to the east had major affiliations with the area, had expressed their desire to return to the area, and had stated their intention to reside there as soon as the Settlement was actually established.

From an Aboriginal point of view, the establishment of Docker River was welcomed. Not only were people able to return to an area of great importance to them after many years of absence, but it was seen that their intrinsic relatedness to the land had been acknowledged and supported by the Government. Acknowledgement and support was made manifest by the provision of their own Settlement in their own 'country'. Ownership and, hence, jurisdiction was implied from the beginning, by virtue of the people's pre-settlement relatedness to the land.

Those Aborigines who were explicitly encouraged to come to Docker River and those who, from an administrative point of view, had primary rights to the Settlement were people who were: (1) 'from' the Petermanns 'originally' and who were (2) previously (and usually) resident in the Northern Territory. Others were directly and indirectly discouraged from coming to Docker River.

The *fact* of the new Settlement in the Petermanns, however, encouraged the return of people who, although related to the area, had for a number of reasons been residing within other administrative boundaries, i.e. Western Australia and South Australia. Consequently, *different* people considered themselves to be actual or potential Docker River people from those whose initial rights to reside at the Settlement had been officially under-written.

In addition, *more* people actually came to Docker than those directly encouraged by the Administration to return to their 'country'.

It is significant that the 'area' as defined by administrative boundaries to be relevant to residence at Docker was different from Aboriginal definitions of that area. For example, the Northern Territory-Western Australia border is only ten track-kilometres (six track-miles) west of Docker River. And, although the Petermanns barely extend into Western Australia at their south-western extremity, the Schwerin Mural Crescent and the Rawlinson Ranges which comprise the western end of the Central Ranges area, are closely linked indeed with the Petermanns, but lie fully within the administrative jurisdiction of Western Australia. The gross distinctions between, for example, 'Western Australian people' *versus* 'Northern Territory people', or 'Areyonga people' *versus* 'Warburton people', were employed as labels connoting major territorial affiliations and implying rights (or lack thereof) to permanent residence at Docker River. These labels and many others based on similarly defined distinctions were frequently used by Settlement staff and taken up by the Aborigines themselves when rights to Settlement services and privileges were contested.

Such rights were frequently contested, but their assertion and recognition were nearly always substantiated in terms of relatedness to land throughout the wider western Central Ranges area, not just within the Petermanns, not just within the Northern Territory.

It is important to keep in mind that all people who *returned* to Docker River had some experience with other places *like* Docker River, i.e. other settlements, missions, ration depots and the like. Although experience with and expectations concerning settlement-like places varied considerably, there was no question but that such installations should necessarily provide at least minimal services and that unencumbered access to such services should be available to those people most closely associated with the Settlement.

Thus people came to the new Docker River, having expectations concerning its function *qua* settlement and how it should operate with respect to the rights of its resident population. At the same time they considered that they had come *back* to their 'country', to land *already related to them* (see Stanner 1965:14) in a number of acknowledged traditional ways.

Although the act or stated intention of returning to one's 'country' constitutes an important and often ritualised social statement, relatedness to land is ubiquitous and many-levelled; and the specific elements of relatedness to land and people which any individual or group manifests or asserts at a particular time depend, to a considerable extent, on situational factors. As indicated above, the Settlement itself must be seen as partly defining the situation; and it will be useful to consider briefly some aspects of that definition.

The term 'Settlement' refers to Docker River Settlement specifically, or to any government settlement and, as such, constitutes an example of the category 'settlement'. The latter is used generically at Docker River to include any installation which is seen as sharing, to some extent, the following characteristics:

(a) A settlement is established, administered, and maintained for Aborigines by non-Aborigines.

(b) It is known or assumed by the Aborigines to be supported and maintained by non-private, external agencies.

(c) It is assumed to be permanent.

(d) Its purpose is the provision of a range of services specifically for Aborigines and to which they have irrevocable rights.

(e) One of the services provided specifically for Aborigines is the settlement staff.

(f) The Aboriginal population constitutes a majority, a definable core of which is considered to have jurisdiction over the place and is associated *primarily* with that place.

HIERARCHY OF CATEGORIES OF 'PLACE'

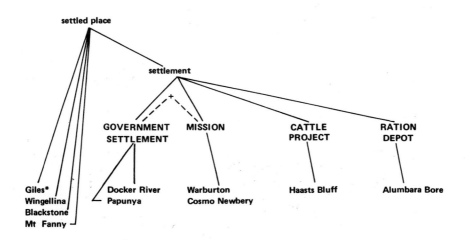

+ = 'Community' in the sense of recent Government development programmes
* The locations mentioned here are intended as examples only and are not inclusive

Examples of settlement, then, include government settlements, missions, ration depots, out-stations, and some cattle projects[6] (see diagram). The category settlement, as defined above, excludes towns and 'fringe'-areas, as well as town reserves which, together with most pastoral properties, are generally assumed by Aborigines to be 'owned' by and administered for non-Aborigines.

From an outside point of view, it could be argued that a settlement is a very different kind of place from, for example, a mission. Different external agencies are involved, and the rationales by which each kind of settlement is established and by which each continues (or continued) to administer often differ widely and at a fundamental level.[7] The Aborigines in this area, however, do not consider such criteria to be relevant points of distinction.

Although it is widely acknowledged by Aborigines that living on a particular mission is, to some extent, different from living on a particular settlement, distinctions are not made in terms of intrinsic differences in *kind* of establishment or *kind* of place, as defined by administrative policy or development rationale. The important differences are articulated in terms of cumulative individual experience of both the type of personnel with which each kind of settlement is generally staffed and the range of specific services each settlement is seen to make available *to the Aborigines*. Activities related to the teaching of Christian doctrine, or conspicuously defined in terms of it, are considered to be characteristic of the type of personnel attached to any settlement, not as one of the services that a particular *kind* of settlement makes available. To my knowledge, there was no instance of any Aboriginal person coming to or leaving Docker River because it was *not* mission-run.

In so far as Docker River is conceived of as an example of the category 'settlement', it partly defines its residents' environmental context. Another element in the definition is that of Docker River as a kind of place with respect to traditional conceptions. A settlement is not sufficiently defined by a point on the map via topographical reference, nor by reference to political or economic functions. Docker River Settlement is land already related to people, and the structure and content of the relatedness in part define it as a *kind* of place.

Consider the term 'settled place' which, as a category, subsumes 'settlement', which in turn subsumes, for example, any 'settlement' and any 'mission'. As a category 'settled place' can be seen as:

(a) a specific location to which people come,

(b) intending to reside permanently or to make it their permanent living base, and

(c) attempting to assert and have commonly acknowledged a range of traditionally defined affiliations and associations with that place which will support their individual and collective, prior and primary, rights to the place and its services, to the area and its resources.

Although all instances of the category 'settlement' can be seen as examples of 'settled place', all 'settled places' are not necessarily 'settlements'. This latter point is well illustrated by the groups of people periodically residing at such places as Giles and Wingellina (both in Western Australia) and by efforts of these and many other groups who have been at pains to convince the Government(s) of their primary rights to a particular area with the expectation that a 'settlement' will be established for them by virtue of their *demonstrated* relatedness to the land. It is significant that, to the Government, relatedness is seen to be demonstrated, at least in part, by residence.

The essential characteristic of 'settled place' is the aspect of permanence which applies not only to actual or intended residence at a particular place but applies also to expectations of a usually resident population component. In other words, 'settled place' implies a *particular, enduring social context*. The general elements of this more or less permanent context, although informed by traditionally recognised kinds of relatedness between people and land, are unaffected by pre-settlement exigencies.

Extra-human factors which previously modified the formation, continuity, and distribution of groups of various size are no longer of vital effect. Yet the social and religious categories which relate people to one another and to the land and which previously would have described a group in any specific social context are still relevant.

Ideally, the traditional complex of such inter-relationships made it possible for people to travel with relative freedom over a very large area of land, forming and re-forming groups of different composition depending upon conditions and occasions and providing the criteria by which the weight of an individual's credentials for being in a certain place in certain company could be assessed. Although everyone[8] who came to Docker River with the intention of residing could claim legitimate, traditionally defined credentials for being at Docker, legitimacy was asserted on the basis of widely differing pre-settlement times, occasions, social contexts, and specific assessments. Taken separately, any of the claims ideally provided sufficient reason for being at Docker. When taken as a whole, however, and directed toward residence and jurisdiction over the Settlement, there was continuing debate as to how such claims could be assessed when taken *all together, in the same place, at the same time.*

Docker River as a 'settled place' stands for — represents — a large area of land, as defined above. In that sense, and with respect to relatedness to land within that area, people did return to their 'country' (see also Yengoyan 1970:82). In another sense, however, residence at Docker River connoted return to and residence in a number of different 'countries' which, in pre-settlement times, had been identified in part by the habitual movement of people over land, between and around a number of uniquely defined *estates* (see Stanner 1965).[9]

Previous residence in the immediate Docker area in pre-settlement times occurred within a variety of social contexts and represented specific groupings of a population distributed over a much wider area. To continue with Stanner's conceptualisation (*ibid.*): the people who returned to Docker as their 'country' attempted to claim prior rights to the Settlement by asserting its pre-settlement location within the range(s) or domain(s) of particular estates to which they were directly or indirectly[10] related.

Relatedness to an estate, especially if connected with an important ritual-mythological centre, is uncontestable although it is unclear to what extent such relatedness ever actually characterised specific groups (see, among others, Berndt 1959; Birdsell 1970; Hiatt 1962, 1966, 1968; Yengoyan 1970). The relatedness of a person to an estate is inalienable and is not significantly affected by his long, or even permanent absence.

It is important here to recall that people returned to Docker after a very long time of both being away from the area and of being in other areas and other 'settled places'. During this time (of up to three decades) all but the most intrinsic relationships, i.e. with estates, had been weakened and modified; and, conversely, relationships with other areas had been established, strengthened, and expanded. The cognitive map of the area, so to speak, had shrunk, had constricted around the various estate locations; and those areas and locations previously relatable to estates as domain and range had become unfocused because unattended. They no longer functioned as life spaces and had not for many years been subject to more or less habitual use.

The reconstruction of pre-settlement *and* pre-settlement social contexts and of particular configurations of group composition can be seen as a concerted effort, on the part of the Aborigines at Docker River, to *re-people* the land. Re-peopling involves the substantiation of relatedness of a number of kinds, by virtue of having gained, or the possibility of having claimed, pre-settlement credentials in the vicinity of Docker River.

The weight of such credentials in the past was highly dependent on the composition of any particular group as well as on the group's location with respect to any estate area. Both freedom of movement and fluidity of group membership have been amply attested to. Balancing such freedom, however, were (and are) qualitative differences between *being in* a place and *belonging to* it (Stanner 1965:2). Strehlow (1965:128) highlights my intended point here:

> The willingness of all group members to return to their proper group areas after temporary absences made it possible for local groups living in more favoured localities to extend hospitality to less fortunate groups during the recurrent droughts.

The general assumption of such willingness, sustained by a range of ritual, social, and emotional attachments to land (see, among others, Strehlow 1965; Peterson 1972) is widely articulated at Docker River but is most clearly demonstrable with reference to estates, more specifically to the immediate area of important ritual centres. As I have indicated, the interactional referents to any individually relevant 'group area' had to be re-located, both conceptually and physically.

Relatedness to estates in the vicinity of Docker River was seldom a matter for debate, whereas claims of relatedness to 'country' which was *possibly* within the range of a particular estate applied to the initially 'unfocused' 'country' which Docker River Settlement connoted but did not define. The Settlement itself was not clearly anyone's estate, and credentials for ever having been in the immediate area did not identify or imply the existence (past or present) of any specific residence grouping.

Assertion of relatedness appropriate to Docker 'country' and re-enactments of what were said to be actual (or similar to) pre-settlement social contexts took place with increasing frequency. The process of re-peopling initially took the form of lengthy, often heated discussions of situations remembered, attested to, and likely. In addition, there was concerted individual and group activity wherein re-enactments of such contexts were actually carried out at appropriate locations. The result has been the gradual extension of social, ritual, and territorial networks of a range and complexity not remembered to be characteristic of the local pre-settlement situation.

In attempting to assert prior and primary rights to Docker River so as to gain and maintain jurisdiction over it, people claimed a range of degrees of relatedness to 'country' in the vicinity of Docker which, by definition, was traditionally within the 'proper' group area of each of their estates. Because of the fluidity with which estate-based groups of people could move over large areas of territory, definition of range and, hence, of domain is most usefully seen in terms of frequency of residence in and use of particular areas. For a number of reasons the larger areas had been uninhabited for many years or, rather, not inhabited according to traditional patterns. Thus all but the most intrinsic ties with land had been modified and had to be socially re-asserted. Re-assertion via particular instances of pre-settlement interaction established relatedness to 'country' in which interaction took place, but it also re-affirmed the inter-relationships and, hence, the inter-relatedness of the people who had participated in that interaction.

Occasional and periodic points of intersection between small, relatively enclosed social networks in the pre-settlement situation have now been defined as points of connection whereby a much more extensive network has been formed which operates in terms of the conceptual and territorial focus of 'settled place', i.e. Docker River Settlement.

The result, conceptually speaking, is rather like a large domain, composed of a number of estates together with their (now) shared range, which includes the Settlement. Docker River 'country' now *means* the principal estates which are 'close'[11] to it, and jurisdiction over the Settlement is negotiable through the aggregate claims of relatedness to one or a number of 'close' estates. The range and, hence, domain of Docker River 'country' is extendable outwards from the Settlement to less proximal estates and is being asserted and acknowledged in terms of frequency of present use, linked relatedness with estates, and extension of kin or kin-like ties.

Docker River 'country' has become a focal point for and an interconnecting link in the wide-spread network of social and territorial relationships which characterise the separate but equally unique settlements throughout the Central Reserves. In addition the establishment of Docker River as a new settlement provided the opportunity for the re-peopling (in the sense in which I use it above) of areas farther afield from Docker River 'country' which are potentially other 'settled places'.

Acknowledgements

I would like to thank W. E. Greble, R. G. Locke, and S. J. Hallam for reading an earlier version of this paper and for providing useful and constructive comments.

Notes

1. I define 'traditional' as pertaining to those elements of life and living which the Aborigines themselves trace, directly or indirectly, to pre-settlement conditions *and* which define 'things Aboriginal' as distinct from 'things non-Aboriginal'. Admittedly this definition is loosely cast. It implies, however, the background of qualitative assumptions by which Aborigines in this area evaluate others' knowledge, experience, and behaviour; and its application is well illustrated by the use of such localised terms as 'the Wanggayi way'.

2. My fieldwork at Docker River was supported by the Australian Institute of Aboriginal Studies and involved three field periods: six weeks in 1969, eight months in 1970, and the last five and one-half months of 1971.

3. I conform here to the A.I.A.S. convention for spelling. The alternative and, perhaps, more widely used spellings would be: Pitjanytjatjara, Ngaatjatjara, Ngaanyatjara, and Pintupi. See, for example, Douglas 1964; Glass and Hackett 1970; Hansen 1974; and ten Raa and Woenne 1970-74.

4. See Northern Territory Administration, Welfare Branch, *Annual Report* 1967-68, p. 128, and subsequent reports.

5. It is not possible here to discuss the complexities of the people's previous involvement with other specific settlements. The primary residential focus of people from the east was Areyonga, Northern Territory, although a number of other places were significantly involved. See Long 1963.

6. For example, those which have been established and are run as adjuncts to other, previously established, installations such as Haasts Bluff, Northern Territory.

7. See, among others, Long 1966:5, 1970:176-88; Hiatt 1965:286-7, 294-5. In addition, overall applied rationale pertaining to *settlements* has been modified from time to time over the years. At present the implementation of plans for community development via the principle of self-determination results in the place label, 'community'. This label, in theory, subsumes both settlement and mission as a *kind* of place; but it remains to be seen whether the functional connotation of the label 'community' will be translated into social action thus, in fact, making Aboriginal communities different in kind from the settlements and missions of the 'past'.

8. There are a few exceptions which do not, however, modify the present point.

9. It is impossible here to consider some important implications of Stanner's (1965) model. For this discussion I go no further afield than his definitions of estate, range, and domain, all of which are well known.

10. Other than patrilineally.

11. The referents to spatial and conceptual distance have demonstrably changed over several generations, most particularly in terms of reckoning the degree of 'closeness' of country and of actual kin.

References

BERNDT, R. M. 1959 The concept of 'the tribe' in the Western Desert of Australia, *Oceania*, XXX:81-107.

BIRDSELL, J. B. 1970 Local group composition among the Australian Aborigines: a critique of the evidence from fieldwork conducted since 1930, *Current Anthropology*, 11:115-42.

DOUGLAS, W. H. 1964 *An introduction to the Western Desert language*. Oceania Linguistic Monographs 4 (revised). Sydney.

GLASS, A. and D. HACKETT 1970 *Pitjantjatjara Grammar: a tagmemic view of the Ngaayatjara [sic] (Warburton Ranges) dialect*. Australian Institute of Aboriginal Studies, Canberra.

HANSEN, K. C. and L. E. HANSEN 1974 *Pintupi dictionary*. Summer Institute of Linguistics, Darwin.

HIATT, L. R. 1962 Local organization among the Australian Aborigines, *Oceania*, XXXII: 267-86.

——1965 Aborigines in the Australian community. In *Australian society* (A. F. Davies and S. Encel eds), pp. 274-95. Cheshire, Melbourne.

——1966 The lost horde. *Oceania*, XXXVII:81-92.

——1968 Ownership and use of land among the Australian Aborigines. In *Man the hunter* (R. B. Lee and I. De Vore eds), pp. 99-102. Aldine, Chicago.

LONG, J. P. M. 1963 Preliminary work in planning welfare development in the Petermann Ranges, *Australian Territories*, 3:4-12.

——1966 The numbers and distribution of Aboriginals in Australia. In *Aborigines in the economy* (I. G. Sharp and C. M. Tatz eds), pp. 1-15. Jacaranda, Brisbane.

——1970 *Aboriginal settlements*. Australian National University Press, Canberra.

MEGGITT, M. J. 1963 Social organization: morphology and typology. In *Australian Aboriginal studies* (H. Sheils ed.), pp. 211-17. Oxford University Press, Melbourne.

NORTHERN TERRITORY ADMINISTRATION, Welfare Branch, 1967/68 *Annual Report*. Darwin.

PETERSON, N. 1972 Totemism yesterday: sentiment and local organization among the Australian Aborigines, *Man*, 7:12-32.

STANNER, W. E. H. 1965 Aboriginal territorial organization: estate, range, domain and regime, *Oceania*, 36:1-26.

STREHLOW, T. G. H. 1965 Culture, social structure and environment in Aboriginal central Australia. In *Aboriginal Man in Australia* (R. M. and C. H. Berndt eds), pp. 121-45. Angus and Robertson, Sydney.

TEN RAA, E. and S. T. WOENNE 1970-74 *Research dictionary of the Western Desert Language of Australia*. University of Western Australia, Nedlands. (Computer print-out.)

YENGOYAN, A. A. 1970 Demographic factors in Pitjandjara social organization. In *Australian Aboriginal Anthropology* (R. M. Berndt ed.), pp. 71-91. University of Western Australia Press, Nedlands.

5 Aboriginal self-regulation and the new regime:

Jigalong, Western Australia

Robert Tonkinson

This paper discusses aspects of socio-economic change at Jigalong, a Western Desert fringe settlement, in the four years since it was relinquished by the Apostolic Church and became a government-run project.[1] This is a tentative statement for two reasons: I have been in the field only ten weeks so far, after a four year absence; also, it is little more than six months since the appointment of a resident Community Adviser and Jigalong's change in status to an incorporated community, so a fair assessment of these important developments is not yet possible.

The transition from colonialist paternalism to a significant measure of Aboriginal self-government has only just commenced at Jigalong, so it is not yet possible to tell what adaptive strategies the Aborigines will employ in coping with the new responsibilities and attendant pressures that are being thrust upon them.[2] This paper suggests that, while the new developments are bringing about alterations in many Jigalong Aborigines' perceptions of the wider society and its agents, their primary concerns remain centred on problems of self-regulation that have little direct relevance to the current community development programme.[3]

Role-stereotypes and the old regime During the twenty-four years that the Apostolic missionaries were at Jigalong, the local Aborigines developed strongly negative stereotypes of them. This negativism arose mainly because of the Aborigines' markedly tradition-oriented outlook, exhibited most clearly in their value system, social organisation and religion.[4] Because of the strength of this tradition, the Aborigines resented missionary attempts to turn their children against them and undermine their Law in order to replace it with a culture based on a fundamentalist version of Christianity. Initial culture contact with frontier white men led the Aborigines to perceive these later arrivals as an aberrant group whom they eventually labelled 'Christian', a category quite distinct from 'white-fella'. They stereotyped 'Christians' as, among other things, anti-Aboriginal, anti-Law, tight-fisted, joyless and unwilling to be friends with them; whereas 'white-fellas' were judged individually, as good or bad or a bit of both, depending on the nature of their treatment of Aborigines.

Aboriginal-missionary relationships were conflict-oriented much of the time and were characterised by very poor communication and a mutual unwillingness to understand the other's viewpoint. By the time of their withdrawal in 1969 the missionaries had only one firmly committed convert (a woman) as well as the sympathy of a number of the local women. This poor showing is not surprising in view of the foregoing comments, but there were additional reasons. Interaction between the adult Aborigines and the missionaries was minimal, formal and confined mainly to the work situation. Also, the missionaries made no attempts whatsoever to involve the Aborigines in decision-making that affected them, regarding them instead as primitive wards to be paternalistically and firmly controlled. They concentrated their evangelising and 'civilising' efforts on the schoolchildren, who submitted to the dormitory discipline but rejected the Christian message. (Negative reinforcement, especially as a socialisation technique, was not characteristic of the traditional culture.)

The Aborigines had experienced relatively little contact with the wider society and knew little about the 'government'. They believed it to be a powerful agency and were concerned that its representatives, particularly the police whom they fear greatly, might act to suppress certain of their traditional activities and customs. Its agents rarely ever consulted with them and were thus seen as working against rather than for them. The missionaries played on Aboriginal fears by periodic use of the threat of 'government' intervention to maintain their control over the schoolchildren and pensioners, on whose government subsidies and social service income they depended heavily for the operation of the mission.

The Aborigines successfully discouraged missionary interference in their internal affairs and excluded them from their ritual life. This vitally important aspect of the traditional culture had actually been strengthened as a result of their settling at Jigalong on a permanent basis. Although made up of members of several different linguistic groups that were once scattered over a wide area of the desert, the Aborigines had successfully subjugated factional interests to become 'the Jigalong Mob', a community unified by its shared Law and its firm opposition to any whites or more sophisticated Aborigines who advocate the modification or destruction of this Law, which is their Dreamtime heritage and the source of all power and pride. In their dealings with the missionaries the Aborigines felt strongly that they held the upper hand much of the time and that they were in control of their own destiny, despite their economic dependence on whites.

Jigalong as government settlement   When the state Native Welfare Department (now AAPA) took control of Jigalong on 1 January 1970, the Aborigines were pleased with what they took to be their triumph over the 'Christians' but were uncertain as to their future under the new regime. The two or three previous years had seen a marked downturn in their conflicts with the missionaries, as dwindling staff numbers had forced the abandonment of the dormitory system. Certain other reforms, such as the full payment of pensions, had been implemented and thus defused potentially disruptive situations. But after the takeover, government proposals to shift the settlement as a solution to the chronic problem of inadequate water supply perturbed the Aborigines. They were aware of the benefits afforded by their relative isolation, so they were — and still are — reluctant to move from what has become their permanent home. They say that they suffer badly from *gudjilba* 'homesickness' if they stay away from Jigalong too long, and their yearning is for the 'country' as well as for their relatives.

For at least the first three years, a combination of continuing staff and finance shortages precluded much developmental activity, although there had been much talk by government agents about Jigalong's eventual economic self-sufficiency and Aboriginal control. In the last year or so, however, Jigalong has been allocated considerable sums for community development and has received a great deal of attention from both state and commonwealth agencies. This has led to many visits by government officials, and more meetings with outsiders than the Aborigines had ever experienced. Many promises have been made and many plans for the future of Jigalong have been discussed.

Inaction and malaise have given way to a flurry of activity. The white staff has been brought to full strength, and ambitious building and station improvement programmes have been implemented, thus increasing the workforce of Aboriginal males. When Jigalong became an incorporated community, an administrative council composed of eight local Aborigines came into being as the governing body. This council acts for the community and has *de jure* control of decision-making in a wide range of matters concerning community development. In its work the council is advised by the Enterprises Officer, who supervises and co-ordinates economic development and maintenance activities, and the Community Adviser, who assists the council and promotes community social development. The councillors have only limited formal education (if any) or experience of the complexities of the outside world, so they must rely heavily on the knowledge and integrity of their advisers in important matters pertaining to planning and expenditure. Although the matters brought up for discussion by the councillors tend to be of more immediate concern (e.g. the use of community vehicles, control of dogs), they are keenly interested in certain larger concerns, such as the provision of Aboriginal housing and other services.

Meanwhile, in the camp (most of which is at least 200 yards from the main settlement on the opposite side of a large creekbed), very little has changed since the mission days, at least in terms of the physical environment and the general life-style of the Aborigines. They now have some toilets and showers, but continue to live in humpies, iron huts or behind windbreaks. As before, about twenty per cent of the Jigalong Mob is away at any given time, working on pastoral stations in the surrounding area; and a few now work in the town of Port Hedland. Of those remaining at Jigalong who are not pensioners, some make a living producing artefacts for sale to whites (Newman township is a lucrative market only 160 kilometres [100 miles] away). A small minority has no visible means of support and must rely on the generosity of relatives, since no unemployment benefits are paid locally.[5] Almost all the money in circulation is eventually spent in the community store.

Among the older Aborigines of both sexes, there is little interest in what is happening across the creek as long as their pensions arrive, there is food in the store and no one is seen to be threatening their Law. Most refer to themselves as *ngura* 'camp' blokes, who keep to their side of the creek and spend very little time in the main settlement. These older people seem content to leave bureaucratic dealings with whites in the hands of the councillors, on whom they rely to safeguard community interests. They are satisfied as long as their representatives 'fight for this country and the Law'.

Changing conceptions

(a) *The government*. In the abstract of this paper, written before entering the field, it was suggested that four years was perhaps long enough for Aboriginal stereotypes of the government workers (white) at Jigalong to have been formed, such that they are categorised, ascribed certain characteristics and evaluated positively or negatively. No such stereotypes have yet arisen, however. Instead, the local whites are classed as 'white-fella' and are assessed individually as good, or not bad, or no good, according to varying criteria, such as friendliness, fairness, general disposition, working ability.

Aboriginal assessment of most local whites is favourable most of the time. This may be in part a consequence of their markedly altered perception of the role of 'the government', from fear that it would interfere in their Law to an awareness among many Aborigines that it is the principal source of their income and appears to be interested in helping them. The most significant and valued conviction acquired by the Aborigines from their many contacts with visiting officials in the past few years is that no attempts will be made to force them to modify their Law or prevent them from following its dictates as they see fit. On the contrary, they maintain that they have been urged to actively retain their traditions. Such encouragement was never forthcoming from the missionaries or most other whites in the past. Belief in such assurances is an important factor in their retention of a strong sense of identity and pride in their heritage.

Although aware of their dependence on government moneys for continued subsistence and for community development, the Aborigines who show an interest in such matters are decidedly ambivalent in their attitudes to the government. Of all the money that has been invested in the Jigalong project recently, very little is seen by the Aborigines to have benefited them in any direct or significant way. Many promises, particularly those relating to the building of an Aboriginal 'village' and other facilities, remain unfulfilled after years of discussion. There is strong dissatisfaction among some Aborigines about the lack of progress in this matter. To date the new 'village' consists of a water tank and one trial house, which many Aborigines criticise for being little more than a tin shed. They point to the rapidity with which new 'proper' houses (transportables) for white staff members are supplied, and say that these are what they want to live in, not empty tin boxes. The whites have electricity and houses with plumbing, running water, coolers and so on, but still the Aborigines have none of these. Many Aborigines are quite disinterested in such material things but for others the contrast in living standards between them and the whites would not continue to be a feature of the contact situation if the government were really sincere about helping them.

Councillors and other men who regularly attend council meetings have a fair idea of the changes that have occurred in their position *vis-à-vis* their white supervisors since incorporation and in the government's plans for eventual Aboriginal ownership and control of the settlement. But the majority of Aborigines have no conviction that the whole enterprise will one day be theirs, so in effect all that is across the creek is still as much the 'white-fellas' business' as it ever was. The proposed new workshops, store, garages and so on are no more felt to be theirs than are the station stock or the windmills. This deeply embedded attitude of dissociation, which is hardly surprising when one considers the history of Aboriginal-white culture contact, will continue to hamper community development and the transition to Aboriginal self-government until the local people can have the fact of their ownership of such property demonstrated to them. For their part, many whites find it equally difficult to cease being paternalistic in their interaction with Aborigines.

(b) *Christians.* One notable change of attitude since the mission period has been an increased conviction among local Aborigines that not all 'Christians' are like the missionaries of old, and that individual 'Christians' may not be a threat to the Law. This willingness to set aside their negative stereotype of 'Christians' clearly stems from the removal of what they saw as an institution dedicated to the breakdown of their traditional values and behaviours. The Aborigines now seem willing to judge people who identify themselves as 'Christians' as they would 'white-fellas'; i.e. on an individual basis. Almost all of them are favourably disposed toward the Apostolic pastor who spent three years at Jigalong (1970-73) and still visits periodically. His approach was deliberately in marked contrast to that of his predecessors: he learned some of the local language, spent a lot of time in the camp and was low-keyed in presenting his message. He is now widely accepted as being pro-Aboriginal, as is the American S.I.L. linguist who has worked at Jigalong from time to time since the late 1960s.

Among some of the local women, particularly, there is evidence of nostalgia for the mission days. Many were then in employment, whereas today very few of the women work in the main settlement. Most women enjoyed attending the weekly singsongs, partly out of sympathy for the female missionaries, partly for the tea and biscuits served at the end of the meeting, but also perhaps because such gatherings added a touch of harmless variety to an often monotonous existence.

Without a doubt, the local Aborigines have forgiven much, but they certainly have not forgotten. Any future return of the 'Christians' in force, or concerted attempts to sabotage the Law, would quickly invoke the old negative stereotype. The Aborigines, particularly the men, are adamant about not wanting to fight the same battle again.

Problems of self-regulation A vital element in the relatively successful adjustment of the Jigalong Aborigines to the contact situation has been their maintenance of a strong sense of independence and autonomy in the conduct of their internal affairs (cf. Tonkinson 1972, 1974). The people felt that they alone made decisions on the questions that mattered to them most, and this bolstered their belief that, despite their economic dependence on agencies of the wider society, they still controlled their own destiny. Their conviction has been strengthened since the mission period by governmental reassurances of non-interference, and more recently by the settlement's change of status to an incorporated Aboriginal community, complete with its own constitution.

Just as the Aborigines' sense of self-regulation during the mission period was illusory to the extent that government decree could have put an end to much of their Law at any time, the rule of the community council is also largely illusory. Although there is often considerable discussion and presentation of alternatives to councillors, it is inevitable that most important initiatives and proposals come from the white advisers or outside agencies, such as the community's management consultants in Perth. These are presented in many cases as *faits accomplis* for the council's ratification. Nevertheless, the Aborigines are now being consulted about most matters affecting them at the local level and this innovation is of considerable importance to a people who were *never* thus consulted before. Also, the fact remains that no matter who originates new proposals, it is the council of Aborigines alone which votes on them. Many local Aborigines as yet are unaware of the significance of the recent political changes, but for council members and other men who regularly attend their meetings, this system is seen as a step in the direction of eventual local self-government.

Although many Aborigines have shown keen interest in the new local developments, it cannot be concluded that their dominant concerns are currently focused in this direction. Instead, they are preoccupied with several problems over which they feel they have inadequate control: (a) liquor, which they perceive as a real threat to the Law; (b) deficiencies in social control, with the related problem of police intervention; and (c) the major problem, which is the threat to their autonomy and community solidarity posed by certain of their Aboriginal neighbours.

(a) *Liquor.* The local people have long been acutely aware of the effect of liquor on Aborigines living in towns, and many comment on what they consider to be the rapidly deteriorating situation in Wiluna, whose Aborigines are now said to be losing their Law.[6] They cite several recent drink-related deaths there as proof of liquor's power to turn Aborigines away from their Law and thus ruin them. But, while all appreciate this threat, Jigalong people repeatedly show the depth of their ambivalence about liquor by eagerly drinking it whenever some of their number bring it onto the settlement. There is not yet a steady supply, but whenever drinking occurs at Jigalong fights seem to follow. Then, once everyone is sober again, there are renewed and heartfelt calls for a ban on the importation of liquor — until the next batch arrives, when the cycle repeats itself. There is much concern that there will soon be deaths as a result of drunken drivers crashing their vehicles. The council has acted positively by formally requesting both sources of supply (the hotel in Newman and the roadhouse at Kumarina, 240 kilometres [150 miles] south) not to sell Jigalong Aborigines flagons of fortified wine, only beer. This request seems to have been heeded, but some flagons still reach Jigalong. Probably as a result of their ambivalence, the Aborigines have not yet decided on any other strategies to deal with the drinking threat, but they continue to talk about the problem, and it is one important reason why they do not want to move the settlement closer to Newman.

(b) *Deficiencies in social control.* In traditional times, the most common sanction invoked against adults who broke the Law was spearing, but this is frowned upon by the police who will not condone it as a method of social control. In recent years there have been several occasions when the community has decided on some other form of punishment for an offender, only to have the defendant refuse to accept it. Whereupon the matter was dropped or, if a fight and injuries were involved, the police were called in. Both courses of action are equally condemned by the Aborigines: ignoring an offender's refusal to accept community sanctioned punishment sets a bad example for future offenders, and calling in the police surrenders highly valued sanctioning powers to an outside agency. The Aborigines are unanimous in their fear and resentment of police intervention, yet they see it as inevitable if they cannot control their own trouble-makers effectively. A related and currently unsolvable problem is the recent outbreak of vandalism by small children in the main settlement area. Beatings have not worked, so the adults are still searching for an effective sanction.

(c) *Conflict with Aboriginal neighbours.* This problem stems from a longstanding dispute between the Jigalong Mob and certain Aboriginal groups to the north, mainly Don McLeod's Pindan Mob, which allegedly modified certain features of the Law in ways that were regarded by Jigalong people as dangerously weakening it.[7] In the past, representatives of the Pindan Mob repeatedly but unsuccessfully attempted to recruit local people as permanent members of the workforce in their mining ventures.[8] The Pindan Mob eventually split into several groups, one of which, the Nomads, still led by McLeod, has settled on Strelley station, near Port Hedland, the property having been purchased for them by the government. Since the government takeover of Jigalong, relations between the Aborigines there and the Strelley Mob have deteriorated to such an extent that the once solidly and strongly ethnocentric Jigalong Mob has been split. Some one hundred and ten out of about five hundred people identifying themselves as Jigalong Mob members are now living at Strelley, and some of these migrants now claim Strelley, not Jigalong, as their home.

With the assistance of a few early converts from Jigalong, the northerners have managed to divide the community along its line of weakest resistance: the basic 'tribal' division between Mandjildjara and Gadudjara speakers. A majority of the once numerically dominant Mandjildjara group is currently at Strelley, leaving some seventy of their number at Jigalong (out of a present population there of about two hundred and fifty). The physical separation of the two main camping areas at Jigalong is now more definite and there appears to be less interaction and more distrust between the two groups than formerly. Part of this increase in social distance stems from the Gadudjara people's suspicions that most Mandjildjara are now Strelley sympathisers— which is not the case among the majority, who have been at Strelley but prefer life at Jigalong.

During visits to Jigalong to recruit more members, the Aboriginal 'bosses' from Strelley have been very critical of the local people for allegedly aligning themselves with the government and submitting to white supervision. As propounded at Jigalong, the Strelley viewpoint strongly opposes government 'control' of Aborigines, the presence of white 'bosses' on Aboriginal settlements and white involvement in Aboriginal self-regulation. The Strelley influence can be discerned among a few of the Mandjildjara still at the settlement. Although most local men agree that the northerners should not interfere as they have in Jigalong affairs and have overstepped traditional bounds in their criticisms, there is still a reluctance on the part of Jigalong's spokesmen to defend themselves publicly against this attack on what they value most highly: their integrity and autonomy. Most local people are well aware of the heavy dependence of Strelley on government moneys, and of the anomaly that the northerners are themselves led by a white, albeit a charismatic figure highly regarded by most Pilbara Aborigines.[9] Despite this, the Jigalong leaders have chosen not to point out these inconsistencies to the Strelley visitors because they are most anxious to heal the breach if they possibly can. As long as open conflict is avoided, they feel that they can work towards the return of their missing members. This conflict appears to be *the* abiding concern of most Jigalong people, and all that is happening across the creek remains of secondary importance.

Jigalong people still speak of McLeod as a man who wishes them no ill-will; instead, they blame his Aboriginal managers for what has happened. The unfortunate aspect of this situation is that other Aborigines have succeeded in doing what almost a quarter century of missionary endeavour was unable to do: they have divided a formerly well-integrated community against itself. In the long run, this schism could do as much as the liquor and social control problems to hasten a breakdown of the Law at Jigalong.

Notes

1. This paper is based mainly on research in progress at Jigalong. For financial assistance in making this work possible, I thank the Research School of Pacific Studies at the Australian National University and the Australian Institute of Aboriginal Studies. For many valuable comments on an earlier draft of this paper I wish to thank my wife Myrna, who is also engaged in anthropological research at Jigalong.

2. Jigalong is an 'institutional community' (Long 1970: 5-6), located in what Rowley (1970:1-26) describes and characterises as 'colonial Australia', which embraces the deserts and sparsely settled northern areas of the continent.

3. Rowley (1970:109-36) has recently discussed the implications of this transition process for institutional communities (see also Long 1970:176-88 for a brief, general treatment of the same subject). Berndt and Berndt (1970:53-79) summarise social and cultural changes in Western Desert Aboriginal fringe communities up to the mid-1960s. But as yet there is little data available on the actual dynamics of the assumption of major self-regulatory powers by Aboriginal communities in colonial Australia, so I am unable to offer any comparative comments in this paper.

4. For detailed accounts of traditional cultural elements and the culture contact situation at Jigalong, see Tonkinson (1966, 1970, 1974).

5. Currently, *per capita* Aboriginal income at Jigalong is approximately one dollar per day.

6. See the paper by Sackett in this volume for an account of Aboriginal drinking and related problems at Wiluna.

7. The Pindan Mob is discussed in detail by J. Wilson (1961). Some of these modifications to the Law are referred to by K. Wilson (1970:340-41).

8. Wilson (1961) gives an account of some of the Pindan Mob's unsuccessful attempts to recruit labour from Jigalong.

9. The pivotal role played by McLeod in the development of Aboriginal initiative in the Pilbara district since the early 1940s is discussed by several authors (cf. Biskup 1973, Rowley 1970, J. Wilson 1961).

References

BERNDT, R. M. *and* C. H. BERNDT 1970 Some points of change in Western Australia. In *Diprotodon to detribalization* (A. R. Pilling *and* R. A. Waterman eds), pp. 53-79. Michigan State University Press, East Lansing.

BISKUP, P. 1973 *Not slaves not citizens.* University of Queensland Press, St. Lucia.

LONG, J. P. M. 1970 *Aboriginal settlements: a survey of institutional communities in Eastern Australia.* Australian National University Press, Canberra.

ROWLEY, C. D. 1970 *The remote Aborigines.* Australian National University Press, Canberra.

TONKINSON, R. 1966 Social structure and acculturation of Aborigines in the Western Desert. M.A. thesis in Anthropology, University of Western Australia, Perth.

——1970 Aboriginal dream-spirit beliefs in a contact situation: Jigalong, Western Australia. In *Australian Aboriginal Anthropology* (R. M. Berndt ed.), pp. 277-91.University of Western Australia Press, Perth.

——1972 Nga:wajil: a Western Desert Aboriginal rainmaking ritual. Ph.D. thesis in Anthropology, University of British Columbia, Vancouver.

——1974 *The Jigalong mob: Aboriginal victors of the desert crusade.* Cummings/Addison-Wesley, Menlo Park.

WILSON, J. 1961 Authority and leadership in a 'new style' Australian Aboriginal community Pindan, Western Australia. M.A. thesis in Anthropology, University of Western Australia, Perth.

WILSON, K. 1970 Pindan: A preliminary comment. In *Diprotodon to detribalization* (A. R. Pilling *and* R. A. Waterman eds), pp. 333-46. Michigan State University Press, East Lansing.

6 Change in spiritual and ritual life in Pitjantjatjara (Bidjandjadjara) society, 1966 to 1973

Noel M. Wallace

My research has centred on the Amata (government) and Ernabella (mission) settlements with numerous visits to neighbouring areas of cultural exchange. The Pitjantjatjara people have intermarried with Ngatjatjara (Ngadjadjara) people from the west, and Yankuntjatjara (Yangundjadjara) people whose country the Pitjantjatjara now occupy. Yankuntjatjara influence is particularly strong at Fregon, forty miles south of Ernabella, and extends through Mimili to Indulkana to the east (see map).

In this contribution, I am concerned with ritual only in general terms: all descriptions of a secret-sacred nature have been omitted.

Direct cultural and religious communication extends from Amata and Ernabella to Indulkana in the east, to Docker River in the north-west, and to Warburton Ranges in the west. Other more distant areas are occasionally included. Also, before the Docker River settlement was established, Areyonga was more regularly visited. Extracted from the sixty or so years of materially significant contact between Pitjantjatjara people and white invaders, the period from 1966 has undoubtedly been the most critical in its effect on their spiritual and ritual life. Prior to 1966, the primary external influence was the Ernabella Mission, established in 1937, although the original charter of that mission, at least ideally speaking, permitted Aborigines who did come there to continue much of their traditional life. More recently, the Amata government settlement was established and has been steadily developed, while Indulkana has grown from an Aboriginal camp into a small town. Lavishly equipped schools have been built. A money economy was introduced in 1966, bringing with it the necessity to work for wages or go hungry, and this inevitably meant a diminution of ritual activity.

At first, material change was not indicative of spiritual change. The notion that a particular ritual must suffer deterioration simply because clothes are worn or emblems are constructed from alien materials is of doubtful validity. Aboriginal philosophy has mostly been to use what is available; and this includes European-style clothing, and coloured wool instead of human or animal hair string. Objects of ritual importance made from wool are also sung over during their making: they too receive, hold, and then transmit the *kurunpa* (spirit) given them by the makers and other relevant persons who are present at a ritual. Much pride is demonstrated in making a 'pretty one' (emblem): and in instances where it is important that the traditional hair string be used, this is done. Traditionally, spun string and other such materials were used, not because of any innate religious significance, but because they were the only materials available. Objects made from 'new' substances are just as sacred, significant and important as

74

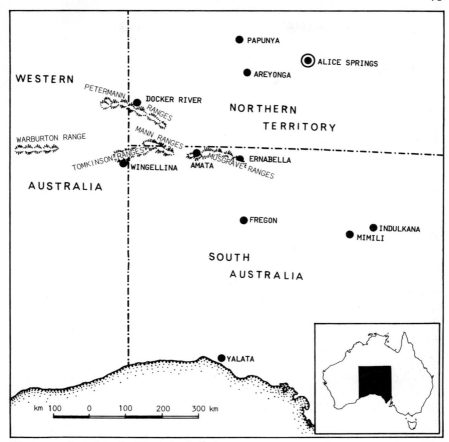

Figure 1 : *Location of settlements studied*

those made the 'old' way: it is the ritual which provides them with their sacred qualities. And whatever such emblems are made of does not detract from their significance — except in the eyes of a purist who is looking for the spectacular rather than the *tjukurpa* (that which has to do with the Dreaming).

The teachings of the spirit ancestors (or mythic beings), held in sacred trust by the knowledgeable elders of the 'tribe', are regarded by them as being unchanging and unchangeable. However, the last three years have seen the older people vainly trying to retain their dignity and authority, in spite of eroding influences which they can neither understand nor control.

Man-making rituals

These rituals are the most vital in the spectrum of Pitjantjatjara religious life. Men themselves claim that the Red Ochre ritual is more important. But it is obvious that, should man-making rituals lose their socio-religious significance, the basis upon which so much other ritual is constructed is undermined. No significant change took place in traditional man-making rituals from 1966 to about 1971. Even changes in the mode of transportation from foot travel with camels, horses and donkeys carrying supplies, swags, etc., to motor vehicles did not materially affect traditional ritual in terms of its unchanged depth of meaning and social relevance.

To evaluate this and subsequent changes it is necessary to look at the whole series of man-making rituals as they were carried out a few short years ago and to compare them with today's manifestations.

The nyi:ṇka and wati mi:nu   When the elders decided that the time had come, soon after puberty, for a boy to commence his training as a candidate for circumcision, he joined the group of *nyi:ṇka* at their strictly segregated camp. These boys were permitted no contact with women or girls, or with their fathers — actual or 'tribal'. A novice was expected to fend for himself, except that his mother would sometimes prepare food and leave it out for him to take, surreptitiously, during the night. Should a person inadvertently see a *nyi:ṇka* during the day, it was invariably at a distance, when he would avert his face, shielding it with a branch of green leaves carried for that purpose. The *nyi:ṇka* camp was always a considerable distance from the main camp area, and their only real contact with the others was through smaller boys who served as messengers and runners and who had relatively free access to the initiatory camp during the day. In this way, these smaller boys were psychologically prepared for their eventual segregation and admission to what was, to them, the desirable company of older boys.

Also segregated, with their own camp, were the *wati mi:nu,* who had been circumcised at previous rituals. They were the instructors of the *nyi:ṇka* in their own songs, myths and rituals, while the older men prepared them (the *nyi:ṇka*) for what followed by tooth evulsion, which was the first stage of their initiatory sequence. The segregation of the *wati mi:nu* was as complete as that of the *nyi:ṇka*, although they were distinguished by the *yakiri,* a headband worn by men, with a chignon or *pukuṭi* on the back of the head. The *inma* (ritual) ground of the *nyi:ṇka* was usually quite secluded. There, the *wati mi:nu* instructed the novices in the teachings of specific spirit ancestors, in relation to their present situation and future advancement. They also taught them the correct forms of body painting, songs and relevant dances, all of which had been originally revealed by those particular spirit ancestors. The boys learned enthusiastically — the dancing was soon performed expertly and they held their rituals almost nightly. Here again we have the situation of the younger boys associating with those a little older and more knowledgeable, with potential admission to the company of *wati mi:nu* being something to be looked forward to.

During the segregation period, the *wati mi:nu* were themselves exposed to further instruction. As totemic secret-sacred rituals were held, the *wati mi:nu* were brought to them, and were told when they had to lie with heads covered (learning through listening and not seeing) and when and where to look. The meaning of what they saw was then explained to them by their guardians.

So, instruction continued; and by the involvement of all men in such rituals, their importance was enhanced and religious totemic knowledge became the most significant factor in their lives. By the same socio-psychological process — that is, through the creation of a powerful desire on the part of the novice and postulant to become one of those whose knowledge and expertise in ritual were superior to his own — they were prepared for the next physical ordeal, the first stage of subincision.

The ulpuru When some of the *nyi:ṇka* were deemed to be ready for circumcision, one of their number was chosen as a messenger, or *ulpuru*. He would be taken by at least two men to distant camps, to call the people to come and bring with them their own *nyi:ṇka* to the forthcoming circumcision rituals. Their mode of travel was unimportant, ranging (through the years we are speaking of) from walking to the use of camel, horse, motor car, and even chartered aircraft, as on one occasion from Areyonga to Amata. In all cases, traditional ritual was observed: the *ulpuru*'s carrying of the all-important hair belt (*nanpa*) and wooden staff (*tjutinpa*); the conventions relevant to departure from his home camp and his arrival at each camp visited, and his leaving for the next destination — events always attended by the whole camp.

The minyma manngiri At the ultimate destination of the *ulpuru*, the people prepared for their journey to the host camp. The men conducted rituals during the day and at night: *pintjila* rituals relating to betrothal were sung by men and danced by women. From among the women, two were chosen as *minyma manngiri*, a role that carried considerable status, since the *ulpuru* would be in their care from daybreak until about midday every day of the return journey: it was their responsibility to see that he returned safely to his home camp.

The tjilkatja The two or more men who accompanied the *ulpuru* were called *tjilkatja*. When the return journey commenced, every able-bodied person would join the party, and all men, women and children became *tjilkatja*. As other camps previously visited by the *ulpuru* were visited again by the travelling *tjilkatja* their populations joined and also became *tjilkatja*. The route to be travelled and the particular *inma* to be sung had already been predetermined, so the same *inma* was sung by all persons joining the travelling group. It was absolutely forbidden for anyone except a *wikaru* to travel along the track toward the advancing *tjilkatja*, hence the predetermined route was inflexibly adhered to. It was also absolutely forbidden for anyone to travel by an alternative route.

The wikaru If it was deemed necessary to call people from camps situated in a different direction from that taken by the *ulpuru*, two men, called *wikaru*, made the journey to these carrying a *nanpa* in a manner similar to that of the *ulpuru*. Additionally, should it be necessary for someone from the host camp to meet the *tjilkatja* in order to assist them, two *wikaru* could go. Having met the *tjilkatja*, they would then become *tjilkatja*, and would remain so for the rest of the journey and for the ensuing rituals.

The journey of the tjilkatja During the return journey of the *ulpuru*, accompanied by a growing number of *tjilkatja*, rituals were held daily. In the early morning, the *ulpuru* (who had camped near the men's camp with other *nyi:ṇka* being brought for circumcision) was taken to the *minyma manngiri*'s camp and placed in their care. At no time was he more than a few feet away from them until about midday, when he was ceremonially handed over to the men, with the entreaty that they should take good care of him until the following day. During that time the *nyi:ṇka* were nowhere near, travelling, still segregated, apart from the others.

After accepting the care of the *ulpuru*, rituals commenced when part of the circumcision *inma* 'line' (or mythic track) was sung, along with part of the *ulpuru*'s own totemic 'line'. He travelled with the men for the rest of the day: and more songs were sung each night. In these circumstances, progress was slow, because of the daily rituals: at the same time, women had to forage for food in order to augment supplies brought with them. This created a balanced situation relative to the time factor. Groups of men were allocated the task of hunting for meat, not so much to provide for all the *tjilkatja*, as to aid those obliged to provide blood for the daily rituals. These, performed by male *tjilkatja*, obviously had the effect of disseminating and consolidating expertise in a variety of totemic rituals as men from various camps joined the party.

The time taken for such a journey was not dependent on the mode of transport. The controlling factor was the frequency and length of rituals held en route. The final camp was made twelve or fourteen kilometres (eight or nine miles) from the host camp. Body painting and ritual then took several hours of the morning. Next, *pintiyalpa* were made from the stems of tecoma bushes and placed in the *yakiri* headbands. Slow progress was made to within six or eight kilometres (four or five miles) of the host camp, by all the *tjilkatja*. Then the men, painted and decorated, formed into lines, carrying spears (point in left hand, shaft resting against left shoulder), and commenced the final advance, walking and running, stopping only when near their destination to gather bunches of eucalypt leaves, to carry in their belts at the back and in their right hands.

The party stopped when the host camp was just in sight — stopped until it was clear that they had been seen by a look-out and that the people waiting for them were prepared for the ceremonial arrival. The traditional advance was then made by the two men who had left with the *ulpuru*, singly; followed by a man from a distant camp, at whom a spear was symbolically thrown, aimed to miss. Food and drink were given to each of the new arrivals — all this showing in the traditional way that no grudges had to be settled before the rituals commenced.

Next came the noisy and spectacular advance of the men, throwing of eucalypt leaves on to the prone bodies of the women and children, and their advance to the *inma* ground where a short, spirited *inma* was sung. They then returned to the main camp, and to the area allocated to the visitors: here the men sat and waited until the visiting women and children, and men not directly involved in the ceremonial entry, arrived some time later.

The host camp   After the departure of the *ulpuru*, *inma* had been performed with increasing frequency — men-only rituals during the day, and *pintjila* rituals, involving men, women and girls, at night. Tension mounted as time passed, because the exact day of the arrival of the *tjilkatja* was unknown — since there must be no contact between the two groups until they actually arrived. Positive information had been sent when they commenced the return journey; but no information had been received after that. After a suitable lapse of time, the impending arrival was expected any day, and the direction of approach of the travellers was watched nightly for signs of a signal fire which would reveal their presence. The pre-arrival period was always an occasion of speculation, tension and suspense.

On the afternoon of the day following the sighting of signal fires, every person assembled in the one area, apart from the camp, women and children in a circle, men standing nearby. A watch was kept in the direction of the oncoming *tjilkatja*. When they were sighted the host party carrying spears in a manner similar to the *tjilkatja* men, lined up with their backs toward the advancing group — except for those involved in the symbolic spear-throwing and in the giving of food and drink. Next, the male *tjilkatja* ran in, throwing their bunches of eucalypt on to the prone bodies of women and children, who were then permitted to sit up and look toward the men. The men of the host camp following the new arrivals, ran to the *inma* ground. That night, there would be *pintjila* singing and dancing, involving both the hosts and the visitors.

The ritual The excitement and tension built up over the preceding weeks allowed for no anticlimax. The following morning, before daybreak, women and children had to leave the camp to spend the day well away, in the opposite direction from the men's *inma* ground. There all the men gathered, and singing and dancing commenced. Later that day, the *wati mi:nu* were subincised for the first time, while other men, more advanced, ritually, carried out further subincision rites.

All of the men then returned to the camp, and shortly afterwards were joined by the women and children. After dark, all assembled near the men's *inma* ground, and the singing commenced. These rituals, similar to those described by Berndt,[1] were watched by everyone, and then, on the arrival of the *nyi:ŋka* emerging from the darkness into the light of the fires, the women and children fled, wailing, to a place where they camped, usually a few kilometres away. The circumcision rites were then performed, and the newly circumcised youths — now *wati wankarpa* — were taken away into the darkness. The men returned to the main camp, and the women and children came back the next morning.

The wati wankarpa The symbolic awakening from death, and rebirth as a man, after the act of circumcision, was marked by a period that extended over several weeks and was a time of tension. The *wati wankarpa* occupied two camps, according to generation levels, separated from each other, and some distance away and hidden from the main camp. Each had to be visited by a group of young men — *wati pulka* — morning and night for ritual, and it was absolutely forbidden for a person of the opposite generation level to approach even in the direction of the other *wati wankarpa* camps. Everyone had to remain in his own camp whilst the men involved visited the *wati wankarpa*, assuming normality only when they returned to their own separate camp. During the day, as many hunting parties as possible were organised, as large quantities of meat were required owing to daily blood-letting rituals which took place in relation to the *wati wankarpa*. All visitors from other areas remained — spending their time gossiping with their relatives and friends from other areas.

Yatitjiti ceremony After some weeks, the time came for the next stage in the progress to manhood. In the late afternoon, the whole group moved to a new temporary camp, divided into generation levels, with certain exceptions that have no relevance in this context.

Singing continued all night, not by the people in the camp, whose role it was to listen, but by two groups of men, now hidden behind brush screens, about three-quarters of a kilometre from the camp and well separated from each other. Here the *wati wankarpa* were physically cleansed and through further ritual became *wati mi:nu*, and had their first *yakiri* bound for them. Also their hair was made up into a *pukuti* as a mark of having reached that particular stage, their bodies were decorated, and at daybreak they were presented to the main camp, members of both generation levels simultaneously. This consisted of a brief impressive ritual around two smoking fires, after which, to the wailing and crying of relatives, they ran from the area followed by small boys, for further segregation in the *wati mi:nu* camp. So, the cycle of religious learning and involvement continued.

Man-making ceremony 1971-73

It is necessary now to compare the foregoing with the present situation — a situation that has developed with such rapidity since 1971.

No diminution in the necessity and importance of man-making rituals has been observed. While some other rituals have been performed less frequently, as mobility has increased with the use of motor vehicles, the area of cultural-ritual communication has also increased. It is now common for exchange visits to include the Warburton Ranges to the west, Docker River to the north (which has replaced Areyonga), and Indulkana to the east. Visits have also been made to Papunya, 800 kilometres (500 miles) to the north and to Yalata, 2400 kilometres (1500 miles) to the south. These have not been solely for man-making rituals. Social exchange over a larger area has increased with their greater mobility. Vehicles are used to transport football teams and their supporters, and so the desire to include those distant places in the ritual circuit grows.

There has been no relaxation of the strict law that a male person is a child — *tjitji* — until after circumcision. Men of any age who have, for some reason, not been circumcised and subincised must remain with the women and children during secret-sacred rituals. For an uninitiated man to father a child is a grave crime, for, should the child live, it has no totemic inheritance and so no place in the social structure of the 'tribe'. To be a 'child of a child' is a stigma of the greatest order.

The nyi:nka School at Ernabella, previously presented as desirable, was not however compulsory. Further schools have been opened at Amata and at Indulkana, and the idea that 'white man's education' is vitally necessary to their children is being instilled into the parents: and with this has come compulsory attendance. To induce children to continue, beyond the age of fourteen, an allowance is paid to parents. This in turn, encourages some fathers to resist the authority of the elders in their selection of *nyi:ŋka*, since money has become a dominating factor in the present situation. Nevertheless, many *nyi:ŋka* are selected without argument, and those whose segregation is deferred eventually succumb to 'tribal' pressures within a year or so. But this whole issue does cause tension, dissent, discontent and confusion among the *nyi:ŋka* themselves, and has implications for the future.

After segregation, a *nyi:ŋka* enters the first stage of a continuing cultural vacuum. The traditional instructor, the *wati mi:nu*, is now working for money and is no longer able to occupy his traditional role uninterruptedly. This results in the *nyi:ŋka* having little to do, during a period which in the immediate past was organised in terms of instruction and ritual demonstration. No longer are they able to sustain themselves as, due to the destruction of their semi-nomadic style of existence, game is not available near their camp. Moreover, they have become more dependent on food left out for them by their parents — consequently, the *nyi:ŋka* camp has moved gradually closer to the main camp until segregation has become no more than a token gesture.

The *nyi:ŋka* were — not unexpectedly — the first to become involved in delinquency, their misdemeanours ranging from breaking into a local store in order to obtain food, to joy-riding in local vehicles and petrol sniffing. Mainly, the idle youths are seeking some form of excitement. With the previously strict segregation laws being broken down, there is growing interaction between boys and girls. Inevitably, this has resulted in some *nyi:ŋka* fathering children, the child-mothers being drawn from the same group and not from distant relatives from distant countries as was traditional practice. We are thus presented with the first and most important breakdown in ritual: the neglect of basic ritual training, and the evasion of 'tribal' custom and authority at the beginning of adult life. Younger boys still communicate freely with *nyi:ŋka*; they are still influenced strongly by the older boys, but not to follow the traditional *nyi:ŋka* way — for them the model consists of acts of delinquency and defiance of previously established custom.

It is true that there is still somewhat cursory instruction in the *nyi:ŋka* ritual, but this has carried with it a tragic form of desecration. Unscrupulous *wati mi:nu*, after learning 'men-only' *inma*, have revealed the songs to *nyi:ŋka*, who sing them in defiance of the older men. A few years ago, this would have resulted in their death. Today, Australian-European law disallows punitive spearing, and the elders have no ultimate sanction to enforce their authority over the boys. Without the close association with *wati mi:nu* as teachers, the urge to become one of them is being destroyed. So, the prospect of circumcision as simply a physical act is gaining ground and it is this attitude which results on numerous occasions, in potential *nyi:ŋka* running away to avoid the rite of circumcision.

The wati mi:nu The *wati mi:nu* still wear *yakiri* and *pukuṭi*; but for them segregation no longer exists, except that they usually sleep some distance from the main camp. Every effort is made by Aboriginal Affairs authorities to provide some form of employment — which, as I have said, leaves them little time to instruct the *nyi:ŋka*. They have only the weekends, or after work should they feel so inclined. Similarly, they themselves are available for instruction only after working hours, and this means that they are ill-prepared for their next stage in the rituals. They have attended few rituals and, like the *nyi:ŋka*, the *wati mi:nu* show a keener interest in 'country and Western' music (in guitars, for example) than they do in traditional *inma*.

The ulpuru   In spite of the rapid disintegration of *nyi:ŋka* religious training, there are always some boys who have what can be regarded in this context as 'above average' qualities. Invariably, it is one such boy who is chosen as an *ulpuru* — so that there is some semblance of traditional continuity.

The minyma manngiri   It was once unheard of for those selected to refuse the honour of becoming *minyma manngiri*. Now, external influences have proved stronger, and the authority of the elders has been weakened. Consequently European-derived reasons are put forward to excuse women from accepting. For instance, the children must stay at the settlement in order to attend school, and if their 'tribal' mothers are travelling with the *tjilkatja*, there will be no one to care for them; or the women are employed at the settlement, and pressures are exerted to prevent them from accepting this task. The pressures are applied by Europeans who cannot be told (or if told, would not understand) that such a woman had an important role to play: to them it probably seems that she merely wants to attend ceremonies at some distant place on an irresponsible 'walkabout'.

The tjilkatja   It is the desire of all the older able-bodied people to accompany the *ulpuru* to his home camp, as the rituals to be performed there are still of primary importance. Preparations for such ventures now take a considerable amount of time, where previously it was simply a matter of picking up one's few belongings, calling the children together, and walking off. Now motor vehicles in various states of disrepair must be made mobile, petrol bought and, if the journey is to be a long one, petrol dumps established. Here, the assistance and co-operation of sympathetic administrative staff is essential. It is confusing and quite incomprehensible to the older people that many decide not to go: the reasons given seem to them to be in direct conflict with traditional thinking — as indeed they are.

A major factor here, in the deterioration of religious life, is that the majority of the children do in fact stay behind. And this prevents them from participating in a rich experience, and being involved at an early age in the rituals of their own culture: they are thus missing a vital step in their own religious training.

Once assembled, the *tjilkatja* travel along established roads, in vehicles, knowing that time is limited since many are on short leave from their work. The *ulpuru*, accompanied by *minyma manngiri*, will usually commence each day by walking, according to tradition, but only for a token distance before they climb back into a motor vehicle. Further, the midday ritual may or may not be held, according to the progress and conditions of the vehicles. The final day's ritual before arrival is still held, and there is dancing, singing and body painting; but instead of the long approach by foot, as many as can do so climb aboard a truck to make the ceremonial entry, stopping it in view of the assembled camp populace and then making the traditional advance on foot. Later comes the entry of more vehicles carrying men who are not involved in the ceremony of arrival, together with women and a few children. Camps are made, and discussions are held to determine when the 'big' man-making rituals will be held. Because of work obligations, this will usually be on the following Saturday, unless arrangements can be made for a holiday on the Friday so that the rituals can be completed with less haste. In any case, there will probably be a delay, with a resultant loss of emotional involvement on the part of most of the participants. *Pintjila* rituals are held, with women having to be coerced into attending — and then, when they are, showing little interest in the proceedings and expressing a preference for Western music and the twist! Ritual participation is the minimum which is acceptable to the older people.

The host camp During the preceding few weeks, the older men of the host camp have been trying to hold rituals but, here again, few younger men have attended owing to work obligations. At weekends, however, the 'men-only' rituals are rich and full, with attendance by almost all: the singing is as vigorous and stirring as it ever was, except that particular men with set weekend employment obligations leave to perform their duties. It used to be impossible to come and go in this way during a ritual performance.

During the men's secret-sacred rituals, it has always been the pattern for women and children to leave camp for the whole day, with women teaching the children the strict behavioural responsibilities that are relevant at such a time. Now, however, for the children there is organised sport that precludes them from being exposed to the traditional experience. Instead, they play football with teams coming from neighbouring settlements; and so there is a constant diminution of children's knowledge of, and respect for, their own culture.

For the ceremony of the *tjilkatja* arrival, it is still customary for the whole camp to be present, unless the children are at school. Here, the most obvious change over the last few years is in the behaviour of those children who are present. Previously, there would be no sound from them; now they protest at being so restrained. Older children used to play an important role in the care of the younger ones, and that pattern continued right through their lives; now they also are ignorant of the necessity for strict obedience in accordance with religious laws.

The ritual On the day of the circumcision, the *nyi:ṇka* are under the care of the older men. Through the lack of socio-psychological preparation (some having worked on the settlement the previous day), many are afraid and some actually run away. This is a matter for shame for their respective parents and uncles. During the day, the women, who must leave the camp on account of its proximity to the *inma* ground, make temporary camps for themselves and the children in a selected area; and at night, when the presence of all used to be mandatory for the first part of the rituals, they stay in their secluded camp to avoid joining the exodus when the *nyi:ṇka* are brought in. Hence, the children, except for a few whose presence is necessary, do not experience the spectacle and excitement of this event. A number, somewhere around one-third of the camp population, now remain in their temporary camp, missing the ritual.

The attitude of the men toward circumcision has changed. Where it was a time of sorrow at the symbolic death of the child and joy at his rebirth as a social adult, it now has connotations of pain being inflicted as a punishment for misbehaviour. In spite of this, the atmosphere during this part of the ritual and the earlier phase of subincision is one of absolute involvement on the part of the men, and their concentration on religious law as a shared experience.

The wati wankarpa   The period between the actual circumcision and rebirth as a social adult was subject to perhaps the strictest discipline of all. Life in the main camp appeared relatively normal; but underneath the surface, tension was evident. European-style work obligations have required men to approach too close to a *wati wankarpa* camp of the alternate generation level as contrasted with themselves, with the result that an offender either loses his job for refusing duty, or is soundly beaten if he performs it. Also, it used to be the practice for all visitors to remain in the host camp until after the *yaritjiti* ritual. Today, most want to return to their home camps as quickly as possible, not only to resume work but also to collect social service payments, since the whole community is now dependent on money.

The extreme in eventual breakdown was observed in 1972, when new *wati wankarpa* who had come from a distant camp were removed from the host camp after one day and taken back to their home area — certainly at night, when no one other than the small party of their guardians would see. They were to complete this vital part of their ritual near their own home camp! Great dissent was noted among the old men on this occasion, but the younger men had their way.

The yaritjiti ritual   This vital ritual is always performed at night, and so there is very little conflict with introduced life-styles. To date, very little change has been noted: the ritual is still exciting and the experience is shared by all. But such is the conflict and confusion in the minds of younger people that after the *yaritjiti* some of them who had performed that exacting ritual faultlessly throughout a whole night, were heard to declare: 'That old stuff! We like Western music'.

Totemic ritual   Distinct from 'man-making' mythic ritual, so-called 'increase' or life-renewal and other rituals were previously held at and near sacred sites during the semi-nomadic travels of the people which took them through their totemic territories. The whole country is criss-crossed by the paths followed in the *tjukurpa* by the spirit ancestors or mythic beings, and there is both a 'song line' and a 'story line' relating to particular incidents that occurred at these various, now sacred, places. Therefore, it was traditionally essential that young men be taken to those sites in order to learn their significance. During these visits, the sites themselves were cared for by clearing away the grass, painting particular parts with ochre and fat, placing leaves on or nearby, or other attentions ordained by religious law. The visits enriched both the sacred objects and the visitors, as *kurunpa* was exchanged and strengthened.

The semi-nomadic travels, influenced largely by seasonal fluctuation, developed into a pattern making it customary, for example, to hold Kangaroo totemic rituals at Pilpiriny in summer and Fig rituals at Kunamata in winter. Even so, such sacred places remained significant in religious thought even if not visited for long periods. They were believed to be safe and inviolate, along with the sacred objects concealed in the repositories. After the Aboriginal people settled at mission and government stations, these sacred sites were neglected. The desire to visit them was still present, but the influence of European life-styles made it increasingly difficult for them to do so. Consequently, most of the children and many young adults have never visited their own totemic countries.

The older people's devotion to their spiritual country has not been lessened: they still picture it as it used to be and dream about visiting it again, soon! But it has become evident that these sacred places are no longer safe. A vital Dingo sacred site was bulldozed out of existence at Wingellina. Makiri, the most important Honey-ant site in the area, was desecrated and many sacred stones shattered. A high-spirited survey team blew up a group of rocks frighteningly close to some of sacred significance. Vehicle tracks were found close to other sacred sites. Portable sacred objects were stolen, thus brutally demonstrating just how vulnerable the sites really were.

These incidents and facts, coupled with despair and frustration on feeling the impact of the new attitudes expressed by children and young people, have created a strong desire on the part of the old people to return to their own totemic areas to look after them. This is not and never can be a return to the old life-style, but it is a growing gesture toward preserving their own religious beliefs. Several groups of people have already left Amata and are living in small communities within their own sacred territory, and people from Ernabella and Fregon are making similar plans. Not all are old people, but all those concerned have strong traditional beliefs. Physical protection of sacred sites from outside interference is not the main purpose of their return: they well know that their power is limited in so far as unwanted visitors are concerned. Older men express feelings of guilt for having neglected the sites for so long and believe that, by returning to them and giving them their traditional care and by singing the ancient songs, the *kurunpa* will become strong again, and the people and the religion will survive.

The use of motor vehicles, as I have said, has facilitated the movement of quite large groups of Aboriginal men over large areas of country — distant sites south of the Mann Range and into the Tomkinson Ranges, where rituals may be performed. It would seem that this revival of traditional interest will continue, particularly if government assistance is forthcoming to build roads giving vehicle access, not to, but near, other sacred areas. Thus, over the past eight years there has been a definite revival in this respect, and indications are that this trend is growing. It is doubtful, however, whether it will survive the passing of the present older generation.

Red Ochre ritual Red Ochre rituals occupy such a vital place in the lives of Western Desert people that this part of their religious life has lost none of its importance. Nevertheless, these too have been drastically changed over the last few years.

Red Ochre ritual, so named because of the liberal use of that material in body decoration, is of major significance since, through the teachings of the relevant spirit ancestors, religious knowledge is increased and enhanced beyond the elementary levels taught during the 'man-making' rituals. The *wati tjukutjuku,* Red Ochre postulants, eventually become *wati pulka* through their religious education during this period; but that learning continues through life. Many spirit ancestors and sacred objects containing their *kurunpa,* go to make up the Red Ochre religious complex. Rituals of major importance used to move in a circuit through all the dialectal units — constituting the Western Desert socio-cultural community. Enquiries have established the time involved in a particular Red Ochre ritual cycle completing a full circuit as being somewhere between twenty and thirty years. Hence, a man had to be of considerable age to be knowledgeable in a great number of these rituals, because his Red Ochre education could not commence until five subincision rites had been completed.

As well as these major Red Ochre rituals, others of less importance would move among the local communities. All told, there could be ten or more of these common to an area of, say, 260 square kilometres (100 square miles), most of them concerned with sacred objects hidden and lying dormant in their repositories for considerable periods of time. In 1968, one of the two reputedly most important sets of Red Ochre ritual objects arrived at Amata from Areyonga; the other was at Mimili, having been brought from the Warburton Ranges a few months previously. During the winter of 1969, Red Ochre men took these from Amata to Ernabella and then on to Mimili, where there were rituals that included the Indulkana people. The objects from the north were left at Mimili, while those that had come from the Warburton Ranges were brought back to Ernabella and then, after more rituals, taken on to Amata. Men stated that, after completion of rituals at Amata, the sacred objects would continue their traditional movement west to the Warburton Ranges, and thence to Laverton, Leonora and onwards. The path to be followed by the other set was north to Areyonga and Papunya.

Five years later, these vitally important Red Ochre sacred objects are still in the South Australian north-west. They are not stationary, since they are being moved between Indulkuna in the east and a site near the border between South and Western Australia occupied by a group of men who choose to live in their sacred country, quite close to the site of the mythic origin of a particular Red Ochre spirit ancestor. The men are afraid that if they allow these objects to be taken away from their personal control they will be stolen and so will never return to them. They explain that, these days, too many people break their law: sacred objects were lost some time ago from the Laverton area, and the last lot of objects received from the west were 'all mixed up' — that is, the sets were incomplete and only some, parts of different sets, had been received. They were very distressed about this, because without the sacred Red Ochre objects, this segment of their religion could disappear. It is important to understand that these objects are said to contain within them the complete *kurunpa* of the spirit ancestor, including the teaching, the 'law': there can be no ritual without them, as the essential 'truth' is contained within them. It is *from* the sacred object that the postulant learns, and without Red Ochre ritual, so it is said, there can be no more *complete* men; without them, they believe their 'race' must die.

Distrust between contiguous groups is growing, and many instances are quoted to substantiate this. Naturally, many of these are not proven, but such episodes include a white man in a green Landrover being guided to a cache of sacred objects near Victory Downs, Northern Territory, and these being stolen and sold; sacred objects being sold from the Laverton and Leonora areas; a long sacred object being cut in half so that it could be transported to Perth and sold; and just recently, sacred objects being stolen from an area sacred to the Fig totem people and being offered for sale in Alice Springs. This theft is alleged by Amata men to have been carried out by a Warburton Range man.

The South Australian Museum recently arranged for some Amata men to inspect objects in its custody. Several were identified and returned to their rightful owners. Having observed the joy that resulted from the museum's action, I suggest that this humane act should be commended and copied by other such bodies.

There is a growing resentment against publications that reveal secrets given to various research workers and others in friendship and confidence. This causes antagonism not only toward the offending author, but toward all researchers whether or not they are motivated by scientific aims. More importantly, it causes distrust between various Aboriginal groups, each accusing the other of revealing secrets to someone who has made them public. In such cases, the Aboriginal who revealed such secrets should, ideally, be punished.

The result of this distressing conflict is that the age-old pattern of ritual movement and cultural exchange has been destroyed. Red Ochre rituals are still significant; but they have become more local in character, each constellation of local communities having its own sets of sacred objects. For example, the small Finke (N.T.) community has its own Red Ochre rituals, shared only with local neighbours.

Conclusion

I have attempted to show that, over the past eight years, 'man-making' rituals have not necessarily diminished in importance for the people intimately concerned; that the area of cultural exchange in this respect has increased, but that the quality of ritual and degree of personal involvement have suffered. Conversely, there has been an attempt to revive both ritual and concurrent devotion to religion, specifically as it relates to particular totemic spirit ancestors and to their sites. In the Red Ochre, there has been a considerable withdrawal by individual groups from the wider frame of Western Desert cultural identity, and with this has come the formation of 'insular' communities with a growing distrust of their neighbours.

The deterioration in spiritual and ritual viability is due to a large degree to the imposed withdrawal of children, some of whom are now young adults, from traditional religious practice. This has resulted in increasing juvenile delinquency which, in turn, may be traced directly to the weakened authority of the older men.

The popular notion that the Pitjantjatjara man gains his status as a man through being a hunter and provider needs reconsideration. As a food gatherer, he was unreliable: the women, with their foraging and capture of small animals, were reliable in this respect and were thus the main providers in Western Desert society.

Aboriginal man attains status through his knowledge and practice of his religion. By use of that knowledge, boys became men: laws were kept; and punishments were imposed on those who did not conform. Through totemic ritual, the country provided sufficient fruit, seed and game for all to live in physical and spiritual harmony with their environment. The women gathered the main supplies of food, but men's rituals ensured that it was there for gathering. Rituals and discussions of rituals once occupied the greater part of men's lives: from this sprang their reason for being.

Children no longer visit their totemic countries with their fathers; no longer do they see them as figures of dignity, possessing knowledge of their culture and their own environment; no longer do they see them as being all-important in the life and survival of the 'tribe'. As so many Aborigines have done before them, the children are in this sense entering a 'cultureless' abyss.

Glossary of Pitjantjatjara words

Pitjantjatjara words are used in the text where there is no simple equivalent in English.

inma Ceremony or ritual involving song and dance, or song alone; ceremony or ritual without singing is not *inma*.

kurunpa The spirit of life contained within sacred objects and people, which can be exchanged and strengthened through ritual.

minyma manngiri *Minyma* = a married woman who has at least two children; *minyma manngiri* is a woman chosen from the *tjilkatja* to have custody of the *ulpuru* each day from daybreak until about midday.

nanpa Sacred hair belt; in this case worn by *ulpuru*.

nyi:nka Boy, having reached puberty, selected as a candidate for circumcision and segregated from his group.

pintiyalpa Feather-like decoration, two of which are worn in the *yakiri* behind the ears. They are made by paring wood from tecoma stems against the grain so that it forms curled shavings still adhering to the parent stick. Usually about 22 to 30 centimetres (9 to 12 inches) long. They have varying sacred significance according to the particular ceremony and ritual.

pukuti Chignon, worn by men.

tjilkatja (1) The men, guardians of the *ulpuru*, who travel with him taking news of forthcoming 'man-making' rituals.
(2) All, men, women and children, who return for the rituals.

tjukurpa The time when the spirit ancestors travelled the world; the beginning of Aboriginal religion; the story of that beginning which is eternal. Popularly, the Dreamtime, or Dreaming.

tjutinpa Stick with cutting-stone hafted on to end; carried ritually by the *ulpuru*.

ulpuru One of the *nyi:nka* chosen as a messenger to carry the news of an impending circumcision ritual to other camps.

wikaru One who assists in some way relevant to the forthcoming rituals: for instance, in taking a *nanpa* with news of the rituals to a camp not to be visited by the *ulpuru*, or going to meet the *tjilkatja* in order to assist them on their journey. These duties are tabu to anyone other than a *wikaru*; on meeting the party, he becomes *tjilkatja*.

wati wankarpa	Man, immediately after circumcision. (From *wanka*, life.)
wati mi:nu	Man, next stage: newly circumcised, wearing the *yakiri* and *pukuṭi*.
wati tjukutjuku	Lit. man, small one. Next stage: subincision has commenced.
wati pulka	Lit. man, big one: subincision complete, and has been admitted to Red Ochre rituals.
wiltja	Lit. shade, or shelter.
yaritjiti	Ritual singing, sometimes with other songs, when the *wati wankarpa* becomes a *wati mi:nu*.
yakiri	A man's traditional headband wound from *puturu*, string. Once of hair string, it is now usually made of red wool.

Acknowledgement

Material contained in this paper was collected from 1966 to 1973 during research supported by grants from the Australian Institute of Aboriginal Studies, to study the mythology, traditional religion and sacred sites of the Pitjantjatjara (Bidjandjadjara) people of the Musgrave Ranges, S.A.

Note

1. See R. and C. Berndt 1943 A preliminary report of fieldwork in the Ooldea Region, western South Australia, *Oceania*, XIII(3).

7 Liquor and the Law:

Wiluna, Western Australia

Lee Sackett

The setting Wiluna, Western Australia, located on the edge of the Western Desert some 960 road kilometres north-east of Perth, is regarded as home by approximately 350 traditionally-oriented Aborigines.[1] The majority of adults, who live either on a Seventh Day Adventist mission (eleven kilometres east of town), Aboriginal reserve (five kilometres east of town), or local pastoral stations, were born in the desert, having migrated into the area over the past twenty to thirty years. *Mandjildjara* is by far the predominant dialect, though *Gadudjara, Budidjara, Bidjandjadjara, Giyadjara,* and *Wanman* are also represented.

The total Aboriginal population is only rarely present in the town. Wiluna, situated in the heart of a large sheep and cattle area, offers good (seasonal) employment opportunities to Aborigines. As a result, many men and their families spend much of the year on isolated pastoral properties, visiting town only once every few months, and then merely for short periods. It is at 'race time', in September, and during the slack mid-summer 'hot time', December and January, that most of the people are gathered together. For the remainder of the year a group of about 150 acts as the stable core. This core population is made up of the old or invalided, who are in receipt of social service payments; men, with their families, who are employed in the immediate area, between jobs, or lacking completely in skills which would allow participation in the employment market; plus young school children boarded in the mission dormitories.

The Law Aborigines in the Wiluna area, along with their neighbours throughout the Western Desert, refer to their religious practices, social rules, and total belief system as 'the Law'.[2] Almost everything that is, including the Law, it is believed, stems from the Dreaming *(djugurba)* and the actions of mythic-beings. Aborigines at Wiluna claim that the Dreaming-beings not only gave shape to the previously featureless landscape, but established and laid down a way of life and pattern of social interaction that is changeless, and ideally serves as a model for the present and the future.

The imperative to follow the Law comes from two sources: social pressure (the pressure to conform) and the Law itself. Correct marriages, for example, are encouraged and those persons who disregard the Law in this aspect, and marry incorrectly (or 'wrongly') must face physical punishment and a period of social ostracism. The youth who ignores the Law by avoiding initiation finds himself, as he grows older, virtually without friends; for to the initiated such an individual is but a boy — incapable of having a voice in decision-making processes or even joining in many gossip sessions. Pressure to conform arises from the belief that things established in the Dreaming must continue unchanged (in a way, this subsumes the social imperative). The Law must be followed *or* abandoned — no middle ground is envisaged, and traditionally there was not even an alternative (Stanner 1965:235). Abandonment entails a cessation of society, at least as the Aborigines know it. Thus, to ensure the continuation of all that is known (and all that is good), people follow their elders, learn the Law, carry it, and pass it on to future generations.

If the term 'Law' covers a great deal, it is perhaps most clearly exemplified in the domain of ritual, i.e. in the performance of songs and dances recounting and re-enacting events which occurred in the Dreaming. Through such rituals the Aborigines remain in touch with the Dreaming and the mythic-beings (Berndt and Berndt 1964: 188 and 230). As suggested above, for society to continue this must be done. In return for the demonstration of on-going concern displayed by Aborigines, they expect a reciprocal interest from the Dreaming-beings. To abandon the Law (and the ritual it involves) is to withhold interest and concern, to which the beings can only be foreseen to respond in similar fashion — giving rise to broken reciprocity. The Wiluna Aborigines indicate that such a chain of events has occurred in many locations — e.g. at Leonora and Meekatharra, with disastrous consequences (as could only be anticipated) — and are anxious that it should not happen in their community.

Naturally, contact with Australian-Europeans has produced changes in Aboriginal culture (whether or not these are recognised by Aborigines). But, unlike the drastic changes brought about in the economic sphere, changes in religion and social organisation have been few and more gradual. The adoption of a somewhat sedentary existence on missions, settlements, or near towns has meant that greater numbers are now living together — perhaps more people than were traditionally seen in a lifetime — but, as Tonkinson (1970:278) and Yengoyan (1970:72) have noted, the aggregation seems only to have intensified many aspects of the Law. Additional changes have been within the traditional mould, non-disruptive, and acceptable. For example, even though rituals are now largely confined to the slack mid-summer months, and attendance is facilitated by travel to and fro in an automobile, the important point is that ritual activity continues, as does participation. And the fact that children, now often conceived and born far from traditional countries, occasionally have Dreamings with no traditional Aboriginal relevance (e.g. damper or rock melon) is not as important as the fact that children still have Dreamings.[3] In essence, such changes are of no more moment to the Aborigines than those which occurred prior to contact; making the idea of unchanging and unchangeable Law a fiction (*vide* Stanner 1966:139 and 154).

Liquor Throughout most of the contact period, possession or use of intoxicating liquor has been illegal for most of Wiluna's Aborigines. This is not to say, however, that the majority had not experienced alcohol and its effects at some time in their lives. Some Europeans were often only too willing to supply Aborigines with drink (frequently in return for access to Aboriginal women) and the few Aborigines with citizenship rights supplied kin and friends in order to satisfy obligations or gain personal prestige. The total amount of illicit alcohol to reach Aborigines was relatively small, though, and looked upon as somewhat of a treat.

The introduction of non-restrictive drinking rights, on 1 July 1971, was to alter drastically the earlier situation regarding liquor and to have ramifications throughout the socio-cultural system. Almost immediately, the number of arrests for drinking and associated offences accelerated; from two in June, to fifteen in July, to twenty-nine in August of 1971. Corresponding to this was an increase in fighting, a decrease in spending on essentials such as food, and a general deterioration in ritual activity, camp appearance (owing mainly to broken bottles), and health.

The pattern of Aboriginal drinking follows closely the availability of money. This means that 'pension day', when social service payments are received, and Friday pay-days are also big drinking days. Additionally, the arrival of station employees, carrying large pay packets, encourages a good deal of drinking. The fact that an individual has little or no money does not stop him (or her) from getting liquor — as long as others in the community have funds. This situation holds because the traditional system of reciprocity still operates. A station hand, with more than two hundred dollars in his pocket on arrival in town, may be (and usually is) completely broke within two to three days. Not only has he got drunk, but he has also paid for the excessive drinking of a number of relatives and friends. In return, he can expect to be provided with food and more drink.

Drinking to excess in Wiluna rarely begins until mid-afternoon, though it often happens that camp is deserted and most people are in town by mid-morning. There they congregate outside the general store, opposite the hotel, or at an old house which serves as a meeting place: they gossip, visit each other, and watch the minimal activity which occurs on the main street. Two or three Aborigines may begin drinking when the bar opens, but most continue to relax until the afternoon. Then more and more people begin to gather inside the bar or under the hotel verandah. Not all who are present drink alcohol — some just want to be involved in the excitement which accompanies such activity. By late afternoon, when the local working men arrive, drinking has already commenced, and this continues until about 6 p.m., when most leave for the reserve or mission. Some, who found the bar too crowded, have previously left, perhaps carrying with them a carton of beer to share among their friends and relatives in a creek bed just outside of town.

By 7–8 p.m. 'drunks' begin to arrive in camp — generally with a good deal of commotion. This exodus from town to camp may continue until 1–2 a.m. the following morning, but usually everyone is home by 10–11 p.m. The disturbance created by the return is ordinarily caused by drunken arguing and fighting. These disputes, which begin in the hotel, in the creek bed, or during the walk to the camp, have a variety of origins. Often they may be triggered by the drinking of another person's liquor without his or her permission; accusations that alcohol is being hoarded; and, not uncommonly, suspected adultery or real or imagined slights also lead to violence.

Drunken fights most often begin between two persons, but are rarely confined to them. As they become more and more boisterous, threatening, or violent, the attention of others is attracted. Some come merely to look on, but others (because of kin or friendship ties) may feel compelled either to attempt to halt the fight or to support one or other of the combatants.[4] But to interfere in such a fight, if only to stop it, invariably leads to further conflict. The indiscriminate blows or abuse of the original fighters are likely to fall upon those who intervene, leading to their involvement. Such a chain reaction, once begun, may eventually entangle virtually all the drunks in a 'battle' of all-against-all, wherein the initial reason for the fight is forgotten and would be no longer relevant even if remembered.

Such fights may continue sporadically throughout the night, to stop only toward dawn, when the participants' need for sleep overcomes their desire to carry on. The next day finds people nursing their wounds — e.g. cut scalps, bruised legs, etc. — remarkably few of which are serious. Even more noteworthy is the manner in which the previous night's combatants behave toward one another. All has been forgiven and forgotten, with no hard feelings. The episode is excused because they were all 'full drunk', i.e. not in control of themselves.

This brief picture of drinking and drunkenness is by no means unique to Wiluna. The pattern of people drinking with the express purpose of getting drunk, achieving their stated aim — or at least acting as though they have — and proceeding to start or become involved in a drunken free-for-all where few injuries are serious and all is forgiven the following day, has been noted, at least in part, by Berndt and Berndt (1951), Fink (1960), Beckett (1965), and Millar and Leung (1971) among others. Beckett (1965:39 and 41) observes that Aborigines did drink in spite of restrictive legislation and suggests that such illicit behaviour played a role in the establishment of current drinking practices, particularly the custom of quickly consuming alcohol — originally intended to dispose of the evidence but now a pattern. Millar and Leung (1971:92) concur in Beckett's appraisal; further, they indicate that such legislation also led to the common trait of drinking in seclusion, where the Aborigines were hidden from the eyes of those in authority. No doubt restrictive legislation designed to keep liquor from Aborigines did play a part in the development of drinking patterns, but the effects of the exemplars (the Europeans) must also be recognised (vide MacAndrew and Edgerton 1969: 136). Remember, traditionally Aborigines had no equivalent to alcohol and thus no established pattern regarding alcohol consumption. Without such a consumption pattern of their own, Aborigines looked to the hard-drinking miners, station hands, and drifters of rural Australia for the primary drinking example. These Europeans, even today, consume their liquor quickly, often in seclusion, and in many instances drunken fighting follows. To some extent, Aborigines are simply following a pattern set by their models.[5]

Fighting, the inevitable outcome of drinking in so many Aboriginal communities, is claimed by Fink (1960:165) to result, in part, from the loosening effects that alcohol has upon aggression-control. But drinking, in cross-cultural perspective, does not always mean that fighting is to follow. More than likely, the fighting observed in conjunction with Aboriginal drunkenness is a combination of a relaxing of aggression-control and the fact that drinking, in itself, involves particular norms (vide Washburne 1961: xviii). That is, fighting is expected to occur among drunks; and as there is little or no stigma attached to such combat, and the 'moral alibi' (Beckett 1965:45) of having been 'full drunk' may later be used to absolve one from any blame, fighting is lightly undertaken.

That fighting is easy to participate in does not mean that untoward consequences never result from such activity. For, though Aboriginal culture
contained no rules governing the use and abuse of alcoholic beverages (or
similar substances) — making it all but impossible to control the time or
place of drinking and drunkenness — a few, as yet not completely formed,
standards covering drunken fighting have evolved. One such rule arises from
the fact that not everyone drinks and even the drinkers are rarely all drunk
at any one time. Indeed, on most occasions the majority of the population
is sober — though the visibility and boisterousness of the drunken minority
might make it appear otherwise. Because sober people should try to refrain
from fighting, the drunken combatants must avoid attempting to involve
non-drunks in disputes. Though seldom broken, this rule is occasionally
tested by a drunk 'growling' at a non-drunk. The test may come to a climax
in one of two ways: the non-drunk might instruct the offender to leave —
which the latter usually does — or, if the pestering becomes too great, the
sober individual will lose patience and simply, quickly and efficiently subdue
the other.

A second rule is that only traditional, or traditional-like, weapons are to
be used in drunken combat. Owing to pressure from the police, fights in
town are largely confined to bare knuckles. In contrast, those which take
place in the camp escalate to more dangerous arms, for men and women
alike find it difficult to resist reaching for sticks, boomerangs, and the like
when they are angered. The only modification to this rule requiring traditional weapons involves the use of steel bars or beer bottles (full or empty) in
lieu of wooden clubs. If a bottle is used, it is not to be broken first to form a
knife, though they do often break on impact, leaving a nasty slash wound.
By and large, however, both sexes prefer the strictly traditional implements
to introduced objects of any kind, even when the latter are readily available.

A final rule to be discussed here concerns the injury one may do to one's
opponent(s). To inflict a serious injury is generally frowned on. This helps
to account for the small number of truly crippling wounds encountered.
It is fair to cut open scalps, bruise legs, etc., but against the rules to break a
leg, knock down and beat an opponent unconscious, and so on. This is not
unlike the *'within limits clause'*, i.e. there are limits beyond which one should
not go, noted by MacAndrew and Edgerton (1969:67 — italics in original).
The inability of persons to subdue their opponents contributes to the length
of most Aboriginal fights. There is, in following the rules, no real victor
because an antagonist is always capable of continuing — with the fight
ending only when the combatants tire of screaming and running about and
desire to sleep. Further emphasis of this rule is found in the fact that onlookers,
when at last they grow weary of the commotion, never suggest that one
combatant knock out or shut up another, only that everybody get some rest.

Liquor and the Law   The introduction of free and easy access to alcoholic
beverages has had, overall, rather devastating effects on Aboriginal socio-
cultural systems. The fact that drinking and general drunkenness has created
a deterioration in European-Aboriginal relations is of no great concern to
Wiluna Aborigines. Some do, however, comment on the decline in general
health among heavy drinkers and the lack of proper care and attention
shown to a number of children by habitually intoxicated parents. It is noted

that prior to 'drinking rights' people looked after themselves, spent more money on ammunition and petrol, and made certain the children and old folks had plenty of fresh meat to eat. But the area of primary attention is the adverse effects drink is having on the Law, in both its social and religious domains.

On the social side, the Law is seen to be most endangered by men and women, not viewed as eligible or potential spouses, who sometimes pair off for drunken sexual activities. Even more disturbing to Aborigines is the occasional drunken woman who offers herself for group intercourse. Additionally, there is the abuse of the system of reciprocity by heavy drinkers. Traditionally the principle was basic to social living, and even in the contact situation the system continues largely unchanged. A station hand, it will be remembered, supports friends and relatives in drinking, and in return can expect to be later provided for himself. Where reciprocity encounters difficulties is when persons who have spent all their money on drink approach non-drinkers for food, tobacco, and so on. As yet, few such requests have been openly rejected but increasingly there are complaints on the part of non-drinkers regarding such demands.

Corresponding with the increase in drinking has been a deterioration in ritual life and associated activities. No longer, except on rare occasions, do men gather in the secret-sacred area to discuss Law matters, view ritual paraphernalia, or plan future events. Free time is now spent in town, close to the pub, or in actual drinking. Added to this is the sacrilege more and more frequently displayed toward the secret-sacred domain by drunks (1) uttering secret terms in the presence of women, the uninitiated, and children or (2) intruding on sober persons who are in the process of performing rituals. Both offences cause great consternation among the non-drunks and have been known to lead to bloodshed.

There is also the increasing problem of carrying rituals through to completion. Just as in the past, rituals must be planned to ensure attendance by necessary males and a sufficient number of participants. Normally, these days, plans are made during the week to hold any one of a number of rituals, termed 'Law business', at the weekend. If, for example, young men are to be initiated into more advanced stages of the Law, the custodians and close kinsmen of the initiates must be consulted. This done, discussions need to be held with the men who will 'grab' the initiates to ensure they do not leave the area or go into town. Quite often it will be arranged that a ritual will begin on a Friday morning, with the young men being grabbed, the grabbers beginning the preparations for the ritual, and the working people going off to their jobs. Ideally, the ritual should be well under way by the time the workers join the activities in late afternoon, upon completion of their work day, and continue throughout the weekend and perhaps into the next week.

Plans are not always followed, however, as the lure of the pub is sometimes too great to resist. After grabbing the initiates, the men may decide there is ample time to go into town for a quick drink prior to beginning the ritual preparations in earnest. Once they are in town, the prospect of the long walk back to the reserve and the coolness of the beer tempt the men to stay until it is (1) too late to begin the ritual and (2) they are too drunk to do so anyway. Such a state of affairs disrupts the ritual schedule, often necessitating an abbreviated performance so that certain men may return to work the following week.

There is also the danger that, if the ritual does go off as planned and the men decide to extend it or even to begin another directly upon completion of the first, many men will absent themselves after the initial period of hectic eagerness to begin drinking again. This means that drunks return to camp to interrupt the activities, or that, owing to the number of absentees, the performance cannot be properly concluded.

Men are not the sole offenders on such occasions. Women are just as likely to create disruptions in a ritual schedule. It has happened that the men have attended bush activities all day, returning to the camp in the afternoon to join the women for their complementary participation, only to find the area deserted. The women have become impatient and gone off to town.

That situations like these arise is undoubtedly linked with the absence of rules governing use (and misuse) of liquor within the society. A man may excuse his non-participation in Law business by simply claiming he was drunk — the fact that he was not drunk when he left for the pub knowing that a ritual would be held or was in progress is commonly overlooked. There is, of course, great concern among the people for their Law and the effects alcohol consumption is having on it. Women, who are on a whole more vocal in this respect than men, point out that during Law business all the men should be present — not some drinking and some in the secret-sacred area. They also decry the lack of attention shown initiates during their seclusion period — they should be looked after by their guardians; instead the men would rather drink.

The men, on their part, recognise that drinking is disrupting their life. Sober men often talk about the dangers of drunken fights, the sacrilege of drunks using secret-sacred terms in the camp, and the deleterious effects that drinking to excess is having on ritual activities generally. But that same evening may find those men drunk, fighting, publicly using secret-sacred words, and disrupting a ritual. Although some rules have evolved in regard to certain aspects of drunken combat, all efforts (mostly through informal discussion by men) aimed at establishing a code governing when to drink have failed. In fact, the only consistent behaviour in liquor use — that a candidate for circumcision should be grabbed while drunk (having one last fling prior to seclusion) — is itself harmful to the Law. Drinking and Law business become associated, an association the older men have helped to foster. The men complain about drunkenness among the younger people, but youth is only following the pattern set by the elders.

At present Wiluna's Aborigines are between two extremes; the Law on one side and liquor (Law abandonment) on the other. This fact makes the Wiluna position rather unique. In this area of the Western Desert there are those groups localised at places like Jigalong, Warburton, and Docker River, where the Law is strong and alcohol is virtually absent; and there are Leonora and Meekatharra type communities where liquor is readily available and where the Law is all but gone; Wiluna is alone in having both a strong Law and easy access to drink. Left alone, in all probability, the situation at Wiluna would rapidly deteriorate to a point where the Law was effectively abandoned. The older people would turn more and more to drink as they interpreted the apparent disinterest on the part of young men as a sign that the new generation was (1) no longer worthy of learning the Law, and as they would not do so (2) there would be no reason to continue the tradition — no one would be in a position to follow it anyway. And the younger generation, seeing the abandonment of the Law by the elders, would take it as a sign that the older people no longer recognised the validity and relevance of the traditions and would themselves lose interest in it.

However, Wiluna is not an isolated community. There is constant contact with other Aboriginal populations, most importantly with the various Law centres of the area. Not only is there frequent traffic of families or small parties of men between these locations. There are also movements back and forth of large sections of the populations during the summer ritual season. In these movements Wiluna plays a most pivotal role. Each year, people travel from as far away as Docker River, ostensibly, at least, to conduct rituals in Wiluna; the unique position of the community, as both a Law centre and a drinking location, acts as a strong attraction. The fact that Aborigines throughout the area condemn liquor as a destructive influence, does not mean they do not like to drink. Indeed, it is usually the case that the most vocal opponents of drinking are also the heaviest drinkers (perhaps such people are attempting to compensate for their own transgressions). By travelling to Wiluna to perform rituals, the Aborigines certainly have in mind the prospect of drinking. Important also is the notion that any drinking done should take place in the congenial atmosphere of friends and relatives having a similar socio-cultural system. At drinking locations where the Law has been abandoned—as well as much else that is traditional — i.e. at all nearby spots save Wiluna, they cannot feel at home, at one with everyone else.

So, while alcohol is by and large a deteriorating influence on Wiluna culture when viewed in a microcosm, easy access to it offers compensating advantages in an area-wide perspective. People from neighbouring Law centres travel to Wiluna with two aims; to have Law business, and to get drunk in a relaxed atmosphere. In so doing they put pressure on the Wiluna Aborigines to continue following the Law — for the well-being not only of the Wiluna community, but of the neighbouring groups as well. At present, the advantages and disadvantages of liquor in Wiluna appear to be in a balanced state, but it is unlikely that this situation can continue indefinitely. The equilibrium exists because no other Law centre in the area has the easy access to alcohol Wiluna enjoys. If liquor is introduced into additional centres, then (1) the necessity of travelling to Wiluna to drink (and have rituals) will disappear, and (2) the decline in the Law will accelerate throughout the area. For the moment, the only hope for the continuation of the Law in Wiluna rests on its remaining the sole traditionally-oriented drinking spot in the region.

Conclusion The introduction of liquor has profoundly affected Aboriginal socio-cultural systems. Aborigines, particularly traditionally-oriented ones, have been largely unable to cope with the new element; for it has no traditional referent, and thus, no established pattern of usage. This means the failure to check excessive drinking (in an attempt to hold on to the Law) is partially a product of the Law itself. For while the use and abuse of alcohol

is having harmful influences on the Law, in both its social and ritual manifestations, the latter contains no sanctions regarding the former. People may
persist in drinking and drunkenness because of the Law, not in spite of it.
Furthermore, all attempts at instituting a drinking code have failed. True,
at Wiluna, a few rules governing drunken fighting have been evolved;
however, these can also be seen as being little more than a continuation of
traditional practices in a new setting, i.e. having nothing to do with drinking
but simply modifications of the old model of combat. The overall failure to
react against drinking and drunkenness could very well be because it might
be more a disregard of the Law to create new rules (even to cover a non-
traditional element) than to allow the persistence of excessive consumption.
And even if instituted, any new rules would lack the authority of tradition
and, in all probability, make inroads into the personal freedom provided for
by the Law. That liquor has not brought about an abandonment of the Law
at Wiluna is accounted for by pressures stemming from outside the community. Although Wiluna Aborigines have as yet been unable to control
alcohol use effectively, people from nearby centres, who regularly visit the
town to participate in ritual and drinking activities, continue to exert
pressure on the group to hold to its traditional ways — to remain a Law
community in spite of the liquor problem — and in so doing have counter-
balanced the detrimental influences of drink.

Acknowledgements

The fieldwork on which this paper is based was carried out with the aid of a Fulbright-Hays
Fellowship (Australian-American Educational Foundation) and grants from the Australian
Institute of Aboriginal Studies and the Department of Anthropology, University of Western
Australia. I wish to thank Professor Ronald M. Berndt and Dr Robert Tonkinson for com-
menting on an earlier version of the paper.

Notes

1. The town has an average European population of seventy-five.

2. Here I follow Wilson (1970) and Tonkinson (1974) in using Law, with a capital L, when
    referring to Aboriginal matters; reserving law, without capitalisation, for matters per-
    taining to European legal institutions.

3. The attributing of Dreaming status to introduced items such as rock melons appears to
    be a not uncommon practice. Tonkinson (1966:240) notes a similar occurrence at Jigalong,
    Western Australia.

4. Berndt (1965:172) has noted that there is an 'assumption that someone will try to halt
    a disturbance before it goes too far', at least as regards quarrelling among sober people.
    Perhaps drunken combatants, in bringing attention to their argument, are operating in
    part under a similar premise.

5. With regard to rapid consumption, Hiatt (personal communication) suggests there may
    be a good deal of the traditional in the pattern. For example, some Arnhem Land
    Aborigines, using Indonesian pipes, smoke tobacco quickly and achieve a knock-out
    effect. The suggestion receives further support from MacFarlane (1974:5), who notes the
    ability of Western Desert males to drink two litres of water in thirty seconds.

References

BECKETT, J. 1965 Aborigines, alcohol, and assimilation. In *Aborigines now* (M. Reay ed.),
    pp. 32-47. Angus and Robertson, Sydney.
BERNDT, R. M. 1965 Law and order in Aboriginal Australia. In *Aboriginal man in Australia*
    (R. M. and C. H. Berndt eds), pp. 167-206. Angus and Robertson, Sydney.
——and C. H. Berndt 1951 *From black to white in South Australia*. Cheshire, Melbourne.
——and——1964 *The world of the first Australians*. Ure Smith, Sydney.

FINK, R. A. 1960 The changing status and cultural identity of Western Australian Aborigines. Ph.D. thesis in Anthropology, Columbia University, New York.

MACANDREW, C. and R. B. EDGERTON 1969 Drunken comportment. Nelson, London.

MACFARLANE, W. V. 1974 Aboriginal palaeophysiology: ms.

MILLAR, C. J. and J. M. S. LEUNG 1971 Aboriginal alcohol consumption in South Australia. In A question of choice (R. M. Berndt ed.), pp. 91-95. University of Western Australia Press, Perth.

STANNER, W. E. H. 1965 Religion, totemism and symbolism. In Aboriginal man in Australia (R. M. Berndt and C. H. Berndt eds), pp. 207-37. Angus and Robertson, Sydney.

——1966 On Aboriginal religion. Oceania Monograph No. 11, Sydney.

TONKINSON, R. 1966 Social structure and acculturation of Aborigines in the Western Desert. M.A. thesis in Anthropology, University of Western Australia, Perth.

——1970 Aboriginal dream-spirit beliefs in a contact situation: Jigalong, Western Australia. In Australian Aboriginal anthropology (R. M. Berndt ed.), pp. 277-91. University of Western Australia Press, Perth.

——1974 The Jigalong mob: Aboriginal victors of the desert crusade. Cummings, Menlo Park.

WASHBURNE, C. 1961 Primitive drinking. College and University Press, New York.

WILSON, K. 1970 Pindan: A preliminary comment. In Diprotodon to detribalization (A. R. Pilling and R. A. Waterman eds), pp. 333-46. Michigan State University, East Lansing.

YENGOYAN, A. A. 1970 Demographic factors in Pitjandjara social organization. In Autsralian Aboriginal anthropology (R. M. Berndt ed.), pp. 70-91. University of Western Australia Press, Perth.

8 From camp to village:

some problems of adaptation

Isobel M. White

The social advantages of mobility   In assessing the many difficulties met by Aborigines in adjusting, even partially, to modern Western culture, it is immediately obvious that a change has to be made from impermanent to permanent settlement, from mobile camp to village or town. Some of these difficulties have been noted and recorded (e.g. Rowley 1970:22), but here I propose to examine some further problems.

Much has been written about the composition of the groups which owned or occupied defined territories in Aboriginal Australia, and about the size and boundaries of these territories (e.g. Berndt 1959; Hiatt 1962; Birdsell 1970). Little attention has been paid to those social relationships within each group which may be reflected in the occupation of space at successive camp sites. When a new site is occupied, is the arrangement of families an exact duplication of that at the last site? A recent paper by P. Hamilton (1973) records details of the typical use of space by a community of about 70 people closely related to, and speaking the same language as, the Yalata Aboriginal Reserve community of over 300 which I studied. The smaller community would be closer in size to the traditional group in pre-contact Aboriginal society, but nevertheless his description of the *wildja*s (old-style shelters) and their distribution over the camp site would apply to Yalata, except that the Yalata arrangement of the *wildja*s is much more scattered and untidy than his model diagram. I have already described the use of space for sleeping within a *wildja* and the way it can be adapted as the size and composition of the family change (White 1975). Hamilton describes the use of the *wildja* itself and the space around it for daytime activities, and this coincides with my observations at Yalata.

Silberbauer (1973:96–98) has recorded within G/wi Bushmen bands the existence of 'cliques' which he describes as 'unstable groups which may undergo partial or complete reconstitution with each move the band makes to a new camp site . . . Cliques consist of a seemingly random range of kin and friends of all ages'. Each clique occupies 'a distinct cluster of from two to seven huts', and interaction is higher between members of a clique than between members of different cliques. There may be no apparent friction within the cliques before a move but nevertheless after it there may be new clique formations.

I have noted something of the same phenomenon in the camp sites on the Yalata Aboriginal Reserve in South Australia. Their situation must not be seen as identical with the traditional one, as there are at Yalata about 300 Aborigines moving within an area of about 1000 square kilometres (400 square miles) instead of the traditional situation in the Western Desert where bands of 30 to 40 might be semi-nomadic over many thousands of square miles (R. Berndt 1959; Birdsell 1970; Gould 1969). However, the Yalata customs probably have a traditional component, and in any case my arguments apply to the Yalata people today since they may have to face the change to permanent settlement some day.

From written reports and from questioning colleagues, I gather that Yalata is unusual among today's Aboriginal settlements in that the whole camp moves several times a year to a new part of the reserve, which may be as far as 30 kilometres (20 miles) from the Yalata Lutheran Mission, but more often 6 to 20 kilometres (4 to 12 miles) away. This unique situation comes about through the active co-operation of the mission superintendent and his staff (some of whom are Aboriginal), who undertake the considerable task of organising transport between camp and mission, because they see the advantages of using a large part of the reserve instead of only a small fraction of it. By far the most common reason for moving is the death of any camp member other than an infant. A new site is chosen by the camp leaders (the mature family men) in consultation with the mission superintendent, and the mission trucks are made available to transport the people and their meagre possessions. (Today each household owns a very heavy tarpaulin, which is used as a cover for the old-type shelter and makes it wind and weatherproof.) The water tanks, which are mounted on trailers, are also dragged to the new site, and so is the medical caravan, in which the nursing sisters hold clinics.

The requirements for the new site are, first, that it should be along one of the dozen or so tracks that radiate from the mission, for there is continual traffic between camp and mission; for example the school bus takes the children to school and back in two loads, thus making eight trips a day; either the truck goes out to the camp to bring people to buy food at the store five days a week and to buy beer at the canteen three days a week, and to church on Sunday; or these facilities are taken out to the camp. The nursing sisters and the welfare officers make daily visits to the camp.

The second requirement is that the site should not have been used before (because of the death tabus), and this in itself means that the camps tend to go out further and further along the tracks. Thirdly, it must have plenty of good trees to provide shelters and firewood, and particularly there should be good stands of western myall (acacia sowdenii), used for most of the artefacts, whose manufacture and sale provide the main income of the Aborigines. There is mallee (eucalyptus oleara) everywhere for the less frequently made spears and carrying dishes.

The traditional requirements that a camp site should be near supplies of water and food are met by the large water tanks which are kept filled by the mission trucks, and by the mission store, although some of the food is still supplied by hunting activities (White 1972).

There exists also, within a mile of the mission, what is called 'the little camp', where live the dozen or so men and youths employed by the mission together with their immediate families and certain old and sick pensioners, for whom the nursing sister exerts special care. This camp also moves when a death occurs within the camp itself, but never very far.

In addition to the two camps there are half-a-dozen or so houses on the mission site, occupied by the most acculturated Aborigines. This number is growing as more of the younger couples choose this type of living, but the growth is slow, and there is always the possibility that such a house may be abandoned permanently (or even burnt down) if someone dies inside it.

All the residents of both camps and of the houses regard themselves as kin and use a small range of kinship terms to refer to each other, and all interact with each other to some extent, although there are certain quite definite divisions, which may break out into active hostility during brawls. For example, on such occasions one can hear abuse and accusations between the Bidjandjara and Janggundjara who make up the two main dialect groups within the camp.[1]

To return to the movement patterns of 'the big camp'; on arrival at the new camp, family sites are chosen, and usually each family will have some neighbours different from those in the old camp. As Silberbauer reported for the G/wi, there seemed no evident friction between neighbours before the move. However, there is no evidence of the clusters he describes for the G/wi, the dwellings at Yalata being rather evenly spread over the whole site.

Some groupings maintain a permanent nucleus, for example where young married couples always live close to one set of parents. At Yalata there are a few cases where young wives camp next to their mothers. The more traditionally oriented older women say that this is wrong because of the rule of mother-in-law/son-in-law avoidance and that the young couple should live right across the camp. However, others regard such an arrangement as permissible provided that formal avoidance rules are kept, such as no direct conversation or sitting down together. The family I know best consists of a middle-aged couple, three young children, and two married daughters, both of whom always have their shelters close to their parents', but behind it, so that the mother-in-law is symbolically turning her back on her son-in-laws. (Though Aboriginal indigenous type shelters can be quickly re-oriented if the wind changes, on the Yalata Reserve the shelters have their backs to the south almost all year round because of the prevailing cold southerlies in winter and the regular strong afternoon southerly sea-breeze in summer.) The immediate neighbours, with whom most interaction takes place, are usually the close 'sisters' or 'mothers' of the middle-aged wife. The husbands would all be 'brothers' or 'fathers', 'mothers' brothers' or 'sisters' sons', in the Western Desert kinship terminology, with its stress on generation levels, but it is the close relationship between the women which is emphasised. However, a 'sister's' or 'mother's' family which was next door in one camp site might be across the camp after the next move.

The relation between physical and social distance   During the six years I have been visiting Yalata I have noticed marked differences in the total area over which the main camp is spread, and believe that this reflects the harmony/conflict situation. The largest total area of about a square kilometre (half-mile square) was in August–September 1971, a period of the utmost social and political stress. This camp was over 20 kilometres (12 miles) from the mission. Shortly before my visit two of the community's most influential men, who were frequent companions and called each other brother, had become involved in a drunken quarrel and one had died as a result. The dead man was one of the most important ritual leaders and also the most universally liked man in the camp because of his happy and helpful disposition. Though an Adelaide jury acquitted the other man of murder, I was told by both Aborigines and whites at Yalata that he was undoubtedly guilty and that he had not returned to Yalata because he would be killed in revenge whenever he was found. (This in fact happened shortly after I had left Yalata.) There was quite evident tension in the camp, though no obviously defined partisan groups, nor did I hear anything about the murder mentioned during the brawls which I witnessed.

Some weeks after I arrived it became time for the annual rain rituals and the camp was moved to an area about three-quarters of a kilometre (half a mile) from the ritual ground so that the whole community could participate. Since this ground is near the mission and the airstrip, the area of this camp site is limited, certainly less than half the size of the former site. During the period of preparation and performance of the rituals, about a week, all quarrels are forbidden, and in the normal course of events a return would have been made to the former camp site immediately the rituals were completed. It happened, however, on this occasion that the South Australian Department of Health wished to make a health survey involving the whole community, so the camp leaders were asked to delay the move back for a week or two. With the rituals over, there was no check on either excessive drinking or quarrelling and during this period there was brawling and fighting almost every night. The more peaceful inhabitants (the vast majority) were looking forward to returning to the more spacious and distant site. During this time a direct attack by a drunken man on my own property caused me to leave earlier than I had planned so I did not witness the return, but I would guess that peace and comparative sobriety immediately prevailed.

It is quite evident that moving the camp has a salutary effect on physical, mental and social health. Since the camps lack sanitation and garbage collection, the physical effects of a new clean site need not be detailed. Moreover, daily tasks are made easier by the vicinity of untouched supplies of wood for fires and artefacts. I have noticed too that the social climate improves, and that there is more friendly interaction; and certainly there may be social advantages in being able to change one's neighbours frequently.

A different kind of living　　I am not sure that all students of Aboriginal societies fully appreciate the central importance of personal relationships. I want to discuss here what I see as *first-hand living* as opposed to *second-hand living*. First-hand living I define as one's own experiences, one's own actions and personal relations and those of one's kin, neighbours and friends. Second-hand living I define as vicarious interest in the doings of other people, real or imaginary. The proportions of time spent by an individual in first- and second-hand living are vastly different in Aboriginal compared with industrial society. The only second-hand living experienced by traditional Aborigines is in hearing news from other Aboriginal communities and in telling and acting out myths. Industrial man on the other hand spends much of his time in second-hand living, through reading, schooling, listening to radio, watching television, attending cinemas, theatres and so on. Among Aborigines, variety in first-hand living through moving camp and changing neighbours adds interest to a life which might otherwise prove monotonous. It also explains the obvious enjoyment derived by the Yalata group of Aborigines from the camp brawls which occur normally every ten to fourteen days.

These are ritualised and dramatised and might be seen as a substitute for a weekly visit to the cinema. (However, objection is taken, as in 1971, to too frequent brawling, particularly if drunkenness causes dangerous violence.) Some observers of Aborigines report that much time is spent in gossiping. (Sharp 1934:430; R. and C. Berndt 1942–45:209.) This again must be seen as part of first-hand living where gossip takes the place of what in our society is filled by the news media, the telephone or letter writing, and any derogatory meaning for the word 'gossip' must not be imputed.

The change to living privately in a house may prove quite traumatic to those used to the variety in personal relationships which a movable camp can offer. If a village with permanent houses were to replace the movable camp and the transitory dwellings, the Yalata people would face some difficult adjustments, notably:

(1) From the native-type *wildjas* to houses. Most of the Yalata women do not want to live in houses. I was once sitting with a group of eight or nine women in the Yalata camp when we were visited by an Adelaide architect, wishing with the best will in the world to design a house that these women would like. When he asked them in turn if they would like to live in a house, to his chagrin all but one (the youngest woman present— in her twenties) said 'No'. When asked why the rejection, after a long pause one woman dared to say 'We'd have to keep it clean', a statement which was greeted with murmurs of agreement. Now this does *not* represent the racist's stereotype of the lazy, feckless Aboriginal woman. Rather it indicates a rejection of white values, particularly those centred around the ownership and careful maintenance of property. Moreover, it may well mean that these Aboriginal women have evaluated and rejected the role of their white counterparts, so much of whose time is involved in the never-ending task of house cleaning.

(2) To houses that cannot be moved, or even subjected to internal rearrangement. The *wildja* is flexible; it can be quickly altered in size and shape, or turned round completely for a change of wind. Unlike the *wildja*, a house has doors between rooms and doors to outside. These shut the occupants in, so that they are cut off from each other and from their neighbours.

(3) To permanent neighbours. Admittedly movement from one house to another might be possible, but the flexibility of the short-stay camp would have gone completely. How many of us in white society can expect a change of neighbours several times a year? In a settlement such as Maningrida between 1958 and 1960, a condition further from the traditional than at Yalata in the early 'seventies was found by Hiatt, who reports 'I judged that *changes in residential association* were less frequent at Maningrida than in the past because of the labour people invested in the construction of modern bark huts.' (Hiatt 1965:35, my italics.)

(4) To a permanent environmental space instead of one which can be changed whenever the community wishes.

In order to make the transition easier, some substitution of second-hand for first-hand living is essential. But second-hand living requires certain skills and facilities, namely, ability to understand spoken and written English and the possibility of being able to buy radio and television sets, newspapers and books. Otherwise the reduction of first-hand living without an equivalent increase in second-hand living must end in social disorder.

Note

1. The old designation of Andagarinja (or *Antingari* as the Berndts heard it called) among the Ooldea people in the 1940s (R. and C. Berndt 1942-45:1) seems to have disappeared, which might mean that this group of the Ooldea population moved elsewhere in 1953 when the Ooldea mission was abandoned and most of the population were moved to Yalata.

References

BERNDT, R. 1959 The concept of 'the tribe' in the Western Desert of Australia, *Oceania*, XXX: 81-107.

——*and* C. BERNDT 1942-45 A preliminary report of field work in the Ooldea region, Western South Australia, *Oceania*, XII-XV.

BIRDSELL, J. B. 1970 Local group composition among the Australian Aborigines: a critique of the evidence from fieldwork conducted since 1930, *Current Anthropology*, 11:115-42.

GOULD, R. 1969 Subsistence behaviour among the Western Desert Aborigines of Australia, *Oceania*, XXXIX:253-74.

HAMILTON, P. 1972 Aspects of interdependence between Aboriginal social behaviour and the spatial and physical environment. *Aboriginal Housing*, Royal Australian Institute of Architects, Canberra.

HIATT, L. R. 1962 Local organization among the Australian Aborigines, *Oceania*, XXXII: 267-86.

——1965 *Kinship and conflict*. Australian National University Press, Canberra.

ROWLEY, C. 1970 *The destruction of Aboriginal society*. Australian National University Press, Canberra.

SHARP, L. 1934 The social organization of the Yir-Yiront tribe of Cape York Peninsula, *Oceania*, V:401-31.

SILBERBAUER, G. B. 1973 Socio-ecology of the G/wi Bushmen. Ph.D. thesis, Monash University.

WHITE, I. M. 1972 Hunting dogs at Yalata, *Mankind*, 8:201-5.

——1975 Sexual conquest and submission in the myths of central Australia. In *Australian Aboriginal mythology* (L. R. Hiatt ed.), pp. 123-42. Australian Institute of Aboriginal Studies Canberra.

9 Walk-off (and later return) of various Aboriginal groups from cattle stations:

Victoria River District, Northern Territory

J. K. Doolan

This paper is a factual account of events which took place on pastoral properties within the Victoria River District during 1972–1973, a period during which Aboriginal people of the area have probably done more through their own efforts to secure for themselves a better way of life, as they see it, than during any other period since occupation by whites in the early 1880s. It is written with the idea of providing material for discnssion and to point out that Aboriginal priorities in many cases are quite different from white priorities, and that perhaps in some cases we may, in our ignorance, be trying to impose on them a way of life and a sense of values which are essentially 'ours' but not 'theirs'. In approaching this problem I illustrate three main points:

(i) An actual instance of strong, independent action being taken by Aboriginal groups, as opposed to their previous submissive acceptance of the white man's ideas and attitudes and conforming with conditions imposed on them by employers in rural areas;

(ii) The type of employer for whom Aborigines prefer to work; and

(iii) The Aboriginal concept of running a pastoral property, as opposed to the European concept.

The establishment of Dagaragu As a background to what has been happening in the Victoria River District, it is necessary to go back to 1966 when there was a mass walk-off by Aborigines from all Vestey's stations in the District, in protest against conditions and treatment which they were forced to endure. A camp was set up at Wattie Creek, known to the Gurindji people as Dagaragu. Many of these people have since returned to Vestey's stations under far better conditions than they had previously enjoyed, and perhaps more important to them, they are treated with more respect now than ever before. They have not returned, however, to one of Vestey's stations. The reason they give for this is that they dislike the manager and will return only when he leaves. There are important Dreaming sites on this station property which they are concerned about: they are prepared to sit and wait for a change in management.

Despite the fact that many did return to all but one of the stations, there remained a hard core (mostly of middle-aged to old people) who continued to live at Dagaragu. The older men, the most outspoken of whom is Vincent Lingiari, maintained a watchful eye on events and on what was happening to Gurindji people on the various properties, acting as mediators in minor disputes between management and employees, and in many cases (especially in so far as Vincent was concerned) were held in high regard by employers

106

in the district. Dagaragu, in addition to its headquarters and post office role, is also used as a wet-season camp during the 'lay-off' period so that Gurindji people, no matter how far afield they may work, never really lose touch with one another. The hard core, however, insisted that they would not return until they got back at least some of their traditional tribal lands; and because of that attitude, Dagaragu has become a symbol of protest throughout the whole of the Victoria River and East Kimberley Districts, and beyond.[1]

In March 1972, the Aborigines living on Victoria River Downs and its outstations (Moolooloo, Pigeon Hole and Mt Sanford) decided to follow the precedent set by the Gurindji and suddenly walked off these stations and headed for Dagaragu.

At this stage, some reference should be made to the role of various Europeans involved in this movement. The Victoria River Downs management is convinced that it was instigated and organised by a white woman who had been living at Dagaragu with Gurindji people and, indeed, she herself has claimed the credit for inducing the people to leave. It cannot be disputed that they were certainly encouraged by her and by other Europeans in the area. However, after spending a considerable period camping with and talking to members of this group, I am equally convinced that it was a decision the Aborigines made themselves. Perhaps she acted as a kind of catalyst, but I am doubtful of that.

The Victoria River Downs people were shortly afterward joined by another group from the adjacent Humbert River Station. They also arrived at Dagaragu, swelling its population to over two hundred and thirty. The stock season was in full swing at the time and pastoralists in the area were desperately short of labour.

The reasons given for this 'walk-off' were as follows:
(a) Dissatisfaction over the failure to provide adequate housing for Aborigines although houses for European employees were being constructed;
(b) A firm belief that Aborigines were not receiving the level of wage to which they were entitled;
(c) A belief that Social Services cheques were not being seen by people who were entitled to them;
(d) That the Victoria River Downs manager was unapproachable;
(e) A feeling of antipathy between Europeans and Aborigines which was not discouraged by the European management; and
(f) A resentment that, although both Aboriginal men and women were 'treated like dogs' in daylight hours, Aboriginal women were considered good enough to sleep with European employees at night.

At the time they left Victoria River Downs, the undisputed leaders of this movement were Charcoal Dulung and Big Mick Ganginang. As members of the group told me, Charcoal was the 'manager' and Big Mick the 'lawyer'. There were two other very old men who had previously played an important part in both 'tribal' and everyday affairs, but because of their age they had relinquished their leadership. However, since the Victoria River Downs group were visitors at Dagaragu, Vincent Lingiari was still considered to be the boss of the entire camp. The Victoria River Downs and Humbert River groups (contrary to newspaper reports of the time) are not one people: they are drawn from several different 'tribes' — e.g. Ngaliwuru, Ngarinman, Bilinara, Djamindjung, Mudbara, Garangburu and others.

The 'labour pool' About a month after they had left Victoria River Downs, some of the men told me that they would like to return to work, provided it was not on that station. Employment was sought and obtained for a good number of them on various pastoral properties in the area. For instance, I would return to Dagaragu and announce that 'Inverway wants three stockmen', 'Mistake Creek, five stockmen' and 'Waterloo, a camp cook', and so on. They should be pleased about this and say that first they would have to ask Vincent Lingiari if they could go to work. Vincent in most cases was happy to see the Dagaragu population decrease, but occasionally he would refuse permission because the man in question had two wives and children and he did not want them left behind while he was away. He even forbade Charcoal Dulung to take up employment on the grounds that, as he was the 'manager' of the Victoria River Downs mob, he must remain behind to look after his people.

Some of the aims of the Victoria River Downs group were already being achieved. Apart from the fact that they had shown initiative in leaving the pastoral properties where conditions had become intolerable, they had now created a 'labour pool' which was the only source available in the district from which the pastoralists and mustering contractors were able to obtain men for the cattle industry. Pastoralists obviously resented this situation, but they were left with no alternative if they wanted employees. Some were prepared to offer higher than award wages to obtain labour, and no doubt their wives were missing the almost unlimited supply of domestic help they had had in the immediate past, the quality of which was often complained of when it had been available. Nevertheless, there was a constant effort by employers visiting Dagaragu to obtain labour. The reactions of the people to the pastoralists' requests were most interesting. They would listen politely, discuss the matter among themselves, then come up with an answer such as: 'Yes, you can have men. If you want more later, come back and see us and we will give you more.' In other cases, they would reply: 'No, we are sorry that we can't help you, Mick. You have been a hard man in the past and we do not trust you.' The really fascinating part of this was that those who were regarded as 'hard men' sometimes offered above award wages and better conditions than men who were often only 'battlers' and could offer little in the way of extra remuneration (and, in the case of mustering contractors, no accommodation at all) — yet the latter usually obtained unlimited labour because they were 'good blokes', while the others obtained nothing at all.

One mustering contractor whom the Aborigines regarded as a 'good man' even secured a team of stockmen to go back and muster on Victoria River Downs. The Aborigines regarded this as being reasonable, because they were not working for that station's management — only for a contractor whom they liked. I do not mean to imply that they would assist only the 'battler'. On the contrary, sometimes they would refuse to aid this type of person because he was not popular with them; on the other hand, they would be prepared to assist a wealthy pastoralist whom they held in high regard. The point I am making is that Aborigines in this area (and for that matter in other areas in which I have worked) will invariably work for a person who they believe has some regard and feeling for them, even if he is not able to pay high wages and provide good accommodation, rather than for someone who pays very well and provides excellent accommodation but who obviously regards them as something less than human — and they are not unperceptive in this respect.

A typical example of this was brought home to me when Aborigines on another station (which I will call Station A) walked off the property in July 1972 and joined the others at Dagaragu. The owner of that station is an elderly man, born in the district, whom the Aborigines have known all their lives. He had been absent for some time on another of his properties in the Alice Springs area and had appointed a manager and head stockman in his absence: the local Aborigines could not agree with either of these men, who in their opinion had little regard for them. On hearing that Station A people had left, the owner flew back and was given the manager's version of the reasons behind the walk-off. However, he was not prepared to accept this until he had visited the people and listened to their views. Having heard the other side of the story, he returned and told the manager that all of the people would be returning within the next few days: the manager replied that if they returned he would leave. The owner said he could make his own choice, but that the Aborigines would be returning. When the owner returned to Dagaragu to take back what he referred to as 'his blackfellows', it was quite a moving spectacle to observe the emotional scenes that followed. The people themselves were overjoyed to be returning 'home', and the owner in turn was happy to bring them back, for reasons that obviously were not merely mercenary. As they told me, they 'belonged' to that station.

The whole exercise was most interesting, providing as it did an insight into 'black-white' relationships in this area. It was a near-perfect example of the old paternalistic-type employer who succeeds in having Aborigines return to his station despite the effects of various militants at Dagaragu to have them remain there. Yet housing, normal facilities and amenities at Station A are not good — and never have been. While the owner of Station A was arranging for 'his' group to return, the owner of another nearby station (which I will call Station B) was also at Dagaragu endeavouring to secure men for employment. He, however, was unsuccessful and left complaining bitterly. Yet Station B has excellent housing and associated facilities for Aboriginal employees.

The significant difference is obvious. At Station A there is mutual communication between employer and employees and their families. Despite comparatively poor housing and facilities, they are able to exist as family groups and retain their personal identity as people. At Station B there is little or no communication between employer and employee. Despite better housing and conditions, Aborigines, when they can be persuaded to work there, are strictly employees only — not really viewed as 'people'. It seems obvious therefore, on the basis of these examples, that the retention of their own identity and an ability to communicate with their employer are more important factors to the Aborigines than living in pleasant homes while ceasing to exist as people. I do not mean to imply that Aborigines do not appreciate good housing and facilities. At Wave Hill settlement (Libanangu), Gurindji and Wailbri people are living in 'normal' Housing Commission-type homes, managing to keep them neat and tidy and apparently enjoying what they have to offer. What I do mean, however, is that if they have a choice between

good housing with an employer whom they dislike and sub-standard accommodation with an employer whom they regard highly, they will invariably
opt for the latter.

Recognition of Dagaragu With the change of federal government,
prospects for the Gurindji people of obtaining a block of their own came
closer to becoming a reality. In June 1973, a combined group of pastoral
consultants, Gurindji, and Vestey representatives together with Department
of Aboriginal Affairs officials from both Darwin and Canberra took part in
a survey of over two thousand five hundred square kilometres (a thousand
square miles) of Wave Hill Station, Lord Vestey having tentatively agreed
to relinquish an area of that station, west of the Victoria River. The consultants, acknowledged experts in this field, decided that new bores should
be sunk, new paddocks fenced, and stock yards built. Vincent Lingiari and
Jerry Rangaiari agreed with these suggestions.

After this survey was completed, the Gurindji people were asked how
many Europeans they thought would be necessary to run the proposed
station. 'None', was the reply. The consultants were astonished. They asked
again: 'Who will build the yards, sink the bores, do the fencing, sell the cattle
and cull the herds?' The answer was 'We will'. Vincent finally agreed that
perhaps they might need a bookkeeper, but as for a manager, head stockman,
yard builder, horse breaker, saddler — well, they had worked out long ago
who would be in charge of these various jobs! The consultants were perplexed.
They could not understand how Vincent and his men by themselves would
ever run a viable economic enterprise, in competition with and along the
lines of neighbouring properties. The point is that the Gurindji do not want
to become serious competitors with their neighbours (at least not at this
stage) when they do eventually get the lease of the property, hopefully in the
near future. Once again, it is European priorities rather than Aboriginal
ones which are really being looked at. What the Aborigines want is to get
back some of their former land so that they can 'sit down' and enjoy their
own ceremonies and rituals, eat their own beef, turn off enough cattle to
provide the necessities of life as they see it, and work at their own pace.
Perhaps in the very distant future some descendant of Vincent Lingiari may
aspire to being elevated to the peerage, but I know that, at this stage, Vincent
himself has no desire to emulate Lord Vestey and become Lord Lingiari! In
this Aboriginal society, he is in a unique position as an undisputed leader of
the Gurindji.

They have now fenced off a twenty-square-kilometre (eight-square-mile)
paddock, over which they have been granted a lease without prejudice to
their larger claim.[2] It was necessary to arrange for this smaller lease, which
the previous government had agreed to, before they could be given a distinct
cattle brand — 'G.D.T.' (which refers to the Gurindji, the Dagaragu camp
on Wattie Creek and the cattle). Yards have been constructed and the
Gurindji are 'in business', even if only in a small way.

The founding of Yarralin While these events relating to the Gurindji
people were taking place, the Victoria River Downs and Humbert River
groups made a bid to get back part of their own 'tribal' country. In early
October 1973, a meeting was held at Victoria River Downs between repre-

sentatives of the owners, Hooker Pastoral Company, the local Aborigines, and Department of Aboriginal Affairs officials. An 'on the ground' inspection was carried out, and after considerable discussion between the Aborigines and Hooker representatives it was agreed that the people would return to a place which they call Yarralin. This is close to an abandoned Victoria River Downs outstation known as Gordon Creek, and about twenty kilometres (twelve miles) from the homestead. Here there was a dilapidated building which could be repaired. The owners have tentatively agreed to relinquish about two hundred and thirty square kilometres (ninety-odd square miles) of good country, the lease of which is now under negotiation. A small grant was given by the government for building materials to erect a temporary wet-season camp. We commenced the move in mid-October, about a week after the initial negotiations. The Aborigines Benefits Trust Fund had provided a small truck and the Wave Hill settlement (Libanangu) loaned a five-ton truck. In a week, eighty-four people with their dogs and belongings had been moved from Dagaragu to Yarralin. Gangs of men were sent out to cut coolibah for posts, others began digging a deep-pit toilet, some commenced repairing the old homestead — all of this being organised amongst themselves. Their greatest disappointment was that they could not start to build a fence around their block, and it took a considerable amount of explanation on my part before I could get through to them that this would not be possible until a lease was granted over the area. Until the wet season closed the road, I paid visits to Yarralin almost every week until late December. By that time the old homestead had been waterproofed and nine small houses constructed. As the stock season had finished, the number of residents had increased to about one hundred and forty. The Victoria River Downs management proved quite helpful in permitting the use of its store and medical facilities, while Charcoal Dulung had come to an arrangement with the manager regarding beef. Apparently, Victoria River Downs badly needed five men to work at various jobs, and Charcoal had supplied the men in consideration of free beef for his people; in addition to this, the men were paid wages.

The leadership of the total group presents an interesting study. There are no less than nine different 'tribes' represented among those people who took part in the original move from Dagaragu to Yarralin. When they first walked off Victoria River Downs, Big Mick Ganginang (a Ngaliwuru man) and Charcoal Dulung (a Garangburu) were the leaders and spokesmen. Since then, Big Mick's health seems to have deteriorated and a younger man, Alan Young Nadjakbai (a Ngarinman) has emerged as spokesman for the group. Alan has a pleasing personality and has become popular with Europeans who have had some involvement with this group. He is always ready to talk of his own and his people's hopes and aspirations to anyone with a sympathetic ear, and has certainly met with some success in achieving results through this ability to convince people of his obvious sincerity. His position is also supported by the fact that, as a member of the Ngarinman 'tribe', he is in his own country. Charcoal Dulung, on the other hand, is handicapped to a certain extent by the fact that the country is his only by adoption, as the Garangburu are more closely associated with the Mudbara. But it is Charcoal who organises the working parties in their various activities and ensures that they carry out their appointed tasks: his authority is unquestioned. Nevertheless, Alan is now referring to the truck as 'my truck' and the proposed station as 'my station'. There is no real power struggle taking place between them; but it seems that Alan would like to be, and talks as if he were, the 'boss', although Charcoal is really the boss and is quite content to let Alan do all the talking for him.

It has been most rewarding to see the change which has taken place in this group. I saw them in late 1971 before they left Victoria River Downs, and they were a most apathetic and dejected group. When I visited them again in April 1972, following the walk-off, they were quite elated over the direct action which they had taken. Between then and October 1973, the mood of elation had left them and they were once again beginning to look and act in a dejected way. Now that they are back again and full of hope for the future, they are again a happy people, making all sorts of plans for the cattle station which they hope one day soon to be operating by themselves. They boast about how they will have a better station than 'that Gurindji mob'. Dagaragu is referred to as 'a proper hungry place' and Yarralin praised as a good place for bush tucker, fish and hunting — which in fact it is. In all the years that I visited Dagaragu I seldom heard a corroboree, but at Yarralin they are an almost nightly occurrence.

Conclusion   The present aim among Aborigines in the Victoria River District seems to be to secure some land of their own, preferably at least part of their own 'tribal' land, where they can work at their own pace, enjoy their rituals and ceremonies, and live as close to their traditional mode of life as present-day conditions will permit. In many areas, it is no longer possible to hunt game, as the country has been denuded of its natural fauna. However, mustering and working cattle serve as substitutes, at least to some extent, for the thrill and challenge of the hunt and for achieving status that was previously accorded a good hunter — which is probably why they enjoy and usually excel at stock work. Nevertheless, they regard the concept of running a successful cattle property as secondary to the acquisition of land. Both the Gurindji and Victoria River Downs groups have made it clear that they wish to have as little contact as possible with Europeans in the future. The same view has, to my knowledge, been expressed farther north by the so-called Brinkin people at the Daly River, where another cattle project is being developed. On the other hand, consultants are interested mainly in seeing the various groups run successful cattle stations with European advisers. Although this attitude is understandable, as government funds are being used to purchase properties for Aboriginal people, nevertheless there is a conflict of ideas.

Since the movement by the Gurindji and Victoria River Downs people, other significant follow-on events have taken place in the district. Kildurk Station was handed over to the Aborigines living on that property, the government having purchased the entire station for them in April 1973. Aborigines living on Nicholson Station (just over the Western Australian border from the Northern Territory) are making a bid to acquire Turner Station, which adjoins that property. Further north, a group of people, mainly Ngarinman, have set up an independent camp at a place called Bulla, on the East Baines River, and have been negotiating for some time with Auvergne Station for a block of their own.

It is obvious therefore that the idea begun by the Gurindji and later followed by the Victoria River Downs group has spread, and that it will probably continue to grow in this area, as in others.

Points (ii) and (iii), which I mentioned at the beginning of this paper, tend to indicate that Aboriginal people wish to preserve their own traditional socio-economic structure rather than be influenced by, and eventually succumb to, European ideas and values.

Notes

1. See R. Berndt (1971:34–5) for a brief discussion of this situation. The earlier period, relevant to conditions of Aboriginal employment on pastoral stations in this area, has been discussed in some detail by R. and C. Berndt (1946). See also Stevens (1974).

2. On 16 August 1975, the Prime Minister, together with other federal ministers, press men and various officials, assembled at Wave Hill for the 'historic handing over of tribal land to the Gurindji Aborigines at Wattie Creek'. The Prime Minister handed the lease for 3100 square km of land to Vincent Lingiari.

References

BERNDT, R. M. 1971 The concept of protest within an Australian Aboriginal context. In *A question of choice: an Australian Aboriginal dilemma* (R. M. Berndt ed.). University of Western Australia Press, Perth.
——and C. H. Berndt 1946 Native labour and welfare in the Northern Territory. Privately distributed, ms.
STEVENS, F. 1974 *Aborigines in the Northern Territory cattle industry*. Australian National University Press, Canberra.

[Notes and References were added to this article by the Editor.]

10 Decentralisation trends in Arnhem Land

W. J. Gray

My purpose here is to present information relating to a social movement in Arnhem Land which has been labelled 'decentralisation'. The term 'decentralisation' in this context refers to groups of Aboriginal people who have chosen to move away from the established centres of population which are administered by either the Australian government or church missions. These smaller groups have settled themselves in country with which they claim to have traditional affiliation. In moving away from the larger settlements, they resume relative independence, free from non-Aboriginal supervision and control. Although I restrict my discussion to the movement as it appears in Arnhem Land, it should be kept in mind that the same trend occurs in other parts of the Northern Territory. The movement represents an adjustment which is being made by these Aboriginal groups, in response to pressures of living in a cross-cultural institutionalised environment. Although it is as yet young, there are already some common features to be found in all of these decentralising groups. I will, therefore, provide information on population and location of these decentralised communities and discuss various factors related to motivation. I will also describe the methods of communication adopted by the Department of Aboriginal Affairs in liaising with these communities and make some comment on the possible future of these small independent communities.

Background   There are approximately 7000 Aboriginal people living in that area of the Northern Territory known as Arnhem Land. The majority of them live on the eight church mission and three government settlements located within the 96 262 square kilometres (37 167 square miles) of that area. The first of these communities was established in 1908 on the Roper River and the most recent at Maningrida in 1957. Several of the mission stations administered until very recently by the United Church in North Australia, are located on islands along the north coast of Arnhem Land. It was church policy at the time of their establishment to obtain the greatest degree of isolation from external influences, which were considered to be of an undesirable nature. As a result, many of the Aboriginal people now living on these missions originally came from mainland areas. Until very recently, the populations of these mission and government settlements were regarded by some of those responsible for the administration of Aboriginal Affairs as single communities which would develop along the same lines as would be expected of any other rural town elsewhere in Australia.

The current situation   Today, we have the same number of settlements operating in Arnhem Land but there is reason to believe that they may not

114

develop according to the previous aspirations of church and government administrators. In all of these centres of population, there has been an increasing desire on the part of Aborigines to return to their 'own country'. It is becoming clear that the people of these settlements cannot be considered to constitute unified communities. They are in fact members of different local descent groups, who tend to place priority on the satisfaction of their own particular needs rather than those of others. Contrary to the opinion of some outside observers, these groups do not necessarily see themselves as sharing common attitudes or common goals with other groups living within the same location — i.e. on the same settlement.

To the best of my knowledge, there are some twenty-nine communities throughout Arnhem Land which have now established themselves as independent groups in country with which they have traditional affiliations. The accompanying map indicates their location, and the Department of Aboriginal Affairs has been in regular communication with them. The number of people living on these various small-scale settlements represents approximately 10 per cent of the total Aboriginal population of Arnhem Land. It is probable that the coming dry season will see a significant increase in the number of people moving away from the larger settlements. To provide some idea of the significance of this movement, here are two examples. During the 1974 wet season, 25 per cent of the total population of Yirrkala moved to various satellite communities within this north-east Arnhem Land region. It is expected that possibly half the population of Yirrkala will eventually move out by the end of the next dry season. In north-central Arnhem Land, at Maningrida, approximately 450 people have moved to satellite communities: this represents approximately 35 per cent of the total population of that settlement and, again, as with Yirrkala, it is expected that there will be a significant increase in such movement in the immediate future.

Such population movements raise a very real question regarding the future role of the larger settlements and mission stations in this region. I believe that these places, which already have facilities such as stores, hospitals, schools and recreation centres, will be used by members of the outlying communities as 'resource centres'. In nearly every case, members of the smaller communities have expressed a desire to have these facilities duplicated on a small scale so that they can be operated by the people themselves while more sophisticated facilities can be provided in the larger centres. Underlying this approach is the wish to minimise the need for non-Aborigines to live in the small communities. Those non-Aboriginal people who are required by virtue of their special skills will live in the larger 'resource centres' and act in the capacity of visiting specialists when the need arises; and that need should be determined by the people living in the satellite communities.

Motivation The most obvious question to ask is why an increasing number of Aboriginal people are moving away from the established settlements and mission stations, with all they have to offer, to areas where few services or facilities are available. No doubt there are many motivating factors involved: but I think we can single out some of the major ones, common to all the groups concerned. The first of these has to do with land affiliation. There is no need for me to emphasise the important relationship that exists between Aborigines and their land. Even so, it is a fact that many of those responsible for the establishment of mission and government settlements did not have any clear understanding of that relationship. In establishing these settlements, the criteria against which the suitability of a location was judged, related almost solely to administrative and geographical considerations — e.g. the need of a good harbour, isolation from the mainland, availability of water, and so on. Factors involving Aboriginal land and Aboriginal rights in it were never really given any serious consideration — if for no other reason, as I have already mentioned, than that they were not understood. Typically, once the settlement personnel were there, Aborigines were either directly or indirectly encouraged to leave outlying areas and to settle in the new establishment to create a 'new community'. Those who accepted the 'invitation' were eventually and inevitably subject to social pressures which originated not only in the cross-cultural context but from within their own culture as well.

As a settlement was established on land of which a particular group claimed ownership, all other Aboriginal people living there, in varying degrees, found it necessary in certain contexts to defer to the authority of the local group. Additionally, the Aborigines as a whole were subject to the authority of non-Aboriginal administrators who were responsible for the running of that settlement. The importance of a local land-owning group in a particular area is often reflected in the membership of village councils and other associations which have become part of institutional living in Arnhem Land. One example of this comes from Yirrkala, where the village council president is a member of the clan and dialectal unit upon whose land the mission is situated. Another example comes from Maningrida, where the president of the council is also a prominent member of the 'tribe' or language group upon whose land that settlement is situated. As a consequence of this, it would seem that until such time as the other Aboriginal groups return to their own countries they will continue to be subject, at least to some extent, to differing authorities. In my opinion, until such time as these Aboriginal groups are able to return to their own traditional countries they will be unable to develop to their full potential. And also I believe that there is a growing realisation by the Aboriginal groups concerned that the restrictions on their own development will be removed only by returning to their own land, where their authority will be recognised by others.

A second major factor influencing people to return to their country has been the increasing activity of mining interests in the Arnhem Land Reserve. There has been, since 1964, an intensive prospecting programme conducted by many companies operating in the area and (to date) in two areas actual mining is in progress. Aboriginal people living in such areas have come to realise that they have had, and still have, little chance of influencing any decisions about prospecting or mining programmes, and they have become increasingly worried about the intrusion by non-Aborigines into their traditional country. One solution of this problem, as they saw it, was to occupy that country in an attempt to control the eroding alien influences.

A third factor of some importance has been the decision of the Australian Government to recognise Aboriginal land rights, and the subsequent enquiries made by the Woodward Royal Commission of Enquiry which took in many areas of Arnhem Land. This, I believe, has caused an acceleration of the movement to occupy land. While it is not an 'Oklahoma land rush', it does represent a genuine indication of their feelings about their own land and the stake they have in it.

A fourth factor relates to the improvement of services and supportive amenities given to communities which have chosen to move away from the established centres. The Australian Government has responded to this situation and has provided services which were not previously available in outlying areas. Throughout Arnhem Land roads have been improved and allow access by 4 x 4 vehicles to areas which were hitherto reached only on foot. Both the United Church in North Australia and the Church Missionary Society provide regular air services to the small remote communities, taking in supplies and providing a much-needed system of communication. With these facilities available, it is now possible for Aborigines to review realistically their priorities as to where they want to live and to assess seriously the social cost of living in (or away from) the larger institutionalised centres. No doubt there are other reasons which motivate people to return to their own country, but these four are, to my mind, among the most important.

Contact and liaison Underlying our approach to these problems is the acceptance of certain basic assumptions which are the basis of community development. These may be stated as:

(1) All people have a strong desire to better themselves, no matter how unambitious they may appear to outsiders. All people have personal and community needs, and they suffer when those needs are not met and wish that something could be done to meet them.

(2) The personal and community needs are not met because, under present conditions, the difficulties militating against their fulfilment are too great for the human and technical resources the people have. Backwardness is not caused by laziness or lack of ambition. It is caused by inability to see the opportunity to meet those needs; to know how to achieve the desired results. Given help in seeing the opportunity and the means of meeting their needs, such people will become active and will progress.

(3) All groups can do something to help themselves when given the opportunity to do so on their own terms. The local people must be given the responsibility of determining the direction of their own efforts and must set their own priorities for action.

(4) Where the need for change is urgent, it is important that government services seek to co-ordinate their programmes in order to influence each area of local activity according to the readiness and wishes of the local people.

In liaising with and supporting these communities, the Department of Aboriginal Affairs focuses its attention on three major areas: (a) commitment; (b) felt needs; and (c) response.

In consulting with groups which have indicated a desire to return to their traditional country, they are made aware that there must be some tangible evidence that enough people within the group are committed to the project before the Department will become involved in assisting them with it. In some cases, the accumulating of an amount of money through the group's own resources may serve as sufficient indication of commitment. In other cases, the organising of unpaid labour on some construction project such as a road may prove sufficient indication, but it depends very much on the circumstances of the case. We believe, however, that it is essential to have tangible evidence that can be seen by the group and by those working with them that there is a commitment toward the establishment of their own community. Expenditure of effort through a voluntary organisation is regarded as an important criterion.

Already, there have been literally miles of roads and thousands of feet of new runways established in many areas of Arnhem Land through the expenditure of voluntary effort. The amount of work carried out by Aborigines in outlying areas has amazed many people who have had years of experience supervising Aboriginal workers on mission and government settlements. The work output far exceeds that which was expected of the same people when they were living on those larger settlements.

We regard the issue of 'felt needs' as being of major importance in determining the success or failure of this kind of community project. The needs the Department is interested in and responds to are those recognised and put forward by the community itself. We realise that, during the initial stages of such development, short-term projects are important in that the community must begin and continue to secure results. We believe that, once the members of the group have attained a degree of confidence in their ability to achieve positive results, they will be less reticent in undertaking longer-term projects.

I have already indicated that the decentralising groups have made it clear that they do not desire an influx of non-Aboriginal people into their communities. They have, however, indicated a need for local services such as health and education. In response, the Departments of Education and Health are experimenting with a programme whereby local Aboriginal teachers and health officers are supported, on request, by visiting non-Aboriginal teachers, nursing sisters and medical doctors.

Perhaps the most important aspect in the development of these smaller communities is the establishment of permanent and reliable communication links with major resource centres. Many of them now have their own vehicles and boats; others have built airstrips and are serviced on a regular basis by light aircraft. In this way, continuing contact can be maintained with major centres. Also, a number of the groups operate their own radio transceivers.

All these communities require some kind of cash inflow in order to maintain themselves at a subsistence level. The need for money arises from the pattern evident in all decentralising communities: they must purchase the greater part of their carbohydrate requirements from a general store, while their protein requirements are derived from local resources — such as shellfish, fish, fowl, and wallabies. Buffalo and cattle, in some areas, are occasionally caught and slaughtered, but less frequently so than the others. Cash is mainly derived from the sale of artefacts and from Social Service payments. Money also finds its way into these communities through relatives working in the major centres, who contribute to the purchase of supplies.

Once the Department's field officer has established a community's 'felt needs', it is necessary for the Department to demonstrate its ability to react positively and quickly to the community's requests in order to maintain its confidence in the Department as a resource agent. In this regard, it is important for such field officers to know what the Department's capabilities are at any particular time before offering assistance to any community.

Recent events (in the 1974–75 period), which have received much publicity, highlight a very real problem with which the Department of Aboriginal

Affairs is faced when trying to respond positively and quickly to Aboriginal needs. I would suggest that, until there is some satisfactory resolution of the basic conflict which is evident between the ideal of 'quick and positive response' and the reality of Treasury regulations and audit requirements, there will be a danger of such communities losing confidence in the Department. Field officers, too, will remain confused as to the ability of their agency to respond to community needs without extensive and debilitating delays.

Land rights As I have mentioned, there has been considerable interest in the visits of the Woodward Royal Commission to various centres in Arnhem Land, and it might be of some interest here to consider some of the possible recommendations as they relate to the decentralising groups.[1]

One of Mr Justice Woodward's preliminary recommendations related to the establishment of a Northern Land Council consisting of a number of Aboriginal people drawn from many centres of the 'Top End' of the Northern Territory, including Arnhem Land. The purpose of this Council was to discuss proposals relevant to land-ownership. One recommendation of the Northern Land Council to the Commission[2] was that matters of land-ownership could be decided only by the traditional owners. It stated:

> by whatever name the group should be known and by whatever manner the group should be constituted, the group which constitutes the focus of the land rights scheme ought to be that group which traditionally had the spiritual and material connection with the land.

Traditional ownership was seen to rest with what was referred to as the local descent group. Professor Berndt gives as examples of such units:

> the north-eastern Arnhem Land *mada-mala* (dialectal unit-clan) combination, the *gunmugugur* of Western Arnhem Land, the collective *njinanga* ('land-based kin group') of the Aranda, the un-named local descent groups of the Western Desert, and so on.[3]

The Land Council recognised some difficulties in administering land through local descent groups and recommended the establishment of local land boards. These Boards would be constituted and incorporated and be vested with a title to an estate in fee simple subject to alienated interests in all the reserved lands, a separate Board being constituted in respect of each of the existing reserves. It also recommended that the Northern Land Council be constituted to give expression to Aboriginal opinion as to the management of land vested in the Land Boards in order to protect the interests of traditional owners of land vested in these Land Boards. The Council would employ officers who would ascertain the wishes of traditional owners with respect to land vested in the Land Boards.

In so far as the decentralising groups are concerned, the scheme as recommended by the Northern Land Council would recognise the rights of those which established valid claims of affiliation to particular areas of country in Arnhem Land. These groups would then be granted leases over their land by the local Land Board. Should any conflict arise over land claims between contending local descent groups, the Northern Land Council would see itself as assuming the role of adjudicator and obtaining, if necessary, specialised advice in order to resolve the matter. In the event that conflicting claims could not be resolved, it would be possible for the matter to be referred to the Supreme Court of the Northern Territory for final resolution. It should be emphasised that at the time of writing this paper these proposals had been recommended by the Northern Land Council to the Woodward Commission and had not then been formally accepted.[4]

A passing phase It has often been suggested to me that decentralisation is only a passing phase. Whether it is or not will depend in large measure on the attitude taken by those who administer and determine government policy and its translation into action. If services and resources (financial and otherwise) are restricted to the established settlements and mission stations, then no doubt decentralisation will have a limited future. On the other hand, if our organisation (i.e. the Department of Aboriginal Affairs) is designed to be responsive to the needs of Aborigines, as determined by them, then we will be committed to assisting these groups in their endeavours to re-establish themselves in their own traditional countries. If we are successful in this, I cannot see decentralisation as 'a passing phase'. On the contrary, I would see an increasing number of communities choosing to re-establish themselves in that way.

Finally, I should underline that I believe decentralisation constitutes one of the most positive steps taken by 'tribal' Aborigines to regain their independence and, most importantly, to re-establish their relationships with the land.

Location and population details of well-established groups*

Western Arnhem Land
  (i) Place — Maningordil
       Location — Gumardir River [Gumadir]
       Language — Gunwinggu
       Population — 45–50
 (ii) Place — Gubolum-bolum
       Location — Gumardir River [Gumadir]
       Language — Gunwinggu
       Population — 12–15
(iii) Place — Nabalakordbo (Table Hill)
       Location — 24 km west of Liverpool River
       Language — Gunwinggu
       Population — 20
 (iv) Place — Murragolidbun (Muragulidban), [Margulidjban]
       Location — 7 km west of Liverpool River
       Language — Gunwinggu
       Population — 70–80
  (v) Place — Mormega [or Mumenger]
       Location — junction of Mann and Liverpool Rivers
       Language — Gunwinggu
       Population — 50

Central Arnhem Land
  (i) Place — Kopanga (Gubanga)
       Location — western bank of Blyth River
       Language — Gidjingali [Burara]
       Population — 100

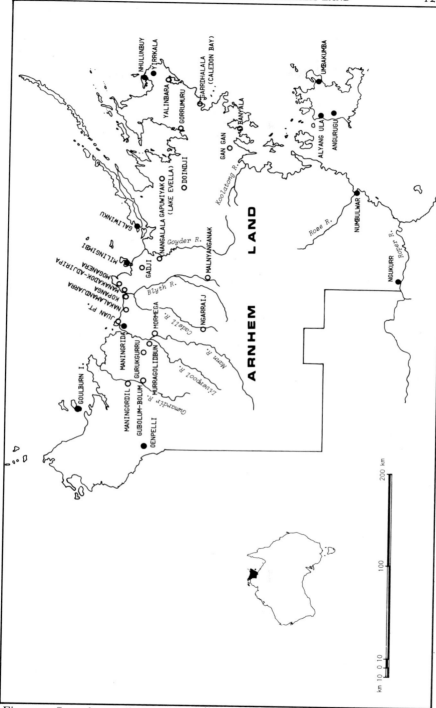

Figure 1: *Some decentralised communities in Arnhem Land.*

(ii) Place — Manakadok-Adjiripa
      Location — eastern bank of Blyth River
      Language — Gidjingali
      Population — 30
(iii) Place — Moganera
      Location — Cape Stewart Beach
      Language — Gidjingali
      Population — 30
(iv) Place — Kojanjindidi
      Location — Cadell River
      Language — Gunadba
      Population — 100
(v)   Place — Guyun
      Location — 32 km south of Maningrida
      Language — Rembarrnga [Rembarnga] and Gungorogoni [also
        Gungoragoni, Gungorolgongi, Gungerawoni]
      Population — 50
(vi) Place — Nakalamandjarra (Navy Landing)
      Location — Anamaiyara Creek, 15 km east of Maningrida
      Language — Nagara
      Population — 40
(vii) Place — Ngarraij [Ngaraidj]
      Location — 105 km south of Maningrida
      Language — Dangbon [Dangbun or Gundangbun]
      Population — 25
(viii) Place — Malnyanganak
      Location — 48 km south of Nangalala
      Language — Rembarrnga [Rembarnga]
      Population — 20

Eastern Arnhem Land
(i)   Place — Garrdhalala
      Location — Caledon Bay
      Language — Djapu [Djabu *mada*]
      Population — 80
(ii) Place — Gorrumuru
      Location — south Arnhem Bay
      Language — Dhalwongu [Dalwongu *mada*]
      Population — 25–30
(iii) Place — Baniyala [Banyala]
      Location — Myaoula Bay [Myaoola Bay]
      Language — Munyuku Madapa [Mararba *mada;* Munyugu *mala*]
      Population — 50
(iv) Place — Gan Gan [Ganganingur]
      Location — 80 km south-west of Yirrkala
      Language — Dhalwongu [Dalwongu *mada*]
      Population — 25–30
(v)   Place — Yalinbara [Yelangbara]
      Location — Pt. Bradshaw
      Language — Rirratjingu [Riradjingu *mada*]
      Population — 25–30

*Names in square brackets indicate alternative spelling or form. [Editor]

Notes

1. See the *Aboriginal Land Rights Commission* reports (the first on 19 July 1973 and the second in April 1974), Australian Government Publishing Service, Canberra, 1974. The second report contains the main recommendations.

   As a background to this subject, see the brief statement by R. M. Berndt in The Concept of Protest within an Australian Aboriginal Context, in *A Question of Choice: an Australian Aboriginal Dilemma*. (R. M. Berndt ed.). University of Western Australia Press, Perth, 1971:35–7 *et seq*.

2. See the *Aboriginal Land Rights Commission: submission by the Northern Land Council*, January 1974. Among others, there was also the special submission on behalf of the Gunmugurgur known as Na-Madjawarr, Na-Murrwan, Na-Mirrar and other members of the Aboriginal community at Oenpelli, February 1974.

3. See R. M. and C. H. Berndt, Relationship of Aborigines to their land, with reference also to sacred and/or traditional sites, pp. 14–29 in the *Submission by the Northern Land Council*, January 1974. The quotation is from page 21.

4. The recommendations by the Northern Land Council were accepted in principle. While this is not the place to embark on a critical assessment of the Woodward final report (April 1974), it should be noted that the Federal Government has been slow in implementing those it did accept, and (to date, September 1975) there is no indication that the States will adopt, in full or in part, the basic premises accepted by the Woodward Commission. [Editor]

11 Pitjantjatjara decentralisation in north-west South Australia:

spiritual and psycho-social motivation

Noel M. Wallace

Decentralised Aboriginal communities, though receiving considerable attention at the moment, are hardly a new phenomenon. The motivation for decentralisation has been present for many years and communities have been 'decentralising', in one way or another, for as long as there has been the means to do so — ever since European influence caused them to leave their traditional hunting and foraging grounds and congregate around mission and government settlements. However, the desire to decentralise certainly seems to be increasing. (See Coombs 1974:135-43.)

Motivation for decentralisation comes in many forms; all must be considered, as concentration on one or two can result in an over-simplification that can only be misleading. Some of them may appear contradictory until, gradually, the overall picture begins to emerge with a little more clarity: it will still not be clear-cut, because many of the factors involved are based on cultural confusion resulting from alien contact. Undoubtedly, the most important motives to be considered are of a spiritual and psycho-social nature. These arise from the fulfilment and contentment that comes from close association with one's own country, particularly when this is linked with a strong emotional component which relates to the effect of living where one's spirit ancestors have travelled, where they remain eternally, and where the teaching of the religious law can take shape in a meaningful context. That motivation is still a strong force today.

History of decentralisation Aborigines came in to make more or less permanent camps at or near fringe settlements: and they remained because, among other things, life seemed to be easier there. Food did not have to be gathered or hunted, and white people's clothing made cold weather more bearable. Nor can one overlook the pressures that were brought to bear on those living their 'tribal' lives, which forced them to move into such settlements. One example of this was to clear Aborigines away from large areas of the Desert to make way for rocket testing at Woomera and another for nuclear bomb testing at Emu Junction and Maralinga. (See Grayden 1957.) Some of these settlements into which they came or were brought were near their 'tribal' lands, but in other cases the people were up to, and sometimes more than, 160 kilometres (100 miles) distant from the sacred totemic tracks of their spirit ancestors. They still visited those areas when they could, for the holding of rituals and ceremonies of various kinds; but this was done under restrictions imposed by nuclear bomb and rocket testing requirements.

As the people became more and more sedentary, with a growing number of Aborigines being employed and paid wages, visits to 'tribal' areas became even less frequent. Then, the desire to return to their own 'tribal' countries grew and so, when the opportunity arose, another decentralised camp was formed. Sometimes the reason for its establishment was a European one, such as the decision of Ernabella Mission to establish (in 1961) an outstation, Fregon, which is located 70 kilometres (44 miles) to the south. The intention in this case was to provide more industry and employment for their cattle station. It is significant that the Aborigines who moved there were totemically associated with that place and the nearby country. Now these same people, or the next generation, are making plans to 'decentralise' once more in order to live right in the territories of their spirit ancestors. It seems likely that a number of small settlements will spring up to the south of Fregon, Mimili and Indulkana.

Also in 1961, a government settlement, then called Musgrave Park, but renamed Amata in 1968, was established 96 kilometres (60 miles) west of Ernabella. (See Hilliard 1968.) Those who were the first to go and live there were six families whose totemic country was in the west — in the Mann Ranges and beyond. When these original settlers were asked why they had been willing to leave Ernabella (although they still loyally refer to Ernabella as 'a good place'), they replied simply: 'This is near our country'. The land of their spirit ancestors is farther to the west and so, recent movement falls within that pattern: people are leaving Amata to live, not only near, but *in* their own country.

One can see certain similarities between these examples and the converse situation — the formation of communities at Indulkana and Everard Park (now Mimili). Indulkana camp was established before there was a European-style settlement. Men of the *Malu* (kangaroo) totem went there from cattle stations, from Finke, Oodnadatta, Ernabella and beyond, because of its importance in the *Malu* 'Law'. The road leading there runs within yards of sacred sites and there are many other sacred sites in the ranges nearby. Indulkana is now a large government settlement, but it has grown from a decentralised camp. The same may be said about Mimili. There, centralisation from north, east and south-east has combined with decentralisation from Fregon and Ernabella to form a group living close to their own most sacred areas and, incidentally, away from the strains and tensions of settlement life.

Settlement life and destruction of culture Aborigines who came to live in settlements were able, for some time, to continue their lives with relatively minor change to their religious culture. (See earlier chapter by Wallace.) Gradually, outlying totemic areas became neglected, some were endangered, some desecrated and some even destroyed by Europeans exploring for minerals, or by members of survey parties, or other activities important to Europeans. Aborigines came to realise that they had been neglecting their sacred places. Earlier, 'man-making' rituals had been held in nearby totemically significant sites; later they were held in areas near the settlements. Other totemic rituals that could be held away from the sacred country were held there, and they lost little because of that — because the ritual life was rich and full. But life at the settlement was something apart, and philosophically unimportant. On the other hand, there are rituals that can be held only at the relevant site, and these became more and more neglected.

Gradually at first, then at an increasing rate, the European (Australian-European) life-style has been forced on to these people. They had to conform, at least in part: not because they wanted to, but because it was made abundantly clear to them that unless they did, they would not receive help. Financial aid from the government would not be provided unless they became 'properly constituted communities'. To comply with this they had to have councils, delegates, representatives, a legally correct constitution, community bank accounts, and so on. There is no Aboriginal at Amata who can speak fluent English, let alone read it! Two men at Ernabella can read simple English — none in any area we visited could understand a legal document.

Councils, committees, appointment of delegates and representatives to speak on behalf of the whole community, are all European concepts. Not only have they no place in Aboriginal thinking (not at the formal level), but they must inevitably destroy the traditional culture. It was quite incomprehensible to them that a young man could speak on behalf of older men. He would not ordinarily presume to do so, and he would even be afraid to do so in case he had not transmitted their information and wishes correctly. There would be many things that he, being a young man, had not yet learnt since traditional education, especially in religious matters, continues all a man's life. Even one old man could not speak on behalf of the whole community, or for all the elders. Traditionally, all affairs have to be discussed by the whole camp. One could see small groups of men sitting talking; then one, or maybe two or three, would move from that group to other groups. Each group would consist of men belonging to a particular relationship or totemically affiliated group — each would have its own viewpoint, based on special knowledge in a particular area or subject. So there was communication between all, all had knowledge of whatever problem had arisen, and all had a voice in deciding what must be done. All this would take time, of course — maybe days, particularly if someone of importance was absent and his word was necessary to the group. And whether consensus was achieved is another matter again.

There was no overall leader, no general spokesman, but each totemic group had a major role in deciding what was to be done about matters that concerned it most. For example, decisions relating to certain central areas of the Mann Ranges, or concerning people from those areas, would be made by men of the *Kalaya* (emu) totem, certainly conferring with men of the *Wanampi* (rainbow serpent) totem to the east, or *Tjangara* and *Wayuta* (possum) men from the west, and others directly concerned. *Mala* (hare-wallaby) men from Ulkiyanya and Uluru and *Tjala* (honey-ant) men from Aparanya would probably be only indirectly involved, but they would know of the discussions, would be part of them, and would be given as much authority as their situation warranted.

Now we have the false authority of elected councils whose members collectively make decisions; and even of the chairman of the council having government-approved authority to make decisions alone when it is not convenient to call a council meeting. The chairman, much of the time, is spokesman and representative of people who do not and cannot recognise his authority. Much of the time, too, the body of people in the community are not aware of what is being decided on their behalf. Under these circumstances the older men, who were in the past the strength of the 'tribe', have their authority eroded. They lodge no protests; they simply withdraw, ignoring the council and its decisions, and unhappily long for a return to traditional law. They have lost their authority, their dignity and their status as men and leaders of their people. The decision-makers today may or may not have attended many rituals; and so the gulf between the learned and the ignorant or partially so grows and grows.

One often hears from those who support the formation and continuation of councils that 'natural leaders emerge'. Should one *natural* leader 'emerge', this means that ten or a dozen *true* totemic leaders have been repressed.

Most of those who are elected to councils try their best to carry out their tasks. The main qualification of those elected (and, incidentally, the reason for their election) is their reputation of being able to speak some, if only limited, English. Those elected are forced into making decisions, and those in (white) authority have taken no action to ensure that they have some idea of the consequences of their decisions, in European terms. Those on councils and committees are striving to do what is right without having been properly prepared, and so experience anxiety. When their decisions prove to be doubtful, those anxieties become unbearable.

Let us look at some of the problems concerning just one group. White people have decided that the most urgent requirement in settlements is housing according to European standards: and so this thought is transmitted to the Aborigines. Housing committees are formed, and the people are asked to decide what kind of houses the community requires. Their experience is limited to the casual knowledge of staff houses within the settlement — so, on what do they base their decisions?

Certainly, transition from bush shelters and huts to European-style housing must be regarded as experimental; but experiment should be carried out on a basis of knowledge and experience. Often, the desirability of living in a house soon fades when the occupants realise that, not only does it have to be kept clean and hygienic (which a European woman knows is practically a full-time task), but houses create a barrier of walls between the occupants and their friends and relatives. This creates a whole new life-style for those who choose to live in houses, and again the strain may build up to unbearable proportions.

During a recent field trip to Amata (July-August 1974) we found Nganyintja, probably the most forward-thinking person at Amata, living in a *yu*, a traditional brush shelter, with her family, in a camp of about twenty families about 1½ kilometres (a mile) from the main settlement. Nganyintja and her family have lived in houses since 1968; first in a two-roomed galvanised iron shack, later in a small but well-built house. She told us that she had left her house many weeks earlier and was having a holiday. There was too much worry. Yes, she would return to her house some day but not yet. She was a member of the Housing Council, and it was worrying her. She did not know when she would go back to her house again; she was happy in this camp where she could feel the wind on her body, and she was constantly near her relatives and friends. She expressed a strong desire to lead her relatives back to a bush camp in her late father's and her own country near Piltati in the Mann Ranges.

Sometimes attempts are made to provide information to assist in making decisions. Often the person providing this assistance lacks the basic understanding of Aboriginal philosophy which is necessary in order to be able to help meaningfully. A few months ago, members of the Amata Housing Society were taken to Alice Springs to inspect various types of dwelling. Two families decided on caravans, having been shown only luxury holiday-type caravans. They were not shown commercial types such as those used by road construction workers or other government organisations: hence they had no knowledge of the many advantages of that robust type of caravan. In all probability, caravans are an answer to many of the problems surrounding transition to houses by people whose 'tribal law' requires that they must move from one place to another at certain times; but, before making their decision they should have had certain things explained to them:

1. Some types of caravan may be more suitable than others for their needs.
2. The electric light that worked in the demonstration caravan in Alice Springs would not work in a camp situation.
3. Water flows from the pump in the caravan only after the tank has been filled, and there will be no facilities to fill the tank in camp.
4. The refrigerator and gas stove will work only if the gas supply is kept up, and gas is expensive at Amata. (Further, no provision was made for use of the larger, 100 lb. gas cylinders, the only ones available at Amata.)
5. The refrigerator will keep working only if it is serviced at least twice a year in that dusty situation.
6. Gas is dangerous if children turn the taps on.
7. Tourist-type caravans usually have Holden wheels, much in demand to keep the Holden cars of one's relatives mobile.
8. One cannot light a fire in a caravan.

Perhaps, after learning of all these disadvantages, the decision would be to purchase one anyway. That would be their own legitimate decision — it would not be an uninformed one. Hector, the owner of the first caravan to arrive at Amata, was proud and delighted when it arrived. On the following morning, when asked how he liked it, he replied: 'Too cold. We slept on the ground outside by a fire.' His joy at its arrival had faded to disillusionment in less than twenty-four hours.

The trauma of failure after failure due to European short-sightedness or neglect in not explaining consequences, does not affect the white man who goes away saying that he did his best — but has a profound effect on Aborigines who have to stay and contend with compounding strain and tension. The only escape is to go away, back to the relative simplicity of living their own way, in their own spiritual country.

The tragedy of cultural destruction is nowhere more evident than in the lives of the children. This alone is a major factor in the motivation of parents to leave the settlement for their totemic country, or for that matter for any country far away from settlement strains and stresses. Children attend school: and so they miss sharing their parents' experiences of being part of their own totemic country. A few years ago, children were constantly in their parents' company: they learnt about traditional life and regarded their elders as being knowledgeable in all things which concerned them. Now, the persons of knowledge and importance are school teachers, who teach things their parents know little or nothing about. Not only are the children not learning about their traditional culture and religion; they no longer see their parents as persons of dignity and education. When they leave school, they are not equipped to enter the white man's world; nor are they equipped to remain meaningfully within their own — they have moved toward the edge of their own heritage. The segregation of teenage boys during initiation is now perfunctory in spite of the effects of the elders to restore 'the law' to what it used to be. (See earlier chapter by Wallace.) This, coupled with juvenile delinquency, has convinced the elders that things have gone too far — they cannot communicate with the young people because their authority has been eroded. Perhaps the answer lies, so they reason, in leaving the troublesome settlement and returning to their old ways: their thoughts are, 'Everything will be all right if we leave all this behind and go back to living the way we used to and care for our law properly'.

The return to sacred country   In considering the question of returning to live in or near their own and their spirit ancestors' country, it is important to emphasise Aboriginal motives for doing so. If European-derived values are the only ones considered, the conclusions would be most misleading.

A common notion is that Aborigines return to their country in order to protect it: and so, some have a mental picture of men with *kulata* (spear), *miru* (spearthrower) and .22 rifle guarding their sacred sites from invading whites. The truth of the situation is more complex than this. Aboriginal men who, as mentioned earlier, have lost both their dignity and their authority in the eyes of children and young adults, blame themselves for the many changes they see about them, which are inevitably destroying their culture. They feel that their 'sins of omission', so to speak, have made the land and its people vulnerable in the face of threat from outside. They have neglected their country; they have not cared for and tended the sacred sites; they have not held 'increase' rituals; they have not strengthened the *kurunpa* (the spirit of life itself) within the sacred rocks and ritual objects — and so their whole culture has been weakened and is in danger of disappearing.

When a group of men visit a sacred site, their pattern of behaviour is always the same. The 'owners' go forward while newcomers (i.e. those Aborigines and trusted Europeans visiting for the first time) stand back, sometimes out of sight. The 'owners' place their hands briefly on each object and walk around and see that everything is in order. Should the visit be for ritual purposes, the area around the sacred objects will be cleared of grass, fallen stones replaced, ochre applied, and green leaves put in position. Then, and only then, the ritual begins. Then, too, the newcomers will be led to the site, guided to the objects (which contain within them the *kurunpa* of the spirit ancestor: see R. and C. Berndt 1943) and instructed to place their hands on them, or whatever the ancient ritual demands. Afterwards, the meaning and religious significance of the objects is explained to them. Should the visit not include ritual, the newcomers will be called forward to help with the clearing of the sacred site etc., preceded by the placing of hands on the sacred objects. The placing of hands on the objects is believed to give one's own *kurunpa* to the spirit ancestor, and, in return, the person receives the *kurunpa* of that ancestor. Both human and mythic beings are strengthened; and the refurbishing of the site itself and the holding of ritual

strengthens the spirit ancestor's *kurunpa* still more. Further, the sacred object
is the spirit ancestor: he or she is just as much alive today as in the beginning
— they are joined eternally through the concept of *tjukurpa* (the Dreaming):
And if these rituals are neglected, all mankind (that is, Aboriginal mankind)
will suffer, and may even die out.

The only way that desecration can be righted is through spiritual com-
munion: and the only way that Aboriginal 'Law' can be retained and
strengthened is through ritual and spiritual renewal. This is what the older
men believe, and their return to their sacred country is the only means that
they have of preventing cultural destruction.

Their physical presence in the area does have some importance: but, as
already mentioned, many factors must be taken into account, each in its
correct perspective.

The relative unimportance of physical protection alone can be understood
only if one takes into account the traditional means of protecting these sites.
The Aborigines did not live in one place; neither did they wander haphazardly. They had more or less regular directions to take, from rockhole to
rockhole, from sacred site to sacred site. So, each site was left unattended for
relatively long periods of time — maybe years. They knew the location of all
the major sites, but portable sacred objects could be moved after inspection,
attention and ritual to a new *kulpi* (cave) or crevice in the rocks, each considered a better hiding place than the last. Such repositories made it quite
obvious to later visitors where the objects were hidden — by arranged stones,
by the breaking down of certain tree branches and, in the case of some of the
Red Ochre objects, by marking rocks with blood. By so doing, they ensured
that those persons entitled to see and use the objects could go directly to them;
and those not entitled to go near them were immediately aware that they
were in the presence of objects not of their own cult or totem, and would
leave the area. Additionally, such signs would warn women and children,
and the uninitiated, that they were near objects containing strong *kurunpa*
and, if they came near, that power would cause illness and even death.
Under such circumstances and with this protection, the totemic owners
knew that their sites and the objects hidden there would be safe.

It seems strange to many Europeans that, these days, Aborigines elect to
have fences placed around such sacred sites to protect them, thus showing
plainly where they are and so making them vulnerable to desecration.
However, it must be realised that this is virtually the same kind of marker that
has been used for thousands of years — except that in this case it is one that
can be read by white men. Of course, the Aborigines know that a fence may
be climbed. It is not put there to keep other people out, but to indicate that
they may not come in!

A closer look at the camps

Wingellina: Though it is not geographically in South Australia, one must
consider Wingellina, which is 20 kilometres (12 miles) over the border in
Western Australia. It has major associations with the Amata people (240
kilometres [150 miles] to the east), and also strong ties with the Warburton
people (225 kilometres [140 miles] to the west). The totem given most
prominence in that area is *Papa* (dingo), because there are several important

sites in the vicinity belonging to *Papa* people. At Wingellina, one such site has been bulldozed out of existence by Europeans mining for chrysoprase and moss agate. At the same time, nickel exploration was proceeding nearby. Test bores were sunk and samples were taken. There are large deposits of lateritic nickel (the Aboriginal people know it as yellow ochre); but until nickel prices increase, it will remain in the ground. Should the proposed open-cut mining proceed, three other major sites will disappear. In 1966 two or three families were living there, but over the next few years the population grew to about sixty-five persons, who had come from Amata and the Warburtons.

It has been said by some Europeans that Aborigines 'invented' the idea of sacredness in relation to such sites because of the intrinsic value of the gemstones. However, the integrity of the totemic owners of the country has been demonstrated on a number of occasions: moreover, the people wanted to live there for the variety of reasons which have already been noted. That wish was made possible because some employment was available there. They could buy some food from a small store; and a woman with nursing experience cared for the health of the community. Firewood, water and game were available too. At that time, they received no aid from government settlements in South Australia, Northern Territory or Western Australia. Both mining projects are now closed, and no white people have been living there for a year. The Aborigines receive Social Service payments and some other help from the government settlements, as at last it has been recognised that they live there because they want to be in or near their own country. They have, however, now moved from Wingellina (as the bore was fitted with an engine and pump, not with a windmill or hand pump) to Lirunnga rockhole, about 8 kilometres (5 miles) to the west, and the community is larger than ever. Although their existence is to some extent precarious, they have achieved their goal of physical as well as spiritual linkage with their country. All people living at Lirunnga have totemic connections with it; there are no exceptions. Mythic beings represented there include not only *Papa* (which has received most attention), but *Nyi-nyi* (painted finch), *Anumara* (an edible grub), *Kalaya* (emu), *Ngapala* (a small lizard), *Partjata* (native cat), *Wintalyka* (mulga seed), *Pukara* (desert thriptomene), *Milpali* (goanna), *Wayuta* (possum) and possibly others. The sacred areas involved extend from Mt Davies, Wingellina, Mt Aloysius, Blackstone Range, Cavenagh Range, Mamutjara, Pukara, Bellrock Range and beyond. And there are many more people who want to leave Amata and live, not with those already living there, but in their own country farther south.

Puta-puta: This was the first camp to be established after the label 'decentralised camp' was coined, and so it is claimed by some to be the first decentralised camp in the Desert area. It is located 193 kilometres (120 miles) west of Amata, and was formed in the latter part of 1971 when four men and three women led by Kata, a man of high authority in the *Malu* (kangaroo) totem, had their request granted and were given assistance to live in their own sacred country. The Mines Department of South Australia had previously put in a bore there, so that a supply of good water was assured. That bore, and their camp, were situated in the midst of some of the most secret-sacred *Malu* totem country, which therefore was, and is, vulnerable to encroachment by white people who are ignorant of the traditional background. There are sites sacred to men, and others sacred to women. The Aborigines know where they may or may not go; non-Aborigines do not.

This area was endangered first when Beadell put a road through it in the course of looking for a suitable site for a weather and observation station. (see Beadell 1965). (A direct result of this was the formation of the Giles Weather Station, which was to cause the destruction of Aboriginal culture in the Rawlinson Ranges.) The road was the first in the area, and Beadell put in others, equally destructive; such roads were required for rocket testing from Woomera and nuclear bomb testing at Emu Junction and Maralinga (Beadell 1967.) People seem to have forgotten that there were at least five nuclear bombs fired in the Central Desert area of South Australia. Beadell's roads certainly should not have been put where they were; but then, he did not work with Aborigines.

Supporting the contention that spiritual, not physical, protection is the motivation for the formation of decentralised camps, there is no one living at Puta-puta now. The people have moved to Pipalyatjara, about seven miles farther west. The reasons for this change of location are important, and should be noted by those who are employed to put in bores to assist people to return to their own country.*

There are three basic requirements for an Aboriginal camp: water, dry firewood, and living trees and shrubs to provide *wiltja* (traditional shelter) material. Lack of any one of these makes the area unsuitable and even impossible to live in. The length of time that the camp can be inhabited will depend on how soon those requirements are exhausted. Usually, it is firewood that goes first, as it has to be within reasonable carrying distance from the bore. Firewood has always been scarce at Puta-puta. Now, lack of firewood has made it 'a bad camp', that can no longer support a community. A bore is useless without firewood, except to supply the passing traveller. Pipalyatjara is a good camp, since all three necessities are there in abundance. Also, it is not too far from Puta-puta, and many sites of both *Malu* and *Papa* totems which can easily be visited on foot. Most bores have been drilled with no thought at all of the Aborigines' total requirements. The drilling has been carried out in accordance with white man's thinking — drill for the maximum water availability, even if no one can use the water! Far better to look for water where there is timber for fires and shelter; far better that just sufficient water be located where it can be used, rather than arranging for an ample supply where it is useless to Aboriginal people.

Yalu-yalu: The next site to be occupied by a small group was Yalu-yalu, 37 kilometres (23 miles) east of Puta-puta and 156 kilometres (97 miles) west of Amata, also on the road put through by Beadell. At Yalu-yalu, an extremely secret-sacred area as a whole, the South Australian Mines Department put a bore right through the middle of one of the most secret-sacred sites. One could elaborate considerably on the effect this desecration had on people from all over the Western Desert area. This particular site is impor-

---

* Since writing this, and as I observed in September 1976, Pipalyatjara has deteriorated into becoming a dust-bowl, and a small group made up of seven families had moved back to Puta-Puta. The camp was situated about 2 km south of the bore, on the edge of a stand of dry firewood. As the wood is used, the camp must move further away from the water supply. (N. M. Wallace, December 1976.)

tant in the Red Ochre cult mythology and the distress at this desecration, accidental as it was (since it was due to ignorance and carelessness, and could have been avoided) involves many thousands of people. In the official records of the South Australian Mines Department is the statement that, when good water was found there, the Aboriginal men were no longer worried by this desecration!

Four or five old people live there from time to time. They are emotionally divided and confused. There is a great need to counteract the spiritual destruction which has taken place. However, it is a place where, traditionally, visits were made by men, never by women; and no one ever camped there. All the living trees are sacred (including the ones destroyed when the road was made); so *wiltja* must be made from dead wood, which may be freely used. Women must not approach the bore on the sacred hill, so all water must be carried by the men. Two years ago, when no Aborigines were at the Yalu-yalu camp, a group of visiting school teachers from the Warburtons passed there. A few days later, I was visited by a group of Aboriginal men who had just returned from that area; they told me that they had found a white woman's footprints by the bore on the sacred hill and asked me to tell them on their way back not to let women go near the hill and bore.

Kunamata: This place, of primary importance to people of the *Ili* (fig) totem, has not yet suffered desecration, as it is not directly on any road or track. It is about 96 kilometres (60 miles) by air south-west of Amata, but much farther by road. It is tabu to camp at or near the sacred areas of Kunamata, of which there are many. It is desecration even to break leaves off living *Ili* trees, as all are sacred. The traditional camping place is at Mingapiti, $1\frac{1}{2}$ kilometres to the east, but little firewood is left there now. The present camp is close to a bore north of Kunamata which produces only a couple of gallons of water an hour, and firewood is scarce. Consequently, the camp is occupied only intermittently. Men of the *Ili* totem probably experience less spiritual guilt than most others, as rituals have been held there relatively recently and the area is regularly visited. Because there has been as yet no desecration by white people, there is a more relaxed atmosphere surrounding that camp and the people who occupy it. A visit there is regarded more in the light of a 'happy holiday', with the contentment that comes from being in one's own country. Those who go there stay for only a short time before returning to Amata, where they look forward to returning again to Kunamata. But for Kunamata to become a major camp, water must be found farther east, where there are large stands of dead mulga for firewood.

Mintjara and Wilu: These are 'holiday' camps about 16 and 24 kilometres (10 and 15 miles) north of Amata. Totemically they are unimportant, but they are pleasant places to spend a few days at, or even a few weeks. There is plenty of firewood, material for building *wiltja,* and water, as well as plenty of rabbits, all within easy distance of Amata but far enough away to escape from settlement worries and tensions.

Walinynga (Cave Hill): The first camp at Walinynga was established on 23 July 1974, when men with stated totemic rights settled there to protect those rights and also in anticipation of largesse from hypothetical tourists coming through this area. Other Aborigines, too, were pressing their claims for the tourists' dollars. This is perhaps the most distressing motive yet encountered and it is one that is causing, and will continue to cause, conflict and destruction of culture at an increasingly rapid rate. Ironically, the opinions of the true owners of the site, who live about 225 kilometres (140 miles) distant, remain unheard.

The death of a 37-year-old man of great importance both socially and totemically at Amata, caused all of the Aborigines to leave that place. In one day, the Walinynga camp grew from eleven adults and eleven children to over two hundred. The situation is worrying to all who regard the traditional culture as something of vital significance to the well-being of the Pitjantjatjara people, and see only disaster from the manipulation of Aborigines to serve the ambition of white people.

The future   A report (W. D. Scott 1972) prepared by a team of business consultants includes these words:

> If Aborigines insist on returning to their totemic areas then it should be made quite clear to them that they must provide their own transport for personnel and supplies. Under no circumstances should Government vehicles run supplies to such groups of Aborigines living away from Settlements.

Fortunately, the present Amata staff deal with this problem with more understanding and with less of the 'great white father knows best' attitude expressed in that report. They *do* take people to the decentralised camps, they *do* provide regular patrols, and they do everything they can to assist the people to live in places where they will experience spiritual contentment.

People living at Amata who came from the Mamutjara-Pukara areas west of the South Australian-Western Australian border are most anxious to return to their country. Men making this request are leaders of their totems and are responsible persons; they should be helped to achieve that aim. The difficulties, however, are profound. They want to retain their links with Amata in preference to the Warburtons in Western Australia. They do not recognise State borders, of course, but government authority does. Distances are great: they would certainly need, and have asked for, a four-wheel-drive vehicle. They would also need access to servicing facilities at Amata: one of their number has an unrestricted driving licence and is employed in that capacity at Amata. Four-wheel-drive vehicles are supplied to Aborigines, but for projects agreed to by or, more particularly, of benefit to white people and their special projects, not to assist Aborigines to live in their sacred country. That, and their use of vehicles and requests for vehicles, are regarded as irresponsible.

Another group wants to live at Kulpitjata, about 40 kilometres (25 miles) north-west of Amata, in the Northern Territory. There are official moves to make this possible. There would be little difficulty in making a road, there are good stands of firewood and live trees to the north-west of Kulpitjata; but they would need a bore. A camp there would no doubt be a popular move, although the major difficulty could be that it would prove too popular.

Kulpitjata is of importance to the people of the *Kalaya* (emu) totem: there is, however, little that is secret-sacred and hence tabu to women and to children. *Kalaya* people are strongly attracted to this place. Not far away to the west and north-west are places of major importance to the *Malu* and *Wayuta* people, who would gain great satisfaction from being able to visit and tend those sacred sites from Kulpitjata, which could serve as a base.

Makiri (Wallace 1975:125-7), desecrated by a survey team in 1969, is another place to which the Fregon people wish to go — that is, to decentralise to the west. Their plans include establishing cattle stations so that they may be financially independent: and their training at Fregon has given them the confidence to run cattle efficiently. They would also be sufficiently near to Fregon to send cattle to established markets. The men state that, should they receive the assistance they have requested, they would be capable of protecting their own country, both spiritually and physically, from further alien inroads. Additionally, they want to join with the people from Mimili and Indulkana in living in a series of camps and so protecting their country south of those settlements, which contains totemic sites of extreme importance which are at present highly vulnerable. Already, they are subjected to pressures to permit oil exploration, right in their most sacred country.

It must be accepted that no decentralised camp can be permanent. As firewood is burnt, as trees are cut down for *wiltja,* the people living there must move to new sites. The alternative is, of course, to provide the 'decentralised camp' with trucks, tractors, and trailers in order to go more and more miles out to collect firewood. Then, of course, a garage, mechanics and streets with staff houses, become essential. So do a school, hospital, electricity generating plant, airstrip, radio telephone, and the like. And then it is necessary to have a properly constituted 'Incorporated Community Council' with delegates, representatives, committees, etc. Then we are back again, full circle, to the strains and tensions of a large and ever-growing community. The older people decide that their culture is still being destroyed, so they leave, with the fragments of their spirit ancestors' law — to form yet another decentralised community!

Note

An earlier version of this paper was presented at an informal seminar in Canberra at the Australian Institute of Aboriginal Studies on 15 October 1974. It has been included in this collection so that Western Desert material on decentralisation may be compared with that from Arnhem Land. [Editor.]

References

BEADELL, L. 1965 *Too long in the bush.* Rigby, Adelaide.
——1967 *Blast the bush.* Rigby, Adelaide.
BERNDT, R. M. *and* C. H. BERNDT 1943 A preliminary report of fieldwork in the Ooldea region, western South Australia, *Oceania,* XIII (3 and 4); XIV (1).
COOMBS, H. C. 1974 Decentralization trends among Aboriginal communities, *Search,* 5:135-43.
GRAYDEN, W. 1957 *Adam and atoms.* Daniels, Perth.
HILLIARD, W. 1968 *The people in between.* Hodder and Stoughton, London.
SCOTT, W. D. *and* Co. 1972 Report on the Western Desert, prepared for the Department of Aboriginal Affairs.
WALLACE, N. M. 1975 Living sacred sites. In *The preservation of Australia's Aboriginal heritage* (R. Edwards ed.), pp. 125-27. Australian Institute of Aboriginal Studies, Canberra.

12 Aboriginal involvement with the Australian economy in the Central Reserve during the winter of 1970

Nicolas Peterson

In early 1970 it seemed likely that a mining operation and township would be established in the Tomkinson Ranges of Central Australia. The only permanent residents in the region at that time were sixteen hundred Aborigines living in the four institutionalised communities of Docker River, Warburton mission, Amata and Ernabella mission (see map). The proposed township would have brought in three thousand or more whites to develop a nickel mine, locating them halfway between Warburton and Amata. I was asked to make a rapid survey of the region and to provide some suggestions as to how Aboriginal community interests might be safeguarded in negotiations with the mining company concerned in the project.[1] As things worked out the mine did not go ahead and recommendations were not required, but during the course of making the survey I collected some information on the sources of income in each of the four communities. While the figures cover only two week periods and are no more than reasonably accurate estimates, they do give a fair picture of the nature of the involvement with the Australian economy at that time and the comparison between them is interesting.

At the time of my visit South Western Mining[2] had an exploration camp at Wingellina on the site of the nickel deposit, 10 km south-south-west of the point where the borders of the Northern Territory, Western Australia and South Australia meet. One hundred and thirty-seven km to the north lay the Docker River community, 241 km to the west the Warburton mission and 225 km and 322 km to the east, Amata and Ernabella mission respectively. To the south the country was unoccupied and inhospitable. Rough but graded roads linked the communities to each other and the outside world. The nearest towns were Laverton 692 km to the south-west of Wingellina as the crow flies and Alice Springs 547 km to the north-east.

Docker River   Docker River was opened by the Northern Territory Welfare Branch at the beginning of 1968. It was established to relieve crowding at some of the other Northern Territory settlements and to encourage permanent settlement among the people who regularly moved between Areyonga, Amata, Ernabella, neighbouring cattle stations and Warburton by providing facilities for them at an acceptable place.

The settlement proved more popular than expected. The original plans were for a population of 150 people but it grew to around 300 in June 1970. The majority of the people seem to have come from Areyonga where the population dropped from an average of 450 to about 250. Others came from Warburton.

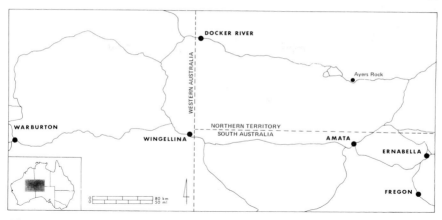

Figure 1: *Map locating the communities visited during survey*

At the time of my visit there was a white staff of eight. A manager, a store-keeper/kitchen-supervisor, a farmer, a clerical assistant to the manager, two teachers, a craft organiser and a prospecting advisor. A health sister flew out from Alice Springs for two to three day visits every three weeks.

At 31 March 1970 there were 322 Aborigines resident at the settlement. This represented the usual number of people living there, although the population fluctuated widely. The day I arrived, 150 people left on a semi-trailer[3] for a ceremony at Warburton but most of them returned within a month or two. The age structure of the population was somewhat unusual for Aboriginal communities in the Northern Territory, being marked by a low proportion of people under 16 years of age. This was due to a large number of single men and young married couples coming to Docker River to benefit, either directly or indirectly, from the high wages.

Age	M	F	% Total Pop.
0–16	36	42	24
16–65	129	84	66
65+	14	17	10
	179	143	100%

Table 1: *Census figures for Docker River as of* 31 *March* 1970

Work was offered to all who requested it provided they indicated their intention to stay on the job for at least a fortnight. Male employment was organised around three bush gangs, numbering between ten and twenty men each, which were taken out on Mondays and picked up on a Friday one or two weeks later. The gangs cut and erected fence posts and prospected over their mineral lease area.

Other jobs in the settlement were for drivers, camp orderlies and odd-job men. The women were mainly employed in the school kitchen (3) and to clean the school shower room (2). Numbers employed fluctuated markedly, ranging from 40 to 110 with the usual number around 80; only 30 people remained on the payroll regularly.

Most men received the standard wage of $48.90 per fortnight although odd individuals earned up to $98.95. Women were paid at the rate of $40 per fortnight. Both rates of pay were high for Aborigines in institutionalised communities at the time and attracted a fluctuating number of between 75 and 150 people from Warburton mission where there was little work and less money.

Besides employment there were three other regular sources of income: sale of craftwork to the craft shop, pensions and child endowment. Twenty to thirty people, mainly women, made carvings in their own time and received cash payments totalling between $150–$200 a week. The main outlets for the craft were passing tourists and the Jay Creek tourist enterprise.

By 1969 all Social Service payments were made directly to the people, so no exact record existed of the amount coming into the community each fortnight. However, the Welfare Branch census required the superintendent to list the number of pensioners; there were 31 recorded in the March 31st census. Pension rates were then $30 a fortnight for a single individual but the rates varied from $26.50 each for married pensioners to sums above forty dollars where pensioners had dependent children. In calculating the income of the community I have used the $30 figure.

Income from child endowment was harder to assess since it was not possible to get details on family size. The rates in 1970 were $2 a month for one child; $6 for two children; $12 for three children; $19 for four children; $27 for five children and $36 for six children. I assume that on average there would be three children to a family and that the income would therefore be $6 per fortnight.

The latest period for which records were available was the fortnight from 11–24 March 1970; income figures are set out in Table 2.

Wage (75 employees)	..	..	3,259
Pensions 31 at $30	..	..	930
Child endowment	..	..	156
Craft at $30 a day	..	..	300
			_____
			$4,645

Table 2: Estimated income during the fortnight 11–24 March 1970 at Docker River

Using these figures in conjunction with the census the estimates set out in Table 3 can be arrived at:

Income per head per fortnight	$14.43
Non-employment income per head: employment income..	$4.30:$10.12
Pensioners as % of population	10
Pensioners' income as % of total income	20
Non-employment income as % of total income	30
Workers as % of population	23
Workers' income as % of total income	70
Actual male workers as % of potential male workers	50

Table 3: Docker River: some calculations on income and population

The figure for actual male workers to potential male workers is derived from the census which shows 65 of the employed 75 as men and lists 129 men between the ages of 16 and 65.

Warburton mission   The mission was established in 1934 by the United Aborigines Mission (U.A.M.). The location seems to have been determined by the Aborigines who used to gather there for ceremonies in good years, but the motivation for establishing the mission is not entirely clear. The U.A.M. organisation was in contact with Pitjantjatjara, Ngatatjara and closely related peoples through their Oodnadatta and Mount Margaret missions and its members are said to have felt that it was better to minister to them in the isolation of the desert than on the fringes of white settlement. For a great number of desert Aborigines, Warburton has been their first point of contact with the outside world.

The mission staff numbered three men and six women. There was an acting superintendent, an acting works manager, a sister, a store keeper, a book-keeper, a clothes maker and three missionary linguists translating the Bible. There was also a farmer and his wife on a working holiday trying to get the stock into some kind of order. Besides mission employees there were five government employees, four school teachers and a projects officer.

At 30 June 1970 there were 453 Aborigines residing at the mission. This figure was about average for the previous four years in spite of the migration to Docker River. This was because a killing of a man on Laverton reserve had caused a number of people to move away from the town back to the mission. The census figures are clearly set out in the estimate of the numbers of people up to 65 years of age and over (see below).

Age	M	F	% Total Pop.
0–16	104	100	45
16–65	114	118	51
65+	9	8	4
	227	226	100%

Table 4: Census figures for Warburton mission as of 30 June 1970

The employment situation was in marked contrast to Docker River: there was neither money available to pay people nor projects for them to work on. Only ten women and two men had regular employment. Up to ten other men were employed casually during the mornings on rubbish clearing, fencing, sanitary work, grass cutting and odd jobs for which they received no more than $2 a day. The permanent female employees worked as domestics in the kitchen for school meals, the shower room and school. A sandalwood cutting operation was just getting underway when I arrived but it was not expected to do more than cover costs and provide some pocket money. There was also a modest craft industry paying out $40 a week to craftsmen for items transported for sale in the towns.

The store opened during the mornings and was the only source of food. There was no game near to the mission in 1970, and gathering by the women was negligible because of the poor condition of the immediately

surrounding country. Some idea of the quantities and kinds of food eaten
can be seen from a normal morning's sale (see Table 5).

Flour	..	..	..	.. 30 × 25 lbs.
Sugar	..	..	..	75 lbs.
Tea	..	..	..	5 lbs.
Tinned Meat	..	..	..	96 tins
Spaghetti and meatballs		..		48 tins
Jam	..	..	..	24 tins
Fruit juice	..	..	..	72 cans
Biscuits	..	..	..	96 packets
Plum pudding		..	..	36 tins
Tinned vegetables	..		..	24 tins
Tinned milk	..	..	..	24 tins
Kraft cheese	..	..	..	48 $\frac{1}{2}$ lb. packets

Table 5: *A normal morning's sales at Warburton mission store*

Fresh fruit was available twice a month and fresh meat irregularly. Other
items most frequently bought were petrol for cars, patent medicines, clothes,
plastic containers for water and blankets. No tobacco was sold in the store.

Although there were no accurate records, the sources of income were few.
The main feature was that about 45 people were receiving pensions although
only 17 appear on the census as aged 65 and over. This discrepancy results
from many of the ages of older people being ascribed more or less arbitrarily
and low consistency being maintained between different contexts. Table 6
sets out the estimated income.

Wages ..	..	..	..	..	210
Pensions (45 at $30) ..		..		..	1,350
Child endowment (70 families with					
3 children each)	..		..	..	420
Craft	..	..	..	..	80
					————
					$2,060

Table 6: *Estimated income during the last fortnight of June 1970 at Warburton
mission*

Table 7 sets out the figures on per capita income and the work force in the
light of the census.

Income per head per fortnight	..	..	..	..	$4.55
Non-employment income per head: employment income..					$4.08:$0.46
Pensioners as % of population	..	..	..	..	10
Pensioners' income as % of total income	..	..	..	66
Non-employment income as % of total income	..	..	90
Workers as % of population ..	..	..	..	..	5
Workers' income as % of total income	..	..	..	10
Actual male workers as % of potential male workers	..	11

Table 7: *Warburton mission: some calculations on income and population*

Amata   The South Australian Department of Aboriginal Affairs established Amata in 1961 primarily as a training centre for cattle management. Seventeen white staff ran the settlement which on 16 June 1970 had an Aboriginal population of 339. This population was a little higher than normal.

Age	M	F	% Total Pop.
0–15	65	69	40
15–65	95	79	51
65+	11	20	9
	171	168	100%

N.B. The first two age categories are slightly different from those used in the Northern Territory and Western Australian censuses: they divide at 15, not 16.

Table 8: Census figures for Amata as at 16 June 1970

As at all the other communities the size of the work force varied considerably, but just over half of the people available to work were usually employed at any one time. Jobs ranged from fencing and pastoral work to settlement maintenance, domestic and medical work and serving in the store. Pay rates for men were $24 a week and for women $21.

The craft industry was flourishing as a result of reorganisation. $250–$300 was being paid out to craft workers, more than two thirds of whom were women. Although work was on a casual, self-planned, self-directed basis and payment made per item, the rate of pay worked out at around a $1 an hour. Individual payouts averaged between $2–$8 a week.

In the month before I arrived, the store had been reorganised to operate self-service style with all items on open shelves and the butcher's shop incorporated in the store building.[4]

From the records it was possible to make an accurate estimate of income from known sources.

Wages	2,185
Pensions (35)[5]..	1,012
Child endowment	248
Craft	597
Dingo scalps	16
	$4,058

Table 9: Estimated income during the fortnight 3-16 July 1970 at Amata

Table 10 sets out the figures on per capita income and the work force in the light of the census.

Income per head per fortnight $11.97
Non-employment income per head: employment income $5.53:$6.45
Pensioners as % of population   10
Pensioners' income as % of total income   25
Non-employment income as % of total income   46
Workers as % of population   12
Workers' income as % of total income   54
Actual male workers as % of potential male workers   ..   32

Table 10: *Amata: some calculations on income and population*

Ernabella mission   The mission was founded in 1937 as a direct result of the efforts of the Moderator of the Presbyterian Church, Dr. Duguid. He advocated the mission as a buffer between the nomads of the desert and the whites living on and around the railway line to Alice Springs. From the outset it was stipulated that training and education were to be given to the Aborigines within the context of Christian service but that there was to be respect for the customs, language and traditions of the people. In 1961 an outstation for cattle rearing was established 64 kilometres (40 miles) to the south of the mission at Fregon.

The white staff numbered 18: a superintendent, two administrators; three pastoral workers; a mechanic; two craft supervisors; four teachers; three sisters; a builder; and a trade teacher.

The Aboriginal population of Ernabella and Fregon combined was 516 on 15 June 1970.

Age	M	F	% Total Pop.
0–15	112	112	43.5
15–65	136	123	50.1
65+	20	13	6.4
	268	248	100%

Table 11: *Census figures for Ernabella as at* 15 *June* 1970

The population is normally smaller than this at around 400 but a ceremony was being planned at Fregon.

Forty-nine men and ninety-three women were employed at the time the census was taken. This ratio of male to female workers is unusual but derives from the emphasis on craft work at Ernabella and the fact that the women who are spinning at home on piece rates are counted as workers. Of the men, ten worked with sheep, thirteen with cattle, thirteen on building, two as leading hands, five as gardeners, one baking bread, one teaching and four part-time artefact making. Of the women, eighty-four were craft workers, four minded sheep, one worked in the hospital, one baking, one teaching and two as domestics.

Wages were subsidised by the South Australian Department of Aboriginal Affairs. Males were paid $21 a week. Female rates varied considerably because of the piece work, spinners being paid 10 cents per pound for coarse wool and 15 cents per pound for fine. The interesting point about the women's involvement with the craft work is that it led to substantial sums of money passing straight into their hands; this amount was always above $200 a week *in toto*.

The mission records payments made per four-week periods so the figures for July were divided in two to get the figures in Table 12.

Wages ..	..	..	..	..	2,350
Pensions (40 at $30) ..		..	..		1,200
Child endowment	..	..	..		412
Craft ..	..	..	..	..	229
Spinning (women)	..	..	..		188

$$\$4,379$$

Table 12: *Estimated income during a two-week period in July* 1970 *at Ernabella mission*

Table 13 sets out the figures on per capita income and the work force in the light of the census.

Income per head per fortnight	$8.49
Non-employment income per head: employment income..	$3.93 : $4.55
Pensioners as % of population	8
Pensioners' income as % of total income	27
Non-employment income as % of total income	46
Workers as % of population	28
Workers' income as % of total income	54
Actual male workers as % of potential male workers ..	36

Table 13: *Ernabella: some calculations on income and population*

Discussion   By comparing the figures on income and population in the four communities it is clear that even with the low levels of *per capita* income the people had substantial amounts of cash surplus to their subsistence needs. The figures from Warburton make this clear.

There, the known income per head per fortnight was $4.55. This sum, plus free meals for school children and the minor contribution of gathering and hunting — 1970 was a drought year — were the only regular sources of subsistence. In round figures therefore the people were living on $5 per head per fortnight. This they managed to do by subsisting on a diet of flour averaging out at 1.3 lbs. per day per person. A 25-pound sack then cost $2 ($3 at Docker River) so that the cost of flour for the fortnight per person was $1.45, leaving $3.55 for other food stuffs and clothing.

There is no doubt that the Aborigines like flour for even at Amata where the income was $11.97 per head per fortnight, the consumption was still on average .9 lb. per person per day. While at Warburton I did hear complaints from Aborigines about the lack of fresh meat in the shop, but apart from that they did not raise any other criticisms of the food available to them during the short time I was there.

It can be seen then that it was quite possible for people in the Central
Reserve to live on $5 per fortnight per head and not feel that they were at
starvation point, although undoubtably if the people had had more money
some of it would have gone on food.[7]

Using this $5 figure it is interesting to look at the amounts of non-employ-
ment to employment income per head per fortnight in the four communities
as set out in Table 14.

	Non-employment Income	Employment Income
Docker River	$4.30	$10.12
Warburton Range	4.08	0.46
Amata	5.53	6.45
Ernabella	3.93	4.55

Table 14: *A comparison of non-employment and employment income in the four
communities*

In all cases non-employment income was more than 75% of minimum
subsistence requirement which, with the exception of Warburton, was raised
well above this amount by employment income.

There is good evidence that the Aborigines were earning more money
than they thought necessary for subsistence needs. This is indicated not only
by the fact that only half of the potential male work force was in employment
at Docker River where work was available for all, but more dramatically in
the high involvement with motor cars. It is impossible to provide any accurate measure of this involvement but an indication is given by the number of
derelict and working cars seen during the survey.[8] The derelict ones, it must
be pointed out, had been accumulating for about five years but the rate of
accumulation had certainly increased with the direct payment of Social
Service moneys in full in 1968. Table 15 sets out the number of working
and derelict cars seen in the 18-day survey. The derelict cars were mainly in
old car dumps at the edge of the communities.

Place	Derelict	Working
Docker River	7	3
Warburton	40	8
Amata	24	7
Ernabella	6	4
Along the road	12	(included in above figures)
	—	—
	89	22

Table 15: *Derelict and working cars seen during survey*

The most common sum paid for cars was said to have been around $200,
though many were not worth it. Besides the capital cost of buying cars,
expenditure on petrol was considerable. Even at Ernabella where the number
of cars was small the Aborigines were spending between $75 and $100 a
fortnight.

While all the figures in this paper have to be treated with caution, since they are not based on long term observations, I think they do express quite accurately the nature of the pattern of income and expenditure treated mathematically. The figures are misleading however in that they imply that the income was evenly distributed within the communities whereas it was not.

Pensioners who formed about 10% of the population in each community received between 20% and 66% of the total income; in three of the communities less than 37% of the males between the ages of 15/16 and 65 were earning at any one time and child endowment, though relatively small, passed directly into the hands of those women with children. Money was therefore being introduced into the community most unevenly.

Redistribution of the money appears to have taken place mainly through card playing, the meeting of demands for support from close relatives and in ceremonial life where cash payments are regularly made.

In a situation in which traditional values are paramount, the existence of such redistribution mechanisms leads to much direct Aboriginal involvement with the Australian economy being largely short term and for specific ends. In particular labour turnover tends to be high and the incentives used to induce whites to stay on the job, such as holidays, weekends, long service leave, superannuation, overtime and the like, are less than adequate for the Aborigines. Higher pay often leads to a more rapid turnover, since men who are target working to save enough for a car, or other purpose, reach their goal more quickly.

Target working is not confined to Aborigines. Many whites in the Centre and North Australia are also explicitly target working. Labour turnover in Northern Territory business is high, with a figure of 300% per year not unknown. But there are at least two differences between European and Aboriginal target workers. The Europeans have no 'second economy' to fall back on and they have different notions of capital.

European notions of capital are primarily concerned with money and material things. If properly curated, both may increase in value and give added security to the owner. For the Aborigines capital is in social relationships which also have to be looked after. Properly cared for they ensure security, in a way that material things such as houses, cars, clothing, cooperative businesses and bank savings never can and which because they are not seen as capital are expected to 'wear out'.

Until such time as Aborigines start to value material capital more highly than social capital, it can be expected that their direct involvement with the Australian economy will be unsatisfactory from an administrative point of view.

Notes

1. I made this survey on behalf of the Council for Aboriginal Affairs between 20 July 1970 and 15 August 1970. I spent either two or three nights in each community. The survey would not have been possible without the ready co-operation of the town and field staff of the Department of Aboriginal Affairs in South Australia, the (then) Department of Native Welfare in Western Australia and the Welfare Branch in the Northern Territory. Thanks are also due to the staff of Warburton and Ernabella missions, Susan Woenne and Graham Harrison.

2. This company is a subsidiary of International Nickel Southern Exploration Limited of Canada. At the time of my visit there was also a small company, misleadingly called 'Wingellina Nickel', mining chrysoprase on a 49-acre lease in the middle of South Western Mining's lease.

3. The semi-trailer was hired at a cost of $800 about $500 of which was raised in cash and the rest signed out of future pay.

4. Most of the Aboriginal income was passing through the store but there was no way of establishing exactly how much since some of the white staff also purchased a proportion of their food requirements at the store. The figures are set out below, however, and show the amount spent on fresh meat separately; this amount ranged from 5%–7% of total expenditure.

Month	Store	Fresh Meat
April	7,643.06	594.15
May	6,973.58	408.25
June	8,048.45	465.95
July	9,280 (approx.)	600.00 (approx.)

An important breakdown of store expenditure that was also not available was the proportion of purchases of food to non-consumable items. This store like the others sold clothes, a variety of utensils, blankets, torches, guns and other items.

5. Exact figures are known here. By rule of thumb calculation the sum would have been $1,050, or over-estimated by $38. 12 people received $30; 1 received $14; 1 received $35; 19 received $26.50; 1 received $57 and 1 received $43 per fortnight.

6. Store turnover was calculated in three-month periods. In the most recent three-month period before my arrival the turnover had been $29,100, averaging out at $9,700 a month. The 18 staff families were buying food at the store, spending an estimated $10 per week each. This would indicate that almost all the Aboriginal income was passing through the store, though doubtless the percentage would vary from week to week and bear some fairly direct relationship to departures from the mission for town.

7. Little comparative data on other Aboriginal communities are readily available. However, Taylor (this volume) indicates that the mean expenditure per head per fortnight on food at Edward River in Cape York during 1970 was $4.36. Undoubtably the diet of many people in this area would have been supplemented by some weekend hunting and gathering in the surrounding rich environment.
    Per capita income is estimated by Coombs (1974:139) for the Bardi at One Arm Point in Western Australia at $11.50 per head per fortnight in 1973; 91% of their income was from non-employment sources. The significant difference between the Bardi non-employment income and that of the communities described here is that 38% came from unemployment relief which was not paid to Aborigines in Central Australia in 1970.

8. By late 1972 involvement with cars had grown as a result of increases in wage levels. In October of that year the population of Docker River rose to around 2,000 for a week when, according to the settlement manager, 55 cars and 7 trucks converged on the place for a series of initiation rituals. The size of this gathering underlines one of the dimensions of intensification of ritual life that has taken place with settled life.

References

COOMBS, H. C. 1974 Decentralization trends among Aboriginal communities, *Search*, 5:135-43.
TAYLOR, J. C. In this volume, pp. 147-58.

13 Diet, health and economy:

some consequences of planned social change in an Aboriginal community

John C. Taylor

Over recent years, a number of medical workers have reported the exist-tence of high levels of malnutrition among Aboriginal children on remote communities and settlements throughout Australia (e.g. Kettle 1966, Propert *et al.* 1968, Maxwell and Elliot 1969, Jose and Welch 1970, Best 1971, Best *et al.* 1973). Malnutrition was most evident in children between the ages of six months and three to four years. It usually manifested itself in growth retardation of varying degrees of severity. Anaemia caused by iron deficiency was ten to twenty times more common in Aboriginal children than in their white counterparts (Moodie 1972:194) and occasionally other specific deficiencies due to shortages of vitamin A, vitamin D and vitamin C have been observed (Jose and Welch 1970). Malnutrition on the settlements studied was a major health problem. There was a strong association between growth retardation and infant mortality. Aboriginal children who died from gastroenteritis or pneumonia often had a history of growth retardation. Further, it was suggested that children who suffered growth retardation in early life might be intellectually handicapped in later life because of retarded brain development.

The malnourishment of infants and children was not simply a matter of their inadequate food intake. Intestinal malabsorption resulting from frequent bouts of infection (so-called endogenous malnutrition) was also implicated. Most fieldworkers would have agreed with Moodie (1973:188) that the problem was set in the '. . . complex interrelationships between socio-economic circumstances, parental attitudes, the physical environment, infection, health behaviour (with respect to health and medical services) and nutrition.'

The health ecology of the remote Aboriginal communities could be characterised by the following model to which most of the communities studied more or less conformed (Moodie 1973:244-47). The socio-economic environment of the communities was typified by low income levels. The staple diet of damper, black sweet tea and occasional meat, lacking chiefly in protein, calcium, vitamin A, vitamin C and sometimes calories, provided poor nourishment for women during pregnancy so that they tended to give birth to low weight babies. At birth, the babies had less than optimum body stores of nutrients and, as a consequence, their capacity to survive nutritional and infective stress was low. After weaning from breast milk, the children graduated to the staple and nutritionally deficient diet of the settlement and entered its unhygienic, usually overcrowded, and certainly highly patho-genic environment. Here they acquired repeated respiratory and gastro-intestinal infections which, if they did not prove fatal, may have impaired the children's ability to absorb nutrients from the diet. Thus the problem was compounded and a vicious cycle seemed to be set up in which the survivors of the process proceeded to adulthood to rear more children under the same circumstances.

In response to the situation, state and commonwealth government agencies intervened principally by establishing feeding centres to provide supplementary nutrition to children up to the age of six years, by appointing education officers to specialise in Aboriginal health education and by organising health teams to work exclusively among Aborigines. Income levels on many Aboriginal communities also rose. Cawte (1973:225) has referred pointedly to the poverty levels of income that made it necessary for the Pitjantjatjara to subsist on a basic diet of flour and sugar — a criticism that implied that increased levels of income might be beneficially reflected in improved dietary standards. However, the relationship between diet and income is not necessarily a straightforward one. This paper[1] traces the origins of present food consumption patterns at Edward River and examines the effect of rising levels of income on diet. It demonstrates how the planned social development of the community has had the unintended effect of fixing the community's dietary levels at their present nutritionally inadequate standard.

Edward River — health and nutritional status

The Edward River settlement lies on the western side of Cape York Peninsula on latitude 14 degrees 54 minutes south and longitude 141 degrees 37 minutes east. In July 1972 its population consisted of 287 full-blood Aborigines, 15 persons of mixed Aboriginal-European descent and one person of Aboriginal-Island descent. Since 1969 the children of Edward River have been under intermittent medical surveillance by teams from the University of Queensland Department of Child Health or the Queensland Institute of Medical Research. The teams reported some degree of anaemia among the children and significant signs of growth retardation. Many children had heavy parasite loads while gastro-intestinal disorders, middle ear and respiratory tract infections were prevalent.

In order to assess the relationship between diet, income and the nutritional status of the community, the writer conducted household budget surveys in February 1970 and in July 1972 (Taylor 1973).[2] Between the two survey periods the purchased diet had remained much the same. Mean weekly per capita expenditure on food had risen from $2.18 in 1970 to $2.67 in 1972 but this increase of 22.5 per cent was more apparent than real since, on average, local store food prices had risen by 24.3 per cent. The purchased diet lacked variety. Seventy-five per cent of the money outlaid on food went to buy fresh meat, refined sugar, white flour, tinned meats and tea. Per capita sugar consumption was high, standing at 1.417 kilos (3.1 lbs.) per week in 1970 and 1.714 kilos (3.75 lbs.) per week in 1972. The nutrient shortfall from recommended levels is indicated in the accompanying Table.

The Table shows some variation between the two survey periods. The 1972 intake of protein, iron and niacin was lower than in 1970 and while the values for retinol activity (vitamin A) and ascorbic acid (vitamin C) show increases, both values are substantially below the dietary allowances recommended for use in Australia (Thomas and Corden 1970). If anything, the diet of 1972 was less nourishing than the diet of 1970 and the extremely low values for iron, retinol, ascorbic acid and low values for calcium and niacin indicate possible areas of deficiency in the overall diet.

Nutrient				Actual Intake ———————————* Recommended Intake	
				February 1970	July 1972
Calories	..	..	..	103.3%	117.5%—117.2%
Protein	..	..	..	105.8%—89.3%	92.3%— 73.9%
Calcium	..	..	..	48.9%—24.1%	57.7%— 25.9%
Iron	..	..	..	72.7%—73.1%	33.3%— 32.7%
Retinol activity	..	..		9.9%	23.9%
Thiamine	..	..	..	259.8%	233.1%
Riboflavin	..	..		56.4%	69.5%
Niacin equivalent		..	..	70.5%	53.3%
Ascorbic acid	..	..	..	10.9%	27.6%

*Expressed as a percentage

Table 1: Mean daily nutrient intake Edward River

Thus Edward River conformed to the model described above and exhibited a maladaptive diet, evident signs of malnutrition and high levels of infection. Yet to the casual observer in 1970 or 1972, it was paradoxical that there should have existed any nutritional problem at all. Since the settlement's inception, the care and welfare of the indigenes had been constantly under the guidance and supervision of well-intentioned Europeans. The local store was well stocked with a variety of foodstuffs at relatively low prices considering its isolation from suppliers. Aboriginal community wages had risen steadily over the recent years and if they were low in comparison with normal Queensland standards (see Figure 1) they would appear to have been sufficient to purchase the kind of diet enjoyed by other Queenslanders. In 1970, Queenslanders spent a weekly average of $4.62 per person on food (Queensland Year Book 1971-1972) while the weekly per capita income of Edward River in January 1970 was $6.06. The explanation of the paradox lies in the history of the community and in the ways in which people adjusted to the social developments planned for their benefit. The history of the community is best discussed from the point of view of two distinct eras of policy and development — the mission era and the subsequent government era.

The mission era 1938-1967 As early as 1922, the Church of England missionaries debated the means of assimilating the coastal Edward River peoples into the mission framework that had already been established in the area. In their 'uncivilised' state they were troublesome to missionaries and pastoralists alike. They caused fights among the settled inmates at the

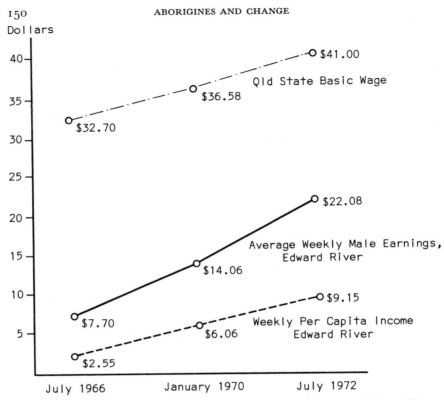

Figure 1: *Average male weekly earnings and weekly per capita income, Edward River*

Mitchell River mission when they came visiting and occasionally speared cattle belonging to the stations that bordered the reserve. The three tribal groups involved shared a similar culture and spoke related dialects. They were: the *Yir Yoront* (Sharp 1934) whose lands lay between the Mitchell and Coleman Rivers and were more commonly called *Koko-menjen* by their neighbours; the *Thaayorre* (also variously spelt *Taiyari, Taiyor, Taior* and *Tyore*) whose country extended from Malaman Creek to the Edward River; and the *Munkan* as they are called locally — but are referred to as *Wik-nantyara* (McConnel 1939, 1940) or *Wik-ngentjin* (Sharp 1940) — whose lands lay along the coastal fringe between the Edward and Holroyd Rivers.

In 1935, the total population of the three groups was 370, and of these, 260 were completely dependent on the bush for their livelihood (Sharp 1940). After a number of exploratory trips and several false starts, the Edward River mission was finally established with the consent of the local land-owning groups at its present site by J. W. Chapman in 1938. At this time most of the remaining 'bush' *Yir Yoront* elected to live at Mitchell River mission so that the Edward River settlement was (and still is) composed largely of *Thaayorre* and *Munkan* speakers with a sprinkling of outsiders.

The long term aim of the missionaries of the Diocese of Carpentaria was to create at Edward River a settled, self-sufficient and Christian community of Aborigines. In physical terms they envisaged something akin to the life-styles of the neighbouring Torres Straits Islands. The Aborigines were to support themselves from gardens, coconuts and cattle. Cattle raising and the coconut groves were eventually to supply the cash inflow into the village. Additionally, the cattle herd was to serve as a training ground from which men could graduate to find employment on the Peninsula cattle properties. Other men were to be trained as seamen on the mission luggers whence, perhaps, they would enter the Torres Straits pearling industry or engage in fishing enterprises.

For Chapman the immediate problem was to prepare a place where the tribesmen could ultimately settle down. How he did this is one of the Peninsula's sagas of survival, for the war years intervened and there was a great lack of funds and personnel to put the Church's ambitions into effect. With the help of the local people for the next fifteen years, Chapman planted gardens (potatoes, yams, taro, cassava and sugar cane), fruit trees (paw paws, bananas, mangoes and custard apples) and coconuts. During the first decade of the mission's life, fresh meat and fish had still to be obtained by hunting since the cattle herd had not reached the numbers necessary to sustain domestic killing. The introduction of wire-pronged spears and metal fish hooks improved the efficiency of indigenous techniques while large fish traps and canoes further augmented traditional methods and increased the food yield. European foods (flour, rice, tea, sugar and salt beef) were rationed out of the mission's small supply to supplement what food shortages occurred in the local environment. Tobacco and clothing were also distributed.

In 1956 the people of Edward River were still being officially described as nomadic (Report D.N.A. 1956). Nonetheless, the majority were living more or less permanently at the mission site in palm thatch houses. From time to time they went out to exploit the seasonal abundances in the bush but for the most part they were obtaining their food requirements from the mission ration system and gardens or from the nearby bush and beach.

From 1956 onwards, the availability of more funds and staff made it possible for the Church to embark on a modestly ambitious community development programme to consolidate Chapman's labours. (Chapman himself retired in 1957.) From then on all Aboriginal men and women who were willing to work were employed on a variety of jobs ranging from building projects, road making, airstrip construction, water supply and plumbing and the development of the reserve as a cattle property. A token wage system was introduced to accustom the people to the use of money and wage earners were expected to buy their food at the local mission store. Rates of pay were based on domestic responsibility and family need rather than on effort, skill or job responsibility. On the mission wage sheets, married workers were differentiated from single men and received higher rates of pay. If a married man's wife worked, he then received the single rate irrespective of the nature of the work. Those who had no job but had family responsibilities were classed as 'indigents' and were given rates of pay similar to those of single men. The mission's efforts were directed toward distributing their limited funds as fairly as possible in order to give the maximum number of people a cash income of some sort to manage. Aspects of the ration system remained. Clothing, blankets and other items were still issued free and infants and school children were given breakfast and a midday dinner together with vitamin supplements during school days. As the variety of projects increased, work on the community gardens lapsed.

On 3 February 1964, the cyclone 'Dora' descended on the mission and destroyed the church, six staff houses and twenty-five of the villagers' thatch houses, the store and the school, and uprooted fruit trees including most of the coconut grove. The Queensland state government immediately rebuilt the store and developed a plan for rehousing the people of Edward River in three-bedroom prefabricated aluminium dwellings. On the basis of this plan the community painfully commenced the task of rebuilding. In May 1967, the Church handed over the administrative control of the mission to the state's Department of Aboriginal and Island Affairs (D.A.I.A.).

The government era 1967-1972   During recent years, the policy of the D.A.I.A. has been guided by the general policy of assimilation formulated by state and commonwealth ministers in 1965. At a more specific level, the Director of the D.A.I.A. indicated his department's plans for the reserves in a newspaper article (Abschol 1968). These are worth quoting at length:

> Killoran: The Department's policy is, simply stated; 'to work itself out of a job'. This will be achieved in a number of ways which might include:
> (1) Training of Aboriginal Queenslanders to take over and manage all of the functions necessary to maintain normal towns within Queensland;
> (2) Develop the economic viability of the reserves to such a degree that they can be converted into some form of organisation which will ensure a living standard for all of the residents.
> (3) Education and training of all community and reserve residents to the extent that they may choose to move into either rural or urban environments with suitable work opportunity, accommodation etc. and become integrated into the broad social strata of Queensland.
> (4) Reorientation of present reserve structures to enable them to be converted and owned by either people of Aboriginal racial origin or alternatively an admixture of all Queenslanders irrespective of racial origin.
> . . . It is the desire of the Department that in the ultimate each of the reserves and towns will merge, no longer as special areas but as normal towns within a normal society in Queensland functioning on similar levels as all other towns . . .

At the time of the government takeover, Edward River was still a long way from realising these aims. The officers of the D.A.I.A. pressed on with restoring the cyclone damage, providing essential community services and completing the housing programme. A cash economy was introduced and the people were given total responsibility for managing their own cash incomes. Virtually all aspects of the ration system were eliminated including the issue of clothing and the communal feeding of children with the exception that several unsupported women who were not then entitled to any form of Social Service benefit were issued with rations weekly and given clothing. A new wage and job structure was instituted with margins for skill, effort and job responsibility irrespective of marital status and household income. The community development programme ensured that there would be enough jobs available to maintain full employment. All social service cheques were given directly to the recipients instead of being deposited in their departmental savings bank accounts.

Wage levels were low (Figure above) but the D.A.I.A. justified the low rates on the basis that the reserves were still deemed to be training and pre-employment establishments and that it was not

> . . . economically possible to provide all with full employment on Award rates and conditions . . . Indeed, such a proposal would generally discourage and defeat the Department's policy for Aborigines and Islanders to face the problems of living and working in the general community of Queensland as fellow-Australians. (Report D.A.I.A. 1970:8.)

However, real income was higher than the money rates indicate. Rents for the new prefabricated houses were low, $3.00 per week. A more realistic rental based on the cost of construction would be nearer $10.00 per week. Store prices too were low since freight costs (other than air freight) were not added to retail prices and the departmental costing system resulted in a lower than usual mark-up on wholesale prices. In 1970, prices in the store were, on average, 8.4 per cent lower than comparable Brisbane store prices. Adding the cash value of these components to, say, the top money wage paid in 1970 brings the real value of the wage up to $32.40 and by comparison much nearer the state basic wage. Additionally medical and dental services and air transport for sick people were free — important factors considering the high levels of morbidity in this remote region. Finally a Commonwealth Savings Bank agency provided an alternative to the departmental banking system which was then coming under increasing criticism because of the controls it exercised over depositors' moneys.

The people of Edward River appeared to adjust to these changes cheerfully and for the most part responsibly. Whatever minor irritations occurred before the new system was understood were offset by the fact that money income was increasing. Most persons, on the urging of local D.A.I.A. officers, placed their savings with the Commonwealth Savings Bank from which they could withdraw freely and without departmental restraints.

Having established these background facts it is now appropriate to consider the factors relevant to food selection.

Traditional attitudes to food The consumption of natural animal and plant foods was constrained by a system of food tabus as well as by pragmatic considerations of ripeness and quality. There were tabus attached to places where some or all of the natural resources of a given locality were forbidden to all except certain old people. Then there were restrictions on the kinds of foods that could be eaten when a person was in some special condition. The most important of these special states occurred during pregnancy, in the course of the parent-child relationship and during mourning observances, initiation and other ritual. The Edward River belief system stressed the sicknesses that followed when the tabus were breached. That is to say, the tabus postulated a link between food consumption and bad health. On the other hand, the writer could discover no indigenous equivalents to the positive values Europeans place on foods when they associate nutrition and good health. Except for certain brief periods during ceremonial activity when hot or burnt food must be avoided by the participants, Edward River people regarded Western food as lying outside the tabu system. Indeed, they turned to Western food with relief when traditional prescriptions were heavy. They uncritically accepted European foods in all their forms as good for eating.

Introduction to European food   The first kinds of Western foods to which the Edward River people were introduced were those of pioneer Australia — the flour, sugar, tea, rice, tinned meat and salt beef regimen of the outback. These foods were cheap, portable and easily stored and thus recommended themselves to the missionaries with their limited funds and storage facilities. During the entire mission era the store rarely contained stocks of much else. These European foodstuffs were easily fitted into the indigenous classification of foods. They also fitted in well with the existing open fire and earth oven cooking techniques. They required a minimum of preparation and only a few extra utensils — usually a billy for boiling tea and a basin for mixing damper. The new kinds of vegetable foods produced in the mission's gardens were either eaten raw or else cooked in the ashes along with other bush tucker.

Since 1960 most food has been bought in the store. Damper and, to a lesser extent, home-made bread, tea, meat and rice have become the confirmed staples in the diet. The trend to restricted variety was accelerated as the community gardens were neglected in favour of other projects. The devastation caused by the cyclone of 1964 marked the end of any further serious gardening activity. After 1967, an increasing range of foodstuffs has been introduced into the store including refrigerated smallgoods and dairy foods, fresh fruit and vegetables and a greater variety of tinned fruits and vegetables.

Changing roles   In the role structures associated with obtaining and preparing foods, there have been changes. As Aboriginal men became more involved in the development of the mission, hunting became an after-hours pastime rather than a daily chore. The traditional household dichotomy of man-the-hunter, woman-the-gatherer, could only be seen on weekends when family groups made short excursions to the bush or beach near the village. Women on the other hand became totally responsible for obtaining the food supply from the community store and cooking it. Therefore the food intake of individual families and the overall nutritional status of the community depended largely on how much women had to spend in the store and on what kinds of food they bought.

Budgeting behaviour   How much the Edward River housewife spent on food was determined by the alternative uses she had for her income. Food was but one of a number of items that made demands on her dollar income. There had been a dramatic expansion in the scale of material wants at Edward River that coincided with the transition from the self-contained and independent economy of the bush natives to the dependent cash economy of the settlement. The demand for various kinds of consumer goods and services was influenced in many diverse ways.

Perhaps the earliest set of demand pressures resulted from attempting to realise traditional usages more efficiently. In 1970, spears, spearthrowers, fighting sticks and shields were almost entirely made with a set of tools of European origin — axes, tomahawks, pocket knives, rasps and sandpaper. Rifles and shotguns, nylon fishing nets, handlines and knives were used in the interests of more efficient hunting. Camping out was the more comfortable for the use of swags, blankets, bushnets, tent-flys and camp ovens. Boats equipped with outboard motors gave men greater access to coastal waterways. Almost every man nourished the ambition to buy his own four-wheel-drive vehicle in order to transport himself and his kin to and from the bush, together with all the impediments that seemed, somehow, to have become indispensable to camping out.

With the completion of the new school, children needed more clothing because the school teacher required them to be cleanly and decently dressed. When free issues of clothing ceased, men had to outfit themselves for work. Mostly they chose the long-wearing, albeit expensive, apparel of the outback stockman. The outback ethos had clearly fashioned musical tastes as well, and Messrs Slim Dusty, Johnny Cash *et al.* provided the daily background music from a growing assortment of record players, tape recorders and radios. Traditional gift-giving obligations tended to find expression in rugs, clothing and rifles rather than in the food, tobacco and spears of the immediate pre-mission era. When the all-weather airstrip became serviceable, the settlement was included on the regular flight schedules of the local bush airline. This in turn meant that relatives on other settlements could be visited or holiday trips made to Cairns to buy things the local store lacked and also, of course, to smuggle liquor illicitly into the community.

The building of the three-bedroom houses had also created new sets of needs that did not exist before. At the time of occupation, the houses contained little more than a few items of furniture. There was a wood-burning stove, perhaps a table and a few chairs, bedframes and possibly mattresses. The simple bush housekeeping that sufficed in the palm thatch houses no longer sufficed in the new houses. From time to time they were subject to hygiene inspections. In order to maintain proper standards of cleanliness, there was a continuing expenditure on brooms, mops, buckets, scrubbing brushes, soaps and household disinfectants. This expenditure was unnecessary in houses with dirt floors. If the houses were to attain a level of creature comfort comparable with the models provided by the houses of the D.A.I.A. staff, then a considerable outlay on consumer durables was necessary. The stove involved a new style of cookery which required other kinds of cooking and eating utensils. China crockery tended to replace the enamel ware that gave good service in the bush. Refrigerators became desired objects. Bedrooms required sheets, pillow slips, blankets and curtains rather than bedrolls. The sitting room needed easy chairs. Within the survey period, few families had managed to furnish their homes even partially. To the present time, the wants that had been engineered into the houses remain as a backlog of deferred consumer expenditure awaiting the chance of realisation when the more immediate demands on income have been met.

Edward River people were acutely aware that they lacked worldly goods. They often depreciatingly referred to themselves as 'poor people' but within the limits of their incomes they strove to remedy the situation. Household budgeting and food buying behaviour therefore took place within a framework of competing wants and was approached from the point of view of rational calculation.

The budgeting behaviour of most households conformed to the same general pattern. Having paid the rent and perhaps banked a little money in his savings account, the head of the house turned the remainder of his wages over to his wife only retaining some for gambling. As a means of capital accumulation, one might describe gambling and banking as rival financial institutions. In time, steady saving resulted in modest capital accumulation. Saving could be particularly effective when a group of brothers pooled their savings for some joint project. But there was always the temptation to spend a growing bank balance prematurely, or to lend it to an importunate relative. On the other hand, for the risk of a few dollars, a lucky streak could produce individual wins sometimes amounting to several hundred dollars since the game of chance played tended, in the long run, to concentrate the cash of many into the hands of a few. In other words, gambling functioned as a lottery that randomly distributed large amounts of capital to a few players. Most men preferred this avenue of obtaining large sums of money to steady saving. Almost invariably, large gambling winnings were immediately spent on consumer durables or else used to finance a holiday trip to Cairns.

The bulk of household purchasing in the store was done by the Edward River housewives armed with their husbands' earnings, their child endowment allowances and what contributions unmarried sons and daughters and pensioner dependents could make. Planned expenditure in the store was difficult since many items such as clothing, household furnishings, materials and fabrics, hardware and other durables, arrived at the store in unpredictable bulk lots owing to the isolation of the community, the requirements of government ordering methods and the vagaries of transport. The Edward River women adopted a simple strategy in order to give themselves the greatest scope for purchasing these articles as and when they appeared. They simply spent as little as they could on their recurring needs and held the rest in reserve. They sternly resisted the impulse to buy the exotic and (relatively) expensive new foods that appeared on the shelves of the store and they ignored the posters pasted on the walls of the store and hospital exhorting them to eat more nutritiously.

Conclusion

In short, between the years 1970 and 1972, the Edward River housewife chose the diet she did because, on ideological grounds she did not believe it to be harmful; she and her family had grown accustomed to it; it was cheap and filling and allowed her to reserve her money for goods more highly valued. If she needed further reinforcement for her food buying behaviour, she had only to reflect that what she ate was typical of what most Aborigines almost anywhere else in remote Australia also ate. In the immediate future there was little likelihood of any change in dietary standards. Increases in wage scales would tend to be diverted toward the satisfaction of deferred consumer demands rather than be spent on foods that might make good the deficiencies that existed in the diet.

The hunger for material things is such at Edward River, that the writer is almost tempted to predict that rare economic phenomenon — a backward-bending demand curve for food. That is to say, the total demand for food would actually lessen with substantial increases in wages. If wages rose substantially, more goods would enter the realm of what could be bought and capital accumulation via savings might become more attractive *vis-à-vis* gambling. In their haste to save more money to acquire more things, Edward River people could well starve themselves. In fact individual families have done this in the past. It would be a bitter irony if, in the belief that they were going to correct a deficient diet at Edward River, social planners increased wage levels and inadvertently increased the problems they were trying to solve. This is not to be taken as an argument against increasing income levels. Obviously income increases are necessary if the Edward River people are to satisfy their felt needs. One hopes that in the process of fulfilling these needs they also learn something of Western food values to enable them to make a nutritionally more rational choice among the foods offered at the store.

Notes

1. The research upon which this paper is based was carried out during two periods. The first was in 1968-1971 when the writer was a full-time Ph.D. candidate with the University of Queensland. The second was during 1971-1973 when the writer joined the Queensland Institute of Medical Research as Anthropologist. The writer wishes to thank the Aboriginal people and the officers of the D.A.I.A. at Edward River for their good humoured tolerance. Dr Malcolm Calley, Mr Athol Chase, Dr Ralph Doherty, the Venerable Michael Martin, Dr Bruce Sommer and Mr John von Sturmer all made useful criticisms and suggestions when presented with earlier drafts. The writer also gratefully acknowledges the financial assistance provided by the office of Aboriginal Affairs.

2. Community members purchase their food requirements from the community's single store and butcher's shop. During both budget surveys it was a relatively easy matter to note all purchases by individuals and to write these up on individual purchasing cards. The completed cards could then be grouped into household purchasing units in order to determine individual household consumption patterns or else they could be aggregated to yield the total community food intake. The nutritional content of all food items purchased by Aborigines was calculated using *Tables of Composition of Australian Foods*, Thomas and Corden 1970. By means of 'Dietary Allowances for Use in Australia — 1970 Revision' (Thomas and Corden 1970:53) it was possible to construct an 'ideal' daily nutrient intake level for a community of similar age and sex structure and to compare this with actual community food intake levels. These are the results presented in Table 1. There are some limitations to this method and caution should be exercised in interpreting the results. Every attempt was made to assess the nutrient requirements of the community including the special needs of pregnant women. People who were absent during any part of the survey (e.g. stockmen who were supplied with meals in their camps) were noted and two women who still received rations were omitted from the survey altogether. However, no reasonable way to estimate body weights and activity levels could be arrived at and so the 'reference men and women' of the food tables (Thomas and Corden 1970:53) had to suffice as average models for body weights and activity levels. Apart from the milk given to children at school there was no way of estimating the amounts of food consumed that were derived from other sources. The food distributed at the infant feeding centre, although strategically important, was small in comparison with the daily food intake of the community. For simple physical reasons, the writer was unable to assess how much food came in from the bush during the actual surveys. Other investigations showed that it was doubtful whether the bush and beach would supply more than one meal of animal protein food per head per week. The gathering of local rootstocks has all but disappeared and only the children now occasionally eat the local wild fruits when they are in season.

    Errors leading to an underestimation of actual nutrient intake may arise because there are incomplete analyses of foodstuffs in the tables themselves while on the other hand there has certainly been some overestimation of nutrient intake since no account has been taken of food wastage or nutrient depreciation during cooking processes.

    As a final comment, it should be noted that what is presented in this paper is an estimate of the overall community food intake. What individuals actually receive varies. Some households are obviously better nourished than others. For example, in 1970, household expenditure on food ranged from $1.21 to $4.63 per head per week, the mean being $2.18 per head per week.

References

ABSCHOL 1968 Director meets the press, *Aboriginal Quarterly*, 1 (3):10-11.
BEST, J. C. 1971 Aboriginal child health, *Queensland Institute of Medical Research*, 27th *Annual Report*:17-19.

——J. S. WELCH, L. McPHEE *and* C. FILIPPICH 1973 Aboriginal child health, *Queensland Institute of Medical Research, 28th Annual Report*:22-6.

CAWTE, J. 1973 Social medicine in Central Australia; the opportunities of Pitjantjara Aborigines, *Medical Journal of Australia*, 1:221-33.

COMMONWEALTH BUREAU OF CENSUS AND STATISTICS 1972 *Queensland Year Book 1971 and 1972.* Government Printer, Brisbane.

JOSE, D. G. *and* J. S. WELCH 1970 Growth retardation, anaemia and infection, with malabsorption and infestation of the bowel. The syndrome of protein-calorie malnutrition in Australian Aboriginal children, *Medical Journal of Australia*, 1:349-56.

KETTLE, E. S. 1966 Weight and height curves for Australian Aboriginal infants and children, *Medical Journal of Australia*, 1:973-77.

MAXWELL, G. M. *and* R. B. ELLIOTT 1969 Nutritional state of Australian Aboriginal children, *American Journal of Clinical Nutrition*, 22(6):716-24.

McCONNEL, U. H. 1939 Social organisation of the tribes of Cape York Peninsula, North Queensland. Part one, *Oceania*, X(1):54-72.

——1940 Social organisation of the tribes of Cape York Peninsula, North Queensland. Part two, *Oceania*, X(4):433-55.

MOODIE, P. M. 1973 *Aboriginal Health.* Australian National University Press, Canberra.

PROPERT, D. N., R. EDMONDS *and* P. A. PARSONS 1968 Birth weights and growth rates up to one year for full-blood and mixed-blood Australian Aboriginal children, *Australian Paediatric Journal*, 4:134-43.

QUEENSLAND 1956 *Annual Report of the Director of Native Affairs.* Government Printer, Brisbane.

——1970 *Annual Report of the Director, Department of Aboriginal and Island Affairs.* Government Printer, Brisbane.

SHARP, R. L. 1934 Ritual life and economics of the Yir Yoront tribe of Cape York Peninsula, *Oceania*, V(1):19-42.

——1940 An Australian Aboriginal population, *Human Biology*, 5(12):481-507.

TAYLOR, J. C. 1973 Anthropologist's report, *Queensland Institute of Medical Research, 27th Annual Report*:26-7.

THOMAS, S. *and* M. CORDEN 1970 *Tables of Composition of Australian Foods.* Commonwealth Department of Health, Canberra.

14 Cultural pattern on an Aboriginal settlement in Queensland

Klaus-Peter Koepping

> *But while both humanisation and dehumanisation are real alternatives, only the first is man's vocation. This vocation is constantly negated, yet it is affirmed by that very negation. It is thwarted by injustice, exploitation, oppression, and the violence of the oppressors; it is affirmed by the yearning of the oppressed for freedom and justice, and by their struggle to recover their lost humanity.*
>
> (Paulo Freire, 1973:21)

> *Australian Aborigines are people. Their cultures are sets of ordered behaviours, systems of interrelated categories, images, and statements in terms of which people interact, understand one another, themselves, and the physical environment. Tearing people from culture makes the one an animal, the other a more or less abstract set of relations. Yet man is an animal who can articulate his dreams, who quickens both his existential relations with others, and the environment which provides the relations with significance, with the ambiguity of his dreams.*
>
> (K. Burridge, 1973:242)

Preamble

Although it has to be admitted that the proliferating specialisation in the science of man in recent times makes it a difficult task to pursue the objectives Freire has advocated as the main axiological problem of man — that is, the pursuit of the humanisation of man — it is hoped that anthropological reporting will in some way or other contribute to this final goal. Since it was the concern of anthropologists from the start to record the infinite variety of man's self-expression in relation to his fellow men, this endeavour may hopefully in the end lead to a better understanding of 'the other' and with it to a liberation even of the anthropologist himself, who could be considered a member of the 'oppressing' class, as far as the origins of his particular discipline and his present position in Western societies is concerned.

To fulfil the humanistic request implied in Freire's writings, it is important to remind ourselves of the indictment of anthropological research on Australian Aborigines to which Burridge in his recent publication is addressing himself.[1] Being scholars and bound by a certain code of professionalism, we should not forget the people behind the structures we are trying to uncover — be it structures of the human mind, of man's relations with his fellow men, be it those of how he relates to his natural environment.

In this article, I try to convey some aspects of the social life of Aborigines and of their attitudes and values on a government settlement in Queensland,[2] located about 290 kilometres (180 miles) north-west of Brisbane. It was established in 1905 as Barambah Station, but has been known since 1931 as

Cherbourg: it now has about 1,260 inhabitants, according to the 1973 *Annual Report* of the Department of Aboriginal and Island Affairs. The actual fieldwork on this settlement was carried out during 1973 and 1974 for about four months. I admit that the size of the population as well as the relatively short duration of field observation militate against the aim of a complete picture of all aspects of the social life in the community. However, I hope that this generalised survey will fill a particular gap in the literature on Aborigines. Up to now, there is available a rather extensive literature on urban situations, as well as on traditional cultural variations among Aborigines; and there are also some glimpses into local history, some general surveys (Long 1970), and the remarkable collation on the history and conditions of Aborigines by Rowley (1972). However, the settlements of Queensland have not been dealt with from the point of view of their internal organisation and the value attitudes of their inhabitants. On Cherbourg in particular, we have a relatively early anthropological report by Tennant Kelly (1935:461-73) which does not go much beyond an evaluation of the then still-prevailing modes of traditional social organisation. Here, I address myself to the following problems:

(a) the ethnohistory of the settlement, including statistical evidence and pronouncements by government officials as to the aims of the settlement policy in Queensland;
(b) the fieldwork approach and concomitant difficulties;
(c) the social structure of the settlement, exemplified by a selected case through the application of the concept of 'network'; and
(d) the generalised values expressed by members of the community.

The ethnohistory of the settlement

The importance of Cherbourg among Queensland settlements — government-controlled as well as church-sponsored — becomes apparent by looking at population statistics. With its 1,260 inhabitants, it is the second-largest government-controlled reserve in Queensland, surpassed only by Palm Island with about fifty more. This represents a considerable increase from the last published figures by Long (1970:105), who reported 928 individuals for the year 1965. Without Torres Strait Islanders, the number of Aborigines on government settlements for 1973 is 6,801 (for nine reserves). The Cherbourg figure makes up about 18 per cent of the total Aboriginal population under institutional governmental control in Queensland. On the other hand, Cherbourg is representative in many ways of a great number of similar institutions all over Australia through its 'ethnic' composition. Through the removal policy, which after 1897 replaced the so-called 'policy of dispersal' (a euphemism for cultural genocide), a variety of 'tribal' groups or remnants of such was brought together in those settlements. What makes Cherbourg interesting in this respect is the fact that this conglomerate of many different ethnic units has existed now for almost seventy years. It is therefore of some importance to assess what kind of social structure has evolved during this time, and that in turn can serve as an indicator of the tremendous resilience and potential for continuous adjustment of the Aboriginal population. I think that the Cherbourg situation is almost unique in Australia, as there were already present in 1934 (Tennant Kelly 1935:462) members of 28 'tribal' or linguistic units. As for the contemporary composition, I was able to identify the following 26 tribal groups as represented on the settlement (the numbers and the spellings of Tennant Kelly are given in parenthesis): 1. Gallali (No. 16, Kalali), 2. Gabbi-Gabbi (No. 24, Kabi-Kabi), 3. Badjala (No. 28, Badjela), 4. Gureng-Gureng (No. 27, Gurang-Gurang), 5. Gudjal-barra, 6. Wakka-Wakka (No. 23, Waka Waka), 7. Kaandju, 8. Waamin, 9. Dadjalacka, 10. Koko-Minni, 11. Wackai, 12. Yirradjali, 13. Guarmalgu, 14. Birrigabba (No. 4, Birigaba), 15. Tarrumbul (No. 8, Dharumbul), 16. Gangalu (No. 9, Khangalu), 17. Gunggari (No. 20, Kungeri), 18. Yugambi or Yugumbi, 19. Kokoyellanji or simply Yirlandji, 20. Dagunji, 21. Gamnel-roi (obviously the Kamilaroi of anthropological literature), 22. Bidjera (No. 3), 23. Watjumbarra, 24. Kokowarra, 25. Koko-imiji, 26. Ulgulu.

Out of the 28 groups mentioned by Tennant Kelly, 10 were still identi-fiable either from genealogies or through direct questions to informants as to how many and which tribal groups they remembered as being represented on the settlement. However, this enumeration should not lead to the generali-sation that all these languages are still spoken or exist as viable forms of communication. Through checking I could confirm that the following languages are still used by some members of the community: 1. *Wakka-Wakka,* which is the most prevalent one; a great number of the inhabitants of Cherbourg claim to be Wakka-Wakka, which has particular undercurrents of belonging to the place, being the original inhabitants or the people whose forefathers owned the area around Murgon; 2. *Gallali* is still understood by several people; 3. *Gureng-Gureng* and 4. *Gunggari* seem the next best remem-bered 'lingos', as informants refer to them; 5. *Birrigabba* or for short *Birri* is still spoken by two or three older people; 6. *Yirlandji,* the only northern language, is still fluently spoken by one informant whose knowledge of his tribal language was far superior to any of the others mentioned. The difference from the list of Tennant Kelly, i.e. the finding of sixteen language units which she did not mention and the non-identification of eighteen additional groups which she found forty years ago, seems to indicate a strong variation in the population groups over the last generation. Many people were transferred by the government to other settlements (such as Palm Island or Woorabinda and Yarrabah), a point which is corroborated by some of the genealogies I collected and by often rather sarcastic and even bitter recollections of infor-mants that they were sent to other settlements as 'incorrigibles', as the government agents have labelled people for any infraction of the 'rules'. On the other hand, there was obviously a considerable influx of people from other areas of Queensland during this time, mainly from two sources: being transferred from northern areas and settlements (such as Yarrabah or Palm Island) for the same reasons as people were moved from Cherbourg to other reserves, or from stations and towns where they were picked up and committed to these institutions for a variety of reasons; and, secondly, from the settle-ments which were closed in the period between 1934 and now — as, for instance, Woodford (about 48 kilometres [30 miles] from Brisbane), Deebing Creek and Purga (both near Ipswich).

In general, the inhabitants of Cherbourg today perceive their ethnic composition in a tripartite division. They speak of three 'lots' of people; (a) the *Wakka-Wakka,* the inhabitants of the Murgon-Kingaroy area and the region called the South Burnett; (b) the *Sun-downers,* from the west of Queensland, covering a huge area from St. George, Cunnamulla and Thargomindah to Winton, including the Blackall/Springsure and Emerald/Clermont regions, whose populations can be found in a greater percentage on Woorabinda settlement; and (c) the *Northerners*, from Townsville to Cape York.

The population figure of Cherbourg is furthermore of some importance if one looks at the surrounding country towns in the area. The town of Murgon, which emerged about the same time as the settlement of Barambah Station, has not more than 2,500 inhabitants, and it is obvious that its economic basis rests to a large extent on the spending power of Aborigines at Cherbourg.

The life-statistics of Cherbourg since 1905

The official story of Barambah Station starts with the *Annual Report* for 1905, where we read of:

> . . . a satisfactory arrangement having been come to with the committee of the Deebing Creek Mission, under whose auspices this settlement had originally been founded and successfully carried on. Situated conveniently to two stations, Murgon and Wondai, on the Kilkivan extension railway line, this area is about 7,000 acres, containing some excellent grazing and farming country . . . (*Annual Report* 1905:15)

It becomes clear in the description that a number of Aborigines from Deebing Creek and from an earlier reserve were brought first to Barambah Station. The other reserve in question was Durundur, 24 kilometres (15 miles) from the Caboolture Railway Station, which had been founded in 1897. The initial population of Barambah Station was about 250 in 1905 (see also Long 1970:102). The growth of the settlement in the following years appears in the statistics of the *Annual Reports* as follows:

1905 Removal of 35 women and 29 men ('half-castes') to Barambah.
1907 Barambah is declared self-supporting.
1908 Pictures of Aboriginal dances and of boxing exercises are included in the *Report*.
1911 Population estimate given as 437; if outside employment is taken into account, the figure might be between 500 and 600; 19 births recorded, but also 46 deaths.

Statistical survey for the years 1912-1972 for Barambah Station

Total Population		Births	Deaths	Removals to Station
1912	: 460	?	51	46
1913	: 550	16	59	72
1915	: 530	39	43	144
1916	: —	—	—	158
1917	: —	—	—	54
1918	: —	—	—	57
1919	: —	26	120 (87 from influenza)	—
1920/21	: 664	34	37	?
1922	: 692	—	—	33
		(of these 233 male, 183 female, 276 children)		
1926	: —	—	—	40
1928	: 729 (of these 220 Full-Bloods)			

Total Population		Births	Deaths	Removals to Station
1937	: 945 (of these 207 male Full-Bloods, 125 female Full-Bloods)			
1956	: 1,010 (of these 139 Full-Bloods, 871 'Half-Castes')			
1957	: 1,045	63	29	—
1959	: 1,167	—	—	—
1961	: 1,207	61	24	—
1962	: 1,240	—	—	—

In the following years there appears finally a decline to 930 in 1965, but a steady increase afterwards, as indicated by the figures for 1970 = 1,201, 1971 = 1,235, and 1972 = 1,271.

Though the statistics of the *Annual Reports* are rather uneven, and emphasise different criteria from time to time, the following observations can be deduced from the figures. In early years, at least until 1920, the death rate considerably surpassed the birth rate, and the actual increase in the total population came about mostly through the removal of people from other areas. A further significant feature of the population movement is the relatively low number of so-called full-blooded Aborigines, with little opportunity for establishing endogamous units among full-blood people. This did not seem to be perceived as a problem by Aboriginal informants. But it might be taken as one major factor responsible for the fast disappearance of traditional cultural traits. The relatively slow increase of the population between 1937 and the 1970s is difficult to explain. It might be due to the increased number of people who have taken the opportunity to move away from the institutional community under the provisions for exemption from the so-called 'Queensland Act'. But since the Department of Aboriginal and Island Affairs does not publish a detailed break-down on out-moving people, this factor is difficult to assess, at least until a clear picture of genealogical information for all households in the settlement is obtained.

I was not able to obtain an accurate demographic picture of the present community, since such information is alleged not to be available. I was asked to provide information about density of households as well as about age-pyramidical structures of the whole settlement by the present liaison-officer, who was obviously unable to gather this himself. Long (1970:104-5) provided a break-down of the community by age, indicating that 63 per cent of the population was under sixteen years old. That situation has not changed much. However, I cannot support his rather optimistic statement concerning the housing situation. For 1965, he says: 'The standard of housing on the settlement, as on other Queensland settlements, was relatively high and with the recent decrease in numbers there could be little overcrowding'. At present there are between 110 and 120 wooden cottages of the 2-3 bedroom variety on the settlement; and I found the occupancy range to be between three and sixteen, with a great number among the 40 households contacted averaging between six and ten members each.

Statements by Queensland government officials on Aborigines and settlements between 1896 and 1973

About the starting of governmental reserves and the reason for the establishment of settlements, Archibald Meston said in the *Annual Report* for 1896:

Specially entitled to practical sympathy are the aborigines scattered
among the settled districts and wandering about the towns. They have
lost their old habits and customs, abandoned their old hunting life, and
descended gradually through various stages of degradation to a condition
which is a reproach to our common humanity. They require collection
on suitable reserves, complete isolation from contact with the civilised
race to save them from that small section of whites more degraded than
any savage; kept free from drink and opium and disease, the young
people and the able-bodied taught industrious habits, and to raise their
own food supplies; the old people being decently cared for, and receiving
the modest amount of comfort they require, or all that is necessary in the
declining years of their existence. Even acceptance of the 'doomed race'
theory can in no way absolve a humane and Christian nation from the
obligations they owe to this helpless people, or our solemn duty to guide
them kindly across the period which spans the abyss between the present
and the unknown point of final departure (*Annual Report* 1896:5).

This is no doubt a very significant statement about the beginnings of the
Queensland settlement policy, revealing an almost 'anthropologically'
comparative approach to the two worlds of the black and the white man —
although it is worded in the language of evolutionary thinking of the turn of
the century. The candidness of Meston appears again in the same report
(1896:12-13) when he says: 'The average aboriginal drunkard is no worse
than the white, and he rarely reaches the same maximum depth of debase-
ment.' Meston's recommendations at that time are of considerable interest,
in particular points 1 and 7. These were:

> 1. Total abolition of native police. [He advocates instead a white police
> with unarmed trackers.] And: No native police officer under the old
> system and no constable in any way connected with that system, should
> be retained for police duty . . .
> 7. That 'Aboriginal Reserves' be created in South, Central and North
> Queensland . . . This principle of isolation on reserves, and the total
> exclusion of whites, has long been adopted by the Canadian and Ameri-
> can Governments towards the Indians of both nations.

But Meston was obviously one of the very few 'enlightened' persons of
his age in the service of the government. A countervoice can be heard in the
person of the Commissioner of Police, W. E. Parry-Okeden, in the Report on
the North Queensland Aborigines and the Native Police for 1897, where he
states, for instance:

> They (the Aborigines) have many weirdly childish superstitions which
> act as the underlying cause of their tribal feuds and personal quarrels
> (*Annual Report* 1896:16). [Further on, he comments on the introduction
> of cattle killing.] The facilities thus afforded for gratifying their carni-
> vorous instincts has had considerable effect in lessening the prevalence
> of cannibalism.

In the *Annual Report* for 1901, W. Roth remarks, after enumerating several
cases of Aboriginal girls having been sent to missions or settlements:

> I cannot conscientiously blame the young aboriginal women allowing
> themselves to get into trouble. I do not expect, that in one, or even two

generations, there can be instilled into them . . . all the moral virtues and mental restraints that it has taken ourselves something like 2,000 years to learn — not necessarily to possess . . . (1901:8).

The 1912 *Annual Report* supplies some pertinent information on Barambah Station itself. Lipscombe notes that 46 Aborigines were removed to the reserve for 'leading an immoral and idle life, being old . . . or for tribal quarrelling' (1912:30). And about the specific problems on the reserve he remarks:

> It seems impossible to stop the gambling, for, if interfered with in the camp, they retire to the bush, and this makes matters worse, as they lose their money to unscrupulous white sharpers.

In general, perusal of the *Annual Reports* gives the impression, in particular if one reads the very elaborate essays by Meston and later by Roth, that the settlement-scheme was established for purely humanitarian reasons. A careful reading of the figures mentioned in these reports indicates, however, that the settlements in the early years of their establishment were also a considerable asset, not only to the state government but in particular to the farmers and graziers in the surrounding areas. Male and female labour was constantly drawn from Barambah Station during those years, and even a comparison of the expenditure incurred for Barambah Station with the revenues received does leave the government with a deficit of only about one thousand pounds (for instance, for 1912 and 1913).

The *Annual Reports* are also testimony to the unfortunate distinction made between 'full-blood' and 'half-caste' Aborigines, which does not seem to have left any overt signs of resentment in the population of the settlement, as far as their attitudes are concerned. The *Annual Report* for 1937 says in this regard:

> Where it has been evident that certain half-castes were by breed, intelligence, and character able to maintain themselves respectably in the civilized community and had the ambition to better themselves, certificates of exemption have been issued releasing them from the control of the Department (1937:12).

In the same context the language becomes even more blatantly discriminatory, when it reads:

> The intellectual superiority of the islander over the mainlander must be recognized as placing the former in a distinct class, with claims to special encouragement and assistance to achieve their ambition to win a position as self-dependent citizens (1937:13).

From the earlier purely protective (but nevertheless exploitative) policy, the new catchword after the Second World War became 'assimilation'. The *Annual Report* for 1956 sees it this way:

> The age of our civilization is immaterial to this subject. Whether we base it from B.C. or A.D. has little comparable relationship to the civilization of the aboriginal. Suffice it to say that ours is a particularly ancient one, theirs as the aboriginal knows it now is a new civilization covering not more than a century (1956:2).

So much for an introduction to comparative cultures! But the report goes on to spell out what is required from Aborigines:

> There is no argument against the fact that the Queensland aboriginal must adapt himself to those things which constitute the civilization of the white if he is to survive and become a useful member of the community . . . That is the path which must be trodden by him and that is the path to which he must reasonably be kept by us consistent, of course, with his psychology, mentality, industry, and capability of assimilation . . . The white civilization of thousands of years is nominally willing to accept people differing in colour and with a civilization of one hundred years (1956:2).

The discussion on policy in the *Annual Report* ends on the note that the only road to complete assimilation is through education.

The same condescending attitude (to use a moderate term) is used regarding Aboriginal arts, although the following statement admittedly is directed toward the commercialisation of Aboriginal art, a difference which seems to escape the writer:

> Our aboriginals and likewise our Torres Strait Islanders are capable of an arts and craft production equal to any by coloured people of their age and civilization . . . (*Annual Report* 1960:7).

With minor variations, the attitude adopted up to the present seems to be formulated in the *Annual Report* for 1964, in the wording of a conference of federal and state ministers held at Darwin in July, 1963, on assimilation:

> As defined at the Conference the Policy of assimilation aims at ensuring that 'all aborigines and part-aborigines will attain the same manner of living as other Australians and live as members of a single Australian community enjoying the same rights and privileges, accepting the same responsibilities, observing the same customs and influenced by the same beliefs, hopes and loyalties as other Australians' (1964:3).

Such statements appearing in official government documents give some indication of how far the Queensland policy has 'progressed' from 1897 to the 1970's. We are obviously still 'prescribing freedom', and I admit that anthropologists are not the least free from this existential problem, which is apparent in some of the recent publications on Aborigines. This problem confronts every so-called 'specialist' when he is asked to advise on policies or alternative forms of action. It is with this precaution in mind that statements like the following should be read:

> Settlements cannot be abolished overnight but their continued existence should be made dependent upon the demonstration of two necessary conditions: (1) that they serve the long-term interest of the aboriginal people rather than administrative convenience, historical accident or the preferences of missionaries and churches; and (2) that aborigines are significantly involved in their local government, with Europeans acting as resource persons and not as controllers (Broom and Jones 1973:79).

What is of interest in the context of the governmental documents is the fact that they do not answer the central problem as propounded by Freire (1973:25-6): 'How can the oppressed, as divided, unauthentic beings, participate in developing the pedagogy of their liberation?' It would be a quite legitimate question to ask an anthropologist who is working with minorities anywhere in the world how far he is willing to commit himself. This is the basic question we will have to cope with in this century, namely the question of the 'radical posture' which Freire describes as follows:

> Discovering himself to be an oppressor may cause considerable anguish, but it does not necessarily lead to solidarity with the oppressed. Rationalising his guilt through paternalistic treatment of the oppressed, all the while holding them fast in a position of dependence, will not do. Solidarity requires that one enter into the situation of those with whom one is identifying.

One might disagree with Freire, but anthropologists in particular will be confronted constantly in the modern world with this existential question and will have to solve it, everybody for himself, since they are using one of those methods which lead to an entering into the situation — i.e. participant observation (see also Koepping 1973).

The fieldwork situation

This particular project was undertaken with the help of an older Aboriginal informant from the Brisbane area who had spent his youth on Cherbourg as well as on Palm Island and had kinship ties in that settlement. These were my first contacts with members of the Cherbourg community itself. Because of administrative regulations and the crowded conditions there, my informant and I had to stay in the area where the white administrators lived: we were thereby removed spatially from the community as a whole and were unable to participate around the clock in its activities. Since it was necessary for me to interrupt the observation-period several times because of the family obligations of my informant, I used one field period to stay at the home of a family which we had got to know quite intimately. But although the hospitality extended was wholehearted, the sleeping conditions of the other family members led me to give up a prolonged stay in that household. Of course, the 'segregated' living quarters had an advantage in that I was able to retire to write down impressions of a day's observations; but it also had definitely the disadvantage of my not being a member of the community. On the other hand, no member of the Aboriginal community ever — even when invited — 'dared' to approach the area in which the administration personnel were quartered. Although access was not restricted by any regulation, people would constantly say, 'What will the manager think of it? He knows everything.' The image of the manager of the settlement had an almost magical quality in the eyes of the people. My time on the settlement was spent mostly in walking around, talking to people, knocking at doors of households we had not visited before or with which the main informant had no direct kin contact.

At first these visits were rather informal, and not much was written down in the presence of Aborigines. Later it was possible to go through a rather loosely formulated questionnaire, and in the end even tape-recordings were taken during discussions. In some houses we spent half a day or more at a time. Many households later became a kind of 'headquarters'; after breakfast, tea or dinner, neighbours and friends of families who had extended the invitation were visited. On the whole, the response to enquiry was positive. Several members of the community became main informants after a while by taking me personally around to their friends. This was necessary, because I encountered quite early the apprehension of people who were approached by myself without the aid of an Aboriginal face around. People were obviously — and many admitted this indirectly — 'afraid', full of anxieties, and some we were never able to contact: they would in some way or other see us coming and literally 'run away' — i.e. visit a neighbour, go shopping or indicate that they had no time. But these incidents were extremely rare, although sometimes I would be involved in a forceful argument as to the purpose of my visit. I explained that I was mainly interested in three aspects: traditional knowledge, kinship relations and living conditions of the people on the settlement. 'What good will that do us?' was a common response, which was and is — as every researcher who does not have any illusions about his influence upon policy-making knows — one that causes great difficulties. It became apparent that 'pure research' was not possible. People had questions, and after they began to trust me to a degree, would ask for favours of different sorts. A car trip to Murgon became a normal feature (a taxi ride cost, at that time, $3.00 for the return trip!). More difficult to answer were questions relating to pensions, social welfare benefits, working conditions, deserted wife's pensions, etc. In these cases, we would either enquire from the administration or refer the case to the liaison officer. We were rather fortunate that this person was new to the community and very eager to follow up these problems. This was rather revealing in two respects: it showed that the Aborigines were afraid to go to some administrators to ask for such information, and in many cases did not know precisely what to do, or how to fill out forms, etc. Secondly, it corroborated an impression which was gained from questioning informants directly, namely, that no white official ever came around to enquire into their personal problems. While this exercise did not itself directly lead to an understanding of the community, it proved the point that 'participant observation' under these circumstances had to be action-oriented; or, as two researchers (Valentine and Valentine 1970:418) in a black ghetto in the United States observed cogently:

> It brings home most forcefully and concretely the need of effectively combining empirical accuracy of a high order with a genuine commitment to humane valuation of community interests and welfare.

The danger of 'over-identification' was avoided through a constant rechecking of the data in question. In any case, we could not avoid becoming genuine participants by being located in a given network of relationships (see also Vidich 1955:355). Involvement became more obvious when we observed people playing cards or drinking alcohol. This led to a certain difficulty between my own objectives of observing the 'real' daily life, and my main informant's desire not to be involved in an 'unlawful' activity (since card-playing as well as alcohol are still forbidden on the reserve, Cherbourg being one of the very few in Queensland not having a canteen). A total neutrality in these respects was, of course, impossible (see Vidich 1955:358, and Koepping 1973): non-interference in pursuits which were by regulation forbidden was made the easier through observation of a certain 'double standard' on the part of white officials on the settlement, who had of course a quite 'reasonable' justification for their own behaviour.

The network of social relations

To elucidate the structural properties of the settlement, I chose to apply the conceptual tool of the 'network' as it was developed by Barnes (1954:39-58 and 1969:51-76) and made useful later through the studies of Bott (1957/ 1971), as well as by other authors. To comment here on the analytical usefulness of the concept and its theoretical implications, as well as on the problems of quantification of portions of a network, would surpass the limits of this article. I am employing the definition of a network as an analytical tool, as given by Mitchell (1969:2) when he states that it is:

> . . . a specific set of linkages among a defined set of persons with the additional property that the characteristics of these linkages as a whole may be used to interpret the social behaviour of the persons involved.

In short, the network approach has been used extensively in urban environments, often in conjunction with sociometric analysis: and it has, as Martin observes (1972:304):

> . . . become a valuable tool for coaxing order and pattern from the seemingly chaotic stuff of city-living, and so shedding fresh light on the meaning of community in an urban environment.

Ideally, a person in a particular community, within his life-sphere, can have innumerable relationships with other people — i.e. through kin-ties, through marriage, through neighbourhood, through his work-situation, etc. These ties with other persons will, of course, differ in terms of duration, intensity, and so on. By mathematical reasoning, a person on the settlement of Cherbourg could conceivably have some kind of relationship with about 1,200 other persons; but although people may know one another, the relationships between them will rarely be meaningful beyond a certain circle. All possible relationships between all persons in a community would constitute the total network. A partial network in the terms of Barnes (1969:55) would be that portion of the total network which is based on some criterion applicable throughout the whole network.

For the study of the community of Cherbourg, I chose to observe and solicit information about the partial network of kin-relations. This was a quite natural choice, not only because kinship has been one of the traditional fields of social anthropologists, but because of remarks people would make in the initial stage of our conversations. Whenever I enquired about a person not known to me, the answer would almost invariably be 'Oh, that is Bill X, they are a big mob, you know'. This reference to 'mob' seemed to be of some significance. People clearly identified other persons not with a house or a region, or where they came from or what job they were connected with, but by their belonging to a unit of people who were related by descent. The term 'mob' seemed to reflect most often the classical type 'lineage', but sometimes it obviously included also persons who had married into it— thus approximating what one could refer to as a *cognatic group* or the *kindred*.

The household and its ties — one typical case Both husband and wife were married for the second time — i.e. living in a *de facto* relationship. They have living with them, at present, three children. The age of the husband, who is an invalid, is 51; his wife's, 44; and the respective ages of the children are 20, 19 and 11. The eldest, a son, is mostly around only during the weekends when he comes home from his job as a ringbarker in the countryside. Four other children of the couple had died earlier, three as babies and one who was in a centre for permanently disabled children in Brisbane. Neither of them had children from former marriages. The first wife of the husband was still living on another settlement, while the first husband of the wife had died. One additional person was living most of the time in this household: a young man of about 35, who had been adopted as a child by the wife's mother and was employed as a teacher's aide in the state school on the settlement.

The house was a typical three-bedroom wooden cottage, well furnished and decorated, but definitely overcrowded. After fitting into two bedrooms either one bed and a drawer-dresser or two beds and a table as well as a television set, there was little room left for movement. A third bedroom was so small that only one bed could be put into it. The living-dining room was furnished with a table and chairs, a radio and record-player unit, and well decorated with pictures. Additionally, there was a long kitchen and a roomy porch and, separated from the living quarters, a unit for washing and a rest-room. Besides the television set, the record-player and radio combination, there were a washing machine, a fridge, and other minor electrical equipment. This seemed to be the average range found in most households on the settlement. The wooden walls and ceiling of the house were unsealed, however, and whenever there was heavy rain driven by wind some of the living areas would get wet. The crowded conditions and the smallness of the rooms would not have allowed any additional or more comfortable furniture, and clothing had of necessity to be hung over the bedroom doors. The general appearance of the house was one of extreme cleanliness and orderliness under the circumstances. Visitors (sometimes ten persons during the day) were accommodated in the living room or on the porch. The couple managed to live on the husband's invalid pension of $44.50 per fortnight. Rent for the house was $8.00 a month, and payments to merchants in Murgon amounted to approximately $30.00 per month. Although other family members who earned a wage contributed to the household budget. it seemed difficult at times to get by. The couple also tried to improve its fortunes by betting on horses, a widely practised leisure-pursuit on the settlement.

The kinship network

	Husband	Wife
Total of remembered kin (excluding children and spouse)	approx. 55	approx. 51
Consanguineal relatives still living on settlement	5	2
Contact with other households on settlement through all kin-ties	8	4

This household conforms in every respect with others on the settlement. Some persons would remember and be able to name up to 100 relatives, but the average seems to lie between 35 and 50. The important point is, that through any household on the settlement a researcher would be able to contact at least about ten other households. Particular generalised features of the social structure of interpersonal relationships between the households are as follows: a highly integrated, not a radial, network of relationships has emerged over a period of time. Multiple marriage ties are to be found in almost every household, whereby the official or church-sanctioned marriage would be the exception: there is also a high number of *de facto* relationships.

The *de facto* relationship is not necessarily taken as being less binding in regard to emotional ties. In the case we are discussing, the mother of the wife had had one official marriage and one *de facto* marriage. The first husband was still living on the settlement in a separate household by himself. But from time to time he would drop in at his daughter's home and also meet his former wife, and conversation would be quite easy: whenever he needed financial assistance, his former wife would accommodate him. Another person who had close relations to her was her 'stepbrother'. Both were in their seventies, but still healthy and vigorous. She had been adopted by this man's mother; and she, in turn, had adopted the son of her step-brother's sister. This younger, adopted man, would also live in this house-hold. Nevertheless, since the mother of the wife of this sample-household was living across the street, the kin-relationship could become at times strained when the couple of the house had a disagreement.

I would subscribe to Bott's statement (1971:296) about the ambivalence of the kin-group in regard to the conjugal relationship: kin has the double interest, of maintaining a marriage and of breaking it up. In many house-holds the men are out at work, often outside the settlement, and the burden of maintaining the house and caring for the children rests on the shoulders of the women. This seems to create considerable stress in families. It also represents a continuation of the old practice of outside employment procured by the administration. It seems to have led to a strongly matrifocal family. A further feature of the structure is the maintenance of contact with many relatives outside the settlement. In general, the network within the community is a connected or interlocking one (Laumann 1973:113), which means that the persons linked by kin-relationships to a particular 'ego' are also known to one another. In summarising, I would say that the interconnectedness of personal relations within the settlement would tend to lead to a strong community feeling and a similar outlook in terms of values and attitudes.

Nevertheless, it might be difficult to deduce from the interlocking nature of the network what Laumann describes (1973:114) as follows:

> In general, we expect an interlocking network to be composed of a set of individuals who are alike in a number of important social respects on the grounds that similarity of social attributes tends to imply similarity of social attitudes and personality characteristics and therefore mutual attraction.

This seems to be a tautological statement: i.e. because people share the same values they are prone to create an interlocking network, and having found such a network, we can assume similarity in values. The particular complication in this settlement, not so much for the application of the network concept, but for any deductions and correlations, lies in the characteristics of the 'community' itself. It has not grown naturally out of economic or other interests of the participants: the community has been artificially created. Furthermore, many members of the community have had until recently no chance to 'break' the almost endogamous local unit by marrying outside their own 'colour', because of prevailing attitudes in the white society. Again, this could be misleading, since in most cases we find in the local genealogies, reference to a white man, Chinese or South Sea Islander in the father's or grandfather's generation. But the circumstances surrounding these unions are mostly not known to the present generation. It seems to me undeniable that something of the feeling which Max Weber postulated (1974:136) for the communal relationship which is 'based on a subjective feeling of the parties . . . that they belong together' is definitely present. This brings us to a consideration of certain key-values and attitudes among the people of Cherbourg. It should be stressed, however, that these and the following generalisations are to be seen in the context of a community which in actuality consists of a plurality of opinions and attitudes. There is definitely no strong unified body of custom or values which binds together all individuals.

The generalised values of the settlement population

The settlement   Concerning the settlement as a living unit, the feeling is ambivalent. People give contradictory statements. Some say: 'Look, this is the only thing we have', or 'I would rather be among my own people'. On the other side, people dismantle dwellings which are no longer inhabited, using the materials for firewood or for other purposes. Informants claim that some members of the community charge their 'fellow' blacks a great deal of money for driving them to town or to work. This ambivalence of feeling toward the settlement as a community might have to be seen in connection with the dichotomy of responsibility: white men are administering everything; the land, the houses and the facilities do not belong to the members of the community—they are, in the real sense of the word, 'alien' to them. Many people complained: 'What good is it, to care for the garden, to keep a fence in order, when the administration can shift me around any time into another house?' This ambivalence in regard to the community seems to be connected more with the place and the administrative set-up than with the social relationships among its members. A further comment is often made: 'The manager seems to care more for the pigs than for people'. This and similar statements refer to the fact that the white administration

is very keen on the economic viability of the settlement, and has expressed
that view several times. People on the settlement feel in some way neglected,
or even cheated. The roads are in bad condition. All houses have to contend
with rain seeping in or with wind blowing through the rooms, and this is
responsible for a number of chronic diseases. People will not buy expensive
furniture, because the rain would ruin it. And the attitude of the administration that the people can fix everything themselves, does not appeal to
them. Many are old or sick. Others work outside the settlement and refuse
to renovate their homes, even if material is provided. In a free enterprise
economy, this point of view would probably change slightly: the outlook
of the people would certainly be different if they could consider the houses
as being their own property.

The traditional culture Much of the traditional culture of the 'tribal'
groups brought together here is of course forgotten. There are, still, older
people who will talk in the 'lingo' among themselves, but the younger
generation refuses to learn anything about it (with one single exception in
my whole sample). A revival of Aboriginal culture seems fruitless. The
attitude toward traditions is very mixed. People in their seventies enjoy
talking about the things they remember; but some refuse outright, even if
they are known to be experts. The ambivalence toward their own traditional
culture seems to be connected with a strong antagonism between the generations. A number of attitudes among the people above fifty years of age seem
to be derived from some internalised values of their white 'masters': for
example cleanliness, orderliness, strict rules, strong punishment for infraction,
belief in authority, and at the same time the attitude instilled into them in
regard to their own past — that Aborigines were uncivilised, etc. Strong
missionary influence, as well as long periods away from the home area, in
outside employment, have eroded much of the genuine knowledge of the
past. Many old-timers revel in what they consider to be 'their past': the life
on pastoral stations, the rodeos, the droving and so on: and these things
still attract younger people as well, although they ridicule the traditional
Aboriginal culture. The last 'corroborees' were abandoned about five years
ago, the reason being 'that the young men would laugh about us'. However,
there is a strong identification with so-called 'country and western music' —
a tradition which points to their white station 'masters' and to Australian
country life.

Attitudes toward work The attitude of a great part of the white
populace about the laziness of Aborigines is reiterated within administrative
circles. The main problem on the settlement is to get younger people to
work on the training farm, in the housing workshops or in other manual
fields open to them. Since there are not enough applicants for available
jobs, blame is put squarely upon the Aborigines. They, in turn, counter
with the telling argument that they, or at least the young men, can earn
more outside than inside the settlement. Furthermore, the training received
on the settlements is not acknowledged outside. This is a vicious cycle:
there are not enough men available on the settlement for carpentry or
prefabricated housing work—therefore the existing craftsmen cannot cope
with the building demands there. A common complaint is that the available

working crews are not put to work on repairing old or building urgently
needed new home units but are sent to build houses in other parts of Queensland. The counter-argument of the administration is that 'the employment
of skilled carpenters etc., outside the settlement gives the Aboriginal people
a lot of prestige'. But even if the same wages were to be paid in the near
future on settlements like Cherbourg, it is doubtful whether the situation
would change appreciably. There remains the way out for the administration to classify the work force according to its 'skill'. A person who by
age and experience could easily be a manager of a sawmill, is simply classed
as a sawyer—so that by the time he is past forty, a man knows that he has
no chance outside the settlement any more.

Attitudes toward the native police force   One of the major complaints
of people living on the settlement concerns the native police. This is one of
considerable frustration. Many former policemen who kept their integrity
and are now in their seventies agree with the general view in arguing that
'the native police had no training, they are drinking, they don't lead a
moral life, why should we obey them?' The turnover of the individual
members of the native police is quite astonishing. An additional complication arises out of the network relationships themselves. It is difficult to
imagine that any policeman who is related to a certain percentage of the
community could perform his duties with scrupulous fairness, even if he
had the willpower and the training to do so.

The Aboriginal council   This institution, which is supposed to serve as
an intermediary body between the population as a whole and the administration, is looked upon by the majority of the people with suspicion, disgust
or plain cynicism. The members of the Council may, as individuals, be held
in high esteem, but their powerlessness makes them the butt of ridicule
among a large proportion of the people. Any initiative they show is either
thwarted by the administration or, because of the build-up of suspicion on
the part of the community, meets with a lukewarm response. The position
of the Council members is, therefore, extremely difficult — not least because
they are not all freely elected by the people, and the same people remain
on the Council for many years. Nobody seems keen to take over this responsibility. Under the circumstances, Council members who do have good
intentions about achieving something worthwhile, are defeated from both
sides. That no one is eager for the position is, of course, again interpreted
in terms of 'the apathy of the Aborigines'. It is not difficult to imagine why,
under the circumstances, most of the people show signs of social anomie—
which is revealed in their attitude toward alcohol, whenever they are outside
the legal realm of the settlement.

The churches on the settlement   There are at present three church
buildings, representing the Australian Inland Mission (A.I.M.), the
Catholic Church, and the Church of England. For several years, the A.I.M.
was the most active group, producing very outspoken, energetic and self-
reliant personalities who became famous as preachers in other parts of
Australia. In terms of the number of church services, the A.I.M. seems to
be the strongest group on the settlement. In some persons, adherence to it

seemed to have influenced behavioural patterns, at least in the short term: one older man claimed, and others supported this, that he had given up his drinking habits. Since he was also a compulsive, but very reliable driving fan, the A.I.M. gave him the opportunity to fulfil his personal ambition, and he was able to drive down to Brisbane with other church members for meetings and rallies. The behaviour-modifying attraction of the A.I.M. seems to lie in the creation of positions of prestige for Aborigines who would participate in and plan meetings; and whenever a white preacher could not come, a black lay preacher of considerable talent would also double as singer and organ player during the service. The reproach of a young Aboriginal woman who was extremely active in the organisation of programmes for children and who is now living in Brisbane, would be taken very seriously even by her elders. This does not imply that there is no criticism of the A.I.M. Many people accuse it of 'cliquishness', in statements such as: 'Oh, the A.I.M. people care only for their own members, the Catholic sisters are quite different, they really visit every home, even if we are not members.'

Conclusion

It is difficult to make any recommendations or predictions about the settlement situation in Queensland. Much more detailed research and analysis is needed, before any policy can be decided. Although I have been dealing with only one settlement, I have visited others for short periods of time. The impression gained from these comparative experiences is that each settlement has its own history and hence its own, often very different problems, although there are overt similarities in certain behavioural norms which show features of what has sometimes been labelled the 'culture of poverty', 'anomie', 'alienation' or the manifestation of 'marginality'. Each settlement differs considerably as to its internal factions, its social environment, its proximity to white society, the age composition of its population, and its attitudes. Some settlements have had a rapid turnover of white administrators, each trying out a different approach within the frame of general policy. Reasons for the so-often mentioned and perceived 'apathy' of the people of these settlements are not difficult to discover, as I have already indicated. Whether we can speak of the behavioural manifestations of persons from these settlements as signs of marginality, mental sickness or anomie, is questionable. We could just as well identify such manifestations (in particular, apathy) as an indication of an adjustive psychological approach of persons who are resilient enough to survive policy changes, the uprooting and extermination of their cultural heritage, and the whole brutalising effect of a majority culture which has systematically suppressed their own humaneness. In short, all the outer manifestations of Aboriginal behaviour patterns could be seen as the only possible way of remaining 'sane' under insane social conditions and in what appears to them to be, at times, an 'insane society'. That form of reasoning is no less defensible than making the suppressed minority into a scapegoat for faults which are not necessarily of its own making: and that view has been persuasively argued by the anthropologist and psychiatrist Jules Henry, by a whole school of psychiatrists from R. D. Laing on, and by educational reformers like Paulo Freire within our own so-called Western

societies. I can only agree with Rowley when he makes the point that we
have actually stereotyped Aborigines to live like another stereotype, the
white Australian, and that European colonial powers have used oppression
and violence because they could not charm the conquered (Rowley 1966:
345). As Archibald Meston said in his report of 1896: 'If we treat the aboriginal as a dangerous wild animal, what wonder if he occasionally acts the
character forced upon him?' (1896:3).

I would not, however, subscribe to Rowley's statement (1972:127) that
separate settlements should disappear as soon as possible. The structural
elements of social relationships between people on such settlements seem to
have developed into a viable basis for communal living. How it can be put
to use, be carried on or transformed into a different life-style, those are the
questions which have to be considered with great care.

Notes

1. It might be useful to readers to refer to a review of this book in *Anthropological Forum*
    (Vol. III, Nos. 3-4, 1973-74:331-3).

2. The research was supported by a grant from the Australian Institute of Aboriginal
    Studies and by research funds from the Department of Anthropology and Sociology,
    University of Queensland.

References

ANNUAL REPORTS, GOVERNMENT OF QUEENSLAND 1896 *et seq*. *Reports on the Aboriginals of
    Queensland*; later as *Annual Report of the Chief Protector of Aboriginals*; continued until the
    present as *Annual Reports*.
BARNES, J. A. 1954 Class and committees in a Norwegian island parish, *Human Relations*,
    7(1):39-58.
——1969 Networks and political process. In *Social networks in urban situations* (J. C. Mitchell
    ed.), pp. 51-76. Manchester University Press, Manchester.
BOTT, E. 1957/1971 *Family and social network*. Tavistock, London.
BROOM, L. *and* F. L. JONES 1973 *A blanket a year*. Australian National University Press,
    Canberra.
BURRIDGE, K. O. L. 1973 *Encountering Aborigines*. Pergamon Press, New York.
DAVIES, A. F. *and* S. ENCEL (eds) 1972 *Australian society*. Cheshire, Melbourne. Second ed.
FREIRE, P. 1973 *Pedagogy of the oppressed*. Pelican Book, Harmondsworth, Middlesex.
GANS, H. J. 1965 *The urban villagers*. The Free Press of Glencoe, New York.
KELLY, C. TENNANT 1935 Tribes on Cherburg settlement, Queensland, *Oceania*, V:461-73.
KOEPPING, K.-P. 1973 Participant observation: problem and promise of a research method,
    Occasional Papers in Anthropology, No. 1:31-67. University of Queensland.
LAUMANN, E. C. 1973 *Bonds of pluralism: the form and substance of urban social networks*: New York.
LONG, J. P. M. 1970 *Aboriginal settlements*. Australian National University Press, Canberra.
MARTIN, J. J. 1972 Suburbia: community and network. In *Australian society* (A. F. Davies *and*
    S. Encel eds), pp. 301-39. Cheshire, Melbourne.
MITCHELL, J. C. (ed.) 1969 *Social networks in urban situations*. Manchester University Press,
    Manchester.
REPORT 1897 *On the North Queensland Aborigines and the Native Police*. Brisbane.
ROWLEY, C. D. 1966 Some questions of causation in relation to Aboriginal affairs. In *Abori-
    gines in the Economy* (I. G. Sharp *and* C. M. Tatz eds), pp. 345-69. Jacaranda Press, Brisbane.
——1972 *The remote Aborigines*. Pelican Book edition, Harmondsworth, Middlesex.
SHARP, I. G. *and* C. M. TATZ, (eds) 1966 *Aborigines in the economy*. Jacaranda Press, Brisbane.
VALENTINE, C. A. *and* B. L. VALENTINE 1970 Making the scene, digging the action, and
    telling like it is: Anthropologist at work in a dark ghetto. In *Afro-American anthropology*
    (N. E. Whitten *and* J. F. Szwed eds), pp. 403-18. The Free Press of Glencoe, New York.
VIDICH, A. J. 1955 Participant observation and the collection and interpretation of data,
    American Journal of Sociology, 60:354-60.
WEBER, M. 1974 *The theory of social and economic organization*. The Free Press of Glencoe,
    New York.
WHITTEN, N. E. JR. *and* J. F. SZWED (eds) 1970 *Afro-American anthropology*. The Free Press of
    Glencoe, New York.

15 A critical appraisal of Anglican mission policy and practice in Arnhem Land, 1908-1939

Keith Cole

Introduction   Anglican mission policy and practice among Aborigines in Arnhem Land has frequently come under attack from anthropologists, government officials, pastoralists and the public at large. Some of these criticisms are justified, but often they seem to arise from prejudice and are not made with a full understanding of the basic facts of the situation. The purpose of this essay is to provide a critical appraisal of some of these basic facts with a view to a more adequate assessment of the contribution that Anglican missions have made to Aboriginal development and welfare. The Anglican mission policy outlined in analytical form in this essay is presented in the form of extracts from mission archival sources (such as they are), which to date have been unavailable to the general public.

The period 1908-1939 has been chosen for a variety of reasons:

(a) The first Anglican mission work in Arnhem Land started in 1908, giving a *terminus a quo*: archival material is not available after 1939 giving a *terminus ad quem*.

(b) The out-working policy on the actual mission stations themselves was very slow, due mainly to the adverse conditions under which they operated, and it was not until the 1930s that they were functioning reasonably well.

(c) The policies of protection and isolationism employed by both missions and governments, were instrumental in Aboriginal communities coming into existence, and formed the basis of later institutionalism and paternalism of Church and State, a circumstance which is subject to considerable scrutiny in these days of Aboriginal 'self-determination'. Although the Department of Aboriginal Affairs may state that these missions and settlements 'invite attention as focal points of the failure of the existing programmes to develop Aboriginal independence' (see the 'Submission of the Senate Standing Committee on the Social Environment', section 13, September 1973), they at least 'in certain areas' preserved the Aboriginal people from destruction and reserved large areas of their tribal land for current right to title.

A critical appraisal of Anglican mission policy during this period, 1908-1939 (so similar in every respect to that adopted by the Methodist Overseas Mission, the only other missionary agency to work in Arnhem Land), is therefore no mere academic exercise, but is of the greatest importance in understanding factors associated with social and cultural change among Aborigines down the years to the present time.

Government indifference and Aboriginal degradation, 1863-1939

Any appraisal of Anglican missionary policy in Arnhem Land must be assessed in the light of the current political and social background of the time.

As Arnhem Land is part of the Northern Territory, this involves a brief review of South Australian administration of the Territory from 1863 until 1911, and then of Commonwealth control from 1911.

South Australian administration of the Northern Territory, 1863-1911

The 48 years of the South Australian administration of the Northern Territory from 1863 until 1911 saw the frontiers of white expansion and occupation extend right to its northern boundary on the Arafura Sea. The reckless speculation in pastoral land in the early 1880s, involving almost the whole of Arnhem Land, coupled with the complete insensitivity of the white South Australian Government and people to any Aboriginal rights to land, led, in theory and frequently in practice, to the dispossession of the very basis of the black Australian's spiritual life and means of livelihood. The aggressive, encroaching white civilisation, which won its way through a superior knowledge of technology, supported where necessary by the brutal use of force, now posed the most serious threat to the Aborigines' hunting and foraging culture. White advancement was accomplished at the expense of the decimation of Aboriginal society. The more remote Aborigines of Arnhem Land did not escape the inexorable march of these white frontiers of 'civilisation'.

Despite the establishment of an administration, the completion of the overland telegraph line, the start of the north-south transcontinental railway and the early promise of pastoral development in the 1880s and 1890s, the final two decades of South Australian administration were years of stagnation and despondency, when little was attempted and nothing accomplished. As Bauer states (1964:194):

> Bitter failure and abject resignation characterised this last 21 years of South Australian control. The pastoral industry of the far north was at a very low ebb ... Mining ... production dropped rapidly. The attempts to establish small farms were complete failures ... As far as the Territory itself was concerned there was no improvement at all in the administration. The only enterprise which operated with reasonable satisfaction throughout the period was the railway, and even that lost money.

Aborigines and the Arnhem Land pastoral industry (1890-1910)

The expanding pastoral industry in the 1880s and 1890s had a most deleterious effect on the Aborigines. Numbers were attracted to European towns and pastoral stations by curiosity, and the craving for tobacco, alcohol and other Western commodities. Some came and went, but others remained to adopt what Elkin has termed 'intelligent parasitism'. Simple rations and a few necessities of life were provided by the pastoralists in exchange for work, often done poorly and without interest or enthusiasm. The sexual use of Aboriginal women frequently was implicit in the arrangement. Formal employment contracts were usually absent and the government made no effort to regulate the conditions of labour. The position in the towns was even worse.

The more remote Aborigines were not much better off. In the early 1880s, the whole of Arnhem Land was under lease. While the important Florida station established on the Goyder River was abandoned in 1893, within a decade the Eastern and African Cold Storage Company had leased the entire eastern half of Arnhem Land (49,858 sq. kilometres or 19,250 sq.

miles) to attempt what became known as the Arafura and Blue Mud Bay experiment. Although the experiment failed within six years on account of the unsuitability of the grass and inadequate mustering facilities, the effect on the Aborigines was most damaging. In retaliation for cattle spearing, the Eastern and African Cold Storage Company, with callous indifference to human life, from time to time employed two gangs of from ten to fourteen Aborigines, led by a European or 'half-caste', systematically to hunt and shoot at sight any Arnhemlander, man, woman or child, whom they encountered. The older Aborigines of the former Roper River Mission (now Ngukurr) tell vivid tales of those terrible times.

Summarising the situation of Aborigines during the 1890-1910 period, Bauer (1964:192-4) states:

> The position of the aborigines constitutes one of the most culpable matters which may be laid at the door of the South Australian Governments during this whole period . . . The aboriginal problem was to prove one of the thorniest passed on to the Commonwealth in 1911, and much of the later difficulties may be traced directly to the complete lack of regard for the rights and responsibilities of this people during the early years.

Arnhem Land Aborigines and the Commonwealth (1911-1939) The three decades of Commonwealth administration of the Northern Territory, from the transfer of authority from the South Australian Government on 1 January 1911 until World War II, were marked by a steady decline from an initial enthusiasm, through the stages of frustration and disillusionment to a low level of resignation and decadence, equalled only by the worst years of South Australian administration. The reasons for this deplorable state of affairs were numerous and diverse. Ignorance and misguided enthusiasm in the south was not helped by seven changes in government and thirteen changes in portfolio between 1911 and 1930. Moreover, the Federal Government was not prepared to invest full power in the Northern Territory Administrator, and certainly did not back him up when he was forced to make unpopular decisions. The demands of World War I led to a depletion of manpower and shipping and the shelving of different projects, while the depredations of the economic depression of the early 1930s hit the Territory as hard as, or even harder than, the Australian States. Then there were the continued problems caused by the two contrasting seasons of the 'wet' and the 'dry', the physiological and psychological problems which Europeans experienced through living in these semi-tropical conditions, and the isolation, which to date has found some answer only in the aeroplane. To compound these difficulties, there was the ignorance of Aboriginal culture on the part of administration and the white population in general.

These first three decades of Commonwealth administration saw an initial improvement in government attempts at Aboriginal welfare, in contrast with the poverty of those of the South Australian government. Legislation was introduced on the basis of Baldwin Spencer's report, which aimed at suitable education and employment and more adequate medical care for Aborigines in Darwin and on pastoral stations. Generally speaking, the welfare of Aborigines in Arnhem Land was left to the missions working there, evoking Bauer's comment (1964:257):

Mission stations in the back country seem to have had a generally beneficial effect on the aborigines with whom they came in contact, but these were a minority of the Territory's population. Being concerned primarily with the aborigines' souls, such groups chose their fields of labour as far from the detrimental effects of civilisation as possible . . . On the whole the missions were only partially successful in providing the aborigines with an introduction into European ways of making a living.

Bauer concludes his survey by stating (*ibid.*:259):

The whole aboriginal problem was one with which the Commonwealth tried, after a fashion, to come to grips; but despite some progress, especially in general health, little real advance was made in the direction of integrating the native black into European ways of life. The basic problem has not changed in the intervening 32 years; how to provide a naturally simple folk with an incentive to accept and adopt a more complex culture when their own has largely been destroyed.

In summary, the background to missionary enterprise in Arnhem Land was the almost complete indifference to Aboriginal culture and land rights on the part of the government, the economic exploitation of Aborigines by the pastoralists, and the almost universal attitude of superiority and intolerance of the white population at large.

Anglican Mission policy

Anglican missions in Arnhem Land have been undertaken solely by the Church Missionary Society of Australia (CMS), a voluntary, self-governing, evangelical society, which had been founded on the 'church but not the high-church principle'. Although the work has been under the jurisdiction of traditionally high church bishops of Carpentaria, generally speaking, theological differences of churchmanship have been eclipsed by the exigencies of the missionary situation and the desperate shortage of missionaries. The strong evangelistic aspirations of the CMS and the inevitable confrontation with Aboriginal culture, however, have posed a number of problems for the missionaries. (See Cole 1971a: Chs. 1 and 9.)

The CMS and the Methodist Overseas Mission (MOM: later incorporated in the United Church in North Australia, UCNA) have both been committed to the principle of mission comity: that is, co-operative agreement on the mutual division of territory into spheres of activity and on non-interference in one another's affairs. As elsewhere, the result of mission comity has been denominationalism by geography, so that Aboriginal Christians are either Anglican or Methodist not by choice, but by the chance of their birthplace.

The first CMS mission in Arnhem Land was commenced at Roper River in 1908. This mission was extended to the Emerald River on Groote Eylandt in 1921 and to Numbulwar on the mainland in 1952. The Emerald River Mission station, concerned until 1933 mainly with 'half-castes', was transferred to Angurugu, about twelve kilometres (eight miles) to the north, in 1943. From 1958 until 1966 the CMS was responsible for the Umbakumba Mission station on Groote Eylandt, until this was taken over by the Welfare

Department of the Northern Territory. The CMS commenced the Oenpelli Mission in the north-western corner of Arnhem Land in 1925, while the Roper River Mission (now Ngukurr) was handed over to Welfare in 1968. The three existing CMS communities of Angurugu, Oenpelli and Numbulwar are now within the Diocese of the Northern Territory, which came into being on 24 February 1968. The administration of the CMS mission stations has become more decentralised over the years. Prior to 1937, however, strict control was exercised by the Victorian CMS over the Roper River and Emerald River stations and by the New South Wales CMS over Oenpelli. From 1937, control of all work was co-ordinated by a Sydney-based committee directly responsible to the CMS Federal Council. Under a new constitution in 1944, the policy of CMS work among Aborigines re-emphasised evangelisation, but stressed the need for educational, medical, agricultural and industrial training which would

> induce the Aborigines to be provident and self-supporting; to develop greater self-respect; to lead them towards effective citizenship in the Commonwealth; and pureness of life as members of the Kingdom of God.

1906 — Humanitarian motive: 'to smooth the pillow of a dying race'

The Roper River Mission was commenced following an impassioned plea for mission work among Aborigines, which was made at the Australian Church Congress in 1906. In his address (Report of the Church Congress . . . 1906:118-21), Bishop Frodsham stated:

> We have an airy way of speaking about Australia being a white man's country. But Australia was first of all, a black man's country, and I have never heard that the black man invited us to take his property from him . . . A previous speaker at this Congress has said that the 'British were put by God into Australia to preach the Gospel to the heathen . . .' I have never heard a more complete condemnation of the stewardship of the Australian people. We have developed the country, and we have civilised it, but we have certainly done very little to preach the Gospel to the people we have dispossessed. The blacks have been shot and poisoned while they were wild and dangerous. They are now left to kill themselves with white vices where they have been 'tamed' — to quote a Queensland expression — but very few have received at our hands, either justice or consideration . . . The Aborigines are disappearing. In the course of a generation or two, at the most, the last Australian blackfellow will have turned his face to warm mother earth, and given back his soul to God Who gave it. Missionary work then may be only smoothing the pillow of a dying race, but I think if the Lord Jesus came to Australia he would be moved with great compassion for these poor outcastes, living by the wayside, robbed of their land, wounded by the lust and passion of a stronger race, and dying — yes, dying, like rotten sheep — with no man to care for their bodies or souls.

It is interesting to note that even at this early date the Church had some concern for Aboriginal land rights.

1908 — 'The benefits of our Christianity and civilisation' Contemporary CMS policy for the new Aboriginal Mission station at Roper River is reflected in the 'Instructions' (CMS *Gleaner,* June 1908) given in July 1908 to the pioneer missionary group:

> In going to the Roper River of the Northern Territory, you, my brethren, are entering upon the service of a distinctly national character. One of the most sacred obligations resting upon the people of this Commonwealth is to give to the original possessors of this Continent — the Aborigines — the benefits of our Christianity and civilisation . . . You are going, then, on behalf of the people of Australia, and specially as the honoured representatives of the Church of England in Australia . . . You are going to a service of great urgency. The Aboriginals need to be properly protected, properly taught various industries, and adequately cared for. Above everything else they require the uplifting influence of the Gospel of our Lord and Saviour Jesus Christ; and your supreme work is to present that to them.

Training of Aborigines 'to live independently' From the outset, the CMS stipulated that the Mission should be industrial and agricultural, as well as educational, medical and spiritual. This is reflected in the Mission minutes of the period, and is reiterated in the farewell Charge (CMS,A, *Minutes,* March 1913) given to H. E. Warren and W. G. Vizard on 11 March 1913 before leaving for the north:

> You are to give yourselves, at the outset at any rate, to this branch (agricultural) of the Mission, which, we repeat, must be specially developed . . . And we wish most earnestly to warn you against the fatal mistake of doing the work yourselves instead of training the Aborigines to do it . . . The Committee . . . is convinced of the absolute necessity of encouraging industrial work amongst members of child races such as the Aborigines of Australia . . . so that men and women connected with the Mission may soon be placed in their own homes and upon their own plots of ground, and be so taught that they shall eventually be able to live independently of material help from the Association . . .

In connection with industry, the Charge stated that:

> Aborigines have a liking for mechanical pursuits . . . Arrangements must be especially made in the daily time-table, which will permit of you taking some of the boys and the young men for definite practical instruction in carpentering, iron, and leather work, and such other simple technical occupations which commend themselves to you. We desire you to understand that we look to you for the early development of this department . . .

Institutionalism The basic policy adopted by the CMS (and other missions and subsequent government settlements) for the accomplishment of its aims was institutionalism. This is again reflected in the establishment of a mission station at Roper River and the subsequent Charge (*ibid.*) delivered to Warren and Vizard in 1913:

We are sure that one of the present outstanding needs of the Mission is the early erection of reasonably comfortable buildings for the use of the Staff, and for the Aborigines living on the Mission. It is possible that building material is not easily available, and that extra labour may be required for this. We expect the Staff to immediately consider this question, and to take such steps, or to make such recommendations to us as will afford the ordinary comforts which are necessary for effective work; and also give such good, simple, accommodation to the Aboriginal children as will help to inculcate those habits of order and self-respect which are so essential to healthy spiritual development...

This policy was reiterated as late as 1939, when the Victorian CMS General Secretary wrote (CMS *Open Door*, November 1939):

As bearing on such work as this, the Bishop of Carpentaria's reference to mission methods for aborigines in his recent address to his Synod are singularly apposite ... Whilst our work among these people is primarily evangelistic . . . we have also to try to lead them away from their nomadic food hunting stage of culture when they can live happily in village communities and produce their own food supply . . . This training takes infinite patience, for it is no use trying to advance too quickly by using implements that in his generation the aboriginal will never be able to purchase for himself.

Extension of mission activity by further missions (institutions)

The need for expansion of the work into other areas was emphasised in the Charge (*ibid.*). This in turn would lead to the establishment of further mission stations as institutions:

You are to remember that the Mission Station at the Roper was deliberately established to be the base for the extension work. The Staff is expected to constantly pray over, and be making preparations for the establishment of one or more outstations in the near future. A strong, progressive, and safe forward policy must dominate the Mission. We have an urgent extension responsibility to those other sheep, especially those to the North of the Roper River, and we shall look forward to receiving recommendations from the Staff on this important matter without unnecessary delay.

Work among 'half-castes'   Largely through the exploitation of Aboriginal women by non-Aboriginal men (whites and Asians), by the 1930s the Territory had a 'half-caste' problem of major dimensions. A police census in 1929 listed 469 such 'half-castes' north of latitude 20°S. Bauer states (1964: 259) that the 'Commonwealth's reaction to the problem, with its obvious moral overtones, was largely on an emotional basis'.

The CMS and the MOM shared with the government in the care of 'half-caste' children. These children had become wards of the State, were taken from their Aboriginal mothers, and were placed in homes or on mission stations. Anglican policy in Bishop Newton's letter to the CMS Victorian Branch on 12 August 1918 (CMS,A, Victorian Branch 1918) read in part:

It is important that the half-caste children be treated and dealt with separately, distinct from aborigines. There must be a separate establishment for half-caste children and the teaching of trades must be the most important part of the teaching and training, next of course to religion. The tendency of the half-caste is to sink to the level of aborigines . . .

Comments

(a) The mission attempted the care of Aborigines when government did not. This action was a significant factor in the preservation of the life (though perhaps not the culture) of the Aboriginal people.

(b) Prior to 1908 little had been done by the CMS for Aborigines, even though the CMS Auxiliary was formed in 1825 for this specific purpose. (Cole 1971a:7.) Marsden's Parramatta Seminary taught half a dozen Aborigines for several years; the Black Town School was undertaken by the mission for just over a year; the two settlements at Wellington Valley (NSW) and Moreton Bay (Qld) lasted for only about a decade. Work started in Victoria at Lake Condah and Lake Tyers in the late 19th century continued into the 20th but employed a chaplain only. Thus, between 1892 (when the Australian CMS became autonomous) and 1907, of the 80 Australian CMS missionaries sent out to various places in (for example) Africa, Asia and China, only two were sent to work among Aborigines (in Victoria).

(c) CMS policy was rigidly administered from the south, leading sometimes to misunderstanding and questionable decisions, despite periodic visits by mission officials and by the Bishop of Carpentaria.

(d) The siting of the first mission station at Roper River was unfortunate, as it was virtually a no-man's land — or rather the meeting place of about ten different tribal groups. There was thus no major tribal language which could be learnt. No anthropological study had been made (or perhaps could have been made) prior to the decision to commence the mission there, which might have suggested a more clearly defined tribal area.

(e) The motives for mission work were, then:
    (i) evangelistic;
    (ii) humanitarian — 'to smooth the pillow of a dying race', dispossessed of its land;
    (iii) to provide 'the benefits of our Christianity and civilisation';
    (iv) to train Aborigines 'to live independently, for employment in industry and agriculture'.

(f) The means employed to accomplish these ends was institutionalism, in early years through the teaching of children and young people in dormitories. Such a policy, however, laid the foundation for the settled welfare communities of the 1950s and 1960s, contrasting greatly with the semi-nomadic hunting and foraging of Aborigines.

(g) Pioneering mission work in these early days was little short of heroic, and required great dedication and personal sacrifice. Material comforts were few, and all buildings had to be constructed from local timber which the mission milled; food was frequently short; and there was isolation. Government support throughout the 1920s and 1930s was a mere £250 for the educational work — the rest came from voluntary church donations.

Institutionalisation for 'civilisation'

Mission institutions (and later, government settlements) were seen to be vehicles of Christianity and civilisation. By implication, mission, government and the white population in general, considered Aboriginal culture and life-style to be primitive, degrading and uncivilised. Conversion to Christianity and education to become citizens of the Commonwealth (with assimilation-ist presuppositions) was the basic philosophy.

The mission at this early stage concentrated on children and their education in the dormitory and in the school. Aboriginal family groups camped on the fringe of the mission stations and came and went at pleasure, leaving the children in the dormitory or taking them away as they wished. Aboriginal families did not start to settle on the stations in any numbers until the late 1930s, were dispersed during the war years, and did not become fully insti-tutionalised until the time of the massive welfare assimilationist programme of the 1950s.

Official, non-mission attitudes to Anglican mission institutionali-sation Conflicting official non-mission attitudes to institutionalised Arn-hem Land missions come from the Bleakley Report (1928) and from Thom-son's Reports (1936, 1937).

(a) *Bleakley Report* (1928:24-29): Bleakley spoke warmly of the Oenpelli and Groote Eylandt Missions and, rightly, less favourably of the Roper River Mission. After reviewing these and other missions, he strongly defended the need for institutions and the advantage of the mission system:

> These missions are all working on right lines; the officers making themselves conversant with the native language and customs and en-deavouring, without pressing the white man's civilization upon them, to induce them, by the education of the young, to see the advantages of the settled and industrious life . . .

He went on to say:

> Objections are frequently voiced against the establishment of mission stations as a measure for the protection of the primitive aboriginal. Anthropologists have expressed the view that such institutions, by encouraging them to leave their tribal grounds for the reserve, cause disintegration of their tribal life and eventual extinction . . . The contention of the objectors is that, beyond reserving for their use suitable and sufficient country and protecting them from outside inter-ference, nothing should be done to interfere with their living their own life in their own way.
>
> These views, though born of sincere desire for the welfare of the natives and worthy of earnest consideration in any measures for the betterment of the race, apparently overlook certain important facts. The native, once having come into contact with the white man or alien and acquired a taste for his foods and luxuries, is not likely to remain a contented savage. There are few places now left of which it can be said that the natives are absolutely uncontaminated . . . The disintegration of tribal life, already encompassed by the encroachment of the white man, has created the need for something more, in the way of protection and relief . . . And this need can best be served by experienced men, with benevolent motives . . .

In outlining the advantages of the mission system, Bleakley stated:

> In the first place, the cost of management is less, and the missions can obtain the type of worker who undertakes the work from missionary, and not mercenary, motives and is likely to have more sympathy with the people.
> The Government, with its tremendous task of developing the country, would be unwise to burden itself . . . with the worry of management of a number of charitable institutions . . . The mission bodies now operating are keen to undertake such work and co-operate with the Government for the betterment of the people.

Bleakley then spoke about training programmes and the great need for subsidies, and suggested that 'Special encouragement should be given to genuine effort to successfully develop the industrial and social side of the work.'

Bleakley went on to say that the most difficult problem was that of the 'half-castes' — 'how to check the breeding of them and how best to deal with those now with us'.

> All half-castes of illegitimate birth, whether male or female, should be rescued from the camps, whether station or bush, and placed in institutions for care and training . . . The education should be simple in nature, but aimed at making them intelligent workmen and fitting to protect themselves in business dealings.

He summarised his recommendations regarding 'half-castes' as:

> To check as far as possible the breeding of half-castes by:
> (a) strict enforcement of laws for protection and control of female aboriginals;
> (b) encouraging immigration of white women into the Territories;
> (c) removal of obstacles to having married men in positions of control over, or on places employing, aboriginals. Collect all illegitimate half-castes, male and female, under sixteen years of age, not otherwise being satisfactorily educated, and place in Aboriginal Industrial Mission Homes for education and vocational training.
> Make education of all half-castes under sixteen years of age compulsory . . .
> Transfer those with preponderance of white blood to European institutions at early age, for absorption into the white population after vocational training . . .

(b) *Thomson Reports* (1936, 1937): Thomson's recommendations were first made in 1936 (followed by further ones in 1937), following two very important events for the future of Aborigines which I discuss later — namely, the proclamation of the Arnhem Land Reserve in 1931 and the manifest injustice of applying a white judicial system to Aboriginal cases, following the Caledon Bay killings. Thomson recommended:

> That the remnant of native tribes in Federal Territory not yet disorganised or detribalized by prolonged contact with alien culture be absolutely segregated, and that it be the policy of the Government to preserve intact their social organization, their social and political institutions, and their culture in its entirety.

That the native reserve Arnhem Land be created an inviolable reserve for the native inhabitants, and that steps be taken at once to establish and maintain the absolute integrity of this reserve . . .
That the whole policy of administration of native justice be revised . . . that special courts, suitably constituted, be established to deal with natives and native offences. That the change of policy of the Commonwealth Government be marked by the establishment of a separate Department of Native Affairs under a trained director . . .

In his 1936 Report, Thomson attacked the institutionalisation of Aborigines:

It is assumed almost invariably, that the first essential in dealing with Australian Aboriginals is to curtail their wanderings, to settle them either in a compound or an institution, or to remove their children from their custody to these places in order that they shall grow up without any knowledge of the life and customs of their own people . . . It can truly be said that the road to progress of the white man in the Northern Territory is paved with the tombstones of the Aboriginals.

His attack on institutionalism naturally included missions. He wrote:

The social structure *in toto* should be preserved as an essential factor in the life of these people . . . the nomadic habits of these people must be regarded as an integral part of their culture. The collecting of natives, not detribalised, into compounds or institutions should be prohibited. If it is desired to teach Christianity to these people, it should be insisted that the Christian teacher or missionary be prepared to visit the people in their own country, and not to gather them about a station or Mission school.

CMS response to the Bleakley and Thomson Reports The CMS reacted favourably to recommendations of the Bleakley Report. The missionaries' preoccupation with 'half-caste' work at Roper River and Groote Eylandt, however, came under censure from the mission executives in Melbourne, leading to the unfortunate recall of the leading missionary, Rev. H. E. de M. Warren (Cole 1971b). The change in emphasis from a 'half-caste' to a full-blood mission enterprise on Groote Eylandt was not easily achieved, and it was not until the station was transferred to Angurugu in 1943 that direct work among the full-bloods of Groote Eylandt became effective.

CMS reaction to Thomson's Reports is reflected in the Mission's 'Commission of Delegation' which visited the mission stations in July-August 1940. After investigating the Arnhem Land stations, the CMS Commission observed:

That the present station method is essential for the stable continuance of our work. We have found encouraging indications of the desire as well as openings for more evangelistic, educational and ameliorative ministrations from the stations as centres. The 'going bush' method should be fruitfully possible in adapted form during the favourable seasons of the year, when small bands could camp among and influence parties of nomad blacks . . . That our missionaries should devote at least one hour each day in applied study of a tribal dialect, even at the expense of urgent station responsibilities. It would be foolish to suggest that the usual method of intercourse in English has been fruitless, but the harder way of acquiring and using aboriginal speech and thought would be speedier and more effective. The use of 'pidgin' English should be avoided.

Comments

(a) In summary, Bleakley favoured institutionalism for 'civilisation'; Thomson, segregation for the preservation of Aboriginal culture. Bleakley favoured missions for cheaper service and more dedicated personnel; Thomson recommended that missions should close their institutions and 'go bush' with the Aborigines. Both Bleakley and Thomson deplored 'the half-caste problem'.

(b) Mission preoccupation with the education and training of young Aborigines and 'half-castes' left contacts with adults for the work situation as casual meetings. This emphasised the institutional aspect of the missions and lessened the sense of urgency of the need to study Aboriginal languages and culture.

(c) The CMS Commission recommendation that missionaries should 'go bush' in the dry season and achieve some facility in the local Aboriginal language was hampered in the first instance by lack of staff, aggravated by the disruption of the war years. Continued use of English, expansion programmes in the Welfare decades of the 1950s and the 1960s, and academic incompetence put language study and speech in the background until very recent times. The CMS stands culpable in this, which has made its central task of evangelism less effective.

(d) Thomson's advocacy of 'inviolable reserves', implying complete segregation and isolation, was and is no answer. To put a stop to the atrocities committed by European beachcombers and Japanese pearlers at 'watering stations', yes; but complete segregation to the extent of not allowing Aborigines to go outside the reserve would have been an infringement of their basic human rights and contrary to their ultimate welfare.

As the Berndts remarked (1954:184) about Thomson's recommendations:

> . . . complete segregation is today only an ideal, which could not be put into practice. It would, moreover, be unsatisfactory to the natives themselves, and especially to these coastal Arnhem Landers who have had so many long years of alien contact. The most enlightened course is to bring about their gradual adjustment to changing conditions, trying to keep the best elements in their traditional culture, and at the same time introducing them to the new culture and society to which they must eventually adapt themselves.

Isolation the first step toward assimilation or integration or apartheid?

The proclamation of the Arnhem Land Reserve in 1931 meant the preservation of the Arnhem Land Aborigines; it also provided the basis for land rights claims, and could lead to eventual community self-determination. Reference to the philosophy underlying the proclamation of Aboriginal reserves is of importance.

Mission reserves   The CMS (as with other missions) obtained mission leases, usually over about 200 square miles of territory in which the settlement was situated. This enabled the Society to erect buildings and carry on their work.

Aboriginal reserves   As far as can be determined, the Bishop of Carpentaria was the first to advocate the proclamation of the whole of Arnhem Land as an Aboriginal reserve. He wrote to the Victorian CMS in 1918 (CMS,A, letter, August 12, 1918):

> I would suggest a bold and big policy, I would suggest that the authorities be approached and asked to declare the whole of the North East of the Territory a reserve for aborigines from about the Rose River on the South to the Alligator River on the West and hence to the coast. I do not know what native population there is in that corner, but I fancy that if there were many anywhere it is there. I would suggest that the whole of that area be closed to white settlement for at least fifty years and that Missions be established to get in touch with and influence the people before the country is opened to settlement and then policy can be defined . . .

The proclamation of such a reserve was also advocated by Bleakley (1928:35). He was not in favour, however, of the proposals being made in some quarters for 'a self-governing Aboriginal State'. Nor could he support the idea of the 'complete segregation of all wandering natives'. Rather,

> the shielding of the race from the evils of contact with the civilized races is urgently necessary, but until, through the education of the growing generation, the tribes are induced to voluntarily seek the sanctuary of the benevolent institutions established for their care, it will be better to concentrate effort on the amelioration of the lot of those suffering from detribalization and the tightening up of the machinery for moral protection. Any wholesale herding into reserves in strange country would be unwise.

The National Missionary Council of Australia, comprising the major non-Catholic mission societies and boards, at its annual meeting on 11 April 1930 called 'the attention of the Missionary Societies to the excellent report issued by Mr. J. W. Bleakley on the aborigines in the hope that this will be utilized as fully as possible for educational purposes'. The NMCA (NMC,A, *Minutes*) also urged action regarding the proclamation of the Arnhem Land Reserve: 'That the whole of Arnhem Land, when available, be made an aboriginal reserve if possible, or the unalienated portion of it be set apart as a sanctuary for aborigines.' Thomson's advocacy of complete segregation of Aborigines and that the inviolability of the reserve be guaranteed has already been noted.

Comments
(a) The Arnhem Land Reserve was created to try to prevent unauthorised *entry* of non-Aboriginal people, but not to restrict Aborigines from moving out from and back into the Reserve. Thomson advocated complete segre-

gation and isolation, and prevention of Aborigines from moving out of the Reserve, to keep them from the detrimental effects of foreign culture contact. (b) What was the purpose of the Reserve? For Thomson, segregation for the preservation of the Aboriginal and his culture and social structure *in toto*. For *Bleakley* (followed by the CMS and Welfare), segregation for the preservation of Aborigines, so that they might be trained, 'by the education of the young, to see the advantages of the settled and industrious life.' (c) The use of the Reserve in subsequent history:

(i) The Reserve has been used to implement Bleakley's views. Government policy in the 1950s was clearly assimilationist. Thus, the reserves were for the preliminary training of Aborigines in the wider Australian way of life until they could be ushered into and absorbed into that way of life. This attitude came under criticism from the National Missionary Council.

(ii) The Reserve has protected land which now can form the basis for claims to it, as traditionally owned land, put forward by Aboriginal communities: i.e. the basis of Mr Justice Woodward's recommendations.

(iii) The Reserve has protected communities, which can now become self-determining under current government policy. These communities are not necessarily homogeneous.

(iv) The Reserve has protected tribal land, which enables families to decentralise and to move back 'to their own country', a feature of current government policy.

(d) The Reserve, then, does not necessarily represent isolation as the first step to assimilation, but could be the means for forwarding policies of assimilation, integration, self-determination, or even apartheid.

Culture conflict

Culture includes anything in the life of an ethnic group which points to its historic traditions as the expression of its particular ethos among other peoples of the world. Aboriginal culture is therefore that particular expression of the religious and social life of Aborigines which is distinctive from other life-styles. Aboriginal culture speaks of the life of Aborigines in the world, the corporate ideas and emotions which influence them, their links with the past, and their desire to express themselves in material creations of their own as well as in language, religion and art. *Acculturation* refers to what goes on when cultures meet. Students of acculturation distinguish a number of different acculturative processes — such as, addition, loss, substitution syncretism, invention and rejection. Acculturation, generally speaking, is dependent upon:

(i) the degree of difference between the two cultures that are in contact;

(ii) the circumstances and intensity of contact;

(iii) the relative prestige enjoyed by the two cultures;

(iv) the particular representatives or agents through whom the cultures meet; and

(v) the direction in which cultural influences are encouraged to flow.

Bearing these factors in mind, it is not surprising that the dominating, aggressive white culture backed by vast economic, technological and scientific resources should have had an immediate, devastating effect on

Aboriginal culture. Thus the preservation of the Aboriginal culture (and the people themselves) could be effected in the first place only through isolation and protection.

Anglican missions and Aboriginal languages It would be untrue to say that, in the early years, the Anglican missionaries in Arnhem Land were not interested in the language and the life-style of the Aborigines among whom they were working. On the other hand, it would be equally untrue to say that very much was done regarding language study and systematic research into their culture. In contrast to other parts of the world where they were working, hardly any attempt was made by Anglican missionaries in Arnhem Land to learn the local languages. This was due to a variety of reasons:
(i) The non-tribal site at the Roper Mission and the detribalised state of the Aborigines who camped there from time to time.
(ii) The emphasis on 'half-caste' work on Groote Eylandt until the latter part of the 1930s.
(iii) The necessary preoccupation of the early missionaries with 'bread and butter' matters of supplies, sawing and milling timber for houses, building construction and rebuilding after floods, growing food and generally maintaining the life of the station.
(iv) General missionary activity being centred mainly on the education of children and young people, the teaching being done in English.
(v) The inability of the missionaries, through lack of training and academic background, to 'reduce' a spoken language to writing, to prepare dictionaries, grammars, primers etc.

The situation at Oenpelli (which became a mission station in 1925) was the one exception. Here the Aborigines were tribally more homogeneous, and through the efforts of a CMS missionary, Mrs G. R. Harris, assisted by A. Capell (then of the University of Sydney), parts of the New Testament and the Liturgy were translated into Gunwinggu in the late 1930s and early 1940s.

In general terms, however, CMS missionaries, until recent years, have relied solely on English as the general means of communication, education and religious instruction; and this has been a great handicap to a full understanding of the culture of the Aborigines with whom they have been working.

Anglican missions and Aboriginal culture Generally speaking, although CMS missionaries were interested in Aboriginal life-style and customs, they considered that Aborigines were 'a dying race', that their culture was uncivilised and their religion completely depraved. This again was accentuated by the detribalised state of the Roper River Aborigines where the first mission was established. N. B. Tindale (then of the South Australian Museum), accompanied the missionaries who founded the Groote Eylandt Mission in 1921 and 'spent some fifteen months on and around Groote Eylandt and in the Roper River District, paying special attention to entomology' (1925-26:61). His research at that time was important, as was that of F. Rose (1960), who did his research at Umbakumba in the late 1930s. Some interest was displayed by Messrs Perriman, Dyer and Lousada on Groote Eylandt, but they had neither the training nor the time to undertake any serious study of the Warnindilyaugwa. Thus, anthropological studies, even of an elementary nature, were not undertaken by CMS missionaries. It was left to A. P. Elkin in the 1930s to draw the attention of the Society to the necessity of anthropological training. Even this training frequently went by default because of staffing pressures.

With little understanding of Anthropology, the effect on Aboriginal culture of the mission's policy of seeking to establish village communities 'to try to lead them away from their food hunting stage of culture' was just not realised. Yet there is a dilemma here. The Aborigines traditionally have migrated to any place where Western commodities could be obtained, even outside the reserves. As a result, they would have come into contact with Western civilisation whether or not the missions had been there.

The early missionaries seemed fairly ignorant of the 'secret' life of Aborigines and of their ritual, stemming as it did and does from their belief in the all-pervasive forces of creation and fertility, as exemplified in their singing of the great totemic heroes and of the land in which they lived: and the rituals they performed ensured the continuity of a life they knew and appreciated. The early missionaries, however, did not try to interfere in these matters when they did know about them; rather, they sought to supersede these ideas with Christian beliefs.

The effects of white civilisation on the Aboriginal life-style was more apparent in everyday life, rather than in the religious realm. The mission, work patterns, ration supplies, housing, gardening, industry, iron tools, guns and clothing, dramatically changed the traditional hunting and foraging pattern of their social existence. Also, mission pressures for (what they perceived to be) a more equitable distribution of women, mainly to provide wives for unmarried men and so lessen fighting and quarrelling over women, were not felt to any great extent during the period 1908-1939. This was left to the later stage, when Aborigines adopted a more settled way of life on the mission settlements.

Comments

(a) While it was obvious that acculturation was taking place at the material level, the deeper implications of settled life on the social patterns of the Aborigines were not apparent to the Anglican missionaries working in Arnhem Land. This was due largely to their lack of understanding of local languages and of their religious beliefs and rituals.

(b) When trying to assess the extent of acculturation, it should be realised that the numbers of Aborigines involved were very small.

(i) Thus in a report on *Roper River,* published in December 1939, it was stated: 'On the station there are 75 Aborigines, mostly children, young people and 18 half-castes' (CMS *Gleaner,* December 1939). (I have not the exact figures of the baptism of full-bloods up to 1939, but probably not more than 10 would have been baptised before that date.)

(ii) On *Groote Eylandt,* the first baptisms of full-blood Aborigines did not take place until 1949. Moreover, at the special service for the unveiling of Wynne Evan's Memorial, the exceptionally large congregation made up of 'staff, half-castes, station and bush Aborigines, numbered 105, made up of 69 Aboriginal men, 10 Aboriginal women, 24 half-caste boys and girls, and 11 staff workers and half-caste helpers'.

(iii) At *Oenpelli*, the October 1939 report reflected the average number of Aborigines on the station: 31 men, 25 women, 12 girls, 11 boys, 8 old people and 6 babies, a total of 93. By that time, only 14 Aborigines, 8 men and 6 women had been baptised.

The 1930s — the 'new look' thwarted

The 1930s were significant for Aboriginal development in Arnhem Land for a variety of reasons. The missions had overcome their initial founding problems and were settling down as benevolent, paternalistic institutions. The Reserve had been proclaimed in 1931, but continued alien contact on the coast was having a detrimental effect upon the Aborigines, leading to killings by Aborigines in eastern Arnhem Land. The remarkable CMS 'Peace Expedition' and the subsequent farcical trials, brought the plight of the Arnhem Landers before the notice of the Australian public in a very dramatic way, leading to Thomson's 'Pacification Expedition' and greater government concern for Aboriginal welfare. The use of aeroplanes by the missions, by the Flying Doctor and by the Qantas flying boat base at Umbakumba, became a significant factor in breaking down barriers of isolation. At the same time, it brought Aborigines into closer contact with the outside world. The influence of Elkin's work was beginning to usher in a new age for Aborigines. The promised 'new look', however, was rudely shattered by the outbreak of World War II, the bombing of Darwin in 1942, and the fortressing of Australia's northern frontiers: the dawning of a new day was to be delayed for some time yet.

Mission paternalism   During the 1930s, the Anglican missions in Arnhem Land were just starting to become focal points of contact between Western civilisation and Aboriginal culture. This is reflected in the report of the CMS delegation (CMS,A,1940) which visited the three missions in July and August 1940, following the destruction of the Roper River settlement by a flood in 1940. Recommendations in the report include:
1. That the Society's work among Aborigines and Half-castes is worth while.
2. That the present station method is essential for the stable continuance of the work.
3. That our missionaries should devote at least one hour each day in applied study of a tribal dialect.
4. That experience indicates that the aborigines can be encouraged to successful community effort in producing food under conditions that will tend to effect happy village community life.
5. The present staff situation is tragic.
6. Re Child Marriages, Tribal: 'When the girls on the station are married — very often to men much older than themselves — much of the work of the missionary is lost. In view of our experience we would urge that the missionaries explore the possibilities of 'purchasing' if necessary, the right of consent to marriage . . .'

The suggested general policy for the future re-emphasised the chief aim as being evangelisation. It recognised that this can be accomplished when missionaries learn the language and customs of the people and Aborigines are taught the gospel. It underlined the importance of medical work and that 'Europeanising of the Aborigines as regards food and clothing is to be kept to the simplest standards compatible with progress', and that 'To induce the aborigines to be provident and self-supporting (thereby maintaining self-respect) suitable industrial measures are to be adopted, tending towards effective citizenship in the Commonwealth and purposefulness of life as members of the Kingdom of God.'

Violation of the Arnhem Land Reserve The proclamation of the Arnhem Land Reserve of 96,262 square kilometres (37,167 square miles) took place in 1931. Government records and those of the Methodist Overseas missions on the north Arnhem Land coast, together with the research of Donald Thomson, indicate the extent to which that Reserve was being violated by unauthorised aliens, including white Australians; and they also made clear the deleterious effect that these contacts were having on Aborigines. The bitterness engendered by these undesirable contacts came to a head with the killing by Aborigines of five Japanese pearlers at Caledon Bay in September 1932, followed by the killing at Woodah Island, in August 1933, of Constable McColl, a member of the police party sent to investigate the earlier incident. In the following November two white beachcombers were also killed on Woodah Island. When these events became known, there was an immediate outcry, and a demand for a police punitive party to go and 'teach the Caledon Bay Aborigines a lesson'.

CMS Arnhem Land 'Peace Expedition' The remarkable CMS Arnhem Land Peace Expedition of Messrs Warren, Dyer and Fowler from November 1933 until March 1934 brought peace to the troubled western coast of the Gulf; the self-confessed killers were contacted and gave themselves up, and were taken by Dyer and Fred Gray to Darwin. The supposed Aboriginal uprising which was taken to be threatening the white population of the Northern Territory was nothing more than a rumour. The subsequent trials of the killers revealed the complete inadequacy of the judicial system in dealing with Aboriginal cases of this kind. The harsh sentences, subsequently quashed, drew the plight of Aborigines to the attention of the general Australian public more effectively than anything else could have. (See Berndt 1954:Chs. 13-18; Cole 1971b: Ch. 9; and Cole 1972:Ch. 7.)

Thomson's 'Pacification Expedition' The killings and the unsettled state of the east Arnhem Land Aborigines also led to Thomson's 'Pacification Expedition' in 1935-1936. His valuable observations and reports have already been noted; but the complete absence of any reference whatsoever to the contribution made by the missionaries (see above), can only lead to the conclusion of unwarranted bias and prejudice on his part against missionaries. The discussions inside and outside government circles resulting from Thomson's reports nevertheless added considerably to the growing interest and concern for Aborigines of eastern Arnhem Land.

The use of the aeroplane The 1930s saw the use by missionaries of the aeroplane in trying to combat problems of distance and isolation. As far as the CMS was concerned, this experiment was first undertaken by Keith

Langford Smith, who, despite a variety of mishaps and adventures, flew the 'Sky Pilot' from 1930 until the final crash at Oenpelli in 1933. Fenton's Flying Doctor service had also pioneered this aspect of medical work about this time. The establishment of the Qantas flying boat base at Port Langdon on the north-eastern corner of Groote Eylandt, accompanied by the formation of Fred Gray's Aboriginal settlement at Umbakumba, was a further significant point of contact between Groote Eylandters and white culture. Initially, the proposal was viewed by the CMS authorities in the south with some alarm, in their concern about undesirable contacts with Aborigines of the Reserve. Through the National Missionary Council, however, the CMS was able to gain assurance from the Minister of the Interior that the interests of the Aborigines would be protected. (See Cole 1971b:38.)

A. P. Elkin's writings   The writings and lectures of A. P. Elkin (who was then head of the Department of Anthropology, in the University of Sydney), in the late 1930s, had a profound influence on governments, mission executives and missionaries, anthropologists, churchmen and the populace in general. Many were seeing, as they had never done before, the social conditions of Aboriginal people and the necessity for additional missionary support along with the need for radical changes in government policy. The latter is demonstrated by the Initial Conference of Commonwealth and State Aboriginal Authorities held in Canberra, 21-23 April 1937. (See Aboriginal Welfare 1937.)

The 'new look' shattered   The promise of 'a new deal' for Aborigines (which had been materialising during the 1930s and seemed destined to herald a new day for Aboriginal welfare), was rudely shattered by the outbreak of World War II. Although delayed until the era of post-war reconstruction, interest in Aboriginal matters was further quickened by the contact which many servicemen had with Aborigines during the war years. The 'new look', when it did come, proved to be the commencement of a vast government welfare programme, in which the missions were to be heavily subsidised and almost all Aborigines became members of settled communities. Few Aboriginal family groups remained semi-nomadic after that time.

Conclusions

Mission commitment   Even though certain aspects of mission policy and practice may come under criticism, the fact remains that the early missionaries really cared for Aboriginal people. They may have been somewhat paternalistic, but they did show kindness and concern in a practical way for a people who had been hunted and massacred in the bush, despised and kicked around on the pastoral stations, or were killing themselves with white vices in the towns. The policy may have been rather colonial, but the first missionaries worked alongside Aborigines from dawn to dark, under the most 'primitive' conditions, for a mere pittance even for those days, while the womenfolk dispensed medicine, taught in the school, ran the dormitory and cared for their own families. They were people of compassion.

Missions and incipient self-determination   Incipient Aboriginal self-determination was inherent within early mission policies. Aborigines were taught trades and agriculture to enable them to become self-supporting, and in this sense self-determining. The first stage was that of instruction, which required institutionalisation. The next stage was employment, not outside the Reserve (which would have been detrimental), but on or near the mission stations. This was a most difficult undertaking, because of the scarcity of appropriate natural resources within the area.

Moreover, on mission settlements Aborigines were free to come and go as they wished. The only compulsion lay in the attraction of the mission stores and rations, for which Aborigines had to work. Thus C. D. Rowley, in my judgement, overemphasises mission 'control' and underestimates the 'work role' of Aborigines when he states (1970:251):

> It was, however, much easier and cheaper (for Governments) to delegate difficult functions to the missionaries, who were ready to assume them. It was also easier where former nomads had 'sat down' and come to regard living off the land as a hardship, to drift into the institutional situation where the missions set up, legally or otherwise, a theocracy in the reserve, so that eventually it controlled the people by controlling the assets, and especially the stores and rations.

Living off the land was hard, very hard, for much of the year, otherwise the people would not have camped on mission station fringes. Again, Aborigines had to work for their rations, especially in the earlier days. It was not so much control by a mission, as the demand for stores, rations and Western-derived foods that was the operative factor in Aborigines coming to mission stations. But, again, it was self-determination.

The education and training of 'half-castes' on the Anglican mission stations at Roper and Groote have enabled most of them to assume positions of responsibility in Australian society, and have given them a great measure of self-respect and certainly of self-determination.

Mission institutions and Aboriginal culture   Several comments need to be made on the highly controversial question: 'To what extent have mission institutions destroyed Aboriginal culture in Arnhem Land?'

The Aboriginal hunting and food-gathering economy was very uncertain, demanding constant movement from place to place, with times of hardship and hunger. It is not surprising that semi-nomadic 'communities' should camp from time to time at any place where food and commodities were available. Nor is it surprising that later they should settle permanently around mission and government settlements — with the freedom to go on temporary 'walk about' to visit other 'communities' and temporarily to hunt and gather food. All Aboriginal informants tell me that they do not wish to return to this way of life: they still want to hunt and fish from time to time, but consider that they could not support themselves permanently in this way. Current decentralisation moves by Aborigines back to their own country do not constitute a return to their former way of life. Decentralised small communities are currently seeking government subsidies for vehicles, equipment, housing, education, health and employment projects. These are miniatures of the larger communities from which they had come, but with localised control by themselves. Their activities are supported only to a limited extent by hunting and foraging. Moreover, the great advantage of small community self-determination could be offset by the 'power of the purse' moving from the benevolent (though perhaps paternalistic) mission to a remote government bureaucracy. This is the Achilles' heel of contemporary self-determination policies for communities of any size.

Anglican mission communities, as already noted, were very small indeed before the late 1930s, becoming larger and more settled only in the 1950s. Even then, each community was hardly what Rowley terms 'a theocracy on the Reserve' — although mission paternalism had Utopian overtones, seen in attitudes to polygyny, discipline for moral offences and the regimentation of conduct.

Cultures do not remain static, and the processes of acculturation are accelerated by intensity of contact. Current self-determination policies are giving a new sense of freedom and self-respect to Aboriginal people, but they are not reverting to their pre-European contact life-style and do not wish to do so. But, as with the case of earlier 'Macassan' contact (see Berndt 1954), they are in the process of skilfully adapting their culture to meet the demands of the present situation. Instead of destroying their culture, the missions have provided a focal point of community, which gave the Aborigines breathing space to prepare themselves to face the onslaught of Western civilisation. As Rowley comments (1970:246-7):

> Destruction of Aboriginal populations was eventually arrested, partly by the efforts of the missions on the large reserves . . . These missions saw their social and educational function as preparing the people, by their efforts in tuition and conversion, to participate in European society. In practice their great material achievement was to present, within the tribal lands, enough of the counter attractions needed in food supplies, clothes, steel and other industrial goods to keep people there. By so doing they made possible an interim process of adjustment based on Aboriginal purposes.

It should also be noted that the 'secret' and religious life of the Aborigines has continued while they have lived in mission communities. Rituals which were frowned upon were held elsewhere, while circumcision, mortuary and other rites have always been commonplace on Arnhem Land mission stations.

Christianity and Aboriginal culture Only a few observations on this complex subject can be made here. The inevitability of some 'rice Christians' and the identification of Christianity with education, clothing, speaking English and a Western life-style, is acknowledged, although it does not appear to have been as widespread as some have claimed. From the figures given above, the large increase in baptisms did not take place until the late 1940s through the 1960s. Thus evangelisation from a mission viewpoint has been slow, and has shown fruit only within the last twenty years. From the viewpoint of the non-Christian Aboriginal, twenty years is an extremely short time to expect any serious attack on his age-old traditions. A more realistic threat to Aboriginal religion does not come from Christianity, but from a growing materialism and the clamour for motor vehicles, transistors, tape recorders, alcohol and Western films. These are the things capturing the minds of the younger generation of Aborigines, now made more possible through the availability of much more money.

While earlier missionaries denounced all Aboriginal religious belief and ritual as being 'of the devil', modern Christian theologians are realising that Aboriginal traditional beliefs can be thought of as preparatory for Christian faith. They are what Capell has called the 'Aboriginal Old Testament'. Thus, far from denigrating all aspects of Aboriginal traditional religion, there is now the realisation that this can be used to lead Aborigines to an understanding of what Christians would claim lie behind their ideas of creation, life, fertility and the land.

References

Archival Material:
CMS,A   CMS archives in Sydney and Melbourne.
CMS *Gleaner* CMS monthly missionary magazine, the name later being changed to the *Open Door*.
NMC,A   National Missionary Council of Australia archives at the Australian Council of Churches, Sydney.

Reports:
REPORT of the Church Congress held at Melbourne, 19th to 24th November 1906.
The Aborigines and Half-Castes of Central and North Australia. Report by J. W. Bleakley, 1928. Cmd paper 1929. (Bleakley Report.)
INTERIM GENERAL REPORT of Preliminary Expedition to Arnhem Land, Northern Territory of Australia, 1935-36, by Dr Donald Thomson. Canberra, 1936.
RECOMMENDATIONS of Policy in Native Affairs in the Northern Territory of Australia, by Dr Donald Thomson. Melbourne. 1937.
ABORIGINAL WELFARE — Initial Conference of Commonwealth and State Aboriginal Authorities held at Canberra, 21-23 April, 1937. Commonwealth of Australia, 1937.
SUBMISSION to the Senate Standing Committee on the Social Environment Policies and Programmes in Aboriginal Affairs. Department of Aboriginal Affairs, Darwin 3 September 1973. Circular Mem. No. 55 of 1973/74.

Publications:
BAUER, F. H. 1964 *Historical geography of white settlement in part of Northern Australia. Part 2, The Katherine-Darwin Region.* CSIRO Divisional Report No. 64/1. Canberra.
BERNDT, R. M. and C. H. BERNDT 1954 *Arnhem Land: its history and its people.* Cheshire, Melbourne.
COLE, K. 1971a *A history of the Church Missionary Society of Australia.* Church Missionary Society, Melbourne.
——1971b *Groote Eylandt pioneer.* Church Missionary Society, Melbourne.
——1972 *Oenpelli pioneer.* Church Missionary Society, Melbourne.
ROSE, F. 1960 *Classification of kin. Age structure and marriage amongst the Groote Eylandt Aborigines.* Deutsche Akademie der Wissenschaften zu Berlin, Berlin.
ROWLEY, C. D. 1970 *The destruction of Aboriginal society.* Australian National University Press, Canberra.
TINDALE, N. B. 1925-6 Natives of Groote Eylandt and the west coast of the Gulf of Carpentaria. Parts 1 and 2, *Records of the South Australian Museum,* III(1):61-102; III(2):103-34.

16 Patterns of role consensus in a culture contact situation

D. Williams

Introduction In 1965-66 and again in 1969 a study was made of children's roles at Elcho Island (now Galiwinku) in Arnhem Land, where 'tribal' Aborigines have been in contact with European missionaries for more than thirty years (see Williams 1971). The study revealed that the home, the peer-group and the school were three significant social systems in the lives of 14-16-year-old children. Parents, European teachers and children were found to be three important categories of people in the systems and were therefore used as subjects. Their thinking about children's behaviour in each of the systems provided the basic quantitative data for the study. Items of behaviour in the role instrument were selected on the basis of role conflict.

This paper deals with an aspect of the role study. Role consensus is examined from a sociological point of view by dealing with patterns of agreement and understanding which exist among the main categories of people. To examine agreement on norms, subjects' personal views about what children 'should do' are compared. Likewise, agreement on what children 'actually do' is studied. To explore patterns of understanding about children's behaviour, the study looks into the statements in which they attribute thoughts and feelings to others. For example, children's views about what European teachers feel are compared with the views expressed by European teachers, as a basis for determining whether children understand European teachers.

The patterns of agreement and understanding illustrate the complex nature of social and cultural change. Some suggestions are made for improving understanding in culture contact situations.

In 1969, Elcho Island had a population of approximately 1,000 Aborigines and 80 Europeans. Since the meagre beginnings of the Elcho mission station in 1942, the tradition-directed Aborigines have witnessed the growth of a township with its church, school, hospital, houses, local industries and service facilities. The children, on whom this study is focused, were completing post-primary education at an age when 'tribal' sanctions were becoming increasingly significant to them. It was, therefore, necessary to explore several dimensions of the culture contact situation, particularly in relation to items of behaviour which were likely to cause problems for these children. One major finding showed that children spend most of their waking time in three major social systems, namely the home, the peer-group and the school. Parents, European teachers and children are three important categories of people in these systems. They perceive that certain codes of behaviour for children vary significantly from system to system. In effect, children are expected to be home-like at home, peer-group-like in the peer-group and school-like at school. Modifying one's behaviour to meet the differing constraints of social systems is an important way of resolving role conflict.

Research problems   This contribution also examines the views of parents, European teachers and children in some detail. Although they basically concur on the effect of social systems on behaviour, there are likely to be marked differences in the views expressed by the three categories of people. For example, there is frequently a marked generation gap between parents and their children in modernising societies. Furthermore, Aborigines are likely to differ from Europeans in their views about children. These likely differences need to be considered in relation to (a) the home, where Aboriginal parents meet their children, (b) the peer-group, where children are away from adults, and (c) the school, where European teachers meet Aboriginal children. To focus the study, the following problems are posed:

1. Do parents, teachers and children share similar views about appropriate behaviour for children? Do parents exert a marked influence on children's views about appropriate behaviour in the home and, likewise, do teachers exert a marked influence on children's views about appropriate behaviour at school?

2. Do parents perceive accurately the views which teachers and children have about appropriate behaviour for children? Likewise, do teachers and children perceive accurately the views held by each of the other two groups?

Theoretical orientation

In order to examine the above problems, some theoretical concepts are discussed below and related research findings are cited as a basis for generating hypotheses.

Basic concepts   The term 'position' is used to refer to a unit in the social structure while the term 'role' is regarded as a unit of culture. In this study 'role' is used as a general term to refer to a set of cognitions about behavior. First-order cognitions are those maintained by social observers about real world events. Expectations and norms are of this order.

> A descriptive orientation applied to the behavior of another is called an expectation. This may be defined as a cognition consisting of a belief held for a characteristic of a person or position. The prescriptive orientation deals with value, with statements of 'ought to do', or with right or wrong. A prescriptive-orientation applied to the behavior of another is called a 'norm'. (Rosencranz and Biddle 1964:244.)

When the social observer maintains cognitions about the cognitions of others, we are dealing with second-order cognitions. Statements about perceived consensus, such as attributed norms, are of this order. For example, children may attribute norms to their parents, thereby stating what they feel are the views held by parents.

Central to the consideration of cognitions about behaviour are the concepts of consensus and dissensus. Gross, Mason and McEachern (1958), in their study of the school superintendent's role, effectively demonstrated that degrees of consensus are empirically problematic issues in role studies. Bible and McComas (1963:225-33) go so far as to say that the concept of role is incomplete without the concept of consensus. The whole question of patterns of consensus and dissensus is extremely complex. Biddle and Thomas (1966:33) define consensus as the degree of agreement of individuals on a given topic. They show how consensus, polarised dissensus and non-polarised dissensus in either overt or covert form can exist for the selected behavioural partitions of prescription, evaluation, description and sanction. The matter becomes even more complicated when, for example, a distinction is made between own[1] and attributed cognitions. Comparing two sets of own cognitions is not the same as comparing a set of own cognitions with a set of attributed cognitions.

Scheff (1967:32-46) claims that there are two main traditions in the study of consensus, one based on individual agreement and the other on the co-orientation of individuals in a group toward a statement. He feels that both of these traditions should be incorporated in any exploration of consensus. His formal definition of a social system model of consensus is as follows:

> . . . complete consensus on an issue exists in a group when there is an infinite series of reciprocating understandings between the members of the group concerning the issue. I know that you know that I know, and so on. This is the definition of *complete* consensus. In actual research, one might find it difficult to locate a single example of such complete consensus, and of demonstrating that it occurred if one did find it. For actual situations, one can derive various degrees of partial consensus, depending upon the level of co-orientation achieved. (*Ibid.*:37.)

Scheff has suggested ways in which this definition may be operationalised. Two of his key terms have been taken and modified to suit the nature of the research reported in this paper. The general term 'agreement' is used to describe any consensus which exists when two sets of own cognitions are compared. For example, we may ask whether teachers agree with parents on norms (for children with respect to a particular behaviour in a particular context) by comparing teachers' own norms and parents' own norms. The general term 'understanding' is used to describe any consensus which exists when attributed cognitions are compared with the own cognitions of the persons to whom cognitions were attributed. For example, we may ask whether teachers understand parents by comparing the norms that teachers attribute to parents (for children with respect to a particular behaviour in a particular context) with the own norms held by parents. The two general terms, 'agreement' and 'understanding', are employed to avoid using a profusion of terms.

It should be noted that the terms 'agreement' and 'understanding', as defined above, deal with comparisons of sets of cognitions from two categories of people such as parents and children. Inter-category comparisons are always involved when the terms are used. It is another empirical issue to determine the degree of consensus among the individual responses from a single category of people such as teachers.

As mentioned earlier, consensus on norms and expectations may vary from context to context. The social systems of the home, peer-group and school are associated with distinct physical settings and social situations which, as

Biddle, Twyman and Rankin (n.d.:20), and others have shown, may have marked effects on behaviour. One dimension of a social situation which could be significant in culture contact studies is the power field effect of a member of one ethnic group on members of another group. In field theory terms, a power field (e.g. Deutsch 1968:458-59) can induce changes in the life space within its area of influence. Normally its source is a person whose area of social influence induces changes in the life spaces of other individuals. For the purposes of this study the concept of background or context is broad and embraces both physical setting and social situation.

Formulation of hypothesis 1   The first research problem asked whether parents, teachers and children share similar views about appropriate behaviour for children. This may be examined with respect to behaviours chosen on the basis of role conflict. As role conflict implies that subjects hold inconsistent cognitions for an object person or persons, the items in the role instrument should reveal a marked degree of disagreement on norms. The research problem therefore deals with an aspect of this disagreement. One way to examine the nature of the agreement or disagreement is to compare the norms of parents, teachers and children and note how children's norms differ from those of parents and teachers. Parents and teachers could, in the home and school respectively, exert marked power field effects on children.

The discussion which follows deals with the possible power field effects of parents in the home situation and teachers in the school situation.

Doob (1960:27-34) suggests that in a less 'civilised' society the roles assigned to people tend to be relatively rigid. They make greater demands upon the individual than roles in a more civilised society. If traditional roles are relatively rigid, there could be a considerable amount of agreement between parents and children on norms and expectations for traditional behaviours. When discussing the nature of traditional roles, Doob points out that in less civilised lands the size of the groups within which the individual interacts with others is relatively small. Elcho Island is a small community, but in the culture contact situation, children are separated from their parents for schooling. High levels of agreement between parents and children on norms and expectations for traditional behaviours could be limited to family and camp life.

The comments by Doob and others about tradition-directed societies suggest that high levels of agreement will exist between parents and children in the perception of traditional roles. However, there is some evidence to show that this agreement can, in part, be dependent upon the age at which roles are learnt.[2] As the role study at Elcho Island dealt with 14-16-year-old children, this matter could not be explored. There is also some evidence to suggest that agreement between parents and children may vary for different types of behaviours.[3] This study deals specifically with role conflict behaviours.

The discussion to date has considered the possible relationship between parents and children in the perception of essentially traditional roles. With the advent of contact, European roles have been introduced. Aborigines and Europeans are likely to exhibit varying degrees of agreement on these roles. Rae Sherwood's study (1958:285-316) of the Bantu clerk illustrated how white supervisors and the clerks themselves held different views about the clerk's role. The data she collected confirmed her hypothesis —

that the role expectations[4] of the efficient Bantu clerk, as perceived by the two criterion groups, white supervisors and Bantu clerks, will differ from each other both in the relative importance which each group attributes to the qualities selected, and in the range of qualities selected. (*Ibid.*: 311.)

Sherwood's study has shown that differences in perception can and do exist between two ethnic groups in a culture contact situation. In the school at Elcho Island, with its curriculum defining the behavioural outcomes in subject areas, children are likely to become very familiar with European norms. Furthermore, they are likely to conform to a certain extent to European norms in the presence of European teachers at school.

Parker's work (1964:325-40) affords a good example of the power field which Europeans may exert. When working in two Eskimo villages, he asked respondents to tell stories about five pictures designed to elicit stories about relative ethnic identity. He found that:

> . . . the adolescent characters in the Kotzebue stories exhibited different attitudes towards Whites, depending on whether the environmental setting was Eskimo or Western. (*Ibid.*: 336.)

The research problem referred to codes of appropriate behaviour and therefore stressed normative agreement. A logical extension of the problem is to ask whether there is agreement on expectations as well as norms. In extending the problem it should be noted that the degree of consensus which subjects exhibit on a norm may differ significantly from the degree of consensus they exhibit on an expectation.[5]

To sum up, there is some theoretical basis for suggesting that parents and children will show high levels of agreement on norms and expectations for essentially traditional behaviours at home. Likewise, teachers and children may show high levels of agreement for essentially European behaviours at school. Because the power field effects of parents and teachers in the home and school respectively are likely to be strong, the levels of agreement may apply generally and not separately to either essentially traditional or essentially European behaviours. The hypothesis which follows therefore does not differentiate between traditional and European behaviours.

Hypothesis 1
(a) There will be closer agreement between children and parents than between children and teachers with respect to norms and expectations for children's behaviours at home.
(b) There will be closer agreement between children and teachers than between children and parents with respect to norms and expectations for children's behaviours at school.

Formulation of hypothesis 2   The second research problem asked, *inter alia*, whether parents perceive accurately the views held by teachers and children. It is concerned with patterns of understanding and misunderstanding.

In a study of the role of the public school teacher, Biddle *et al.* (1966) showed that patterns of shared inaccuracy exist. Parents, teachers, pupils and school officials were asked, among other things, to give their own norms for teacher performances in given situations, and then to attribute norms to people in general, teachers and school officials. Subjects were asked to choose one of five behavioural alternatives to indicate their own or attributed norms. The scale ranged from: (1) teachers should do a little or no (e.g. 'watching pupils during a study period') to (5) teachers should do a great deal of (e.g 'watching pupils during a study period'). When sets of responses were compared, it was found that shared inaccuracies or pluralistic ignorance existed. The design of the research reported in this paper follows closely the design developed by Biddle.

When reporting the research mentioned above in a discussion of roles, goals and value structures in organisations, Biddle (1964) set out several propositions dealing with the aetiology and maintenance of pluralistic ignorance in the school system. His two propositions relating to the genesis of pluralistic ignorance were as follows:

> *Proposition* 14. Pluralistic ignorance results when behavioral observation is curtailed, discussion of norms or expectations is restricted, clearly stated tasks are at a minimum, and/or discussion of norms is slanted.
> *Proposition* 15. Pluralistic ignorance is more likely to occur for positions in the public domain than for positions defined privately in the organization, more likely for public organizations and for organizations or professional societies having poorly stated purposes. (*Ibid.*: 169.)

His three propositions dealing with the effects of pluralistic ignorance were as follows:

> *Proposition* 16. Pluralistic ignorance leads to the restriction of communication and the slanting of normative discussions.
> *Proposition* 17. For members of the position to which pluralistic ignorance is applied (teachers), pluralistic ignorance leads to the establishment of behavioral standards at odds with own norms, to the restriction of behavioral standards, and to dissatisfaction.
> *Proposition* 18. For members of positions holding pluralistic ignorance (school officials, parents), pluralistic ignorance leads to the establishment of inappropriate behavioral standards, to reduction of the status of their own position, and to dissatisfaction. (*Ibid.*: 170.)

In the culture contact situation at Elcho Island, where two distinct ethnic groups speak different languages, there could be curtailment of behavioural observation and restrictions on the discussion of expectations and norms. These conditions could generate pluralistic ignorance which might lead to the restriction of communication and the slanting of normative discussions.

In England, Musgrove (1967:61-8) and Musgrove and Taylor (1969) have done a considerable amount of work on studying the teacher's role. One study conducted by Musgrove and Taylor (1965:171-78) was carried out among 470 teachers in grammar, modern, junior and infant schools. It endeavoured to find out how widely or narrowly teachers conceived their role. The instrument listed six commonly accepted educational aims which teachers were asked to rank as they themselves valued them and also as their experience led them to believe that parents in general valued them. A sample of 237 parents was also selected and they were asked to rank the objectives as they thought they should weigh with teachers in charge of their children. The study revealed that teachers generally misunderstood parents.

But the area of discrepancy between teachers' aims and what they imagine to be parents' is still very large. On the whole, teachers take an unflattering view of parents (and their own aims are remarkably idealistic), seeing them as indifferent to moral training but very concerned with social advancement. In fact, parents were substantially in agreement with teachers. The area of (unnecessary) tension might be considerably reduced if parents and teachers established more effective means of communication. (Musgrove and Taylor, 1965:178.)

Musgrove and Taylor cite the work of Biddle and his associates who carried out a comprehensive study of teachers' role cognitions and conflicts in England, Australia, New Zealand and the United States.

One of the instruments used in this research was a list of ten problems of teacher behaviour, e.g. 'Your having an occasional drink at a local hotel or bar', 'Emphasis on social advancement in your instruction (preparing pupils to "get ahead in life")', 'Emphasis on a broad range of goals in your classroom instruction (i.e. teaching the whole child)'. Respondents rated on a five-point scale their degree of approval or disapproval of these behaviours. They also rated the level of approval or disapproval which they felt would be exhibited by school officials, headmaster, other teachers and parents. (Musgrove and Taylor 1969:58.)

Biddle found that conflict between parents and teachers was greater in England than in any of the other three countries. The data suggested that there was considerable social distance, or perhaps hostility, between parents and teachers in England. The findings of Musgrove and Taylor, which were cited earlier, are in line with those of Biddle. Biddle describes the effects of pluralistic ignorance in terms of restrictions on communication and the slanting of normative discussions. Scheff's (1967:32-46) analysis of aspects of consensus led him to suggest the following proposition:

The type and extent of consensus is dependent on the type and extent of coordination required between the members of the group. (*Ibid.*: 41.)

For illustrative purposes he considers three dimensions of co-ordination — formalisation, complexity and type of payoff. One of the examples he gives to show how the structure of consensus derives from the nature of the co-ordination required deals with the social integration of Negroes and whites in America. He shows how it is possible for the consensual structure to be asymmetrical in respect of particular behaviours. There can be agreement between two groups on a behaviour, but this can be coupled with understanding of agreement on the Negro side and misunderstanding on the white side.

Bledsoe and Wiggins (1973:131-6) in a study of 100 adolescents and their parents from a south-eastern university town in the U.S.A., found that parents' perceptions of their adolescents' self-perceptions are more favourable than the adolescents' self-perceptions. Parents seldom understood their adolescent children. If misunderstanding of this order can be found in an American city, it is likely that greater degrees of misunderstanding will exist in a culture contact situation where non-literate parents from one culture are sending their children to a formal school conducted in another cultural tradition.

In the culture contact situation at Elcho Island where a formal, European-type school has been introduced into a tradition-directed Aboriginal community, it is likely that marked pluralistic ignorance will exist. Parents, many of whom never attended a formal school, are likely to have little appreciation of 'school'. They have only a limited scope to observe school behaviour and their poor knowledge of the English language does not enable them to communicate readily with teachers. Likewise, European teachers, in spite of the mission's policy of expecting its teachers to learn the vernacular and acquire a knowledge of Aboriginal culture, are likely to be ignorant of much of the traditional way of life. Aboriginal children who attend school grow up in two cultural worlds: the Aboriginal and the European. Parents freely observe children's behaviour at home in the camp while teachers are restricted in this regard. In a similar manner, teachers freely observe children's behaviour at school while parents have little opportunity to do so. These restrictions on communication and behavioural observation suggest the following hypothesis:

Hypothesis 2
(a) Children's understanding of parents will be greater than teachers' understanding of parents with respect to norms for children's behaviours at home.
(b) Parents' understanding of children will be greater than teachers' understanding of children with respect to norms for children's behaviours at home.
(c) Children's understanding of teachers will be greater than parents' understanding of teachers with respect to norms for children's behaviours at school.
(d) Teachers' understanding of children will be greater than parents' understanding of children with respect to norms for children's behaviours at school.

Research design and methodology

The following is a brief outline of the research design and methodology. Samples in the study included:

(a) a random sample of twelve boys and twelve girls from a population of forty-six post-primary children in the 14-16-year age range.
(b) a random sample of twelve male and twelve female parents of 14-16-year-old children. (There was therefore at least a generation gap between parents and children.)
(c) eight European teachers.

The role instrument contained 33 items which were selected on the basis of role conflict.[6] Where possible a behaviour was set, in turn, in settings and social situations characteristic of the home, the peer-group and the school. Only fifteen behaviours were relevant to all three social systems and twenty were common to both the home and the school. For each of the children's behaviours in a particular social situation, each subject was asked to indicate his:

(a) own expectation
(b) own norm
(c) norm attributed to parents
(d) norm attributed to teachers
(e) norm attributed to children

The following is a list of the 33 items included in the role instrument. Behind the abbreviated statement of each item the social systems in which it was examined are shown.

1. Keeping noses clean (home, peer-group and school)
2. Taking things without asking (home and school)
3. Covering coughs (home, peer-group and school)
4. Saying personal names of deceased (home, peer-group and school)
5. Gurrung and rumaru mukul* saying each other's personal names (home, peer-group and school)
6. Excelling (home, peer-group and school)
7. Boys saying their sisters' personal names (home, peer-group and school)
8. Obeying parents/teachers (home and school)
9. Keeping things tidy (home and school)
10. Keeping hair combed (home, peer-group and school)
11. Remaining silent when questioned (home, peer-group and school)
12. Covering heads when sleeping (home)
13. Looking after the fire (home)
14. Gurrung and rumaru mukul* looking straight at each other (home, peer-group and school)
15. Cleaning wax out of ears with an object (home, peer-group and school)
16. Use of 'please' (vernacular: home, peer-group and school)
16a. Use of 'please' (English: school)
17. Running through yards (home)
18. Sharing possessions (home and school)
19. Asking others to help with work (home and school)
20. Informing people when unable to keep an appointment (home, peer-group and school)
21. Looking after younger brothers and sisters (home)
22. Following the promise system for marriage (as this item was not well-suited for use in a research design concerned with the frequency of occurrence of behaviours, it was not included in the study)
23. Using lavatories (home, peer-group and school)
24. Dancing in secular 'corroborees' (home)
25. Being shy toward Aboriginal strangers (home, peer-group and school)
25a. Being shy toward European strangers (school)
26. Boys hitting their sisters when sisters sworn at by someone (home and school)
27. When sick asking to have body rubbed (home)
28. Boys staying home at night (home)
28a. Girls staying home at night (home)
29. Participating in bukulup† ceremonies (home)
30. Pregnant girls drinking hot tea (home)
31. Girls eating fish during their menstrual periods (home)
32. Drawing plants and animals which are totems (school)
33. Drinking out of 'used' vessels (home)

Individual interviews with parents and children were conducted in the vernacular except in one or two instances where an item implied that the medium of communication would normally be English. A pencil and paper questionnaire was completed by European teachers. A four-point scale was used to record cognitions about the frequency of occurrence of a behaviour. In English the scale points were as follows:

* *Gurung* (daughter's husband); *mugul-rumurung* (wife's mother) — i.e., tabu-ed relatives. (Editor)
† *Bugalub* 'normalising' rites, designed to restore goodwill. (Editor)

1. a little or not at all
2. a fair amount but not a lot
3. reasonably frequently
4. a great deal or all the time

School children were asked to complete a whole series of scaling exercises in an endeavour to probe the meanings of the vernacular terms used in the scale. The two main issues investigated were the perceived universe of possible occurrences of a behaviour and the method of partitioning the universe to form a scale.[7] Because the sample of teachers was considerably smaller than the sample of either parents or children, it was not possible to test certain aspects of the hypotheses rigorously. The situation was further aggravated because the number of teachers who responded to questions occasionally varied.

In order to examine the data, two methods were used. The first method examined each item separately and involved the comparison of sets of cognitions using Sign and Mann-Whitney U tests for ordinal data. Because the sample of teachers was relatively small, significant differences between (a) parents and teachers and (b) children and teachers were more difficult to obtain than those between (c) parents and children.

The second method used to examine the data was based upon mean differences between subjects' sets of cognitions for each item. For example, from the mean differences for particular items it could be seen whether children's cognitions were closer to those of parents or those of teachers. The null hypothesis was that there would be no difference in the overall frequency with which children's cognitions were closer to those of parents than those of teachers. For an item where children's cognitions were equidistant from parents' and teachers' cognitions, 0.5 was added to each frequency tally. A simple Chi Square test was used to determine whether the observed frequency was significantly different from the expected frequency.

Results

To simplify the presentation of results, detailed statistical tables are omitted from this paper which provides only summaries of the findings.

Test of hypothesis 1   There is a considerable amount of support for Hypothesis 1 (a) with respect to norms only. *With regard to norms for children's behaviour at home, children agree more closely with their parents than they do with teachers.* With parity in sample sizes, this agreement could have been more significant. For 22 out of 32 items children's norms are closer to parents' norms than teachers' norms. This observed frequency *vis-à-vis* the expected frequency is significant at the 0.05 level. As far as expectations are concerned, there is no support for Hypothesis 1(a). However, there is a strong trend in the predicted direction.

The data provide no support for Hypothesis 1(b) but indicate a nonsignificant trend in the direction opposite from the one predicted. In other words, *for both norms and expectations in the school, children's cognitions tend to be closer to parents' cognitions than to teachers' cognitions.* When the hypothesis was being formulated, the work of Doob (1960) and others suggested that there would be a high level of agreement between parents and children. It was felt, however, that this agreement might be limited to cognitions about behaviour in the home situation where parents and children frequently interact. For behaviour in the school situation, it was predicted that children's cognitions would agree more closely with those of teachers. This proved to be incorrect. The fact that these basic assumptions have not been confirmed does not automatically validate other *post hoc* assumptions. The explanation which follows might well be *non-sequitur,* and hence it should be subjected to empirical investigation before it is accepted. It appears that the power field effect of Europeans is recognised by all Aborigines who have developed patterns of behaviour appropriate for European-dominated situations. On the basis of this knowledge parents form their norms and expectations for children's behaviour at school. As a result, parents and children show a reasonably high level of agreement on norms and expectations for behaviour at school. An interesting exception to the general pattern of agreement is illustrated in Figure 1 which shows how teachers and children are in close agreement on expectations and norms for the item, 'Saying personal names of deceased'.

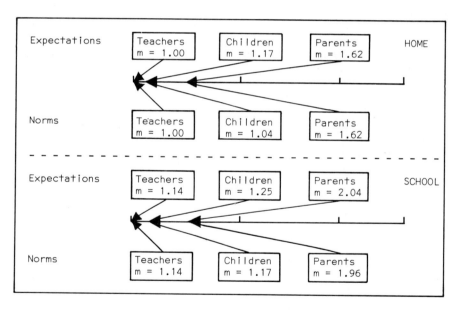

Figure 1: *Patterns of agreement/disagreement on the item 'Saying Personal Names of Deceased'*

To simplify the presentation of results, items are not treated separately but are reviewed collectively. Means and mean differences between sets of cognitions are used as a basis for compiling Tables 1 and 2 which follow. Although mean differences are shown in the Tables, it should be noted that tests of significance based on the Mann-Whitney U Test involve ordinal data only and do not involve means.

Setting and Social Situation	Home			Peer group			School		
Comparison of one group of subjects' own expectations/norms for children and another group of subjects' own expectations/norms for children	Parents' Own Expectations/Norms & Teachers' Own Expectations/Norms	Children's Own Expectations/Norms & Teachers' Own Expectations/Norms	Parents' Own Expectations/Norms & Children's Own Expectations/Norms	Parents' Own Expectations/Norms & Teachers' Own Expectations/Norms	Children's Own Expectations/Norms & Teachers' Own Expectations/Norms	Parents' Own Expectations/Norms & Children's Own Expectations/Norms	Parents' Own Expectations/Norms & Teachers' Own Expectations/Norms	Children's Own Expectations/Norms & Teachers' Own Expectations/Norms	Parents' Own Expectations/Norms & Children's Own Expectations/Norms
A. COMPARISON OF EXPECTATIONS ($p \leqslant .05$ using a Mann-Whitney U Test)									
(1) Total number of items	30	30	32	15	15	15	22	22	23
(2) Number of items with significant differences between subjects' cognitions	9	10	10	9	6	3	12	9	9
(3) Average of absolute mean differences for items referred to in (2) above	1.01	.89	.68	.74	.94	.51	.97	.81	.50
(4) Percentage of items with significant differences	30%	33%	31%	60%	40%	20%	55%	41%	39%
B. COMPARISON OF NORMS ($p \leqslant .05$ using a Mann-Whitney U Test)									
(1) Total number of items	30	30	32	15	15	15	22	22	23
(2) Number of items with significant differences between subjects' cognitions	19	16	15	4	5	5	7	6	5
(3) Average of absolute mean differences for items referred to in (2) above	1.11	1.03	.56	1.19	1.06	.43	.62	.70	.44
(4) Percentage of items with significant differences	63%	50%	47%	27%	33%	33%	32%	27%	22%
C. COMPARISON OF EXPECTATIONS ($p \leqslant .05$ using a Chi Square Test)									
(1) Total number of items	32	32	32	15	15	15	23	23	23
(2) Average of absolute mean differences	.49	.48	.34	.57	.49	.27	.65	.51	.28
(3) Number of items where children's cognitions are closer to parents' than teachers'	18			11			15		
(4) Number of items where children's cognitions are closer to teachers' than parents'	14			4			8		
(5) Chi Square test. Observed frequencies for (3) and (4) as against expected frequencies	$x^2 = .50$ Not significant $(.3 < p \leqslant .5)$			$x^2 = 3.27$ Not significant $(.05 < p \leqslant .1)$			$x^2 = 2.13$ Not significant $(.1 < p \leqslant .2)$		
D. COMPARISON OF NORMS ($p \leqslant .05$ using a Chi Square Test)									
(1) Total number of items	32	32	32	15	15	15	23	23	23
(2) Average of absolute mean differences	.84	.72	.30	.52	.54	.25	.34	.36	.22
(3) Number of items where children's cognitions are closer to parents' than teachers'	22			10			16		
(4) Number of items where children's cognitions are closer to teachers' than parents'	10			5			7		
(5) Chi Square Test. Observed frequencies for (3) and (4) as against expected frequencies	$x^2 = 4.5$ Significant $.02 < p \leqslant .05$			$x^2 = 1.67$ Not significant $(.1 < p \leqslant .2)$			$x^2 = 3.52$ Not significant $(.05 < p \leqslant .1)$		

Table 1 : Patterns of agreement

Columns	Understanding Parents (1)		Understanding Teachers (2)		Understanding Children (3)	
Sub-columns	a	b	a	b	a	b
Comparison of one group of subjects' own norms and another group of subjects' attributed norms to sentient-objects (i.e. to the first group of subjects)	Parents' Own Norms and Teachers' Attributed Norms to Parents	Parents' Own Norms and Children's Attributed Norms to Parents	Teachers' Own Norms and Parents' Attributed Norms to Teachers	Teachers' Own Norms and Children's Attributed Norms to Teachers	Children's Own Norms and Parents' Attributed Norms to Children	Children's Own Norms and Teachers' Attributed Norms to Children

Based on a study of items which revealed significant differences using a Mann-Whitney U Test

Setting and Social Situation	HOME					
(A) Number of items with significant differences between own and attributed norms	12	7	10	11	17	11
(B) Total number of items	30	32	30	30	32	30
(C) (A) as a percentage of (B)	40%	22%	33%	34%	53%	37%
(D) Average of absolute mean differences for items which revealed significant differences	1.09	.52	1.10	.81	.76	1.06

Setting and Social Situation	SCHOOL					
(A) Number of items with significant differences between own and attributed norms	15	12	7	4	9	11
(B) Total number of items	21	22	22	22	23	22
(C) (A) as a percentage of (B)	71%	55%	32%	18%	39%	50%
(D) Average of absolute mean differences for items which revealed significant differences	1.04	.56	.92	.60	.67	.89

Based on a study of all items

Setting and Social Situation	HOME					
(A) Total number of items	32	32	32	32	32	32
(B) Sub-column a: Number of items where a > b / Sub-column b: Number of items where b > a	24	8	17.5	14.5	15	17
(C) Chi square Test: Observed frequencies for 'a>b' and 'b>a' as against expected frequencies	x^2=8.00 Significant .001<p<.01		x^2=.28 Not Significant		x^2=.13 Not Significant	
(D) Average of absolute mean differences — all items	.66	.26	.56	.50	.49	.60

Setting and Social Situation	SCHOOL					
(A) Total number of items	22	22	23	23	23	23
(B) Sub-column a: Number of items where a>b / Sub-column b: Number of items where b>a	18	4	18	5	7	16
(C) Chi square Test: Observed frequencies for 'a>b' and 'b>a' as against expected frequencies	x^2=8.91 Significant .001<p<.01		x^2=7.35 Significant .001<p<.01		x^2=3.52 Not Significant (.05<p<.10)	
(D) Average of absolute mean differences — all items	.86	.36	.50	.31	.31	.57

Table 2: Patterns of understanding

Further exploration of data   Only fifteen items deal with behaviour in the peer-group. With such a small number of items it is difficult to reveal any significant patterns of agreement. The study of fifteen items indicates that children's norms and expectations tend to be closer to those of parents than those of teachers for behaviour in the peer-group. Notwithstanding this tendency, some items show that children's norms can be closer to those of teachers than those of parents for behaviours in the peer-group. The sub-culture of the peer-group is a mixture of traditional and European cultures. A broad classification of items into two categories — 'traditional' and 'European' — does not reveal any clearly defined patterns of agreement.

Test of hypothesis 2   There is a considerable amount of support for Hypothesis 2(a). *Children have a greater understanding of parents than do teachers on norms for children's behaviour at home.* On 24 out of 32 items children show greater understanding than teachers and this is significant at the 0.01 level using a Chi Square Test. It is interesting to note that the items on which teachers show greater understanding than children are items with well-defined norms in traditional culture. Because this observation is based on mean differences and involves only seven items, it needs to be interpreted cautiously.

Hypothesis 2(b) is not supported by the data. *The evidence suggests that teachers and parents differ little in their understanding of children's norms for behaviour at home.* This is an interesting finding because teachers have little opportunity to observe children's behaviour in the camp and to discuss it with Aborigines. As restrictions on observation and discussion were important considerations when Hypothesis 2(b) was formulated, it is appropriate to digress and specu-late on the lack of support for the hypothesis.

A superficial interpretation of the above finding might lead one to believe that teachers have a remarkable understanding of children's behaviour at home in the camp — so remarkable that it equates with the understanding parents have. An alternative explanation is more plausible. The data suggest that parents' understanding of children is poor — so poor that it equates with the understanding teachers have of children's behaviour at home in the camp. The lack of support for Hypothesis 2(b) could therefore be attribu-table to a lower-than-expected level of understanding by parents rather than a higher-than-expected level of understanding by teachers.

There is some support for Hypothesis 2(c). *Children have a greater understanding of teachers than do parents on norms for children's behaviour at school.* For 18 out of 23 items children's attributed norms to teachers are closer to teachers' own norms than are parents' attributed norms to teachers. This observed frequency is significantly different from the expected frequency at the 0.01 level. The significant differences between own and attributed norms, determined by using a Mann-Whitney U Test, do not indicate the same degree of support for the hypothesis.

Hypothesis 2(d) predicts that teachers will have a greater understanding of children than will parents on norms for children's behaviour at school. The basis for this prediction is that parents have little opportunity to observe behaviour in school and that discussion of school norms can take place only at home in the camp. There is no support for Hypothesis 2(d). The data actually show that *parents have a greater understanding of children than do teachers* ($p \leqslant 0.1$). These results suggest that the theoretical assumptions and considerations which gave rise to the hypothesis should be re-examined.

At home in the camp, parents and children have the opportunity to discuss norms and expectations for children's behaviour at school. Such a discussion, if it takes place, could be part of a larger discussion which might deal with appropriate and actual codes of behaviour for all Aborigines when they are in the presence of Europeans. In other settings and social situations, such as church and Sunday School, parents and their children gain first-hand experience at behaving in the presence of Europeans.

On the basis of this experience and the possible discussion of school life by parents and children, parents may develop an appreciation of how children feel they should behave in school. This explanation is based on conjecture and cannot be substantiated with the data obtained in the present study. However, it does suggest some issues which should be investigated in any subsequent study of understanding.

The tests of Hypothesis 2(b) and (d), when considered together, indicate that predicting patterns of understanding in a culture contact situation involves more than just a consideration of restrictions on the observation of behaviour and the discussion of expectations and norms. Such variables as the relationship between subjects (e.g. between Aboriginal parents and their children) and the nature of behaviour settings need to be considered as well.

Further exploration of data   Hypothesis 2 does not deal with subjects' understanding of teachers' norms for children's behaviour at home, nor does it deal with subjects' understanding of parents' norms for children's behaviour at school. Because children spend more time with teachers than do parents, there is some basis for predicting that they will have a greater understanding of teachers. The greater amount of time spent with teachers affords more opportunity to discuss expectations and norms for children's behaviours at home. The data show a slight degree of support for this prediction; but it is not significant.

In a similar manner, it could be predicted that children will have a greater understanding of parents than will teachers for children's behaviour at school. They spend more time with their parents than do teachers. The data provide general support for this prediction. For 18 out of 22 items, children's attributed norms to parents are closer to parents' own norms than are teachers' attributed norms to parents. This observed frequency differs significantly from the expected frequency ($p \leqslant .01$).

A significant degree of misunderstanding exists for almost every item. This applies to both the essentially European and the essentially traditional behaviours. As the items were selected on the basis of role conflict, a considerable amount of misunderstanding is to be expected. It should be noted that behaviour settings and social situations have a marked effect on patterns of understanding. If subjects display understanding of norms for children's behaviours at home, this does not necessarily mean that they will understand the norms for children on the same behaviours at school.

A study of mean differences without reference to the distribution of scores is an untenable statistical procedure. Furthermore, in this particular study the concept of a mean is suspect as there is no basis for assuming an interval level of scaling. With these factors duly acknowledged, Table 3 is presented as a basis for speculation about patterns of understanding. The average of absolute mean differences shown in the Table suggests that, in general, children possess a greater degree of understanding of others than either parents or teachers do, and that parents have a greater degree of understanding of others than teachers have.

Subjects (who attribute norms to sentient-objects)	Sentient-Objects (whose own norms are compared with norms attributed to them by subjects)	Mean Differences between own and attributed norms (ignoring signs)	
		HOME	SCHOOL
Children	Parents	.26	.36
Children	Teachers	.50	.31
Average Mean Difference:		.38	.34
Parents	Teachers	.56	.50
Parents	Children	.49	.36
Average Mean Difference:		.53	.43
Teachers	Parents	.66	.86
Teachers	Children	.60	.57
Average Mean Difference:		.63	.72

Table 3: *Relative degrees of understanding possessed by parents, teachers and children (based on a study of all items)*

At this juncture it is appropriate to compare patterns of agreement with patterns of understanding. The test of Hypothesis 1(a) showed that children's own norms for behaviour at home are significantly closer to parents' own norms than teachers' own norms. The test of Hypothesis 2(b) showed that there is no significant difference between parents and teachers in their understanding of children's norms for behaviour at home. In the exploration of the data it was suggested that parents reveal a lower-than-expected level of understanding of children's norms. From the data used to examine Hypotheses 1(a) and 2(b), the picture which emerges is this: Parents tend to agree with children but generally misunderstand them on norms for behaviour at home. Children, on the other hand, tend to agree with and also understand parents on norms for behaviour at home. These observations are based on a superficial treatment of the data and should be treated cautiously. They do suggest matters to be investigated in subsequent research.

A comparison of patterns of agreement with patterns of understanding for behaviour in the school situation reveals a complex picture. Parents' level of agreement with children appears to be higher than their level of understanding of children. Likewise, children's level of agreement with parents is higher than their level of understanding of parents. For 12 out of 22 items, children's attributed norms to parents are significantly different from parents' own norms. An analysis of these differences shows that children generally think that parents are more conservative than they really are with regard to the relaxation of traditional norms and the acceptance of European norms for behaviour at school. The same can be said of teachers who tend to regard parents as conservative, and who generally misunderstand parents' norms. In Figure 2, the above patterns are clearly illustrated.

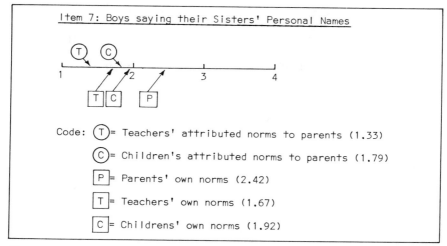

Figure 2: *Patterns of agreement and understanding for Item* 7 *in the school situation*

Discussion: educational implications

This study has shown that patterns of agreement and understanding are quite complex in the culture contact situation at Elcho Island. Children are in closer agreement with their parents than with teachers on what constitutes appropriate behaviour for them at home, and, to some extent, at school. However, this pattern of agreement is not matched by corresponding patterns of understanding. For example, children have a better understanding of their parents than parents have of their children with respect to children's behaviour at home. If curriculum developers and teachers want to achieve higher levels of understanding among various categories of people, it will be necessary to develop programmes —

(a) which involve all categories of people in the community and not just children;

(b) which maximise discussion of norms and increase observation of behaviour in the major social systems;

(c) which involve Aborigines and Europeans working together to study each other's cultures.

In the educational world at present, the merits and demerits of specifying behavioural objectives are being discussed. This study suggests at least two important considerations for teachers and educationists who are prescribing goals for Aboriginal children.

(a) Consensus is a key factor in understanding behaviour. Children should be taught that people may differ in their views on what constitutes appropriate behaviour.

(b) For a particular behaviour, norms and expectations may vary considerably to suit the demands of the various social systems in which it is performed. For example, the prescribed curriculum outcome, 'Uses toilet facilities', needs to be considered in a variety of contexts. Satisfactory use of toilet facilities at school may be matched by little or no use of them at home. Norms may reflect this marked difference in performance.

The findings of this study have implications for the research worker. For example, when describing a kinship role in a culture contact situation, glib statements such as, 'Aboriginal males should not say the personal names of their sisters', may be an over-simplification of the role. There is a need for researchers to explore additional dimensions of the concept of consensus, particularly those dimensions which explore intra-group as opposed to inter-group consensus.

Notes

1. This use of the word 'own' accords with Biddle's use of it (see B. J. Biddle *et al.* 1966). 'Own cognitions' may be compared and contrasted with 'attributed cognitions'.

2. Since Spiro (1955:1240-52) and Bruner (1956:191-99) clearly enunciated the early learning hypothesis over a decade ago, several theorists have examined it in acculturation situations. Leis' (1964:32-42) discussion of Ijaw enculturation contains a summary of the various attempts to test the early learning hypothesis. In brief, the hypothesis states that what is learned and internalised in infancy and early childhood is most resistant to change in culture contact situations. Conversely, what is learned late in life is least resistant to change. Many claim that the hypothesis provides an explanation which is at best fortuitous, while others, such as Bruner himself, regard it as a partial explanation of the process of change. When planning the present study of roles at Elcho Island, consideration was given to examining the age at which norms were learnt by children, to see whether this bore some relationship to the patterns of agreement and disagreement between parents and children. The age at which roles are learnt was found to be a difficult concept to operationalise. A pictorial age chart was used to enable informants to indicate the ages at which children learned particular norms. The validity of this method was considered to be suspect, and only a limited amount of data was collected. It could be that children's norms and expectations agree more closely with those of parents for items of behaviour which are learnt early in life.

3. Dohrenwend and Smith (1969:30-39), in attempting to develop a theory of acculturation, place a considerable amount of stress on deviations from the well-defined norms in a society. Although their comments about individual acculturation do not deal specifically with patterns of agreement and disagreement, they do suggest (*ibid.*: 35-36) important implications for the present study. For example:

    > That individual is most acculturated who deviates furthest from the norms of the strongest, that is, the most exclusive, orders of structured activity in his culture. Conversely, that individual is least acculturated who conforms most closely to the norms of the strongest or most exclusive orders of activity in his culture. In this view, deviation from norms of the weak institutions has little consequence for *individual* variation in acculturation relative to the strength or weakness of the culture in the contact situation.

    If Dohrenwend and Smith are correct, it becomes important to know what are the strongest and most exclusive orders of activity in Aboriginal culture. The significance of any patterns of agreement and disagreement between parents and children on role cognitions could be dependent upon the nature of the behaviours selected for study. There is no basis for assuming that a sample of role conflict items deals with the most exclusive orders of activity in Aboriginal culture.

4. 'Role expectations consist of shared attitudes or beliefs held by relevant criterion groups about what role occupants should or should not do.' (Sherwood 1958:285.) In this paper, the term 'expectation' has a different meaning.

5. The fact that consensus on norms may be different from consensus on expectations is shown in Bible and McComas (1963:225-33). In a study of the effectiveness of the vocational agriculture teacher, Bible and McComas were basically concerned with perceptions of role expectations (referred to as norms in this paper) and role performances (referred to as expectations in this paper). One of their hypotheses (*ibid.*:227) was as follows:

    > There will be greater agreement on perception of role expectations among vocational agriculture teachers and among school administrators than on their perception of role performances for the vocational agriculture teacher's position.

In order to test this and other hypotheses, data were collected from thirty vocational agriculture teachers and thirty administrators in ten central Ohio counties. Subjects were asked to state their own perceptions of role expectations on a five-point scale ranging from 1: 'Definitely should be obligated' to 5: 'Definitely should not be obligated') and role performances on a four-point scale (ranging from 1: 'always' to 4: 'never') for each of seventy role-definition items describing behaviour in which the Vo-Ag teachers may or may not be expected to engage. The data obtained corroborated the hypothesis. For example (*ibid.*: 230):

> Both vocational agriculture teachers and their school administrators had higher consensus on perception of role expectations than on perception of role performances. For the teachers, consensus was higher (lower variance) for 83 per cent of the items when perceived as role expectations compared with only 17 per cent of the items when perceived as role performances. For administrators the percentages were 89 and 11 per cent respectively. This is in support of Homans' hypothesis that, 'members of the group are often more nearly alike in the norms they hold than in their overt behaviour.'

Unlike the study by Bible and McComas, the present study is concerned with agreement among categories of persons and not the degree of consensus within each category. However, the nature of the distribution of responses within each category will have an effect on inter-category comparisons.

6. Biddle, Twyman and Rankin (n.d.:32) define role conflict as follows:

> Role conflict is any of several possible relatively enduring disparities between role elements exhibited by persons in a social situation which result in problems for one or more of these persons as individuals.

The same authors have isolated four basic forms of role conflict:
(a) Behavioural Pressure Conflict
(b) Individual Cognitive Disparity Conflict
(c) Multi-person Cognitive Disparity Conflict
(d) Behaviour-Cognition Conflict

With Aboriginal teaching assistants acting as informants, items were selected which could be expected to produce multi-person cognitive disparity conflict for children. Items of behaviour were therefore chosen if teaching assistants felt that the norms for children held by at least two of the three groups of people in the positions of parents, teachers and children were disparate in either the home, the peer-group or the school situation. In addition, they were asked to select items of behaviour where disparate norms would create problems for children when it came to actual performance. It is possible that the norms teaching assistants attributed to parents, teachers and children may not have always coincided with the 'own norms' held by the three groups of people.

It should be noted that it is another empirical issue to determine whether norms match expectations or the real world situation. Furthermore, the norms children attributed to parents, teachers and other children need to be examined to determine whether children perceive accurately the cognitive structure of others. The 'own norms' of parents, teachers and children may be disparate, but children may be unaware of this and hence not experience role conflict.

It was not always possible to interview each teaching assistant before an item was selected, and this no doubt affected the construction of the role instrument. Aboriginal teaching assistants were chosen as informants because it was felt that they would be in a position to select items of behaviour which were relevant to either or both of the cultures involved.

7. The problems associated with establishing a scale are discussed in the paper, 'Ordinal Scaling of Prescriptions and Descriptions of Behaviour in an Aboriginal Community', presented at the symposium on cognition, Australian Institute of Aboriginal Studies, Biennial Conference, 1974.

References

BIBLE, B. L. *and* J. D. McCOMAS 1963 Role consensus and teacher effectiveness, *Social Forces*, 42.

BIDDLE, B. J. 1964 Roles, goals and value structures in organizations. In *New perspectives in organization research* (W. W. Cooper, H. J. Leavitt *and* M. W. Shelly eds). John Wiley, New York.

——*et al.* 1966 Shared inaccuracies in the role of the teacher. In *Role theory: concepts and research* (B. J. Biddle *and* E. J. Thomas eds).

——*and* E. J. THOMAS eds 1966 *Role theory: concepts and research.* John Wiley, New York.

——J. P. TWYMAN *and* E. F. RANKIN n.d. *The concept of role conflict.* Arts and Sciences Studies. Social Studies Series No. 11, Oklahoma State University.

BLEDSOE, J. C. *and* R. C. WIGGINS 1973 Consequence of adolescents' self-concepts and parents' perceptions of adolescents' self-concepts, *Journal of Psychology*, 83.

BRUNER, E. M. 1956 Cultural transmission and cultural change, *Southwestern Journal of Anthropology*, 12.

DEUTSCH, M. 1968 Field theory in social psychology. In *The handbook of social psychology* (G. Lindzey *and* E. Aronson eds) Vol. 1. Addison-Wesley, Massachusetts.

DOOB, L. W. 1960 *Becoming more civilized*. Yale University Press, New Haven.

DOHRENWEND, B. P. *and* R. J. SMITH 1969 Toward a theory of acculturation, *Southwestern Journal of Anthropology*, 18.

GROSS, N., W. S. MASON *and* A. W. McEACHERN 1958 *Explorations in role analysis*. 2nd ed. John Wiley, New York.

LEIS, P. E. 1964 Ijaw enculturation: a re-examination of the early learning hypothesis, *Southwestern Journal of Anthropology*, 20.

MUGSROVE, F. 1967 Teachers' role conflicts in the English grammar and secondary modern school, *Educational Science*, 2.

——*and* P. H. TAYLOR 1965 Teachers' and parents' conception of the teacher's role, *British Journal of Educational Psychology*, 35.

——*and* —— 1969 *Society and the teacher's role*. Routledge and Kegan Paul, London.

PARKER, S. 1964 Ethnic identity and acculturation in two Eskimo villages, *American Anthropologist*, 66.

ROSENCRANZ, H. A. *and* B. J. BIDDLE 1964 The role approach to teacher competence. In *Contemporary research on teacher effectiveness* (B. J. BIDDLE *and* W. J. Ellena eds). Holt, Rinehart and Winston, New York.

SCHEFF, T. J. 1967 Toward a sociological model of consensus, *American Sociological Review*, 32.

SHERWOOD, R. 1958 The Bantu Clerk: a study of role expectations, *Journal of Social Psychology*, 47.

SPIRO, M. E. 1955 The acculturation of American ethnic groups, *American Anthropologist*, 57.

WILLIAMS, D. 1971 A study of children's roles in a rapidly changing Aboriginal community. Unpublished Ph.D. thesis, University of Queensland.

17 The teaching of Aboriginal children

C. F. Makin

Preamble   Information was sought late in 1972 about problems encountered by teachers in schools with a fairly high proportion of Aboriginal children. For this purpose a questionnaire was designed to elicit information about the school situation, the surrounding community, enrolment, age and experience of the teaching staff, actual pedagogical problems encountered and methods of dealing with them. Another principal aim was to ascertain the extent to which the curriculum had been adapted to local situations and to determine what implications this might have for pre-service and in-service training.

The present contribution outlines some of the findings of the survey. Conclusions are necessarily tentative, since it became increasingly obvious as the results were tabulated that there was need for further and more detailed analysis of particular findings.

The survey questionnaire sought information in the following general areas:

Teachers: their age, sex, and teaching experience.
Schools: their location, type and enrolment.
Educational policies: their nature, comprehension, perceived effectiveness, and adaptation in the field situation.
Training of teachers: whether there is need for specialised training either in pre-service or in in-service training.
Pedagogical problems: those encountered in the actual school situation and methods of dealing with them.
The Aboriginal in the community: his/her opportunities, aspirations, economic assimilation and associated problems.

The questionnaire was directed to schools in the following regions of the State of Western Australia: (1) Kimberleys, (2) the North-West, (3) the Eastern Goldfields, and (4) the Great Southern. The actual schools included in the overall survey do not necessarily form a representative sample but, it is considered, they are representative of the general problems of learning and teaching in them. (There is no such thing as 'learning and teaching' or general problems in the abstract, of course. There are, rather, varieties of learners and teachers, a wide range of objectives for learning and teaching, different contexts and methods, and even different views about relevant outcomes and appropriate ways of evaluating these outcomes. It is hoped that this survey indicates something of the range of these teaching and learning problems.)

An endeavour has been made to summarise and make relevant comments on the information elicited from the questionnaire. The actual tables and comments upon which these summary findings are based and the questionnaire itself, which illustrates in more detail the purpose of the survey and the type of questions employed, is available from the Graylands Teachers College, Graylands, Western Australia.

Summary findings

Profile of teachers   Approximately 75 per cent of the teachers who responded to the questionnaire were under the age of 35: about half were between 26 and 19. Although the teachers were relatively young, the majority were not inexperienced. There were 20 to 25 per cent who had taught for less than one year (with the exception of 44 per cent of the teachers from the Eastern Goldfields, who had taught for less than one year). (The figures from the Eastern Goldfields should be regarded with caution, for the percentages are based on responses of only 9 teachers and 4 schools and may not be statistically significant.) There were slightly more females than males among the respondents, with the percentage of female teachers being highest in the large schools located in towns.

About a fifth of the respondents were headmasters. The majority of respondents (both teachers and headmasters), however, had taught for at least five years or more. Most had taught either composite classes or junior primary grades, with a smaller proportion of respondents responsible exclusively for the middle and upper primary grades.

In sum, most of the teachers were young, with between 1-10 years' experience and in charge of the junior primary grades.

School and its surrounding community

a. *Type and location of schools sampled:* All of the schools sampled from the North-West and the Great Southern regions were situated in towns. In contrast, the majority of schools in the Eastern Goldfields were on mission stations (again, a note of caution must be raised in the light of the low rate of response from this area). The schools in the Kimberleys were fairly well distributed between mission, pastoral station and town locations.

b. *Educational facilities for Aborigines in the community:* The responses suggested that pre-school facilities were available in most centres but, although the Australian government paid fees for Aboriginal children and 'home makers' have endeavoured to attract pupils, attendance was still low in most areas. Some communities still lacked kindergarten and other pre-school facilities.

The provision of educational programmes for adult Aborigines needs investigation. According to the respondents, there was an appalling under-utilisation of adult programmes, particularly in the North-West. Why are such facilities not used?

Opinions concerning in-service educational policies

a. *Knowledge of policies and need for changes:* The majority of teachers responded that they understood some but not all of the Education Department's current policies concerning Aboriginal education. The existing confusion is apparently due to the overlapping functions of different Commonwealth and State government departments involved in Aboriginal education. Most of the teachers expressed the opinion that new government policies on Aboriginal education were needed.

There was not the same confusion about school policy guidelines. These were frequently established by the staff itself, and changed when necessary to meet prevailing conditions. Teachers responded that they were informed of school policy through staff meetings, discussions with the headmaster, a written school policy, or staff information sheets.

Teachers were asked to comment on the duration of appointment that should be required for teaching in a predominantly Aboriginal school. Eighty per cent of the teachers suggested that a two-year minimum limit should be set for both headmasters and assistants. Several respondents considered that two years could be too long for unsuitable teachers. Others were of the opinion that greater inducement should be offered to suitable teachers to encourage longer periods of service beyond a two-year minimum. With the exception of teachers in the Kimberleys, the majority of respondents were opposed to a maximum time limit. Forty-five per cent of the teachers in the Kimberleys suggested that a maximum time limit should be set, but that the length of time should vary, depending on the rank of the teacher and the location of the school.

b. *Adaptation of curriculum:* Most teachers believed that the present curriculum contained an adequate source of learning experiences for Aboriginal children. However, at the same time the majority saw a need to adapt the curriculum to local situations. The subject areas in which they felt most adaptation was necessary were English language studies, social studies, and mathematics. Respondents claimed that generally most teachers do adapt curriculum content for Aboriginal children, but pointed out that special training was needed to carry out more effective adaptation. They agreed that a special curriculum for *all* Aboriginal children would not be practicable since there was such a wide variation in Aboriginal cultures throughout the State. It was argued that special curricula suitable in, say, Gnowangerup in the Great Southern could be totally unsuitable for Aboriginal children located in the North-West, for example.

Several questions dealt with the 'Project Courses' which have recently been introduced at the secondary school level to teach pre-vocational skills. Response to these questions was low, since few schools at the time of the survey had actually begun to teach the courses. These limited replies seem to suggest that they have been fairly successful. Thirteen headmasters reported that the courses had been effective in achieving the goal of acquiring vocational skills. However, six headmasters of other schools were still uncertain about this. They commented that more specialised training of teachers was needed, and that the courses suffered from lack of equipment.

c. *Overlapping of staff on appointment:* The majority response of teachers was that overlapping of staff was highly desirable. It was thought to be a good idea for new staff to have some discussion with previous teachers. However, in most cases there was limited accommodation in school districts; as well, the long summer vacation created some practical problems in this regard.

d. *In-service training course for teachers of Aboriginal children:* Most of the teachers reported that they had never attended an in-service course dealing with Aboriginal children. This was a significant fact revealed by this survey.

Those who had attended such a course (less than 15 per cent) suggested that the practical aspects of teaching methods and accounts of actual experiences were the most valuable parts of the course. They agreed that more lectures and discussions by experienced teachers and Aboriginal leaders should be added to future courses. They also believed that in-service programmes should have more of a sociological and anthropological basis.

In response to a question concerning the relevance of the W.A. Education Department's *In-Service Book for Teachers of Aboriginal Children* (1971), a large percentage of the teachers replied that they had not even seen the book. Of those who had, most felt it contained information that was relevant to their teaching situation. There were requests for more information on problems of discipline, Aboriginal health, housing, prejudice, how to adapt the curriculum, and practical ideas and aids suitable for Aboriginal pupils.

e. *Planning:*

1. *Planning at the Education Department level:* Responses to a question about general planning for Aboriginal education were varied, but fell into these four main areas of need:

(i) *Material assistance — school level:*

More finance needed to counter lack of parents-and-citizens associations.

More equipment, based on research into special needs.

More expeditious supply of necessary material.

Supply of simple workbooks for reading, phonetics, mathematics.

Simple reading series related to children's needs.

Recognition of the need to provide facilities to meet special requirements of Aborigines.

Special 'readiness' material needed.

More sport and physical education equipment needed.

More camp-school opportunities.

(ii) *Advisory assistance — teaching and techniques:*

In-service conferences needed by all.

More regional in-service conferences.

Special curriculum for Aboriginal children.

Guidance officers to plan remedial teaching.

Appointment of advisory superintendents or teachers in Aboriginal education.

Encouragement of teachers to adapt curricula to meet Aboriginal needs.

Reduction of District Superintendent's load to enable more advisory visits to be made.

Development of more 'project type' courses, and extension of these into the primary school.

More realistic approach to planning of courses. Planning based on experiences.

(iii) *Facilities for Aboriginal children and adults:*

More government and community action, to meet needs of Aborigines.

More pre-schools.

More hostels.

Better housing for Aborigines.

(iv) *Staff:*

Avoid appointing teachers fresh from teachers college.

Smaller pupil-teacher ratios.

More careful selection of staff.

Greater promotional opportunities for headmasters of Special Native Schools.

2. *Planning at school level:* Suggestions for planning at this level can be grouped conveniently into four main categories:

(i) *Courses — curricula — methods:*

Special classes for Aboriginal children.

Teaching in vernacular.

Ability-grouping rather than grade-placing.

Flexible timetabling (scheduling).

Cross-grading.

Definite policy needed to bring Aboriginal children to achievement level of European-Australian children.

Awareness needed of limited conceptual development of Aboriginal pupils.

Emphasis on activity and practical teaching.

Adaptation of syllabus to suit local needs and conditions.

Provision of curriculum guides, and suggestions as to levels of expectation.

(ii) *Teachers and general staffing:*

Staff need to approach problems as a team.

Need for frequent staff discussions.

More than 'youthful enthusiasm' needed.

Experienced staff needed for remedial work.

Fewer staff changes — overlap needed.

Smaller classes.

Need for greater effort to encourage, motivate and provide incentives for success.

More in-service courses.

Teachers required to have special training.

(iii) *General Aboriginal welfare and health:*

Provision of meals at minimum cost.

Need for communication with parents.

Supervision of home environment and hostels to achieve punctuality, adequate nutrition and sleep.

Need for special emphasis on health and hygiene.

Encourage responsibility in Aboriginal children — use as leaders.

(iv) *Materials:*

Adequate display space needed.

Better facilities needed for adequate training in health and hygiene.

3. *Planning at teacher education level:* Responses could be grouped into three major areas:

(i) *Courses in Aboriginal education at teachers colleges:*

Special pre-service courses needed.

Knowledge of problems to be encountered — contact with experienced teachers.

Need for anthropological background.

Training in remedial techniques.

Practice-teaching in schools with Aboriginal children.

Knowledge of psychological and social background of Aboriginal children.

Need for college staff with experience in teaching Aboriginal children.

(ii) *Specifically mentioned courses:*

Language study needed.

Training in educating 'deprived' children.

Provision of short courses in Aboriginal education for teachers appointed.

Methods of adapting curricula.

English as a second language.

(iii) *Remedial teaching techniques:*

This area was seen as the most essential item of training for teachers of Aboriginal children.

f. *Mixed Aboriginal/European-Australian school:* There was general consensus that the children who are most often neglected in a mixed school are the slower students — both Aboriginal and European-Australian. Although some teachers felt that Aboriginal children were occasionally neglected in order to cater for the needs of European-Australian children, in general, the teachers believed that the main differences in the classroom were ability levels and not 'racial' ones. Ability grouping, unit progress and other methods of individualising syllabi were suggested ways of meeting individual needs. But it was recognised that teachers cannot devote all the time that is ideally required to meet the special needs of children at either extreme of achievement.

The final question in this section was: 'Do you believe that, in many cases, Aboriginal children might just as well not be going to school at all?' Approximately 75 per cent of the teachers answered 'No'. Teachers from the Great Southern region were less sure. Only 58 per cent of them responded 'No'. In other words, a fairly substantial number of teachers from the Great Southern agreed that, in many cases, Aboriginal children might just as well not be going to school at all. In general, the comments from the teachers indicated that although progress in cognitive learning might be minimal, the socialisation process resulting from school attendance was considered 'worthwhile'.

g. *Remedial teaching:* More than 70 per cent of all teachers agreed that there was a 'great need' for 'concentrated remedial teaching'. Those who did not agree suggested in their comments that there was a greater need for 'readiness' teaching, rather than 'remedial'.

The period of an Aboriginal child's schooling generally seen as the most critical was that of pre-school and junior primary. However, upper primary and early secondary were cited by many teachers as critical in another sense. At this time, it was suggested, Aboriginal children became increasingly aware of their disadvantaged position and began to question the value of education for themselves.

h. *Mastery of English:* Responses indicated that except in remote districts all children spoke a form of 'English' but that this was deficient in most cases. This was not simply 'poor English'. Linguists are currently referring to this speech as 'Aboriginal English', which is defined as a dialect with an English vocabulary but having a structure, grammar and intonation that relate to a 'superseded' vernacular form of speech.

i. *Vocational training and employment opportunities:* The general consensus of teachers was that employment prospects for Aboriginal school leavers were poor. Present avenues (those mentioned most frequently), were as follows:

> For Aboriginal boys: Labourers (shire, wharf, water supply and road); station work; stockmen and general hands; gardeners and semi-skilled tradesmen.
>
> For Aboriginal girls: shop assistants; domestics; nursing aides; office jobs; kindergarten helpers.

Their answers highlight the need for vocational training which prepares Aboriginal children for general employment in their home districts. 'Project-type' courses with tradesmen instructing were most frequently suggested. Provision of hostels in larger centres and government action to provide employment were also seen as necessary.

There was evidence of the negative effect of dearth of employment opportunities on Aborigines, principally in their attitudes toward continuing education. Teachers mentioned also the adverse effects of the situation in camps and reserves, where many were able to live on welfare payments without working. Creation of employment and the necessity to change community attitudes toward employing Aborigines were seen as two essential factors in reversing the present poor employment situation for Aborigines.

j. *Health:* Responses showed very strong evidence of poor health and nutrition and their adverse effects on the education of Aborigines. The main effects seen in the classroom were frequent 'day-dreaming', inattention, short attention spans, poor concentration, apathy and restlessness. Many schools have endeavoured to overcome these problems with school health programmes involving shower facilities, and the provision of milk, protein biscuits and vitamin tablets.

Opinions about teacher education

a. *Teaching of English as a second language:* The teaching of English as a second language was seen to be of greater importance in the Kimberleys and Eastern Goldfields schools than in the North-West and Great Southern regions. This was undoubtedly due to the greater deficiency in English reported for the Kimberleys and Eastern Goldfields school children.

b. *Education motivation:* Motivation was assessed as strongest in grade 1 and weakest in grade 7. The lack of long-term aspirations appeared to lead to a depreciation of the value of education and consequently decreasing motivation to learn.

c. *Discipline and behavioural problems:* Aggressiveness and absenteeism were more frequently mentioned as behavioural problems in the Great Southern and Eastern Goldfields than in the Kimberleys and the North-West regions. On the other hand, withdrawal and shyness were more common in the latter regions. Present living conditions, permissive child-rearing, parental disinterest and peer-group influences were thought to be at the basis of the behavioural problems associated with Aboriginal children, but were areas in which school influence was minimal.

In dealing with behavioural problems, teachers rated positive methods (praise and reward) as more successsful than negative ones (detention and corporal punishment). Many teachers commented that Aboriginal children did not regard 'staying in class' as a punishment.

d. *Aboriginal culture as part of curriculum:* About 75 per cent of Kimberley and North-West teachers and 50 per cent of Eastern Goldfields and Great Southern teachers suggested it was desirable to impart knowledge of Aboriginal cultures to all children (both Aboriginal and non-Aboriginal) in school. It is likely that the higher value attached to 'tribal' customs in the northern areas of the State was the reason why teachers from that area expressed the need for Aboriginal cultural values to be taught at school.

The majority of teachers did not think that the existing materials used in their schools had any ethnocentric bias against Aborigines. However, it was pointed out by one teacher that European-Australian books with predominantly 'white' values assumed that these were *good,* and that by inference other values (including many Aboriginal values) were bad, or at least, not as good.

e. *Special training for teachers of Aboriginal children:* The majority of teachers considered special training to be desirable for teachers of Aboriginal children. The importance of learning remedial teaching techniques and having practical experience teaching Aboriginal children were stressed.

f. *Attributes of teachers who were considered effective with Aboriginal children:* Female teachers were considered more effective in junior primary grades (1 and 2), while the converse was true for the upper grades (6 and 7). This seems to reflect educational policy and practice more than anything else, for certainly the attributes needed for effective teaching at any level would not necessarily be sex-oriented. Understanding, adaptability, fairness, patience and firmness were all rated essential for effectiveness in teaching Aboriginal children.

g. *Parental contact with school:* Generally, parents were informed of their children's progress once a term through their report forms. Usually the parents or guardians were informed of school activities orally through their children, or through newsletters and circulars sent by the school. The main problem with this last mode of communication was that most Aboriginal parents could not read the newsletters. Another reason for minimal parental contact with schools was their reported indifference to education; this was considered to be a consequence of their perceiving few benefits likely to derive from it. Teachers say they have had only moderate success in trying to involve Aboriginal parents directly in the school and in the education of their children. Displaying children's work at school at frequent intervals met with the greatest success.

h. *Motivating Aboriginal children to continue their education:* The ways suggested in the questionnaire for encouraging Aboriginal children to continue their education were thought by the teachers to have a possibility of only moderate success. Trying to encourage them through monetary incentives, free housing or vocationally-oriented courses would not be convincing, teachers suggested, if the real opportunities for employment were not made available to Aborigines.

i. *Acceptance of Aboriginal in local community:* The responses to the question: 'What present problems do you consider prevent the complete acceptance of the Aboriginal in the local community?' were divided into two main categories:

1. *Behaviour seen as originating in the Aboriginal* (listed in order of frequency mentioned):

Lack of personal hygiene.

Unreliable work habits; do not keep jobs; indolent; lazy.

Excessive consumption of alcohol.

Anti-social behaviour, delinquency, 'permissiveness', immorality.

Reliance on 'handouts', easier to live on welfare handouts.

Lack of ambition; very low aspirations; apathy.

Indifference to dress and appearance; lack of self-respect.

Inability to manage own affairs.

Lack of interest, ability and responsibility.

Shyness; lack of confidence; inferiority complex.

2. *Problems not attributed to Aboriginal descent:*

Prejudice and traditional non-acceptance by prospective employers.

Lack of adequate housing; over-crowding; living on reserves.

Language barriers.

Inability to attain or achieve standard of education or literacy.

Lack of employment opportunities and low socio-economic status.

Health factors.

Different values; education and material goods not valued.

Lack of human understanding on the part of 'white' people.

Those who have accepted 'white' standards are accepted.

'White' resentment of welfare handouts.

j. *Effect of home environment on Aboriginal children's education:* Children from town houses, hostels, mission stations and camp reserves were rated on a number of items as measures of the interaction of family background and adaptability in school. These covered level of nutrition, personal hygiene, interest of parent or guardian, educationally stimulating environment, desire for self-advancement, English vocabulary, adjustment to school, occupational expectations, self-esteem, co-operative attitude, and respect of adults for academic achievement. Children living in hostels were rated highest in terms of these values, in contrast to those living on reserves, who were rated lowest. Those living in town houses and on mission stations were ranked in between those from hostels and reserves. This would appear to follow logically from the fact that the hostel environment would be most like the school environment, the reserve one least similar to school life.

k. *Leisure-type activities for Aborigines:* In most communities there are youth and church clubs, organised sports (including swimming), and libraries for children. There are also special adult education programmes and Aboriginal centres. Although these facilities exist in most towns, they are not always utilised. One major problem appears to be the lack of transportation from camps and reserves to the town itself where most activities are located. It was reported that this was exacerbated by the fact (or 'myth'?) that Aborigines did not like to walk about in the dark.

l. *Effect of linguistic and cultural background on education of Aboriginal children:* Several questions were included to ascertain the effect of language and cultural background on the educational progress of Aboriginal children. Responses from the Kimberleys and North-West schools indicated that between one third and one half of the pupils of grades 1 to 7 were adversely affected by their linguistic-cultural background. This negative effect is considered either to inhibit practically all learning or to be a major difficulty in coping with a normal education programme. The negative effect on learning was not considered peculiar to any one grade. It was, of course, shown as 'high' in most junior primary grades. Another feature of the responses to this question was the high incidence of reporting of the retarding effect in grade 7 and in post-primary grades. This was probably due to the higher verbal content of the syllabus and greater dependence on study-reading, where language deficiencies become a particularly telling factor. It may be significant that the high adverse effect of language deficiency in grade 7 and post-primary classes matched the low level of motivation among Aboriginal children in these grades, mentioned above. It could well be that these figures illustrate the cumulative effect of cultural-linguistic deficiencies and a continual pattern of failure. Failure to learn in this sense is not so much a result of lack of motivation; rather, lack of motivation is a result of failure to learn, or what is to be learnt is not seen as immediately relevant.

In North-West and Kimberleys regions the adverse effect of language/cultural background was reported to hinder the progress of Aboriginal children as follows:

Approximate percentage of children adversely affected:

Reading	80%
Oral English	90%
Written Expression	80%
Social Studies	80%
Mathematics	75%
Adjustment	75%

A similar situation exists in both the Eastern Goldfields and Great Southern schools. This raises the question of the relative effect of each of the two components — language on the one hand and cultural background on the other. The great majority of Aboriginal children and adults in the Great Southern region speak and use English as the means of everyday communication. The same applies to a lesser extent in the Eastern Goldfields. Yet the teachers' estimates of the combined effects of language-culture are remarkably similar throughout the State. This may suggest that in the Great Southern the divergent socio-cultural background of Aboriginal pupils was as inhibiting to learning as both language and socio-cultural barriers in other areas. It may also mean that the socio-cultural values of people of Aboriginal descent are (or, are seen as) a more inhibiting factor than language *per se* and that what was thought to have been the effect of language has actually been largely caused by basic socio-cultural differences.

Certainly within each region there are considerable variations in the living conditions and the family values of Aborigines. It was mentioned above that teachers could distinguish among children who live in town houses, missions, hostels, or in camps on the outskirts of town or in reserves. Teachers indicated that in each educational area assessed, the lowest range of abilities involved children from camps and reserves where living conditions were extremely poor. However, even among the better-housed families the socio-cultural 'lag' could be deleterious to Aboriginal children's progress at school. The Watts-Gallacher Report (1964:36) suggests that, although there is growing conviction among Aboriginal parents that education is a 'good thing' and they are making some endeavour to provide a favourable climate toward education, they are limited by their own deficient background.

m. *Mental ability of Aboriginal children:* Several questions endeavoured to ascertain the estimated vocabulary level of Aboriginal children. Figures supplied indicated a very wide range of abilities. In a few returns, while the chronological age and the estimated vocabulary age were very close, the majority of teachers noted retardation. From the information supplied, it is estimated that Aboriginal children in the North-West, Kimberleys and Eastern Goldfields areas in the 5-7 year age range have their vocabulary range $1\frac{1}{2}$ years retarded, and at the age of 12 years this retardation has extended to an estimated $2\frac{1}{2}$ years. The estimates made by teachers in the Great Southern District are similar for the 5-7 year age group, but at 12 years the retardation appears to be lower, and Aboriginal children of upper primary and post-primary grades have a reasonably good command of everyday English.

The implication seems clear — that pre-school education for Aboriginal children is essential. The effect of home conditions on the development of vocabulary revealed that children from camps and reserves were rated lower on vocabulary than children from town houses and hostels.

n. *Reading material:* The survey sought teachers' opinions on the principles governing content and structure of reading materials for Aboriginal children in the 5-7 and 7-12 year age groups who were beginning to read. Teachers were asked to assess the relative value of producing reading material related to:

   (i) Local Aboriginal 'folklore';
   (ii) European-Australian nursery rhymes or cultural heritage;
   (iii) Experiential backgrounds in both cultures;
   (iv) Experiential approach to the learning of reading.

Seventy per cent of Kimberley and North-West teachers saw value in relating reading material to Aboriginal 'folklore' for both the 5-7 and 7-12 year age groups. No teachers from the Eastern Goldfields schools agreed that this would be 'most' valuable. A few saw some possible value, but most were in disagreement. Great Southern teachers appear to be evenly divided between seeing some value, and disagreeing with the suggestion.

Opinions relating reading to European-Australian cultural heritage and nursery rhymes were fairly mixed: few teachers had strong opinions either way, although about 50 per cent of teachers saw some possible value in developing an understanding of European-Australian cultural heritage as assisting in the assimilation of Aboriginal people. For linguistic development of the Aboriginal child, some of the nursery-rhymes heritage of European children must of necessity be introduced. However, integrated with this could be nursery rhymes based on Aboriginal children — i.e. Mary and Elizabeth Durack's collection.

Responses indicated that teachers in all parts of Western Australia were overwhelmingly in favour of having reading material related to a planned experiential approach to the learning of reading and incorporating elements of both cultures. This attitude is in keeping with the recommendations of the Watts-Gallacher Report (1964:129): that is,

> . . . this reading material should reflect the Aboriginal culture and also the European culture to which the Aboriginal child is being introduced

and also,

> . . . recommends that a series of readers be constructed on the basis of vocabulary and structure control reflecting elements of both Aboriginal and European cultures.

(The reading material referred to above is for the use of Aboriginal children at the end of stage III of the Northern Territory's reading development programme.)

Teachers were asked whether the reading material currently available, and in use, related to the interests of Aboriginal children. The majority of responses suggested only a moderate or low relationship. The low interest level clearly warrants the development of new material.

An indication of the availability and use of locally constructed experience readers was sought. Although 'yes' responses were low, the recent teacher interest in the making of experience readers (as outlined in the 1973 In-Service Education publication *Developing the Child*) should result in an increase in functional reading material of much more interest to Aboriginal children. (A short course in the construction of 'On the spot reading materials' using polaroid cameras was developed in the final term of 1972 for graduating students at Graylands Teachers College, and in 1973 there was considerable development of this scheme.)

Teachers listed reading material in current use (end of 1972), shown in descending order of frequency, as follows:

Happy Venture
Readers' Digest
Wide Range
Endeavour Series
S.R.A. and W.A.R.D.S. Reading Development Programme
Janet and John
Cowboy Sam
Young Australians
Bush Books
Beacon Series
McKee Readers

In addition, a wide range of further reading materials was listed, suggesting that teachers are experimenting and diversifying their reading programmes. These were:

Words in Colour
Locally produced material
Dragon Series
Epic Prose
Far and Near Readers
Far West Readers

Look Ahead Series
Kennet Readers
I.T.A.
Advance Series
Dulch Readers
Yamadji Readers
Dolphin Series
Ladybird Readers
Schonell Readers
Vanguard Series

Responses showed that in 1972 the basic reading material in use reflected European-Australian interests and values — i.e. Happy Venture, Wide Range, Readers' Digest and Endeavour Series being the most commonly used. The fact that teachers used these readers although they have little or no cultural interest value to the Aboriginal child, particularly in more remote areas, further emphasises the need for new materials that conform with the principles of vocabulary and structure control, and high interest for Aboriginal children. On the whole, the Endeavour Series is seen as best meeting some of these needs.

There appears to be some evidence that teachers in more remote districts are not aware of new reading material as it becomes available, so they have very limited opportunity for examining this at first hand. Some scheme whereby new reading (and other) materials could be introduced to teachers in their schools appears to be needed. If special advisory teachers are not considered warranted, some form of 'Travelling Box Scheme' (similar to the Hadley Library boxes of former years) may give outback teachers the opportunity to see 'what is new'. There seems to be a need also to construct (or modify) existing language development 'boxes' of the Peabody, Distar and S.R.A. type to suit the needs of Aboriginal children.

o. *Knowledge of local Aboriginal dialects:* The value, to teachers, of knowledge of local Aboriginal dialects was seen as of 'some value' by half of the teachers responding; the other half were about evenly divided between considering this to be of 'great value' and of 'little value'. The key to this pattern of response, except for remote districts, appears to be that all children speak some form of 'English' even if it is deficient.

Just as the *amount* of dialect used is known to vary considerably from place to place, so is the *nature* of the dialect, making a teacher's knowledge of one dialect viable in one place but almost useless in another. (The mission station at La Grange serves an Aboriginal population speaking five different dialects.) The question arises here of where the teacher is to acquire a knowledge of local Aboriginal dialects. The best place is probably in the district where it is commonly used; but if the present pattern of staff transfer continues, teachers would become acquainted with a particular dialect only when they were preparing to go elsewhere, in all probability to a place where the acquired language skill would be either useless or not required. Watts-Gallacher (1964:100) recognise the desirability of education in the vernacular, but also recognise the practical problems involved. That is, 'that it would be impossible to require all teachers to master an Aboriginal language.' Perhaps the solution may lie in the training of apt Aboriginal pupils as teaching aides for schools in their language area. It is important, however, that they be employed as aides and not teachers, if Aboriginal education *per se* is not to be devalued by being in the hands of untrained teachers.

p. *Knowledge of Aboriginal culture:* In response to a question concerning the need for teachers to have a knowledge of Aboriginal culture, teachers indicated that there was a need for a background and understanding of Aboriginal culture in general. Some of the problems attendant on knowledge of dialect are also applicable here. Cultural patterns vary from place to place. However, the transfer of staff is not of such significance in this respect. Teachers may move, but schools usually stay; and it should be an interesting and not too difficult task for teachers, over the years, to build up a useful account both of local traditional culture, and of local (and other) problems of social and cultural change. This record, of course, should stay in the school. This approach may open up many ways of bringing the Aboriginal adult population closer to the school.

General comments on problems encountered in various subject areas
a. *Spoken English*
    1. *Problems:* Getting the children to vocalise was a major problem in all regions. Approximately 50 per cent of teachers from each district marked this as an area of difficulty. Lack of success in school, poor vocabulary, pronunciation difficulties and lack of incentives for the use of 'normal' English outside the school were also rated as exacerbating the problem. Generally, the responses indicated that Aboriginal children commence school with a variety of non-standard English dialects which inhibit or create great difficulties for the development of English language.
    2. *Remedies:* Teachers' responses suggest very clearly that visual stimuli of all kinds, particularly those related to the child's environment, are most successful in promoting speech. Informal situations, activity approaches and the use of audio-visual aids of all kinds rank highly in listed 'successful ways and means'.
b. *Written English*
    1. *Problems:* A limited vocabulary and poor technical and grammatical skills are major reasons given for retardation in written English. Lack of experience outside the immediate environment (hence a limited range) was also rated fairly high. Poor spelling ability, home environment, infrequent attendance, and limited concentration span were also seen as limiting ability in written English.
    2. *Remedies:* The problems of written English reflect the problems of spoken English. Suggestions for improving skills in this area include:
        (i) Activities based on relevant experience and the immediate environment.
        (ii) Use of colour slides, pictures, etc. as providing motivation.
        (iii) Avoidance of lengthy topics.
        (iv) Re-telling of actual happenings, well-known stories, etc.
        (v) Group production of verse or story.
c. *Mathematics*
    1. *Problems:* Most teachers seem to consider the 'cultural environment' area to be a major limiting problem in all regions in the State. The minimal use of numbers in the vernacular and the subsequent difficulty

entailed in establishing basic number facts and processes, increase the difficulty in developing abstract number concepts.

2. *Remedies:*

    (i) Practical, concrete approach to basic number concepts.

    (ii) Mathematic 'games' to consolidate processes.

    (iii) Shorter periods to cover lack of concentration span.

    (iv) Relating mathematics to practical situations involving local area.

    (v) Group and individual tuition for early remediation.

    (vi) 'Shop' and play money for money practice.

Conclusions

From the point of view of the classroom teacher, it seems reasonably clear that Aboriginal children, whether 'tribally' oriented or otherwise, reveal many of the attitudes toward education reported for lower-class Western Europeans — that is, they reflect socio-economic circumstances and perceptions as much as they do 'Aboriginal' ones. Particularly does this seem to be the case for urbanised Aboriginal children at these socio-economic levels. For example, these children are more likely to respond to concrete, tangible, immediate and particular properties of things, rather than the more abstract, categorical and relational properties more characteristic of middle-class values which foster aspirations for academic and vocational 'success' and the patterns of deferred gratification necessary to achieve these (see generally Ausubel 1969). Aboriginal children (and their parents) apparently do not perceive education as being instrumental to future success. To them, the future is always vague and uncertain and guidelines for present action are never clear. These differences in perceptual disposition are carried into all the areas leading to 'success' in the school situation — numeracy and literacy skills and the like. Teachers, by virtue of their training and middle-class origin, place greater emphasis on the learning of abstract relationships and on the abstract use of language. Consequently, Aboriginal children on the whole experience much greater difficulty in mastering the curriculum (and its interpretation by the teacher) than do their non-Aboriginal counterparts. Aboriginal school children are quite clearly handicapped by a lower level of intellectual functioning than is typical of comparable European-Australian children of the same age. Many of these intellectual characteristics are typical of children living in what has been termed 'a culture of poverty' situation. Material impoverishment in the home is matched by intellectual impoverishment at school. Retardation in this sense stems largely from the poor standard of English spoken in the home and the general lack of books and other 'educational resources' — including aspirations for success — in the wider society.

The basic problem for teachers (given realistic operational goals) is really the solving of the problem of intellectual retardation — mainly, the poor development of verbal and mathematical skills and the concomitant absence of intellectual aspirations. The solution is equally basic: provide 'better than average' teachers, and utilise teaching strategies that are generally effective and specifically appropriate when dealing with Aboriginal children. By 'better than average' teachers is meant 'educators' in the sense that their role is seen less and less in terms of inculcating 'knowledge' and more and more in encouraging thinking and in facilitating education (e.g. see UNESCO Report 1972).

For the average classroom teacher, the following points appear to be important as suggesting operational guidelines:

1. The establishment of empathy and rapport between teacher and child.
2. The realisation by the teacher that he or she is a facilitator, director, or co-ordinator of a learning situation and that, particularly with children of this background, a formal approach may not be conducive to optimal learning.
3. Learning materials should be geared to a state of 'continual readiness' — i.e. ascertaining as carefully as possible what the learner brings to the learning situation and how he perceives it.
4. On-going tasks should be mastered (internalised) before new areas are introduced. Emphasis should be on consolidation. Slowness with intellectual tasks should not be confused with dullness. Planning should ensure adequate time for the completion of tasks.
5. Structured learning situations could possibly facilitate learning at these levels. 'Programmed' learning materials, for example, are carefully researched and planned, sequentially arranged, use small steps, and provide for self-pacing and for feedback, and so on.
6. Arrange for frequent evaluation and feedback so as to enhance consolidation by confirming, clarifying and correcting previous learning.
7. Provide for individualisation (self-pacing).
8. De-emphasise a verbal approach. Emphasise visual and manipulative skills: programme 'learning by doing' experiences.
9. Emphasise the present — not the future or the past. Relate learning to its relevant application, the solving of real problems in the children's environment. Structure activities to experience success.
10. Perceive the overall task within the framework of education as a lifelong process.

The problem of Aboriginal education   For decades, social scientists have carried out research into problems confronting minority groups in various societies. Their studies have centred on the possible causes for unequal relationships between majority and minority groups. Whether they conclude that the causes are economic, psychological or socio-cultural, they generally can be reduced to basic inequality in status and power relations that pervade society. It is obvious in Australian society that people of Aboriginal descent are a minority group occupying an inferior status and are mostly cut off from majority values and the benefits that the wider society enjoys. This position of inferiority has clearly many implications for the education of Aboriginal children. What can educators do to change the existing position of Aborigines in Australian society?

Educators in various societies have generally approached this kind of question from two divergent points of view. On the one hand, there have been those who have looked upon schools as agents of social and cultural change and approached the problem of inequality through the educational system. They have urged greater emphasis on compensatory education (for members of minority groups) and increased equality of access to educational opportunities. On the other hand, there are those who have been more sceptical about using schools to induce change and focus their attention on forces outside the schools where, they suggest, the source of inequality is located. Foster (1966:143), for example, in referring to the impact of educational institutions in African countries, comments:

> . . . schools are remarkably clumsy instruments for inducing prompt large-scale changes in under-developed areas. To be sure, formal education has had immense impact in Africa but its consequences have rarely been those anticipated, and the schools have not often functioned in the manner intended by educational planners.

A recent study in the United States by Jencks *et al.* (1972:*passim*), that re-assessed the effects of family and schooling in determining position in the occupational hierarchy, concluded that prevailing inequities are a part of society and institutions such as schools cannot erase them. It suggested that all the resources and energy devoted to improving the educational system of the minority groups in the United States had not resulted in decreasing the income gap between the rich and the poor. In effect, even when controlling for I.Q., amount of education and family background, there was still a disparity of income between 'white' and 'black' males.

Australia is facing many of the same problems that confronted the United States in the last decade or so. However, the situation is certainly not identical and the decisions to be made have to take into account these main differences. Perhaps many of the questions that are being asked are more like those in developing nations. Should the curriculum be adapted to local conditions and be more relevant to Aboriginal culture and experiences, or should it be geared toward the values of European-Australians? Should educators be concerned only with educating Aboriginal children, or also with teaching adult Aborigines? What should be the nature of schooling: boarding schools to remove the children from the influences of their families, day schools catering for children but not for adults, or community schools which try to educate all members of a community?

The question is whether one can separate the Aboriginal from his (her) role as a member of his own community, his family or even society at large. If the goal of education is to change the Aboriginal's role in society, it might have greater chances of success if not only the individual were educated for this change, but also his family, the surrounding community and society at large.

Further, not all education takes place in schools. Perhaps educators ought to be more concerned with the part played by informal or out-of-school education. This is an area still requiring research, since little is known about 'education' outside the formal school system. How do Aborigines learn to be gardeners or stockmen or to take up the various roles within their own community?

It has been suggested that more vocational training is needed for Aboriginal children, ostensibly because they tend to leave school at an early age and do not have the necessary skills to obtain jobs. To avoid this situation, teachers have suggested in their responses that vocational skills should be taught during the upper 'primary and secondary grades. But if this course of action were taken instead of educating the children in 'academic' subjects, would this not be training Aboriginal children to take up lower positions in society?

Finally, a more important question is, who should make the decisions about how Aborigines should be educated? How can the educators encourage the Aborigines to become involved in the educational system and in the major decisions that will affect their future? Much could be gained by investigating the methods used by Paulo Freire (1972a, 1972b) and his approach to adult education. His philosophical insights demand a method of discovering the people's significant themes, and then returning the themes to the people and the basic education programme. The need to involve Aborigines in designing education curricula and educational decision-making is at issue.

Aborigines need not necessarily merge into the wider population. But in coming to a decision about this, it is what they want to do which is important. Some will undoubtedly seek their future, and that of their children, within a largely European-Australian framework and perhaps play down their Aboriginal heritage. On the other hand, particularly since many of the social and legal constraints discouraging participation in the wider society have been removed, many may well retain a healthy pride in being Aboriginal. Some, because of discrimination in particular communities, may have little real choice. The main point, surely, is that they should be free (in this sense) to make the same choice as do other Australians. In a democratic society this must be the starting point for their education.

Note: This chapter was adapted from a Graylands College report: 'A survey of Aboriginal education in selected Western Australian schools' by C. F. Makin and D. Ibbotson, edited by J. Currie. The questionnaire which was used in this survey is available from the College.

References

AUSUBEL, D. P. 1969 *Readings in school learning.* Holt, Rinehart and Winston, New York.
EDUCATION DEPARTMENT OF WESTERN AUSTRALIA 1973 In-service course for teachers of Aboriginal Education, *Objectives in Aboriginal education — Developing the child.*
FOSTER, P. J. 1966 The vocational fallacy in development planning. In *Education and economic development* (C. A. Anderson *and* M. J. Bowman eds), pp. 142-66. Cass, London.
INTERNATIONAL COMMISSION ON THE DEVELOPMENT OF EDUCATION, UNESCO 1972 *Learning to be: the world of education today and tomorrow.* Harrap, London.
JENCKS, C. *et al.* 1972 *Inequality: a reassessment of effects of family and schooling in America.* Basic Books, New York.
FREIRE, P. 1972a *Pedagogy of the oppressed.* Penguin Books, Harmondsworth.
———1972b *Cultural action for freedom.* Penguin Books, Harmondsworth.
WATTS, B. H. *and* J. D. GALLACHER 1964 *Report on an investigation into the curriculum and teaching methods used in Aboriginal schools in the Northern Territory.* Report to the Minister of State for Territories, Parliament House, Canberra.

18 Language problems, language planning and Aboriginal education

Susan Kaldor

The rapidly growing body of sociolinguistic writings on language planning[1] reflects an increased awareness by many people all over the world of the fact that language issues are of great importance in the life of nations, that they require close attention by governments and that governments need the advice of specialists for developing language policies. Such awareness has typically been more characteristic of the 'developing' nations (Fishman *et al.* 1968), than of the 'developed' ones. To regard language issues as matters of national importance is an attitude which is new to the majority of Australians. However, recently formulated policies in relation to migrant education and Aboriginal bilingual education[2] are gradually bringing questions of language into the public consciousness. This paper examines language problems and their treatment in relation to Aboriginal education. An attempt is made to outline a systematic framework in which potential and actual language planning for Aboriginal education may be investigated. Areas which have so far received inadequate attention will be specified within this framework.

Language problems in education may be defined as 'problems caused by differences in language, dialect, style (in sum, "code-differences") between persons who need to communicate with each other in order to proceed toward the fulfilment of educational goals'. Such problems are likely to be experienced, at some stage, by most of those who participate in Aboriginal education, directly or indirectly, both at the 'receiving' and the 'imparting' end of the educational process.

The children's language problems Let us take first the 'receiving' end of the educational process, the target population of any educational programme directed at Aborigines, the Aboriginal learner. Aboriginal learners may be divided into (1) pre-school, (2) primary, (3) secondary, (4) tertiary students and (5) adults who are potential or actual participants in adult education schemes. This paper focuses on the problems of category No. 2 — the primary school child.

In order to function successfully in and outside school during his primary education, a child needs to be able to communicate successfully (a) with his parents, other kinsmen and generally members of his household, (b) his classmates, (c) children in other classes, in his own school or in other schools, (d) his teacher/s, (e) members of the wider community in the region and (f) members of the wider community outside the region. We may call such links the child's 'lines of communication'. If he has difficulties in any of these lines of communication due to differences between his language/dialect/style on the one hand, and the language/dialect/style of other persons in his environment, then the child may be said to have language problems.[3]

Aboriginal children in Australia may experience language problems along several of the lines of communication outlined above. The particular configuration for each child depends on a number of factors, *viz.* a condition which I shall call the child's own 'linguistic state' (whether monolingual in an Aboriginal language, bilingual in an Aboriginal language and a non-standard form of English, monolingual in a non-standard form of English, monolingual in 'standard' Australian English, etc.), the type of school he enters (whether education is monolingual or bilingual, whether the school population is predominantly Aboriginal or non-Aboriginal) and the position of the school in the wider community (whether in a large city, country town, in an isolated desert community, at a pastoral station, etc.).

Table 1 shows how language problems along the various lines of communication (shown here as a, b, c, d, e, f) may vary according to the children's linguistic state and the type of school they enter.

		Type of School				
		Monolingual (English) Education			Bilingual Education	
		School Population				
Child's linguistic state		Predominantly non-Aboriginal	Mixed	Predominantly Aboriginal	Language same as child's	Language different
Monolingual	Aboriginal language	b,c,d,(e),f	b,c,d, (e),f	d,f	d_2,f	(b),(c),d_1, d_2,(e),f
	Non-standard English	d,f	d,f	(b),(c),d,f	—	—
	Standard English	Ø	(b),(c)	(b),(c)	—	—
Bilingual	Aboriginal Language/ Non-standard English	d,f	d,f	d,f	d_2,f	d_1,d_2,(e),f
	Aboriginal Language/ Standard English	Ø	Ø	Ø	Ø	(b),(c),d_1, (e)

Ø = no language problems d_1 = communication with d_2 = communication
— = not applicable   Aboriginal teacher   with non-Aboriginal teacher

Brackets indicate that the child may have language problems only with certain sections of a category of speakers representing a particular line of communication, e.g. monolingual speakers of an Aboriginal language will have difficulties in communicating with only non-Aboriginal members of their regional environment.

Note: This table represents much oversimplification and can only serve as a rough indication of differences among groups. Divisions are, of course, not watertight (e.g. between 'mixed' and 'predominantly Aboriginal' or 'predominantly non-Aboriginal'). Relatively severe problems are shown, while relatively less severe problems are not (e.g. a speaker of non-standard English may have problems along 'b' and 'c' in monolingual schools, where the school population is predominantly non-Aboriginal, but these are not likely to be as severe as his problems along 'd' and 'f').
The above categories of speakers may be further subdivided into speakers with varying degrees of proficiency in either of the languages (see Douglas 1973).

Table 1: Language problems along lines of communication 'a'-'f'

Thus, when a child who is monolingual in an Aboriginal language enters a monolingual (Australian-English-medium only) school in a community where his own vernacular is spoken and where the school population is predominantly Aboriginal and monolingual in the same language, he is likely to encounter language problems only along lines of communication 'd' and 'f'. If he enters a bilingual school in the same community, then line 'd' has to be subdivided into two branches: line 'd$_1$', that connecting him with the Aboriginal teacher and 'd$_2$', that connecting him with the non-Aboriginal teacher. The child's language problems are then restricted to 'd$_2$'.[4] If a child who is monolingual in an Aboriginal language enters a school which has a predominantly non-Aboriginal population, then he will experience language problems also along lines of communication 'b', 'c', and 'e', in addition to 'd' and 'f'.

Lines 'd' and 'f' are the paths which lead to further education in the majority language of the nation, 'standard' Australian English. Line 'd' is to be interpreted as comprising not only communication with the teacher, but also, passively, at the decoding end, with all writers and producers of textbooks and educational programmes in different media which reach the school. Line 'f' includes writers, speakers, producers, editors and others who are responsible for the general output of the mass media.

The problems of language planners   The planners' problems arise out of the realisation that the children's language problems must be solved and that this is an issue of significance at governmental level.

The term 'planner' as used here refers to all those persons — politicians, administrators, linguists, educationists, anthropologists or other specialists — who are engaged in planning, designing, or advising on the design of education programmes involving language.[5] It is beyond the scope of this paper to discuss differences between the problems of each of these categories of persons in the course of planning processes — we shall be concerned only with broad goals which may be assumed to be relevant to all categories.

The requirements of language planning for Aboriginal education are shown in a summary outline in Table 2, where planning areas are related to various aspects of planning. The discussion which follows is an elaboration of this outline.

English   Table 1 shows that almost every type of speaker needs help in the promotion of the flow of communication along lines 'd' and 'f', through the medium of 'standard' Australian English, hereinafter to be referred to simply as 'English'.[6]

The development of English has been of central concern to the various State and Commonwealth education authorities since the earliest days of Aboriginal education. However, the assumptions on which the teaching of English rested, have undergone drastic revision in recent years. Although the history of English teaching in Australia is probably well-known to the majority of readers, it is worth recalling it here for the purposes of further discussion. The earlier — and, in some parts of the Commonwealth quite recently held — philosophy was that English is acquired by all children alike in Australian schools no matter what ethnic and linguistic backgrounds they

			Aspects of Planning			
Planning Areas			Research priorities	Teacher training	Source materials	Evaluation
For monolingual _and_ bilingual programmes	English (standard)	as a second language				
		as a second dialect				
For bilingual programmes only	Other languages	role definition				
		graphisation				
		standardisation				
		modernisation				
	Co-ordination of two components of bilingual programmes					

Table 2: Outline of proposal for language planning

come from. Children were expected to 'pick up' the language of the school without any trouble, as, indeed, in some cases they did. This earlier educational philosophy has been, gradually and with varying timing in individual States, giving way to a new approach originally developed by the Commonwealth Office of Education for use in the Northern Territory. The new approach leans heavily on Australian experience in migrant education and is based on principles developed in the branch of applied linguistics known as the Teaching of English as a Second Language (TESL).

The field of TESL developed all over the world primarily to meet the demands of children whose mother tongue is a language other than English and who live in a country where the national language is a dialect of English. We need not go into the well-known principles on which TESL practices rest beyond recalling that the basic assumption of all second language teaching is that first and second language acquisition are fundamentally different processes and that the average learner who had acquired his first language 'naturally' in his social-cultural environment, does need specialist help in second language learning, when the circumstances of first language acquisition no longer apply and when he has to counteract the forces of interference from the mother tongue.

TESL methods were, until recently, not considered relevant to the language problems of the child whose mother tongue and only language is a non-standard form of English. In the past, in English-speaking countries and elsewhere where standard dialects were taught to speakers of non-standard dialects of the same language, such teaching used to be considered 'remedial'. The child's own dialect was regarded as a defective and distorted replica of the standard dialect. 'Incorrect' pronunciation, 'incorrect' grammatical and vocabulary usage were to be 'eradicated' and the child was to be taught to 'speak and write correctly'. Recent work with Negro children and children of other ethnic minorities in the United States has brought into focus the futility and often harmful consequences of the educational principle of 'eradication'. Specialists in the education of speakers of non-standard dialects now urge that the child's own dialect be regarded as a resource rather than an obstacle, a linguistic system in its own right in which the child underwent his early cognitive development and which served him as an adequate means of communication in his immediate environment during the early years of his life. According to such new principles, the child is to be allowed to express himself freely, without fear of being branded a 'lazy speaker', someone whose own speech and whose parents' and friends' speech is inferior. The standard dialect is to be taught as a second dialect which the child at first associates with the school and later uses for various other functions in the wider community, while he can still continue to speak the non-standard dialect (e.g. Black English, Puerto Rican English, etc.) with his school mates, members of his family and other persons in his immediate environment. The child is made aware of the fact that there may be several dialects of a language and that there is no cause for anyone to be ashamed of his own. Such principles have resulted in the development of the educational /linguistic field of Teaching Standard English as a Second Dialect (TSESD) (Allen 1968).

TSESD is still very much in its infancy. In the first period of enthusiasm specialists tried to adopt TESL principles. It soon became evident, however, that while the two teaching tasks have a great deal in common (*viz.* that they are both based on contrastive analyses between the learner's language/dialect and the target language/dialect, that the teaching of the target language/dialect must be structure-centred, that no value judgements must be attached to the learner's own mother tongue), they require different teaching methods and different skills on the part of the teacher (Allen 1970). A child whose mother tongue is some form of English has little patience with repetitive drills which characteristically form an essential part of TESL methods. He does not get a sense of achievement when he takes a small step forward in acquiring standard English which to him does not seem as different from his own dialect or as novel as it would if it were a completely new and foreign language form.

A further difference between TESL and TSESD is that in the latter, the teacher is likely to meet with great sensitivity when referring to non-standard English in any form. Children and parents themselves often regard a non-standard dialect as inferior if, indeed, they recognise its existence, and may interpret any reference to it as mockery and insult.[7]

The importance of TSESD has been pointed out by Australian linguists (Flint 1973) and some very valuable materials have been prepared for helping young children with their English language development along TSESD principles in Queensland (Department of Education, Queensland, 1972). However, TSESD as a field is far from being widely known among Australian teachers. A great deal more information than is at present available will have to be collected on Aboriginal English in general and on Aboriginal children's speech in particular from all parts of Australia before further advances can be made in this field. Data are already available from some areas (Flint 1968, Douglas 1976, Sharpe 1974, Department of Education, Queensland 1972), work in other areas is under way (Kaldor 1973), but much more is yet to be done.

Other languages The use of languages other than English in formal education in English-speaking countries has emerged as a result of the realisation that the teaching of English alone is insufficient for opening up lines of communication 'd' and 'f' with children who are monolingual or near-monolingual in a minority language. It was this realisation which was instrumental in the formulation of the bilingual education programme for Aboriginal children in the Northern Territory in December 1972.

The launching of bilingual education in Australia came about at a time when a wealth of material based on overseas experience had already accumulated. Since, in the early nineteen-fifties, a group of specialists from all over the world agreed on the basic need of every child to begin formal education in his mother tongue (Report of the UNESCO Meeting 1951), scores of bilingual education programmes have sprung up all over the world. The rationale for bilingual education is usually considered to be threefold: (1) bilingual education provides a continuation of the child's early experience 'with the world through language' and thus promotes cognitive development, (2) it promotes the child's lines of communication 'a', 'b', 'c' and 'e' and thus reinforces his ties with his own society and culture and (3) it 'builds a bridge' between the child's early experiences in his mother tongue on the one hand and education in the medium of the national language on the other, thus aiding communication along lines 'd' and 'f'. For example, literacy in the mother tongue promotes literacy in the national language.[8]

While few linguist-educators would question the desirability of bilingual education for children of minority languages in certain settings, some warn about the 'difficulty in translating bilingual education from theory to practice' (Sanchez 1973). Just how complex a field is subsumed by the term 'bilingual education' has been aptly illustrated by Mackey who set up a typology distinguishing some 90 different types of bilingual education schemes (Mackey 1972).

It is hardly surprising that difficulties arise when languages are assigned functions which they had not fulfilled before. The Australian situation is no exception. The dimensions along which careful planning is required, are analogous to those outlined in the literature of language planning mainly in relation to national languages. These are: role definition, graphisation, standardisation and modernisation.[9]

Role definition. When a language is assigned new functions, planners need to foresee, as far as possible, the role which the language may be expected to play in the life of communities, regions or perhaps as a *lingua franca* in wider areas. They need to be familiar with the roles that individual languages play in given regions prior to planning; they also have to predict possible changes in these roles which may occur as a consequence of the launching of language programmes.

In the recommendations for the Northern Territory (Department of Education, Canberra 1973) the matter of the selection of languages for bilingual education rested, understandably and justifiably, mainly on practical considerations. Bilingual education was a major departure from former educational practices and the advisers[10] had to do pioneering work in setting up a scheme within a very short time. Their report stated that, ideally, every child should receive his initial education in his own first language, but recognised that such an ideal cannot be achieved for all. The criteria employed for priorities were, firstly, the wishes of individual communities, and secondly, the concentration of a sizeable group of speakers of a single language, the availability of linguistic descriptions, of resident linguists (attached to missions or to the Summer Institute of Linguistics) as consultants and of Aboriginal teachers.

The role of the languages thus selected was seen mainly as a medium of early education, a language which provides the bridge between the child's first experiences and those gained in formal schooling, a language which thus represents cultural and linguistic continuity. For later years, the Aboriginal language was envisaged as a medium of education in the 'Language Arts of that language and for Aboriginal Studies' (*ibid.*: 11).

It may well happen, however, that, after a while, and particularly in successful programmes, some of the languages may assume a broader role. Children may well want to discuss topics relegated by the planners to the English component of the programme with their Aboriginal teacher, just as they may, on occasion, want to talk about 'Aboriginal matters' with their English-speaking teacher.

This brings up the question as to whether some Aboriginal languages are to be maintained and supported further than the role assigned to them in the early phases of the bilingual programmes would require. If so, manpower and material resources may have to be pooled to concentrate on some of the languages which would then have to be developed as languages of education higher than the first few primary grades.

In the States where bilingual education has not yet been launched on a large scale, planners are in a position to decide on one of two alternative courses of action open to them, if they wish to introduce bilingual education. One is to support a small number of languages to a higher degree of development and thus define an increasingly significant role for them. The other is to give limited and minor support only to all languages in which bilingual education is desired by the community and feasible on practical grounds.

Languages may, of course, be supported by educational programmes other than bilingual education in the primary schools. Language courses which teach an Aboriginal language as a foreign language (TAFL?) to non-Aborigines or Aborigines who do not speak it — such as the Adelaide course in Pitjantjatjara and the Perth course in Ngaanyatjarra — may go a long way toward changing the role of particular languages. Adult literacy programmes are also most important factors in promoting language maintenance and development.

Graphisation. This term was suggested by Ferguson (1968) to refer to the introduction and regular use of writing in a speech community. The very first step in graphisation is the development of suitable orthographies. The graphisation of Aboriginal languages to meet the demands of bilingual education was made possible by the great advances which had already been made in this field by the linguists attached to the Summer Institute of Linguistics and which culminated in a proposal for alternative choices of symbols for all areas of the continent (Leeding and Gudschinsky 1974).

While the graphisation of Aboriginal languages is thus, due to the vast amount of energy and expertise channelled in this direction by the Summer Institute of Linguistics, much more advanced than could have been expected within a year of launching bilingual education, many problems still remain.

The linguistic ideal for orthographies toward which most writers of literacy programmes strive is a strict phonemic alphabet.[11] However, as has been recognised by Leeding and Gudschinsky (*ibid.*), there may be various pressures at work in some communities which necessitate departure from this ideal and the use of partially allophonic (sub-phonemic) alphabets. This is likely to occur where speakers have some fluency in English and where they are influenced in their conception of their own sound system by their acquaintance with the sound system of English. In some instances partially allographic alphabets may be necessary, for similar reasons, as certain letter combinations may lead to an 'anglicised' reading of the Aboriginal word. The particular choice of symbols may, for some dialects, depend on the orthographies of neighbouring dialects and may consequently not be the most appropriate phonetic approximation of the sounds which they symbolise.

All this is likely to lead to the development of scores of slightly different orthographies throughout the continent. A further complicating factor is that the Australian Institute of Aboriginal Studies standard for the writing of tribal and language names (A.I.A.S. 1973) differs from the Summer Institute of Linguistics conventions and recommendations.

As things stand at the moment, the graphisation of Aboriginal languages must present a rather bewildering picture to the non-linguist. I cannot share the optimism of Leeding and Gudschinsky when they state that the difference between conventions 'does not seem . . . to be a problem'. It must be remembered that large numbers of linguistically untrained persons, Aboriginal and non-Aboriginal, will need to refer to both sets of standards. The linguist's recourse to a common phonetic framework for comparison is not available to the layman. Even linguists sometimes have to dig deep in their stocks of unpublished materials received from other linguists before they can make decisions about symbols to be used when referring to languages in which they are not area specialists.

Some of the symbols contained in the Leeding and Gudschinsky recommendation are likely to require modification.[12] Such modifications should probably be effected before orthographies become widely spread.

Thus, graphisation is, at this stage, far from being a closed book. There is an urgent need for much further work in this area, particularly in helping educators and members of the general public (Aboriginal and non-Aboriginal) to find their way around orthographic systems.

Standardisation. There are three types of standardisation processes relevant to language planning for Aboriginal education. These are: (1) intradialectal/intralanguage, (2) interdialectal and (3) interlanguage standardisation.

Intradialectal/intralanguage standardisation involves the identification and promotion of model speech and written varieties (Ray 1963:70) within one dialect or language. The Aboriginal teacher and other members of Aboriginal communities will have to provide a rich stock of spoken and written language output for the development of such models.

Questions of interdialectal standardisation may come up in the work of developers of literacy programmes as well as in the work of writers of teaching courses in Aboriginal languages for non-Aboriginal learners (TAFL) in areas where several dialects are spoken in the same speech community or in neighbouring speech communities. Some of these questions involve matters of 'purism'. Should the writer of texts and teaching materials keep dialects 'pure' where the speakers themselves mix dialects? Or should he 'codify' dialect mixture and thus promote the emergence of a new regional standard?

Interlanguage standardisation relates to the development of uniform approaches to features which are common among the various languages. The similarity of the phonological systems of Australian languages made it possible to devise the orthographic standards to which we have already referred. Other areas which lend themselves to standardisation are approaches to the teaching of reading (standardised approaches are already under way following methods developed by Dr Sarah Gudschinsky) and the developing of new vocabulary. We shall discuss this latter area under the next heading, 'Modernisation'.

Modernisation. This term, as commonly used in the literature of language planning, refers to at least partial 'intertranslatability' of languages which require planned development, with 'developed' languages, in this instance, with English. The matter of modernisation has so far not received attention in relation to Aboriginal education. Just how relevant this aspect of planning is to Aboriginal education, depends partly on the role definition of individual languages. Where further education in the vernacular is envisaged, some guidelines will undoubtedly have to be developed for the expansion of vocabularies. Even in cases where the Aboriginal language is used for limited functions only (*viz.* for initial literacy in the early years of primary school and thereafter for 'Aboriginal Studies'), some modernisation processes will become necessary. New vocabulary is required simply to talk about school and classroom life and activity — a field of discourse new to languages which have, until recently, not been media of formal education. Some of the questions to which answers will have to be sought, are: From what sources will the new vocabulary items come? Where words are borrowed from English, what changes will they undergo?[13]

Co-ordination of the two components of bilingual programmes

Much of the success of bilingual education depends on the effective co-ordination of the two components of the programme. The importance of co-ordination has received strong emphasis in published recommendations (Department of Education, Canberra 1973 and Department of Education, Darwin 1973). The fully qualified English-medium teacher has been allocated the responsibility of providing in-service help to the Aboriginal team member; both teachers have been encouraged to devise methods and set time aside for exchanging information and for developing common teaching strategies; headmasters have been assigned the task of co-ordinating the two components.

The role of educational linguists attached or to be attached to Departments of Education is going to be a crucial one in this respect. They will have an overview of all the problems and of the various approaches taken toward solutions. They will be in a position to establish links of communication between teaching teams and between Departments in various States. Hopefully, they will have some time left to keep abreast of advances in linguistic theory and practice overseas and at home. They will be the persons on whom planners will ultimately have to rely in finding the ideal balance between the two components of the programme.

We have so far considered the planning areas as set out on Table 2. In the final part of this paper, I propose to relate some aspects of planning to the various planning areas.

Research priorities All the language education tasks outlined in the foregoing call for a vast amount of information concerning languages, dialects, language teaching method, language learning styles and many other topics. Some of this information is available, but much more is yet to be obtained. In order to pinpoint priorities, planners will be faced with the task of scanning and analysing the research output of such organisations in Australia as the Australian Institute of Aboriginal Studies, the Summer Institute of Linguistics, the universities, the teachers colleges, the Commonwealth and State Education Departments as well as of overseas universities, and other research institutions. This task, once again, brings into focus the need for highly qualified educational linguists in positions where they can be of maximal assistance in language planning.

The type of research required in particular planning areas varies considerably.

TESL is a well developed field with a vast literature from all over the world. However, the specifics of teaching English as a second language to Aboriginal children in Australia need careful investigation. The research requirements of this planning area include the study of the sociolinguistic and linguistic characteristics and developmental sequences of the speech of the average Australian-English-speaking child; the contrastive study of standard English and Aboriginal languages and the testing of various TESL methods and techniques from the point of view of their suitability in Aboriginal education.

TSESD, being a much more recently emerging field, requires research not only in relation to its specific application in Australia, but in the very development of a comprehensive theory and methodology. The Australian experience with speakers of Aboriginal English may contribute significantly to the future shaping of this subfield of applied linguistics. As mentioned earlier, descriptive statements on Aboriginal English from all parts of the Commonwealth are a prerequisite to developing TSESD methods and techniques.

As for Aboriginal languages, basic descriptive work is still lacking in some areas, while excellent materials exist in others. The basic interests of research organisations which sponsored work on Aboriginal languages in the past were different from those of educational linguistics. From an educational point of view priorities must be given to languages which are assigned important roles in language planning.

As mentioned already, the questions of role definition, graphisation, standardisation and modernisation have not yet been fully explored in relation to Aboriginal languages.

The importance of research on psycholinguistic and sociolinguistic aspects of first and second language acquisition by Aboriginal children must be stressed here as relevant to all planning areas. Cognitive categories, learning styles, patterns of language socialisation, linguistic factors in problem solving are some of the topics in which significant research has already been undertaken.

Teacher training The importance of training teachers to enable them to handle children's language problems cannot be over-emphasised. The best teaching materials and the most reliable research results are of real value only in the hands of the skilled and confident teacher.

Before we can consider the requirements of teacher training for Aboriginal education, it will be helpful to summarise the linguistic aspects of the teachers' tasks in all types of schools where different categories of Aboriginal learners are enrolled.

In the bilingual schools, the non-Aboriginal member of the teaching team has to help the Aboriginal teacher develop the Aboriginal component of the programme. He has to help in the preparation and editing of teaching materials in the language. He must have a knowledge of TESL and understand the specific interference phenomena which occur in his pupils' English speech and written composition. He has to understand the advisory linguist's recommendations and the rationale underlying orthographies and reading courses.

The Aboriginal teacher has the highly important task of imparting initial literacy — the transition to English literacy depends heavily on how successful his work has been. He has to help the children develop their language and so build a bridge between a six-year-old's language competence and that of an adolescent in his mother tongue. He has to have insight into the English side of the programme in order to appreciate his pupils' general progress. He, too, has to understand the principles on which literacy materials are built and the advisory linguist's recommendations.

In the monolingual schools, the teacher has to have some knowledge of the structure of languages that are the mother tongues of his pupils.[14] He has to be aware of the nature of the non-standard form of English some of his pupils may speak as their mother tongues. He has to be able to pinpoint the problem areas some children have with English, whether they are speakers of other languages, or of non-standard varieties of English. He has to be familiar with TESL and TSESD principles.

In all situations, teachers must have some knowledge of developmental stages of language acquisition by the standard-English-speaking child, so they can evaluate language progress made by their bilingual or bidialectal pupils (the initially monolingual child, of course, gradually turns into a bilingual in the course of his schooling.)

School heads have no fewer linguistic problems. Whether in charge of a bilingual or monolingual school, school heads increasingly have to deal with matters of language, as they guide, direct, help and co-ordinate the work of their teachers. They must be well aware of what goes on in relation to languages in their schools and in other Australian schools.

It is evident that the work of all teachers of Aboriginal children requires a linguistic awareness not hitherto demanded of the Australian teacher. The teacher has to be able to make constant snap decisions in the detailed implementation of Commonwealth or State language education policies. Where such policies are well formulated and explicit, he has to translate them into everyday action. Where policies are non-existent or vaguely formulated, he has to take it upon himself to map out his own course of action to cater for his pupils' communicative needs.

It follows from the above that the more effectively problems are solved at the planners' end, the fewer the teachers' problems are going to be. The situation calls for massive and concentrated activity on the part of linguists in order to bring linguistics to the school teacher in the form of (a) simplified texts in applied linguistics oriented toward the specific requirements of the Australian teacher; and (b) training courses, correspondence courses and in-service courses.

Whether there is a sufficient number of linguists around at the moment to fulfil such a demand, is a further question to be explored by planners. A recognition of the need for such personnel by education departments and other organisations could do a great deal to channel talented young linguists into the field of educational linguistics. Until recently, only on rare occasions could one encounter advertisements for positions in which qualifications in linguistics were required, although it cannot be doubted that in many educational and administrative appointments such qualifications would have been of considerable value.

A number of teachers colleges in Australia now offer courses in applied linguistics and some very important developments have recently got off the ground involving the provision of linguistic training to Aborigines at the School of Australian Linguistics in the Northern Territory. However, there are still many teachers passing through various colleges throughout the Commonwealth who are not in any way exposed to linguistics in the course of their training. Language planning in relation to Aboriginal education would be a simpler task if it could be assumed that every Australian teacher has had basic training in applied linguistics. The specific requirements of Aboriginal education could then be based on more solid foundations. If all teachers were trained, not as linguistic specialists, but as 'general linguistic practitioners' who understand the nature of languages and of language problems, they could address themselves to their tasks without constant recourse to the help of advisory linguists. There would be the added bonus of a better understanding of the standard-English-speaking child's language development.

A basic course in applied linguistics would benefit teachers even if they are transferred to schools where there are no Aboriginal children. There are hardly any schools now in Australia where there are no children at all with some kinds of language problem.

Source materials   The writing of source materials and texts for bilingual programmes is an area of lively activity at present. Readers are being produced in a number of Aboriginal languages. Here, once again, the role definition for particular languages could determine the extent to which materials are to be developed in them. Already, in some languages there is a demand for advanced reading materials. In others, progress is slower and such demands do not yet arise.

As mentioned earlier, some special materials in English are also available for use in both bilingual and monolingual schools. However, there is by no means an adequate choice of readers in English specially designed for Aboriginal learners of different categories.

It may be useful to examine also the ordinary readers which are used by all children in Australian schools from the point of view of the child with language problems. It is particularly important for such children that all reading materials be linguistically well graded and that their content should be sociolinguistically sound. All too often, readers contain discourse which would not be natural in a real life situation among speakers of standard Australian English. The monolingual English-speaking child can more readily dismiss such discourse as a manifestation of 'textbook language' (even if he does not consciously formulate such an opinion), as he can use the speech of members of his environment as models for everyday speech patterns. For the bilingual child, school readers should serve as models for the development not only of written, but also of oral-aural language skills.

Source materials for Aboriginal education must also extend to textbooks for the training of teachers. I have already touched on this problem under the heading, 'Teacher training'. Suitable materials for training Australian teachers in applied linguistics are extremely scarce. The literature of Aboriginal linguistics is highly academically oriented. Much of the literature of English linguistics is steeped in controversy on highly abstract issues of linguistic theory. It is up to Australian linguists to 'translate' and simplify these complex fields so that textbooks for teachers can economically include all the essential information which has immediate relevance to class room work.

Evaluation Last, but not least, evaluation must form an integral part of any planning programme. The recommendations for the bilingual education programme contained a plea for '. . . research . . . in the area of evaluation' (Department of Education, Canberra 1973:59). I would like to conclude this paper by calling attention to the need for the continuing evaluation of the *total range* of educational activities related to languages and dialects in Aboriginal education. This would need to include language development programmes also in monolingual schools.

Evaluation can help planners in sharpening their definitions of goals (Rubin 1971), in establishing orders of priority for the allocation of resources and in seeing achievements and frustrations in relation to long-range aims.

Notes

1. See Rubin and Jernudd (1971).

2. For a comparison of the two, see Kaldor (1976).

3. Differences in 'style' are to be interpreted as those over and above expected and acceptable differences between the speech styles of children and adults.

4. Brandl (1973) has, however, drawn attention to an intralanguage problem arising out of bilingual education schemes: that of the child communicating with an Aboriginal teacher of his own community with whom he was previously in a different well-defined relationship possibly involving tabu restrictions.

5. Jernudd and Das Gupta (1971) mention that 'the broadest authorization for [language] planning is obtained from the politicians. A body of experts is then specifically delegated the task of preparing a plan'. The terms 'politician' and 'administrator' as used here include representatives and council members of Aboriginal communities.

6. While we are, at the present time, not in a position to refer to any authorative linguistic description of 'standard' Australian English, it seems reasonable to assume that such a dialect exists and that it is used by the large majority of teachers and by the majority of students who communicate successfully with the teachers.

7. At a conference on TSESD at Georgetown University a young woman objected to the use of the term 'non-standard English' as being discriminatory and insulting (Alatis 1970:197).

8. For a recent review of bilingual education in relation to the requirements of Aboriginal children, see Glass (1973).

9. In the use of the terms graphisation, standardisation and modernisation, I follow the scheme developed by Ferguson (1968). I regard these as 'planning areas' rather than 'resultants of planning' as suggested by Fishman (1973). The topics which I discuss here under the heading 'role definition' are mostly dealt with under the heading 'selection' in the literature. 'Role definition' seems to me to be a broader, more encompassing term than 'selection' which usually refers to selection for a single role, that of a national language.

10. B. H. Watts, W. J. McGrath and J. L. Tandy.

11. Although this ideal has been challenged in recent years as a sequel of new developments in phonological theory, no alternative suggestions have so far been proposed for literacy programmes. Yallop (1974) urges Australian linguists to collaborate with psychologists in carrying out research into the psycholinguistic aspects of alternative orthographic principles.

12. Dixon (1974) has pointed out some problem areas and has offered alternatives for some of the symbols.

13. Compare the words 'hospital' and 'kapaman' (government) in the Ngaanyatjarra Language Learning Course (Hackett, 1974).

14. These considerations, of course, apply to the language problems of migrant children as much as they do to those of Aboriginal children.

References

A.I.A.S. 1973 Convention for representation of tribal and language names. Australian Institute of Aboriginal Studies, Canberra.

ALATIS, J. E. ed. 1970 *Report of the twentieth annual Round Table Meeting of Linguistics and Language Studies.* Georgetown University Press, Georgetown.

ALLEN V. F. 1968 Teaching standard English as a second dialect. In *Developing programs for the educationally disadvantaged* (A. H. Passow ed.), pp. 207-23. Columbia University Teachers College Press, New York.

——1970 A second dialect is not a foreign language. In *Report of the twentieth annual Round Table Meeting . . .* (J. E. Alatis ed.), pp. 189-202.

BRANDL, M. 1974 The role of teachers involved in bilingual education programmes, *Developing education,* 1(5).

DEPARTMENT OF EDUCATION, Canberra 1973 *Bilingual education in schools in Aboriginal communities in the Northern Territory.*

DEPARTMENT OF EDUCATION, Darwin 1973 *Handbook for teachers in bilingual schools.*

DEPARTMENT OF EDUCATION, Queensland 1972 B. van Leer Foundation Project. *Research report on some effects of an Experimental Language Development Programme on the performance of Aboriginal children in their first year at school.*

DIXON, R. M. W. 1974 Comment, *Australian Institute of Aboriginal Studies, Newsletter,* New Series No. 1:31.

DOUGLAS, W. H. 1976 *The Aboriginal languages of the South-West of Australia.* 2nd ed. Australian Institute of Aboriginal Studies, Canberra.

——1973 The problems experienced by vernacular-speaking Aboriginal children when English only is used as the medium of their formal education. Paper read at Bilingual Education Seminar, Kalgoorlie. (Mimeographed.)

FERGUSON, C. A. 1968 Language development. In *Language problems of developing nations* (J. A. Fishman *et al.* eds), pp. 27-35. John Wiley, New York.

FISHMAN, J. A. ed. 1968 *Readings in the sociology of language.* Mouton, The Hague.

——ed. 1972 *Advances in the sociology of language.* Mouton, The Hague.

——1973 Language modernization and planning in comparison with other types of national modernization and planning, *Language in Society,* 2(1):23-44.

——C. A. FERGUSON *and* J. DAS GUPTA eds 1968 *Language problems of developing nations.* John Wiley, New York.

FLINT, E. H. 1968 Aboriginal English. Linguistic description as an aid to teaching, *English in Australia,* 6:3-21.

——1973 Language planning in relation to the education of bidialectals and bilinguals. Paper read at the Annual General Meeting of the Linguistic Society of Australia, Brisbane. (Mimeographed.)

GLASS, A. 1973 Bilingual education for Aborigines, *Aboriginal Affairs Planning Authority Newsletter,* 1(3):1-17.

HACKETT, D. 1974 *Ngaanyatjarra Language learning course.* Western Australian Institute of Technology. Tapes and teaching notes.

JERNUDD, B. *and* J. DAS GUPTA 1971 Towards a theory of language planning. In *Can language be planned?* (J. Rubin *and* B. H. Jernudd eds), pp. 195-215.

KALDOR, S. 1973 Studies on the language problems of Aboriginal children, Department of Anthropology, University of Western Australia. (Mimeographed.)

——1976 Issues for language planning in Australia, *Linguistic Communications*, 16: 89-98.

LEEDING, V. J. *and* S. C. GUDSCHINSKY 1974 Towards a more uniform orthography for Australian Aboriginal languages, *Australian Institute of Aboriginal Studies Newsletter*, New Series No. 1:26-31.

MACKEY, W. F. 1972 A typology of bilingual education. In *Advances in the sociology of language* (J. A. Fishman ed.) pp. 413-32.

RAY, P. S. 1963 *Language standardization.* Janua Linguarum Series Minor, No. 29. Mouton, The Hague.

REPORT OF UNESCO MEETING OF SPECIALISTS 1951 The use of vernacular languages in education. In *Readings in the sociology of language* (J. A. Fishman ed.). Mouton, The Hague.

RUBIN, J. 1971 Evaluation and language planning. In *Can language be planned?* (J. Rubin *and* B. H. Jernudd eds), pp. 217-52.

——*and* B. H. Jernudd eds, 1971 *Can language be planned?* The University of Hawaii Press, Honolulu.

SANCHEZ, G. 1973 Position paper on bilingual education. In *Bilingual children* (M. Saville-Troike ed.). A resource document prepared for Child Development Associate Consortium Inc. Washington, Center for Applied Linguistics.

SHARPE, M. C. 1974 Notes on the Pidgin English Creole of Roper River, *Australian Institute of Aboriginal Studies Newsletter*, New Series No. 2:2-12.

YALLOP, C. 1974 Phonology and orthography. Paper read at the Annual Conference of the Linguistic Society of Australia. (Manuscript.)

19 The construction of a part-Aboriginal world

Robert McKeich

Introduction Only part-Aborigines can really know their part-Aboriginal world. It may be considered arrogance on my part, first to claim to know that world, and secondly to attempt to explain it. But until such times as part-Aborigines are themselves able to 'tell it like it is', this tentative approach at understanding will raise some of the important issues and place them within at least one theoretical framework. At the outset it is recognised that the view from the outside-in may be quite different from the view from the inside-in, and this of course includes the view from the inside-out. Granted that participants in a game are often too engrossed with the play (or, at the very least, their own section of the play) to appreciate the totality of the game, they at least have insights into the nuances of the various strategies they apply, and experience the emotional excitement of participation. Nevertheless, informed spectators from the vantage of indirect emotional involvement and with a wider perspective may observe features of the game hidden to the players.

The National Workshop on Aboriginal Education (Watts 1971:13) recommended:

> That a study be made of Aboriginal world views and the relevance of these views to educational aims, teacher training and teacher strategies; e.g. the study of attitude and belief systems; systems of logic; ways of presenting the social cultural and physical world, the operational value of this system; linguistic research; and examination of the various Aboriginal sub-cultures that influence the child's world views.

My comment is that such a study is necessary and long overdue, not only for educational purposes, but also for an understanding of every aspect of Aboriginal and part-Aboriginal life within their own socio-cultural setting and in adjusting to the wider Australian communities.

Most social anthropological studies to date can be categorised under two headings, ethnographies and problem areas. Ethnographic descriptions tend to be couched in structural-functionalist terms; they demonstrate unique features of Aboriginal and/or part-Aboriginal cultures, or else they highlight cultural differences by making cross-cultural comparisons. Problem areas usually focus upon difficulties encountered by people of Aboriginal descent in adjusting to European-Australian contact. Special interest is paid to the major institutions of 'white' society (e.g. health, education, employment, housing, crime, and the like), and these so-called underprivileged people are seen to *have* problems, or they *are* problems, because 'their ways' are different from 'our ways'.[1]

In addition, from a psychological perspective, attempts have been made to study and analyse intelligence (de Lacey 1971; Fowler 1940; Elkin 1932; Porteous 1931, 1933, 1937, 1965; McElwain 1969; Kearney 1966), concept development (de Lemos 1969; Seagrim 1971), language (Douglas 1968; Nurcombe and Moffitt 1970; Flint 1968; Harris 1968; Teasdale and Katz 1968), attitudes (Dawson 1969; Gault 1969), motivation (Duncan 1969; Milliken 1969) and problems of behaviour and identity (Berry 1970; Cawte, Bianchi and Kiloh 1968; Nurcombe and Cawte 1967). Apart from giving general consideration to 'innate' characteristics, early socialisation, culture contact and cross-cultural comparisons, none of these studies examines in detail either the developmental processes or how they are 'built into' the Aboriginal or part-Aboriginal world.

This paper is an exploratory study into the nature and development of what I conceive to be a part-Aboriginal world — in regard both to the process *per se* and to its end product. The end product is seen in terms of a world of social relations and a world of knowledge; the processes are examined as means by which these relations and knowledge are transmitted to members of a part-Aboriginal 'society'. Note that the concepts of sub-culture and sub-society are not recognised here. Part-Aboriginal 'society' and 'culture' are seen as complete, integrated and consistent systems relevant to their members — not merely as a truncated (or castrated) version of any other socio-cultural systems.

As a background to this study I draw on the work of Mannheim (1936), Merton (1967), Goffman (1959), Garfinkel (1967), Cicourel (1973), Becker (1971) and Louch (1969). Those who have read Berger and Luckmann (1967) will recognise that I borrow both my title and the general orientation from that source. In essence this is a timid journey into the relatively unexplored regions of ethnomethodology and phenomenology (see Psathas 1968) through a 'sociology of knowledge' approach.

Social structure — roles or meanings? If we consider social structure to be an ordered arrangement of positions and roles, then part-Aboriginal 'society' has a structure (e.g. see Barwick 1963; Bell 1965; Fink 1955; Gale 1964; Inglis 1961; McKeich 1971; Reay 1964; J. Wilson 1958; K. Wilson 1958). There are childhood, adolescent and parental roles; roles *vis-a-vis* educational, economic, religious, judiciary and similar institutions in the wider society; roles appropriate to wage-earners and dependants; roles relevant to various social strata within a part-Aboriginal community; roles for mobile members; sick roles, drinking roles, gambling roles, prostitution roles; as well as wedding, funeral, entertainment, accommodation, and nepotism roles. In fact, to the superficial observer what appears to be disorder, is seen on closer examination to be a well-integrated social system, functioning adequately to meet most of part-Aboriginal needs.

A question arises as to how part-Aborigines learn the roles appropriate to each social situation. I have suggested (McKeich 1971) that significant others and generalised others (in the Mead-Cooley tradition) form the reference individuals or groups for modelling behaviour. My thesis merely states that reference groups constitute a focus of orientation but does not indicate *how* the transfer takes place.

The fact that their own society is ordered and that their world 'makes sense' is taken for granted by most societal members. Each person learns that there are typical ways of behaving. Habits and routines perform dual functions, of providing familiar landmarks and cues for social interaction as well as giving ready-made models for action. When 'problems' arise they can be solved within that system; or, if they fall outside the range of special knowledge or habitual responses, there are always other ways of dealing with such problems (e.g. denying that a problem exists, withdrawing from the social situation, categorising the problem within a familiar framework, creating a new and untried response, etc.). But social interaction is more than a system of roles, of typified behaviour; it is also an integrated system of knowledge which constitutes the source of all meaningful behaviour. Blumer (1970:284) says:

> In order to act the individual has to identify what he wants, establish an objective or goal, map out a prospective line of behaviour, note and interpret the actions of others, size up his situation, check himself at this or that point, figure out what to do at other points, and frequently spur himself on in the face of dragging dispositions or discouraging settings.

The question is, how does this body of knowledge, which is utilised in making behavioural decisions, come to be part of an individual's repertoire for social action? Does it emerge from the various reference features of existing society? To answer 'yes' to the second question is only partially correct; it neglects important features of human relationships such as mechanisms of socialisation, individual selectivity and creativity, sanctioning devices, definitions of a situation, available linguistic apparatus, and so on. There is a range of available resources, from reflex responses to complex philosophical or ideological abstractions. These form the social reality of everyday life. Berger and Luckmann (1966:33) sum up the points presented so far:

> The social reality of everyday life is thus apprehended in a continuum of typifications, which are progressively anonymous as they are removed from the 'here-and-now' of the face-to-face situation. At one pole of the continuum are those others with whom I frequently and intensively interact in face-to-face situations — my 'inner circle' as it were. At the other pole are highly anonymous abstractions, which by their very nature can never be available in face-to-face interaction. Social structure is the sum total of these typifications and of the recurrent patterns of interaction established by means of them. As such, social structure is an essential element of the reality of everyday life.

Language   A 'continuum of typifications' for part-Aborigines would begin within the immediate family, through the wider kin and friendship groups, merging eventually into the wider European-Australian society, and finally incorporating sets of values and ideologies, possibly gleaned from Aboriginal, part-Aboriginal and European-Australian sources. It is suggested that part-Aborigines are not cognitively aware of such a continuum but nevertheless take it for granted as reality: the world is mediated to them through thoughts and actions. In this connection language plays a vital part. Language not only objectivates their world, filling it with meaningful objects, it also serves as an index of subjective meaning; furthermore, it enables part-Aborigines to live in a 'common world' as they communicate with one another. Language, here, includes verbal symbols as well as gesticulations, bodily attitudes and movements, clothing, badges, social situations — in fact, everything which is given symbolic meaning within part-Aboriginal society.

One advantage of language is its ability to supersede immediate biological impulses, to vault outside the 'here and now' or the face-to-face situation. Language gives the objective world its meanings and permits the subjective world to be expressed (and communicated) symbolically. People can talk about matters and objects that are not present, and discuss situations which individuals might never experience directly.

Language possesses a quality of reciprocity within two subjective systems of communication — the system of communication with others and the intra-subjective communication with the 'self'. Both of these systems do not merely bark out words but convey meaning, and it is meaning which carries the social world.

In a part-Aboriginal society special, almost esoteric meanings are attributed through the language which is used; the meanings of words (gestures, situations, objects, etc.) are frequently not reflected by their European-Australian counterparts. Part-Aborigines dwell, as it were, in a different symbolic universe.

Within a particular culture, meanings are inherent in the words used — 'a thing is what it is called and it could not be called anything else' (Berger and Luckmann 1966:59). Language is thus coercive in the sense that it forces people into a linguistic mould if they are to communicate adequately or interact successfully. Meanings are not merely object-oriented or situation-bound; they form an integrated meaningful whole for every 'normal' individual, constructing his own personal world view. They also combine into a gestaltic patterned system to form a collective world view. The dynamic nature of human society introduces problems into this semantic ideal, and of course there are misunderstandings through faulty communication. Nevertheless, social systems are distinguished as much by patterns of meaning as they are by their social structure. A part-Aboriginal social system has its own unique language system (perhaps it might be better called a 'semantic system') which can be categorised as a 'part-Aboriginal world view'.

I illustrate this with reference to what can be regarded as examples of typical part-Aboriginal families. One feature of these families is the relatively large number of children found in most households. Children reared in these circumstances learn to interact with several siblings of various ages and both sexes; they take each other into account. As they proceed through their developmental stages, these occur with reference to older or younger persons whose behaviour and linguistic ability are at different functioning levels; they assume roles vis-à-vis their parents and siblings so that their 'self' concepts are moulded in these terms. Ideas about such matters as sharing, 'good' behaviour, modesty, ownership of personal possessions, family responsibilities, means of self-expression, obedience to authority and the like, become part of an individual's personality. Attitudes toward institutions relevant within the family and those within the wider society are communicated via personal experiences and through accounts given by other family members. A whole host of factors influences the world view of these children, merely by being members of large families; and these contrast with the world views of children with fewer siblings. Where there are inter-family contacts with relatives and non-relatives who also have large family settings, the above responses are reinforced so that they become built into a total cultural milieu. A structural and functional examination of part-Aboriginal families (indeed, of any family) does not provide a full understanding of the meaning of family relationships for its members and within a wider social context.

The complexity of 'meaning' is not overlooked. The meaning of 'family' to each member may be quite different: a young child, an adolescent, male or female, husband/father, wife/mother may all have their individual cognitive and emotional viewpoints, but these will all be part-Aboriginal in context and therefore worthy of special study. I refer to a statement made earlier in this paper: that the 'inside' view may never be completely understood, either by the participants in the zone of action or by the most skilful, sympathetic or well-trained observer. Nevertheless, it is this kind of reality which we must examine if we are to move toward a fuller understanding of mankind, specific or generalised.

The above example of the family is one of many possible institutions which can be studied, and family size is only one of a range of criteria examined. The meanings of work and leisure, religion, economic activities, rites of passage, socialisation processes and sanctions, health and hygiene beliefs and practices, and many others, also carry their own definitions and meanings. And, I emphasise again, the total body of knowledge constitutes a world view — not necessarily without some cognitive dissonance, but sufficiently homogeneous and integrated to enable part-Aborigines to distinguish themselves and to be recognised from outside their ranks, as part-Aborigines.

World view — macropedagogy Earlier on, the following question was formulated: 'How does this body of knowledge, which is utilised in making behavioural decisions, come to be part of an individual's repertoire for social action?' The answer could be given at two levels. First, how is this knowledge generated within a group of people in such a way that it emerges as their ethos or world view? Second, how is such an ethos communicated and how is it absorbed or assimilated by its individual members? Although it is obvious that these two features are concomitant, we shall examine each of them separately.

Let us turn to the problem of the development of world views. In modifying ideas expressed by Berger and Luckmann (1966:47-116), I am assisted by two diagrams which are really alternatives to each other. While concentrating on Figure 1, we may like to consider the 'perceptual' impression of Figure 2 and make our own interpretation of its meanings.

Such consideration begins outside the diagrams themselves. Human beings may make random acts which have no apparent communicable meaning (e.g. stroking a beard, blinking, scratching, sitting, flexing muscles, clenching fists, licking lips, etc.). When these acts become associated with solving a particular 'problem', they immediately take on a particular meaning; but while they remain unique, temporal and unattached to any special need, they may not enter meaningfully into the wider social world. Examples of behaviour with nascent meaning are picking up a match, removing a rock

INTEGRATION	WORLD VIEW
	CULTURE
PREDICTION	LEGITIMATION
	SOCIAL CONTROL
BIOGRAPHY (HISTORY)	TYPIFICATION
	HABITUATION

Figure 1: *Social processes of reality construction*

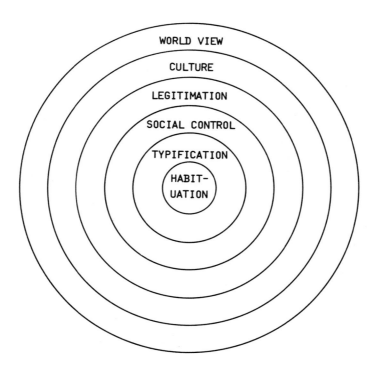

Figure 2: *Social processes of reality construction*

from a pathway, gazing at a sunset, scratching to relieve an itch, etc.
Frequent recurrence of a 'problem' may lead to a selection of a habitual
behavioural response in order to deal with it. The act becomes associated
with a regular need and is therefore patterned toward meeting that need. We
now enter Figures 1 and 2, at the level of *Habituation*. At this point, we are
focusing on the behaviour of an individual; but when others also develop
identical habitual ways of dealing with similar problems, responses emerge
which become typical of a group — thus, group habituations are called
Typifications. We have just considered the 'historical growth' (biography)
of typifications within a society. It would be very unusual if such typical
behaviour emerged 'out of nothing', so that research into the details of such
a biography would possibly reveal links with other typifications. For the
purpose of continuing the paradigm, let us leave it at that point. When
typifications become accepted into the routines of everyday life, they become
predictable as standard responses to particular problems. More than that,
they may be reckoned to be the only acceptable ways of behaving in particular circumstances and hence contain a sense of 'rightness' — that is,
a moral or ethical evaluation is now added. Attempts at varying the formulae
initiate social control mechanisms (which could themselves become habitual
and typical, thus throwing them back to stage one of the paradigm). Social
control requires support in two ways — the typification being sanctioned
must be legitimated and, also, the mechanisms of social control themselves
need legitimation. *Legitimation* formulae and procedures emerge, which not
only indicate to persons why they *should* perform one action rather than
another, but also establish why things *are* what they are. The realm of meaning
is thus being expanded as 'knowledge' grows from a simple behavioural act
to meet a particular need, into compelling expectations with wider social
relevance.

So far our frame of reference has been based upon the hypothetical
solution of a particular 'problem' or 'problems', but these are not isolated
or discrete events. Social living is complex and integrated. Certain patterns
or clusters of behaviour, called institutions, are associated with a number of
zones of meaning (Berger and Luckmann 1966:41) which themselves become
integrated into the totality of culture. *Culture*, therefore, may be described in
these terms as a meaningful universe which is shared and socially articulated.
That is, people within the cultural system 'know' what they are doing and
have a consensus of agreement about it all. The implications of this statement are very wide. There is the knowledge of belonging to a group which
shares a mutuality about what is important; in-group/out-group sentiments
emerge; a social world is created which provides stability and security for its
members; a real and meaningful world is constructed by means of culture,
which is not only a means to social identity, but also is the end product.
Culture is thus a self-supporting, self-perpetuating reality system within
which all participants live. But it lacks one thing. Culture as such is a closed
system; it is encapsulated within a particular society. (This is abundantly clear
in all definitions of 'culture' which use societal boundaries, and conversely all
definitions of 'society' which specify cultural boundaries.) The social world
(cosmos, or universe) does not consist only of inward-looking and self-
consistent cultures. A *World View* is complete only when one looks 'outside' as
well. The degree of relevance of this statement varies considerably from one

culture to another — but it is recognised that there are few societies, if any, which live in total socio-cultural isolation. Others who do not subscribe to *my* way of life cannot be ignored, even if they impinge only indirectly into *my* culture; and therefore they must be taken into account in *my* stock of knowledge, *my* world view.

Paradigms are never entirely satisfactory. While they serve to represent models, they must be regarded as points of departure for criticism and for further analysis of what they claim to portray. They are too simplistic and seldom seem to convey the idea of dynamic processes, or the full reality of their stated purpose. In this context, Figure 1 should be seen as a 'process' model showing, step by step, development from habitual acts to the social construction of a world view. Figure 2 is more static, but has the advantage of demonstrating that each level, from its centre, is already embraced by what it anticipates. That is, the world view encompasses each level right through to habituation. A kind of feed-back operates, whereby habituation is influenced by typifications; and so on through social control mechanisms, legitimation beliefs, cultural integration, and the world view already in existence or in the process of being formed.

In this context, too, a macro-level application of the above to the construction of a part-Aboriginal world view poses a number of difficulties. One difficulty is the limitation imposed by the length of this paper; an associated problem is the selection of simple yet adequate examples. Nevertheless, I will trace out hypothetical stages and processes in the emergence of a part-Aboriginal world view.

For the purpose of illustration, I will assume the birth of a part-Aboriginal child who enters a social setting where he is rejected by, or excluded to a large extent from, both Aboriginal and non-Aboriginal 'societies'. By trial and error he learns that certain kinds of behaviour provide him with an element of satisfaction, or at least reduce the impact of negative sanctions which he believes are applied against him. Through repetition, such items of behaviour become habitual ways of dealing with the problem of rejection. He may withdraw physically or psychologically from threatening contact situations; he may develop aggressive behaviour, or some other form of action. So far, his behaviour is individual and idiosyncratic.

If he discovers he is not unique and there are others who in fact share that rejection, they may confer together (formally or informally) and find mutual support. Shared behavioural habits become typical of people with similar problems — in this case, rejection because of their being part-Aboriginal. In order that social solidarity may be sustained among them, the 'group' of fellow-sufferers may begin to establish rules of conduct and to formulate means for social control, including sanctions. Moral or ethical values lend support for, or give legitimation to, the 'rightness' of selected behaviour. But legitimation is not simply a matter of abstract values; it implies knowledge both of the values themselves and of the logical (or otherwise), mythical, precedential, or situational circumstances which lend support to these values. At this point the 'sociology of knowledge' becomes relevant and world view construction begins to emerge.

These persons have now built for themselves a nomic world with high relevance to their particular needs as rejected part-Aborigines. That world has little attraction for non-part-Aborigines, because the needs which give rise to such particularised behaviour are not necessarily located in their social experience. Cultural patterns (and boundaries) begin to emerge. Behaviour, beliefs and a range of material objects within this socio-cultural system are now considered to be particularly part-Aboriginal. An awareness of cultural self-identity is thus born. As with personal self-identity (in true Meadian/Cooley style), true 'self'-hood requires an alter (or an 'other'); so, part-Aborigines, as such, require non-part-Aborigines to validate their identity. In fact, a cycle has been completed. The out-group, by rejecting the primary subject, gives rise to a part-Aboriginal world view, and is now included in that world view and serves to reinforce it. The store of knowledge not only encompasses what part-Aborigines 'know' about themselves; it also takes into account what they 'know' about non-part-Aboriginal society and culture. What they 'know' about outsiders is coloured by their experiences with them, or, more particularly, by their definitions of the relevant situations which they encounter.

The above illustration may not of itself seem very convincing. When one adds to the initial proposition of social rejection such problem areas as discrimination, housing, employment, paternalism, segregation, marriage restrictions, education, absence of material goods, and a host of other things, the power of significance of this model increases.

World view — micropedagogy   Socialisation and educational goals and processes are reasonably well known, so I shall concentrate upon some specific points relevant to my general theme. By what processes is the socially constructed world, which I have been discussing, internalised in individual consciousness?

All individuals have a quality of uniqueness, and yet no individual is entirely autonomous. All live within an institutional order which emerges from the typifications noted above. The institutions themselves have no meaning or relevance unless they are represented in society through roles — that is, the institutions are played out and thereby reified, by the individual actors themselves. Berger and Luckmann (1966:75) say:

> The institution, with its assemblage of 'programmed' actions, is like the unwritten libretto of a drama. The realization of the drama depends upon the reiterated performance of its prescribed roles by living actors.

Institutions are also represented by 'linguistic objectifications' (Berger and Luckmann 1966:75): that is, by becoming verbalised directly or indirectly; they may be represented also by physical objects which have acquired symbolic meanings. Unless they are given life by human actors they disappear from the world of knowledge and become irrelevant. Institutions and roles are both complementary and integrated; it is:

> by virtue of the roles he plays the individual is inducted into specific areas of socially objectivated knowledge, not only in the narrower cognitive sense, but also in the sense of the 'knowledge' of norms, values and even emotions. (Berger and Luckmann 1966:76.)

In a previous study (McKeich 1971), I outlined the relationship between roles and reference groups and applied them directly to part-Aborigines; I developed a Mead-Cooley perspective and discussed the application of Mertonian (Merton 1967) propositions. Developmentally, a child becomes a member of society first by being aware of a world 'out there' — one which is distinguishable from himself and with his own person being distinguished from it. What follows, is a growing recognition of a 'meaning' associated with that world 'out there'. Internalisation is the process whereby symbolic meaning is communicated by others and then adopted as the basis for the individual's own symbolic interaction with others: he takes over the world of others in a dialectic involving a process of reciprocally defining shared situations, whereby the same world is mutually understood — and, more than that, participants share in each other's 'being'.

Significant others are important in this process and, in early years when particular others are imposed upon a child, he accepts their definitions of reality as his own. The social world is filtered through them and takes shape with an added boost of emotional associations. Berger and Luckmann (1966:131-38) label this process 'Primary Socialization' and state that it:

> ends when the concept of the generalized other . . . has been established in the consciousness of the individual . . . (when) he is an effective member of the society and in subjective possession of a self and a world.

Of course, this process never really ends, but the importance of early life experiences cannot be overemphasised. In contrast, 'Secondary Socialization is the internalization of institution or institution-based "sub-worlds" ' (Berger and Luckmann 1966:138). It involves the acquisition of role-specific knowledge and vocabularies, and proceeds without a great deal of emotional identification with the role-teachers or role-examples. I am not entirely happy with the dichotomous model, and would prefer a continuum if that were possible. Nevertheless, differences between significant and less-significant others are recognised.

Neither 'primary' nor 'secondary' socialisation proceeds smoothly, for two reasons. First, there may be disagreement or inconsistency between the 'knowledge' imparted by the two systems, requiring resolution by the individual. Second, when confronted with choices individuals are not entirely predictable so that the outcome may not be socially conforming. People in marginal positions such as adolescents, mobile members of society, those with a stake in 'two worlds', and the like, are frequently labelled as deviant, mentally sick, ignorant, depraved, or criminal when in fact such behaviour may merely reflect the opportunities of choosing from two or more realities or zones of meaning.

Finally, we are led to the consideration of identity. The question 'Who am I?' is rooted in man's humanity, in his capacity to ask that very question. Identity is socially constructed via the dialectic between man and society — it is socially bestowed and socially maintained. A man knows himself, or is known by, the company he keeps, or the company that keeps him. He belongs as much to his world view as his world view belongs to him.

Part-Aborigines are identified as such because they have constructed for themselves a part-Aboriginal world. Primary socialisation, and some secondary socialisation, takes place among significant part-Aboriginal others. It is therefore inevitable that a part-Aboriginal reality is located and perpetuated within their own ranks and can be understood only in terms of their special vocabularies. Language, in that context, is not a problem to them because it is an expression, in an overt and objective way, of the subjective reality of their world view.

A part-Aboriginal world   Only part-Aborigines can really *know* their part-Aboriginal world. A survey I conducted in 1965/66 (McKeich 1971), gave part-Aboriginal high school children in the south-west of Western Australia the opportunity to state some of their goals and values. The report of that research included cross-cultural comparisons between the statements made by the part-Aborigines and those made by two distinct European-Australian control groups. The part-Aboriginal world, as such, is the focus of this paper; therefore, contrasts between these other groups will not be made here.

Earlier in this paper reference was made to work done by Barwick, Bell, Fink, Gale, Inglis, Reay, and J. and K. Wilson. I also mentioned the large family size (an average of 6.3 children per family; see McKeich 1971:187), and have made brief references to problems associated with discrimination, housing, employment, paternalism, segregation, marriage restrictions, education, relative absence of material goods and other features of part-Aboriginal living.

A part-Aboriginal world view is composed of a totality of features forming an integrated whole. The fact that a non-part-Aboriginal world impinges into or is imposed upon it does not diminish the validity of the claims made here. Two important issues are raised. First, in simple terms, a part-Aboriginal world view is both a creative internal socio-cultural system, and a response to external influences such as the informal and institutional impact of the 'outside world'. Second, the 'outside world' has its own interpretation of itself; it has its own body of knowledge, and it embraces its own reality, imparting symbolic meanings in its own terms. Part-Aborigines interpret the 'outside world' in different terms; 'outside' objects, behaviours, situations, ideologies and the like, carry different symbolic meanings for them.

Bearing these points in mind, we may now consider data from questionnaires administered to part-Aboriginal high school students. Part-Aborigines preferred to associate socially with other part-Aborigines. In an open-choice sociometric survey, the responses were as follows:

3 part-Aborigines	.. 65.38%
2 part-Aborigines 1 non-part-Aboriginal	.. 14.90%
1 part-Aboriginal 2 non-part-Aboriginal	.. 7.69%
3 non-part-Aborigines	.. 12.03%

Table 1: *Socio-choices by part-Aborigines*

Ten important characteristics of an 'Ideal Person' in rank order are listed:

Positive	*Negative*
1. Has a job	Drink
2. Polite, well-mannered	Smoke
3. Tidy, clean, neat	Fight
4. Good-looking, attractive	Lazy
5. Kind	Bad language
6. Hard worker	Gamble

7. Prefer part-Aboriginal   Dishonest, Liar
8. Colour optional   Snobbish
9. Sociable   Larrikin
10. Has character and personality   Selfish

Table 2: Characteristics of an ideal person given by part-Aborigines

The criteria for the 'Ideal Person' were not structured for the students and there is some difficulty in interpreting these data. Nevertheless, however interpreted, a pattern of priorities is noted.

As this was an educationally-oriented research project, students stated the length of time they wished to remain at school. A follow-up survey in 1969 of the same students revealed the actual levels attained.

Aspiration	*Achievement*
8.84% wished to leave school on completion of 1 year High School	25.00%
32.10% wished to leave school without entering 3rd year level	59.69%
51.16% wished to remain at school for 3 years	35.72%
83.26% wished to leave school before or at end of 3 years	95.41%
10.70% wished to remain at school for 5 years	4.08%
2.32% aspired to tertiary education .. ..(No figure on achievement)	

Table 3: Educational aspirations and achievements by part-Aboriginal high school students

The pattern of future occupational preferences indicates that their world view excludes any great participation in professional fields.

High managerial and professional	1.19%
Skilled trades, clerical, lower professional etc...	47.72%
Labouring, unskilled trades, service etc. ..	28.07%

Table 4: Occupational preferences by part-Aborigines

Actual employment in 1969, according to official figures, is as follows:

Males		*Females*	
1. Professional	3	Professional	18
2. Clerical and commercial ..	10	Clerical and commercial..	31
3. Tradesmen	39	Skilled occupations ..	17
4. Rural workers	738	Unskilled occupations ..	66
5. Industrial workers	740	Domestics	101
6. Mining industry	0		
7. Pastoral industry	0		
8. Pearling and fishing industry	2		
9. Self-employed	17		
10. Apprenticeships	30		
Total	1579		233

Table 5: Part-Aboriginal employment as at 30 June 1969

I have purposely not drawn any implications from the above Tables, nor have I qualified them by commenting further. At least, part-Aborigines have been given the opportunity to indicate some features of their own world. The focus has been upon the *construction* of a part-Aboriginal world, not upon the qualities of that world. Nevertheless, the above information should raise a number of questions as stimulation for further research and provide a little background to the more theoretical issues raised here. The 'so what?' question is partially answered by the earlier material in this paper.

In conclusion, although very little that is new in social Anthropology has been added by the material presented here, some important issues have been raised. While not decrying cross-cultural studies, insufficient attention has been paid to part-Aboriginal society and culture in its own right. Structural-functional analyses are limited in their usefulness. The study of 'problems' is somewhat piecemeal. It is necessary for those engaged in medical, educational, housing, and economic welfare, but requires a much broader perspective than that usually encountered. This paper has stated that part-Aborigines *have* a world view, and has given some attention to its construction. Ethnoscience, ethnomethodology and phenomenology (see Psathas 1968) have barely been touched upon but would represent a logical progression in any examination, particularly if the content of a part-Aboriginal world is to be revealed and understood.

Note

1. But of course the term 'problem' in its social scientific usage implies theoretical consideration of specific issues, and not necessarily a problem in applied anthropological terms. (Editor)

References

BARWICK, D. E. 1963 A little more than kin: regional affiliation and group identity among Aboriginal migrants in Melbourne. Ph.D. thesis, Australian National University.

BECKER, E. 1971 *The birth and death of meaning*. The Free Press, Glencoe, Illinois.

BELL, J. H. 1965 The part-Aborigines of New South Wales: three contemporary social situations. In *Aboriginal man in Australia* (R. M. *and* C. H. Berndt eds). Angus and Robertson, Sydney.

BERGER, P. L. *and* T. LUCKMANN 1966 *The social construction of reality: a treatise on the sociology of knowledge*. Doubleday, New York.

BERRY, J. W. 1970 Marginality, stress and ethnic identification in an acculturated Aboriginal community, *Journal of Cross-Cultural Psychology*, (I)3:239-52.

BLUMER, H. 1970 Sociological implications of the thought of George Herbert Mead. In *Social psychology through symbolic interaction* (G. P. Stone *and* H. A. Farberman eds), pp. 282-93. Ginn-Blaisdell, Massachusetts. (Also in *American Journal of Sociology*, 1966, 73:535-44, 547-48.)

CAWTE, J. E., G. N. BIANCHI *and* L. G. KILOH 1968 Personal discomfort in Australian Aborigines, *Australian and New Zealand Journal of Psychiatry*, 2(2):69-79.

CICOUREL, A. V. 1973 *Cognitive sociology: language and meaning in social interaction*. Penguin, Harmondsworth.

DAWSON, J. L. M. 1969 Attitude change and conflict among Australian Aborigines, *Australian Journal of Psychology*, 21(2):101-16.

DE LACEY, P. R. 1971 Classificatory ability and verbal intelligence among high-contact Aboriginal and low-socioeconomic white Australian children, *Journal of Cross-Cultural Psychology*, 2(4):393-96.

DE LEMOS, M. M. 1969 Conceptual development in Aboriginal children: implications for Aboriginal education. In *Aborigines and education* (S. S. Dunn *and* C. M. Tatz eds), pp. 244-63. Sun Books, Melbourne.

DOUGLAS, W. H. 1968 *The Aboriginal languages of South-West Australia. Speech forms in current use and a technical description of Nyungar*. Australian Institute of Aboriginal Studies, Canberra.

DUNCAN A. T. 1969 Motivation for achievement in an industrial society. In *Aborigines and education* (S. S. Dunn *and* C. M.Tatz eds), pp. 192-20. Sun Books, Melbourne.

ELKIN, A. P. 1932 Social life and intelligence of the Australian Aborigine, *Oceania*, 2(1):101-13.

FINK, R. A. 1955 Social stratification: a sequel to the assimilation process in a part-Aboriginal community. M.A. thesis, University of Sydney.

FLINT, E. H. 1968 Aboriginal English: linguistic description as an aid to teaching, *English in Australia*, 6:3-21.

FOWLER, H. L. 1940 Intelligence among Australian Aborigines, *Nature*, CXLIX:195.

GALE, F. 1964 *A study of assimilation: part-Aborigines in South Australia*. Libraries Board of South Australia, Adelaide.

GARFINKEL, H. 1967 *Studies in ethnomethodology*. Prentice-Hall, Englewood Cliffs.

GAULT, E. 1969 Attitudes of Aboriginal adolescents in Victoria: a preliminary study. In *Aborigines and education* (S. S. Dunn *and* C. M. Tatz eds), pp. 202-18. Sun Books, Melbourne.

GOFFMAN, E. 1959 *The presentation of self in everyday life*. Doubleday-Anchor, New York.

HARRIS, J. K. 1968 Linguistics and Aboriginal education: a practical use of linguistic research in Aboriginal education in the Northern Territory, *Australian Territories*, 8:24-34.

INGLIS, J. 1961 Aborigines in Adelaide, *Journal of the Polynesian Society*, 70(2).

KEARNEY, J. E. 1966 Aboriginal ability, *Journal of Christian Education*, 9(2).

LOUCH, A. R. 1969 *Explanation and human action*. University of California Press, California.

McELWAIN, D. W. 1969 Some aspects of the cognitive ability of Aboriginal children. In *Aborigines and education* (S. S. Dunn *and* C. M. Tatz eds), pp. 264-72. Sun Books, Melbourne

McKEICH, R. 1971 Problems of part-Aboriginal education. Ph.D. thesis, University of Western Australia.

MANNHEIM, K. 1936 *Ideology and Utopia*. Harcourt and Brace, New York.

MERTON, R. K. 1967 *Social theory and social structure*. The Free Press, Glencoe, Illinois.

MILLIKEN, E. P. 1969 Social and cultural factors influencing achievement of Aboriginal children. In *Aborigines and education* (S. S. Dunn *and* C. M. Tatz eds), pp. 219-27, Sun Books, Melbourne.

NURCOMBE, B. *and* J. E. CAWTE 1967 Patterns of behaviour disorder amongst the children of an Aboriginal population, *Australian and New Zealand Journal of Psychiatry*, 1(3):119-33.

——*and* P. MOFFITT 1970 Cultural deprivation and language defect: project enrichment of childhood, *Australian Psychologist*, 5(3):249-59.

PORTEOUS, S. D. 1931 *The psychology of a primitive people: a study of the Australian Aborigine*. Longmans, Green, New York.

——1933 Mentality of Australian Aborigines, *Oceania*, 1(1):30-36.

——1937 *Primitive intelligence and environment*. Macmillan, New York.

——1965 Problems of Aboriginal mentality, *Mankind Quarterly*, 5(3):123-30.

PSATHAS, G. 1968 Ethnomethods and phenomenology, *Social Research*, 35(3):500-20. [Also in *Symbolic interaction, a reader in social psychology* (J. A. Manis *and* B. N. Meltzer eds). Allyn and Bacon, Boston, 1972.]

REAY, M. ed. 1964 *Aborigines now: new perspective in the study of Aboriginal communities*. Angus and Robertson, Sydney.

SEAGRIM, G. 1971 The cognitive development of Aboriginal children. In *Report of the National Workshop on Aboriginal Education. Priorities for action and research* (B. H. Watts ed). Department of Education, University of Queensland.

TEASDALE, A. R. *and* F. M. KATZ 1968 Psycholinguistic abilities of children from different ethnic and socio-economic backgrounds, *Australian Journal of Psychology*, 20(3).

WATTS, B. H. 1971 *Report of the National Workshop on Aboriginal Education. Priorities for action and research*. Department of Education, University of Queensland.

WILSON, J. 1958 Cooraradale. B.A. Hons. thesis, University of Western Australia.

WILSON, K. 1958 Kinship at Cooraradale: a part-Aboriginal housing settlement. B.Sc. Hons. thesis, University of Western Australia.

20 Basic value orientations, change and stress in two Aboriginal communities

R. G. Hausfeld

This paper reports, in part, a study of an Aboriginal community (Coasttown) in south-eastern New South Wales and related studies of Forestville Aborigines in north-eastern New South Wales, and three groups of Whites (College, Pilot and Commune) from a metropolitan area (Hausfeld 1972, 1973; Frith 1975; Frith, Hausfeld and Moodie 1974). Fieldwork was carried out between January 1966 and August 1971.

The communities

Coasttown is the pseudonym for a coastal town which is the commercial and social centre for a dispersed community of 750 people of Aboriginal descent of whom 33 did not identify as Aborigines; 659 Aborigines in 106 households agreed to co-operate in the study. The area covered was about 30 km east-west by 55 km north-south and had a total population of about 22,000. First contact with Whites was in 1791 but settlement was not until 1822 when the Aborigines were described as 'ferocious'. Despite violence on both sides, by 1836 Aborigines were employed as farmhands and sawyers. By the 1840s the area was closely settled by farmers and timber-getters. The Aborigines were changed from landholders to employees and servants.

Dairy farming, and later tourism, provided the area's economic base until the 1940s. Industrialisation commenced after the Second World War with the establishment of two factories, but during the study period the area was still essentially rural and agricultural.

In 1966 Aborigines were about 3 per cent of the Coasttown population. Discrimination against Aborigines was not marked despite some restrictions on their access to the lounges of some hotels. By comparison with some towns in north-eastern New South Wales, ethnic relations at Coasttown were good. Stereotypic prejudice in Whites against Blacks and Blacks against Whites did exist, but this was seldom manifested in discrimination.

The relaxed racial atmosphere at Coasttown is evidenced by the 20 per cent of co-operating households with one White spouse — the figure for total Aboriginal households was 30 per cent. Genealogical evidence shows that intermarriage has been occurring for at least three generations.

Coasttown Aborigines in 1966 were living on settlements, in fringe camps, rural areas and in the township itself. Prior to 1966 there were two Aboriginal stations in the area, but by the study period one had reverted to Crown land status though the Aborigines continued to live on in the same houses; the other reserve was no longer under the full-time management of an officer of the Aborigines Welfare Board.

The average number of Aborigines per household was 6.1, however the median household of four rooms was occupied by between seven and eight people. The median number of bedrooms per house was two and the median number of persons per bedroom was four, but there were eight instances of more than six persons per bedroom. Serious overcrowding occurred where extensions to the primary family, or a large number of children, made available space inadequate. Half the children lived in households with four or more other children, 56 lived in households with eight or more other children and only nine lived in households as only children.

There was no evidence of marked 'matri-focused authority' at Coasttown. Eighty-nine per cent of households had a cohabiting couple in charge and men tended to make crucial decisions and exercise final authority, but this was in a situation of extreme permissiveness in child-rearing. Male children tended to assert autonomy at about the age of puberty and females a year or two later.

Of the study population (659 persons at 30 June 1966) 54.1 per cent was under the age of 15 years and only 1.6 per cent was over the age of 65 — the equivalent figures for Australia as a whole are 28.9 per cent and 10.0 per cent (*Commonwealth Year Book* 1972:137).

There were 121 males for each 100 females — under 15 years there were 117 males for each 100 females. This shortage of females is reflected in the fact that out of 80 males over 29 years of age, 25 had never established a permanent conjugal relationship. Unattached adult males were almost all of a group of Aborigines referred to by Whites as 'no-hopers', and the same group was grossly overrepresented in the unemployed.

Of the 279 who had completed their education 1 per cent had never attended school, 61 per cent had primary education only and only 3 per cent had received an Intermediate Certificate — the highest educational achievement at that time. Since 1966 more Aborigines have gained a School Certificate than in the whole previous history of the area.

The potential Aboriginal workforce (post-school, under retiring age and not engaged in domestic duties) in 1966 was 242 of whom 65 per cent were employed at interview, 19 per cent were unemployed and 16 per cent were in receipt of a pension of some kind.

The Coasttown people are derived from the tribes which occupied the coastal strip between Sydney and south-eastern Victoria, with the addition of an extension across the Great Dividing Range on to the south-west slopes in New South Wales. Within that area 95 per cent of the 1966 population had been born, indicating the continued high rate of localisation of Aborigines in rural areas.

Traditional culture is virtually a thing of the past at Coasttown. Very few speakers of any Aboriginal language remain alive and they do not use their languages in day-to-day communication. There is little or no knowledge of the local country. However, kinship bonds remain strong and functional in the organisation of support and sharing systems within the community.

During the six years the community was studied no fundamental change was observed — their personal interactions, community structures and economic conditions were a continuance of former patterns. Within that general framework many minor changes occurred as many residential changes took place which brought the people into closer contact with the White majority. Table 1 summarises the population changes over the five years from 30 June 1966 to 30 June 1971.

Table 2 records the housing changes for the same period. Grade 1 houses are 'shacks' and Grade 3 houses have all the normal facilities; Grade 2 houses are intermediate between the two extremes.

My impression is that I have studied Coasttown at a time when the traditional is finally departing. This is perhaps the reason why so many of those interviewed seemed troubled with identity problems, finding it difficult to express clearly their Aboriginality. 'Blood', even a tiny proportion of Aboriginal ancestry, was the major claim to Aboriginality. Being an Aboriginal seemed to be important to almost all — it provided an identity and I suspect, an excuse.

Categories	Sex		Sub-	Adjusted
	M	F	totals	totals
Recorded Aboriginal population at 30/6/1966	361	298	659	
White spouses of above	13	5	18	677
*White migrants out to 30/6/71	3			
*Migrants from Aboriginal children's home to 30/6/71	8	5		
*Aboriginal migrants out to 30/6/71 ..	39	59	114	563
Deaths from 1/7/66 to 30/6/71	20	6	26	537
Births ,, ,, ,, ,, ...	56	61	117	654
Aboriginal migrants in as spouses from 1/7/66 to 30/6/71	7	3		
White migrants in as spouses from 1/7/66 to 30/6/71	8	2		
Non-Aboriginal-non-White migrants in as spouses 1/7/66 to 30/6/71	1			
Migrants in to children's home to 30/6/71 ..	5	5	31	685
*Other known Aboriginal migrants in from 1/7/66 to 30/6/71	40	44	84	769
Known study population at 30/6/71 ..				769
Total White spouses at 30/6/71	18	7	25	
Total other non-Aboriginal spouses at 30/6/71	1		1	
Aboriginal population at 30/6/71	402	341		743

*Births and deaths for these groups not included in calculations.

Table 1 : Coasttown Aboriginal study population changes between 30 June 1966 and 30 June 1971

Locality	House Grade	Period 1966	1971
Town	1		
	2		
	3	13	30
Settlement	1		
	2	15	
	3	20	30
	Caravans		2
Fringe	1	24	8
	2	5	5
	3	20	30
	Caravans		2
Totals	1	24	8
	2	20	5
	3	53	90
	Caravans		4
Grand Totals		97	107

Table 2: Housing comparison of Coasttown Aboriginal households, 30 June 1966 and 30 June 1971

Forestville is the pseudonym for an area inland from the coast in north-eastern coastal New South Wales. A census of Aboriginal households in February-March 1969 recorded 201 Aborigines living in 34 locations. One household of five people declined to co-operate in the study (an old antagonism between the household head and myself made this refusal understandable). Forestville Aborigines were between 6 and 10 per cent of the total population of the research area of about 35 km². Australian census districts did not coincide with the research area, so it is not possible to be precise. In one extreme village there were 64 (20%) Aborigines in a total population of 309 (1971 census figures).

Forestville was first crossed by Whites in the 1830s and settlement of big holdings by pastoral squatters came a decade later at a time when Coasttown was already closely settled by farmers on small holdings. The Forestville area was not subdivided into small holdings until the years between 1905 and 1920.

Early contact at Forestville was violent and all the areas around were involved in serious conflicts in which ancestors of the Forestville people were shot, poisoned and driven off their lands, and Whites were ambushed and killed by Blacks in retaliation. Violence continued until about 1870, but thereafter Aborigines were incorporated into the economics of the cattle stations and the timber industry which was exploiting the rich stands of cedar in the area. The situation for Aborigines worsened after closer settlement when their labour and presence was no longer necessary to the family settlers on small holdings.

There is much evidence of discrimination by Whites against the Forestville Aborigines throughout the present century. In early 1969, at the request of the Aborigines, I negotiated with a hotel licensee to have him admit Aboriginal men in his public bar. He eventually did so, but reluctantly. The incident is indicative of the unfavourable ethnic relations at Forestville. Aborigines at Forestville react strongly against White-Black sexual relationships and until recently excluded from their community any woman who had a relationship with a White man.

Whites, even when most numerous, were never at the relative strength they have at Coasttown. The White population is now declining steadily as mechanisation of farming and timber-getting drastically reduces the available jobs. Between 1966 and 1971, the total population declined by about 8 per cent at a time when the Aboriginal population was increasing at about 2 per cent per annum (net). In only one of the households was there a White spouse — a man who came from outside the area as the *de facto* husband of an Aboriginal woman who could pass in most circumstances as White.

Aboriginal life is centred on the one reserve though households were also located in three villages and in some isolated rural places. There were, on average, 5.9 persons per household, with the median house of four rooms being occupied by six people — a figure well below the seven to eight persons noted for the median Coasttown household. At Forestville the median house had two bedrooms with three persons per bedroom, and there were only four cases with four or more persons per bedroom. In 1969 more than half the houses were sub-standard, but in terms of space the people were better off than those at Coasttown. Since 1969 the building of fourteen new houses and eight aged persons' units has radically improved the housing at Forestville, but has placed a considerable strain on the people who have to pay rent — in many cases for the first time in their lives.

Though overcrowding was not so severe at Forestville as at Coasttown, 56 per cent of the children lived in households with at least five other children and 31 per cent lived in households with at least seven other children. Only four children were living as only children.

Generally, authority is focused in the men; and this holds even in two cases where the men concerned might be judged ineffectual by ordinary White standards. In 21 (90%) households with children, a cohabiting couple was in charge, so there was no evidence of matri-focused households being over-represented.

Of the study population of 196 at 31 December 1968, 53.1 per cent was under the age of 15 years and only 3.5 per cent was over the age of 65. The sexes were fairly equally distributed but there were imbalances in certain age groups; for example, between 15 and 40 years there were 15 unattached males but only 5 unattached females.

Ninety Forestville Aborigines had completed their education and of that number 4 (4.4%) had received no schooling, a further 62 (68.9%) had received only primary education — mainly to fourth class — and only 1 (1.1%) had received a Junior Certificate. Information received from the schools suggested no immediate improvement of that dismal picture was likely.

The potential Aboriginal workforce at Forestville in 1969 was 58 of whom 33 (57%) were employed at interview, 12 (21%) were unemployed and 13 (22%) were in receipt of a pension of some kind.

Basically, the people derive from a single tribe whose tribal land surrounds the study area, 90 per cent having a direct link with the tribal country and a further 5 per cent were linked to it by marriage, whereas only one household (5%) was not directly linked to the immediate area by either birth or marriage. This family was moved into the area by a State authority to provide accommodation in an emergency and was already planning to return to Queensland during the study period. Forestville people are more tribally homogeneous and geographically restricted in origins than those of Coasttown.

While in no sense can Forestville Aborigines be thought of as 'tribal', there is ample evidence that the traditional past maintains an influence on their life-style and particularly on their thinking. In 1969, a 20 per cent stratified random sample of those over 15 years was drawn and 18 of the 19 were interviewed in depth. Of that number, seven (average age 54 years, youngest 34) reported themselves as speakers of the Aboriginal language; five (average age 31, youngest 19) reported themselves as being able to 'speak a little'; whereas only six (average age 23, eldest 27) reported themselves as non-speakers. Only two (a boy and his sister) reported that neither of their parents was or had been speakers of the local language.

In more immediate ways the traditional past remained very real for Forestville Aborigines. During an earlier study (Hausfeld 1960) all the tribal clan countries in the area were mapped, and within clan boundaries many of the patrilineage areas were recorded. The location of sacred and increase sites was known and respected and a considerable body of mythology associated with the sites was known. Kinship and marriage rules were still recognised as important.

However, by 1969 there were two legally sanctioned marriages which were very 'wrong' by traditional standards. These were excused by a strong supporter of the Aboriginal Church group by reference to the fact that the Queen had married her cousin. A further breakdown of the hold of the past is occurring as old and important carriers of tradition die without passing on their knowledge to the young people who no longer speak the local language.

Nevertheless, it is clear that Forestville is much less acculturated than is Coasttown, despite the changes that are taking place at an increasing tempo. Some demographic changes between 1959 and 1968 are shown in Table 3.

Some summarised comparisons to support the claim that Coasttown Aborigines are far more acculturated than those at Forestville are presented in Table 4. The differences show Forestville as a community suffering marked disadvantages in the general community. For example, the percentage of the Australian population (1968-69) over 15 years of age in receipt of some form of pension was about ten (*Commonwealth Year Book* 1970) compared with Coasttown 13 per cent and Forestville 22 per cent — this despite the fact that in both Aboriginal communities the percentage of old people is lower than in the Australian population.

Categories	Sex		Sub-	Adjusted
	M	F	totals	totals
Recorded Aboriginal population at 31/12/59	92	77		169
*Migrants out to 31/12/68	32	25	57	112
Deaths to ,, ...	13	3	16	96
Migrant spouses in to 31/12/68	7	2	9	105
Births to 31/12/68	27	32	59	164
*Aboriginal migrants in to 31/12/68 ..	20	17	37	201
One white spouse to be excluded	1			200
Four occupants of house not co-operating ..	1	3	4†	196
Co-operating population at 31/12/69 ..	99	97		196

*Births and deaths for these groups not included in calculations.
†The non-co-operating household is shown (see above) as having five occupants, but one of these was not a member of the 1959 household.

Table 3: Forestville Aboriginal population changes between 31 December 1959 and 31 December 1968

Workforce	Coasttown	Forestville
% unemployed	23	27
% casually or seasonally employed ..	20	20
% regularly employed	57	53
% who were pensioners		
(post-school, all types)	13	22

Population		
Natural increase per annum	3.0%	3.5%
Crude birth rate per 1,000	38	48
% net increase in population		
per annum	2.5	2.1

History		
First settlement	1820s	1840s
Closer settlement	1840s	1900s

Ethnic relations		
Intermarriage with Whites	Common and accepted	Rare and not accepted
White-Aboriginal interaction	Fair to good	Poor to bad

Tradition		
Knowledge of Aboriginal language ..	Virtually nil	Commonly known to those over 30 years
Knowledge of tribal country and mythology	Virtually nil	Considerable

Table 4: Coasttown-Forestville comparisons

White control groups The *College* group was selected because it was generally representative of successful middle-class, and because its members were in training for work in official programmes with Aborigines. All students available at the time of interview co-operated.

The *Commune* group was selected to contrast with College; and, before interview, was thought of as disenchanted middle-class. In fact, only about half the Commune members derive from the middle-class. All the residents and individuals closely associated with the Commune house in an inner-metropolitan suburb, available at the time of interview, co-operated.

The *Pilot* group was similar to the College and was used in pilot-testing the schedules about two years prior to recording College and Commune data. Demographic data were not recorded for the Pilot group.

A comparison of College and Commune demographic data is given in Tables 6 and 7. The average age of the groups is comparable (22 and 20), as is their marital status; otherwise there are important differences. All College members were career workers with government agencies, whereas

	College	Commune
Average age:	22	20
Church attendance: Does not attend	2 (11%)	9 (45%)
Attends sometimes	9 (50%)	8 (40%)
Attends regularly	7 (39%)	3 (15%)
Marital status: Single	15	19
Married	2	1
Deserted	1	0
Place of Birth: Metropolitan	11 (61%)	16 (80%)
Rural	6 (33%)	3 (15%)
Not stated	1 (6%)	1 (5%)
Foreign born	1 (6%)	4 (20%)
Employment: Teachers-in-training	10	
Welfare Officers-in-training	8	
Teachers		1
Nurses, student nurses		5
Students		6
Screen printer, computer operator		1 each
Labourer, kitchen maid		1 each
Unemployed		4
Average income:	$3,000	$2,100
Educational achievement: Degree		1
Some university		8
Higher School Certificate	18	7
Junior School Certificate		4

Table 5: White control groups

Commune members were variously employed and unemployed. The average income of the College group is 50 per cent above that of Commune workers, but Commune paternal average income was double that of College fathers. One College member was foreign born, whereas this applied to four Commune members.

The College group's fathers' occupations were generally solid middle to lower middle-class, whereas those of Commune fathers were split between upper middle-class and working-class.

College members, by job selection, had sought security and respectability; whereas Commune members, by life-style, had dropped out of the system, rejecting its goals of ambitious achievement and material acquisitiveness. Most Commune members had experimented with drugs (hard and/or soft) and about 60 per cent were marihuana smokers. Commune members were not political activists, but could be described as passivist humanitarians.

College	Commune
3 x farmers	1 x professor
2 x station managers	1 x doctor
1 x agricultural adviser	1 x architect
1 x design engineer	1 x anthropologist
1 x school teacher	1 x veterinary surgeon
1 x mechanic	1 x E.D.P. manager
1 x hairdresser	1 x wholesale butcher
2 x production supervisors	2 x public servants
2 x office managers	1 x warehouse manager
1 x toolmaker	1 x taxi driver
1 x carpenter	1 x factory foreman
1 x defence forces police	1 x cable jointer
1 x deceased (unknown)	1 x mail officer
	1 x clerk
	1 x council workman
	1 x labourer
	1 x shed cleaner
	2 x retired (unknown)

Fathers' average income:

$4,300	$8,100

Table 6: *Fathers' occupations — white control groups*

Value orientation   The conceptualisation of values used here is that of Kluckhohn and Strodtbeck (1961:4). They define value orientations in the following way:

> Value orientations are complex but definitely patterned (rank ordered) principles, resulting from the transactional interplay of three analytically distinguishable elements of the evaluative process — the cognitive, the affective, and the directive elements — which give order and direction to the ever-flowing stream of human acts and thoughts as these relate to the solution of 'common human' problems.

This conceptualisation of value orientations differs from earlier ideas in that it sees value orientations as rank ordered sets, rather than as single dominant values. They are variable only within limits. The variation is in patterning only. That is, they propose a field theory (with variation within the field boundaries) rather than a two-dimensional or linear theory.

They argue that the *directive* aspect of the value orientation process is of first importance, and that the *complex principles* are on an implicit-explicit continuum.

Certain assumptions are made by Kluckhohn and Strodtbeck and these are set out as follows:

That: 1. there is an ordered variation in value orientation systems;
      2. there is a limited number of commom human problems for which all peoples at all times must find some solution.

The common human problems proposed by Kluckhohn and Strodtbeck deal with (1) the nature of human nature; (2) man's relation with nature; (3) man's relation with man; (4) man's temporal focus; and (5) man's modality of activity.

For all values except *human nature* they see a *three-point range of variation* involved in the rank ordering of orientations (Kluckhohn and Strodtbeck 1961:13). The *human nature* value is complicated beyond the orientation of good, evil and neutral by secondary principles of mutability and immutability; and also by the logical position of a *mixture of good and evil*. They failed to solve the problems involved in such a complex patterning, and this value has not been further considered in this study.

The Kluckhohn and Strodtbeck conceptualisation of the *man-nature* value included the concept of 'supernature' along with 'nature' in a single value orientation set. Since it is logical for man to hold the view that he lives in a lawful universe without invoking the supernatural as a causal explanation, I take the view that two values are involved — not one. Consequently, in modifying their schedule for use in Australia with Aborigines, I removed the notion of supernature from their man-nature set of items and developed another value set which I called *World View* — with the orientations of *Spirituality, Materiality* and *Balance*. This value expresses man's relation with supernature.

Consequently, a set of five values remained and a schedule of 25 items was developed (five items per value) to explore respondents' orientations to the

Orientation	Postulated range of variations		
man-nature	Subjugation-to-nature	Harmony-with-nature	Mastery-over-nature
world view	Spirituality	Balance	Materiality
time	Past	Present	Future
relational	Lineality	Collaterality	Individualism
activity	Being	(Being-in-Becoming)*	Doing

*Not used in this study.

Table 7: Value orientations and postulated variations

values. Wherever applicable, the schedule items closely followed those developed and validated by Kluckhohn and Strodtbeck. The values examined and the postulated range of variations are set out in Table 7.

With the exception of the *Activity* variations perhaps, the items are self-explanatory. Neither I nor Kluckhohn and Strodtbeck managed to develop satisfactory items to cope with the concept of *Being-in-Becoming* and consequently I followed them in using only *Being* ('a spontaneous expression of what is conceived to be "given" in the human personality') and *Doing* ('a spontaneous expression in activity of impulses and desires'). (Kluckhohn and Strodtbeck 1961:16.)

The results of the analysis of the responses of the four major groups [(1) a 10% stratified random sample of Coasttown adults — over 15 years; (2) a 20% stratified random sample of Forestville adults; (3) all the College group; (4) all the Commune group] are given for the five value orientations in Figure 1. The method of analysis set out by Kluckhohn and Strodtbeck (1961:Ch.IV) is used for the combination of sets of five items for each value orientation, with the exception of the *man-nature* orientations which will be discussed separately. In order to present graphical comparability, m (the number of respondents) was standardised at 20 in each case by a simple method of proportions. However, to ensure statistical precision, all calculations were made on the actual number of respondents in each case.

The hexagonal graphs, while not commonly used, are excellent for the presentation of the relationships between three dependent variables. They are simply read. The centre point represents the position where no preference is shown for any of the variables. The distance of a point from this neutral position is an expression of the strength with which a group holds a particular variation. Where m (the number of respondents) is 20, as in this case, the maximum strength is represented by a value of 4.5, consequently dotted hexagon represents the boundary of the field within which variation can occur. The arcal position of a particular point within this field represents the relationship between the variations. For example, in Figure 1(b) C1 (College) falls in the segment of the graph which indicates that *Individualism* is preferred to *Collaterality* which is preferred to *Lineality*; the distance of C1 from the centre indicates that this position is strongly held by the group, and the arcal position indicates that C1 is roughly one-third of the way between outright *Individualism* and outright *Collaterality*. The particular strength of any variation can be read by dropping a perpendicular to the desired variation scale (the numbered diameters).

Looking at Figures 1(d) and 1(e) it can be seen that items 4 and 19 [grouped in 1(d)] indicate that three of the four groups express a ranking of preferences Subjugation-to-nature preferred to Mastery-over-nature preferred to Harmony-with-nature, BUT items 9, 14 & 24 [Figure 1(e)] show all four groups expressing the variation Harmony-with-nature preferred to Mastery-over-nature preferred to Subjugation-to-nature, a position which is diametrically opposed to that expressed by the other two items. Either the schedule items are poor measures of the variations or the value orientation *man-nature* remains conceptually weak despite the removal of the notion of super-nature from the original Kluckhohn and Strodtbeck conceptualisation. In either case, the results represented in Figures 1(d) and 1(e) are problematical and will not be further considered here.

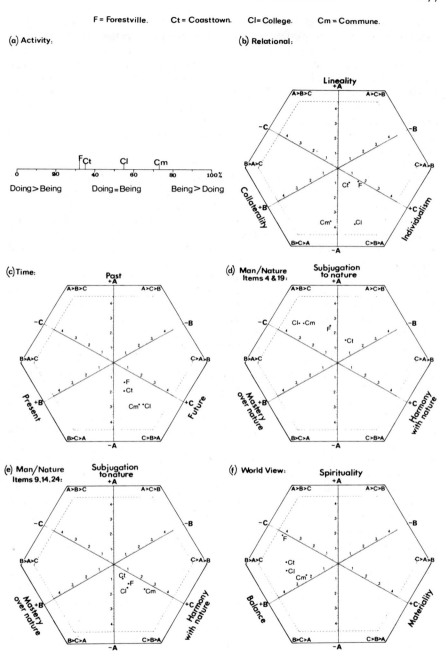

Figure 1: *Total groups. Comparison on combined items*

An examination of the remaining results shows that there would be little to choose between the groups if only the segmental locations of points were considered. However, as indicated above, the strength with which a particular variation is held is also indicated and the further analysis of the results will show that this factor is vital in comparing the value orientations of different groups; but first it is necessary to consider the question of stress.

Stress   *Stress,* as used in this study, is an external force acting to produce strain in the individuals of a group. Such a force cannot be measured directly, but if a way is available to measure the results of strain, then this can be accepted as an indicator of stress. One such measure is the Cornell Medical Index Health Questionnaire (CMI) — a diagnostic instrument of 195 questions relating to both physical and psychiatric symptoms as perceived by a respondent. This schedule has been used in this study.

The CMI is divided into 18 sections (A–L) covering all the bodily systems, and six sections (M–R) dealing with moods and feelings. (Brodman *et al.* 1949). The CMI Manual specifically suggests the uses to which the CMI is put in this study:

> . . . to compare the probable number of individuals with specified symptoms, medical disorders, or emotional disturbances in one population with the number in others. (*Ibid.*:3.)

The CMI is here used in three different ways:

1. as a measure of stress acting on the individual to produce strain which is manifest in symptoms as revealed by 'yes' answers over the whole CMI;
2. as a measure of emotional disturbance — the Manual says:

> A medically significant emotional disturbance may be suspected when any of the following is evidenced on the CMI: a syndrome of 'Yes' answers clinically suggestive of a psychological disorder; thirty or more 'Yes' responses on the entire CMI; three or more 'Yes' responses on the last page (Sections M–R) of the CMI; or four or more questions not answered, answered both 'Yes' and 'No', or with changes or remarks written in by the patient . . . When a patient has a significant emotional disturbance, more than one of these evidences is usually found. (*Ibid.*:7.)

CMI Sections			Average number of 'yes' responses			
			College	Commune	Coasttown	Forestville
A–L	..	..	13.1	14.8	17.8	22.6
M–R	..	..	6.6	6.6	6.7	11.7
A–R	..	..	19.7	21.4	24.5	34.3
			% emotionally disturbed			
More than 29 on CMI *and* more than 2 M–R	..	..	17%	20%	21%	63%

Table 8: *CMI average scores and per cent emotionally disturbed*

The measure of emotional disturbance used here is a combination of 'more than 29 Yes responses on the whole CMI' *and* 'more than 2 Yes responses on Sections M–R of the CMI'. This measure was chosen because it satisfies the Manual's requirements but does not call for any medical skill in its analysis.

3. as a measure of *self-perceived morbidity* — the whole CMI is used for a total measure, sections A–L are used as a measure of physical symptoms, and sections M–R are used as a measure of moods and feelings disturbance.

The results obtained from an analysis of respondent's responses to the CMI are summarised in Table 8.

The concept of value dissonance   Two things are necessary to relate the level of stress to the differences observed in value orientations:

1. some standard against which particular value positions can be measured;

2. some way in which all the differences between groups can be summed to provide a single measure of value orientation difference.

The first of these problems was solved by dividing each group at its median CMI score and then assessing separately each sub-group so formed. The results of this procedure are illustrated in Figure 2. It will be seen that in 14 out of 16 cases the high-to-low direction is the same for each group. Fourteen confirming cases out of a total of sixteen is statistically significant at the one per cent level (binomial analysis).

From this analysis an Ideal Type value orientations pattern for Australia can be developed, by taking the extreme position indicated by the high-to-low directions in Figure 2. The resulting Ideal Type pattern of value orientations is as follows:

Activity: *Doing* preferred to *Being* 100% of the time.

Relational: *Individualism* preferred to *Collaterality* preferred to *Lineality* 100% of the time.

Time: *Future* preferred to *Present* preferred to *Past* 100% of the time.

World View: *Balance* preferred to both *Spirituality* and *Materiality* 100% of the time; and *Spirituality* equally preferred to *Materiality*.

Using this standard it is possible to determine for each variation-pair the percentage of each group holding a particular preference and to compare that percentage with the percentage expected to hold the same preference in the Ideal Type pattern. Such an analysis was carried out for each possible value orientation variation-pair (for example, for the pair 'Past preferred to Present' for items 3, 8, 13, 18 and 23 of the schedule for each of the groups). The result of this analysis is given in Table 9, where the expected percentage for the Ideal Type is also given in each case. To obtain a measure of difference in any case it is only necessary to take the absolute value of the difference of a group from the Ideal Type. It is then possible to sum all the differences from the Ideal Type for a particular group to obtain a measure of total difference. This measure I have called *Value Dissonance*.

H= High CMI.   L= Low CMI.

F = Forestville.   Ct = Coasttown.   Cl = College.   Cm = Commune.

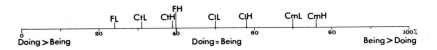

a Activity:

b Relational:

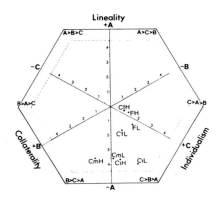

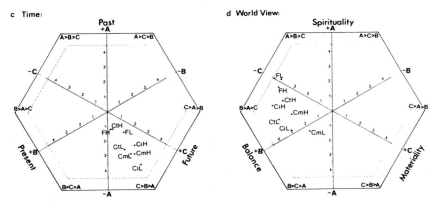

Figure 2: *HIGH/LOW CMI sub-groups' value orientation comparisons, by combined value items totals, by group*

Table 9: *Percentage of responses for value orientation pair preferences*
$>$ = *preferred to*

Value orientation preference	Item	% of responses choosing preference (Total Groups)			
		Forestville	Coasttown	College	Commune
Being>Doing	1	42	30	6	65
	6	37	58	31	50
Ideal Type (I.T.	11	37	30	94	100
% = 0)	16	16	36	67	90
	21	26	22	72	60
Lineality>Collaterality	2	47	39	6	5
	7	68	55	0	0
(I.T. % = 0)	12	16	39	11	10
	17	26	12	11	15
	22	79	72	17	5
Lineality>Individualism	2	16	15	0	5
	7	42	42	0	8
(I.T. % = 0)	12	21	21	6	20
	17	32	27	17	20
	22	53	63	6	10
Collaterality >Individualism	2	5	12	0	20
	7	11	27	24	70
	12	47	36	39	60
(I.T. % = 0)	17	58	67	50	65
	22	37	50	33	65
Past>Present	3	32	12	0	20
	8	42	18	17	10
(I.T. % = 0)	13	26	36	17	5
	18	47	52	47	40
	23	37	48	67	48
Past>Future	3	16	6	0	10
	8	32	21	11	20
(I.T. % = 0)	13	26	9	0	20
	18	74	67	18	5
	23	21	18	0	0
Present>Future	3	11	15	39	10
	8	26	36	39	35
(I.T. % = 0)	13	37	30	28	65
	18	79	73	12	5
	23	37	42	0	5

(*continued on p.* 282)

(continued from p. 281)

Value orientation preference	Item	% of responses choosing preference (Total groups)			
		Forestville	Coasttown	College	Commune
Spirituality>Balance	5	58	33	12	30
	10	26	30	11	20
(I.T. % = 0)	15	37	15	44	35
	20	42	15	6	25
	25	68	36	22	15
Spirituality>Materiality	5	100	82	77	60
	10	95	79	83	55
(I.T. % = 50)	15	90	64	72	70
	20	100	64	56	48
	25	100	88	67	55
Balance>Materiality	5	95	91	88	80
	10	95	88	94	70
(I.T. % = 100)	15	95	91	89	80
	20	95	91	83	63
	25	100	91	89	75

The Value Dissonance for each group, arrived at in this way, is: College: 1032; Commune: 1340; Coasttown: 1551; and Forestville: 1745.

By using this Ideal Type, it is possible to rank all four groups relative to the Ideal Type.

Value	Rank order totals			
	Forestville	Coasttown	College	Commune
Activity (5)	10	10	12	18
Relational (15)	47	46	20.5	36.5
Time (15)	48.5	42.5	30	29
World View (15)	43	36	35	36
Totals (50) O =	148.5	134.5	97.5	119.5
Expected E =	125	125	125	125
E–O =	− 23.5	− 9.5	+ 27.5	+ 5.5

m = 50   S = 1429   p<.01

Ranking order: College, Commune, Coasttown, Forestville.

Note: number in brackets is number of pairs involved.

Table 10: Rank ordering of dissonance from Ideal Type value orientation pattern, by value totals for individual item value orientation pairs comparison

Table 10 gives a summarised result of such a procedure, showing the rank totals by value. Only the calculation, of Kendall's Coefficient of Concordance, for all values combined is shown. The result is significant at one per cent, and provides us with the rank ordering: College, Commune, Coasttown, Forestville with respect to relative distance from the Ideal Type pattern of value orientations.

Other correlations Table 11 shows the relationships between Value Dissonance and scores on the CMI, by groups and sub-groups. There is a remarkable consistency in these results with the exception that Forestville males and young have higher CMI scores than might be expected, and Forestville females have a lower CMI score than expected.

It was pointed out earlier that Forestville was a situation of poor ethnic relations with evidence of discrimination against Aborigines. The males and the young are forced into contact with Whites in school and economic relationships and it seems reasonable that the increased stress of these contacts

Group or sub-group	Value dissonance from Ideal Type	Average CMI scores by sections		
		A–R	A–L	M–R
College				
males	928	16.6	11.9	4.8
total	1,032	19.7	13.1	6.6
females	1,168	22.1	14.1	8.0
Commune				
females	1,318	19.1	12.3	6.8
total	1,340	21.4	14.8	6.6
males	1,370	23.7	17.3	6.4
Coasttown				
young	1,492	21.3	14.2	7.1
non-sett.	1,519	22.4	16.9	5.4
males	1,523	19.4	14.8	4.6
total	1,551	24.5	17.8	6.7
sett.	1,573	27.4	18.9	8.4
females	1,574	30.5	21.3	9.2
old	1,602	27.4	21.2	6.2
Forestville				
males	1,629	36.7	24.8	11.9
young	1,679	38.3	23.6	14.6
non- sett.	1,690	32.1	20.3	11.8
total	1,745	34.3	22.6	11.7
old	1,796	31.5	21.8	9.6
sett.	1,800	36.8	25.1	11.7
females	1,908	31.0	19.5	11.5

Table 11: Groups and sub-groups listed in ascending order of value dissonance from Ideal Type, showing average CMI scores by sections

is reflected in the heightened CMI scores for these sub-groups. Females, on the other hand, can avoid many such contacts to a significant extent and withdraw into their own community where their intensive involvement in Church activities may prove stress-relieving and account for their lowered CMI scores.

Figure 3(a) shows the result of plotting Value Dissonance against total CMI scores for the four groups. The line, which provides a reasonable fit to the points, was arrived at by taking the theoretical position of the Ideal Type (zero dissonance and zero CMI) as one point and the combined College and Commune groups (value dissonance = 1,210 and CMI = 20.6) as the other, thus indicating that the Aboriginal groups are under the same influences as other members of Australian society — that is, there is no necessity to appeal to a racial (genetic) factor to explain either their high value dissonance or their high levels of self-perceived morbidity.

Figures 3(b), 4(a) and 4(b) show the regression of the four groups College, Commune, Coasttown and Forestville for total and grouped CMI scores. All results are statistically significant at the five per cent level, and the regressions successfully predict the Pilot group's results in each case within the five per cent boundaries represented by the dotted lines.

Further supporting evidence is given in Table 12 where a number of measures are brought together. With such perfect correlations no statistical procedures are necessary to support the assertion of high significance.

	College	Commune	Coasttown	Forestville
Value dissonance	1,032	1,340	1,551	1,745
% Emotionally disturbed ..	17	20	21	63
Level of morbidity .. .. (average CMI)	19.7	21.4	24.5	34.3

	Australia			
Age corrected death rate ..	9		17	25
Birth rate	19		38	48
% Invalid pensioners (pensionable age) ..	1.8		5.8	10.8
% of workforce unemployed	2?		23	27
Average I.Q.	100		85	76
Average years of educational retardation (teacher estimates)	0		1.4	2.8
Average days absent from school — 1 year	5?		27	59

Table 12: *Some comparisons*

All these results lend substantial support to the hypothesis that: *In a society, the life chances of the members of a sub-cultural group are inversely proportional to its value dissonance.*

(a) Prediction of Coasttown(Ct) and Forestville(F), from Ideal Type and combined College(Cl) and Commune(Cm).   Total CMI(A-R).

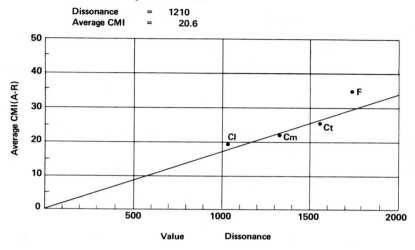

(b) Regression of College, Commune, Coasttown and Forestville to predict Pilot.

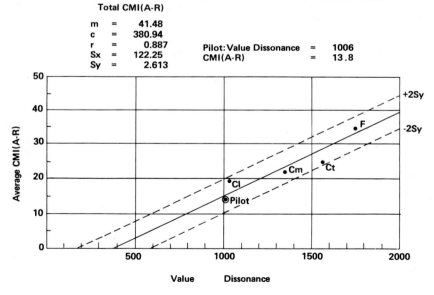

Figures 3(a) *and* (b)

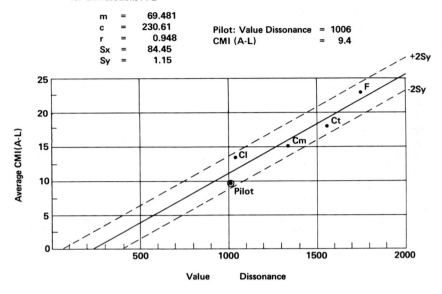

(a)   **Regression of College, Commune, Coasttown and Forestville to predict Pilot for CMI sections A-L**

$m = 69.481$
$c = 230.61$
$r = 0.948$
$Sx = 84.45$
$Sy = 1.15$

Pilot: Value Dissonance $= 1006$
CMI (A-L) $= 9.4$

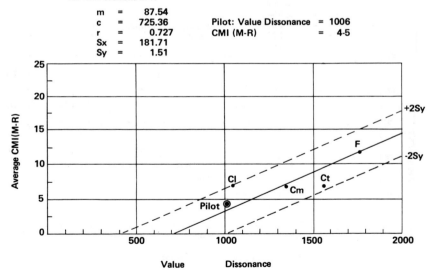

(b)   **Regression of College, Commune, Coasttown and Forestville to predict Pilot for CMI-sections M-R**

$m = 87.54$
$c = 725.36$
$r = 0.727$
$Sx = 181.71$
$Sy = 1.51$

Pilot: Value Dissonance $= 1006$
CMI (M-R) $= 4-5$

Figures 4(a) *and* (b)

Conclusions The study demonstrates that the concept of *value dissonance* is heuristically valuable in that:

1. it ranks sub-cultural groups in accordance with sociological facts;
2. it provides a measure which successfully predicts levels of stress, self-perceived morbidity, probable morbidity (see Hausfeld 1973), and levels of emotional disturbance in groups.

Further, it has been shown that the disadvantages Aborigines suffer can be adequately explained by sociological facts alone and no recourse to genetic explanations is necessary.

It has been shown also that stress does not result from change but rather from its absence when the environment demands it.

These facts offer no comfort in the Australian scene because we know of no way to change basic value orientations embedded in basic personality structure (Berger and Luckmann 1966). The result of this impasse is that we can do no more than ameliorate the situation for Aborigines by developing as many stress-relieving situations as possible, and waiting for time to bring about generational change. Short of a special kind of revolution in society, miracles of change are not available.

Acknowledgements

I wish to thank Edgar Ford, who prepared the Figures, and Fran Hausfeld whose incisive comments improved this paper.

References

BERGER, P. L. *and* T. LUCKMANN 1966 *The social construction of reality: a treatise in the sociology of knowledge.* Doubleday, New York.

BRODMAN, K., A. J. ERDMANN *and* H. G. WOLFF 1949 *Manual: Cornell Medical Index Health Questionnaire.* Cornell University Medical College, New York.

COMMONWEALTH YEAR BOOK 1970, 1972 *Official Year Book of the Commonwealth of Australia.* Government Printer, Canberra.

FRITH, N .C. 1975 *Experiences in public health nursing.* Australian Government Publishing Service, Canberra.

——R. G. HAUSFELD *and* P. M. MOODIE 1974 *The Coasttown project.* Australian Government Publishing Service, Canberra.

HAUSFELD, R. G. 1960 Aspects of Aboriginal station management. M.A. thesis, University of Sydney.

——1972 Value orientations, change and stress. Ph.D thesis, University of Sydney.

——1973 The social prediction of self-perceived morbidity, *Medical Journal of Australia,* 2:975-78.

KLUCKHOHN, F. R. *and* F. L. STRODTBECK 1961 *Variations in value orientations.* Row, Peterson, New York.

21 Group organisation and identity within an urban Aboriginal community

A.-K. Eckermann

Introduction Past research into the way of life of Aboriginal people living in urban areas[1] has always presented the minority as a depressed group, prone to alcoholism, in need of special social, economic and educational programmes. In order to explain the situation authors have variously pointed to historical circumstances; a persistence of traditional attitudes and values; the minority's inability to cope with an industrial system and its values, or its unwillingness to adopt 'white man's ways' as a form of passive resistance against the overwhelming white majority. Here I hope to present additional information about Aboriginal people in urban areas in order to dispel some of the misconceptions and ignorance about their social and economic life-style.

My data indicate that Aboriginal people in this community live in socio-economic circumstances very similar to those found among working-class people generally, and can consequently be labelled 'assimilated', 'integrated' or 'acculturated'. Nevertheless, a strong and positive sense of being Aboriginal persists and is perpetuated. I believe this identification to be due to a number of factors, most importantly those associated with child-rearing practices, common historical experiences and a rich and flourishing system of folklore.

Research for this report was carried out over a period of two and a half years from June 1969 to December 1971 among a group of Aboriginal people living in a non-metropolitan urban area of south-east Queensland.[2] In 1970-71 the total Aboriginal population in 'Industrial City' numbered 320. This included 145 children — that is, persons under the age of sixteen — and 175 adults. During the two and a half years of fieldwork, 4 per cent of the total adult population left the area permanently, while a further 6 per cent moved out but returned before December 1972.

Ninety per cent of the Aboriginal population belong to one of six major kindreds, or 'clans'[3] as they call themselves. The other 10 per cent are divided among seven independent families who are only now beginning to inter-marry with the 'clans' of longer residence. Each of the 'clans' and three of the isolated families have, at one time or another, been associated with an Aboriginal settlement before the turn of the century, and a later church mission which operated on the outskirts of 'Industrial City'. Most people obtained their exemption papers[4] before the mission station closed down in 1940. Those thought to be unfit to be exempted from the provisions of the Act were sent to a government community.

Like any other institution of its kind, 'Mission Town' was directive and restrictive in its dealings with Aboriginal people. However, in many respects it was unique. Aboriginal men and women were continually moving between the mission and various forms of *outside* employment. There is no suggestion that 'Mission Town' ever attempted to employ its population fully — rather, farm activities were carried out to train the young, and supplement its other means of subsistence. As such, individuals in 'Mission Town' were never 'institutionalised' in the sense that present inhabitants of government settlements and church mission stations are 'institutionalised' today. Nevertheless, as long as the mission station was operating, Aborigines were 'placed' — jobs were found for them, and they were required to remain in their employment until their contracts had expired. They returned to the mission station for their holidays, to get married, to have their babies and, at times, to die. Therefore, by the time 'Mission Town' was abandoned, Aborigines connected with it considered the area their 'home', although their forefathers had come from all areas of the state south of Rockhampton.

The clans Table 1 notes 'clans' by area of origin and language, and lists some traditions as they are remembered. It must be stressed that where a

Clan	Area of origin	Language spoken	Traditions remembered
A	South-west Queensland	*Gungari* (also known as *kungeri*) Kelly (1935:462)*	A case of 'singing'
B	Dawson and Upper Burnett Rivers	*Wakka-Wakka/ Gurang Gurang*	Some 'tribal' traditions
C	Unknown, though central Queensland is claimed through association	*Wakka-Wakka*	—
D	Communities in New South Wales and Queensland	—	—
E	South-west Queensland	*Wakka-Wakka*	A case of 'singing'
F	South-east coast of Queensland and New South Wales	—	—

* According to Mathews (1898), the area was occupied by the *Kogai-Yuipera* 'nation' as well as the northern groups of the *Kamilaroi* nation. Kelly (1935), however, maintains that this district was inhabited by the *Kuam* around Mitchell, the *Kambuwul* near Roma and the *Kungeri* in the St George area.

Table 1: Origin and traditional background of clans

vernacular language is spoken, this is confined totally to the older female members of groups. Further, the predominance of *Wakka Wakka* is due to the fact that this was the *lingua franca* of 'Mission Town'. Traditions remembered are explained in detail later; however, those of 'clan' B can be singled out at this stage to illustrate the pattern.

'Clan' B's male founder is said to have been *gungil* — a 'clever man' — and is reputed to have handed some of his power and knowledge on to his daughters. The sisters believe that their 'clan' belongs to both the *Wakka Wakka* and the *Gurang Gurang,* though they consider themselves *Wakka Wakka* and call their language *gudang gudang*. Consequently they claim the Dawson-Upper Burnett area of Queensland as their 'country'. Their paternal great-grandfather was one of the early settlers or convicts from England, while their grandfather belonged to the *Gugurapu* tribe (or clan) from the Fassifern area around Mt Walker. The sisters were familiarised with tribal traditions although they were reared in 'Mission Town'. However, unlike many children who were brought up in dormitories, they lived in the camp section; thus their parents greatly influenced their upbringing. Some of the things they remember are:

> In the tribal days, unmarried girls were not permitted to prepare food — this was perhaps related to the taboo on food preparation by menstruating women.
> They speak of brother/sister avoidance; they believe that brothers were not permitted to speak face-to-face — this may originally have been related to respect relationships between older and younger brothers.
> They have been told that girls were not permitted to sleep with their mothers, while no such restriction was applied to boys. Further, they claim, children were never tolerated at the same camp fire as adults.[5]

Although the extent of their knowledge about traditional life is small, the sisters have retained their language as well as many folk-beliefs (to be discussed later). Their children, however, show no interest in traditional matters, including language, and the sisters are sure that all reminiscences will die out with them.

Those aspects of traditional life handed down to the members of 'clan' B have no effect on their style of life in the present. On the basis of this knowledge, however, they consider themselves to be different from other Aboriginal groups in 'Industrial City'. They believe that their awareness of 'old ways' and contact with the 'old people' provides them with certain insights which are not shared by other Aborigines. The prevalence and significance of this 'knowledge' will be discussed in the section on folklore.

Most of the 'clans' are female-oriented, if not female-dominated. 'Clan' A is presided over by one senior female; 'clans' B and C are organised around a group of sisters; 'clans' D, E and F are dually grouped around a dominant male and female who are either siblings ('clans' E and F) or mother and son ('clan' D). In 'clan' D, for example, female-centredness is limited to some extent by the fact that at the present time it is composed of two large, and relatively independent, extended families. One of these is centred around the 'matriarch' and her younger children, married and single. The other is grouped around her eldest son, whom she placed in 'Mission Town' when he was very young, and his children, married and single. There is only limited contact between the groups. No doubt this is due to the fact that the eldest son developed independently of his family in 'Mission Town'. In 'clan' E the greatest influence is exerted by the oldest surviving brother and the youngest sister, while 'clan' F is composed essentially of two extended families centred around an older sister and her younger brother.

Although the 'clans' are composed of numerous nuclear families, the 'clan' does serve as a unit of identification. Members consider themselves part of a 'clan' because they are all related to the original founding pair, in which most emphasis is placed on the female. Take, for example, 'clan' A. The daughters and sons of the founding matriarch have all married, thus dividing the 'clan' into a number of interrelated families. The sons are of minor importance to the group and lead lives relatively isolated from it. The daughters' daughters still consider themselves part of their families of orientation, into which their husbands are also incorporated. Overall identification for both daughters and sons as well as for their respective children is, however, with 'clan' A, and it is this identification which is stressed by them outside 'Industrial City'.

The same principle applies to all the 'clans'. In 'clan' C, however, the only unifying forces are the four sisters — even though there have been many disagreements within the group, and especially among the sisters themselves, which have resulted in physical violence as well as in the complete breaking-off of relations between individual families for many months. However, 'clan' C forms a definite out-group in 'Industrial City' today. Its members have a reputation for drinking and brawling; until the middle of 1971 they lived in the poorest accommodation in the area; they are reputed to be continually 'sponging' on their own relatives as well as on anybody who 'is fool enough' to help them. Consequently, they have little interaction with the rest of the Aboriginal community. Although they do not form a particularly cohesive group in themselves, they are forced to identify with their 'clan' because anyone belonging to it is treated as such by the rest of the community.

Relations between groups   There are strong ties between five of the six 'clans'. An analysis of intergroup ties is presented in Diagram 1. In general, people strongly resent non-recognition of actual or imaginary relationships and kin ties. For example, one person was insulted because he had not been informed of another's illness — for, 'after all, he's my cousin'. These ties are reinforced in times of other crises, especially funerals. All kinds of kin relationships are then quoted and people come to sympathise, give advice, and offer help. However, even within the 'clan', ties are not strong enough to cope with financial disaster. When this happens the individual family is very much on its own. When financial aid is given, this takes place only between parents and children and between siblings. But economic conditions are usually so difficult that, even in 'good' weeks, this type of assistance is rare. Although people claimed, as did those quoted by Barwick (1962) and Beckett (1958), that they would give a helping hand to anyone, white or black, who needed a new start, this ideal is not realised in practice, and a large proportion of arguments within the nuclear family arise because of financial problems. Only three examples of parents providing extended financial aid to children have been recorded, while there have been no cases

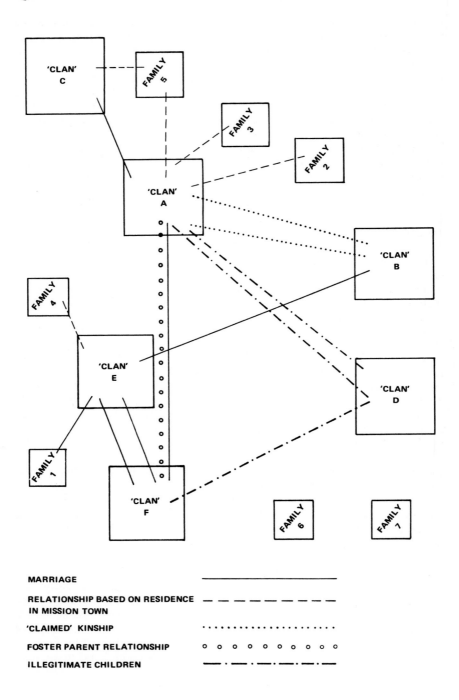

MARRIAGE	———————————————
RELATIONSHIP BASED ON RESIDENCE IN MISSION TOWN	— — — — — — — —
'CLAIMED' KINSHIP	· · · · · · · · · · · · · · · · · · ·
FOSTER PARENT RELATIONSHIP	o o o o o o o o o o o
ILLEGITIMATE CHILDREN	—·—·—·—·—·—·—

Diagram 1: *Interaction of groups*

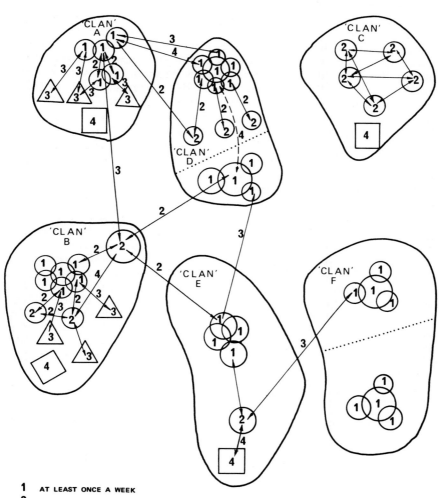

1 AT LEAST ONCE A WEEK
2 AT LEAST ONCE A MONTH
3 LESS THAN ONCE A MONTH
BUT MORE THAN ONCE EVERY 3 MONTHS

4 LESS THAN 3 MONTHS

Diagram 2: Patterns of interaction between and within 'clans'

of children supporting parents. Thus, the ideals of sharing and communality are present, but are applied only to the immediate family.

Similarly, regular visiting (that is, interaction at least once a week) is confined to parents and their children. Visiting between siblings of opposite sex belonging to the older generation (that is, those brothers and sisters who were reared in 'Mission Town', especially in the dormitory) is restricted to once a month or less. Visiting between siblings of the present younger generation (male or female, married or single, or older siblings of the same sex who were therefore reared in the same dormitory) is much more prevalent. This may be due to the fact that children in 'Mission Town' were not encouraged to maintain family ties, but their children have grown up in ordinary homes with a great deal of interpersonal contact and parental affection.

It is possible to set out diagrammatically patterns of interaction between 'clans' as well as interaction between the family units. Diagram 2 shows clearly that a number of isolated families have contact less than once every three months with members of their own 'clan'. This, again, emphasises the lack of cohesiveness within the 'clans' themselves. In two cases, isolated 'clan' families keep apart because that is their own choice; in the other three cases, bitter arguments in the past have led to a break in cordial relations.

Contact between 'clans' is based exclusively on propinquity, rather than on kin ties. Where 'clans' occupy the same 'territory' (that is, live in the same suburb), their members meet at stores, children go to the same schools, and women intervisit at 'tupper-ware' parties and on similar occasions. Relationships formed on these bases are not particularly strong or long-lasting, though they may at times be quite warm if individual members have shared the same experiences at 'Mission Town'. In all cases, anyone (either black or white) marrying into one of the 'clans' is claimed by it and socially classed by the rest of the Aboriginal community as belonging to it. In this manner, 'clans' maintain group identity even though intermarriage with whites is common. Table 2 presents marriage patterns of Aborigines with Europeans in 'Industrial City', 1944-1971.

Clan	European men married to Aboriginal women		Aboriginal men married to European women	
	Before 1965	Since 1965	Before 1965	Since 1965
A	0	3	0	2
B	3	2	0	4
C	1	2	0	2
D	0	4	0	0
E	1	0	0	0
F	0	2	0	0
Total	5	13	0	8

Table 2: Marriage patterns of Aborigines with Europeans: 'Industrial City' 1944-71

Twenty-six of the 48 marriages are with European partners. Only five mixed marriages were entered into prior to 1965, while 21 have been contracted since then. The first five intermarriages were all of Aboriginal women to European men. At present, the ratio of Aboriginal women marrying European men compared with that of Aboriginal men marrying European women, is 13:8. In 1970, the ratio was 8:8 (*de facto* unions excluded). These findings contrast sharply with results from other studies. For example, Beckett in his 1958 study of rural New South Wales reported on eighteen mixed marriages from a total of 115 recorded unions. Of these eighteen,

Skilled	16–30 years	31–39 years	40+	Frequency
Liaison officer			1	
Diesel mechanic	1			
Bank teller	1			
Butcher			1	
Licenced drainer			1	
Total	2		3	5
Semi-skilled				
Meatworker	10	3	1	
Fork-lift driver		1		
Truck driver		1		
Garage attendant			1	
Total	10	5	2	17
Unskilled				
Labourer	32	5	11	
Railway fettler			1	
Total	32	5	12	49
Unemployed	2	3	1	6
Pensioners			3	3
Students	3			3
			Total	83

Table 3: Employment of Aboriginal men in 'Industrial City': frequency by age groups

fourteen were of Aboriginal women to European husbands, while only four were of European women to Aboriginal husbands. Similarly, Barwick (1963) found in Melbourne that only 11 per cent of married Aboriginal men but 27 per cent of married Aboriginal women were living with European spouses. Inglis (1964) adds further weight to these findings by reporting, from her South Australian research, that while 13 per cent of Aboriginal women were married to European men, only 1 per cent of Aboriginal men were married to European women.

In 'Industrial City', mixed marriages account for approximately 54 per cent of all Aboriginal marriages; about 36 per cent of these are of Aboriginal women to European men, while about 17 per cent are of European women to Aboriginal men. No member of isolated families residing in 'Industrial City' has married a European.

These figures suggest the following: 'Industrial City' has had contact with people of Aboriginal descent for over seventy years; while the mission station was operating, actual social contact between the ethnic groups was confined to an employer-employee relationship, although this did not prelude casual sexual liaisons between Aborigines and Europeans. Once the mission station was abandoned, and Aboriginal families returned to 'Industrial City' from

Skilled	16–30 years	31–39 years	40+	Frequency
Clerk-typist	4			4
Semi-skilled				
Factory worker	2	1		
Meatworker	4	1	1	
Assistant nurse	2			
Total	8	2	1	11
Unskilled				
Domestic	1	1	3	5
Unemployed	9			9
Housewife	20	12	21	53
Pensioner		1	2	3
			Total	85

Table 4: Employment of Aboriginal women in 'Industrial City': frequency by age groups

their various farm jobs, they were forced to settle in sub-standard accommodation with correlated low standards of education, hygiene and dress. In this period, lasting to the mid-1950s, social contact between the two ethnic groups seems to have come to a virtual standstill. Certainly, only five inter-marriages took place between 1944 and 1965, and all were of white men to 'coloured' women. Since the mid-1950s, socio-economic standards in the Aboriginal community have improved steadily; yet only after 1965 has relative acceptance of these changes by Europeans become evident in marriage patterns, especially in the sharply rising number of Aboriginal men marrying European women, as well as the fact that most European partners are recruited from the area itself.

Analyses of the inter-ethnic marriage patterns usually include assessments of whether the partners married 'up' or 'down' in the social scale. Where Aboriginal men have married European women in 'Industrial City', both of the partners have come from the same socio-economic background (that is, a working-class background), characterised by semi-skilled and unskilled employment, existence on the basic award wage, and a minimum of comforts in the home. The same applied to Aboriginal women marrying European men. That Aboriginal people in this urban area may be classified within a broad working-class framework is evidenced by their standards of housing, employment, education, recreational activities and so on (see Eckermann 1973). Tables (3, 4 and 5) on educational standards and employment are included here, since many writers see these two factors as important indicators of class membership.

Standard	Age and sex*						Total
	16–30		31–39		40+		
	M	F	M	F	M	F	
No education					2	2	4
Primary	36	27	12	16	17	25	133
Some secondary	16	8					24
Junior	4	7					11
Senior**	2	1					3
Total	58	43	12	16	19	27	175

* Not including persons under 16 years of age still at school.
** One of the men completing Senior also attended university although he did not finish his degree.

Table 5: Educational standards of Aborigines in 'Industrial City' (1971)

Child-rearing practices The next two aspects, child-rearing practices and folk-beliefs, are important interrelated factors in determining group and self-identity within this urban Aboriginal minority. Through socialisation, the urban minority perpetuates the values and beliefs which distinguish it; through socialisation, it ensures that its members are not lost to the majority and that its children, while being 'acceptable' to the majority, will also 'fit into' their own group. Description of child-rearing practices among Aboriginal people in 'Industrial City' suggests many similarities with those of working-class whites, Negroes in the U.S.A. and other minority groups.

As might well be expected, parents tend to perpetuate the type of socialisation practices which they themselves experienced. Children in 'Mission Town' grew up in an atmosphere of authoritarianism on the one hand and protection on the other. Decisions were made for all by the European staff; Aborigines were encouraged to 'become civilised', acquiescent to their fate, and models of respectability in order to offset the ideals and practices of the past. Usually, Aborigines were quite prepared to co-operate because it provided them with acceptable guidelines and norms of behaviour which proved advantageous in their dealing with Europeans. The ideal propagated by the mission was to be a 'Christian'. A Christian was one who did not swear, at least not in the presence of Europeans, one who did not drink, was clean and neat, employed in a steady job, obedient to authority, resigned to his 'station in life', did not gamble and went to church every Sunday. The emphasis was on what one did, on social behaviour, rather than on belief. Further, the behaviour advocated corresponded with ideal rather than actual practice.

No Aboriginal really attempts to adhere to these ideals today, and possibly never did. The mission goals of 'respectability', obedience and acceptance are, however, still prevalent in the community's values today and find ready expression in socialisation practices. In general, Aboriginal children in 'Industrial City' have a fairly similar social and physical environment. Thus, the child is a member of a family where there are three or four other children. The father is usually employed as a labourer and the family often subsists on the basic wage. Overcrowding of houses is not acute, yet available facilities are often inadequate to cope with the number of persons using them. Beds are frequently shared, although electrical appliances and television sets are generally present, being purchased on time-payment.

The father is usually away at work during the day, and rarely interferes in the running of the home when he is present. Further, in thirteen households there is no 'father figure' in the normal sense. In six of these cases young women and their children live at home or with a married sister; these children are influenced by some kind of father figure. In four other cases, separate households have been established where no father figure is available; and in a further three cases, recurrent separations and reunions mean that there are no stable father figures.

Mothers are rarely employed outside the home, and are the dominant influence in the family in most matters except financial ones. Matri-focal family organisation has been documented by Lickiss (1971), Rowley (1967) and Kitaoji (1971), among others. Most writers explain this female-centredness by reference to a deterioration of traditional organisation and the predominance of *de facto* relationships or unstable marriages. Rowley (1967:96), however, suggests that matri-focal organisation is a feature of the 'culture of poverty', where men are away from the home in search of employment for long periods and the household often faces insecurity of tenure: 'The matri-focused family is part of a cycle of poverty; which must further handicap large families on low income . . .' Certainly, among Aborigines in 'Industrial City', women hold the family together. They are the ones who worry about their children's education, ration the weekly food, maintain most of the intergroup ties through intervisiting, are most active in voluntary organi-sations, and deal with trouble such as conflict with the law or with school authorities. A number of men are reported to beat their wives; on the other hand, a large number of women are said to torment their husbands by making use of physical violence as well as by shunning and shaming them. Practically all separations are initiated by women, who either leave their spouses or throw them out of their own homes.

The following quotations are typical of female attitudes toward separation from their spouses:

> Soon as he got in the door I knew he was drunk, so I let'm have it with the loaf of bread I had in my hand. Should've seen the look on his face. . . said, 'O Mum you hit me' . . . so I let'm have it again . . .

> He tried to hit me so I just packed my kids and took off to my parents. He come round every night and wanted to 'see the kids' but I let'm sweat it out for two weeks . . . He's never gonna try that again . . .

Further, women take great care that the resources of the family are not depleted by irresponsible spending or lending. For example:

> Goes and wants to build a hi fi set with his mates. There's me and my kids starving and he reckons he can spend $40 on that.

Women are also prepared to fight for their children:

> . . . those coppers, they reckon 'just because you're black they can pick on the kid'. I went to see the headmaster about them making trouble for the boy at school. *He* didn't have much to say for himself but he listened to the coppers before. You gotta get justice for the boy or he'll think no one's sticking up for him.

Thus, women are the mainstay of the family and the chief socialisation agents for the child.

Parents generally stress independence and self-reliance in bringing up their children, after an initial period of complete indulgence. Physical punishment predominates over verbal chastisement in inducing a child to fit into a mould of 'respectability' where he accepts the authority of his elders. Ready use is made of outside agents to frighten a child into submission. Ridicule, too, plays an important part in teaching a child not to take himself too seriously and not to 'think too much of himself'.

Considering these aspects, it becomes necessary to ask to what extent socialisation practices in this community are typically 'Aboriginal'. Most of the characteristics described here are found in many other groups in the non-Aboriginal society, and Watts (1968), for example, has drawn attention to this. There is, however, one typically 'Aboriginal' aspect of socialisation. From earliest toddler-hood, children are made aware of terms like 'black boong' and 'blackfellow'. The terms *black, coloured* and *dirty* are emphasised again and again. People playing with a child will tease him about being a 'little black boy', or tell an older child to have a bath because 'we don't like dirty blacks in this house'. In fact, a large part of the attention and affection lavished on small children takes the form of gentle teasing and deliberate 'baiting' to provoke the child into an expression of temper or embarrassment which is enjoyed by all. Once a child has been placed in an especially uncomfortable situation, the circumstances are told to everybody's amusement. As the child grows older, teasing takes on a more serious note; anyone who becomes too upset is ridiculed even more because 'he can't take a joke'.

Teasing by adults and among siblings ensures that a child never forgets that he or she is an Aboriginal; this 'colour consciousness' is emphasised more as he grows older and social contact makes him aware that he is different from the other children in his group. By the time he might be seriously hurt by such derogatory remarks, he is accustomed to them, uses them himself about members of his own group, and has become emphatically 'Aboriginal'. On the other hand, a child is also taught that not everything 'Aboriginal' is wrong, bad or valueless. Thus, he is taught that Aborigines have a better sense of humour than Europeans, are more trustworthy, kinder and warmer, readier to share, and are more interested in people.

Whether or not such ideals are actually prevalent in the Aboriginal community is not really important. What is important is that through believing them a child receives comfort and an acceptable self-image to help him should he meet prejudice from Europeans. Thus, the Aboriginal group seeks to protect itself against possible slights by instilling defence mechanisms into the child's perception of his environment at an early age. Obviously, too, teasing plays a major role in developing children's awareness of their 'Aboriginality'.

Lickiss (1971) reports that numerous Sydney suburban Aborigines try to 'pass' into the wider society, while others display ambivalence in their identification. Similarly, Docker (1964:16-17) maintains that among the Walgett Aborigines:

> The town-dwellers have virtually repudiated their Aboriginal inheritance. They have gone 'white men's way'. Determinedly, almost desperately at times, they seek to identify themselves completely with what is most European in them.

Barwick (1962) also draws attention to the fact that individuals in Melbourne try to 'pass', but adds that this is deeply resented by other Aborigines who see this as a threat to their self-esteem. No such attempts to 'pass' or ambivalence in relation to self-identification are evident among Aborigines in 'Industrial City'. Even if it were possible to 'pass' in this community — which has had continuous and stable Aboriginal settlement for over seventy years, and where there is little mobility into or out of the area — the child is *not* encouraged to deny this ancestry. Socialisation makes repudiation in this respect unlikely, since a child's Aboriginal rather than his European ancestry is emphasised. His earliest contacts 'drum' into him that he is an Aboriginal, that he is therefore different from others, that there is no reason to be ashamed of this difference (that, in fact, Aborigines are much better *people* than Europeans), but that there are misguided persons who do not understand Aborigines and must therefore be treated warily. His process of 'initiation' by his own people, as well as by his family is not always easy. It may well be argued that a child may actually become ashamed of his origins and oversensitive to friendly or malicious quips from members of his own group and come to regard 'colour' as being bad. One woman expressed her concern by asking:

> Do you think we really mean it, I mean when we call each other 'black boongs' and 'dirty Abos'? you think we really mean it? Always thought it was just joking, Aboriginal humour you know, but sometimes I wonder, really.

Two adult men in 'Industrial City' have reacted in a negative fashion. They are preoccupied with the question of 'colour', and reject relatives and even their own children with darker skin colour; they 'show off' children with fair colouring, emphasise European friends and court European favours. These men are held up to ridicule by the rest of the Aboriginal community.

Folk-beliefs Closely related to the question of Aboriginal identification is a person's adherence to particular sets of folk-belief. Such adherence lends a distinguishing consciousness to this group of urban Aborigines, which believes it to be peculiar to themselves, and to provide real or imaginary links with a common past about which so little is remembered. Certainly, continual reference to such folk-beliefs within the family circle plays an important part in instilling in the child an awareness of his Aboriginality. None of these elements, however, has any bearing on the life of the community as such; that is, they do not influence the individual's economic or social activities within the wider European society.

Traditional beliefs retained some importance during 'Mission Town's' early history, as the following example illustrates. One man reared in 'Mission Town' had this to say about the power of the old men:

> You don't wanna take any notice of that — that's just old blackfella's talk. See, there might be this old blackfella and he knows that there's good fish in that pond. Now, he's too old to go hunting, or go to work or anything, so he gets all them young fellas and puts the fear of God in'm and they're scared and don't go near that pond. So, when they're away, he goes and fishes and gets a good catch. See, they reckoned that this waterhole near here was *gundil* [a common term in 'Industrial City' for anything which had supernatural powers], and they reckoned that anyone who'd go near'd drown — said that there was this bullock driver and he gave his bullocks a drink there and they all went under, cart and all — and this proved it was *gundil*. Well, they pumped that pond dry and I went to have a look. There was nothing there — you don't wanna take notice of that . . . Once these old fellas, they showed me this burial ground and I picked up this thigh bone and took it back the to camp. Well, you should've heard all the old fellas scream. They got real upset,

told me my hand'd get all mouldy and the sore'd never heal up. So I got
sick of it and chucked the bone into a ploughed field. Well, that was
even worse. They got even more upset — said that'd be my friend now
and that I had to have him near me and couldn't just chuck him away.
So I put it where they told me, and this clever man — supposed to be,
anyway — came along and ask me if he could have it, and I said 'sure',
and he burned fat that night. They used to do that at 'Mission Town' —
burn fat to keep the bones away. And he came back and told me that
the ghost of the bloke whose bone I had, come up, and he was 200 year
old and he was his grandfather — what a lot of rubbish. But I believe in
ghosts. I reckon that someone who's been murdered will come back and
tell.

It is quite obvious, from this and other stories, that the old men tried to
maintain some form of authority and control over the young, as against
mission influences — for example, education and Christian religion, which
tended to take decision making and leadership away from the elders. It is
equally certain that they were unable to retain their former power. Nevertheless, some aspects of traditional lore have been incorporated into a contemporary system of folk-belief, and apprehension regarding the inexplicable
and unnatural is still present.

The following stories, experiences and beliefs were recorded in the course
of this research. For example, people remembered two cases of persons being
magically 'sung'. Such stories refer to instances which occurred about sixty
years ago, are separate cases, were not told at the same time, and refer to
different people.

Case 1   One woman is reported to have been 'sung' when she was a girl
living in the Dirranbandi district, which was her tribal area at that time.
Some people maintained that she was 'sung' because her family had killed
or eaten the 'meat' (totem) of another group. Others believed that she
incurred a 'clever man's' wrath because she had refused his attentions. The
reports maintain that the victim dropped into a deep coma. The avenging
clever man's 'meat' was supposed to have been pig and, while the girl was
unconscious, her sister claims to have heard grunting and squealing of pigs
all around the bush hut in which they lived. The girl's grandfather, her
mother's step-father, also a clever man, was subsequently 'sung' into the
camp at Dirranbandi from Noondah, in order to break the spell. It is said
that when the girl's mother was speaking to him she had to avert her eyes,
address him as 'grandfather' and talk to his back.

This clever man asked everybody to leave the hut and to sit around a huge
fire which had been built some distance away. He then massaged the girl
while talking over her, repeatedly raising his hands, open-palmed, to the
sky. After murmuring some spells, he pulled a fishing line, a hook, a pack of
cards, and some half-crown pieces from her body. These he buried some
distance away from the hut and stamped on them. He then whispered some
more incantations over the girl and left. The next morning she had recovered
from her ordeal without any after-effects.

Case 2   The second case also involves a girl being 'sung' because she apparently refused the advances of a clever man. Again, the victim fell into a

deep coma and her group 'sung' its own clever man into camp to 'sing' her back to health. This man carried the girl into the open, laid her on her back, and lit fires all around her. He then stuck a nulla-nulla club into the ground next to her and tied a piece of rag to it. He danced and sang around her and made blood drip on to the rag. This, it was said, was her 'bad' blood, which he was extracting by means of his special power, because she was not bleeding and he had made no incisions on her body. Later she was well again.

The two incidents represent definite links with the traditional past. Mathew (1887 and 1910) records the widespread use of projectile magic along the south-eastern coast of Queensland. Here, specially powerful pieces of quartz were projected into the vital parts of the victim's body. These were known as *kundir*, a word very similar to *gundil*, which is currently in use in 'Industrial City' for anything possessing magical powers. These missiles could be removed in two distinct ways. In one method, the clever man brought into contact with the victim an equally strong or more powerful *kundir*, which would:

> ... afford the patient immediate relief by extracting from him a piece of glass or newspaper, a few yards of hairstring or even a quid of tobacco. . . (Mathew 1910:177.)

In the second method, he could suck blood from the victim in the following manner:

> The clever man is provided with cord made from fur. One end of this cord is placed around the patient at the spot where it hurts, the other is dipped into a vessel with water. The clever man sits between patient and water vessel, holding the cord and rubbing it backwards and for-wards across his gums, causing them to bleed. Saliva and blood are spat into the vessel until it is filled with discoloured liquid; this mixture is said to have been drawn from the patient who finally drinks it. (Mathew 1887:165.)

It is obvious that certain aspects of bone pointing are reflected in both cases as they are remembered in 'Industrial City' today: the clever man removes the projectile which is causing the illness, either in the form of bad blood or by means of concrete objects such as money and fish hooks.

Clever men maintained their power and influence over people in the area for some time, as the following story illustrates.

About forty years ago a young boy, a member of 'clan' B, was suffering from fits. European doctors believed that he would die young and that nothing could be done for him. One day a stranger arrived at the doorstep saying that he had heard of their misfortune and had come to cure the boy. He spent many days talking to the boy and observing him. Then he decided to show the boy's relatives the extent of his power. He rubbed his upper arm, and little bolts of lightning shot from his skin. That night he ordered every-one except the boy to go out. In the course of the evening he told the people that he would bring on a big storm, lightning and thunder would strike, and the boy would be cured. The storm came and they all rushed home. When they arrived they discovered that lightning had struck the tree outside the boy's bedroom. From that day on he had no more fits. The relatives searched everywhere for the clever man in order to thank him, but he had vanished. Reports reached them that two hours after the storm he was seen walking up the main street of Rockhampton.

This incident, it was said, demonstrates not only the tremendous curative powers of the *gundil* man, but also his ability to transport himself over immense distances either by flying or by travelling at great speeds underground. Mathew (1910) reported that the *Wakka Wakka* and *Kabi* people — from whom this family is descended — were well acquainted with such magical powers. A boy told Mathew that during a police raid he had been picked up and thrown one to two miles to a place of safety by a clever man, who had retreated to this place himself by travelling underground. The same boy threatened Mathew that his father, a *gundil* man, would send lightning and thunder to frighten him. Thus the relationship between lightning and clever men appears to have had its roots in traditional belief. This is an obvious association when one remembers that the clever man received his special powers from the rainbow.

Even after the passing of the traditional *kundir bonggan* (clever men), their influence remained. Their position was assumed by less qualified, but nevertheless greatly feared, persons who retained some of that traditional knowledge and were consequently considered to have a great deal of prestige. For example, people refer to the founder of 'clan' B — 'Pop' — who died about twenty years ago, as a *gundil* or clever man. No one claims that he was a *gundil* in a traditional sense, as he was not initiated, but he is reputed to have had special powers. Consequently, he was treated with much respect.

'Pop' was able to drive away ghosts, and to 'smoke' out houses after a death. I mentioned before that during the early mission period the old men 'burned fat' to keep away evil spirits and ghosts. That practice died with them. Later, houses were 'smoked out' with smouldering gum leaves after a death, or if they were believed to be haunted. This was always done by 'Pop'. He lit bunches of green twigs, and after all the inhabitants had left the premises he walked through the house making sure that the smoke penetrated every corner. In this manner, he 'smoked out' a house when two brothers and a sister were being haunted by their maternal grandmother. The 'smoking' was directed especially toward the brothers, who were so frightened by the ghost that they were unable to sleep. Because the 'grandmother' did not bother their sister, it was believed that the ghost had a special interest in the girl, with whom close ties had been established during its lifetime, and that it was now keeping watch over her. The following is a further example of 'Pop's' powers.

When 'Pop' died, his son cut his hair, intending to keep it as a memento. But he 'couldn't hold it'. He felt guilty and uncomfortable as long as the hair was in his possession. So he passed it on to his sisters, who in turn handed it on until it reached the particular sister who could 'hold it'. When one woman became ill, this sister took the hair along on a visit to the hospital. Everybody in the car is reported to have shivered and felt very uncomfortable during the journey. At the hospital, the hair was rubbed over the sick woman's legs so that some of its strength would be communicated to her.

A similar story was told about a special money pouch belonging to 'Pop's' wife. Before she died she gave this to her eldest daughter, who in turn lent it to her siblings, but it was always returned to her because none 'could hold it'. It gave them feelings of guilt, as if they had stolen it. Her brother once won a lot of money at cards while the pouch was in his possession; consequently, he considered it to be a lucky charm. But the pouch disappeared during a fishing trip, and he was unable to find it even after many hours of searching. A week later it was found by someone else, at the exact spot where he had been fishing, and returned to the elder sister.

These events, it was said, prove that the pouch is her *gundil*. In this case the term means 'special charm' rather than an object of magical powers. The charm, as was the hair, is meant for a specific person and not intended to be used by anyone else. This belief also forges a link between 'clan' B and its ancestors, a bond which the members see as a very personal one. Again, the link with tradition is evident in the light of Mathew's (1926) report that it was usual among the *Kabi* to inherit powerful magical objects in the male line.

It is more general, in 'Industrial City' today, for a deceased person's property to be divided equally among his living relatives. Today it is also rare to 'smoke out' houses, although it has been done within the last ten years by the oldest surviving member of a 'clan'.

As I have mentioned, the sisters dominating 'clan' B claim to have inherited some of their father's supernatural powers. They believe that they are in contact with their ancestors, are warned about impending disaster by their 'old people', and can call on them for aid in times of crisis. All of them report seeing apparitions of their father, mother and grandfather during their sleep. Sometimes these bring special messages, at other times they simply want company. But if they appear too frequently and cause annoyance (and one way for a spirit to make its presence felt is to 'freeze' or paralyse a living person), they may be chastised in 'language' (e.g. told to go away). If the spirits want to warn someone of an impending disaster, they 'freeze' him, while a sign comes hurtling toward him out of the sky. The direction from which the sign comes is the direction from which the accident, sickness or death will originate. The nature and time of such disasters are not disclosed, nor does the sign necessarily mean that the person having this experience will suffer — usually it refers to a relative or friend.

That these beliefs are derived from traditional *Wakka Wakka* ones is strongly suggested, for Mathew (1910:168-69) writes that the *Wakka Wakka*:

> . . . acknowledged the existence of supernatural beings who had power to render assistance or inflict injury. They spoke of them with reverence. They also believed in the continued existence of the *nguthuru*, or shades of human beings after death. The *nguthuru* could occasionally be seen, with smiling countenances, as they floated among the foliage at night and peered down upon their quondam fellow mortals.

Mathew reports that many other tribes in the south Queensland area held similar beliefs.

One further practice links members of 'clan' B with their traditional past. Each person, no matter what his admixture of ancestry, is taken to Ban-Ban Springs near Gayndah at the age of two or three years, and baptised there.

The term 'baptism' is their own to describe this practice. They believe that the spirits of their 'old people' live in the springs. All children are therefore submerged in the water in order to introduce them to their ancestors. I have not yet witnessed such a ceremony, but have been told that special 'language' is spoken to introduce the children to the ancestral spirits, who are forthwith expected to watch over them. Rarely, non-members may also be baptised. Once baptised, it is believed that the outsider will be protected by the spirits as if he or she were a member of the group. Cameron (1904) relates that the *Wakka Wakka* used to visit Ban-Ban Springs, where a male spirit (an old *Kowonian*) is reputed to have lived. He also maintains that the *Wakka Wakka* used to walk up to the springs and call out loudly; if the spirit showed itself, they would not drink or bathe there for fear that he would pull them in. Thus the springs were of importance in traditional times, even though ancestral spirits did not appear to have been associated with them. However, Mathew (1910:70) reports on traditional beliefs among the *Wakka Wakka* and *Kabi* linking springs in general with benevolent spirits. He writes:

> Another variety of supernatural beings had representatives of both sexes, *jonjari* (male) and *jonjaringa* (female) who are acknowledged by both tribes. They were benevolent spirits, whose haunts were mineral springs. The healthful influences of the springs were ascribed to them. They protected the blacks, and rendered them happy.

Obviously two separate traditions have been incorporated to form a new, contemporary piece of folklore about Ban-Ban Springs. A similar amalgamation of traditions occurs in the present-day beliefs in the *jonjari* or *janjardi* as he is now known, in south-east Queensland. While 'baptism' is particular to 'clan' B, everyone in 'Industrial City' is familiar with *janjardi*. He is believed to be a little, knee-high, hairy man, who is a friend of children, and will play with and comfort them when they are ill. Adults, however, have to be wary of him and take care he does not carry children off with him to the spirit world. Clearly, here again are several separate traditions that have been amalgamated. Thus the *jonjari* seems to have acquired those qualities for which the spirit *muthar* was feared. *Muthar* (Mathew 1926) was believed to have lived in the sky, from where he would swoop down to earth to kidnap children.

No other 'clan' in 'Industrial City' claims a 'spirit place' like Ban-Ban Springs. There is, however, another contemporary, commonly-known area in 'Industrial City' called Danger Gully. Danger Gully is a ravine situated along the road which used to link 'Mission Town' with 'Industrial City'. It is said that a huge dog used to live in this area. At times it was two-headed, and it was capable of turning itself into a sheep or a red kangaroo. Many people claim to have seen this spirit. Thus one woman tells of an incident when she was driving a buggy along the road in the 1920s. Near the gully, the horse reared and bolted. Turning to see what had frightened the horse, she saw a huge dog, which in turn frightened *her* to such an extent that she 'took off like a black streak of lightnin'. Another woman claims to have seen a two-headed lamb with its throat ripped open, crossing the gully; while a boy was scared by the sudden appearance of a large hairy, ape-like form in the area. The story goes that there is an ancient burial ground in Danger Gully and that the 'dog' watches over it. It is said that a dead lamb indicates when the 'thing' is close by. When questioned as to how long the spirit is supposed to have been in the area, some thought 'as long as there have been black-fellas'; others, that the 'evil spirit was probably chased away when the road was built'.

Equally widespread among the Aborigines is a belief in ghosts and in the return of the dead to visit their relatives. Premonitions, visitations and apparitions are not as prevalent in the total Aboriginal population as among the 'clan' B sisters; yet they occur with enough regularity to ensure that even the young, who generally scoff at the beliefs of their parents, have a healthy respect for 'ghosts'. In contrast to the older members of the groups, the young are easily frightened by visions. Older people welcome them, maintaining that 'the dead won't hurt you, it's the living you have to watch out for'. As most people in the community, young and old, report having had mystical experiences or have been told of them, few people question their occurrence or are prepared to ridicule them. Further, it is believed that spirits associated with a particular place or house may haunt an individual.

So far, this description of folk-beliefs has demonstrated that there are a number of practices, stories and mystical experiences which link members of this Aboriginal population to the traditional past of their own or other groups. In addition to these beliefs, there are others which Aborigines consider to belong to their old way of life, but which are nevertheless of doubtful origin. These include various signs which are thought to herald bad news, such as:

1. The death bird — a crow or 'big black bird' which persistently hovers around a house.
2. A night owl which perches on or near a house and looks straight at its inmates.
3. A mysterious knocking which recurs three times.
4. The howling, not barking, of a dog at night.
5. The recurrence of the same person or thing in three fairly consecutive dreams.
6. The 'black' dream — where the dreamer moves in an atmosphere of complete darkness.

The lack of influence of contemporary folklore on people's social or economic activities in relation to the non-Aboriginal community in 'Industrial City' has already been mentioned. A latent fear of or respect for clever men does not cause members of Aboriginal groups to seek their help rather than that of European doctors; nor does it influence people to supplement European-style medicine with various traditional medicines, charms or potions. Further, the bulk of such 'traditional' knowledge is confined to 'clan' B, primarily because of the influence of the father, 'Pop'.

Belief in many aspects of traditional life is diminishing, especially among the young. While children accept the possibility that supernatural forces may attract them, and some have experienced these forces, they nevertheless refuse to learn 'language' even when they have an opportunity to do so. It is perhaps surprising, then, that despite the reluctance of young people to be associated with traditional knowledge, a number of Aboriginal words, whose origin has long been forgotten, are still used by the whole community

and especially in the presence of Europeans. A list of these words follows in
Table 6. These words, understood by all other Aborigines, at times referring
to normally 'impolite' conversational subjects such as urine, excrement or

Word	Meaning	Origin	Source
andenu:s	children		
anjerebai	children		
banji	lovey		
binang	ear	*Kabi*	*p'inang*—Mathew 1887:199
		Wakka	
		Gurang	*pinna*—Mathew 1913:438
buddu	penis		
bunthi	buttocks	*Kabi*	similar to *bundhur* meaning back—Mathew 1910:226
darri	smoke		
gaemin'	pretending	European	M. J. Calley: personal communication, 1972
gubbi	urine	*Kabi*	similar to *Ka'bur*—Mathew 1910:228
		Gurang	similar to *Kapi*—Mathew 1913:438
guri	black man black woman		
gunang	excrement	*Kabi*	*gu'nang*, meaning bowels—Mathew 1910:227
		Wakka	*ku'nang*, meaning bowels—Mathew 1910:227
		Gurang	*kunna*, meaning bowels—Mathew 1913:438
gu:m	methylated spirits		
jalabai	urine		
jamba	camp		
jin	woman	*Wakka*	*gin* ('g' hard)—Mathew 1910:226
jaramin	horse	*Kabi*	*yeraman*—Mathew 1887:200
		Gurang	*yiraman*—Mathew 1913:439
juri	meat		
mantha	bread		
marri	black man black woman		
migalu	white man white woman		
muggai	ghost		

Table 6: *Words believed to be of Aboriginal origin in contemporary use by Aborigines
in 'Industrial City'*

penis, are used frequently as a badge of identity. Europeans are encouraged to use the terms incorrectly, to everyone's amusement. In this manner, members of the Aboriginal population set themselves apart from the rest of the 'Industrial City' community. Folk-beliefs, gossip about the latest signs, accounts of magical powers exhibited by past clever men, all of these aspects maintain a firm conviction among Aborigines in this area that they have special gifts not shared by Europeans. This conviction strongly supports their identification as Aborigines, and ensures that it is a favourable one.

Relations with Europeans While Aborigines in 'Industrial City' do not hesitate to identify themselves as 'coloureds', their attitudes toward Europeans are ambivalent. On a physical plane, they attend the same churches, buy at the same shops, attend the same schools and picture theatres and, in effect, belong to the same social organisation. This free interaction is, however, hampered by painful memories and traditions of past Aboriginal-European contact which have led, inevitably, to their distrust of 'white people'. All Aborigines in 'Industrial City' have at some time been involved in conflict with Europeans, arising from blatant exploitation, insults and slander, real or imaginary victimisation and degrees of discrimination. Contemporary attitudes toward Europeans may be best illustrated by the following comments by Aborigines: these are reproduced verbatim from tape recordings. Such instances are told and retold by them, especially in the presence of children. For instance, one person recalled with bitterness her treatment by station owners:

> They [the station owners] used to take me visiting, but I never got out of the car. I cottoned on to the idea — they'd say: O, come and have a cuppa' — you'd sit in the kitchen all by yourself, and after, they'd make you do the washing up for their great big dinner. So I rather stayed in the car. I stayed in the car for five hours once, they wouldn't even ask you if you wanted a drink of water.

Another woman expressed her resentment at what she felt was an unusual degree of discrimination:

> Another time I went to see about this job. It was just light housework, more companion type of thing, really. Well, this woman came and said she didn't want a coloured girl to do *her* sweeping. Oh, I must have been about sixteen, 'cause I was fifteen when I went out on the station. I worked among all kinds and nationalities and that sort of thing don't happen too often.

The following demonstrates apprehension on the part of some Europeans at having Aboriginal neighbours, Aboriginal resentment regarding this, and the potentiality of conflict:

> When Mum was expecting 'L', this woman screamed out across the road, 'that black bitch is having another kid'. Me and the boys went up to her place to see about that, but she wouldn't come out, called the cops. The cop told us not to go to her place any more, not to walk past her place so she couldn't insult us. But I told him: 'would you just stand by and let her insult your mother?' I told him I wasn't going up back

streets for anyone. I'm as good as the next one, always have been, always will be. Sometimes I think I'm better, and that's what I'll think till I'm proven otherwise.
When we first moved here, Mrs. B. over the road was singing out to the lady up that way: 'Oh, youse better lock your doors, there's blacks moving in next door'.

An illustration of 'intelligent parasitism' as described by Elkin (1964) is to be found in the following quotation. It is not an attitude readily expressed, even in its sophisticated form; usually, comments of this sort follow accounts of injustices in the past and are expressions of bitterness. This conversation is reported to have taken place between a man from 'Industrial City' and a resident of a North Queensland community.

When I was there this bloke invited me to dinner, and they had all this meat and bread and stuff, so I ask him: 'how'd you like living here, letting the white man look after you?' So this bloke he answers: 'Let the white man look after me, he's doing a better job than I could!'

A similar attitude is expressed in the next statement. It was made in answer to a specific question in which the woman was asked in what way she thought Aborigines differed from Europeans. The issue arose from a newspaper article, under discussion in a group of Aborigines:

Let'm think we are different — we'll take them for everything they'll offer — 'out of the goodness of their hearts'. Me and my kids will take them for every scholarship, every possible handout — as long as they don't realize we're just like them, we're sitting pretty.

The real problem in Aboriginal-European contact is probably expressed in the following statement:

Sometime I look at the white people in church and ask myself, 'Are you really trying to be friends — or are you just doing your Christian duty?'

It should be noted, however, that during my period of fieldwork no evidence of *overt* discrimination against Aboriginal people in 'Industrial City' was documented. Indeed, the Aborigines themselves are quick to point this out when they discuss Europeans and their attitudes. Rather, it seems, the difficulty today lies at the other extreme. Europeans in 'Industrial City', especially those belonging to voluntary associations concerned with Aboriginal welfare, over-emphasise liberal-mindedness and 'love' of Aborigines, which on the receiving end is interpreted as paternalism. Such an attitude engenders Aboriginal colour-consciousness, not of a militant kind, but one which is based on a mixture of feelings of inferiority as well as of superiority — just as surely as did those injustices of the past.

These ambivalent feelings of inferiority-superiority arise because Aborigines see European attitudes as manifestations of ego-satisfaction. Consequently, they feel no qualms in taking advantage of 'hand-outs' (i.e. Elkin's 'intelligent parasitism'), secure in the knowledge that they are not what the white man thinks they are — which underlines their feeling of superiority. On the other hand, they have been indoctrinated with the idea of Aboriginal inferiority for many generations, and have to some extent internalised this. Although they regard such assertions of inferiority as untrue for their own particular group, Aborigines themselves are quick to condemn shortcomings in others not belonging to their group or family. Further, Aborigines are keenly aware of the stereotypes about them prevalent among some Europeans. As one man expressed it: 'If I turn up in my work clothes at the pub, I'd be just another dirty Abo . . . If they see *one* dirty or fighting Murri, all Murris are like that'. (*Murri*, or *marri*, is a Queensland term used by Aborigines to describe other Aborigines; another term of self-identification is *guri*.)

These findings are strongly supported by results from an analysis of the Kluckhohn-Strodtbeck (1961) 'Value Orientation Schedule' (adapted by Hausfeld and Watts), which was applied to this urban minority (see Eckermann 1973). In one question, Aborigines were asked to identify the orientations they thought to be prevalent among Europeans as well as those prevalent among 'other Aborigines'. Aboriginal respondents clearly, and correctly, identified orientations prevalent among both 'other Aborigines' and Europeans. Analysis of the data indicates, however, that a significant proportion of them believe themselves to be different from other Aborigines, and, conversely, to be similar to Europeans (see Eckermann, 1973:231-5). Perhaps this is due to the fact that Aborigines have internalised derogatory values about themselves, or rather, about 'other Aborigines'. Consequently, they tend to reaffirm their belief that they are different from other 'blackfellas'. Identification with correctly perceived European orientations may thus not be incongruous with identification as 'Aboriginal' as such. That Europeans adhere to stereotypes about Aborigines has been documented by others (e.g. Western 1968). That they exist in 'Industrial City' is evident in European ideas about what value orientations they believe to be typically 'Aboriginal' (Eckermann 1973:410). These include the wellworn belief that Aborigines will always rely on their kin to help them when they are in trouble and will think in terms of the present and past rather than the future.

It is certain that awareness of stereotypes, strengthened by feelings of inferiority, leads to strong antagonism against other Aborigines who by their behaviour, reinforce these stereotypes. For example, when asked about their attitudes to a publican who had barred Aborigines from his hotel in South Brisbane, a person in 'Industrial City' replied: 'And rightly too — I don't blame him — you should see the sort of scum that go there'. A similar attitude is expressed in the following remark: 'They [her relatives] could have made her look a bit nicer, you know, dress her up a bit. She looked real tatty — but I guess you can't blame her, coming from the mission and all'. Consequently, a common phrase among Aborigines in 'Industrial City' is, 'Don't go actin' like a Abo'.

In response to the European side of the picture, Aborigines themselves hold certain stereotypes about members of the white majority. These include beliefs that Europeans cannot be trusted, are cold in personal relationships, have no humour and so on; these stereotypes, again, strengthen in-group feelings of superiority. They are, however, not applied to European friends; friends are expected to realise that they are different from 'white people' in general, and should therefore not take offence at the joking, ridicule and disparaging comments about other Europeans.

These 'Aboriginal' stereotypes provide people with an ideology which affords protection against feelings of inferiority. In general, they are features of Aboriginal 'exclusiveness' and largely confined to within the group itself. Thus victimisation and exploitation in the past or present become badges of identity. They also serve as useful warnings to children against whites who are so 'ignorant they don't know any better' and discriminate against 'coloured people'. Only two men reacted antagonistically to all whites purely on the basis of skin colour. The rest of the community describe these men as 'touchy blackfellas'. In the normal course of events, 70 per cent of Aborigines in 'Industrial City' have close and unrestricted contact with a number of Europeans who regularly visit their homes, work with them, or belong to the same clubs. All Aborigines associate with members of the dominant group to some extent because of the high rate of intermarriage. Similarly, it is not unusual for black and white neighbours to visit, to invite each other to parties, to take each other on outings to the football, on picnics or fishing trips. In all cases, European friends come from a similar socio-economic background.

These findings contrast with those of Lickiss (1971:218), who notes a complete absence of black-white neighbourhood interaction in Sydney:

> Interaction with neighbours appears to be slight . . . even in more stable families on no occasion was a neighbour found visiting the household nor was reference made to a visit to a neighbour's, nor was reference ever spontaneously made to the family life of a neighbour.

Similarly, Barwick (1962:21) points out that among Aborigines in Melbourne:

> White workmates and neighbours rarely become friends, for changing jobs and residence makes long-continued intimacy unlikely. Also, whites simply aren't very interesting. They are outside the gossip network and have few shared experiences to joke about.

Both writers maintain that this lack of contact is probably due to the high rate of mobility in the urban Aboriginal population. In contrast, in 'Industrial City' mobility within the Aboriginal population is low; this favours the establishment and maintenance of relationships. The ambivalence and uncertainty as to whether Europeans are trustworthy, whether their motives are honourable, is, however, retained and becomes an important issue in child-rearing. A further example of this is found in relations with the police.

Relations with police   Earliest Aboriginal contacts with Europeans in this area were often confined to police action, which involved forcible separation of individuals from their family group and from residence on the mission reserves. Consequently, Aborigines have distrusted the law, are inept in their dealing with its representatives and are frightened of policemen. Bardsley (1965:15) reports a similar situation in Sydney:

> The memory of the past, when the police exercised almost God-like powers over the lives of Aborigines, and too frequent and often excessive use of their powers, has induced in many Aborigines a fear and dislike of the law, which they identify with the police.

In 'Industrial City' this distrust finds ready expression in accusations that the police 'pick on coloured boys'. Stories are told of police hounding Aborigines from hotels, picking them up for brawling and vagrancy without apparent grounds, and calling them 'black bastards'. Two policemen have so far been assaulted by young Aboriginal men because they made derogatory remarks about their colour and ancestry. Bardsley (1965:15) cites incidents in which policemen allegedly break into Aboriginal homes without entry warrants and make arrests. She says:

> A pattern of plainclothes police driving around . . . picking up Aborigines from the streets and taking them to the police station. There were many allegations of police brutality, both during the arrest and at the police station.

Similar allegations have been made in 'Industrial City'. It is claimed that the police have picked up young Aboriginal men, have driven them to an alley and beaten them up. A European woman in close contact with the Aboriginal community reports that she was told by the police to keep her son from interacting with coloured boys, or he would be in serious trouble. Further, two boys were convicted on evidence which could have been challenged in a court of appeal had they not been induced to make self-incriminatory statements.

These are examples of what some Aborigines claim to be questionable behaviour by members of the police force. There is no concrete evidence for these allegations, but it is significant that even those Aborigines who have had no trouble with the police maintain that the law is apt to 'pick on coloured boys'. Consequently, little stigma is attached to individuals who have been jailed. In fact, one young man decided to go to jail rather than pay a fine for a serious driving offence, even though he could have afforded to do so. He

Age of offender	Frequency and type of offence					
	Drunken-ness	Brawling	Breaking & entering	Assault	Rape	Traffic offence
15–20		1	3*	1*		
21–30	2	4			2	6
31–40						
41–50						
51+						

* In one case the same person was also charged with assault.

Table 7: Aboriginal Arrests: 'Industrial City', 1970-1972

described this as 'having a holiday on the government'. Further, the community tends to sympathise with those who have committed 'crimes' because of the stereotypes held about policemen in general, which are reinforced by the discriminatory behaviour of some members of the force. Table 7 indicates the number of Aboriginal arrests during the period of this study; and shows that a total of eighteen young men have been in trouble with the police. With the exception of the two cases of rape, the offences were of a minor nature or did not lead to conviction.

Since December 1971, a small group of about eight Aboriginal boys aged between twelve and seventeen has been roaming the streets of 'Industrial City' on Saturday nights. Unlike other teenage friendship groups, they are an all-Aboriginal group, and spend their time baiting or fighting with white teenagers. At present, other members of the community condemn them, and the attitude toward them is that 'these little hoods and toughies' make you ' 'shamed to walk down the street, seein' them like that'. Again, there is the fear that all Aborigines will be labelled as troublemakers because of this group's behaviour. While still condemning police action in general, people now say, 'The cops should give them a good kick in the "backside", that's what they need!'

Undoubtedly, as more cases of police action against minors become known, especially action which the Aboriginal group interprets as victimisation, indignation about police brutality will outweigh the fear of shaming. In fact, the Aboriginal crime rate in 'Industrial City' is very low, though conflict with the police is common. As mentioned, even those families who never come into police contact decry police victimisation of 'coloured' people. This, in my opinion, is the essence of relations with the law. Attitudes toward the police have their roots in history, and are an expression of the kind of stereotyped responses which characterise the ambivalence of Aboriginal-European relations. Aborigines are ignorant of the law and, like many other people, are aware only of its punitive measures. Fear leads to suspicion, which is accentuated by alleged injustice. The community does not feel justified in exerting strong sanctions against offenders, because it simply does not trust the law or its officers. So far, little has been done by the police force to alleviate this fear and distrust.

Urban Aborigines in relation to working class people generally
Collation of all ethnographic and survey material about Aboriginal people in 'Industrial City' is a complex undertaking. It is therefore necessary to find some framework in which the material may be analysed. Jessor and Richardson (1968:6) present such a framework within their theory of *proximal* and *distal* environmental variables which influence an individual's behaviour and personality traits. They maintain (*ibid.*:4) that:

> What many authors are referring to as 'crude' or 'gross' environmental variables, e.g. social class, are more properly considered as distal variables, variables whose relationship to behaviour must be considered to be mediated by proximal variables. Thus race or socio-economic status . . . are environmental descriptions relatively remote from psychological or experimental significance. That they have implications for the latter is quite clearly true — that is why they have often been used as relatively effective co-dependent variables. But their implications can

only be taken to be probabalistic in nature: to be Negro in the United States involves a high probability of being exposed to a stigmatising interpersonal environment. The crucial point is that behaviour and development are invariant with the latter, the proximal environment of stigmatising stimuli, rather than with the former, the distal environment of being a Negro.

They continue by emphasising the need in social science for a theory of environment which encompasses the totality of variables and which specifies the structure of relations among the variables.

Thus Jessor and Richardson's (1968:7) model provides a useful tool, and their theory a clear framework by means of which ethnographic material may be ordered, listed, contrasted and examined. The primary concepts of this model are environment, person and behaviour. The authors caution that:

1. The variables in one column cannot be considered as independent from those in another column. 'As a matter of fact one of the important tasks is the identification of the pattern of their relationship under different conditions.'
2. Variables in one column may have implications for several variations in another column. Further, 'While there is a directional implication in the scheme, running from left to right and giving priority to the environment, the region should, over time, be seen as part of an independent system generating complex feedback effects.'
3. The environment plays a dual role. Over time it leads, through socialization and learning, to certain personal attributes; however, at the same time, it interacts with those attributes to generate behaviour.

Thus the model must be seen as an interaction system where distal variables A B C D influence and are influenced by proximal variables a b c d in a circular pattern.

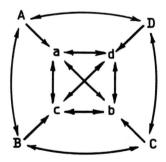

Keeping these qualifying statements in mind, I have endeavoured to present ethnographic and survey material collected among Aboriginal people in 'Industrial City' in terms of the Jessor and Richardson model.

As indicated in Diagram 3, the following aspects have been included in the category of *distal environmental variables*:
1. Ethnic membership
2. Social class
3. History of culture contact

Environmental Attributes		Personal	Behavioural
Distal	Proximal	Attributes	Attributes
Ethnic membership `Social class:	Folk beliefs Within-family interaction,	Self identity: Inferiority/ superiority,	Over-emphasis of 'colour' Intelligent parasitism,
(a) housing (b) employment (c) education History of culture contact	Group Interaction, Relations with majority: (a) paternalism, (b) equal competition, (c) discrimination Child rearing: (a) mother dominance, (b) status oriented control, (c) respectability, (d) 'fitting-in', (e) aquiescence Values, Interests	Group identity: Affiliative attributes, Dependence on mother, Passivity, Compliance, Lack of achievement motivation, Belief in fate, Attitude toward authority, Attitudes to work,	Distrust, Acceptance, Hostility, Incongruence between ideals and behaviour Low school performance, Apathy, Respect for elders, Search for security in group support, 'Steady' rather than highly qualified work

Diagram 3: Distal and proximal variables influencing Aborigines in 'Industrial City' (Adapted from Jessor and Richardson, 1968:6)

Concentrating on just two variables, ethnic membership and history of culture contact, we find that: because of membership in this particular group and its history of contact with whites, Aborigines in 'Industrial City' adhere to certain folklore beliefs which have influenced their concept of group- and self-identity, peculiar to themselves. These have been transmitted through the medium of child-rearing, and this in turn has led to an emphasis on 'Aboriginality'. Yet it is impossible to name just one or two distal variables which, because of influential proximal environmental and personal attributes, lead to behavioural attributes such as aggressive ethnic identification. Jessor and Richardson (1968) draw attention to the dangers of such oversimplification.

One aspect which so far has been mentioned only briefly, but which is obviously of great importance, is that of social class. It is appropriate to extend this analysis now, utilising the Jessor and Richardson model. Numerous writers have set out the salient features of that social category called 'the working-class' — e.g. Havighurst and Neugarten (1962), Goldthorpe and Lockwood (1967), Hyman (1967) Sears, Maccoby and Lewin (1957), Newson and Newson (1970), and Hess and Shipman (1968), Hagan and de Lacey (1971), among others. These writers demonstrate that the kind of socialisation practices prevalent in a group, influence differential attitudes toward education, employment and the whole achievement syndrome. They point out that status-oriented control, lack of verbalisation, lack of adequate models, all contribute toward placing the working-class child at a disadvantage during his earliest school experiences. These proximal variables have a direct bearing on his personal and behavioural attributes and thus his attitudes toward education. These in turn are supplemented by parental stress on 'secure jobs', 'trade in hands', affiliative rather than achievement orientations and acceptance or 'passivity'. Thus Havighurst's (1962) attitude of 'getting by' is extended and will in turn influence occupational status.

Amalgamating the information on working-class characteristics in terms of Jessor and Richardson's (1968) model, it is possible to construct Diagram 4.

Environmental Attributes		Personal Attributes	Behavioural Attributes
Distal	Proximal		
Social class: Working class	Child rearing: (a) authoritarian (b) mother-dominated (c) use of force (d) little verbalisation, status-oriented (e) respectability (f) 'fitting in' Interaction patterns Social evaluation	Affiliative attitudes: Dependence on mother Values of collectivity or 'us' Lack of achievement motivation Passivity Compliance Belief in fate Feelings of inadequacy	Respect Good behaviour Search for security in group support Delinquency Truancy Apathy Aggression Incongruence between ideals and behaviour Low educational attainment
Employment: (a) semi-skilled (b) seasonal (c) dependence on social service Education: (a) low attainment of parents Housing: (a) poor standard (b) over-crowding			

Diagram 4: *Proximal and distal variables influencing the working-class*

These various descriptions of prevalent values, attitudes and practices among 'working-class' persons, are in no way incongruous with earlier descriptions of life-style among urban Aborigines in 'Industrial City'. Thus, it is appropriate to draw attention to the fact that Aborigines in an urban context rear their children in a manner very similar to Europeans within the same socio-economic stratum. Further, they face the same socio-economic problems arising from low occupational status — i.e. financial insecurity and little education. Accommodation pressures, lack of adequate facilities and a minimum of luxuries are similar. Attitudes toward education and ideals of behaviour and achievement correspond, as does the ambiguity between ideal and actual behaviour. Certainly, this ambiguity is *not* uniquely 'Aboriginal'. Research has shown that working class ideals, expectations and goals correspond closely with those of the middle class. However, as Chinoy (1967) has pointed out, the ambitions and desires of working-class youth are tempered by actual experience in their socio-economic environment as young men accommodate themselves to the exigencies of circumstances and as they reinforce ties with those who share their social status and their identity.

Certainly one *distal* variable which really sets Aborigines apart from other 'working-class' people is their ethnic origin. All their problems, similar to those of Europeans in the same economic stratum, are influenced by 'colour'. Whereas working-class people's interaction with other classes may be influenced by a striving 'to be equal', feelings of inadequacy and consequent rejection of achievement-oriented values, Aborigines are influenced by all of these aspects as well as by European paternalism, discrimination, distrust and hostility. For these reasons, urban Aborigines will never become 'just' poor black whites. Further, the whole nexus of folklore, in-group identity and emphasis on 'Aboriginality' provides the individual with a screen through which he can identify himself positively as 'coloured', possessing qualities no white man has.

Notes

1. The term 'Aboriginal' or 'Aborigines' will be used throughout this contribution to describe all persons of Aboriginal descent who identify themselves in those terms.

2. Financial support was provided by the Australian Institute of Aboriginal Studies; and special reference should be made to Drs B. H. Watts, M. J. Calley and R. McSwain (of the University of Queensland), who advised and assisted me in this project.

3. According to strict anthropological definition, these groups do not in fact constitute 'clans'. I have, however, retained the term because of its frequent use by Aborigines in describing their own descent groups.

4. Most Aborigines in Queensland were classed as 'assisted' or 'controlled'. A 'controlled' Aboriginal was a person subject to the provisions of the Acts (such as *The Aboriginals Preservation and Protection Acts, 1939 to 1946*, and later *The Aborigines and Torres Straits Islanders Act of 1965*), usually resident on a settlement or reserve and under the juris-diction of the various Departments of Native Affairs. Aborigines who wished to be 'free' had to apply for exemption papers. People generally had to prove first that they were capable of coping with their own affairs, and could demonstrate sobriety and industry.

5. Mathew (1913:435) adds to this information by pointing out that the *Gurang Gurang* as well as the *Wakka Wakka* were organised on the basis of a four-'class' system. He main-tains that the four classes or sections were grouped into two phratries (or moieties) in the following manner:

Dilbai	m., *bonda*	f., *bondagan*
	m., *dherwain*	f., *dherwaingan*
Kapaiin	m., *barang*	f., *baranggan*
	m., *bandyar*	f., *bandyurgan*

Tennant Kelly (1935), like Mathew, analysed the social organisation as a four-section system; however, she believed that the sections were grouped into exogamous moieties. Both agree that descent was matrilineal, that cohabitation was prohibited between members of the same moiety or phratry, and that children's section membership was dependent on that of the mothers'.

References

BARDSLEY, G. 1965 Aborigines and the law, *Smoke Signals,* December: 15-16.

BARWICK, D. E. 1962 Economic absorption without assimilation? The case of some Melbourne part-Aboriginal families, *Oceania,* XXXIII (1):18-23.

——1963 A little more than kin: regional affiliation and group identity among Aboriginal migrants in Melbourne. Ph.D thesis in Anthropology, Australian National University, Canberra.

BECKETT, J. 1958 A study of the mixed-blood Aboriginal minority in the pastoral west of New South Wales. Ph.D thesis in Anthropology, University of Sydney.

CAMERON, A. L. P. 1904 On two Queensland tribes, *Science of Man,* 7(2):27-9.

CHINOY, E, 1967 The chronology of aspirations. In *The study of society* (P. I. Rose ed.), pp. 393-404. Random House, New York.

DOCKER, E. G. 1964 *Simply human beings.* Jacaranda Press, Brisbane.

ECKERMANN, A.-K. 1973 Contact. M.A. thesis, University of Queensland.

ELKIN, A. P. 1964 *The Australian Aborigines: How to understand them.* Angus and Robertson, Sydney. (Fourth edition.)

GOLDTHORPE, J. H. *and* D. LOCKWOOD 1967 Affluence and the British social class. In *The study of society* (P. I. Rose ed.), pp. 348-71. Random House, New York.

HAGAN, J. *and* P. R. DE LACEY 1971 Social class and compensatory education. In *Critical writings on Australian education* (S. D'Urso ed.), pp. 258-65. Wiley, Sydney.

HAVIGHURST, R. J. *and* B. I. NEUGARTEN 1962 *Society and education.* Allyn and Brown, Boston.

HESS, R. D. *and* V. C. SHIPMAN 1968 Early experience and the socialisation of cognitive modes in children. In *Contemporary issues in developmental psychology* (N. S. Endler, L. R. Boulter *and* H. Osser eds), pp. 519-33. Holt, Rinehart and Winston, New York.

HYMAN, H. H. 1967 The value system of different issues. In *The study of society* (P. I. Rose ed.), pp. 371-93. Random House, New York.

INGLIS, J. 1964 Dispersal of Aboriginal families in South Australia (1860-1960). In *Aborigines now* (M. Reay ed.), pp. 115-32. Angus and Robertson, Sydney.

JESSOR, R. *and* S. RICHARDSON 1968 Psychosocial deprivation and personality development. In *Perspectives on human deprivation: Biological, psychological and sociological,* pp. 1-69. U.S. Department of Health, Education and Welfare.

KELLY, C. TENNANT 1935 Tribes on Cherbourg Settlement, Queensland, *Oceania,* V (4):461-73.

KITAOJI, Y. 1971 *Contemporary Aboriginal families in the Lower Macleay valley.* Preliminary Report on Fieldwork, December.

KLUCKHOHN, F. *and* F. STRODTBECK 1961 *Variations in value orientations.* Row Peterson, Evanston, Illinois.

LICKISS, J. N. 1971 Aboriginal children in Sydney. The socio-economic environment, *Oceania,* XLI (3):201-28.

MATHEW, J. 1887 Mary River and Bunya Bunya country. In *The Australian race* (E. M. Curr ed.), 3:152-209. Ferres, Melbourne.

——1910 *Two representative tribes of Queensland.* Fisher Unwin, London.

——1913 Note on the Gurang Gurang tribe of Queensland, with vocabulary, *Australian and New Zealand Association for the Advancement of Science,* 15:433-43.

——1926 The religious cults of the Australian Aborigines, *Australian and New Zealand Association of Science Report,* 18:524-40.

MATHEWS, R. H. 1898 Initiation ceremonies of Australian tribes, *American Philosophical Society Proceedings,* 37:54-75.

NEWSON, T. *and* E. NEWSON 1970 *Four years old in an urban community.* Pelican. (Second edition.)

RÓHEIM, G. 1925 The pointing bone, *Journal of the Royal Anthropological Institute,* 55:90-114.

ROWLEY, C. D. 1967 The Aboriginal householder, *Quadrant,* 7(6):90-6.

SEARS, R. R., E. E. MACCOBY *and* H. LEWIN 1957 *Patterns of child rearing.* Row Peterson, Evanston, Illinois.

WATTS, B. H. 1968 Equality of educational opportunity for Aboriginal children. In *Ethnic minorities in Australia* (H. Throssell ed.), pp. 113-27. Australian Council of Social Service, Brisbane.

WESTERN, J. S. 1968-69 The Australian Aboriginal: what White Australians know and think about him — A preliminary survey, *Race,* 10:411-34.

22 Aboriginal identity

Instruction and interaction at an experimental training workshop

Margaret Valadian and Diane Barwick

The six-week workshop sponsored by the Commonwealth Office of Aboriginal Affairs at the Australian National University in January-February 1971 had certain unique features. It was perhaps the first extended residential training programme to include both urban and 'bicultural' Aborigines; it was probably the first to provide instruction in Anthropology, Human Biology, Archaeology and other subjects usually taught at the tertiary level; it was certainly the first to be originated, designed and organised by an Aboriginal.

A recent ANZAAS paper (Duke and Sommerlad 1973) criticised the curriculum rather severely and, we think, misinterpreted the purpose of this workshop. As the only 'staff' members who participated in the entire proceeding we can perhaps offer a useful perspective on the project, as well as reviewing its history. Only the twenty-two Aborigines who completed the course can adequately assess its success. We will merely describe the initial aims, discuss the design of the curriculum, and mention some of the special problems which caused alteration of the programme. In conclusion, we will quote some written assessments by Aboriginal participants.

In their description of this workshop the educationists used words like 'educative intervention strategies', 'individuated skill training', 'purpose-designed seminars', 'structured syndicates', 'stimulating learning community' and 'reconceptualised model'. We are not sure we understand these pompous phrases. We are sure this workshop was not intended to be a 'culture course' to somehow re-tribalise the southern folk, or 'foster' Aboriginal culture and identity. The initial programme did not naïvely propose 'leadership training' for 'existing or potential leaders' with the expectation of producing a 'nation-wide network of leaders'.

The project was originally planned to provide assistance and training for those Aborigines already struggling in their own way to work in their own communities, in Aboriginal organisations, and in government departments. The curriculum was designed to give participants an understanding of the historical background to their own and others' situations, to increase their knowledge of current developments in Aboriginal affairs across the nation, and to give them better 'tools' for the work they were already doing.

Participation in a 'workshop' for American Indians, the original model for this project, had demonstrated that the 'non-directive', 'consciousness-raising' or 'sensitivity group' style of unstructured discussion was at best a waste of time for people who wanted and needed to acquire specific skills and information, and at worst a potentially dangerous kind of amateur cross-cultural psychiatry.

During 1970 the workshop idea was discussed with various Aborigines in different regions of Australia. They confirmed this opinion, saying that already many national and regional conferences provided opportunities for meeting and comparing problems and grievances. But these conferences were too brief and 'just talk sessions'. What people wanted was 'more schooling'. In recent years, more and more Aborigines had been examining their own notions about Aboriginal identity and searching for information about their people and their past. But schools, libraries and museums offered little that was useful to them. And by 1970 many middle-aged and younger men and women were obtaining full-time employment as Aboriginal welfare workers. But most felt frustrated and handicapped by their lack of knowledge of community resources and basic paperwork and administrative skills. Many wanted at least a few weeks of formal training to improve their qualifications, and some explicitly wanted a certificate which would help to convince paternalistic employers and colleagues of their abilities.

The design of the workshop curriculum was based on a social worker's professional evaluation of the needs of various Aboriginal communities, plus many years of participant observation. Fostering Aboriginal identity never was the central focus. But detailed information on traditional ways, including regional variation in Aboriginal culture, was included to help overcome the confusion or even embarrassment caused by false impressions of Aboriginal history and heritage, and to help urban folk understand the more conservative communities. Because isolation and ignorance caused so many individuals to despair of solving what they thought were unique problems, it also seemed important to discuss the history of European contact and government policies, the nature of prejudice, and the typical characteristics and values of modern Aboriginal sub-cultures, as well as providing information on comparable ethnic groups overseas, especially Maoris, Canadian Indians and Black Americans.

The course content was thus necessarily 'academic'. Lectures, tutorials, library research, written papers and oral presentations, the experience of formal chairmanship, and examinations to reinforce learning were all seen as essential to provide knowledge and skills that likely applicants needed and wanted. Six weeks seemed the minimum time for effective teaching — and the maximum time that adult workers could leave their jobs and families. Limited money, accommodation and staff meant that twenty-four Aborigines, plus one Maori, was the maximum possible attendance.

Formal administration of the Commonwealth grant for the workshop was undertaken by the Australian National University's Centre for Continuing Education. The Director and several members of the Centre's small permanent staff supervised the preliminary organisation and the recruitment of teachers and students, as well as providing background support services throughout the project. Their expertise and efficiency (and that of the Warden and staff of Bruce Hall, which provided accommodation) were of immeasurable importance to the smooth running of the workshop.

The full-time teaching staff consisted of two highly qualified and experienced adult education tutors recruited from Sydney and Adelaide, plus two 'Honorary Academic Directors'. The latter title covered every conceivable and some inconceivable duties — such as killing and plucking chickens to obtain down for a Tiwi dancer! Forty lecturers (including fifteen members of the Australian Institute of Aboriginal Studies) were recruited —sometimes hastily — to teach specific topics. All of the forty academics, medical experts, media representatives and government officials had some expertise or special interest in the fields of Aboriginal affairs or ethnic relations. We should here acknowledge our gratitude, especially to those recruited outside Canberra, for their eagerness to participate, even when this meant an inconvenient disruption of their work or their holidays. Many made their lectures so enthralling that they had to come back and talk some more, and some followed up with private discussions or tours of laboratories, libraries and museums.

We have outlined the initial aims and the basic organisation of the workshop. What were the special problems and the changes of programme?

The original recruiting circular specified that this was a university study course, but laid down no minimum academic qualifications. Now somehow labelled 'The Culture, Identity and Future of the Aborigines', the workshop programme was specified in detail: sixteen lectures by anthropologists, linguists, prehistorians and ethnomusicologists describing aspects of traditional life during the first fortnight; then two weeks devoted to contemporary problems, including lectures by specialists on history, administration, housing, employment, health, education, nutrition, voluntary organisations, adoption and fostering, legal problems, the land rights issues, and governmental resources and services. Participants were asked to prepare written papers (before their arrival) describing the characteristics and special problems of their home communities, as a basis for extended discussion. The programme for the final fortnight was not specified in detail, but the original aim was to devote this time to individual projects. Guided by workshop supervisors, students were to be encouraged to exercise their increased skills by completing and presenting research reports focused on specific planning of future programmes to suit the needs of their own communities.

This last part of the curriculum had to be modified, as it proved impossible for the burdened staff to plan and supervise twenty-two separate projects in this time span. Moreover, the general standard of literacy was so much lower than anticipated that tutorials, study periods and examination reviews were largely devoted to basic remedial instruction and reinforcement of the formal lectures. Preparation of a second set of individual reports was abandoned; instead, more specialists were recruited during the final fortnight to provide lectures and laboratory sessions on topics specially requested by the students — notably archaeology, human biology, sports, medicine, education, hostel management, linguistics, Aboriginal drama and bark painting, interviewing techniques, and the writing of biographies and community histories—as well as scheduled films and lectures providing comparisons with the experience of ethnic groups overseas.

In any educational project the main 'problem' will be the students! More than seventy applications were received before the deadline, but some others applied too late or were unable to attend for the full six weeks. For fear of discouraging anyone, the recruiting circular had asked only age and occupation, but fortunately many applicants did provide additional background information. The selection process took weeks of agonised discussion, attempting to secure a fair representation by age and experience, sex, and State residence, as well as a balance between urban folk and members of more remote communities. Yet, after all this, last-minute domestic and job crises, plus incredible difficulties in transcontinental communication and the organisation of transportation over the Christmas holiday period, caused withdrawals and substitutions up to and including the first week of the workshop. Never will we forget our vain searches of the Canberra airport (crowded with delegates to the International Orientalists Congress), while debating how best to inform Mr Harry Giese that we had lost five of his Aborigines!

Family and money problems plagued many participants throughout the six weeks, distracting their study and exhausting the staff. Although the Western Australian and Victorian governments generously provided paid leave for employees, workshop funds had to be stretched to the utmost to provide supporting grants for other applicants. Inevitably variations in such grants, and in mode of travel, caused some contention. Fatigue from their long journeys, anxiety about the unfamiliar classroom setting and, even more importantly, continuing involvement in the affairs of their home communities, delayed the initial adjustment of some participants. It is understandable that adult workers, many of whom held responsible positions in their own communities, found it hard to forget the claims of their jobs and families and concentrate on their studies. In the final days before their return home the students were again distracted by this necessary mental readjustment.

Half of the twenty-four participants came from the southern capital cities, including all but one of the seven women. Their ages ranged from seventeen to fifty-four years, and their previous education from third grade primary to second year University level. This variation was not apparently a handicap in comprehending the lectures, for discussion was invariably perceptive and extensive. But lack of practice in English composition and limited technical vocabularies — probably equally characteristic of other rural working-class Australians — made the essay and examination demands of the course difficult for some. Likewise, lack of experience in library research meant that the specially chosen books were not sufficiently used, despite individual supervision and encouragement.

The most serious initial problem, certain southerners' hostility to 'white men who think they can tell Aborigines about our culture' was quickly overcome, largely by the anthropological sophistication of the six truly bicultural and bilingual participants and the obvious expertise, enthusiasm and respect for Aboriginal culture shown by the lecturers. Despite the urbanites' ignorance of traditional values and customs and misconceptions about settlement life, and their tendency to dominate discussion in the formal sessions, relations between them and the representatives of more conservative communities were excellent. The informal interaction of students from different backgrounds was also a form of instruction, and of course every participant had his turn as teacher in formal classes.

When we chose the title 'Aboriginal Identity: Instruction and Interaction' for this paper, it brought to mind a favourite memory of the workshop: watching a Port Hedland man and a Yirrkala man covering the blackboard with genealogical symbols and kinship terminology and explaining to each other the elements of his own system. If only we had possessed a movie camera: the 'Murngin Controversy' might have been settled that day!

One minor problem, in itself a lesson in cross-cultural teaching, was the reluctance of the younger 'tribally-oriented' men to speak until invited to do so, or to precede their elders in debate; an insensitive chairman, unaware of their rather different notions of etiquette, could too easily allow discussion to become monopolised by southerners sophisticated by years of conference participation.

How can one measure the usefulness of such a short-term education project, how judge whether the money was well spent? This six-week workshop did not 'create' a 'nationwide network of leaders'; such a 'king-making' expectation or intention would be utterly naïve. The original aims were rather to provide an opportunity for participating Aborigines to gain a better understanding of their cultural heritage, to become better informed on current developments in Aboriginal welfare, and to add to their working skills and perhaps thereby increase their own self-confidence.

The written comments of some of the graduates provide an assessment of the achievement of these three goals. Rural as well as urban folk praised the workshop as 'a step towards unity' because it had given them 'a chance to understand my people more'. Many wanted more such courses, organised on a regional as well as a national basis. There were no criticisms of the academic curriculum, and in their enthusiasm for learning some even suggested that such workshops should be 'extended to three months or more' as 'the lectures was a bit too squash for that short six weeks'. Some reported feeling a new confidence in their Aboriginal identity: 'I swelled up with pride when I got the first concepts of our traditional culture. For once in my life I was really proud'. A new appreciation of their cultural heritage, plus new skills, increased self-confidence:

> . . . before, I was always somewhat embarrassed when it came to discussions with non-Aboriginal people (about Aboriginal living). Now, since the course I am proud of the Aboriginal way of life. And I can argue and convince people . . .

And some others saw immediate practical results in their work: 'It has given me prestige with my dealings with European people because the respect of the facts of universities go over much easier'.

Professional educationalists might 'measure' the success of the workshop by calculating the numbers who got better jobs, or started new development projects in their own communities, or acquired new local or national renown as spokesmen or leaders. Some students did all of these things.

But it is perhaps more relevant that we succeeded, however briefly, in creating a shared community by living and learning together, and all of us gained, were changed, were educated by this experience. The formal graduation might have seemed to outsiders a pathetic imitation of university ceremony, or merely a display of academic vanity by those entitled to wear robes and regalia. It was Mr Lindsay Burrud Roughsey, honoured that night as teacher of us all, who linked the two cultures represented there by speaking of our shared values, of teaching and learning, of the need for humility and discipline in the initiate's long journey. It was he who transformed that gathering, he who defined it as a ceremony of initiation for all of us. And it was he who reminded us that the ceremony was not an end, but a beginning.

References

DUKE, C. *and* E. SOMMERLAD 1973 Fostering Aboriginal culture and identity — Theoretical and practical problems. ANZAAS, Perth (CCE/73/178, The Australian National University, mimeographed).

23 Aboriginal values in relation to poverty in Adelaide

Fay Gale

The purpose of this paper is to show that Aborigines living in towns and cities retain close ties with their kinsfolk not only because they wish it but also because they are forced to do so by strong economic pressures.

Much has been said about Aboriginal kin loyalties, the strength of their networks and their observance of reciprocal obligations. Several urban Aborigines have expressed pride in what they consider to be the caring and sharing basis of their society and have contrasted it with the individualism of western society. Some white observers have praised the apparent communal basis of much Aboriginal life, although the majority have criticised it as being detrimental to the acceptance of Aborigines into the general community.

But there are economic factors in this pattern of living and these may be as important as the social influences. I am, therefore, suggesting that Aborigines maintain close links with their relatives and frequently live in extended family units not just because they want to, but because they have to.

During 1973 I made a study of Aboriginal poverty in Adelaide, the results of which were given to the Commonwealth Commission of Inquiry into Poverty. The following tables used in this discussion were first published by the Inquiry (Gale and Beviss 1974). To obtain information about the Aboriginal economic situation I drew a random sample of seventy Aboriginal households on a stratified residential basis from a total population of 330 households. Of these seventy households, the adults interviewed in four were either unwilling or unable to give full details about income. The following discussion is therefore based on interviews carried out in 66 Aboriginal households during the middle part of 1973.

Poverty is usually defined as a percentage value below a given figure which is estimated as the minimum income a man requires to keep a wife and two children. The poverty line is thus represented by the value of 100 per cent.

Poverty Level											
Very poor		Poor		Marginal		Low income		Other			
0–79.9	%	80–99.9	%	100–119.9	%	120–139.9	%	140–199.9	%	200+	%
2	3	14	21	19	29	11	17	12	18	8	12

Table 1: Household poverty

Those households with incomes up to 20 per cent below the line are classed as poor and those up to 20 per cent above the line as marginally poor. Table 1 shows the distribution of the 66 households surveyed in relation to the poverty line calculated by the Commonwealth Commission of Inquiry into Poverty.

This Table shows that 24 per cent of Aborigines in Adelaide were below the poverty line and a further 29 per cent were in marginal poverty, that is a total of 53 per cent of the Aborigines studied were poor or marginally poor. Although these figures suggest that just over half of the Aborigines in Adelaide do not receive enough income to maintain an adequate standard of living, other surveys show that Aborigines in Adelaide are actually well off in comparison with Aborigines elsewhere. A similar survey in Brisbane recorded 47 per cent actually below the poverty line and a further 8 per cent in marginal poverty.

During the course of this survey, female householders were asked to give their own assessments of their financial situations. The interviewer asked the householders how they considered they were managing financially. Self-assessment of this kind, and in the circumstances of the interview, namely an inquiry into poverty, is a very subjective process. Much depends upon the type of image which the householder wishes to convey. The assessment is also influenced by the standards which the householder has set for her family. These standards tend to be determined by the knowledge which the inter-viewee has of other households both in her micro-environment (the homes of friends and relatives) and in the macro-environment (the homes of non-Aborigines in the community at large).

Given these difficulties of assessment it seems apparent that most Aborigines have a very clear idea of their financial situation and a quite realistic appraisal of their poverty level.

A correlation has been made between the actual poverty level of the household and the householder's appraisal of that level. Of the sixteen households below the poverty line just over two-thirds said that they were definitely poor and needed more money. One-third, however, said that they were just managing. This suggests that either they were living within their very limited means or that they were obtaining money other than that divulged to the interviewer.

A closer examination of those five poor households, which considered themselves to be just above the poverty line, will explain their particular positions. Two of the households were single income units with only one adult woman receiving a pension. The various allowances, travel, medical, education, in addition to concession rents, enabled them to manage frugally but in their own eyes, adequately. Another was an unmarried mother with similar concessions but also in receipt of much assistance from a voluntary agency. A fourth, a widow on a pension, had a large sum of insurance money received from her deceased husband. The fifth household had three male boarders which the householder said were essential to keep the household above the poverty line.

Such examples support the contention that the Aboriginal householder has a very clear appreciation of her financial situation. This is equally true for households in all categories.

Two-thirds of those in the marginal and low income groups considered that they were just above the poverty line as indeed they were. Their comments could be summarised as 'just managing'. Approximately one-third of these groups (37 per cent of the marginally poor and 33 per cent of the low income group) said that they needed more money to manage adequately.

Householders classified above these levels and placed into the category of 'other' realised that they were reasonably well off. Only two of the twenty householders in this category stated that they needed more money. One was an older widow receiving a pension with a son on a large wage. The combined household income was therefore high. However the widow did not actually share very much of the son's income and she was not as well off as the household level would suggest. The only other householder in this category who said that she wanted more money was a woman on a pension living with a man who was earning. She cared for her sibling's children and felt she was not adequately compensated. She had emotional rather than financial reasons for requiring more money.

It therefore seems evident that most Aboriginal householders assess their financial situations according to their basic needs rather than in terms of the comforts and standards they cannot afford. Generally, they appear to have a more realistic appreciation of their resources than do many members of the white community. Such assessments rather make nonsense of the oft-repeated comment that 'Aborigines cannot manage money'.

If Aborigines do in fact have a realistic appreciation of their economic situation it is to be expected that they will use every means available to them in their fight for economic survival. In this case the maintenance of kinship ties is but one way in which they can advance their economic position. The survey of Aboriginal poverty in Adelaide has shown that households improve their poverty level by living in larger household groupings.

For the purposes of this study the household was subdivided into income units in the same manner as that adopted by the Commonwealth Commission of Inquiry into Poverty (1974). An income unit is defined as any person or group of persons receiving an income whether it be from wages, pensions or unemployment benefits. A family consisting of a husband, wife and dependent children would be classed as one income unit whether or not both husband and wife are working or receiving pensions or benefits. But independent juveniles or adult sons or daughters, working or on benefits, would be classed as separate income units as would other adult relatives such as aged parents. Aboriginal households in the survey contained from one to ten income units.

This study has shown that, on the whole, the larger the number of income units living in a house, the better off will be the household. At first glance this situation appears to be an anomaly. Large households containing more than one family and often several children look disorganised and indeed sometimes quite chaotic. Several welfare officers have described such large households as poor. Although they may look poor, and the house itself is overcrowded and not well maintained, in actual fact the members of that household, on average, are better off financially than many of the smaller nuclear families.

To explain this apparent anomaly the households in this survey are placed into two categories, namely single and multiple unit households. There were 30 single and 36 multiple unit households in the 66 households surveyed. Table 2 summarises the position of these 66 households on the poverty scale.

This Table shows a poverty calculation before and after rent. If house-holders are paying low rents or several income earners are responsible for the rent then their level on the poverty scale is improved. If however the family is paying a high rent and there is only one income to meet it, then that household may go lower on the poverty scale than before a rent allowance is calculated.

Poverty level	Number			
	Single income unit		Multiple income unit	
	Before	After	Before	After
Very poor and poor	11	6	5	2
Marginal	8	12	11	7
Low income	5	5	6	11
Other	6	7	14	16
Total	30	30	36	36

Table 2: Single and multiple income unit households in each poverty level before and after rent

Table 2 shows that even before rent is taken into consideration, more than twice as many single income unit households are below the poverty line as multiple unit households. There is a very favourable rental situation for low income families in Adelaide who live in houses owned by the South Austra-lian Housing Trust. Many poor families are given assistance by the Trust but even so Table 2 shows that multiple income households where rent is shared, benefit far more than do single income unit families. When rent is taken into the poverty calculation, two of the multiple income unit house-holds and six of the single unit households remained below the poverty line even after the favourable rental situation in Adelaide had been accounted for.

It is at the other end of the poverty scale that the value of shared house-holds stands out clearly. A large proportion of the multiple income unit households, namely 14 out of 36, or 44 per cent, were well out of poverty into the medium income ranges after rent was calculated. By contrast only 7 out of 30, or 23 per cent, of the single unit households attained this standard of living even when the favourable rental situation is taken into account.

The differences between these types of household are now examined in more detail in an attempt to explain the reasons for the variations in the poverty level seen in the Aboriginal community.

Eleven of the single-unit households, or 37 per cent, were found to be below the poverty line before rent was adjusted. One was categorised as very poor and ten as poor. Six of these eleven were nuclear intact families. All except one of the fathers was working. That one was receiving a pension. The nuclear families with working fathers were at the lower end of the scale and the pensioner was better off. In fact the only two households in the survey classed as very poor (one a single and one a double unit household), had male household heads working for a state government department. In both cases the families would have been better off if the fathers had left their jobs and taken unemployment benefits.

The single-unit households headed by deserted wives or widows receive more sympathy and financial assistance than do nuclear families. In fact, all of these one-parent families were higher up the poverty scale than five of the six intact, single-unit families. With such supporting evidence it is little wonder that Aborigines are becoming so critical of Western society's norms. They find that legally married, nuclear families with reliable, working husbands tend to be poorer than any other members of their community.

Five of the multiple-unit households or 14 per cent were found to be below the poverty line before rent was taken into account. One of these was in the very poor category and that was a household with only two units. All others were at the top of the poor class almost on the poverty line. Four of the five were intact nuclear households. The household head of the other one was a widower. Three of the four husbands were employed, the fourth being on a pension. The additional units in these households were due to the receipt of a pension, usually unemployment, by one member of the household. However, when rent was distributed and taken into the calculation only one of these multiple-income units remained below the poverty line but seven of the single income unit households remained poor after rent was calculated.

A similar pattern continues as the poverty class increases. There were eight single-unit households in the marginally poor class and eleven multiple-unit households. Of the eight single-unit households, five consisted of nuclear intact families with legally married parents and three contained single or separated women. Two of these were receiving pensions and one was working. All of the married men were employed. One, however, was in gaol at the time of the interview but was said to be usually employed when 'outside'.

Of the eleven multiple-unit households in the marginally poor class, eight were two-unit households only because they had one additional person, usually an older daughter or son, earning or on unemployment benefits. Seven of these were nuclear intact families. Five of these males were employed, the others were receiving pensions. Three of the households in this category of marginally poor were truly extended families containing four or six income units.

There were five single and six multiple income unit households classed in the low income category before rent was allowed for. All of the single units were intact nuclear families. All male heads were employed. Of the six multiple units in the low income group four had household heads who were employed and two depended entirely on pensions. It is ironical that one household of three units had all three persons permanently employed yet it was only just above the marginal poverty line but the five other households which had at least one pension coming in were all higher on the scale.

It is in the medium income groupings classed as 'other' that the difference in household structure is most obvious. There were six single and fourteen multiple unit families in this higher category. All of the single-unit households were at the lowest end of this category, being near 140 per cent of the poverty level. But eight of the multiple-unit households were classed in the 200 plus category.

The six single-unit households were higher on the scale because all were intact families with husbands working. In addition, four of the six wives were also working and a further one was receiving a pension, her union being a *de facto* one. Only one of these six single-income-unit households did not in fact have two incomes going into the one unit.

Only seven of the fourteen multiple unit households contained intact families. The other seven had female household heads, separated or widowed. Only six of the fourteen household heads were employed. The others received pensions. Regardless of whether the household head was employed there were enough members in the house receiving pensions or wages to lift the total household income well above the poverty line.

Generally speaking, then, the greater the number of income units pooling resources within a household the higher is the likely average income level of each unit. The sharing of resources and household costs enables more households to sit above the poverty line than would be possible if all remain in single-unit households.

Many interviewees described this position by comments such as the following: 'Us Nungas always help each other'. 'We always share everything; it is better that way'. 'Sharing is a necessary part of our lives'.

Whilst many social workers are frustrated by the large households which appear to be disorganised and are often mistakenly termed multiple-problem families, the economic justification for large households cannot be overlooked. There may thus be very sound economic reasons why so many Aborigines maintain their kinship ties in the urban location. The extended family is an economic necessity for many. So long as this condition remains, is it really legitimate to discuss such kinship ties solely in terms of traditional or social values?

References

GALE, F. *and* J. BEVISS 1974 *Poverty amongst Aboriginal families in Adelaide*. Australian Government Publishing Service, Canberra.
POVERTY IN AUSTRALIA 1974 *Interim Report of the Australian Government's Commission of Inquiry into Poverty*. Australian Government Publishing Service, Canberra.

24 Social agents as generators of crime

Dorothy Parker

A three-year study of the processes of law enforcement and administration of justice involving Aborigines in Western Australia, suggests that the Aboriginal stereotype held by policemen, judicial agents and prison officers, plays an important part in the amplification of deviant behaviour attributed to Aborigines. The disproportionate number of Aborigines in Western Australian gaols is due, not only to the wide discrepancies in political and socio-economic status which exist between Aboriginal and non-Aboriginal Australians, but also to the expectations of social agents. Values and behaviour which deviate from those of the dominant groups in Australian society are seen as potentially destructive of that society. Policemen, the initiators of the whole process of criminal justice, are on the alert for behaviour which fits their unfavourable stereotype of the Australian Aboriginal, thus demonstrating the truth of W. I. Thomas's dictum that a situation defined as real in a society will be real in its consequences.

The Western Australian system of criminal justice ensures that the policeman on patrol has almost absolute discretionary powers of arrest. These are not always used wisely or responsibly, especially where those on the receiving end are people of low socio-political status. Aborigines are mostly charged with non-indictable offences and appear in courts of lower jurisdiction. Unnecessary and often unjustifiable police action in remote country areas is too often condoned and reinforced by Justices of the Peace with minimal legal training, dependent on policemen's 'superior knowledge of the law'. Magistrates in Courts of Petty Sessions seldom question police actions and statements and defendants are seldom represented by counsel. Conviction is usually followed by imprisonment in institutions where containment and punishment are considered to be far more important than rehabilitation. Aborigines are all too often victims of the 'revolving door' phenomenon.

It is clear that radical changes are required in public attitudes and also in legislative, executive and administrative areas of the system of justice in Western Australia.

Official documents (Comptroller General of Prisons 1970:4) show that the proportion of Aboriginal prisoners in Western Australian gaols is more than ten times as great as the proportion of Aborigines in the general population of Western Australia.

A study carried out in 1970-72 examined the reasons for such a discrepancy and attempted to understand the degree of criminality of Aborigines in Western Australia. Originally this was commenced as research for a higher degree in Anthropology within the University of Western Australia: and was later supported by the then Department of Native Welfare for Western Australia on the understanding that the material could be used eventually for a thesis. The methods and techniques used in this study followed the accepted criminological tradition of the late nineteen-sixties. My first aim was to examine existing official records in order to establish comparative crime rates of Aboriginal and non-Aboriginal populations. There is no doubt that Aboriginal crime rates for all offences except the 'middle-class' offences of forgery, uttering and offences against currency, are constantly and markedly higher than non-Aboriginal crime rates (see Appendix).

Aboriginal crime rates were found to be highest in the area of offences against good order in general, and drunkenness in particular. A closer scrutiny of the severity of the offences committed by Aborigines who had been imprisoned showed, however, that within each class of offence, Aborigines had committed less serious offences than non-Aborigines and were therefore given shorter sentences. These rates were, of necessity, computed on the basis of convictions and not on the numbers of persons convicted. Many Aboriginal men and women were arrested several times within the same year. The imprisonment of Aborigines convicted for minor offences displays a classic example of the 'revolving door' phenomenon.

There are already well-established reasons as to why figures of court convictions and/or prison populations are not adequate bases for the measurement of criminality of any ethnic group. For instance:

(1) Scandinavian, American and British studies have shown that many crimes are not reported to, or recorded by, agents of law enforcement so that a realistic picture of all the criminal activity. in any particular society is never available (Sutherland and Cressey 1966).

(2) Western Australian police records show that a relatively minor proportion of the crimes known to the police is cleared by them (*Annual Report of the Commissioner of Police* 1967-9).

(3) It has been shown in the United States (Piliavin and Briar 1964:206-14; Pettigrew 1964) the United Kingdom (Lambert 1969:430-32; Pearson 1968:30-34), and in Australia (Eggleston 1970) that arrest and sentencing rates show discrimination against coloured minority groups.

(4) Valid comparisons cannot be made of the criminality of two ethnic groups until such factors as income, social class, community participation and social commitment are taken into consideration (Wood 1946-47:249).

When we compare Aborigines with non-Aborigines in Australian society, we have on the one hand a group whose almost total membership has low socio-political status, low educational achievement and low income, and on the other hand a group whose membership covers the whole spectrum of status, education and income.

Socio-cultural, economic and personality factors may well be important components of any explanation of deviant behaviour. But my study of the processes of law enforcement and administration of justice has convinced me that the expectations of Aboriginal behaviour held by agents of law enforcement and administration of justice are actually instrumental in bringing about the so-called 'criminal behaviour' exhibited by those Aborigines who are eventually convicted of criminal offences.

The main contention of my paper then, is that figures of conviction and imprisonment are largely reflections of the beliefs and attitudes held by social agents, who are merely representatives of the wider society, and of the quality of interaction which occurs between people of Aboriginal descent and the wider society. These, in turn, reflect the importance of the dimensions of power in our society: how and why are certain rules made, how and by whom are they enforced and who are the victims of the power game? The exploratory research described in this paper reveals the importance of these last factors.

Law enforcement   The techniques used in this area of my research were:

(1) *Participant observation:* I travelled with policemen on their normal patrols in the metropolitan area in police vans, attending on one or two nights a week over a period of three months. I varied the nights of the week and the shifts I attended to minimise the chance of special provisions being made by senior officers for my benefit. At first I notified them of my visits one day beforehand, later I shortened this period to a few hours. I doubt if my carefully planned variations could have allowed for special arrangements to have been made by the police force. The spontaneity of the policemen's conversation and behaviour soon showed that they had assigned to me the role of a 'harmless' welfare worker who wanted to understand the problems the police had with Aborigines.

There were many drawbacks in playing such a role: I could not use any technical aids in recording interviews or behaviour and I soon discovered that I could not take notes in their presence. The whole situation was extremely delicate, for policemen are very suspicious of social scientists.

Whenever possible I accompanied policemen on their patrols in the country. This proved less easy to arrange than it had been in the metropolitan area, despite my letter of introduction from the Deputy Commissioner of Police, so I had to be satisfied with observation from street corners or hotel windows and balconies.

(2) *Loosely structured individual interviews* and many 'casual' conversations with every policeman I met, either while travelling in the police van, or on official visits to police stations in the metropolitan or country areas.

(3) *Group interviews* in appropriate situations, e.g. when I was asked to meet the 'Women's Police Force', or when I visited larger country town police stations where the sergeant's desk is in the same room as those of his junior staff.

Findings   Before giving a description of police powers, attitudes and behaviour, I will draw attention to the now well documented history of Aboriginal-police relationships in the early days of the state (Hasluck 1970; Biskup 1960; Rowley 1970). These have left indelible imprints on the memory of older Aborigines and of their children to whom they have communicated their fears and hostility. They remember the massacres of Aboriginal groups, the chaining of prisoners to be taken south to gaol, and the removal of children to the missions.

On the one hand, policemen have had various administrative duties in relation to Aborigines, including supervision of health conditions, accommodation and sustenance provided by employers for their Aboriginal workers. On the other hand, these same policemen have had to ensure

Aboriginal obedience to an alien legal system, particularly in relation to the consumption of alcoholic beverages. They also ensured that Aborigines stayed out of towns, lest the sensibilities of European-Australians should be offended by the presence of poor and ill-clad people. This task is still being carried out by police, because many people in country towns regard Aborigines as 'blots on the landscape'. In towns where the concentration of Aborigines is high (as in Gnowangerup or Pingelly), and where they often use the same shops and services as the rest of the townspeople, the feeling against Aborigines is particularly strong. It is, in my view, a complex feeling of prejudice compounded by ignorance, apathy and guilt. And it is always the policeman's implicit duty, in country towns like these, to ensure that Aborigines are as inconspicuous as possible. This was brought home to me by the statement made over and over again by policemen throughout the state: 'I have to make sure they don't hang around the town'.

Policemen then have been protectors, law enforcement agents and, by sheer force of circumstance, prosecutors and gaol warders in country towns. It is with this background of roles and their ensuing actions and attitudes that policemen and Aborigines must coexist and have frequent interaction today.

Present police powers in Western Australia   The discretionary powers wielded by the policeman on patrol duty give him virtual *carte blanche* in his decision to arrest or not to arrest any citizen he observes. The low visibility of such decisions ensures that departmental or judicial review is very seldom applied (Goldstein 1960:543-94), especially in cases where the arrested person has low political or social status.

The policeman's discretion is dependent upon his value system which in turn is the result of his socialisation processes and learning experiences, his measure of intellect and understanding. Particularly in his dealings with people whose social and cultural traditions differ from those of his own community, he should have some elementary knowledge of History, Social Anthropology and Psychology. At the very least he should have acquired a measure of tolerance. This is highly unlikely to be the situation with our Australian police forces. The very nature of the policeman's work is not conducive to making it attractive to well-educated, liberal-minded people. The remuneration offered has improved of recent years but still does not compare favourably with any occupation which requires a modicum of specialised training. At the time of my research, the fortnightly salary offered during training and first year of service was $134.66 increasing by automatic yearly increments to $144.94 for the fifth year of service. On qualifying and completion of five years of service, promotion to First Class Constable assured a salary of $158.13 (*The Independent*, Sept. 20 1970:12).

In a survey of Australian police forces carried out by Chappell and Wilson (1969) it was found that none of the States required formal educational qualifications for entry and that the entrance examination for aspiring candidates consisted of tests in English and arithmetic set at about second year high school level. This was followed in Western Australia by an intelligence test (the Otis Higher Test form C) which was then sent to the Western Australian Education Department's Counselling Service for assessment. But the results of this test were not necessarily final. In the words of the Western Australian Commissioner of Police: 'If they "felt" (*sic*) that the applicant has the ability, with training, to raise the standard of his education they would admit him despite low performance in both tests'. During my own research a senior police administrator told me quite seriously and sincerely that he felt it would be unwise to have highly educated policemen, for they would then be unable to make contact with members of the public!

In Chappell and Wilson's estimation, several Australasian forces accept recruits with intelligence quotients as low as 80. Intelligence tests are notoriously unreliable and they are not necessarily authoritative predictions of a policeman's performance, but it is necesssary to point out that the extremely wide powers of discretion in the hands of the most junior policemen on patrol are not always going to be exercised skilfully or wisely. It is part of police training to suspect anything 'different', anything which does not conform to the ideal type of the European-Australian society which values thrift, cleanliness and acquisitiveness above all other qualities.

Travelling with policemen on their regular patrols through Central and East Perth it became evident that certain characteristics of dress, stance or race spell danger to policemen. Young men congregating in a central shopping area around their motorbikes or at street corners represented a threat to my travelling companions, who could seldom relate specific instances of the boys' misdeeds but who always expected trouble from these groups. Whenever a group of Aboriginal youngsters, whatever their dress, was seen in Wellington, William, Beaufort or Stirling Streets,[1] the police driver beside me would automatically slow down his vehicle and peer hard at the Aborigines.

Trouble is expected and looked for from Aborigines who drink alcoholic beverages. Wine saloons frequented mainly by Aborigines are visited several times in one evening as a routine matter, not merely upon the request of the saloon-owners. A staggering step or a raised voice, is sufficient proof of 'drunkenness'. Where a staggering 'white' man is allowed to find his way home when he states in a reasonably restrained manner that this is his destination, most of the policemen I observed imprisoned the Aboriginal on the grounds that she or he would be safer and better off in a 'clean' cell, where a 'clean' bed and a 'decent meal' would be provided. Indeed in one of the country towns visited a well known solicitor and barrister commented on the fact that when he had had too many drinks in one of the local hotels he would either be driven home or put into a taxi by the policeman on duty, whereas Aborigines would be delivered to gaol in the police van.

On my very first trip with the metropolitan police, I saw a police sergeant arrest four Aborigines in one wine saloon on charges of drunkenness quite early in the evening. Not one of these people appeared to me to be offensively drunk. They had been drinking and some smelled of liquor but they were not staggering or abusive — not one of these cases could have been seriously considered to be a public nuisance. When questioned on his criteria of drunkenness, the sergeant confidently asserted that: 'If a native (sic) has had a drink, he's drunk as far as I'm concerned'. The implication of such a statement is that a policeman has taken upon himself the legislative powers of Parliament. Aborigines, he believes, cannot tolerate alcohol, they should not be allowed to drink at all. He thus overrides the official will of the people expressed through the law which decrees that Aborigines should have the same drinking rights as other Western Australian citizens. This particular policeman was probably a-typical in his rigid beliefs, but similar behaviour and beliefs, varying only in degree, were seen and heard from other policeman.

Another abuse of power was found in the informal private agreement often entered into by country policemen and local publicans. This agreement varied from an 'understanding' that beer only should be served to Aborigines in hotel bars, to a curtailment of the number of bottles which Aborigines should be allowed to buy and take home.

In a court case in which the Western Australian Black Power Movement challenged the right of a publican 'to refuse to serve wine to an Aboriginal without reasonable cause' (*The West Australian*, Feb. 4 1972:4), the president of the Western Australian branch of the Australian Hotels' Association claimed that 'police had asked country publicans not to serve wine or spirits to Aborigines' (*The West Australian*, Feb. 5 1972:3). This claim was refuted by the police officer then in charge of the Liquor Branch. The official position may well be as the officer stated, namely that 'no instruction had been issued to policemen to ask publicans not to serve wine and spirits to Aborigines' (*ibid.*). Such an instruction would have been illegal, therefore it would hardly have been committed to paper. However, this senior officer must have been aware of the realities of the situation if he had any communication with his subordinates. Throughout the state I have heard many policemen asserting proudly that they had little trouble with excessive Aboriginal drunkenness, because they had an 'understanding' with the publican regarding the type or amount of alcoholic beverage to be served to Aborigines. One policeman in the southern division naïvely related his refusal to accept a charge against a local publican of refusing to serve an Aboriginal on the grounds that 'the publican was only doing it to oblige me'. The case was eventually heard and proven in another place and the publican was fined the minimum amount. It is doubtful whether these minimal fines provide any deterrent to publicans who wish to live in harmony with the local policeman.

Aborigines should challenge such abuses of police power by commencing legal proceedings against policemen. Court proceedings, however, are seldom instituted by people who have no funds and no confidence in the existing system of justice. Their lack of confidence after so many years of treatment as second class citizens, their past experiences in courts of justice — these are likely to inhibit such action. With the establishment of movements such as 'Black Power,' some risks might have been taken by Aboriginal members with some political power. But such movements do not live long in Western Australia. The connotations of 'Black Power' frightened most of the old supporters of Aborigines and the movement came to an early demise. However, if the abuse of power by policemen and members of the 'Establishment' continues, there is little doubt that truly militant Aboriginal organisations, hostile to the wider society, will succeed even in Western Australia.

Police attitudes and behaviour The policemen I interviewed in the metropolitan area and in twenty-five country towns ranged from being paternalistic, at the favourable end of the continuum, to openly antagonistic at the unfavourable end. One policeman was honest enough to tell me that his suggested solution to the Aboriginal problem would be 'unprintable'.

Further probing revealed that he would like to be rid of them in a final and irreversible manner.

Many policemen as well as other influential members of the European-Australian 'Establishment' in country towns suggested similar, though less drastic, solutions to 'the Aboriginal problem'. The suggestion, with minor variations, ran like this: a large area of land should be put aside in a remote and uninhabited part of the country for the erection of an Aboriginal commune under the supervision of European administrators. Within the boundaries of this commune, Aborigines should be trained to live like 'civilised people' — to learn all kinds of new physical, mental and social skills, until such time as they were 'ready' to mix with the Australian community. 'They cannot expect to be treated on the same footing as "white" people until they learn to live like us' was the favourite comment.

In the meantime, the approved behaviour of Aborigines should be humble, subservient and patient. In the words of one senior police officer: 'Aborigines have to learn that the meek shall inherit the earth'. The fact that the old 'Uncle Tom' stance has not benefited Aborigines, but has reinforced the arrogant and authoritarian attitude of so many public servants, seems to have escaped senior members of the police force. They firmly believe that the protest movements and the complaints about the unjust treatment of Aborigines which are gathering momentum throughout Australia, are instigated and manipulated by communist-inspired professional agitators. Liberal and progressive thinkers, university students and other European-Australians who advocate reform are labelled 'dangerous stirrers'.

Senior police officers have hundreds and hundreds of well-substantiated complaints of discrimination and brutality in policemen's dealings with people of Aboriginal descent. These complaints have been made on an official basis by the then Department of Native Welfare only after thorough investigation by welfare officers and departmental heads. Each complaint represents only the visible part of the iceberg, for most departmental officers in small country towns are loath to risk the displeasure of the local policeman by reporting him. Thus the Aboriginal complainant has to have remarkable tenacity and courage to persist with his complaint.

Harassment by policemen of 'troublesome' Aborigines is well known. A 'troublesome' Aboriginal, in the eyes of a policeman, is one who is aware of his legal rights and who is confident enough to express such rights. A typical example of such harassment which came to my notice was the case of an Aboriginal community leader who was refused a drink in a hotel bar, though he was respectably dressed and quite sober. He complained to the local policeman, who refused to accept the complaint. When the Aboriginal expressed a desire to take his complaint to higher authorities, the policeman proceeded to inspect the Aboriginal's car, pointing out all its deficiencies, with no attempt to mask his threat of prosecution. It is difficult to prove such harassment in a court of law where the complainant is a member of an oppressed minority group and the judicial agent is anxious to uphold the image of impartial and 'moralistic' law enforcement. The then Department of Native Welfare preferred to deal with such complaints interdepartmentally. An official letter setting out the complaint and its sources was sent by the Department of Native Welfare to the Police Department. After investigation by one of the senior police officers, the policeman who is found to be at fault may be reprimanded or, in extreme cases, sent to another placement. After a thorough perusal of all available substantiated complaints made by the Department of Native Welfare to the Police Department, I did not find one case of a policeman who had been demoted or expelled from the police force on the grounds of harassment of Aborigines. Thus justice is not 'seen to be done', the Aboriginal has not been vindicated or compensated, and other members of the police force have not learnt anything from the episode except that Aborigines can be ill-treated with considerable impunity.

A study of complaints in official files and countless anecdotes told by Aborigines and verified by careful cross-checking, leave little doubt that instances of brutality on the part of policemen are commonplace. The officers I observed were fairly careful, for obvious reasons, to refrain from physical or verbal attack on Aborigines in my presence — but they gave themselves away in many instances.

Example: A routine call at an east Perth wine saloon revealed a well-dressed elderly Aboriginal staggering on the footpath just near the entrance to the saloon. The policemen commented that this man was well known to them for his drinking excesses, therefore two policemen attempted to arrest him. He resisted on the grounds that he was not seriously drunk and that he was about to call a taxi to take him home. Two more policemen in the back of the van stepped out to aid their colleagues and the Aboriginal was brought down to the pavement. He put up considerable physical resistance by kicking out with his legs. He was eventually handcuffed and dragged into the police van by the four policemen. A small crowd of people had gathered to witness this incident. The police sergeant, returning to his front seat beside me, commented to his junior colleague who was driving the vehicle 'you can't *do* [his emphasis] anything to them while there is a crowd watching'. The implications of such a comment are substantiated by eye-witness accounts of what were then called Native Welfare officers and reliable Aboriginal 'leaders' in country towns. Several senior country police officers commented that they were obliged to 'keep an eye' on some of the younger policemen because they used questionable methods of law enforcement where Aborigines were concerned.

Police administrators justify such behaviour on the grounds that policemen are only human and cannot be expected to tolerate arrogance. One may understand such reactions, but this explanation cannot be accepted as an excuse for police brutality.

Policemen wield a great deal of power, especially among people who have low social status, and are unaware of their legal rights and unable to afford litigation. Aborigines living on reserves or on the fringes of country towns in the ubiquitous 'transitional houses', see the policeman as the representative of the state and of the 'white' community. It is incumbent upon such a representative to act in a truly professional way, to control and even submerge his own personal values and emotional reactions just as the doctor, the psychologist or any other professional person must do when faced with a maladjusted or even psychotic client. Policemen should be bound by stringent codes of behaviour which are enforced by an independent, autonomous body. Such a body should have the power to hold public hearings regarding allegations of police misconduct. Private inter- and intra-departmental inquiries are completely unsatisfactory since justice cannot be seen to be done.

Until society is prepared to recognise the responsibilities involved in a policeman's role and offers rewards commensurate with such responsibilities, it is unlikely that we shall have a professional police force. Apart from more selective enrolment and reward for specific educational qualifications, the policeman's salary should encompass the special elements of risk and danger, elements which weigh heavily on the policeman's mind and which, together with his ignorance of cultural differences and historical circumstances, colour his attitudes and behaviour.

The role played by the police is of crucial importance in any problems of criminality. My research has led me to the conclusion that the discriminatory attitudes and actions of many members of the police force are important contributory factors to the existence of a disproportionate number of Aboriginal prisoners in Western Australian gaols.

The administration of justice   Another important factor contributing to the disproportionate imprisonment of Aborigines in Western Australia is the inadequate system of criminal justice which is being administered in our courts of law. It is a system which favours the wealthy, the well-educated urban European-Australian whose confidence in his own civil rights may be reinforced by adequate legal representation at an open court hearing presided over by a judicial agent trained in law. Wherever there is any doubt about the legality of the proceedings, this middle-class European-Australian is able to take his case to a higher court on appeal.

Theoretically, such safeguards are available to all Australians. My own observations of court proceedings, my interviews with Magistrates, Justices of the Peace, Clerks of Court, Aborigines both in and out of prison, and my study of the social history cards and files of Aboriginal prisoners, lead to the conclusion that all men are not equal before the law.

Many of the inadequacies which will be discussed in this section apply not only to Aborigines, but to any indigent and poorly educated person of low social status. As Nagel (1967:3-9) has said:

> Justice . . . may have a blindfold, but it may also have a price, a complexion, a location, and even age and sex; and those with enough money, the right complexion, in the right court, and even sometimes of the right age and the right sex, can often get better treatment.

There are certain factors, however, which compound the injustices faced by the Aborigines, the first one of these being the predominantly rural nature of the Aboriginal population in this state. Because Aborigines in this state are mostly tried and convicted in courts of summary jurisdiction, and because most Aborigines live in the country, justice to Aborigines is frequently administered by Justices of the Peace. Magistrates have to cover vast areas and therefore preside infrequently in small country centres. Any offence 'made punishable on summary conviction', and 'any offence, act or omission' which is not treason, felony, crime or misdemeanour may be heard and determined by two or more Justices in a summary manner (Justices Act No. 11 of 1902, Sect. 20). Complaints for indictable offences or simple offences should be heard by two or more Justices, but, with the consent of all parties concerned, such complaints may be heard by a Justice of the Peace sitting alone (*ibid.*: Sect. 29). Thus in remote country towns we frequently see the Aboriginal defendant appearing before one Justice of the Peace and one policeman — no other witnesses of the hearing, no press: no safeguards.

In the case of a country police court, the local policeman acts as both prosecutor and judge. He presents his case against the defendant, advises the Justices of the Peace (or sometimes one Justice of the Peace) on the relevant legislation dealing with the alleged offence, and often advises on the appropriate punishment. This dependance by the Justice of the Peace on the police is possible and often necessary because the Justice has had no training in law. His decisions are supposed to be based on the Statutes, which he often does not understand (since understanding of legislation so often depends on past interpretations) and on a small manual which purports to cover the most common circumstances he is likely to meet, and on his 'common sense'. I have heard a police inspector extolling the virtues of 'common sense' at a seminar held for Justices by an enterprising Magistrate. 'Common sense beats all academic thinking in my view'.[2] Maybe, but whose common sense, and how defined? A very nebulous concept for the basis of administration of justice.

The Justices Act does not lay down any special qualifications for a Justice of the Peace, but empowers the Governor to appoint as many justices, male and female, as may from time to time be deemed necessary to keep the peace in the State of Western Australia (Justices Act No. 11 of 1902, Sect. 6). In practice, Justices of the Peace are 'men of some public respectability and achievement who give up their time for community service' (Buckley 1966:10). 'Achievement' is measured usually in terms of material success. Thus we find the owner of the town's largest store, the most prosperous farmers, the station owner or the manager of an agricultural firm — these are the Justices of the Peace, together with the Mayor or the Chairman of the Shire who automatically becomes Justice of the Peace upon appointment. Inevitably they represent the vested interests of the town, they are the defenders of the status quo. In my experience these are also the people with the least understanding and tolerance of Aborigines, and with the most prejudicial attitudes toward them.

These then are the men who sit in court and decide the fate of the Aboriginal defendant. Quite often they feel they know the defendant well, and know 'what is good for him' before they have heard the case in court. One station owner who was also a Justice of the Peace told me in an interview held before a court case that he knew the young man well who was to appear before him, since he had grown up on his station. All his troubles, said the Justice of the Peace, stemmed from drink, therefore he would see to it that the defendant should be declared an habitual drunkard and thus prevented from drinking for a reasonable period. He had decided not only on the guilt of the defendant, but also on his punishment before he had heard the case in court. This made a farce of the ensuing criminal proceedings.

There are some Justices of the Peace who are genuinely concerned about Aboriginal offenders. They confess themselves perplexed about the people who come before them so frequently for trivial offences. Fines often cannot be paid, imprisonment, they say, is obviously no deterrent. They ask for guidance in these cases and it is difficult to provide such guidance. The remedy lies with social, legal and economic status. The short-term remedy may lie in the more judicious use of police discretion, but the long-term remedy lies in equal opportunities for Aborigines in the areas of housing, education, employment.

There are also some Justices of the Peace who are aware that they are hampered by their lack of legal training and that they carry great responsibilities. They seek advice from the Magistrate and the latter helps wherever possible, but this involves time and special efforts to establish communication. Far too often, in case of doubt, the policeman's advice is taken because this is the most practical and expedient course of action. At the seminar for Justices of the Peace in Northam, the senior police officer said 'There is great co-operation between Justices of the Peace and the Police Force'.[2] Care must must be taken that such co-operation does not amount to what might be described as collusion.

Legal representation   Because Aborigines are mostly charged with non-indictable offences and because the most frequent charge is that of drunkenness, it is not surprising that most of the court proceedings observed throughout this study dealt with drunken charges or charges arising from excessive drinking, e.g. disorderly conduct, obscene language or breaches of the Licensing Act.

There was a popular 'myth' prevailing within the Department of Native Welfare, that drunken charges were not important and should therefore be ignored by departmental officers. Policemen and Clerks of Court throughout the state told me that they had been given to understand by departmental officers that they did not wish to be informed when an Aboriginal was to appear in court solely on a charge of drunkenness. The argument put forward was that welfare officers are far too busy to attend to such minor charges which only involve trivial punishments and which are almost impossible to rebut. Professional legal representation in such cases is not to be even considered unless, of course, the Aboriginal defendant can provide it at his own expense and on his own initiative.[3]

The official booklet on 'Legal Representation for Aborigines' which was published and distributed by the Department of Native Welfare for the 'Guidance of Field Officers' (1969:1) stated that an Aboriginal 'should be assisted . . . to obtain legal counsel . . . in any circumstances in which an Aboriginal is likely to be involved in legal proceedings, which could have serious consequences to him'.

It is my contention that any appearance of an Aboriginal in a court of law, regardless of the severity of the charge, has 'serious personal consequences' for him — in terms of self respect, reputation, future employment and future involvement with the law. In each and every case the Aboriginal defendant should be represented. The right to representation in defence of a charge made by the state is a right which should be available to every member of our society, whereas in fact it is only a right available to those who can afford to pay counsel.

Having seen the enormous powers of discretion wielded by the police force and having learnt of the attitudes held by most policemen toward people of Aboriginal descent, I deem it essential to provide the latter with a more efficient protective tool such as comprehensive legal representation, regardless of the severity of the charge.

Social history cards of prisoners in both Fremantle Gaol and at Bandyup Training Centre show a large preponderance of first convictions for drunkenness and many a so-called 'criminal career' has commenced with just such a trivial charge. The prevention of imprisonment is highly desirable. There is little doubt that policemen would be less likely to apprehend Aborigines on drunken charges if they knew that such charges would require proof other than hearsay evidence.

But quite apart from the deleterious consequences of unnecessary imprisonment, it is the status of the Aboriginal which is at stake and which should be protected. Rowley's perceptive comment that 'Aborigines are far more in need of lawyers than welfare officers' (1966:343) does not apply only to the situation where they seek to assert their rights to land *vis-à-vis* big companies: it applies to any appearances in court where they are faced by more powerful opponents.

Appearance in a court of law is an awesome and frightening experience for the most secure and confident citizen. There is a set of scales in the Police Court at East Perth upon which are inscribed the following words:

> Justice is a chilly virtue. It is of high importance that we be introduced into the inhospitable halls of justice by a friend . . . The first duty of the bar is to make sure that everyone who feels the need of a friend in Court shall have one . . . a good judge will fill the need if the bar does not.

Magistrates often hold stereotypes of Aborigines which are not unlike those held by policemen. It is understandable that, meeting only those Aborigines who engage in anti-social behaviour, they have a biased view of the Aboriginal population. Magistrates and Judges are products of their middle-class European environment, and nothing in their legal training has prepared them for an understanding of the handicaps of Aborigines or a tolerance for different cultural values.

Research on West Australian attitudes to Aborigines (Taft 1970) has shown that there is a slight tendency for the better educated respondents to be more tolerant on social distance measures and to be less ethnocentric. But there is little doubt of the existence of the Aboriginal stereotype, that of 'an irresponsible, lazy and dirty slob who has the redeeming features of being a good parent and a friendly respectful and generous person' (*ibid.*: 14). This stereotype seems to have deteriorated since Professor Taft's research was carried out in 1965. My non-Aboriginal informants would not have attributed the feature of 'being a good parent' to Aborigines.

A press report of a stipendiary magistrate's decision admirably exposes the prevalent attitudes and beliefs as I found them among the judiciary in the lower courts. A Perth magistrate, faced with the decision as to whether the defendant should be classed as an Aboriginal under the National Service Act, and thus found not guilty of a charge of failing to register for national service, is reported to have said: 'There's no evidence of his living in a native camp and he apparently lives at a normal address in Perth. I must also take notice of his appearance. He is well dressed and well presented and I am going to convict him' (*The West Australian*, June 22 1972). A telling indictment of the Aboriginal's status in Australian society and a clear indication of the magistrate's personal image of Aborigines.

Legal representation should be available to every person who appears in court charged with a criminal offence however trivial, whether he be Aboriginal or European. However, it is clear that an Aboriginal has special disadvantages:

(1) *Low social status.* As we have seen in the preceding section, an Aboriginal is much more likely to be arrested than a non-Aboriginal, since he has no powerful friends to help him.

There have been occasions when Aborigines arrested in the streets and brought to the East Perth Gaol have claimed relationship or friendship with well-known people and have asked that these people should be contacted. Police officers have laughed, winked at me knowingly and ignored these claims and these requests. Yet every prisoner is entitled to make one phone call. It may well be that experience has shown such claims to be false — but this cannot be taken for granted. Every effort should be made to contact 'a friend' of the arrested person, whether he be an 'institutionalised' friend such as a welfare officer assigned to night duty, a member of the family or a personal friend, so that bail may be arranged.

The derision, often good natured, with which Aborigines are treated at what is euphemistically called the 'Lockup' is one more example of the way in which they are denied personal dignity. It is possible that for policemen this ability to laugh and joke at their prisoners provides a release of tension in what would otherwise be too stressful an occupation. Indeed the prisoners often join in the laughter against themselves, to oblige their mentors. Yet the whole procedure is a gross infringement of personal liberty, and many of the prisoners resent it bitterly. 'You wouldn't talk to me like this if I was a white woman', said a middle-aged Aboriginal.

Police officers, on the other hand, point out the frequently undignified behaviour of Aborigines. Aboriginal women especially, they say, lack control of language and action. This, I believe, is simply a fulfilment of role expectations enhanced by the lack of restraint which is promoted by alcoholic beverages.

In the infrequent event of a middle-class 'respectable'[4] person being brought in to gaol, not on a drunken charge (because he can get drunk in his own home or that of his friends, rather than in a saloon or on a park bench) but on a charge of 'driving under the influence of intoxicating liquor or drugs', the treatment meted out to him is very different and he is given every chance to contact his family or his solicitor.

(2) *Low educational status.* The second handicap, not peculiarly Aboriginal, but perhaps most marked in an Aboriginal, is that of a poor standard of education which, together with his low psychological and social status, prevents him from knowing, asserting and defending his rights. Thus, throughout the state he usually pleads 'guilty' to the charge. As one country police officer put it: 'Oh yes, they always do the right thing' when asked about Aboriginal pleading in court.

There is a propensity in the general population for people charged with petty offences to plead guilty, but this is particularly marked in the case of Aborigines. There are several reasons for this:

(i) He has been told that if he pleads guilty, he will be convicted of a simple offence and his punishment will be minimal;

(ii) His wish is to be finished with the whole unpleasant business as quickly as possible. A plea of guilty means a shorter period in gaol, since a plea of not guilty usually means a remand while the police prepare their case. Since he is often unable to pay bail, he would have to spend the intervening time in gaol. A plea of guilty means a shorter period in the court-room and less questioning and exposure to 'white' people.

(iii) A plea of not guilty requires a defence and this involves, ideally, legal representation. For a non-indictable offence, defence by a qualified solicitor and barrister has to be paid out of his own pocket. Aborigines who can afford this luxury are in the minority. Native Welfare Department representation, where available for petty offences, is not usually very helpful. The welfare officers are not trained in law, they lack the confidence to argue with the prosecution, and they do not really understand the role of an advocate in a court of law. It is their belief that if a defendant admits to them personally that he has committed an offence, he should automatically plead guilty and receive his punishment. As one Magistrate explained to me in an approving tone: 'The Native Welfare Department officer defending an Aboriginal is a friend of the Court, rather than a friend of the defendant'. This, of course, makes it very much easier for the prosecution to establish their case and for the defendant to be convicted. The Aboriginal defendant has therefore learnt from his own experience or that of his friends that representation by an officer of the Department is seldom helpful. His rapport with that officer is not always good — once again the simplest course is to plead 'guilty'.

(3) *Ignorance of procedure.* The Aboriginal defendant often lacks understanding of court proceedings. This is especially true in the north, north-western and eastern regions of the state where language difficulties exacerbate the ignorance of court procedure. Clerks of Court and Magistrates in these areas have often remarked that Aboriginal defendants seem to 'remove' themselves mentally from proceedings. They stare out of the window or at the ground and appear to be quite apathetic as to the outcome of the trial. It is obvious that they feel completely powerless in an alien situation, and give up any attempt to follow proceedings. If questions are asked, either for the prosecution or the defence, the answer given is often one which the Aboriginal feels will please his questioner, though it may have no connection with the truth.

Elkin (1947:176) has pointed out that this reflects the adjustment which the traditionally-oriented Aboriginal has had to make to the contact situation. His evidence in court aims to 'satisfy the questioner, to tell him what "the Aboriginal thinks" he wants to be told, and even at times to appear stupid, funny, child-like and pleased with patronizing'.

The traditionally-oriented Aboriginal in the Kimberleys or from the Western Desert presents a very special problem in which language difficulties and very marked cultural differences are highlighted. The case of Regina v Ferguson[5] is an excellent example of this problem as it also points to the conflict of laws which may still occur in our society.

The case showed the strong and overwhelming influence of traditional beliefs held by some full-blood Aborigines. To a greater or lesser degree these beliefs influence the lives of many Aborigines throughout the state and in Robinson's words 'contribute to the feeling that the Australian-European legal system is a thing quite detached from their own conceptions of right and wrong'. In this particular case, an able and interested lawyer saw the difficulties of interpretation and conceptualisation and sought advice from the Department of Anthropology regarding language differences and the meaning and influence of traditional beliefs. The Judge involved, Mr Justice Burt, was sympathetic and interested and welcomed advice from anthropological experts. The welfare officer was experienced, energetic and alert. All these circumstances combined to help the defendant and to minimise a miscarriage of justice. The case has set a precedent in Western Australia for the consideration of the special difficulties encountered by traditionally-oriented Aborigines appearing in our courts of law. I doubt, however, whether such understanding has been shown in many instances by Magistrates or Justices of the Peace presiding in courts of lower jurisdiction. It is difficult for them to envisage the complete lack of understanding of the meaning and function of court procedure for a traditionally-oriented Aboriginal. One Magistrate told me that he took it for granted that the Native Welfare officer appearing in court would make sure that his charge understood the proceedings, and was able to put forward the defendant's explanation of the case. In view of the lack of knowledge of most welfare officers of Aboriginal traditional language and culture, and in view of the existence of many different dialects, it is highly unlikely that welfare officers could be satisfactory interpreters.

Wurm (1963:1-10) has pointed out that an exceptionally qualified interpreter conversant with both European and Aboriginal cultures, is required to convey to the Aboriginal with a 'tribal' background the white man's legal concepts and the principles underlying his court procedure. It is almost impossible to obtain the services of such a man for an ordinary court case and it is therefore unlikely that European juristic ideas and principles can be conveyed to the tribal Aboriginal.

The Native Welfare Act of 1964 presented a safeguard, albeit an unsatisfactory one, to the traditionally-oriented Aboriginal by virtue of Section 31 which prohibited pre-trial admissions of guilt made by traditionally-oriented Aborigines residing above the 26th parallel. The new Act leaves it to the discretion of the court to accept or refuse a plea of guilt. This places a great responsibility on the court. How will they be able to satisfy themselves that the accused is a person of Aboriginal descent 'who from want of comprehension of the nature of the circumstances alleged, or of the proceedings, is or was not capable of understanding that plea of guilt or that admission of guilt or confession' (Section 49[1] of the Aboriginal Affairs Planning Authority Act, 1972).

The Magistrate who heard the committal proceedings of the Regina v Ferguson case did not understand the problems faced by the defendant, in spite of many years' experience in an area inhabited by traditionally-oriented Aborigines. There is room for a special course to be given to law students and to practising lawyers and Clerks of Court. This course should introduce some of the beliefs and values of traditional Aboriginal culture and present the special difficulties faced by Aboriginal defendants.

Since the section applies to 'an offence which is punishable in the first instance by a term of imprisonment for a period of six months or more' we may assume that the defendant will be represented. We must ensure then that both judicial agents and legal representatives are fully aware of the cultural and linguistic difficulties involved. And once again, I am concerned with the traditionally-oriented Aboriginal not covered by Section 49(1) of the previously mentioned Act of 1972 — the Aboriginal who has committed a lesser offence which is not punishable by six months' imprisonment. Are we to condone a miscarriage of justice which incarcerates a defendant for three months, or even for three weeks? In every case where such a person is involved great care must be taken that he understands the charge, the plea and the court proceedings.

In the situation of the so-called 'sophisticated' Aboriginal in the metropolitan and south-western areas of the state, solicitors often consider that Aboriginal witnesses prejudice their own cases. It is only too easy to intimidate the Aboriginal witness. I observed one of the few cases which have been instituted by an Aboriginal against the police for assault, and watched an Aboriginal witness being brow-beaten by an aggressive counsel for the defence. In this case the Aboriginal witness had a measure of self-confidence for he had been accepted (relatively speaking) by European-Australian society for many years. He was well dressed and well spoken, he had a 'steady' job, a conventional house and had not been in trouble with the police. He held a responsible position as a leader and representative of the Aboriginal community — all accolades bestowed upon him by the European society for his identification with and acceptance of Western ways. He risked all this security and respectability in order to appear as a witness for a less fortunate Aboriginal who claimed he had been ill-treated by the police.

It was not difficult for counsel for the defence to brow-beat this witness, to force him into careless and apparently conflicting statements, for the veneer of self-confidence had been carefully nurtured and was not very deep. Counsel for the plaintiff was, as he often is when the Law Society assigns counsel for an indigent client, a young and inexperienced man who could not match the attack of his colleague and who found it difficult to pierce the solid front presented by the two policemen whose evidence had obviously been carefully rehearsed. Outside the court, a welfare officer's comment on the case, addressed to the Aboriginal plaintiff, was revealing: 'You should have had some 'white' witnesses on your side!' So much for our belief in equal justice!

These problems of Aboriginal evidence make it even more imperative that Aborigines should have adequate legal representation.

The most basic and fundamental safeguard for an adequate system of justice is the existence of a stable, egalitarian and well-informed society. While certain sectors of society remain under-privileged and liable to discrimination it is the duty of the political machinery of that society to provide special safeguards. The most immediate requirement for people of Aboriginal descent is the knowledge that they may stand in court armed with the best defence available against the abuse of the state's power. Jerome Skolnick (1970) has said: 'The function of the defense attorney in our adversary system is to provide, as stated by Dean Francis Allen, "constant, searching and creative questioning of official decisions and assertions of authority at all stages of the process"'.

There are many practical difficulties involved in providing legal aid for every Aboriginal who appears in court. The urban situation presents few problems in terms of arranging legal representation, and there would not be too many difficulties in the South-Western and Central Divisions. The real difficulties arise when we come to deal with the northern and eastern parts of this state where legal representation is most essential in view of the special problems of traditionally-oriented Aborigines.

As the number of law graduates in our University is constantly increasing, it may be possible for the Crown Law Department to appoint Public Defenders who would be stationed in strategically placed country centres throughout the state. Their salaries should compare favourably with those of their colleagues who are employed by legal firms but have not reached the exalted station of a partner in the firm. These Public Defenders would be available for all indigent defendants requiring representation. Ideally, they should be contacted by the defendant or by welfare officers before the commencement of a trial. Since this may not always be possible, they should always be present in court in case of need. Such Public Defenders should understand the special difficulties faced by Aborigines, so that they would be aware of the need for expert anthropological or linguistic help wherever necessary. Some realisation of Aboriginal needs and differences is being shown at the Law School within the University of Western Australia. This realisation should be fostered so that a special course of lectures might eventually be given on traditional Aboriginal culture and on the handicaps facing Aborigines in our society. Lawyers should not be expected to be anthropologists but they should at least be aware of the existence of differences in areas of language, beliefs and culture.

Another urgent requirement for a more adequate system of justice is the restriction of the duties of the Justice of the Peace. Magistrates who are obliged to have a measure of training in the law and who, increasingly, are law graduates, should be the only judicial agents in courts of summary jurisdiction. They too should be exposed to some education on the problems of minority groups in general and Aborigines in particular. Many younger Magistrates have expressed concern to me about the frequent appearances of Aborigines in court — it is at this stage before they become inflexible and unsympathetic that we should help them by explaining the background of the Aboriginal defendant.

Aborigines themselves should be informed about their legal rights. It should not be possible for policemen to use insulting language, to break down doors; or shine bright lights into reserve houses. There should be insistence upon the right to contact a friend after arrest in order to raise bail. Many infringements of an individual's liberty could be minimised if trained people could be asked to address Aborigines on these topics, making them aware of their legal rights. Perhaps the talks could be dramatised. There could be role enactments so that the lesson could be brought home to the least educated of Aborigines.

I have often been asked: 'Can "they" ["they" being the authorities] — can they do that to us?' Most Aborigines are afraid to protest at what appears to be unwarranted disrespect or intrusion, for fear that they may incur worse punishments. This fear would be removed (after a transitory period) if they could feel calm and confident about their legal rights.

Concern and embarrassment is often expressed at government level when sympathetic individuals take it into their own hands to awaken Aborigines to their rights as citizens and to the daily infringements of these rights by the dominant society. Such embarrassment could be avoided, and such concern could be more usefully employed in taking the initiative to protect Aborigines from such infringements and to provide such education in civil liberties within the administrative machinery so that Aborigines would look upon the government and its representatives as friends rather than enemies.

All these recommendations involve greater expense. The provision of legal representation throughout the states, the appointment of more magistrates, the special education of the judiciary, of lawyers and of Aborigines — all these will involve more state expenditure. But if we compare the expenditure on these measures with that of keeping a disproportionate and ever increasing number of Aborigines in prison, together with the social service payments which have to be made to the families of those prisoners, it is doubtful whether the new measures would entail a much greater expenditure of public funds.

Conclusion This paper has described some aspects of the processes of law enforcement and administration of justice in Western Australia to people of Aboriginal descent. The term 'social agents' has been limited to policemen and members of the judiciary. I should have liked to extend it to welfare and prison officers since my research took into consideration both representatives of the Department of Native Welfare and of one maximum and one medium security prison. Western Australia has the highest imprisonment rate in Australia while the average period served in days is the shortest in Australia (Biles 1972:621-55). Biles points out that if no Aborigines were imprisoned in Western Australia ('admittedly a whimsical thought' he says) the overall imprisonment rate would drop considerably. He suggests that the high imprisonment rate is due to the geographical isolation of the state which results in a more vigorous condemnation of social deviance in Western Australia than in other Australian states. I suggest that the reason lies in the inadequate welfare facilities in this state, in the attitudes of the Western Australian police force, the dependence of judicial agents in courts of lower jurisdiction on the police, and the apparent ignorance of judicial agents regarding current research findings on the effects of penal treatment which is largely custodial and punitive.

Having carried out this research in the traditional criminological sequence, I have now come to the conclusion that a much more radical approach is necessary, an approach which pays much more attention to the quality of interaction between policemen who have almost absolute power in the exercise of their discretion and Aborigines (or indeed any other disadvantaged minority group) who have no power at all. The whole process of social control should be looked at from an interactionist or transactional perspective (Cohen 1971, 1973:622-25), a sceptical perspective which does not assume that the established order is acceptable and irreversible. Every step in the process of social control should be examined and questions should be asked about who make the rules and why do they make certain rules rather than others, who enforce the rules and how do they carry out such enforcement, what is the effect of such processes on the 'deviant', and how was such a label affixed to him?

It has become clear to me that the study of official statistics is very marginal to any understanding of the process of deviance or crime in a society. When we quote rates of crime we are largely referring to the people without social or political power who have been labelled 'criminals' by social agents who possess too much power.

APPENDIX A[a]

	Aborigines			Non-Aborigines		
Year	No. of [b,c] convictions	Population[d] 10–50 yrs.	Crime rate per 1,000 of pop.	No. of convictions	Population 10–50 yrs.	Crime rate per 1,000 of pop.
(a) Offences against Property						
1961	380	9,507	39.97	4,844	416,197	11.63
1966	860	11,615	74.04	7,622	480,892	15.85
1970	2,428	13,434	180.74	12,031	559,083	21.52
(b) Offences against the Person						
1961	134	9,507	14.10	411	416,197	0.98
1966	293	11,615	25.23	575	480,892	1.19
1970	482	13,434	35.88	916	559,083	1.64
(c) Offences against Good Order						
1961	2,764	9,507	290.73	7,182	416,197	17.25
1966	5,535	11,615	476.54	7,562	480,892	15.72
1970	8,989	13,434	669.12	9,008	559,083	16.11

Table 1: *Magistrates' Courts*

	Aborigines			Non-Aborigines		
Year	No. of convictions	Population 10–50 yrs.	Crime rate per 1,000 of pop.	No. of convictions	Population 10–50 yrs.	Crime rate per 1,000 of ·of pop.
(a) Offences against Property						
1961	8	9,507	0.84	161	416,197	0.06
1966	13	11,615	1.12	211	480,892	0.44
1970	51	13,434	3.80	918	559,083	1.64
(b) Offences against the Person						
1961	7	9,507	0.74	26	416,197	0.06
1966	5	11,615	0.43	64	480,892	0.13
1970	14	13,434	1.04	92	559,083	0.16
(c) Total Number of Offences						
1961	15	9,507	1.58	203	416,197	0.49
1966	23	11,615	1.98	279	480,892	0.58
1970	65	13,434	4.85	1,122	559,083	2.01

Table 2: *Judges' Courts*

a A more detailed explanation of computations is available in the report by D. Parker on 'The Criminality of Aborigines in Western Australia', prepared for the Department of Native Welfare of W.A. (now the Department of Aboriginal Affairs), 1970-72.

b Source: Commonwealth Bureau of Census and Statistics.

c The number of distinct persons convicted is not given in the official records. It must be emphasised that the crime rates represent the number of convictions per 1,000 of population.

d The 'population at risk' is calculated to include persons between the ages of 10–50 years. Wolfgang and Sellin (1964) state that crime occurs predominantly among males between 15 and 50 years of age. Western Australian figures for Juvenile Court convictions suggest that many offences are committed between the ages of 11 and 13 (see Commonwealth Bureau of Census and Statistics, 1970). Therefore I decided to extend the 'population at risk' to those aged 10–50 years. The Aboriginal population figures used as bases for crime rate computations were those used by Schapper (1970:164–65).

Notes

1. The area on both sides of the railway line in the city. It is regarded as the 'wrong' part of the city.

2. Verbatim quotation from a lecture by a senior police officer at a seminar held for Justices of the Peace at Northam, 5 May 1970.

3. Unfortunately, the solicitors of the newly established Aboriginal Legal Aid Services in Western Australia have been obliged to perpetuate this myth, due to the vast distances involved and the paucity of staff.

4. 'Respectable' to the police in 1970-72 meant well dressed — i.e. wearing a suit or a sports jacket, trousers, shirt and tie, haircut of 'short back and sides'.

5. I am indebted to Mr Michael Robinson and Professor R. M. Berndt of the Department of Anthropology, University of Western Australia, for access to details of the case and the recommendations they made in their pre-sentence reports. The Department of Aboriginal Affairs Planning Authority, W.A., has on its files the full transcript of the case together with these recommendations.

References

ANNUAL REPORT OF THE COMMISSIONER OF POLICE 1967-9 Government Printer, Western Australia.

BILES, D. 1972 Australian prisons and their use. In *The Australian Criminal Justice System* (D. Chappell *and* P. R. Wilson eds). Butterworth, Sydney.

BISKUP, P. 1960 Native administration and welfare in Western Australia, 1897-1954. M.A. thesis in History, University of Western Australia.

BUCKLEY, B. 1966 Rough justices, *Bulletin*, Vol. 88.

CHAPPELL, D. *and* P. R. WILSON 1969 *The police and the public in Australia and New Zealand.* University of Queensland Press, Brisbane.

COMPTROLLER GENERAL OF PRISONS 1970 *Annual Report of the Prisons Department.* Western Australia.

COHEN S. (ed.) 1971 *Images of deviance.* Penguin Books, Harmondsworth.

——1973 The failures of criminology, *The Listener*, Vol. 90, No. 2328.

EGGLESTON, E. 1970 Aborigines and the administration of justice. Ph.D. thesis, Monash University, Victoria.

ELKIN, A. P. 1947 Aboriginal evidence and justice in Northern Australia, *Oceania*, XVII (3).

GOLDSTEIN, J. 1960 Police discretion not to invoke the criminal process: low visibility decisions in the administration of justice, *Yale Law Journal*, 69 (4).

HASLUCK, P. 1970 *Black Australians*. Melbourne University Press, Melbourne. (2nd ed.)

LAMBERT, J. 1969 Police discretion, *New Society*, 18 Sept. No. 364.

NAGEL, S. S. 1967 The tipped scales of American justice, *Transaction*, May-June.

PEARSON, N. 1968 Colour and the police, *The Criminologist*, 3(10).

PETTIGREW, T. F. 1964 *A profile of the Negro American*. Van Norstrand, New York.

PILIAVIN, I. *and* S. BRIAR 1964 Police encounters with juveniles, *American Journal of Sociology*, Vol. 69.

ROWLEY, C. D. 1966 commenting on D. Dunstan, Aboriginal land title and employment in South Australia. In *Aborigines in the economy* (I. G. Sharp *and* C. M. Tatz eds). Jacaraadn Press, Brisbane.

——1970 *Aboriginal policy and practice*. Vols. I-III. Australian National University Press, Canberra.

SCHAPPER, H. P. 1970 *Aboriginal advancement to integration*. Australian National University Press, Canberra.

SKOLNICK, J. H. 1970 Black separation and civil liberties. In *Society and the legal order* (J. H. Skolnick *and* R. D. Schwartz eds). Basic Books. New York.

SUTHERLAND, E. H. *and* D. R. CRESSEY 1966 *Principles of Criminology*. Lippincott, New York.

TAFT, R. 1970 Attitudes of Western Australians towards Aborigines. In *Attitudes and social conditions* (R. Taft, J. L. M. Dawson *and* P. Beasley eds). Australian National University Press, Canberra.

WOLFGANG, M. E. *and* T. SELLIN 1964 *The measurement of delinquency*. Wiley, New York.

WOOD, A. L. 1946-47 Minority group criminality and cultural integration, *Journal of Criminal Law, Criminology and Political Science*, 37.

WURM, S. A. 1963 Aboriginal languages and the law, *University of Western Australian Law Review*, 6(1).

25 Aboriginal legal services

Elizabeth Eggleston

The establishment of Aboriginal legal services has been a very recent development. In 1971 it was possible for Richard Chisholm to write an article on 'The Aboriginal Legal Service' which referred solely to the New South Wales Service, as that was then the only one in existence. Since that time a service has been established in every state and the Northern Territory.

In the United States it was found that legal services for poor people were an essential part of the War on Poverty. It has been considered by some commentators that legal services have been the most successful component of the Office of Economic Opportunity's programme. Among these legal services have been offices set up on Indian reservations to cater to a predominantly Indian clientele. It may be that, in the long run, the setting up of Aboriginal legal services will also turn out to have been one of the most significant developments in Aboriginal affairs.

The explosive growth of Aboriginal legal services The pioneering service in New South Wales was set up in 1970 in Redfern. It grew directly from the demands and needs of Aborigines in Sydney. Some young Aborigines deeply resenting police treatment of their people in Redfern, approached Professor Wootten, Dean of the Law School of the University of New South Wales, for help. As a result of their discussions, an organisation was formed to arrange for legal representation of Aborigines. Its council had seventeen members. The constitution provided that at least one-third of its members and at least one of its officers must be Aboriginal. Its management committee also had substantial Aboriginal representation. At an early date a newspaper article appeared, detailing Wootten's concern about injustice meted out to Aborigines. This drew an immediate response from Mr W. C. Wentworth, who was then Minister-in-charge of Aboriginal Affairs. He offered a Commonwealth grant, which enabled the service to employ an Aboriginal field officer, a solicitor and a secretary. But the service also relied to a considerable extent on work done free of charge by the legal profession.

The Victorian Aboriginal Legal Service also grew out of Aboriginal initiative. In this case Mr Stewart Murray, Director of the Aborigines Advancement League, approached law teachers at Monash University for assistance with the increasing burden of arranging legal representation for Aboriginal people. After an abortive attempt to cope with the problem using volunteer law students, the Aboriginal Legal Service was formed at a public meeting in June 1972.[1] It was largely modelled on the New South Wales service. However, it was anticipated that the federal government would not be prepared to make as large a grant as it had made to the New South Wales service. This view was held because of the smaller Aboriginal population and geographical area of Victoria as compared with the senior State. The Victorian service therefore proposed initially to appoint a field officer and a secretary, but not a solicitor. Legal work was to be performed by barristers and solicitors who had volunteered to join a panel; some cases were to be referred to the legal aid agencies which serve the general community (the Legal Aid Committee and the Public Solicitor). First priority was given to selecting a field officer, preferably an Aboriginal with good contacts with Aborigines throughout the state, whose job it would be to inform Aborigines about the established legal aid services, to arrange legal assistance using the lawyers who had agreed to act on an honorary basis and to provide general advice on non-legal matters. In December 1972 the service received grants from both the state and federal governments. This led to the opening of an office in Fitzroy in February 1973 and the appointment of a field officer the same month.

The council of the Victorian service has a majority of Aboriginal members. However, until recently the body which met weekly to oversee the day-to-day running of the service functioned essentially as a non-Aboriginal group.

The Queensland service also started on a voluntary basis (in February 1972). It followed the pattern of the other services in later appointing full-time staff. It was aware of the need to decentralise and by November 1972 had established a committee in Townsville which had a considerable degree of autonomy.

The South Australian Aboriginal Legal Rights Movement was created in November 1971 following a visit to Adelaide by Wootten and G. Foley of the New South Wales service. During the first year the field work was performed by Aboriginal volunteers and the legal work by a panel of lawyers working with the Law Society. The council of the Movement has eighteen members of whom not less than two-thirds must be Aborigines. The Movement, like the other services, was started by Aboriginal people.

The service in Western Australia is conducted by the New Era Aboriginal Fellowship, a multi-racial body dedicated to Aboriginal advancement in all fields. Its activities in the legal area began in 1972. Midway through that year it received an interim Commonwealth grant. However, it employed no permanent staff until May 1973 and its administration was carried out on a purely voluntary basis until then.

At the time of the first conference of Aboriginal legal services, held in April 1973, there was no legal service in Tasmania or the Northern Territory specifically for Aborigines. The Aboriginal Information Centre in Tasmania handled legal matters as well as other functions. Its secretary, an Aboriginal woman, referred cases to lawyers and also personally made representations to the police, which resulted in some charges being dropped. At first this service received no government finance and funds were raised through bottle-drives by the Aboriginal people themselves. The last Aboriginal legal service to be established was in the Northern Territory. Before it was set up, some Aborigines obtained legal representation under the Legal Assistance Ordinance and the Social Welfare Ordinance.

Early developments in each Aboriginal legal service have been briefly sketched above. The accession to power of the Australian Labor Party in December 1972 completely transformed the scene. The Labor Party's pre-election speeches included the promise that any Aboriginal appearing in court would be supplied with legal representation. The new government honoured its commitment by including in the budget for the period ending 30 June 1973 the sum of $850,000 for Aboriginal legal services. For the full financial year from 1 July 1973 to 30 June 1974 the budget amount was $1,500,000. This vastly increased financial provision has enabled the services to expand, both by taking on new staff and by opening new offices. The Victorian service, for example, which started with a field officer, an administrative secretary and a secretarial assistant, now has nine full-time employees, including five Aborigines. It employs two full-time solicitors in its Fitzroy office. It also contemplates setting up a country office in Swan Hill to be staffed by a solicitor and a field officer with part-time secretarial assistance.

The Aboriginal and Torres Strait Islanders Legal Service (Queensland) Ltd. has already decentralised to a considerable extent. It has district committees in a number of country towns and employs field officers in many locations outside Brisbane. Its growth has really been phenomenal. Decentralisation is also occurring in other states. The New South Wales service appointed Neil Mackerras, a leading Sydney barrister, to a position in Moree. Other regional offices have been opened in that state.

Regional conferences have been held in Western Australia to determine where local Aboriginal people think there was a need for the legal service to operate. Following these meetings lawyers were sent to country centres. John Toohey, former President of the Law Society, went to Port Hedland to set up an office of the legal service. He worked with an Aboriginal field officer and covered the north-west region of the state. Another lawyer was given a retainer to cover the south-west of the state. In South Australia a field officer has been appointed at Murray Bridge and part-time field officers at Port Augusta and Port Lincoln. An independent organisation, the West Coast Legal Aid Service, has been set up at Ceduna, a town noted for its bad race relations. The Aboriginal Legal Service Scheme was set up in Tasmania in June 1973. It took over the role previously carried on by Abschol and the Aboriginal Information Centre. A solicitor is now retained by the service on a half-time basis. Two services now operate in the Northern Territory. The Central Australian Aboriginal Legal Aid Service has been operating from Alice Springs since July 1973. Another service has its office in Darwin.

Such expansion has obviously allowed the services to offer legal assistance to many more Aborigines. The finance which has been provided by the federal government was beyond the wildest dreams of those who participated in setting up the original services. But money does not solve all problems. It may be that the sudden accession of wealth has fundamentally changed the nature of Aboriginal legal services and rendered them less capable of achieving some of their basic aims. Even if this has not yet occurred, such a danger may exist. Before considering specific problems confronting the legal services, it is necessary to look at their objectives, their distinguishing characteristics and the principles on which they operate.

Objectives of the Aboriginal legal services The aims of the Aboriginal legal services can be extracted from a document prepared in the Attorney-General's Department and approved by representatives from each legal service at a conference held in Canberra on 9 April 1973.[2] It states:

> This service establishes a legal facility to meet the special needs of Aboriginals and Torres Strait Islanders, with funds provided primarily by the Australian Government. The service is to be operated through an Aboriginal legal service in each State and Territory in Australia on Government grants given on these terms . . .
>
> Each service is to have flexibility in its development, to meet the needs of Aboriginals who stand in need of legal assistance. The facilities are to include, as funds permit, arrangements with legal practitioners in private practice for representing applicants in individual cases, with legal practitioners on a retainer basis where the usual arrangements for individual cases cannot readily be made, and the direct employment of legal practitioners, field workers, social workers and administrative staff. In the latter three cases, preference will be given to Aboriginals or to those persons who show an affinity with Aboriginals . . .

Thus the primary emphasis is on the provision of legal assistance and the means by which this is to be arranged. A policy of preference for Aborigines in employment by the services is laid down but there is no mention of the composition of the governing body of each service. There is no formal requirement of Aboriginal control of the service.

Proceedings at the April conference were largely dominated by the lawyer-presidents of each legal service. Brief statements on the operation of each service were made by lawyers, with the exception of the Tasmanian statement, made by Mrs R. Langford, Secretary of the Aboriginal Information Centre. Mr P. Slicer, a solicitor from Tasmania, raised objections to the whole concept as embodied in the document. As he expressed the key issue:

> Is it to be controlled by experts or technocrats, no matter how well intentioned, or is the real basis of control going to come from the Aborigines themselves?

His fellow lawyers seemed to have difficulty understanding the thrust of his argument. It should be remembered that the constitutions of most of the legal services already provided for Aboriginal majorities on the governing councils, so that presidents of those services were working on the assumption that Aboriginal involvement was assured. But that was not true of every service and it is interesting that this conference did not see any need to write the requirement of Aboriginal control into the basic document relating to the national service. At a later conference, held in December 1973, the matter of Aboriginal self-determination was much more in the forefront of discussion. In response to a threat of take-over by the Australian Legal Aid Office, established by the Attorney-General, delegates stressed the unique features of their service. As one expressed it:

> We are especially capable of running a service for Aboriginals, because we are controlled by Aboriginals, we have Aboriginal personnel, we are capable of communicating to Aboriginals in a way that no-one else in the community is, we are an Aboriginal-oriented Service.

Or as Eric Kyle, the Aboriginal Secretary of the Queensland service said:

> This service has been brought by the people for the people, the Aboriginal people themselves. The Aboriginal people brought this forward

for the Aboriginal people. We do not want a cold-blooded service that this Attorney-General's Department is going to put forward . . . The way the service is going now, the way the service has been set up, it is a warm service and people can approach it.

It is clear, then, that the Aboriginal Legal Services actually have twin objectives. One is to provide legal assistance to Aborigines who need it. The other, equally important, is to promote Aboriginal self-determination by involving Aborigines in the running of the services.

I turn now to an examination of the extent to which Aboriginal Legal Services have reached their objectives. This leads on to discussion of possible conflict between the two main objectives and other problems facing the Aboriginal Legal Services or which may face them in the future.

The objective of providing legal assistance to Aborigines The crudest measure of the success of a legal service is the number of cases handled. Figures may be cited which show a high level of acceptance of the Aboriginal legal services by Aboriginal clients. At the time of the first national conference in April 1973, for example, the New South Wales service was already opening about 1,100 files a year. The case load in Brisbane was running at about 130 a month. By contrast, the general Legal Assistance Committee in that city sees only about eight Aboriginal clients a month. The South Australian Aboriginal Legal Rights Movement had handled over 250 matters since it started in November 1971. After the appointment of a full-time field officer in December 1972 and a full-time solicitor in March 1973 the number of cases increased substantially. In the period from 16 March to 23 October 1973 the movement solicitor personally handled 221 cases of which 115 had been completed. In addition, many cases were referred to outside lawyers. In Victoria 254 files were finalised for the quarter ending 31 December 1973. These included matters handled by the service's own solicitor and those referred to other solicitors.[3]

It is possible that most of these Aboriginal clients would not have obtained legal assistance in the absence of the Aboriginal legal services. No studies have yet been carried out comparing legal representation of Aborigines in a particular area before and after the establishment of an Aboriginal legal service. But earlier research showed a generally low level of utilisation of legal services among Aborigines (Eggleston 1970:V). Also relevant is the fact that the Victorian service, after initially attempting to operate through referrals to the Legal Aid Committee, abandoned the effort, because it found that Aboriginal clients were not able to satisfy the conditions imposed by the Committee.[4]

Another basis for assessing the Aboriginal legal services would be to compare the number of cases taken with the amount of unmet legal need in the Aboriginal community. It is relatively easy to count the number of Aborigines appearing in court who do not have legal representation. Statistics have been produced for some areas in relation to criminal cases (Eggleston 1970:V). It is more difficult to quantify unmet legal need in civil matters and particularly where legal advice is required in relation to matters not involving litigation. The purpose of the Aboriginal legal services is to do for an Aboriginal client all the things which a lawyer would do for an ordinary client.

Legal assistance to Aboriginals is to be available for:

(a) representation in courts and tribunals throughout Australia where the Aboriginal has grounds for such representation;
(b) advice and action (i.e. preparation of letters, documents, registration, incorporation, etc.) on matters in which the Aboriginal has or is likely to have a direct interest whether personally or as a member of a group.[5]

Aboriginal legal services have so far tended to concentrate on criminal cases. In Victoria, for example, of the 254 cases finalised in the quarter ending 31 December 1973 there were 184 criminal cases (72 per cent of the total). The balance between criminal and civil cases is more even in South Australia. In Tasmania the experience has been that more civil than criminal cases are handled. Representation of Aboriginal defendants charged with criminal offences is an area of obvious urgent need. Some people see the main function of Aboriginal legal services as keeping Aborigines out of gaol. But in the long term, the civil side of the work may become more important. The Victorian service, though it has devoted most of its resources to the criminal field, has also performed useful work in civil matters. It drew up the documents of incorporation of an Aboriginal theatre company, for example. The provision of a legal structure within which groups can function should help to strengthen group identity.

Volume of work alone is not a very useful index of the efficiency of a legal service. Attention should be directed also to the results of legal action taken and to client satisfaction. The South Australian Aboriginal Legal Rights Movement provided legal representation in one case which produced profound results in terms of the outcome of criminal charges laid, the sentences imposed and the consequent effect on the morale of local Aborigines. In May 1972 thirteen Aborigines from Yalata Mission were charged with a total of 121 offences connected with an incident at a roadhouse (White 1974). All defendants were represented by the Movement. The presence of legal representatives who challenged the way in which the police had framed the charges, led to the dropping of many of the charges. Finally the group was convicted of a total of eighteen charges. Two defendants were sentenced to imprisonment for up to fourteen days; the rest were fined small amounts. This was one of the few occasions that any Aborigines on the West Coast had pleaded not guilty to any charges. There is little doubt that if these men and boys had been undefended all would have received substantial terms of imprisonment. In view of the trivial nature of some of the charges originally preferred against them, that would have been an unjust result. The South Australian Movement has also observed that as a result of its involvement there has been a noticeable decrease in the number of charges levelled against Aborigines in Adelaide for offences like loitering, begging alms and resisting and hindering arrest. Police respect for Aboriginal rights is increasing in this state and elsewhere.

In the United States the legal services established under the Office of Economic Opportunity have adopted a new philosophy of what legal practice means (Cahn and Cahn 1964; Note, Neighbourhood Law Offices 1967). They developed the idea of the storefront office, strategically situated in poor neighbourhoods to overcome physical and psychological barriers to use by the poor of legal services. To them decentralisation meant moving out from the central city area to poorer areas of the city. They have had little success in penetrating rural areas, with the exception of the Indian legal services on reservations. The Indian legal services were relatively late on the scene.

In Australia the pioneers in developing new concepts of legal service have been the Aboriginal Legal Services. They have been influenced by American ideas but have adapted to local needs and have produced new ideas of their own. Their judgment that 'in the past, we have been the only community law service in Australia' and that the Australian Legal Aid Office is following their lead into this new field is, I think, a fair one. The hope is that the Australian Legal Aid Office will extend to other poor members of the Australian community the benefits of legal assistance which are now beginning to be enjoyed by Aborigines.

Aboriginal legal services set up storefront offices in inner city areas like Redfern and Fitzroy, which are readily accessible to Aboriginal clients. The informality of application procedures and the involvement of Aboriginal employees destroy any inhibitions potential clients might have about approaching a legal office. The services have also seen the need to decentralise into the country, though that has not yet proceeded as far as some states would like. In Western Australia, for example, 80 per cent of the Aboriginal population lives in the country. Many live in areas where there are no practising lawyers. Even where local solicitors have offered to act, the service would prefer to use its own lawyers. The Aborigines do not trust country solicitors, whom they identify with the local white 'Establishment'. Recent moves to decentralise in Western Australia are a step in the right direction but the vast distances involved create enormous problems if the aim is effective representation of every Aboriginal person in the state.

Another important policy of American legal services is participation of the local community in the running of the services. As I have suggested, Aboriginal control of the services is also a key concept in this country. Because of its importance this topic will be more extensively discussed later. There are a number of other innovative features of Aboriginal legal services. One is their willingness to become involved in the field of social welfare. They will give advice on non-legal matters. It is also contemplated that they may employ social workers. The Queensland service employed a social worker for a period but has not been able to replace her since her resignation.

The Department of Aboriginal Affairs has shown concern that some Aboriginal legal services have exhibited a tendency to go beyond legal aid into other areas such as social welfare. It wished to emphasise that grants are given to legal aid services solely for legal aid purposes. Having in the past given grants on flexible terms and having been criticised for it by members of the public and of Parliament, the Department has now become over-anxious about how its grants are spent. The result is, in my view, an unduly narrow interpretation of what is meant by legal services (note that what is at issue is legal services, not legal aid). The lawyer delegates at the Aboriginal legal services conferences refused to accept any narrow definition of their function. It is interesting that lawyers had a wider conception of what a lawyer may properly do than many laymen present. Partly this is due to their realisation that even in traditional legal practice the lawyer often gives advice which is essentially non-legal. After all the client who enters a lawyer's office does not know whether the problem which is bothering him is one for which there is a legal solution or not. Lawyers associated with Aboriginal legal services are also well aware of the rethinking of the lawyer's role which has taken place recently, particularly in America (Note, The New Public Interest Lawyers 1970; Wexler 1970; Ginger 1972). Many lawyers now accept community organisation as a proper function for a lawyer to perform. Lawyers dealing with a poor clientele are forced to a realisation, if they did not know it before, that legal and social problems are inextricably interwoven. It therefore makes sense to have social welfare advice readily available to clients of the legal service. This is not to say that the lawyer himself will necessarily give that advice; nor does it necessarily demand a trained social worker on the premises. But some arrangement for provision of that kind of service is a necessary adjunct of an Aboriginal legal service.

In the same vein are the bail funds established by some of the services and the Half-Way House set up by at least one of them. The bail fund of the Victorian service, for example, has worked extremely well. It consists of money raised by way of subscriptions and donations from members of the community and of the legal profession. It is in the nature of a revolving fund which can be used time and time again as people answer to their bail. It has undoubtedly kept many people out of prison while waiting for trials or appeals to be heard. In most cases the field officer acts as surety. Only three people have failed to appear after having been released on bail. A Half-Way House for persons released from gaol, on bail, or awaiting trial was opened in October 1973 by the Victorian service. It also has contributed to keeping a number of clients out of gaol. However, the policy is that the Half-Way House should be used only for short-term stays. There is still a need for a hostel for released prisoners which would enable them to stay for longer periods during which they could undergo training or find employment. Whether such a hostel would be most appropriately run by the legal service is a matter for the local Aboriginal community. The service itself has given consideration to opening a hostel or home for young boys who would otherwise be sent to a Social Welfare Department institution. It also considered the possibility of establishing a home for alcoholic men, but lack of resources has precluded any further action.

Another innovative project is the employment of duty solicitors by the Western Australian service. These lawyers attend regularly at lower courts in the Perth metropolitan area where a number of Aborigines are brought into court. They are able to appear for any Aborigines who need legal representation; they also arrange bail, advise on the appropriate plea and so on. The services contemplated other activities which were also part of the philosophy of the American Neighbourhood Law Offices, namely preventative law, law reform through test cases and research on Aboriginal legal problems. Quoting again from the document approved at the April conference:

> Research assistance into the special legal problems of Aboriginals is envisaged. So also is publicity about each service's activities, and programmes of education about the legal system and personal rights under it, specifically directed to Aboriginals and persons or groups who deal with Aboriginals.[6]

In these areas the services have fallen short of their own goals. Very little research has been done, other than legal research narrowly directed to the immediate needs of individual clients. Test case litigation has not been consciously undertaken. The American view is that lawyers for the poor should be aiming to restructure society. 'We came in time to conceive of our mission in this way: to find leverage points in the system to bring about a redistribution of power and income more favorable to the poor' (Carlin 1970). Many Australian lawyers working in Aboriginal legal services would accept this view in theory but it is difficult to see what they have done to put it into practice.

Publicity has not been widespread, at least if advertising through the media is considered. But from the point of view of informing Aborigines about the service the most effective means of communication is word of mouth and that seems to be working quite well. What is needed to increase Aboriginal knowledge of the service is more field officers to travel round the countryside and more regional offices. There has been little in the way of educational programmes directed toward Aborigines. Nor has there been much in the way of formal educational programmes aimed at people who deal with Aborigines, such as police officers, justices of the peace, magistrates and judges. However, the mere presence of a legal representative who speaks up for his Aboriginal client's rights can have profound educative influence on officers of the law. Some instances of this effect were noted earlier. The South Australian Legal Rights Movement has probably done most in these areas. It has set up a number of sub-committees to deal with particular matters, including one to report on the inadequacies of the state anti-discrimination law. It has five members on the Police/Aboriginal Liaison Committee. Some of its members have lectured to police officers. The Judges of the Central and District Criminal Court have invited the Movement to prepare material on sentencing to be distributed among them. It is hoped that all services will expand their activities in these areas. Overall the Aboriginal legal services have proved to be remarkably successful in attracting and satisfying individual clients. Have they been equally successful in achieving their second major objective?

The objective of promoting Aboriginal self-determination In the United States the Economic Opportunity Act provides that in community action programmes there should be 'maximum feasible participation' of the poor.[7] In Australia, as we have seen, no similar requirement was written into the document establishing the terms on which Aboriginal legal services were to operate. Nevertheless, it is clearly an aim of the services that Aboriginal control should be encouraged. The American experience has been that the requirement of 'maximum feasible participation' has been difficult to implement. It seems that the degree to which the poor are given control over their own destiny by being allocated seats on the governing bodies of community action programmes and legal services depends on the willingness of the non-poor to give up power to them. I say this although I am aware that complaints have been made about the apathy of the poor, their unwillingness to take responsibility and so on. In the final analysis it will probably not matter that the requirement of Aboriginal control was not spelt out when the national Aboriginal Legal Service was first set up. What will be important is the willingness of the white experts to hand over power and the readiness of Aborigines to assert their rights to manage their own affairs.

Administrative structures provide some clue to the degree of Aboriginal control, though it is necessary also to know who makes the decisions in practice. We have noted already that several of the Aboriginal legal services have constitutions requiring a majority of Aboriginal members on the council. In Victoria, for example, the council of the service has a majority of Aboriginal members. However, the full council met only about three times during the first year of the service's existence. At the last annual general meeting of the service, held on 3 April 1974, the President, Professor Waller, retired from office. The new council of the service is headed by the Aboriginal field officer as President and has an Aboriginal Vice-President, a young law student. Two white lawyers were elected by the meeting to act as Secretary and Treasurer. They had previously been serving in those capacities. The rest of the council is overwhelmingly Aboriginal in composition. It also includes three nominated members: one is the nominee of the Victorian Ministry of Aboriginal Affairs, one of the Victorian Bar Council and one of the Law Institute of Victoria. This new council represents a significant step forward in Aboriginal control of the service. It is interesting that Aboriginal members of the service deferred to white lawyers by selecting them as Secretary and Treasurer. The duties of these positions require general administrative skills rather than specifically legal skills. It is true that lawyers, by virtue of their education, including limited training in keeping accounts, and the nature of their work, are generally more expert in these fields than most Aborigines, who lack formal education.

This brings us back to the question of whether the large government grants have been an unmixed blessing. The size of the government grants and the demand from the government for strict accounting of how the money has been spent tend to exert pressures in favour of the expert and against the Aboriginal non-expert. This is so even though officially federal government Aboriginal policy now stresses Aboriginal self-determination. There is no reason, though, why Aborigines should not be trained to take on the tasks required of the honorary Secretary and Treasurer of the service. Aboriginal legal services can promote Aboriginal self-determination and enhance Aboriginal identity and dignity in a number of ways. First is the membership of Aborigines on the councils and executive committees of the services. Second is the employment of Aborigines in positions of responsibility as field officers, liaison officers, and secretaries. Finally there is the effect on Aboriginal clients of assertion of their legal rights. By learning that they can stand up to injustice, Aboriginal confidence is increased.

Is there then any conflict between the two main objectives of providing legal assistance and of promoting Aboriginal self-determination? If Aboriginal legal services, whether controlled by Aborigines or by lawyers or other experts, are in the business of providing legal services to those who need them, where is the possibility of conflict? On one side it may be said that the demand for Aboriginal control of the services is a demand for non-expertness, for a second-class service for Aboriginal clients. It may be, for example, that Aboriginal people, without the experience of administering a legal office, will not be able to handle the volume of work which could be dealt with if all administrative positions were filled by experts. In Queensland, conflict erupted when an Aboriginal field officer complained that whites were dominating the running of the service, and demanded more power for

Aborigines. Ultimately he was forced to resign. Comments on the incident made by white lawyers indicated that they saw the field officer's actions as playing politics. They thought he had neglected to consider the needs of Aboriginal clients of the service. As one lawyer said: 'The Aboriginal clients could not understand what the fuss was about. Many of them had not heard of [the field officer]. As long as they were getting legal assistance they did not care who controlled the service.'[8]

This approach, which can be used to justify lawyer domination of a service, fails to do justice to the case for Aboriginal control.[9] A distinction needs to be made between administrative tasks and the formulation of policy. American programmes have found that the infinite need for legal services in poor communities requires them to set some priorities about which cases should be taken. There may be, for example, a difference between individual and group needs. The programme may decide to concentrate on test cases which have the potential to affect many individuals in the future rather than on the cases of individuals who happen to present themselves with problems that are unique to themselves. The programme may decide to seek out people who need legal assistance, rather than simply serve those with the initiative to seek out the service. It may decide to allocate a large proportion of its resources to educating Aborigines about the law, so that they avoid trouble in the future, rather than spending all its resources (both of money and staff time) in dealing with the immediate legal problems of individual clients.

These are difficult policy decisions and it is in this area that Aboriginal people are particularly well qualified to act. It should be up to them to determine priorities, since they have a better understanding of the real needs of the Aboriginal community than any white lawyer is likely to have. The Native American Rights Fund in Boulder, Colorado, has an all-Indian Steering Committee which sets policy. It determined that it was important to take test cases on behalf of young Indians who had been excluded from school for wearing long hair. A member of the organisation financing the Fund found this decision difficult to understand but went along with it because it had been agreed that Indians should determine policy. The Indians well appreciated the significance of the long hair cases, as involving the perpetuation of Indian tradition and the right of Indians to remain Indian rather than being forced to assimilate into the wider community. Similarly, DNA, the legal service programme on the Navajo Reservation, derives its strength from the extent to which it involves local Indian communities in decision-making.[10] Some of the Indian representatives are illiterate, yet that is obviously not a disqualification for knowing what the people want. What this implies for the Australian scene is that lawyers should only act in areas where their expertise is essential and that otherwise they should deliberately withdraw. It is difficult for lawyers to understand that their mere presence may inhibit Aboriginal decision-making. At the very least, lawyers should carefully think through their position on Aboriginal control of legal services and try to delineate areas where they feel that a lawyer's involvement is essential. They may not all reach the conclusion to which I have come, that Aboriginal involvement is to be preferred even if it means some loss of efficiency, but they should become more aware of what is at stake.

So far the discussion has concerned mainly lawyers on councils of Aboriginal legal services. The situation of the lawyer employed to do legal work on

behalf of the service is somewhat different and raises further issues. To these
we now turn.

Relationship of the retained lawyer to the council of the legal service

There exists the possibility of clash between what is demanded of the lawyer
by the ethics of his profession and Aboriginal requests for action. One solicitor
raised this question at the December conference when he referred to the
potential problem that could foreseeably exist in an office where the committee attempted to control the professional ability of the solicitor. The
problem was discussed in the context of a direction by the Aboriginal governing body to take on a particular case which the lawyer was ethically forced
to decline, because he was aware that the client intended to commit perjury
in court, for example. Bruce McGuinness, an Aboriginal delegate from
Victoria, said: 'It seems to me that, although Aborigines ought not to impinge
on the professionalism of solicitors, surely the solicitors are in turn answerable,
in the way they conduct their case, to the Aboriginal community . . .' Later
he said: 'We understand that, by saying to a community that on ethical
grounds you cannot take a case, that is ample reason, that is ample excuse,
that is sufficient'. If this view is generally accepted among Aborigines it
provides the basis for a reasonable working arrangement between the
employed or retained lawyer and the Aborigines who control the legal
service.

Nevertheless it seems likely that further incidents will occur in legal
services, when serious divisions of opinion exist between the most militant
Aborigines on one side and moderate Aborigines aligned with white lawyers
on the other. In the Northern Territory, an Aboriginal field officer was
involved in the Nola Garanamba affair. A young Aboriginal girl who had
been fostered with a white family was taken from them on the pretext of a
day's outing and returned to her natural family on an Aboriginal settlement,
where she remains. A lawyer in such a situation will take the view that such
direct action is wrong and unnecessary because there was legal action which
could have been taken to have the girl restored to her natural parents. It is
likely that the majority of Aborigines involved with the legal service will
support that view. After all, trust in a legal service implies a commitment to
working within the law, to accepting the basic political and legal structure of
the society. Similarly, one cannot really expect a lawyer to support the
advocacy of violence as a method of achieving Aboriginal objectives.

Does this mean that the supporters of direct action should be dismissed
from the legal service and their viewpoint forgotten? Is it enough to say that
they are unrepresentative, that they have few followers? It seems to me that,
on the contrary, Aboriginal legal services should endeavour to represent all
shades of Aboriginal opinion from the most moderate to the most militant.
The voice of violence is an authentic Aboriginal voice, even though it speaks
for a minority. It may prove to be impossible to cater for such a diverse
range of opinions within the one organisation. But I believe that we, as
white lawyers, must at least try to understand the depth of resentment
against the legal system and what it has done to the Aboriginal people.

All Aborigines within the locality served by the legal service are members
of the client community, either as present or potential clients. It might be
thought then that representativeness can only be ensured by elections at

which voting is compulsory for all members of the Aboriginal community. But the system operating in Victoria appears satisfactory, even though voting is confined to those Aborigines sufficiently interested to become members of the legal service and to attend its meetings. The question of decentralisation is relevant here too. What is the appropriate size of the unit which should have a board to decide policy for the Aboriginal legal service? DNA appears to work well because it has local committees in 98 of the 101 chapters or sub-districts on the Navajo reservation. There are efficient lines of communication between this grassroots level and the central office. The governing Board of Directors of the programme includes representatives of each of the five administration areas of the reservation. It has twenty-two Navajo members and eight non-Indian members.

There is another compelling reason for ensuring that all shades of Aboriginal opinion are represented on the governing bodies of Aboriginal legal services. It is essential to avoid the entrenchment of an Aboriginal 'Establishment' in the service, responsive only to its own faction and distrusted by other Aborigines. In the United States this problem has been particularly acute on some reservations, where tribal councils have real political power and the ability to disburse large amounts of government money. Allegations of factionalism and corruption in relation to the allocation of resources have been levelled at some tribal councils. The historical development of legal services for Indians was that first the tribal councils obtained counsel; only later did individuals obtain access to Indian legal services. The employment of counsel on a permanent basis gave the tribes hitting power in their dealings with the government (Dobyns 1970), but it did nothing for the position of individual Indians, except to the extent that they benefited as members of the tribe. The OEO Indian Legal Services, referred to earlier in this paper, have redressed the balance, since they act for individuals rather than for tribes. But there is some reluctance on their part to initiate legal action against tribal councils on behalf of tribal members. They believe it is essential to preserve tribal sovereignty, in order to keep tribes strong in their dealings with the federal government. Anything which weakens tribal councils weakens the political power of all Indians. Therefore any such action is strictly scrutinised by Indian legal services.

It is likely that a similar problem, if it occurs in Australia, will arise on one of the reserves where royalties are accruing to a tribal group or where business enterprises produce profits for the residents. With funds advanced by the Aboriginal Capital Fund some groups are hiring lawyers. No information is yet available on relationships between these lawyers and their clients. The possibility that one faction may use its access to a lawyer to entrench its position within the Aboriginal community should be borne in mind. One way to lessen its adverse effects would be to preserve the right of any Aboriginal to use the legal services available in the general community if he does not wish to avail himself of Aboriginal legal services.

Aboriginal legal services in the future: the prospect of change In spite of problems they have faced and will confront in future, Aboriginal legal services have been a remarkable success in their short history. This may surprise people who regard lawyers as members of the most traditional, hide-bound profession. The success story appears to be due to two factors:

first, the fact that Aboriginal communities had already changed to the extent that they included individuals prepared to assert their rights and self-confident enough to approach lawyers for help. The second factor is the changes which have been occurring in the legal profession; the reassessment of their role being undertaken by many practitioners, and a readiness to consider new forms of legal practice. Some lawyers are now anxious to demystify the profession, to make it accessible to all, especially the poor, who at present have least access to it. Though these more radical lawyers are still in a minority, there are enough of them to supply the legal talent needed in the Aboriginal legal services. Even the conventional view of the lawyer's role is conducive to Aboriginal self-determination. The lawyer has traditionally regarded his function as being to act as a mouthpiece for his client. He offers the client advice on the law and then waits for the client's decision as to what action should be taken. Of course, in practice, it does not always work out like that; the lawyer exerts greater or lesser influence, depending on his personality and that of his client. It will be necessary for some lawyers in the Aboriginal field to learn to exercise more self-restraint and truly to accept direction from their clients. Many have already been educated by their experiences in the Aboriginal legal services.

As for the future, it is hoped that developments will proceed in the direction of further Aboriginal autonomy. To preserve the unique virtues of the Aboriginal legal services it will be necessary to resist attempts to incorporate them within other legal services: the battlelines have already been drawn with the Attorney-General's Department but it is not yet certain that the fight is over. Excessively detailed control by the Department of Aboriginal Affairs must also be resisted. To make the services fully effective, they will need to develop programmes of community education and law reform, perhaps by establishing clearing-houses and backup centres. But a good start has been made.

Acknowledgements

The information for this paper was drawn largely from the transcripts of the two Aboriginal legal services conferences which have been held. As these documents are not widely available I have not referred to specific pages of the transcript. The amount of information available on different state services varied.

Dr Elizabeth Eggleston died late in 1976. [Editor]

Notes

1. The scheme using law students from Melbourne and Monash Universities was not successful, primarily because the students were able to attend only on a roster one half-day each week. This did not provide sufficient continuity of service; clients needing legal advice did not necessarily appear at the League's office at the time the students were there. Most matters were too urgent to be held over for the students' next visit.

2. A National Aboriginal Legal Service Government Proposals. 47 Law Institute Journal 239 (1973). The document is there set out in the amended form adopted by the conference.

3. Information supplied to Annual General Meeting of Victorian Aboriginal Legal Service held on 3 April 1974. The other figures are drawn from delegates' reports to the Aboriginal Legal Services conferences. They are obviously not readily comparable, both because of the form of presentation and because some relate to a period in which all work was voluntary while other services had full-time employees.

4. Victorian Aboriginal Legal Service, first year of operation — 1973.

5. A National Aboriginal Legal Service: Government Proposals. 47 Law Institute Journal 239 (1973). Clause 4. Clause 5 provides a limited restriction on the taking of appeals. Though it was agreed at the conference that another proposed restriction would be eliminated, it still appears in guidelines used by the Department of Aboriginal Affairs, which now funds the ALS. This appears to be due to an oversight and the restriction will not appear once the guidelines are amended. It reads as follows: 'actions to be taken on behalf of an Aboriginal community or a substantial Aboriginal group will be considered on an individual basis by the Australian Government following an approach by a Service'.

6. A National Aboriginal Legal Service: Government Proposals. 47 Law Institute Journal 239 (1973).

7. Economic Opportunity Act of 1964. Section 244 (42 U.S.C. 2836).

8. This is not a verbatim quotation, but reproduces the sense of an interview with a lawyer at the Aboriginal Legal Service in Brisbane in March 1974.

9. It is fair to say that this particular controversy involved other strands, including allegations of violence, which may have justified the particular action taken. I am not concerned here with the rights and wrongs of this case but with the general principle of expert control versus Aboriginal control.

10. Information on DNA was obtained on a personal visit and from Mr T. Purcell, Executive Director of the New South Wales Law Foundation. I am grateful to Mr Purcell for making available to me his unpublished report on DNA.

References

CAHN, E. S. and J. C. CAHN 1964 The war on poverty: a civilian perspective, *Yale Law Journal*, 73:1317-52.
CARLIN, J. E. 1970 Store front lawyers in San Francisco, *Transaction*. Reprinted in *The politics of the powerless* (R. H. Binstock and K. Ely eds). Winthrop, Cambridge, Mass., 1971.
CHISHOLM, R. 1971 The Aboriginal legal service, *Justice*, (4):26-33.
DOBYNS, H. F. 1970 Therapeutic experience of responsible democracy. In *The American Indian today* (S. Levine and N. O. Lurie eds). Penguin Books, Harmondsworth.
EGGLESTON, E. M. 1970 Aborigines and the administration of justice. Ph.D. thesis, Monash University.
GINGER, A. F. (ed.) 1972 *The relevant lawyers*. Simon and Schuster, New York.
NOTE, 1967 Neighborhood Law Offices: the new wave in legal services for the poor, *Harvard Law Review*, 80:805-50.
NOTE, 1970 The new public interest lawyers, *Yale Law Journal*, 79:1069-152.
POTTER, C. E., JR. 1974 Poverty law practice: the Aboriginal Legal Service in New South Wales. Research seminar on Aborigines and the Law, Centre for Research into Aboriginal Affairs, Monash University, 12-16 July.
——1974 Poverty law practice: the Aboriginal Legal Service in New South Wales. Australasian Universities Law Schools Association 29th Annual Conference held at Monash University, 19-21 August.
WEXLER, S. 1970 Practicing law for poor people, *Yale Law Journal*, 79:1049-67.
WHITE, I. M. 1974 The Nundroo incident: the trial of an Aboriginal football team. In *Aborigines in the 70s; Seminars 1972-3*. Centre for Research into Aboriginal Affairs, Monash University.

26 Aboriginal political change in an urban setting:

the N.A.C.C. election in Perth

Michael Howard

To anthropologists and political scientists elections have long been viewed as being ideal situations in which to examine a people's politics in that they provide a 'bottle-neck' which concentrates political activities (cf. Mackenzie 1957, and Epstein, Parker and Reay (eds) 1971). They may thus be treated as a 'social situation' in that they lend themselves to being abstracted as a 'temporally and spatially bounded series of events' (Garbett 1970:216). However, an election, much like the bridge opening ceremony in southern Africa analysed by Gluckman (1958), is a special social situation in that political activities are concentrated in them in cases where they are taken seriously. Where elections are newly introduced they provide an ideal situation for analysing the process of political change, as well as of the political system in general, as a people make choices in response to the new situation. Thus, the recent N.A.C.C. (the National Aboriginal Consultative Committee) election in Perth provides an excellent opportunity for examining urban Aboriginal politics in the process of change.[1]

The sociocultural niche To provide background for the analysis of the N.A.C.C. election and an examination of the changes resulting from it, it is first necessary to provide a brief review of the niche occupied by Aborigines in south-west Western Australia within their sociocultural environment in a historical perspective and of the development of Aboriginal politics in response to this niche.[2]

By the late 19th century the Aboriginal population in the area concerned was quite small. Disease and other factors had contributed to a considerable depopulation of the full-blood Aborigines since the first settlement of Europeans in the 1820s. During this same period the number of part-Aborigines slowly increased (from about 600 in the south-west in 1890 to around 3,500 in 1930 and to over 8,000 in 1960) as the number of full-bloods in the area decreased. The living conditions of some part-Aborigines in the late 19th century were not particularly bad, compared to what they were to become, in relation to the non-Aboriginal population. In 1901 nearly one-third were formally literate, many children were attending school and several families owned their own farms. Also, legally part-Aborigines were not in too disadvantageous a position in comparison with the rest of Australian society.

From about 1905 onward, the condition of Aborigines in the south-west in general, and of part-Aborigines in particular, deteriorated. Of considerable importance was the 1905 *Aborigines Act* which broadened the definition of an Aboriginal to include most part-Aborigines. From this date, until after World War II, increasingly repressive legislation was introduced which progressively led to a deterioration of Aboriginal rights and living standards. The adverse reaction to the part-Aborigines may be seen as being related to their increasing number (and hence visibility) and to the deteriorating economic condition following the First World War. By 1915 most part-Aboriginal farmers had lost their land and in almost every sphere of activity they were increasingly discriminated against. Thus, beginning around 1914 Aboriginal children were being expelled from schools at an increasing rate (often to 'protect the health' of the other pupils). In 1915 Carrolup settlement was opened, resulting in the segregation of many Aborigines. Another such settlement was established at Moore River in 1918. In 1922, Carrolup was closed and the inmates were sent to Moore River. Increasingly large numbers of Aborigines were placed in these institutions until by 1922 over 400 were in Moore River (almost 20 per cent of the south-west Aboriginal population). During the remainder of the 1920s and the 1930s this overall trend of increasing discrimination continued and with the 1936 *Native Administration Act* the Department of Native Welfare was given almost complete control over a sizeable proportion of the Aboriginal population.

Changing conditions during and after World War II finally led to a partial reversal of the above trend. During the war many Aborigines served in the armed forces and others found employment in related jobs. Also, world and public opinion became more liberal and the repressive laws regarding Aborigines became increasingly unpopular and embarrassing for Australia. After the war the new Commissioner of Native Welfare in Western Australia (John Middleton, who took over the post in 1948) introduced a policy of more enlightened paternalism and sought to promote the assimilation of Aborigines into Australian society. During the next twenty years many Aboriginal rights were slowly restored (from the perspective of the part-Aborigines) or provided (from the perspective of the full-blood) and educational and occupational opportunities increased. Finally, in 1967, Aborigines were given the same legal rights as other Australians. The importance of this action was somewhat muted, however, by the state of near 'anomie' on the part of some Aboriginal people due to the past nature of their condition and, perhaps more importantly, the continued presence of racism and discrimination. The post-1967 period has, despite these problems, witnessed an increase in opportunity for Aborigines in many areas.

The development of Aboriginal politics Throughout the period covered above Aboriginal politics in south-west Australia tended to develop in response to the changing nature of the sociocultural niche which they occupied. With the introduction of the 1905 *Aboriginal Act* and the increasing deterioration of the rights and conditions of part-Aborigines, protests were mounted by some of the more articulate ones. These protests continued into the mid-1920s and crystallised with the formation of the Native Union, the first part-Aboriginal political organisation in the state. By the end of the 1920s this form of protest had virtually disappeared. From this time until the Second World War the condition of Aborigines generally left little room for mounting organised protests. Aboriginal politics became increasingly 'the politics of the asylum, hospital, camp, or other authoritarian institution' (Rowley 1970b:190, and cf. Goffman 1961) as state control over their activities increased.

One type of Aboriginal spokesman appears to have been present since the earliest contact with Europeans — the cultural broker.[3] Such brokers may be defined as 'individuals who place people in touch with each other either directly or indirectly for profit' (Boissevain 1969:380 and 1973). This category included many of the so-called 'kings', those who worked for the police, various informers or 'stoolies' and numerous other individuals. As cultural brokers these individuals possess what Boissevain calls 'second order resources', which consist of strategic contacts with other people, rather than 'first order resources' which are directly controlled.

Much attention has been paid to the role of the cultural broker in bringing about communication. However, what is often overlooked is that such brokers often hinder, channel, or distort communication through their attempts to maintain their strategic niche. In the case of the early Aboriginal brokers, although a degree of communication was permitted between Europeans and Aborigines, it appears as if it was often necessary for these individuals to structure the flow of information to ensure the maintenance of their position. This required some distortion in many instances, due to the expectations of the non-Aboriginal patrons regarding the kinds of information desired. In many cases, what the patrons desired was to set up some Aboriginal to act as a broker who would in effect feed them information that was not too disparate from their own preconceived notions of the kind of information that should be transmitted — that is, someone who could make the Aboriginal data fit into an often narrow European mould. Although this is communication of a sort, it is of limited utility in discovering the 'truth' (from an Aboriginal perspective) and often creates an invalid picture of an Aboriginal situation. (The above deserves a much more thorough discussion than is possible here; for examples of the problem see Bates 1938 and Salvado 1854.)

An important consideration in dealing with any broker is that he will usually attempt to convert his 'second order resources' into 'first order resources' (cf. Boissevain 1969 and 1973; Eidheim 1963) and to this end create for himself a patronage niche. In an encapsulated situation, such as with the Aborigines, the broker's attempted conversion will often take the form of trying to create a patronage niche through utilisation of a person's contacts in the dominant, or European-Australian, society. This, for example, may take the form of acquiring a job which gives the holder access to first order resources. Such conversions before World War II were quite difficult, if not virtually impossible, due to a number of variables, but have become increasingly accessible in recent years. However, even those Aborigines who are able to occupy such positions often find themselves still dependent upon non-Aboriginal patrons for the maintenance of their niche.

It should be noted that some potential spokesmen did not occupy such brokerage positions since what they sought to communicate was too divergent from what the non-Aboriginal patrons desired of the brokers. Thus, especially before World War II, there was little chance of such 'leaders' being listened to by non-Aborigines (though they might in fact have some standing within the Aboriginal community). Such men were often the 'trouble-makers' who frequently found themselves in jail.

Following the Second World War, and as a result of the changing conditions and the introduction of liberal paternalistic policies, two developments appeared in Aboriginal politics. One was the resurgence of Aboriginal political activity and protest on a modest scale (cf. Berndt 1971). The second was the emergence of Aboriginal brokers to feed information to non-Aboriginal 'liberals' concerning the condition and desires of Aborigines. Again, the nature of this information was often restricted by the expectations of non-Aborigines concerned so that 'true' spokesmen or brokers were usually those who provided information that was not too divergent from the patron's preconceptions. This does not imply that a range of information could not be expressed by Aboriginal spokesmen. Due to variations in the outlook of the various non-Aborigines concerned, Aborigines espousing different views regarding Aboriginal affairs could often find patrons who were in agreement, at least to some degree, with these views. Behaviour and life-style seem to have emerged as an important criterion in maintaining legitimacy in the eyes of the non-Aboriginal patrons. This may be seen as being in part due to the increased stress on assimilating Aborigines in addition to prevalent Australian norms of behaviour.

It should be borne in mind that as conditions deteriorated for the Aborigines before World War II, anyone seeking escape from the hardships virtually required the support of non-Aboriginal patrons. Under the liberalised conditions following the war this, to a large extent, remained the case. The non-Aboriginal Australians had decided upon a policy of assimilation for Aborigines and they were the ones who dictated how this would proceed, what constituted being assimilated (cf. J. Wilson 1964) and who would be given the 'opportunity' to assimilate.

During the post-war period two types of voluntary organisation concerned with Aboriginal affairs emerged. One, represented by the Coolbaroo League (begun in 1946 and reconstituted in 1950) and the Youth Club (begun in 1957), was exclusively Aboriginal in membership with one or more non-Aboriginal patrons (cf. Wilson 1958; Makin 1970). The other type consisted of various liberal non-Aboriginal welfare groups which usually had a few token Aborigines included among their members to serve as brokers (such a position should not be seen as implying lack of motivation to help other Aborigines on the part of those occupying such positions, they may simply be seen as occupying one of the few niches available to them should they wish to help those in need of it). These groups were centralised in 1952 into the Native Welfare Council (due in part to government pressure). Aboriginal organisations faded out by the early 1960s and, in general, non-Aboriginal dominance of the various voluntary organisations and the related patron and broker relationships remained until the late 1960s.

Following the 1967 Referendum there was a marked increase in Aboriginal interest and involvement in political affairs (although the actual number of individuals involved still remained relatively small) as more sought to exploit the wider niche now available for Aboriginal activities. In many of the non-Aboriginal dominated voluntary organisations Aboriginal members have manoeuvred to try to gain control. This has met with some resistance and a few non-Aboriginal members have fought to retain their control through the support of other non-Aborigines as well as their Aboriginal clients. Several all-Aboriginal organisations have also been formed in recent years. These were originally operated on a voluntary basis and were relatively autonomous with little or no non-Aboriginal control. However, most have accepted government financial support to expand their activities and in a Weberian sense volunteerism has given way to bureaucratisation. This process has led to the lessening of autonomy on the part of some of these organisations and at present most are dependent upon government patronage for their survival.

Organising the election As has been indicated previously, the niche available for Aboriginal politics has been very limited. This situation altered somewhat following the 1967 Referendum (cf. C. H. Berndt 1969). With the Labor Party assuming office nationally in late 1972, the political environment was again altered to allow for the potentiality of increasing Aboriginal involvement in Australian political affairs due to the stated policy of the new government. The new Labor government had adopted a policy of reform in Aboriginal affairs and of increasing Aboriginal determination over their own affairs (stated policy and action of course do not always coincide). As part of the new programme of reform the idea was put forward of establishing an elected Aboriginal body to advise on Aboriginal affairs (the actual power and functioning of this body was not tightly formulated at this time and some ambiguity in these respects remains).

The work of setting up this consultative body was begun early in 1973. A steering Committee was established in Canberra for this purpose and to decide in broad terms what its role and function should be. This committee included a few West Australian Aborigines, although, in the main, it appears to have been dominated by easterners. Committee discussions in Canberra began in February and by June the members felt that most of the broad outlines and structure had been worked out. During the middle of June a two-day conference was held by the members of the committee in Perth to discuss these plans with some of the local Aborigines. Thus, throughout the course of establishing the N.A.C.C. there was little interest on the part of the steering committee in guiding their plans according to local feedback. Only once the initial guidelines were established was the plan presented locally. In reality, probably no other method was possible. For, as was indicated in the preceding review of Aboriginal political development, the channels of communication between government (and all non-Aborigines) and Aborigines tend to be limited, depending upon information supplied by cultural brokers and 'experts' on Aboriginal affairs.

During the two-day conference a tentative date of August 11 was set for the election. It was felt by some, however, that this date might be premature (as it turned out, by about two months). In presenting their plans for the N.A.C.C., the steering committee apparently continued to leave the function and power of the N.A.C.C. rather vague. What seemed paramount was that such a body be formed — it could find its feet later. At the local level this degree of ambiguity was to have important repercussions. Thus, some of those enrolling thought that they were voting for an Aboriginal Congress or Parliament. It was also used by those campaigning or trying to enrol people in a variety of ways, to either encourage or dissuade people to vote.

Being a new situation, the election machinery was loosely organised. Copying normal Australian electoral procedures was obviously not entirely possible due to the newness of the situation and the lack of institutionalised political units and procedures (there was some criticism that the organisation was a bit too loose). Briefly, there was a state-wide co-ordinator who was based in Perth. He had an assistant and a secretary. Before the actual election, the co-ordinator's principal tasks were publicising the election and getting people enrolled. Publicity involved a liberal use of the media (especially the newspaper), use of various Aboriginal-related voluntary organisations and passing information informally by word of mouth. In addition, assistance was provided by the various government agencies concerned. The candidates and their supporters were also quite active in getting people to enrol. Though, of course, this was quite selective.

Shortly after the June conference the registration drive got underway and nominations were opened. Enrolment of Aborigines in the Perth area proved to be slow and difficult. Some felt that the N.A.C.C. was yet another meaningless government project which would be of no benefit to Aboriginal people. A few specifically felt this way since the N.A.C.C. appeared to have been given little actual power. Others were suspicious of anything sponsored by the government. Still others were against placing their names on the roll since they felt that a separate body for Aborigines was wrong and contrary to a policy of assimilation. These suspicions were at times exacerbated by some of the individuals campaigning. Such individuals would in some instances inform those who they felt might vote for someone in opposition that those enrolling would lose the right to enrol on the normal roll or that those on the normal roll were not entitled to enrol on the Aboriginal one.

Many of those who did enrol did so at the urging of those actively campaigning (who were often relatives or neighbours). Also, those using the services of the various voluntary organisations were encouraged to enrol. Finally, some enrolled because they felt that they should do so as Aborigines and that the N.A.C.C. should be given a chance. It should be noted that, although it is in regular elections, voting was not compulsory (though a few who had enrolled believed that it was).

Basically, the only requirement for prospective Aboriginal candidates (the broadened definition of 'Aboriginal' was used which included all those of Aboriginal descent) to be nominated was payment of a ten-dollar fee. Eventually, eight candidates were nominated. Some prominent Aboriginal spokesmen chose not to run for a variety of reasons, such as being opposed to the N.A.C.C. on principle (although a few speculated that it was because they were afraid of losing and thus being categorised among the ranks of the 'so-called' leaders). Candidates were almost exclusively drawn from among the small group of Aborigines actively involved with voluntary organisations. Thus, most were among those who had been operating as Aboriginal spokesmen and the election was looked upon by many as a means of validating their claim to leadership by demonstrating positively that they had widespread support within the Aboriginal community.

The candidates and their resources   In any political contest, individual contestants must attempt to convert their personal resources through strategic manoeuvring, dictated by the candidate's ability to perceive his position (cf. Blau 1964) and to forecast responses (cf. Bailey 1969) to his strategy within the relevant sociocultural milieu or political arena, into support. In a highly institutionalised contest, such strategies and forecasts may be relatively clear-cut and predictable. However, in situations of radical change this becomes more difficult in relation to the degree of change or non-

institutionalisation of political activities in those spheres from which the
contestant's predictions are made. As previously stated, until the time of the
N.A.C.C. elections the structure of Aboriginal politics was predominantly
in terms of patronage and brokerage roles in relation to the nature of the
encapsulation of the Aboriginal segment of the population and the power
wielded by non-Aborigines *vis-à-vis* Aborigines. As a result, the Aboriginal
political system had to a degree become institutionalised along these lines,
enabling those involved in Aboriginal politics to formulate strategies and
forecasts within the framework of this patronage and brokerage system.
Thus, non-Aboriginal patronage was often necessary for status as an Aboriginal leader (as recognised in the non-Aboriginal, and to a degree within
the Aboriginal, community) and support and legitimacy came largely from
the non-Aboriginal sector. That is, to be a 'good' Aboriginal leader and a
'true' spokesman, not a 'so-called' leader, a particular Aboriginal had to
behave in an acceptable manner to his patron(s) and express views which
were reasonably compatible with the patron's notions of the nature of
Aboriginal society and its problems. There have been exceptions to this,
especially following World War II. However, development of more independent spokesmen has been very slow and is still made difficult by the present
socio-cultural environment. At its broadest, support and legitimation for
Aboriginal spokesmen had been in terms of the controlling cliques (usually
European-Australians and a few allied Aborigines) of the various voluntary
organisations. Within an Aboriginal community, support was rarely necessary
beyond the bounds of immediate kin and such support was often situational
due to the frequency of cross-cutting ties and the nature of inter-personal
relations between those concerned. Thus, two forms of support and legitimation were available to a potential Aboriginal leader. The first, resulting
from the nature of inter-ethnic relations and the resultant patronage system
had been the most significant and was in some ways in opposition to the
second which resulted from Aboriginal norms of kinship solidarity. This was
largely true since behaviour patterns demanded by non-Aboriginal patrons
were difficult to reconcile with the pressures toward kin-group solidarity and
mutual assistance (cf. C. H. Berndt 1962). Those who were considered by
non-Aborigines (and often by themselves) to be among the *élite* of the
Aboriginal community had difficulty in maintaining the roles required for
each form of support. Many tried to strike a balance, although the individual
strategies varied considerably. In the case of those politically involved,
expectations on the part of the non-Aborigines tended to be more important
for their political status, and the behavioural dictates of non-Aborigines
predominated in such instances at the expense of Aboriginal ones where they
came into conflict. Previously (especially before the Second World War)
the patronage links had been more important. Also, in more recent years
the 'content' (cf. Mitchell 1969:20) of the patron-client links has in many
cases become less restrictive and more freedom of action has become possible.
However, primary dependence upon a wide range of Aborigines for legitimation and support had not developed at the time of the election, although
support of kin and friends was at times important in elections within the
various voluntary organisations, and the patron-client pattern across ethnic
boundaries remained dominant.

Support for the candidates in the N.A.C.C. election was in many ways different from what had been previously required. Candidates who had acquired status through the system of patron-client relations were now forced to muster an often differing set or constellation of resources. The patron-client system was sufficiently institutionalised that forecasting was possible and strategies could be planned according to fairly established determinants. However, in the case of the N.A.C.C. election, such forecasting and strategy formulation was much more difficult. Much of the forecasting was dependent upon various Aboriginal norms which had not previously been tested to any great extent in a political contest. Thus, dependence upon untested norms and experimentation was considerable in the election strategies of the candidates as they evolved throughout the course of the campaign in response to new tactics introduced by other contestants.

Mayer (1963:120-22) mentions four potential sources of support for candidates in elections, which may be of use in analysing the N.A.C.C. election: (1) social relationships such as kinship, residence and friendship; (2) patron-client and broker links; (3) issues or principles and; (4) support due to opposition to someone or something else (the 'lesser of two evils'). The eight candidates in the N.A.C.C. election were forced to construct strategies based partly upon their perceptions of their own and of their opponents' resources as a means of gaining support. A detailed analysis of each candidate's resources is not possible in such a short paper. However, below are outlined some of the most important resources and liabilities of the various candidates. For obvious reasons, no actual names are used.

Candidate

A. A former Department of Native Welfare and A.A.P.A. employee. In 1973 took a job with a local voluntary organisation concerned with Aboriginal welfare. A has a fairly extensive kinship network in the metropolitan area (there are no links through A's spouse, who is not an Aboriginal). A has occupied a brokerage niche for many years and has been relatively dependent upon non-Aboriginal support. The organisation which A now works for is held in low esteem by some Aborigines, and employment by the government is frowned upon by many. A also has a 'drinking problem'.

B. Has been active in Aboriginal affairs for only a few years. In 1972 was employed by another voluntary organisation concerned with Aboriginal affairs (with a less tainted image at the time of the election than the one above). Has an extensive kinship network (again, B's spouse is not an Aboriginal) and B's job involves a considerable amount of brokerage activity. B is a reformed alcoholic.

C. Active in Aboriginal affairs since the 1940s and at present involved in many voluntary organisations. Has a good deal of support in the non-Aboriginal community and had been involved in the patron-broker system. Possesses a relatively large kinship network in the metropolitan area, although C's network is interrelated with those of a few of the candidates below. The oldest candidate, and in relatively poor health.

D. Active in Aboriginal affairs for only a few years. Worked briefly for the government, but not long enough to be identified with it. In 1973 elected president of the organisation which employs A, due in part to support from a growing number of Aboriginal members. Has a fairly large kinship network in the metropolitan area, but the links overlap with some of the other candidates and some have been left fairly dormant over the years. Also, one of D's most influential relatives came out strongly against the N.A.C.C.

E. An ex-alcoholic active in rehabilitation work for a few years. Little identification with local voluntary organisations. A very small and weak kin network in Perth.

F. During the 1950s had been marginally identified with a few voluntary organisations in Perth. A pensioner. During the course of the campaign, tried to form a voluntary organisation in one neighbourhood. Most kin links in Perth through spouse (who has an extensive network, which overlaps with B's). A good deal of gossip about F's personal behaviour.

G. Youngest candidate. Fairly well educated. Active for a short time in some of the voluntary organisations. G had a 'drinking problem', but is now reformed. In 1973 started working with a government department after losing a job with one of the voluntary organisations. Has a fairly large kinship network, but it overlaps with some of the above.

H. Active for several years in various non-Aboriginal organisations and for a short time with the same organisation as A and D. Has made use of patron links over the years. Again, a fairly large kinship network, but overlapping (especially with C).

Each of these candidates was assured of the support of a core of close kin and friends. However, beyond these (especially where such links had previously been neglected) support became increasingly problematical. The main difficulty facing candidates was how to create a wide base of support, since this had not previously existed within the Aboriginal community. In fact, as has been stated earlier, maintenance of spokesman status often meant limiting the 'content' of personal networks involving other Aborigines. Now these links, which had in some instances been allowed to become quite dormant, had to be extended and strengthened.

The campaign   In any campaign, some means of feedback is necessary to determine the effectiveness of one's strategy and to make the necessary adjustments. This often takes the form of an independent source to check on the electorate (cf. Mayer 1963:124). However, due to the newness of such situations as the N.A.C.C. election, in which feedback had previously been within completely different spheres, such a check is extremely difficult. This means that the effectiveness of one's campaign strategy is difficult to assess until after the election (and it may remain so even then). As with Mayer's study of elections in India, so in the Perth case, when kin or friends were asked to vote for someone they would invariably agree. Thus, one person who was related to several of the candidates might promise to vote for each of them. Such a situation requires independent assessment or some sort of 'spying' arrangement to get an accurate picture of one's support.

Initially, the various candidates did very little campaigning. What there was consisted primarily of random personal conversations with friends and relatives requesting support. However, by late September, with the election drawing near (it was at this time set for November 14th) and as it began to appear as if the N.A.C.C. would actually become a reality (scepticism in this regard played an important role in lessening the intensity of the campaign during the previous months), the tempo of electioneering increased considerably.

As pointed out by Bailey (1969:5), campaign strategies are based upon 'pragmatic' rules (or assumptions), which are broadly bounded by general and vague 'normative' ones. These pragmatic rules 'recommend tactics and manoeuvres as likely to be the most efficient' (Bailey 1969:5). Candidates' strategies may also be seen as containing two basic aspects which they try to convey to the voter: (1) why support me (this involves capitalising upon the contestant's resources), and (2) why not to support the opposition (which involves capitalising upon differences and the opposition's liabilities). In both cases these vary according to a person's perception, and situationally according to the audience being addressed. Pragmatic rules dictate the most effective means by which to convey these aims. In the case of the N.A.C.C. candidates, such rules had to be drawn largely from non-Aboriginal politics in an effort to create a wider base of support and modified to fit the Aboriginal situation (in some cases the modifications were not adequate and the tactics proved ineffective in the different environment). The content to be conveyed, however, was relatively specific to the Aboriginal setting. Thus, the content of the strategies was specific to the Aboriginal situation and to Aboriginal values and social relations while, where support was sought over a wide spectrum of the Aboriginal population, the means of conveying it was largely of non-Aboriginal derivation.

The tactics of the various contestants varied individually and over time. Thus, while some candidates maintained a 'low-key', personal type of campaign (which tended not to reach a large number of Aborigines) others developed increasingly 'Europeanised' types of campaign (especially candidates A, B and H). The development of these tactics was largely in response to innovations introduced by individual candidates. In this respect, when one candidate issued a leaflet about himself, others followed in an effort to keep pace with the innovator. The effectiveness of such moves was often difficult to judge, due to the previously discussed uncertainty in forecasting. Most candidates adopted the leaflet approach. One went so far as to place advertisements in a local newspaper. Perhaps the most important innovation, one which was utilised by only a few of the candidates (the recognised front-runners), was the systematic use of campaign workers. This began with one candidate introducing a 'campaign manager', and a few others then organised supporters in various parts of the metropolitan area. The variation in tactics, once either the systematisation of electioneering assistants or the use of leaflets was adopted, is probably related to several factors: the lack of precise rules due to the newness of the situation; realisation on the part of a few of the candidates that they stood little chance of winning (they continued to hope for a fairly good showing, however, to be able to convert it into some post-election spoil) and thus were little inclined to expend too much energy; and the availability of financial and institutional support (in a few cases political parties or various non-Aboriginal organisations provided funds for some of the candidates, owing mostly to the utilisation of pre-existing patronage links). Interestingly, the amount of money spent on the campaigns had relatively little bearing on the outcome of the election.

The content of the campaign message varied personally and situationally.

Some stressed what they had done in the past; others, what they would do in the future. In attacking other candidates, care had to be taken according to the person being addressed. For example, a campaigner might say 'C is your auntie and has done a lot for the Aboriginal people over the years, but her heart is crook and this job will be demanding', when addressing one of C's relatives, while in another context it might be 'What has C ever done for the Aboriginal people? Her ideas are old-fashioned, and all she ever does is go to meetings which don't accomplish anything.' What is of primary importance in considering the above, as well as the entire election, is that a relatively small, fairly well-integrated community is involved in which many of the people know the candidates personally or at least have easy access to first-hand information on them. Thus, the public 'face' claimed by the candidate (cf. Goffman 1967:5) cannot be too divergent from his more private one. In other words. the candidate's private life cannot be easily hidden or transformed as is the case in larger political arenas where there is larger scope for image management. Also, the candidates will probably continue to live in the community after the election and this may place limitations on their activities (e.g. statements about other candidates).

The election The number of people registered for the Perth metropolitan area (District 8 in Western Australia of the N.A.C.C.) by election day was relatively low — less than 900 out of a total population for the area of about 5,500 (A.A.P.A. 1973:24). Polling had been conducted earlier in two out-lying areas and the prisons, and a roving ballot box was provided for some of the more isolated areas. On election day (November 14th), polls were located at six different places in areas of high concentrations of Aborigines. Publicity immediately before the election was relatively widespread. Several of the candidates spent the day taking people to the polls (one visited several of the wine saloons seeking support), and some of the voluntary organisations provided transport for those needing it. Also, the candidates in several instances provided poll watchers to ensure that balloting went fairly. Of those enrolled, less than two-thirds voted (a few were added to the roll on election day as well). As a result of this low turn-out, it was decided to open one poll again on the following Saturday to boost the number. The total number actually voting (501 out of 893 on the roll), however, remained low. The result of the election was as follows:

A. 148 (29.7%)
B. 146 (29.3%)
C. 63 (12.6%)
D. 30 (6.0%)
E. 49 (9.8%)
F. 22 (4.4%)
G. 20 (4.0%)
H. 21 (4.2%)

499 (plus 2 informal votes)

Table 1: Results of the N.A.C.C. election in Perth

The voting was very close between candidates A and B. A was ahead until the counting of the absentee ballots, which put B ahead by 2 votes.

The question now is, why were the results as they were? What were the deciding factors in the election results? To answer this, we must ask why the various candidates received as many votes as they did, as well as why they were not able to garner more. In reviewing the four main sources mentioned by Mayer (cited above) all, in this case, seem relevant to differing degrees in understanding the results. First, social relationships proved to be very important. This seemed especially true due to the social integration of the electorate. Those candidates with relatively few kin tended not to do well; and they were forced to depend upon other resources, which in themselves proved insufficient to generate adequate support. Also, many of the candidates had to compete with each other for the support of kin since their kinship networks overlapped. It should be noted that support of a candidate to whom one is related does not necessarily imply that one is doing so for general reasons of kinship solidarity. In fact, such support was often related to other factors, particularly to patronage and brokerage activities of the candidate. In general, kinship, while being of considerable importance, was in no case adequate by itself to produce sufficient support.

Residence proved to be an important variable. It should be noted that since many Aborigines live in State Housing Commission homes there is often little choice in place of residence. Residence was especially important in the case of candidates A and B, who lived at opposite ends of town, and each managed to carry a sizeable portion of their respective areas. In these cases, this support seems to have also been related to another source — patronage and brokerage. Candidates A, B and E were the ones most directly involved in welfare work for other Aborigines (which involved increasingly large numbers resulting in part from the decentralisation of the Department of Native Welfare). Although the other candidates were also involved to varying degrees in welfare work, for them it was of a more secondary nature, in that they often referred people to others (e.g. to candidates A and B) who were more directly involved. This patron-broker role in welfare work is related to residence in that, since welfare work among Aborigines when performed by Aborigines tends to be a full-time job, much of the work is conducted at home or in one's own neighbourhood. Also, there appears to be a preference in seeking help from those who are either kin or neighbours due to the added familiarity. It should be pointed out that E, with a history of voluntary work in rehabilitation (both A and B worked through voluntary organisations, and this probably enabled them to extend their support more than was possible for E in his voluntary capacity), was able to garner 9.8% of the vote. This was a sizeable showing, considering that E has a very weak kinship network in Perth and that he made little use of the various campaign innovations. His campaign remained on a personal level (he expended more energy in running his campaign than any other candidate), and much of his support came from those he had helped (which often involved brokerage activities).

The 'lesser of two evils' source of support was also evident, though to a limited extent, since most of those not positively committed to an individual failed to register. A few relatively uncommitted persons did register and there were cases of people voting for candidates since, 'although there are a lot of things I don't like about B, at least he doesn't drink and gamble like A'. Such reasoning was also evident in some of the campaigning. 'Why vote for C?

She won't get in, and that ratbag A might win. You know that B is at least better than A.'

To convert these various resources into support, they need to be mobilised and presented in a strategic manner to the public. Thus, the various campaign strategies must also be considered in order to understand the outcome of the election. As stated earlier, a campaign strategy is based upon the candidate's perception of his resources and the political environment, and his ability to make forecasts and adjust them accordingly in response to feedback. It was also noted that forecasts and feedback were difficult to formulate, and that strategies had to be based largely upon untested beliefs regarding social behaviour, and in response to the innovations of other candidates. Thus, F predicted that 'all of the people around here will vote for me. They know me and I'm related to many of them.' In fact, this did not occur. Some did vote for him: but many, although they had promised him their support, voted for others. In this case, F lacked other resources that were necessary to mobilise support in the area. He received only 4.4% of the total vote. Had he been better able to judge the extent and nature of his support, he might have been able to adjust his strategy in a way to make better use of his limited resources (or he might not have run in the first place). E stated that 'all of the blokes in the jails will vote for me.' Again, they had told him that they would, but when it came to their final decisions the other candidates were able to garner a fair number of the votes in the jails through use of a variety of resources, in addition to rehabilitation work. The claims for support by some of the other candidates as it turned out, due often to kinship and friendship, in some instances were more important. Also, their campaign strategies may have been more effective. Basically. what occurred was that candidates were able to assess general sources of support, but they were not able to refine their forecasts.

Candidates A and B were able to gain the majority of the votes (59% between them). They were able to gain the widest spectrum of support, since they had the most significant constellations of resources and were best able to utilise these effectively in generating suppport. Their resources included extensive and largely uncontested kinship networks and the most important patron and broker roles in welfare activities. Also, their campaign strategies were the most systematised, ensuring coverage of a wide segment of the population. Although each of these candidates had liabilities, these were not sufficient to keep them from gaining fairly widespread support (although they did set some limitations). Generally, the other candidates mounted campaigns that were in no way as extensive as these two.

Conclusion From the preceding it is apparent that an analysis of patronage and brokerage within the context of the nature and development of the sociocultural niche occupied by Aborigines in Australian society is central to an understanding of Aboriginal politics in south-west Western Australia. Also, shifts in the nature of this niche and its integration within Australian society have led to some alterations in the Aboriginal political system. The analysis of the process of change in this situation appears to be best handled from an actor-oriented perspective. Thus, change in the political system may be examined in terms of the responses or adaptations and strategies of individuals (e.g. the N.A.C.C. candidates) to their changing environment (cf. Mair 1969:4).

Such a method of analysis has been adopted in recent years by a number of social anthropologists who have addressed themselves to an examination of social process and change. This was in part due to a growing dissatisfaction with the structural-functionalist model of society (cf. van Velsen 1967; Noble 1973) and led to the adoption by some of an actor-oriented perspective in regard to the choices people make in response to the sociocultural environment (cf. Reader 1964). Evans-Pritchard in his pioneering study of Azande witchcraft (1937) demonstrated the importance of what he termed 'situational selection' in witchcraft cases. Later, Firth (1954) wrote on the role of choice-making in social change, though he failed to operationalise this in his re-study of Tikopia (1959). Barth (1966, 1967), drawing upon a theory of exchange derived largely from Homans (1958, 1961) as well as from 'game theory', developed a 'transactional' model of society and social change which placed strong emphasis upon the role of the individual (this was illustrated earlier in a monograph edited by Barth [1963] on the role of the entrepreneur in social change). This form of analysis was further developed by Kapferer (1969, 1972) who utilised a modified theory of exchange derived from Blau (1964) in which the actor's choices are seen as being affected by limited perception and restricted information (such limitations clearly emerge in the election strategies of the various N.A.C.C. candidates). Others, such as van Velsen (1964) and Moore (1970), have dealt with the instrumentality or manipulatability and situational aspects of social relationships, norms and values. Such a shift away from structural-functionalism toward an actor-oriented perspective in the study of politics has led to an increasing awareness of the importance of patronage and brokerage (cf. Strickon and Greenfield 1972).

It would appear that, despite changes in certain aspects of the niche occupied by Aborigines in the south-west since the early part of the century, the predominant political system has remained one of patronage and brokerage (for comparison see Heath 1972). This appears to be the case since, although the sociopolitical niche occupied by Aborigines in the south-west has undergone some changes, the conditions which encouraged the development and importance of patronage and brokerage have remained in force. That is, the niche occupied by the Aborigines has remained a manifestly subservient one with little real political power being possessed by the Aborigines themselves. They remain, to a large extent, dependent upon the gratuity of non-Aboriginal society.

Those who occupied the most central patron-broker positions in the pre-election system in Perth appear to have been best able to alter and expand their bases of support to fit the new system for a variety of reasons. One was related to the nature of the specific social networks of the individuals concerned. Also, due to their positions (e.g. working for voluntary organisations in a liaison capacity) and their knowledge of and contacts within the non-Aboriginal sociopolitical system (which was not a monopoly of theirs, but in combination with other factors proved important) they were able to evolve and activate methods of garnering support from a wide spectrum of the Aboriginal population. Finally, the role of 'leader' in many ways remained the same after the election. Thus, Aboriginal leaders remained primarily cultural brokers. For this reason, those already possessing the most significant resources under the old system were in many ways in an advantageous position to convert this position into an important resource under the 'new' one. Thus, although there was change in such things as lines of support and legitimacy, there was considerable continuity in the overall political system in terms of the roles of leaders and the niche occupied by Aboriginal politics within the Australian sociopolitical arena.

Notes

1. The term Aboriginal (or Aborigines) in this paper is generally used in the broad sense of all those belonging to the ethnic category of Australian Aborigines. This includes those of Aboriginal descent (who constitute the vast majority of the Aboriginal population of the south-west). When reference is specifically to full-blooded Aborigines this is indicated.

2. General overviews of the history and traditional culture of the Aborigines of this area are available in Hasluck 1942; Biskup 1973; Haynes *et al.* 1972; Berndt 1973; and Rowley 1970*a*, 1970*b*. Much of the historical material presented is either from these sources or from the author's own research.

3. The term 'profit' is used in the broad sense, as it is by Barth, Boissevain and others.

References

ABORIGINAL AFFAIRS PLANNING AUTHORITY 1973 *Western Australia Annual Report for the year ended 30 June, 1973*. Perth.
BAILEY, F. G. 1969 *Stratagems and spoils, a social anthropology of politics*. Blackwell, Oxford.
BARTH, F. (ed.) 1963 *The role of the entrepreneur in social change in northern Norway*. Universitetsforlaget, Bergen-Oslo.
——1966 *Models of social organization*. Occasional Papers of the Royal Anthropological Institute No. 23.
——1967 The study of social change, *American Anthropologist*, 69:661-69.
BATES, D. 1938 *The passing of the Aborigines*. Murray, London.
BERNDT, C. H. 1962 Mateship or success: an assimilation dilemma, *Oceania*, XXXIII: 71-89.
——1969 A time of rediscovery. In *Aboriginal progress, a new era?* (D. E. Hutchison ed.), pp. 16-34. University of Western Australia Press, Perth.
BERNDT, R. M. The concept of protest within an Australian Aboriginal context. In *A question of choice* (R. M. Berndt ed.), pp. 25-43. University of Western Australia Press, Perth.
——1973 Aborigines of southwestern Australia: the past and present, *Journal of the Royal Society of Western Australia*, 56:50-55.
BISKUP, P. 1973 *Not slaves not citizens, the Aboriginal problem in Western Australia. 1898-1954*. University of Queensland Press, St. Lucia.
BLAU, P. 1964 *Exchange and power in social life*. Wiley, London.
BOISSEVAIN, J. 1969 Patrons as brokers, *Sociologische Gids*, 16:379-86.
——1973 *Friends of friends: networks, manipulaters and coalitions*. Blackwell, Oxford.
EIDHEIM, H. 1963 Entrepreneurship in politics. In *The role of the entrepreneur in social change in northern Norway* (F. Barth ed.), pp. 70-83. Universitetsforlaget, Bergen-Oslo.
EPSTEIN, A. L., R. S. PARKER and M. REAY (eds) 1971 *The politics of dependence, Papua New Guinea 1968*. Australian National University Press, Canberra.
EVANS-PRITCHARD, E. E. 1937 *Witchcraft, oracles and magic among the Azande*. Clarendon Press, Oxford.
FIRTH, R. 1954 Social organisation and social change, *Journal of the Royal Anthropological Institute*, 84:1-20.
——1959 *Social change in Tikopia*. Allen and Unwin, London.
GARBETT, G. K. 1970 The analysis of social situations, *Man* (n.s.), 5:214-27.
GLUCKMAN, M. 1958 *Analysis of a social situation in modern Zululand*. Rhodes-Livingstone Paper No. 28.
GOFFMAN, E. 1961 *Asylums, essays on the social situation of mental patients and other inmates*. Doubleday, New York.
——1967 *Interaction ritual, essays on face-to-face behaviour*. Doubleday, New York.
HASLUCK, P. 1942 *Black Australians, a survey of native policy in Western Australia 1829-1897*. Melbourne University Press, Melbourne.
HAYNES, B. T. *et al.* (eds) 1972 *W.A. Aborigines 1622-1972*. History Association of Western Australia, Perth.

HEATH, D. B. 1972 New patrons for old: changing patron-client relationships in the Bolivian Yungas. In *Structure and process in Latin America* (A. Strickon *and* S. M. Greenfield eds) pp. 101-37. University of New Mexico Press, Albuquerque.

HOMANS, G. C. 1958 Social behaviour as exchange, *American Journal of Sociology*, 62:597-606.

——1961 *Social behaviour: its elementary forms*. Harcourt, Brace and World, New York.

KAPFERER, B. 1969 Norms and the manipulation of relationships in a work context. In *Social networks in urban situations* (J. C. Mitchell ed.), pp. 181-244. Manchester University Press, Manchester.

——1972 *Strategy and transaction in an African factory*. Manchester University Press, Manchester.

MACKENZIE, W. J. M. 1957 The export of electoral systems, *Political Studies*, 5:240-57.

MAIR, L. 1969 *Anthropology and social change*. London School of Economics Monographs on Social Anthropology No. 38. Athlone Press, London.

MAKIN, C. F. 1970 A socio-economic anthropological survey of people of Aboriginal descent in the metropolitan region of Perth, Western Australia. Ph.D. thesis in Anthropology, University of Western Australia, Perth.

MAYER, A. C. 1963 Municipal elections: a central Indian case study. In *Politics and Society in India* (C. H. Philips ed.), pp. 115-32. Allen and Unwin, London.

MITCHELL, J. C. 1969 The concept and use of social networks. In *Social networks in urban situations* (J. C. Mitchell ed.), pp. 1-50. Manchester University Press, Manchester.

MOORE, S. F. 1970 Politics, procedures, and norms in changing Chagga Law, *Africa*, 40:321-43.

NOBLE, M. 1973 Social network: its uses as a conceptual framework in family analysis. In *Network analysis, studies in human interaction* (J. Boissevain *and* J. C. Mitchell eds), pp. 3-13. Mouton, The Hague.

READER, D. H. 1964 Models in social change, with special reference to southern Africa, *African Studies*, 23:11-33.

ROWLEY, C. D. 1970a *The destruction of Aboriginal society*. Australian National University Press, Canberra.

——1970b *Outcasts in white Australia*. Australian National University Press, Canberra.

SALVADO, R. 1854 *Mémoires historiques sur l'Australie*. Paris.

STRICKON, A. *and* S. M. GREENFIELD 1972 The analysis of patron-client relationships: an introduction. In *Structure and process in Latin America; patronage, clientage and power systems* (A. Strickon *and* S. M. Greenfield eds), pp. 1-17. University of New Mexico Press, Albuquerque.

VAN VELSEN, J. 1964 *The politics of kinship, a study in social manipulation among the Lakeside Tonga*. Manchester University Press, Manchester.

——1967 The extended-case method and situational analysis. In *The craft of social anthropology* (A. L. Epstein ed.), pp. 129-49. Tavistock, London.

WILSON, J. 1958 Cooraradale. B.A. Hons. thesis in Anthropology, University of Western Australia, Perth.

——1964 Assimilation to what? comments on the white society. In *Aborigines now, new perspective in the study of Aboriginal communities* (M. Reay ed.), pp. 151-66. Angus and Robertson, Sydney.

27 Aborigines: political options and strategies

Colin Tatz

I

There is some evidence to suggest that race relations in Australia can only get worse. Changes in political philosophy, abolition of discriminatory legislation, new human rights bills, revamped institutional structures and infusion of money cannot solve three fundamental problems. First, there is the psychological inability of whites to stop talking *about* blacks rather than *with* them, to cease being their proctors and curators, of allowing them to act on their own behalf. Secondly, there is the cultural impossibility, for most whites, of evincing empathy rather than sympathy for black viewpoints on black consciousness and identity, on their frustration, alienation and deprivation. Thirdly, there is the improbability of whites ever comprehending, let alone conceding, that a major avenue for black survival and progress is their rejection of white society, its values and the programmes it mounts for their benefit.

To recognise a group as a 'problem' has the merit of implying the need for action toward its 'solution'. Rowley has portrayed (1970-71) fully the action of neglect, and occasionally the action of concern, until the 1960s. Theses, symposia, anthologies and articles have expounded the variety of welfare and social change programmes this past decade. Social history demonstrates one feature common to both the eras of neglect and concern: that white society unilaterally defines the problems, prescribes the policy dicta, enacts the legislation, creates the administrative machinery and determines the nature, content, personnel and flavour of remedial programmes.

At the national policy level, the conferences of ministers and officials in 1937, 1951, 1961, 1963, 1965 (and those following) decided on philosophies of limited segregation, or assimilation, or integration, or cultural choice, or mongrel mixtures of them all. Until the 1960s, legislatures elected solely by whites enacted what was believed to be in the Aborigines' best interests. The Aboriginal franchise has not affected that situation. Governmental agencies were, and are, so structured as to leave no doubt about who are the administrators and who the administered. Events at the May 1974 conference of the Australian Institute of Aboriginal Studies may change that body's outlook, but the record to date has made plain who are the studiers and who the studied.

Under the 1972 federal Labor government the Woodward Commission (1974) has been a white-centred operation. It is true that land is for whites to give, but it would not have been calamitous to grant persistent Aboriginal demands for a couple of black deputy commissioners. (In 1965, New Zealand had the integrity, or the public relations foresight, to include Hemi Tono Waetford as a junior partner to Justice Ivor Prichard in their inquiry into

Maori land laws and land courts.) The National Aboriginal Consultative Committee was Gordon Bryant's concept and creation. Even the laudable policy precept that 'community self-determination should be the over-riding principle of Government policy' was decided by a seminar of officials and a few missionaries at Batchelor in February 1973.[1]

Innumerable examples show that Aboriginal affairs have always been, and still remain, a white activity. This tradition has become a cultural norm, as deeply ingrained as our acceptance of private schooling or private enterprise in social welfare activity. How does one break this psychological yoke? Some ministers and officials have stated a vague awareness that there has to be a new order of things, namely, the cessation of proctorship and guardianship, the need to cede power, authority, responsibility and accountability to the 'problem' people. But I doubt whether anyone really *believes* it, or in it. Hence the endless token mechanisms of reserve councils, advisory councils, national consultative committees, specially convened seminars and, lamentably at the end of the field, some Aboriginal membership of the Australian Institute of Aboriginal Studies.

One could argue that in some countries the ceding of economic, legal and political autonomy to black people could destroy their present order of social control and social cohesion. Such a cession to between one and two per cent of the population is hardly likely to crumple the walls of the white Australian Jericho. But the conundrum remains: how does white society, the defining group, come to recognise and to *accept* the reverse situation, namely, that by its words, promises, policy slogans, attitudes and actions, *it* is the very essence of the problem?

The second fundamental problem is even less likely of achievement: that a mainstream society can ever have empathy with the depressed minority, the group at the receiving end, the group which voluntarily wishes to identify itself in its own way, its different though (doubtless to many) less comfortable way. One can feel and display sympathy, that is, have compassion for, share *intellectually* another person's emotion or sensation or condition. But can one — never having *experienced* the same kind of frustration, alienation and discrimination — feel empathy, that is, project one's personality into and so fully comprehend another's experiences? I think not.

W. E. du Bois' concept of 'double consciousness' is more than a concept: it is the reality of being forever aware that one is black (or yellow, or female, or Mormon, or Jewish) in a WASP society and aware that the WASPs are aware of one's difference. Those of 'single consciousness' can intellectualise du Bois but they cannot, by definition, experience it or fully comprehend it. Hence the predilection of so many administrators and academics for prescribing a variety of remedies for Aboriginal ills, all of which demand that the price for a better health status, or equality before the law, or equal wages, is the impossible surrender of cultural attitudes, values, beliefs — and being. Cawte (1972:56) has written: 'The truth is that there is no return to an aboriginal culture possible for Aborigines, and *if* health and growth is the aim, there can be no standing still in the present marginal society'. Moodie cites (1972:236-37) the paradox:

If Aboriginal (or part-Aboriginal) cultural differences are tolerated fully . . . then health disadvantages within certain parameters must be tolerated also. If Aborigines must have the same health status as other Australians, then there is no alternative to complete social and economic assimilation, with complete loss of Aboriginal identity.

In the context of deploring guilt as a bad motivator (of governmental action), he 'deplores the tendency by many Australians — including some Aboriginal opinion-leaders — to harp upon the past misdeeds of citizens and governments in the treatment of Aborigines' (*ibid.*: 240).

I have been criticised for misrepresenting their views, for alleging that these academics are demanding that Aborigines *must* have better health and therefore *must* surrender cultural identity. If I have said that (Tatz 1972*a*:20), I retract. But I still contest three points. First, improved health as such is *not* contingent on cultural surrender and consequent assimilation. One can assuredly be an Herero tribesman and healthy, a Sicilian ethnic and healthy, Jewish and healthy. Health in the sense of physical, mental and social well-being is not a state reserved and preserved by definition for white, Western, urbanised, technologically-oriented Anglo-Saxon Protestants and Catholics. Second, there *is* a return to an Aboriginal culture — even if awkward, gross, artificial, diluted or symbolic—on the part of those whom we decree have lost it. Thirdly, these men (and others) reveal that very lack of empathy I have been discussing — a lack of full comprehension that the deeds and misdeeds of the Aboriginal past are an intrinsic part of their folkways and mores. Massacre, persecution, violent clash and culture clash are often part of the social cement that holds an identity together. Identity is rarely an issue for a secure member of the WASP-ish mainstream. The 'let's-turn-over-a-new-leaf-and-start-from-scratch' philosophy is simply not possible.

This contention about empathy has moved some social anthropologists, doctors and lawyers to ask whether I am saying that only 'ethnics with experience of discrimination' should work, as academics or officials, among Aborigines. The answer is no — in such areas of research and administration as archaeology, blood group genetics and running the Aboriginal capital enterprises fund. The other answer is that those who have it are much more likely to succeed in such areas as designing houses to suit Aboriginal family culture, mounting Aboriginal Studies courses for those who want them, establishing special medical and nursing services and giving sensitive legal aid and counsel.

It is highly unlikely that white Australian society can swallow the proposition that black progress is contingent on their rejection of white society. The reasoning that follows here is not mine but that of the 'black consciousness' movement generally. The basic precept is that blacks want to know, and must know, more about who they were and who they are if they are seriously concerned about *whom they intend to become*. Black consciousness is an attitude of mind, a way of life. A basic tenet is that the black man must reject all value systems that seek to make him a foreigner in his own country and which reduce his human dignity. He must build up his own value systems, and see himself as self-defined and not defined by others. As Charles Perkins put it: 'However favourably a white person, or any other racial or national group in this country mingles with Aborigines or looks upon the Aboriginal question, he is just not part of that definition' (see Nettheim ed. 1974).

Group cohesion and solidarity therefore become much more important than ever before. Thus, in order to join the open society on anything like equal terms, black people *should first close their ranks*: not as evidence of anti-whitism, but as an exclusion of whites for the time it will take to realise their immediate aspirations of black consciousness. Rejection is not hatred. Integration is the ultimate goal: but one that cannot be achieved in a suspicious, hostile and distrustful atmosphere. It does not mean assimilation of blacks into an already established set of norms drawn up and motivated by white society. Integration means voluntary separatism first: the development of group cohesion, an awareness of political and economic strength, a feeling of power arising out of knowing who and what they are; followed then by free participation in a given society, *on their own terms*. This is not the kind of integration espoused by some political parties, advancement organisations or academic critics. Their efforts, say blacks, are directed merely at relaxing certain oppressive measures and practices and *allowing* blacks into a white-type society.

Of this emergent philosophy, two prominent South African writers have made interesting comments. Nadine Gordimer sees black consciousness as a revival of the philosophy of Negritude propounded by Aime Cesaire and Leopold Senghor, and as an essential step toward liberation. She views the rejection of whites by blacks as a sign of 'healthy negritude'.[2] Alan Paton states that this philosophy wants to change the order of things: but the order cannot be changed without power. 'How long will the young zealots be satisfied with a mush of culture, mysticism, lyricism and going round saying "haven't I a lovely skin?"'. This philosophy could lead, he speculates, to 'a refusal to believe, on principle, that any white man can speak the truth, and might end up being a twin of white nationalism'.[3] Paton is doubtless the more pragmatic, in terms of ultimate change and the need for power to effect it. But, I believe, Jewish Nadine has a greater empathy and comprehension of where it is at in black minds than has Protestant Alan. Her perception, which I share, is that the 'mush' (if that's what it is) is a pre-requisite to establishing the power needed for change.

II

Where does this leave Aborigines in a white-dominated, decision-making, uncomprehending society, one which twitches neurotically at the mention of separatism for fear of being lumped in the same malodorous category as South Africa? What *political* strategies or options are available to Aborigines, or can be devised by them, which can produce any modicum of change in 'The System'? Our political institutions offer little of comfort or substance to the poor, the disorganised, the uneducated, the religious and racial minorities. Do Aborigines have access to political institutions and do they influence, let alone participate in, decision-making that affects them? The commonplace, moronic response is that by virtue of their franchise they *are* political participants.

Just what does political equality, in the voting sense, mean for such a group? Representation theory in political science is a tortuous concept. Briefly, there are four sub-theories.[4] 'Authorisation' theory holds that a community consciously sets aside one or more men to act on behalf of the whole. Once the representative is so authorised, the principals (constituents) are bound by his actions. This transmission of authority from constituents to representative is sometimes held to embrace a 'doctrine of mandate'. On the other hand, the paradoxical 'accountability' theory is that representatives are *themselves* responsible for their actions to their principals. The underlying notion is that the representative should be kept both responsive and responsible to his electorate.

'Microcosmic' theory reflects the view that in a modern society, all cannot meet to decide on policies best for them. Therefore, elected representatives should meet on their behalf. Thus an assembly of representatives should reflect the composition of the nation, or the region, at large. John Adams, an early U.S. President, once wrote that the legislature 'should be an exact portrait, in miniature, of the people at large, as it should think, feel, reason and act like them'. In most societies such a legislature could only begin to be achieved by adoption, at the very least, of a proportional system of representation. Finally, there is the 'acting for' theory: the notion that we elect a representative to do our politicking for us. He is the specialist, the one who acts efficiently to advance our particular objectives.

If these concepts have any validity for us, which I very much doubt, what meaning have they for Aborigines? A great many Aboriginal population concentrations in north and western Australia are to be found in Country Party controlled electorates. Aborigines there have assuredly not given that Party's candidates a mandate to block attempts at granting land rights, to peg wages on pastoral properties, to create legions of 'slow workers', to inhibit and prohibit the provision of accommodation in crop-picking districts, and so on. Nor, to my knowledge, has any representative of any party — with the possible exception of Gordon Bryant — at state or federal level felt obliged, or been obliged, to account to Aborigines for actions taken for or about them.

In the absence of proportional representation, the Adams concept is just not available for Aborigines (and many other groups). There is simply no way that white representatives (or white officials), of whatever ilk, can think, feel, reason and act like them. This concept doubtless led Bruce McGuinness and Elizabeth Hoffman to stand for the May 1974 Senate, the one political institution that has the vaguest tinge of proportional representation about it. But unlike Senator Bonner, Bruce McGuinness has yet to learn that our system works for the party machines, not for independent, or even symbolically representative, individuals.[5]

Given the overriding consideration in our system of keeping the party machine oiled and efficient, there is little room for the individual representative to politick for us. The party symbol men — the largely unknown but party pre-selected men — do it, in an arena all their own, with an agenda all of their own. That Gordon Bryant — co-founder of the Aboriginal Advancement League in Victoria and the Federal Council for the Advancement of Aborigines and Torres Strait Islanders — became very temporarily Minister for Aboriginal Affairs was simply a short-lived, happy coincidence.

Ironies abound when white society deals with dark people. One particular twist comes to mind. The recent past has heard the cry: 'if only there was an emergent Aboriginal leadership!' But once emerging, the retreat and defence tactic is to deny the 'representativeness' of those who criticise. When confronted with Aboriginal spokesmen from pressure groups or civil services —

notably Doug Nicholls, Charles Perkins, John Moriarty, Harry Penrith, Shirley Smith and Chicka Dixon — the first reaction is to demand of each: 'how representative are *you* of Aborigines?' Unless they can show — and clearly they cannot — that each of them has been given a unanimous mandate, that each has been authorised, is accountable for his actions, is truly symbolic of and each is acting for the total 'grass-roots' community, then they are written off as non-leaders and non-spokesmen. In 1973 Charles Perkins claimed, before an audience of 220 teacher trainees in Armidale, that some departmental colleagues had told him to stop insisting on being consulted — because by virtue of his B.A. degree he was no longer an Aboriginal.

The system of reserve, mission and settlement councils can hardly be accepted as political structures providing participatory decison-making. It must be remembered that these councils operate, not in a normal, open milieu but in what Erving Goffman (1961:11) defines as 'total institutions':

> . . . place(s) of residence and work where a large number of like-situated individuals, cut off from the wider society for an appreciable period of time, together lead an enclosed, formally administered round of life. Prisons serve as a clear example, providing we appreciate that what is prison-like about prisons is found in institutions whose members have broken no laws.

Where councils exist, permissively, in legislation, and more so where they are created by administrative fiat, they are contained and constrained in terms of effective authority and power (see Long 1970 and Nettheim 1973). The spending of canteen profits, the purchase of football equipment, the punishment of those who offend the white system or the tribal system — these are not real powers. In Queensland, especially, there is always an overriding authority in the form of the managership or directorship.

Now, after decades of total institutionalisation and white-imposed programmes, the federal government has announced a policy of 'self-determination' for reserve communities — at least in its Aboriginal jurisdictions of the Northern Territory, South Australia and Western Australia. There is an official resolve to get out of the way of Aboriginal decision-making, to opt for 'non-directive' rather than directed programmes. The February 1973 gathering at Batchelor (N.T.), albeit a wholly white affair, decided that henceforth the fulcrum of policy will be 'self-determination', defined as 'Aboriginal communities deciding the pace and nature of their future development'. Government will have to create the necessary climate and conditions therefor. 'Unwilling communities' should not have other government goals — such as on health, education and housing — imposed on them. Land ownership is 'a fundamental pre-requisite' and 'communities should be free to evolve their own forms of organisations'. Further, 'no decision-making structure should be imposed upon them and they should be free from an externally imposed time scale'. If communities waste money initially, this should be tolerated. Finally, where Aborigines seek funds based on their own view of their needs, 'the merits of the case should not necessarily be judged in European terms'.

There is significance in all this. But what, precisely? First, this wording and thinking is not ministerial or political party gloss, but radical attitude change by *senior* officials in the field. Secondly, as a wave of 'freedom' it embraces the large black populations in the Territory and two states. Thirdly, several points of substance have been publicly pinned to the mast-head, yardsticks for staff to follow and for others to measure, prod, praise or criticise governmental action.

However, several doubts come to mind. Reserve communities in Queensland, N.S.W. and Victoria will continue under the existing constraints.[6] The new dictates apply to very specific communities and say or do nothing of meaning for urban and peri-urban 'non-reserve' Aborigines. Officials believe they can inspire and imbue general field staff with this new ethos. I don't. My scepticism stems from being an 'administration-watcher' from way back: observing the same people, or the same kind of people, administering a succession of segregationist, assimilationist, welfare, wardship and social welfare tenets. The slogans come and go, but the attitudes and behaviour of the men and women who deal daily with Aborigines remain. 'Non-directive' approaches cannot become reality overnight following a Batchelor seminar. Quite often they can emerge from three or four years of 'directive' socialisation in social work degree programmes. Assuredly the field staffs in these three jurisdictions will not be going back to school. Finally, one cannot avoid the cynical comment that it has taken officialdom in Australia 62 years to catch up with President Woodrow Wilson's liberation slogan at Versailles for the oppressed and depressed in Europe.

Writing in 1970, Rowley could say (1970*b*:384-85) that 'the Aboriginal voice is now continuous; and this in itself is indicative of a growing confidence, of a potential for leadership'. But he added, 'as yet these voices are not backed by effective *Aboriginal* pressure groups and organizations'. It is regrettable that there has been no serious research into the origins, aims, personnel, tactics and effectiveness of Aboriginal pressure groups, that is, those earlier dominated by whites, and later, those taken over by blacks. Such research might well conclude that pressure tactics had the effect of highlighting, but not directly preventing or ending, the removal of the Mapoon people, the Woomera rocket range people, the nightmarish drinking laws epitomised by Namatjira's case, and police treatment of Aboriginal 'offenders'. More successful has been pressure on the Yirrkala and other mining situations, on land rights, abolition of the Victorian Aborigines Welfare Board, on the retention of Lake Tyers reserve and on federal responsibility for Aboriginal affairs.[7]

A significant feature of this activity, however, has been the consistent white tactic of asserting that advancement organisations have been manipulated, or infiltrated, or run by the ubiquitous reds, pinks and fellow-travellers. Communism as a menace is now *passé*: it has been replaced, notably in the eyes and utterances of Victorian and Queensland officials and ministers, by academic critics or more loosely, 'do-gooders'. On a recent *This Day Tonight* programme dealing with Aboriginal stoning of white cars in Alice Springs, Tony Greatorex — then president of the Northern Territory Legislative Council — said that he knew blacks very well: 'they have no organisation, they can't organise themselves out of a paper bag; therefore the violence involved must be being organised by someone else'.

Group pressure has, in my view, gained something for Aborigines. But as a strategy it has serious weaknesses: decision-makers can and do accuse the organisations of being puppets for 'other' mysterious and dark forces; they can and do claim that these bodies are not truly representative or that their views conflict with other Aboriginal views; and there is the inability of these groups to pose any real threat to the security of the corporate men in the political or bureaucratic power structure. There is no hard (or even softish) evidence of a cattleman being deprived of his labour for his misuse of it; or of a policeman being dismissed for his ill-treatment; or of an official being suspended, demoted or punished for his graft, or embezzlement of Aboriginal funds, or his gross misuse of such funds, or abuse of his statutory obligations.

The emergence of young, articulate and militant Aborigines, supported by student action groups, civil rights movements and above all, the media, finally made Aboriginal affairs a real political issue at the start of this decade. 'Aborigines' wound up well and truly on the lists of the socially and politically concerned — together with female equality, abortion and homosexual law reform, drugs, the poor and the environment. The 1972 federal election was notable for Labor's priority cry that 'we will solve the Aboriginal problem and we will grant land rights'.

Seventeen months later — after some unholy botching relating to Charles Perkins' public criticisms, land rights commission personnel, abuses of Treasury regulations on disbursements, ministerial changes, turtle farms and on the handling of 'white backlash'— the May 1974 election was notable for some 20 sentences *in toto* on Aborigines. The Opposition said nothing, though it did produce a policy manifesto giving credence to the concept of cultural diversity — from which, presumably, there will not be any turning back when they come to govern. Labor said it agreed *in principle* with the Woodward Commission recommendations: and the Prime Minister, dealing with social policies in a TV speech, lumped Aborigines at the tail end of a list thus: 'Labor will take action to remedy the problems of the poor, the sick, the old, the retarded and the Aborigines'. I suspect Mr Whitlam meant aborigines with a small 'a'. He seemed to be classifying them as a generic group, the way in which the well-to-do and the mentally well treat the totality of those they consider as 'the poor' and 'the retarded'.

There is some surprise in all this. Given that it took so long for Aborigines to become a major issue in a federal election, one can be forgiven for expecting it to remain one for a reasonable period of time. One could have surmised that as more discontent and less 'solution' became manifest under Labor, so the Opposition would have retained 'Aborigines' as an electoral issue. They did not. The conclusion for Aborigines will doubtless be that the party political system has nothing to offer them in the way of real change.

III

Rowley's prescription (1970*b*:422) is that the Aboriginal future rests on the willingness of governments to *negotiate* with leaders 'willing to operate within the political system or face others who have rejected it'. *Negotiation*, he says, is preferable to *reconciliation*, because that would involve 'the admission of injustices by government in the past'. Negotiation requires representative spokesmen: 'and these in turn depend on accepted ways of making decisions which are binding on the group and on recognition of authority held by some individuals to express views based on consensus'. What must emerge then is '*a structure of authority* within Aboriginal groups'. This in turn 'requires that the limits of the groups be defined, probably on the basis of location and common interests'. Finally, new Aboriginal institutions need to be established 'which can be entrusted with property, either in perpetuity . . . or in the form of loans, user rights, or on a rental basis . . . they may also be entrusted to administer government property which is devoted to the requirements of Aborigines'.

Almost as if he had used Rowley's prescription, and as an answer to Aboriginal frustration within our political system, Gordon Bryant announced the creation of a National Aboriginal Consultative Committee in January 1973. Following the (white) policy precept of an N.A.C.C., Aborigines figured largely in the structural details — 'in consultation with specialist advisers from the Australian National University, Chief Australian Electoral Office, Attorney-General's Department, the Legal Profession, Senior Officers of the Department of Aboriginal Affairs and others'.[8] Two meetings of an interim N.A.C.C. and two steering committee meetings spelled out the proposed electoral arrangements. Aborigines within, and seconded to, the Department of Aboriginal Affairs worked out the details: the creation of 41 single member constituencies, covering all states, the Northern Territory and the Torres Straits. Eligibility to vote was confined to persons of Aboriginal or Islander descent who identify as Aborigines or Islanders and who are accepted as such by the community with which they are associated. Voters had to be 18 and voting was not compulsory. An N.A.C.C. electoral roll was compiled. A candidate had to be Aboriginal, at least 18, be on the electoral roll, and resident in the electoral district for at least three months prior to the closing of the roll. A candidate had to be nominated by six other electors and each had to put up a $10 deposit. Single choice, first-past-the-post was the system used. Candidates will hold office for two years and 'be paid a suitable remuneration whilst serving in office'.

The poll result was announced on 13 February 1973.[9] The results are of interest:

State	No. of contestants	No. elected	Total voters roll	Total votes cast	Votes cast as % of roll
N.S.W.	38	8	5,810	4,368	75.18
VIC.	8	3	1,044	846	81.03
QLD.	55	9	11,614	10,398	89.52
S.A.	14	4	2,376	1,929	81.18
TAS.	3	1	354	300	84.75
N.T.	39	8	7,281	5,434	74.63
W.A.	35	8	7,859	4,964	{ 63.16 or 76.71*
TOTALS:	192	41	36,338	28,239	{ 80.05 or 77.71

* One W.A. candidate, in an electorate of 1,065 voters, was returned unopposed. If those electors are omitted, the percentage vote is 63.16 for W.A. and 77.71 per cent for Australia. The Department of Aboriginal Affairs has weighted the unopposed seat in some way, thereby arriving at figures of 76.71 per cent and 80.05 per cent respectively. The overall informal vote was 2.54 per cent.

Even though a white-conceived mechanism, we have here the appearance of all that Rowley says is needed: 41 elected Aborigines, having not one but virtually all the characteristics Hanna Pitkin deems necessary for true representatives (duly authorised, accountable, reflecting the composition of the community and standing or acting for them). An analysis of the voting returns indicates that — within the constraints of a multi-candidate first-past-the-post-system — the majority of those elected have a Pitkin-type 'mandate' or the Rowley-type 'authority to express views based on consensus'. Thus, one successful candidate polled 23 per cent of the total vote[10]; 5 polled between 25 and 29 per cent of the total vote; 14 between 30 and 39; 9 between 40 and 49; 7 between 50 and 59; 3 between 60 and 69 per cent; one over 70 per cent and one was returned unopposed. The limits of the groups were certainly defined on the basis of location and common interests. If not ideally defined according to some Aboriginal critics, the electoral divisions were certainly a brave first attempt.

In short, the N.A.C.C. appears to be a 'structure of authority' from within Aboriginal groups, a new political institution allowing for governmental negotiation with authoritative black leadership. If this is the appearance, what is the reality? Reality, I suggest, hinges on the reconciliation of Aboriginal and governmental perceptions of the purpose, role, powers and function of the N.A.C.C.

Gordon Bryant's January 1973 announcement of the N.A.C.C. indicated that body would 'advise me directly on Aboriginal problems'.[11] Departmental material sent to Aboriginal communities declared the new Committee would 'advise the Government in matters pertinent to Aboriginal citizens'.[12] Senator Cavanagh, having replaced Bryant as Minister, told the first N.A.C.C meeting: 'if your proposals are wise and logical the Government would reject them only at its own peril . . . we want the Committee to be a forum for the expression of Aboriginal people'.[13] The governmental perception is clear: a forum, an advisory role and function, a consultation mechanism, a black 'think-tank' whose views will be listened to — provided the white mind sees them as both wise and logical.

It may have been unhappy coincidence, but the Prime Minister's statement to the N.A.C.C. on official polling day was: 'our most important objective now is to restore to Aborigines the power to make decisions about their own way of life'.[14] The N.A.C.C. would, he added, also take part in the process of transferring responsibility for community affairs from government superintendents and managers to Aborigines. The minutes of the first N.A.C.C. meeting reflect the black interpretation, or misinterpretation, namely, that the N.A.C.C. 'will take part in the machinery of policy-making on all matters affecting Aborigines'. If Mr Whitlam was in fact announcing the 'de-institutionalisation' policy for reserve communities, he chose a peculiar time, place and context in which to do it. The Aboriginal perception is, or was, clear then: a representative body invested with power to participate in decisions on all Aboriginal matters. The extent and strength of this view became clearer early in 1974.

Following the declaration, things began smoothly enough: the Prime Minister met the successful candidates for lunch, and husbands and wives took part in a tour of Parliament House, a visit to the War Memorial, a launch trip on Lake Burley Griffin and a tour of Canberra. The inaugural meeting was held on 13 December 1973. Apart from speeches, discussion took place on salaries and allowances of members. Four members of the Department and 39 N.A.C.C. members met again on 14 December. It began with a mild fracas between a few members and the press. An N.A.C.C. press statement hoped for co-operation but regretted media 'misconstruction to suit the purpose of sensationalism'. The context was the level of salaries being sought by members. Then followed a serious discussion about 'suitable remuneration': delegates sought $7,500 per annum plus $3,000 expenses. (Later the Government agreed to $6,000 p.a., with $2,000 expenses for urban and $3,000 for rural members.) A motion was passed 'that all people other than the delegates be asked to leave the room'.

The problems began early in the new year. On Monday, 5 February, the N.A.C.C. voted to change its name to the National Aboriginal Congress — with all the black nationalistic connotations of the word 'Congress' — and announced its aim of making the Department of Aboriginal Affairs its 'secretariat'.[15] On the 6th, Senator Cavanagh said he would not accept these proposals. They were, he said, spending too much time worrying about their own powers and not enough on voicing the demands of their constituents: 'Whatever they call themselves they are only a consultative committee. Their power is only to advise the Government'.[16] To which the Chairman, Bruce McGuinness, replied that the Minister's statement was 'reactionary': 'We are setting ourselves up as a separate body that is not going to be dictated to by the Government and Senator Cavanagh'.

On 8 February the Congress censured the Senator, accusing him of being 'ignorant of the plight of the Aboriginal people of Australia' and calling on the Prime Minister to take over the portfolio.[17] The Minister's response was to ask his officers to meet with Treasury: to discuss whether delegates could be paid their salaries now that the N.A.C.C. 'had adopted different functions from those described in the Cabinet minute establishing that body':

> I may have no power to pay them in view of the fact that they have changed their name, and become, not a body to consult with me, but a directive body. If my belief is correct, they have put themselves off the payroll.

The *impasse* was resolved by a publicly announced compromise: the Congress would revert to its original name of N.A.C.C. and its members would continue to be paid. Further, the N.A.C.C. would continue its advisory role until the government considers a new constitution for a National Aboriginal Congress.[18] However, said Bruce McGuinness, while the new format would still be advisory, 'we must have a dual role: we cannot operate just as a tool of the government'.[19]

What is the nub of all this? What factors have led to a ministerial decree that they are 'only a consultative committee', with power 'only to advise' and a Congress 'attempting vaingloriously to arrogate to themselves a quasi-parliamentary right of running their own affairs'?[20] The *Australian* suggested that both Gordon Bryant and the Aborigines 'were obsessed by the euphoria of their own idealism and the result was that they over-interpreted the liberalism of a new government which, in fact, is basically as conservative as its predecessors'.[21] Early in 1973 euphoria was rampant: the quick elevation of the new Department of Aboriginal Affairs; its 'victory' after years of defeat by the hard-line, Country-Party-controlled Department of the Interior; the full-circle swing by which a number of key advancement league people — like Gordon Bryant — became *the* decision-makers; the flushness of a vastly greater budget; the Labor tenet of not whether land rights but how land rights would be granted, and so on.

Secondly, there is a real sense in which the psychological climate of the Aboriginal community has run ahead of both ministerial and departmental thinking. Consultation ideas are white ideas: 'Congress' notions and power-sharing are black ones. Thirdly, the Department has decided to invest its eggs in the 'self-determination' basket, a policy essentially for northern reserve-dwelling communities. It envisages a new set of black organisations working out their destiny, at their own pace, in their own terms — new structures which could possibly give greater autonomy and responsibility to local communities than they could obtain from an N.A.C.C. As with the South African Bantustan philosophy, it provides a kind of separate development ethos for reserve blacks. Neither policy takes into account the considerable numbers of non-reservists. Unlike urban Africans, urban Aborigines cannot be fobbed off with the response that if they want autonomy and power-sharing on their own terms they must return to their 'homelands'. The urban part-Aborigines cannot therefore be faulted for seeing the N.A.C.C. as the *only* political vehicle available for them.

There is little doubt in my mind that an important factor in this confrontation is the desire by the then Minister and some of his officials to assert *their* control over Aboriginal policy. It is also a desire for Aboriginal approval of what they decide is in their best interests, for co-operative endorsement, not for hectic criticism — let alone a role reversal by which the Aborigines become the policy-makers and the Department *their* civil service! The vastly expanded new Department of Aboriginal Affairs now has 'territory' — and a pretty grand budget. Like all other Aboriginal administrations before it, it believes it has to expand before it can disappear, 'disappearance' being the age-old cry of them all. Aged 20 months, it is not about to surrender its control, its power, its internal status considerations, and its new-found muscles because a new black princess has been born. It is now hell-bent on yet another reorganisation by the time-and-motion 'management men', introducing procedures that may stop financial abuses but which will assuredly mean less access, 'openness' and response to Aborigines.

The idea of a quasi-parliamentary N.A.C.C. is indeed a vainglorious one. Ministers will not, and cannot, surrender their ministerial responsibility and Parliament cannot surrender its control over allocation of and account-ability for public funds in order to create an autonomous, statutory N.A.C.C. When all these factors and realities sink in, my prediction — for what it is worth — is that by the end of 1975 the majority of Aborigines will write off the N.A.C.C. as a political vehicle and decide to operate their pressure outside our political conventions. There will be a growth of Gary Foley's kind of thinking:[22]

> They [N.A.C.C.] are totally out of their depth in terms of political awareness and have no real grasp of the overall Aboriginal 'problem'. It was to be expected though. I predicted over 12 months ago that to

apply the white man's all embracing concept of democracy to the complex and diversified Aboriginal situation would result in a disaster. I said that generally it would result in the election of the local 'loud-mouth' reserve 'personality'. Sadly, dominant personality types are rarely the politically aware or the persons with their finger on the pulse of a rapidly changing Aboriginal situation. I hate to say I told you so!!!

The story is all too familiar. Advisory bodies of this very type, and born of this kind of motivation, have come to rapid grief in South Africa, Canada and New Zealand. The final words of the Natives Representative Council in South Africa in 1946 seem to me to be *the* portent of what is to come with the N.A.C.C.:[23]

> We have reached a stage when we feel that our coming to Pretoria and pretending to represent the people to place their grievances before the Government is just a waste of time . . . We are using this Council as the only platform we have, but we have come to the stage where we realise that we are wasting our time, and we fear sometimes that unlimited tolerance means the disappearance of all tolerance . . . We have been fooled. We have been asked to co-operate with a toy telephone. We have been speaking into an apparatus which cannot transmit sound and at the end of which there is nobody to receive the message. Like children we have taken pleasure at the echo of our voices . . .

IV

The conclusion then is that the existing political institutions and options available offer Aborigines no hope of real change, and that present institutions (including the new N.A.C.C.) are incapable of yielding to their legitimate grievances. It is not simply that the mechanisms or the structures cannot yield; rather it is the states of mind of the white organisation men — discussed earlier — that prohibit the cessions and concessions being demanded.

What other options are there? Elsewhere I have discussed (Tatz 1972b: 97-109) the possibility of new political and politico-legal mechanisms. Briefly, it is worth considering the New Zealand concept of *Maori Incorporations* under the *Maori Social and Economic Advancement Act*. These legal incorporations, usually but not always based on land and its economic use, provide an umbrella of legal rights, making far more use of lawyers as advisers than welfare officers as guides. The system shows, as it does in Canada with statutorily derived and empowered Band Councils, that decision-makers give greater credence to the 'incorporated' viewpoints of Aborigines than has ever been given to the claims or complaints of the 'naked' individual, no matter how articulate. The present government intends legislating for Aboriginal corporations, and supports several communities already incorporated in this way. It will be of interest to see how soon these incorporations are 'entrusted to administer government property' — as Rowley suggests they should be.

Secondly, the participation-consultation mechanisms that exist are based very much on western notions of representativeness and representative structures. Our idea of committees, councils, chairmen, treasurers, secretaries, agendas and rules of procedure have been foisted upon Aborigines — as if they were the only valid forms or vehicles for decision-making and spokesmanship. One of the reasons for the failure of these mechanisms to 'produce' is that they are intrinsically alien to the cultural configurations of the indigenous societies. With the vast anthropological research material available, it seems a not too difficult exercise to interpret the indigenous system of decision-making and to create structures that have strands of thought and practice substitutive for our equivalent cultural assumptions. The 'self-determination' policy fully recognises this point when it states that communities 'should be free to evolve their own forms of organisations'. One can only speculate about the use officials will make of political science-anthropological expertise in these exercises, or will allow Aborigines to make use of it.

There are a number of legal strategies that may prove valuable in the short and long term. These options may not ignite a new or better set of race relations and they may not obviate or eliminate the three fundamental problems I posed at the beginning. But, as a political scientist, I see more optimism in the legal framework than in the political one. Illich (1974:98-99) talks about the need to 'recover legal procedure':

> Most of the present laws and present legislators, most of the present courts and their decisions, most of the claimants and their demands are deeply corrupted by an overarching industrial consensus: that more is better, and that corporations serve the public interest better than men. But this entrenched consensus does not invalidate my thesis that any revolution which neglects the use of formal legal and political procedures will fail. Only an active majority in which all individuals and groups insist for their own reasons on their own rights, and whose members share the same convivial procedure, can recover the rights of men against corporations.
>
> The use of procedure for the purpose of hampering, stopping, and inverting our major institutions will appear to their managers and addicts as a misuse of the law and as subversion of the only order which they recognise. The use of due convivial procedure appears corrupt and criminal to the bureaucrat, even one who calls himself a judge.

In short, law or legal procedure can be viewed as Illich viewed it, as a convivial (friendly) tool of social change — as opposed to political strategies that are, or become, a violent tool of social revolution. Can Aborigines recover their rights against the corporations, be they Swiss aluminium companies, or federal and state bureaucracies, or mission societies?

Political battles can be won in the legal arena. Often failing, expensive and tortuous, resort to civil law processes has nevertheless won considerable concessions for blacks and Indians in the United States and in Canada. The Aboriginal legal aid programmes have to date shown that their only concern is providing ambulance-type, last minute representation for Aborigines appearing in criminal courts. I am not denigrating this function, but its natural concomitant is counteraction in the civil courts. There is a crying need for this kind of Nader-type or Illich-type function. Aborigines are currently suffering legal and political wrongs for which white society (and other minority groups abroad) has found resolution through actions in contract theory, intentional and negligent torts, the laws of descent and distribution. Recourse has been had to the developing body of international conventions on human rights and the notion of an official tort in the administration of governmental programmes. These areas of action need to be explored by and for Aborigines. The threat of expensive, time-consuming, and very public civil litigation, or the actual pursuit of that litigation, has the remarkable effect of causing institutional men to think twice before acting and above all, to feel a modicum of insecurity for the first time in their lives. Nader has shown just how very effective such civil action can be. The litigation instituted by a group of Methodist ex-missionaries on behalf of the Yirrkala clans in the case of *Milirrpum* (etc.) resulted in the loss of that particular case. But in the end it won the *principle* of land rights. The *reality* of land rights could well come about through civil cases if there is no political action by government.

Finally, there is one other option — one far less theoretical and far more realistic each day: the threat of, or actual violence. In another essay I have dealt at some length with the prospects of civil violence in Australia (see Nettheim ed. 1974).

Civil violence occurs when expectations about rights and status are continually frustrated, and peaceful efforts to press these claims yield inadequate results. Whether frustration or protest erupts in violence depends mainly on the degree and consistency of social control and the degree to which social and political institutions afford peaceful alternatives for the redress of group grievances. One can postulate this syndrome: frustration, then alienation, then withdrawal from the larger society, then violence, or the threat of it.

In Australia we are said to have an 'open' political system. 'Open' implies greater flexibility of the existing channels for redress of grievances — and the creation of new institutions for that purpose. I have shown that our system offers few, if any, peaceful alternatives for Aborigines, and that the new institution, the N.A.C.C., is tailor-made for the creation rather than the diminution of new frustration. Aborigines, in Rowley's words, have always been met with the whip, the lash and the gun, or the threat of them. We now have threats of 'advisory' roles only, and of the cutting off of salaries. For some, there is in turn a recognition that threats of rocks and bottles, or actual rocks and bottles, call more attention to their grievances than any other single tactic.

The erection of the Aboriginal tent 'Embassy' on the lawns outside Parliament House in Canberra on 26 January 1972 was indicative of Aboriginal frustration, alienation and feeling of foreignness in their own country. It was a piece of political genius, a peaceful confrontation that lasted six months. As Harris puts it (1972:viii-x): 'on 20 July the Government's patience, which had much to do with the growing public sympathy with the Aborigines, finally snapped'. The police moved in, producing and provoking, or provoking and producing, considerable violence. A week later, when the tent was re-erected, Bobbi Sykes shouted at supporters protecting the Embassy from police:

> 'What do we want?'
> 'Land rights!' they shouted back.
> 'When do we get them?'
> 'Now!'
> 'And what have we got?'
> 'Fuck all!'

The Harris and other accounts of the Embassy — erected again at this time of writing — illustrate only too well the point being made: that in the end, confrontation and eyeball to eyeball tactics produce hastier — though not always better — results. Much of Labor's rush to formulate new policies stemmed from these events. Certainly it has no wish for more world TV coverage of another round between those armed with weapons and those only with tongues.

Our white philosophy in a democratic system is that effective democracy is equated with stable democracy, that is, that violence is pathological to the system of governance. This philosophy, as expounded in political science textbooks, is not reality. Violence is, in many ways, an integral facet of Western societies, especially frontier societies such as ours. Violence may be abhorrent to those socialised as we are, but we cannot demand that it be abhorrent to, or abstained from by, those people historically at the receiving end of it. That black people see violence as a legitimate political weapon is a reality. Like Nixon's Watergate, one can deplore it, attack it, and wish it were not there: but it is there and we have to learn to comprehend it, even appreciate it. If we fail to do so, we will unleash a shocked, surprised and vengeful violence in return, to the irretrievable detriment of race relations in Australia.

Postscript on the National Aboriginal Congress

Senator J. L. Cavanagh met with eight members of the N.A.C.C. on 2 July 1974 to discuss changes in that body's constitution. The following day the Minister released these comments to the media (Department of Aboriginal Affairs 'Media Release' JC/72):

> Upon adoption of the new proposed constitution, the N.A.C.C. shall be known as the National Aboriginal Congress according to the wishes of its members. The whole basis of operations is to be changed.

> The desire of members is to have an independent congress with permanency, with or without Government support. It is, and shall remain an advisory body to the Government while possessing certain executive powers of its own.

The Minister said that objections to previous constitutional amendments — which vested 'excessive power' in the executive — had been met: there were now 'safeguards' which would make the constitution acceptable, on this point, to Cabinet. The executive would 'head' committees dealing with health, housing, education etc. It would be known as the Executive Council, and its members as Councillors — not 'Ministers' as was previously proposed.

The constitution would provide for the 'setting up of local community groups, which shall select, or appoint, at least one representative to a regional assembly in which the local community group is situated'. These regional assemblies will meet regularly 'to advise and assist the local Congress member, make recommendations and communicate information to the Aboriginal people within the region'.

State meetings of N.A.C. members will meet regularly:
'I believe the formation of these bodies will establish consultation with the Aboriginal people at grass roots level and will better look after the special needs and situations in all areas of Aboriginal settlement'.

In conclusion. I believe the Government will agree to recognise the aspirations of the Aboriginal people as set out in the Constitution.

Among these aspirations is the objective to preserve and promote Aboriginal languages and culture, which is already Government policy.

Among others which the Government would certainly support is the desire to influence State and local government authorities for the betterment of the Aboriginal people.

I believe the N.A.C. could play an important role in Aboriginal Affairs. Now that we have agreed on its Constitution, one major hurdle to its progress has been removed.

This Constitution as agreed upon has to be ratified by the next full meeting of the Committee when it shall then be submitted to Cabinet for approval.

Notes

1. Press Release: Statement by the then Minister for Aboriginal Affairs, Mr. Gordon Bryant, Canberra and Darwin, 29 March 1973.

2. In *Reality*, a South African journal, November 1972.

3. In *Reality*, March 1972.

4. Drawn from H. F. Pitkin (1972).

5. At the completion of primary vote counting in June 1974, Bruce McGuinness had 4,183 and Elizabeth Hoffman 434 — a total of 4,617 primary votes for the Aboriginal Independent Party. (A fair number of non-Aborigines voted for them: we know that the N.A.C.C. electoral roll in Victoria has 1,044 Aboriginal voters.) On the other hand, Senator Neville Bonner gained 17,824 primary votes as number 3 on the Queensland 'Liberal National Party' ticket. (Figures from *Sydney Morning Herald*, 8 June 1974.)

6. These States have refused to place their Aboriginal administrations under the federal Department of Aboriginal Affairs — as W.A. and S.A. have done.

7. Pressure-group activity can produce some interesting bed-, or if that word is inappropriate, soul-mates. In 1967 the federal government joined hands and expenses with the Aborigines Advancement League in Victoria and with F.C.A.A.T.S.I. to make propaganda for a yes vote for the Aboriginal referendum questions. A year or so earlier, I recall Mr W. C. Wentworth and Mrs Doris Blackburn, socialist *extraordinaire* and widow of Maurice Blackburn, socialist *diabolique*, holding hands and singing 'We Shall Overcome'. The setting was a F.C.A.A.T.S.I. meeting; the context a black resolution to cable the U.N. on Aboriginal demands for 500,000,000 pounds compensation for dispossessed land.

8. Departmental circular from Charles Perkins to the chairmen of various Aboriginal Councils (no date).

9. *Aboriginal News*, vol. 1, no. 5, February 1974, a Department of Aboriginal Affairs publication.

10. In that Queensland electorate, there were 7 candidates and a 95 per cent poll.

11. *Australian Government Digest*, vol. 1, no. 1, p. 63.

12. The Perkins circular, see Note 8.

13. *Sydney Morning Herald*, 14 December 1973.

14. *The Australian*, 24 November 1973.

15. *The Australian*, 7 February 1974.

16. *The Australian*, 7 February 1974.

17. *The Australian*, 11 February 1974.

18. A curious point: at the Australian Institute of Aboriginal Studies conference in May 1974, senior Aboriginal Affairs officers insisted on N.A.C. as the current title; but telegrams to the Institute from Darwin where that body was meeting were signed as N.A.C.C.

19. *Sydney Morning Herald*, 13 February 1974.

20. *The Australian*, 12 February 1974.

21. *The Australian*, 12 February 1974.

22. Roneoed paper, *National Aboriginal Congress in Action*.

23. *The Report of the Proceedings of the Native Representative Council*, Pretoria, 14-15 August 1946, quoted in C. M. Tatz (1962:115-6).

References

CAWTE, J. 1972 Racial prejudice and Aboriginal adjustment: the social psychiatric view. In *Racism: the Australian Experience*. Vol. 2 (F. S. Stevens ed.).

COMMITTEE OF INQUIRY 1965 *Committee of Inquiry into Laws affecting Maori Land and Powers of the Maori Land Court*. Government Printer, New Zealand. [Roneoed, 15 December 1965.]

GOFFMAN, E. 1961 *Asylums*. Penguin, Harmondsworth.

HARRIS, S. 1972 *This our land*. Australian National University Press, Canberra.

ILLICH, I. 1974 *Tools for conviviality*. Harper and Row, New York.

LONG, J. P. M. 1970 *Aboriginal settlements: a survey of institutional communities in eastern Australia*. Australian National University Press, Canberra.

MOODIE, P. M. 1972 The health disadvantages of Aborigines. In *Racism: the Australian experience*. Vol. 2 (F. S. Stevens ed.). Australia and New Zealand Book Co., Sydney.

NETTHEIM, G. 1973 *Out lawed*. Australian and New Zealand Book Co., Sydney.

——(ed.) 1974 *Aborigines, human rights and the law*. Australian and New Zealand Book Co. Sydney. [Report of conference sponsored by the International Commission of Jurists.]

PITKIN, H. F. 1972 *The concept of representation*. University of California Press, Berkeley.

ROWLEY, C. D. 1970a *The destruction of Aboriginal society*, Vol. I. Australian National University Press, Canberra.

——1970b *Outcasts in White Australia*, Vol. II. Australian National University Press, Canberra.

——1971 *The remote Aborigines*, Vol. III. Australian National University Press, Canberra.

STEVENS, F. S. (ed.) 1972 *Racism: the Australian experience*, Vol. 2. Australia and New Zealand Book Co., Sydney.

TATZ, C. M. 1962 *Shadow and substance in South Africa*. Natal University Press, Natal.

——1972a The politics of Aboriginal health, *Politics* (special supplement), VII(2).

——1972b Aborigines: law and political development. In *Racism: the Australian experience*, Vol. 2. (F.S. Stevens ed.). Australia and New Zealand Book Co., Sydney.

WOODWARD, A. E. 1974 *Aboriginal Land Rights Commission*. Second Report, April 1974. Australian Government Publishing Service, Canberra. [The Woodward Report.]

Editor's Note

While this volume was in its final page-proof stage, the federal Minister for Aboriginal Affairs announced that the N.A.C.C. was to be replaced by a National Aboriginal Conference. This would comprise 35 elected members. Five of these and five government nominees would be chosen to make up a 'high-level' advisory group.

28 Out of the frying pan..? or, back to square one?

Catherine H. Berndt

This paper is intended as a short statement drawing attention to a couple of points that seem to need underlining in the context of this Symposium.

In one sense the title and subtitle are exaggerated. In another, they are not. The theme is that what remains of traditional Aboriginal society and culture is currently faced with a crisis-situation, not unlike the crisis-situation that confronted Aborigines in their initial contact with Europeans (recognising that such contact was not a single happening but had an uneven time-space spread and that it was not the same everywhere). Of course, there are marked differences between then and now. It is never possible to go back to square one, because square one is not what it was before. Nevertheless, there is enough in common to suggest some interesting parallels.

The vulnerability of Aboriginal tradition   One example is the field of 'outside' attitudes toward Aboriginal culture then and now. Until a few years ago, these attitudes were almost entirely negative. Many people disparaged Aboriginal culture. Even the few who did not, could see no place for any of it in the new style of life that they anticipated for Aborigines. Maybe they still feel the same way — or some of them do. But as a rule they do not say so publicly. Hostility can be concealed in expressions of apparent concern (about the effects of malnutrition or disease or liquor), as well as in legislation that puts Aborigines in a particularly vulnerable position, notably in regard to mining rights over Aboriginal reserves. And for the majority of other Australians, Aborigines are outside the range of ordinary living — irrelevant to it, or regarded as if they ought to be. Nevertheless, the views that are most often or most explicitly expressed today take a double-positive line: i.e. Aboriginal culture is good in itself, and it can and should survive into the future. The actual mechanics of this, how it can be translated into practice, are not usually specified. Especially in regard to the second part (survival-potential), and bearing in mind the total range of traditional cultures, the conceptual framework and implications are very hazily thought out, even where Aboriginal arts and Aboriginal languages are being encouraged and taught. But the principle of retaining 'Aboriginal culture' has been enunciated officially, more *as* a principle, and has attracted a tremendous amount of support.

Ironically, when anthropologists in the 1930s, '40s and '50s pressed for the establishment and safeguarding of Aboriginal reserves, they were accused of supporting a policy of apartheid. As to their motives, they were alleged to be interested only in scientific research and not in welfare — or at the expense of welfare. This claim was especially popular among people who for one reason or another wanted those reserves to be abolished and saw anthropologists as blocking that objective. The term 'anthropologist' was (and is) used rather loosely. But professional anthropologists were actually quite few in number. As far as they were concerned, the major aim, where there is information on this, certainly had strong welfare overtones. It was to provide at least some Aborigines with a spatial buffer against the kind of fate that was overtaking so many others, and to increase Aborigines' chances of being able to decide for themselves what their relations with other Australians might be. The fact that this did not work out so well is another matter. On the other hand, if there had been no Arnhem Land Reserve, it is doubtful whether there would have been even the remote likelihood of a Gove land rights case or any sort of protest about it — with all the implications of that case for other claims, in other areas.

But the Arnhem Land Reserve was maintained as such only with difficulty. Opposition to it came from a variety of sources and for a variety of reasons. The aims were much the same, however: to abolish it, to 'open it up', or to whittle it away. Tourist and other commercial ventures tried to infiltrate it, especially from the 1940s on. One such plan was to set up a tourist village at each mission station, and on a smaller scale there were permit-applications from (e.g.) individual crocodile-shooters. A number of officials in the Northern Territory administration advocated the throwing-open of all Aboriginal reserves, on the grounds that Aborigines no longer needed them but other people did. And welfare bodies in the southern states, including people of Aboriginal descent, saw the Arnhem Land Reserve, and others, as an unwanted and invidious symbol of 'separateness', an example of enforced apartheid. Our plea in 1954 that 'Arnhem Land must remain a country for the Arnhem Landers alone . . . And they must exploit its natural resources themselves' (*Arnhem Land, its History and its People*, Cheshire, Melbourne, p. 201) was unpopular all around at that time, *except* among the Arnhem Landers themselves on whose behalf we had made it. We may have been a bit naive in the way we put this, and at that time the likelihood of intensive mining developments seemed much more remote than the wealth to be derived from the sea. Nevertheless, the main point was the need to block outside exploitation and at the same time help the local people to develop their own resources so that they could deal with other Australians from a position of strength and equality. Those of us who urged that the Arnhem Landers, for instance, should not be compelled to abandon their traditional culture, which was still vigorous although obviously modified, included missionaries as well as anthropologists. Again, how the principle would be translated into practice was another question: but it was advocated in the teeth of such strong opposition that at the time it seemed almost hopeless. It is true that the emphasis was on local situations and local culture, not on an Australia-wide basis. But the 'pride in the Aboriginal heritage' which some of us tried to stimulate has always had this wider relevance.

There was never much doubt about the emotional involvement of older Aboriginal men and women throughout the north and centre of the continent in their own cultural heritage, and their emotional commitment to it. Their difficulties in this respect came directly from outside, from the Europeans who impinged on them with varying schemes for their betterment or otherwise, but also from within their own society — the Trojan Horse of the young people who were enticed by the prospect of brighter lights and greener pastures. Aboriginal children who went (and who go) to country towns and cities for schooling or employment or training are no more likely than other outback children to return permanently to what they come to see as isolated areas — not if they can avoid it.

Traditionally, the Aborigines were realistic about the kinds of process that were important in ensuring the survival of their particular heritage. They did not assume that it would be transmitted mystically or through genetic inheritance. On the contrary, they worked hard at the practical business of teaching-and-learning. They paid special attention to the transition from childhood to maturity, trying to inculcate the information and attitudes they considered necessary for adult life. A fair proportion of their cultural pro- gramme-for-living was devoted to this. Contact with the outside world in all but a few areas shattered those programmes and the continuities they were based on. And the effects have been cumulative. Even where children were not separated from adults for long periods (e.g. where the dormitory system was operating), the *content* of the programme was curtailed or modified. This was most obvious in the setting of initiation procedures, for instance; but it permeated the domestic side too, as generations of parents were influenced, cumulatively, by such changes. Arnhem Land was not immune, although the impact was less conspicuous there (and in the Western Desert) until the advent of miners and oilmen set even more traumatic events in train for all of the Arnhem Landers, both eastern and western.

In Australia generally, for a while, interest in Aboriginal culture seemed to be increasing in proportion as the Aboriginal population seemed to be declining. When it became clear that the population decline had been reversed, it still looked as if the traditional culture was doomed. That trend has been checked too; but the rate of the cultural revival has not kept pace with the expanding public interest in it — or rather in sentimental ideas about it or in congenial bits of it: art and dance, for example, and 'closeness to nature'. Traditionally-oriented Aborigines have achieved a 'good' image. So has their culture, seen as a simple but appealing and ulcer-free type of adaptation to the natural and social environment.

One sign of the current popularity of 'Aboriginal culture' is the pro- liferating number of courses on it, offered in schools and teachers' colleges and in universities and other tertiary institutions. The motivation for these probably rests as much on welfare as on factual or theoretical considerations, if not more so. And some staff members and students do more than talk about it. Along with others, they take an active part in welfare enterprises of various kinds.

The new paternalism　　Aborigines are targets or objects of welfare concern as well as objects of interest. Aside from recognition of individual Aborigines as persons, and establishment of personal relationships with them, or in addition to that, collectively they represent a Cause. As in the case of the early missionaries, dedication is the prime ingredient. Like their earlier counterparts too, some of the new-style welfare missionaries move out to attempt firsthand contacts with people of Aboriginal descent; but for them, outside their home areas or outside the metropolitan regions, these contacts are mostly on a short-term basis. Another point of similarity: technical and practical skills are seen as acceptable and important, but less crucial than dedication.

> Nursing is a field where 'dedication' is virtually built into the image. A recent advertisement sponsored by the 'Australian Department of Health' spells it out in a recruiting drive for the Northern Territory. Of four portraits, one is of Daisy Bates: 'Known as "the great white queen of the Never-Never". Devoted much of her life to helping aborigines, dwelling with outback tribes'. The text adds, 'Nurses with similar qualities wanted for the Northern Territory', and: 'You could find yourself working with an aboriginal medicine man (also employed by us). You may find him easier to work with than matron'. (*The West Australian*, 15.5.74.)

One point of difference is in keeping with today's heightened stress on social relations — on 'getting along with people', rather than on specific accomplishments by themselves. This is the weighting accorded to 'empathy', not always under that label. It comes out in some advertisements for personnel to serve in government departments dealing with Aboriginal affairs.

> In January 1974, for example, the Aboriginal Affairs Planning Authority in Perth, W.A., advertised for 'Community Advisers and Economic Advisers' in the field of 'Community Development', noting that career-opportunities were available 'for people with a sensitive concern for others and an ability to relate in a non-directive manner'. (*The West Australian*, 26.1.74.)

This makes a change, of course, from advertisements for some government posts in the Aboriginal-affairs field not very long ago, where the stipulated requirements were simply a matriculation (or a leaving) certificate and a driver's licence.

> In another example, the 'South Australian Branch Office of the Department of Aboriginal Affairs' sought two Field Officers with the following qualifications: 'A deep and detailed understanding of the aboriginal people and the ability to communicate effectively with aboriginals and to interpret their requirements to the department'.

Two points regarding their duties are worth noting (and I stress them accordingly). These were: to 'Maintain personal liaison with aboriginals and aboriginal organisations to ensure *a complete two-way flow of information* between aboriginals and the department, and *assist in field investigations being carried out by a team of Project Officers*'. (*The West Australian*, 2.2.74.) The first indicates the kind of line of communication — and influence — that is being established between local communities and the central office in Canberra. The second reflects the burgeoning of research carried out by and for government departments. Some departments have expanded their own research units, or turned themselves into combined research and welfare agencies. A few have stepped up their efforts to direct and control all research that might come within hailing distance of their own interests. In this competitive atmosphere, there have even been attempts to restrict or oppose non-government research projects.

A third point emerges from these two advertisements. In the first (again, stress added), 'Community Advisers will be required *to live in the community they are servicing*'; the same ('. . . or at regional centres') applies to Economic Advisers. Also continuously present, in some remote communities, are persons hired through management-consultant teams. The running of some communities has been, in effect, handed over to such teams. Ostensibly they are under Aboriginal control, but much more needs to be said about that. Just because there is no non-Aboriginal authority figure in sight, that does not necessarily mean that none exists. 'Invisible government', 'invisible influence' are not easy to assess — or to control.

Two further advertisements are relevant here, each involving a different firm: one, 'Chartered Accountants'; the other 'Management Consultants'.

First, for an 'Enterprises Officer' for the 'Ngangganawili Community incorporated', of Wiluna.

> 'The person sought for this position should have sound practical knowledge and skills, a proven ability to relate positively to other people and a sensitivity towards the needs of Aboriginal people.' Under the heading of 'Duties': 'The Enterprises Officer is responsible, in an advisory mode, to the Community for the implementation, carrying out and supervision of all enterprises and economic activity, as well as general overall on-site management and financial control of economic enterprises conducted by Ngangganawili Community Inc.' The 'General' heading throws the net even more widely: 'Experience in pastoral activities, irrigation, mechanical and electrical maintenance and book-keeping all advantages.' It adds: 'Ideally, applicants should be married, and employment opportunities will eventually be available for the wife of the successful applicant.' (*The West Australian,* 20.7.74.)

Secondly, under 'Project Staff for the Warburton Community Incorporated'. ('Warburton is being developed as a mainly Aboriginal township.' The Community 'provides power, water, sewerage and rubbish disposal services, it operates a store, bank agency and service station and trades in artefacts'.)

> A 'Construction Supervisor (Position No. 485)' was to 'be responsible for employing the majority of the aboriginal work force on the construction and maintenance of Community facilities', and 'to contract with the agencies operating at Warburton for the use of the Community's plant. Experience in the building or construction industry and a knowledge of earthmoving equipment is required.' (*The West Australian,* 6.7.74.) A slightly higher salary was offered to a 'Project Manager (Position No. 484)'. 'The Manager's position is similar to that of a Shire Clerk/Shire Engineer in Local Government but it also encompasses the management of trading activities. The Manager will work closely with the Aboriginal Council to develop projects which will contribute to the well-being of the population and bring employment and income to the Community.' 'Apart from his responsibility for carrying out the agreed projects, he will *control the routine operations of the Community* through the Construction Supervisor, Maintenance Officer, Store Manager and Book-keeper. The job calls for a man with imagination and tact as well as practical management experience.' (*The West Australian,* 6.7.74 and 17.8.74.) In both cases, 'Furnished air-conditioned accommodation is available at a low rental . . .'

Aside from the issues of technical qualifications and social relationships, and the tricky problem of guidance, advice and authority, these advertisements hint at another feature of the current situation. That is, the growth of the non-Aboriginal population in areas that a few years ago were predominantly Aboriginal. Even on the mission and government stations of those days, the ratio of non-Aborigines to Aborigines was much smaller. The difference between them in range and quality of material goods may have seemed quite large at the time, but it was nothing like the present picture in such areas. Competition for land to build settlements on was muted because the Aborigines either did not realise they were really losing it, or had no effective means of asserting their claims. And competition for housing there was hardly an issue. On both counts, the scene has changed. (Today, for example, it is not just 'Who gets the houses?' but 'Who gets the *air-conditioned* houses?') Contrasts in living standards are much more visible now, not only in places like the Gove Peninsula (contrasts between Nhulunbuy and Yirrkalla) but also in formerly out-of-the-way settlements such as Warburton. Laverton (W.A.) is another example. Until the development of the Windarra Nickel Project, it was the Aboriginal population that kept the town alive. Now, 'The town is being redeveloped to house the workforce', 'new' or 'modern' air-conditioned houses and home units are available, together with a 'modern caravan park', 'in fact the whole new way of life at Laverton W.A.' (*The West Australian*: many entries, e.g. 17.8.74.)

So much for the influx of long-term (or potentially long-term) residents from outside. The faces may fluctuate; but the immigrant population as such, in this new wave of colonisation, is fairly well entrenched. Over and above them, there is a growing stream of official and unofficial visitors; making brief surveys, supplying asked-for or unasked-for advice, or passing through in the course of drilling or mining-exploration trips. Or, sharing 'experiences in drama, music, craft and dance with Aborigines', as Perth's Round Earth Company set out to do on a three months' round of mission and other settlements (*The West Australian*, 16.4.74): 'The company's director . . . said that the group hoped to introduce forms of Western arts to the people of the central desert'. (They also 'hoped to learn something of Aboriginal culture'.) And tourists, of course. Even where travel agents do not specifically offer 'aboriginal culture' as an enticement, as the Pioneer 'Arnhemlander' trip does, it is a concealed inducement in a number of others.

Add to all this the fact that commissions and committees of enquiry have proliferated, alongside such long-standing research centres as the universities and, later, the Australian Institute of Aboriginal Studies. Then, add the imbalance in numbers between Aborigines and non-Aborigines in Australia, plus overseas visitors wanting to see for themselves Aboriginal people and Aboriginal culture. Being the subject or basis of a bandwagon can have advantages, for example in regard to physical welfare, but it can be disturbing in other ways. The sum total, from the standpoint even of Aborigines who are as yet only partly aware of it, can hardly fail to cause alarm and despondency.

And the old dilemma The idea of a generalised Aboriginal culture is useful for people who are anxious to learn or re-learn it, and useful for giving substance to identity-claims. Museums and archives supply information on 'how it was before', or how *some* of it was. But they are not of much help to people who want to keep what they still have, as an integral part of their lives: not just ceremonial displays for the benefit of others, or an assortment of arts and crafts, or retention of the vernacular language in a kind of cultural vacuum. And they want to keep it with a minimum of direction from outsiders, including other Aborigines. At the same time, they want to be able to choose from the outside scene the things and ideas that might be helpful and/or attractive to them and to keep out those that are not.

And this epitomises the dilemma. First: to be able to make choices effectively now, in full awareness of all the relevant factors, calls for a broader frame of reference than is available in most small-scale societies or sub-societies. What was adequate once, is adequate no longer. Moving outside such a society, spatially or psychologically or both, is one way of trying to cope with current pressures, but it has certain consequences for membership in that society. Consciously selecting cultural traits for retention, or rejection, is not the same as participating in that culture as a living reality.

Increasingly, some younger people of Aboriginal descent who have grown up in an environment where their traditional culture has continuity and substance, have been drawn away from it. In turning their backs on the process of *detailed* learning of that culture, they are also rejecting (trying to reject) the authority structure that goes with it. Conversely, a number of those who are endeavouring to recapture what they envisage as Aboriginal tradition are outside the range of authority of traditional religious leaders — or can *choose* to submit to those leaders, on a voluntary and temporary basis. The interplay between these centrifugal and centripetal trends is one factor in the reshaping and redefining of 'Aboriginal culture'.

Secondly, there is the problem of distribution of power and authority, and access to the channels of power and authority. 'Grass roots' today are not what they used to be. Local, shallow-rooted varieties of grass are out of fashion. Some lip-service is still paid to them, and from some angles the new varieties even look the same. Nevertheless, the roots are now being cultivated to draw their main nourishment from a centralised root-system. Concentration of population and power in the south-eastern corner of Australia, and the growing centralisation of power and control in Canberra, have weakened the authority and independence of local towns and settlements and cities elsewhere in the continent, and not only where Aborigines are concerned.

In addition, economic self-sufficiency for small communities is harder to achieve now, even if they want it. Even adults who are prepared to 'live off the land' in their own territories are not content with the range of goods that was traditionally satisfying there. Their children will probably be even less so. Socio-political involvement at some level in extra-community affairs is harder to avoid. More Aborigines now speak English, which (ideally) broadens their perspective but also makes them more accessible — and in some ways more vulnerable. Spatial distance is less effective as a barrier against outside intrusion. Linkages-out are at least as significant, in such communities, as linkages-within.

For example, how much further do the Yirkalla people need to move away from the traditional core that remains to them, before they can make informed judgments about the Nabalco-Nhulunbuy complex and assess its implications for themselves? Or, in regard to Nabarlek: how much information do the Oenpelli people need to have, not just about Queensland Mines but about economic and political issues within and beyond Australia? And how do they get that information? — except, in the first place, through outside advisers whose motives they may not be able to sort out. Or the process of sorting them out successfully, again, leads outward before it leads back into the local scene.

Research involvement provides one sort of answer, though obviously it is not for everybody. (It never is, in any society.)

Generally speaking, Aborigines have not made nearly enough use of anthropologists. There are exceptions, but not as many as there should be. Much of the responsibility for this must rest with anthropologists themselves, to the extent that they have not made clear their research and welfare concerns, their reasons for what they customarily do and how they go about it. But the research aspect, in particular, is not easy to convey in a situation where that kind of tradition is not a cultural theme. It is difficult enough in large sections of other populations, including the wider Australian society.

To be really useful, 'research' must mean more than either unsystematic collection of statements and observations, or systematic collection of opinions or 'facts' without adequate depth or context. And research must be welfare-relevant even where there appears to be no direct connection. Projects with immediate welfare aims are only one facet of this.

Systematic and sympathetic research is more than an academic exercise. The data and the insights deriving from it represent a resource that can (could) be drawn on more positively in regard to the development of Aboriginal socio-political and cultural identity in a changing situation, and the practical considerations and claims associated with it. This research, in fact, represents one of the major differences between 'then' and 'now'. And in what I have called the present crisis-situation no avenue of potential help should be neglected.

On one hand, research expertise and 'professionalisation' have increased at a time when traditional Aboriginal culture (what is left of it) is being rapidly eroded. On the other hand, hazy notions about what is involved have downgraded 'research' to an unsystematic mixture which is often no more than an attempt to get simplistic answers to a few simplistic questions. And applying the label 'anthropologist' to anyone who asks questions of or about Aborigines has further confused the picture.

Some anthropologists have been hesitant about offering advice to Aborigines unless they are specifically asked for it — except in crisis-situations where the need for it seems more than usually urgent. For ourselves, this reluctance has come about through years of seeing Aborigines being told, quite peremptorily, what to do and when (sometimes how) to do it, while at the same time all the main decisions about their activities and their pro-grammes-for-living were made by others. It is true that they were not given enough information about the non-Aboriginal world that was penetrating theirs so drastically; and they needed this kind of information to build up a degree of self-protection against it. But to many of them, a few years ago, that outside world appeared uncongenial in all but a few respects, as well as incomprehensible; they were more interested in their own affairs, accepting the new material goods they wanted without seeing that acceptance as a threat to their own life-style. It is also true that we did not stand aloof from welfare commitments. We tried to intervene in a number of circumstances where we considered that intervention was necessary, because in their relations with the outside world of officials and others, many Aborigines were inarticulate, in two ways. Mostly they were not fluent in English even when they spoke it at all (fluency and oratorical skills in their own language did nothing for them in this situation of contact); and they did not know enough about the overall context to be able to frame a telling statement covering what they thought was going on and what could or should be done to remedy it. Above all, they were powerless to take effective action in cases where they did not see eye-to-eye with non-Aboriginal authorities.

Nevertheless, as the history of Aboriginal contact with Europeans has shown, force and threat are not the only means of changing a culture. The same end can be achieved through transactions in a low key, without obvious intent, and even while paying lip-service to the idea of keeping that culture more or less intact. The line between 'influencing' and 'directing' is quite thin, and in advising people on how to go about making their own decisions the distinction can be thoroughly blurred — in practice, if not at the level of verbal recognition.

For many Aborigines now, the concatenation of events and directives and suggestions is as overwhelming in its own way as the earlier impact was. Mining developments and the surveys preceding and accompanying them have had traumatic and ramifying consequences in once-remote areas. So, in its own way, has tourism — even though its expected expansion has barely got going. Liquor has hit many communities hard. Government and other demands are thicker on the ground, harder to evade, and often totally confusing. These facts alone make up a formidable picture. And the backdrop is a national and global setting with which many people are increasingly disenchanted, but which they find it almost impossible to retreat from.

The survival-potential of more than a token amount of Aboriginal traditional culture and/or of distinctively different (*not* merely spatially separate) Aboriginal communities is even lower than it was. And the prospects for its revival are not bright. Not least, there is the hazard already mentioned. Modelling oneself on the 'adversary' for purposes of self-protection might seem to make good sense, but only up to a point — a point not easily specified. The unintended consequences of that process can be irreversible. The aim of 'protection' may perhaps be realised, at least in part. Separate identity may be sustained too. But the content of that identity will certainly be different — very different — from what it was before. There is no going back to the way things were. Not only circumstances change. People's attitudes and expectations change too.

Over and above this, much of what is happening in the wider world today has no precedents — in the scale of socio-political relations and events, in the communications arena, and in the cumulative expansion of their material and technological base. The implications of what is being done and said now are even less clear than they used to be; and although many people continue to behave as if they knew the right answers as well as the right questions, the outcome in the long term is even harder to predict than it was in the past. Research to date takes us so far, but not far enough, in spite of the fact that in some fields it has become virtually 'big business' in its own right.

To be more effective, to get further away from 'square one', research must be not only more co-operative but also more thoughtfully and sensitively designed. (I am not speaking only about anthropologists.) The dilemma facing people of Aboriginal descent cannot be resolved by throwing out resource-personnel — *or* by succumbing to them. Like the rest of us in the larger 'crisis-situation' that impinges on everyone today (whether or not we use such slogans as 'Spaceship Earth'), Aborigines need all the help and advice they can get.

Contributors

Dr Diane E. Barwick,
    45 Waite Street, Farrer,
    Australian Capital Territory.
Dr Catherine H. Berndt,
    Department of Anthropology,
    University of Western Australia.
Professor Ronald M. Berndt,
    Department of Anthropology,
    University of Western Australia.
Dr Keith Cole,
    Combined Church Training and Research Centre,
    Nungalinya College, Darwin.
Mr J. K. Doolan,
    Department of Aboriginal Affairs, Darwin.
Miss Anne-Katrin Eckermann,
    Department of Anthropology and Sociology,
    University of Queensland.
Dr Elizabeth Eggleston,
    Centre for Research into Aboriginal Affairs,
    Monash University.
Dr Fay Gale,
    Department of Geography,
    University of Adelaide.
Mr W. J. Gray,
    Department of Aboriginal Affairs,
    Northern Territory Division, Darwin.
Dr R. G. Hausfeld,
    School of Public Health and Tropical Medicine,
    University of Sydney.
Dr Michael Howard,
    California Polytechnic State University,
    San Luis Obispo, California,
    United States of America.
Dr Susan Kaldor,
    Department of Anthropology,
    University of Western Australia.
Dr Klaus-Peter Koepping,
    Department of Anthropology and Sociology,
    University of Queensland.

Dr Erich Kolig,
Department of Anthropology,
University of Otago, New Zealand.
Dr Kenneth Maddock,
School of Behavioural Sciences,
Macquarie University.
Dr Clarrie F. Makin,
Graylands Teachers College, Western Australia.
Dr Robert McKeich,
Anthropology, Department of Social Sciences,
Western Australian Institute of Technology.
Mrs Dorothy Parker,
Department of Anthropology,
University of Western Australia.
Dr Nicolas Peterson,
Department of Prehistory and Anthropology,
Australian National University.
Dr Lee Sackett,
Department of Anthropology,
University of Adelaide.
Professor Colin Tatz,
Department of Politics,
University of New England, Armidale.
Mr John C. Taylor,
Queensland Institute of Medical Research, Brisbane.
Associate Professor Robert Tonkinson,
Department of Anthropology,
University of Oregon, Eugene, United States of America.
Miss Margaret Valadian,
Consultant and Adviser on Aboriginal Affairs.
Mr Noel M. Wallace,
23 Ormond Road, Ivanhoe, Victoria.
Mrs Isobel M. White,
Department of Anthropology and Sociology,
Monash University.
Dr Don Williams,
School of Teacher Education,
Canberra College of Advanced Education.
Mrs Susan Tod Woenne,
Department of Anthropology,
University of Western Australia.

Name index

Subject index

Aboriginality ix, xi, 5, 7, 8, 9, 11, 35–6, 43, 48–52, 268, 270; and urban Aborigines ix, xii, 10–1, 35, 48–58, 259–60, 288–318, 321, 322–3, 324, 382. *See also* identity

advice, advisers and/or consultants viii, ix–x, 6, 65, 67, 70, 110, 112, 115, 118, 119, 120, 128, 134, 137, 166, 248, 384, 386, 406, 407, 409, 410, 411. *See also* legal aid

alcohol *see* liquor

apartheid 14, 28, 29, 30, 402, 403. *See also* segregation

arts, the, as means of Aboriginal cultural expression 190; commercialisation and/or professionalisation of 10, 18, 22, 166, 406, 408. *See also* craft

assimilation, policies and/or practice of xi, 1, 6, 14, 19, 21, 25, 26, 27, 29, 30, 31, 149, 152, 165–6, 180, 185, 186, 188, 190, 219, 229, 288, 300, 369, 371, 373, 384, 387, 390; contrasted with 'integration' 14, 28–9, 188, 190, 280, 384, 386, 387; and with two-laws concept 27 (*see* law). *See also* biculturalism; identity

authority, traditional 2, 25, 126, 301, 324, 408; erosion of 20, 26, 70, 71, 75, 80–1, 82, 83, 84, 86, 87, 96–8, 126–7, 129, 173, 302. *See also* leadership

biculturalism 14, 28

card-playing 19, 20, 145, 168–9, 305. *See also* gambling

cash economy vii, viii, x, 18, 19, 23, 67, 72, 74, 80–1, 92, 95, 101, 118, 126, 134, 135, 136–46, 148, 151, 152, 153, 154, 156–7, 162, 170, 172, 197, 226, 291–2, 297, 305, 317, 318, 326–31, 377, 406; accumulation, capital x, 23, 145, 156, cash, as evidence of community commitment 117. *See also* economy

ceremonies ('corroborees') 18, 20, 22, 27, 110, 112, 173, 207, 237; religious *see* religious rituals. *See also* recreation

change: Aboriginal attitudes toward x, xi, 8, 10, 14–5, 37, 45, 52, 66, 90–1, 196–7, 391, 396; Australian-European attitudes toward ix–xi, 6, 234. *See also* government 'welfare' programmes; values

children: and family relationships 76, 80, 94, 128, 153, 171, 183, 185, 199, 200, 202, 206, 208–9, 212–5, 216, 223, 226, 227, 228–9, 235, 254, 255–6, 267, 270, 290, 294, 364; removed to dormitories, schools or other centres 21, 66, 90, 101, 128–9, 183, 186, 187, 195, 202, 235, 288, 290, 294, 334, 404, or in institutions 184, 185, 186, 187, 227, 228, 229, 288, 290, and/or culturally alienated 65, 82, 85, 87, 91, 191, 197, 200, 203, 205, 290, 294, 404, 408. *See also* education; school(s); family; kinship

churches, involvement of 114, 284, 310. *See* missions

citizen(ship) 33, 48, 50, 91, 163, 165, 181, 185, 194, 288, 318, 348

community, use of term 4–5, 6, 24, 63

community development ix, 63, 65, 67, 68, 69, 117–9, 151, 152. 177, 190, 193

communication: changes in x, 2, 64, and widening range of 8, 36, 44–7; and interaction 3–4, 8, 10, 11, 40, 43, 63, 370. *See also* identity; mobility; religion

councils, Aboriginal x, 10, 67, 69, 70, 116, 119, 126, 127, 135, 174, 384, 385, 389, 400

courts, need for special 187. *See* legal aid

craft work 10, 67, 118, 138, 139, 140, 141, 142–3. *See also* arts

'crime' 261, 313–4, 332–51, 357, 358, 397. *See* legal aid; police

crises, continuing, for Aborigines xi, 402, 409, 411

dances, dancing, Aboriginal: publicity for 10, 18, 162; survival of 20, 24. *See also* arts; ceremonies; religious rituals

decentralisation vii, viii–ix, 61, 85, 106, 114–20, 123–35, 190, 196–7; of legal services 359; of mission authority 181

decisions about Aboriginal affairs, Aboriginal control over x, 7, 9–10, 20, 24, 27–8, 35, 36, 65, 66, 69, 72, 107, 110, 114, 115, 126–9, 134, 135, 153, 166–7,